D1008113

THE FOUNDING FATHER

THE FOUNDING FATHER

The Story of Joseph P. Kennedy

Richard J. Whalen

REGNERY GATEWAY
Washington, D.C.

Library of Congress Cataloging-in-Publication Data
Whalen, Richard J., 1935–
The founding father : the story of Joseph P. Kennedy / Richard J. Whalen.
p. cm.
Originally published : New York : New American Library, 1964.
Includes bibliographical references and index.
ISBN 0-89526-733-0 (alk. paper)
1. Kennedy, Joseph P. (Joseph Patrick), 1888–1969.
2. Ambassadors—United States—Biography. I. Title.
E748.K376W43 1993
973.9′092—dc20 93-16484
[B] CIP

Originally published in 1964 by The New American Library of World Literature, Inc.
Reprinted by arrangement with the author.

Published in the United States by
Regnery Gateway
1130 17th Street, NW
Washington, DC 20036

Distributed to the trade by
National Book Network
4720-A Boston Way
Lanham, MD 20706

Printed on acid-free paper.

Manufactured in the United States of America.

10 9 8 7 6 5 4 3 2 1

FOR JOAN

The ambition of the Irish is to say a thing as everybody says it, only louder.

—*Gerard Manley Hopkins*

Contents

Author's Preface to the Regnery Gateway Edition

IN THE SUMMER of 1962, I was twenty-six and a newly arrived staff writer at *Fortune*. The editors asked me to tell the untold story of President John F. Kennedy's father, the elusive Joseph P. Kennedy. I had barely heard of him. Although the elder Kennedy and his family had used publicity brilliantly in their rise, they had also erected formidable defenses against journalists they did not control. When the family met my request for cooperation with stony silence, I embarked on the most exciting investigative reporting assignment of my career.

It led, first, to a 13,000-word profile of Joseph Kennedy published in *Fortune*'s January 1963 issue—the longest piece, my pleased editors said, ever to appear in a single issue of the magazine—and then, twenty-two months later, to this book. On the basis of the *Fortune* article, a dozen book publishers bid for *The Founding Father*. Because this was my first book, the successful bidder, New American Library, insured my life for the advance and imposed tight deadlines for delivery of the manuscript in Dickensian, serial-like installments.

In the middle of the manuscript, word came that President Kennedy had been murdered in Dallas by a lone left-wing sympathizer of Cuba's Fidel Castro—a story I found incredible then and still do not believe.

In that shattering moment, the nation's hunger for the truth about the Kennedys, beginning with Old Joe who had masterminded and bankrolled the clan's drive to power, vanished and was replaced by an understandable but blindly emotional urge to memorialize the slain president and enfold him, his gallant widow, and his entire family in the media-spun haze of spurious legend.

Instead of my reporter's dream of confronting an incumbent president seeking reelection in 1964 with a rigorously factual account of his father's fortune- and dynasty-building, I faced the closed ranks of the Kennedys, their court historians, and their legions of media imitators, all now keepers of the myth of Camelot.

In the year of research and writing that followed the president's murder, I kept before me the same imperative that had guided me from the beginning: to respect my subject and tell the truth, in as fair and balanced a way as I could. While my publisher wavered in the emotional upheaval of the immediate post-assassination hysteria, the editors soon were full of fresh enthusiasm on reading my concluding chapters.

The book was published in November 1964. In a prefatory note, I attempted to strike a tone of sincere yet tactical modesty, declaring that "this narrative, the product of a journalist's independent inquiry, does not pretend to be definitive." The passage of three decades and the scrutiny of many scholars and critics, I'm pleased to say, have removed any need for disclaimers. This sturdy book stands up. While I could add new details to the story that have come to light since the book was first published, this is as close to the definitive account of Joseph Kennedy's life as we are likely to have until, one day, the closely guarded Kennedy family archives are opened unconditionally to scholars.

I can cite no less an authority than Rose Kennedy to support my conclusion. In her library in the family's Palm Beach mansion she kept a copy of *The Founding Father*, its margins filled with her handwritten notes and addenda to the narrative. She used the book to help in composing her own 1975 autobiography, *Times To Remember*, and over the years has shown the heavily annotated *Founding Father* to journalists who were granted interviews. It is not a boastful but strictly accurate statement about Joe Kennedy's tightly compartmentalized life to say that his wife and children doubtless learned much about him and his career, especially his business dealings, from *The Founding Father*.

Despite the vast proliferation of Kennedy literature, there is no evidence that the public's curiosity about the family is flagging. The more we comprehend the Kennedys, the more we know, for good or ill, about ourselves and twentieth-century America. In trying to understand who the Kennedys really are, the key lies in Joseph Kennedy, whose hungers fueled their rise and whose flaws perhaps caused their fall. Here he is.

Richard J. Whalen
Washington, D.C.
January 1993

Author's Note and Acknowledgments from 1964 Edition

This biography is the outgrowth of an assignment undertaken for *Fortune* during the summer of 1962. My editors proposed that I set down what was known, and what could be discovered, about Joseph P. Kennedy's remarkable life and career. The cooperation of my subject and his family was requested, but the requests went unanswered. Therefore, this narrative, the product of a journalist's independent inquiry, does not pretend to be definitive. I have merely attempted to tell, insofar as I could, a story that has gone untold too long.

In the chapter notes I have indicated my indebtedness to printed and manuscript sources. One debt that deserves special acknowledgment, on behalf of myself and others who have written about the Kennedys, is owed to Robert Cantwell, a colleague at Time Inc. It was Cantwell who wrote an unsigned profile of Kennedy, published in the September, 1937, issue of *Fortune,* which was for a quarter of a century the standard reference.

The story of much of Kennedy's life was unrecorded, and existed only in the recollections of widely dispersed associates and contemporaries. Scores of individuals generously assisted my research, among them several who had never before been interviewed. I wish to express my gratitude to the following: Miss Katherine Sullivan, Henry J. O'Meara, Max Levine, Raymond S. Wilkins, Ralph Lowell, Oscar Haussermann, Frank W. Buxton, Richard Babson, Joseph L. Merrill, Thomas G. Corcoran, Burton K. Wheeler, James A. Fayne, the late James M. Landis, Benjamin V. Cohen, James A. Farley, James F. Byrnes, Miss Gloria Swanson, Clarence A. Barnes, Robert G. Steinert, Stuart Webb, John Fox, Francis Currie, Albert Tegan, Mark Dalton, John C. Dowd, John Galvin, William C. Danforth, James G. Colbert, John B. Hynes, John J. Reynolds, Lawrence Dennis, Jeremiah Milbank, Sr., James F. Donovan, Theodore H. Streibert, and William McMasters. In addition, many persons assisted who, for one reason or another, cannot be named.

I am grateful for information and assistance provided by the following persons: Harry Elmer Barnes, William L. Langer, Julius W. Pratt, Charles C. Tansill, Tyler G. Kent, Raymond K. Price, Jr., Miss Ruth Mehrtens, Joseph F. Dinneen, William P. Loeb, William Duncliffe, Raymond Moley, John Chamberlain, George Bookman, Walter Trohan, and Mr. and Mrs. John Henry Cutler. I also wish to express my gratitude for the assistance of Howard B. Gotlieb, former Archivist of the Yale University Library, and Miss Elizabeth Drewry, Director of the Franklin D. Roosevelt Library. I am indebted to Charles B. Parsons and Mrs. George Rublee for permission to examine and quote from unpublished manuscript material. A similar courtesy was extended to me by Arthur Krock, who also suggested the title, *The Founding Father*.

I wish to thank my colleagues on *Fortune*, Max Ways and Louis Banks, for their valuable criticisms of the manuscript. I am especially grateful to Managing Editor Duncan Norton-Taylor for his patience, understanding, and support during this project. In the early stages of research, I was assisted by Miss Nancy Bryan and William J. Gill, both of whom unearthed original and important information. The Index was prepared by Charles W. Wiley. The task of checking the manuscript, under deadline pressure, was skillfully performed by Miss Tracy Tothill of New American Library. I am also grateful to David Brown of New American Library for his unfailing enthusiasm and encouragement.

The debt I owe to my wife, Joan Marie Whalen, is incalculable. For the better part of two years, she conducted research, typed manuscript, criticized drafts, ran down leads, corrected proofs, and somehow simultaneously cared for two small children and a home. Her sacrifice has improved every page of this book; the errors and shortcomings are mine.

Introduction

BY 1960, when John F. Kennedy became the Democratic party's presidential candidate, the Kennedy family had enjoyed several decades of favorable publicity. Joseph P. Kennedy, the family's proud father, had employed writers and public relations experts to furnish the country's leading magazines and newspapers with glowing stories and photographs about himself, his wife Rose, and their nine children. Jack Kennedy's heroism in the Second World War and his numerous political and literary achievements had also brought widespread attention to the family. The Kennedys seemed to be an American ideal: handsome, affluent, intelligent, courageous, loyal, and pious.

The elder Kennedy, it was widely known, had become wealthy at an early age and had enjoyed success in banking, the stock market, the movie industry, and in Washington. President Roosevelt had appointed him chairman of the Securities and Exchange Commission and the Maritime Commission, and had named him ambassador to the Court of St. James's.

To be sure, Joseph P. Kennedy had enemies. They complained about his ruthless business dealings, his isolationism, his hot temper, and his penchant for personal vengeance. He was rumored to have been a bootlegger during Prohibition and a stock market swindler before the Crash. There were stories of numerous marital infidelities. Politicians well understood that there were strings attached to the elder Kennedy's generous political contributions.

Still, the general public had a positive image of the Kennedys, including the *paterfamilias*. Good looks, talent, brains, money, character—they seemed to have it all.

Kennedy family members were highly active in Jack's political campaigns. In the 1940s and 1950s, thousands of Massachusetts citizens turned out at numerous public events to share the charm and energy of this extraordinary clan. By 1960 the Kennedys, including brother Bobby and Jack's wife Jacqueline, were at work nationally to win the White House.

A few insiders, like Harry Truman, Adlai Stevenson, and Eleanor Roosevelt, distrusted Jack Kennedy, considering him simply his father's puppet. They thought Joseph P. Kennedy excessively right wing and personally corrupt. But this resistance quickly dissipated after Jack's stunning victory at the Democratic Convention. Jack was said to be on his own, in every way, and had been for years. Partisans described the elder Kennedy as benign and retired. Jacqueline Kennedy had declared, ". . . actually, he's a nice old gentleman we see at Thanksgiving and Christmas."

Joseph P. Kennedy seldom appeared in the press during his son's presidential campaign. After the election, he stayed away from the White House. A severe stroke in December 1961 appeared to end whatever lingering influence he might have had on the chief executive.

Throughout the Thousand Days, all of the Kennedys enjoyed splendid relations with the media. In part this was due to the president's extraordinary manipulation of the press. The good looks and elegance of the president and his family also played a role.

The tempo of this national and international adulation was intensified greatly, of course, after the assassination. Soon, the myth of Camelot—a thousand days of grace, brilliance, courage, and character—became a staple of American history.

Joseph P. Kennedy's reputation as a wise and loving father, who encouraged but did not tamper with his son's ambitions, continued to be a component of Camelot hagiography. Historian Arthur Schlesinger, Jr., had the elder Kennedy asking Jack "why he wanted to take on the appalling burden of the presidency." Jack answered, "These things have always been done by men, and they can be done by men now."

Not everyone was taken in. In September 1963 conservative journalist Victor Lasky published *J.F.K.: The Man And The Myth*. Lasky described Jack as superficial, calculating, morally obtuse, and reckless. His father was portrayed as a ruthless, imperious, ambitious tyrant who had moulded his children "in his own image" and was entirely responsible for Jack's political campaigns and election victories. The book was weakened by its partisan tone and heavy reliance on secondary sources. It received largely hostile reviews and was withdrawn from print after the assassination.

In 1964, Richard J. Whalen published *The Founding Father: The Story of Joseph P. Kennedy*. It marked the beginning of serious, objective research on the Kennedys. Whalen had done extensive interviewing, worked in manuscript collections (although not the Joseph P. Kennedy Papers, which remain closed), and had consulted an impressive array of solid books, articles, and newspapers.

Whalen largely substantiated Lasky's thesis about the elder Kennedy, and his careful documentation and dispassionate approach proved so compelling that the book was a best-seller for seven months. Joseph P. Kennedy could now be seen more clearly than ever as he really was: extraordinarily interesting, complex, at times emotional, driven, insensitive, domineering, and unscrupulous.

Whalen shed much light on the elder Kennedy's business career, and described his political adventures in considerable detail. One of the most fascinating contributions of the study was the description of how the ambassador mercilessly schooled his youngsters to compete and to excel at all cost. The Kennedy children were an extension of their father's incredible ego and lust for power.

The myth of a tender and unobtrusive father was now exploded, along with the idea that Jack Kennedy had enjoyed more than a tiny measure of independence before his father's stroke. Whalen pointed to Joseph P. Kennedy's crucial and commanding presence in each of his son's political campaigns, observing that principle was of less importance in these contests than practically anyone realized. Evidence also appeared linking the elder Kennedy with numerous decisions, including the appointment of cabinet members, made during the first year of the Kennedy administration.

We now know a great deal more about the Kennedys and the Kennedy administration than we did in 1964. Dispassionate scholars have come to understand that the decades of Kennedy public relations efforts were deceiving; very little of the Camelot myth remains plausible. Joseph P. Kennedy seems more cynical, sinister, lecherous, and overweening than we suspected. JFK, for all his positive features, was the most reckless and morally bankrupt chief executive in our history. He was largely what his father made him.

Our new knowledge of Joseph P. Kennedy and his family has largely substantiated and amplified work done by Richard J. Whalen. The general picture presented in *The Founding Father* was accurate, fair, and responsible. The book is as fascinating to read today as it ever was.

For a clear understanding of the Kennedys, one must start with the dominant figure in the story. And Whalen's volume is the place to begin.

Thomas C. Reeves

BOOK I
THE OUTSIDER

The people, not the bosses, must rule. Bigger, Better, Busier Boston!

—*From a John F. Fitzgerald campaign poster in 1905*

Our present Mayor has the distinction of appointing more saloonkeepers and bartenders to public office than any previous mayor.

—*A clergyman, referring to Mayor Fitzgerald in 1906*

CHAPTER 1

Beachhead in a Hard Land

EXCEPT for the stiff westerly breeze whipping over the marshes of the Charles, the June afternoon was perfect. After a damp, depressing week, the warm sunshine lifted the spirits of the crowd streaming across the bright lawns toward the stadium. The young men in flowing academic gowns, Harvard's Class of 1911, had received their degrees the previous day under glowering skies. Now free of pomp and ceremony and well-wishing aunts, they returned the laughter of the girls on their arms, still aglow from last evening's parties. (The festive Harvard Yard had been the scene of an innovation: Japanese lanterns containing incandescent lights, rather than the traditional candles, had illuminated the canopied bandstands and sparkling fountains.) Swelling the crowd were backslapping old grads, sporting bright-hued bands on their straw hats. They fell into step with classmates and discussed with relish the prospect of Yale's humiliation. Harvard had defeated Yale at New Haven earlier in the week, and a victory today would mean the first Crimson sweep in the Class Day baseball series since 1903.[1]

The gentleman from the *Boston Evening Transcript,* aware that he was covering an event of utmost importance to Proper Bostonians, hurriedly scribbled the pregame story for page one of that afternoon's edition. The grandstand was filled well before two o'clock, and a large overflow crowd stood behind ropes in the outfield. The reporter estimated the attendance at fifteen thousand persons. Also worthy of prominence in his story was the starting pitcher for Harvard: Captain Charles B. (Chick) McLaughlin, playing the last game of his brilliant career.[2] As McLaughlin warmed up, few spectators noticed the rangy, red-haired player who took a seat near the end of the Harvard bench. But his unexpected appearance in uniform drew curious stares from the players. He had failed to make the team that spring, had not appeared at other games, and, so far as anyone knew, wasn't a member of the squad. Yet there he sat.[3]

This minor mystery was forgotten as the game began. Harvard jumped off to an early lead, scoring three runs, then Yale scored a run, but that was all McLaughlin would yield. Pitching smoothly, he set down the visitors inning after inning as volleys of cheers rang from the west grandstand.[4] The ninth inning opened with Harvard leading, 4–1. After retiring the first two Yale batters, McLaughlin turned to the umpire and asked for time. To the surprise of his teammates, he called the redhead from the bench and waved him to first base. The next Yale batter hit a grounder to the infield and was retired at first. As the Harvard team came off the field, McLaughlin, who had assured the last-minute first baseman of his coveted *H,* asked him for the game-winning ball. The substitute shook his head.

"I made the putout, didn't I?"

With that, Joe Kennedy stuck the ball in his pocket and walked away.[5]

The young man on the baseball diamond in Cambridge knew what he wanted. A half century later, the white-haired man in the sun-splashed inaugural grandstand in Washington, sturdy and erect in his seventy-third year, at last had what he wanted.

Wealth, power, and the chance of greatness for his name were the lifelong ambitions of Joseph Patrick Kennedy. The first two goals he achieved to an awesome degree; the last, which came fleetingly within his grasp, eluded him. But the sons he reared, enjoying advantages he provided, retrieved it. In a way that went deeper than ordinary parental pride, their success was his. For Joe Kennedy's children were an extension of himself; they carried his name into the future.

The thread of family also tied him to the past. Himself the son of a determined man in whom the progenitor's sense was strong, he stood between what the Kennedys had been and what they could become. He stepped from a circumscribed world and opened a limitless one to the next generation; yet he seemed always in midpassage, fired by old passions even as he seized new opportunities. He bore the indelible imprint of the time and place of his birth, and of the circumstances in which the Kennedys had started their climb in America.

The baseball letter at Harvard, sought so intensely and taken so coldly, was one prize in a lifetime spent in quest of success, a pursuit bound up with a grandfather he never knew, for whom success was the humble certainty of a full stomach.

The grandfather, Patrick Kennedy, was a tenant farmer, almost the only occupation in Ireland in the middle of the nineteenth century. A wild, beautiful land of cliff-hung coasts, rolling hills, and mist-covered lakes, Ireland was a conquered country and the Irish were perhaps the poorest and most backward people in Europe. Ireland existed to be exploited. The mercantilist design of the English rulers discouraged domestic trade and industry, and took Ireland's produce and livestock for English consumption. The money received was scarcely warm in Irish palms before it was returned to England in payment of cruelly high rents. The great majority of the twenty thousand landlords who owned most of Ireland were absentees;[6] and many, indifferent so long as remittances arrived promptly, passed their lives without once visiting their estates.[7] Aside from maintaining the one-sided trade, the only concern of Her Majesty's Government in Ireland was the maintenance of strong garrisons to check the constant threat of rebellion.

How neighboring Ireland existed, the reality of its daily life, was as much of a mystery to Victorian England as the economy of distant India, a state of ignorance which spared the sensibilities of gentlefolk. For the Irish peasant's windowless mud hut stank—from the manure pile at the entrance, the pig wallowing on the dirt floor, and the nightly crowding of unwashed bodies. His bed was the bare earth, his stove the peat fire, and his food the large, coarse "horse" potato or "lumper."

Wondrously cheap and easily cultivated, the potato was Ireland's universal food, eaten by man and beast alike.

Life was made bearable by the gregarious nature of the Irish, who found frequent excuses to summon the fiddler and dance merrily until daybreak. Or they gathered in the evening around a neighbor's fire to sip poteen, their illicit but plentiful whiskey, and hear the myths of heroism and romance burnished by the tongues of generations of storytellers. Irish women were famously chaste and early marriage was the rule, with the result that by 1845 Ireland's population may well have exceeded nine million persons.[8] Land was valued above gold. Small plots were divided and subdivided, until large families looked for their precarious subsistence to an acre or less of potatoes.

In 1845, a mysterious blight crossed the ocean from North America and the potato crop failed. It struck with dismaying swiftness, seeming to turn sound potatoes black and putrid in a single night. Without the potato, Ireland was destitute. Though the tenant and his family starved, the corn and grain standing untouched beside their ruined potato patch had to be sold to pay rent. Failure to pay in most cases meant merciless eviction and slow death wandering on the roads.

Famine fell upon Ireland like a shroud, closely followed by epidemics of typhus, cholera, and relapsing fever. Ill-prepared British civil servants, brave clergymen, charitable landlords, and such groups as the Society of Friends could do little to mitigate the catastrophe rooted in ancient poverty and misrule. Witnesses reported heartrending scenes: a mother, wasted to a scarecrow, begging the officials of an overcrowded poorhouse to take her children; whole villages torn down and their inhabitants driven into freezing weather by troops serving conscienceless landlords; emaciated figures who rose from the ditches along the coach roads and ran away like panic-stricken skeletons, crawling back later to wait for death to overtake them. Under the scourge of famine, disease, and rack-rent landlords, at least one million Irish peasants died between 1846 and 1849, at least one million more fled in desperation to North America, and an even larger number crossed the Irish Channel to Great Britain.[9]

The Kennedys endured. Their small holding, at Dunganstown, in County Wexford, lay in a corner of southeast Ireland that was prosperous by comparison with the prostrate south and west. Work for wages could be found there, a rare situation, and grain was purchased to replace the potato. But Wexford was compelled to pay dearly for its deliverance. Their rents hopelessly lost in the famine-stricken regions, the landlords turned the screw tighter on the tenants who survived. For Patrick Kennedy, twenty-five and the youngest of three sons, the prospect was bleak. Faced with the scarcity of land and fearfully high rents, he decided to emigrate. In October, 1848, he received the blessing of the priest from the church at Ballykelly, left the tiny, thatch-roofed cottage where he had been born, and followed the dirt track along the Barrow River down to the seaport of New Ross, six miles away.

Busier in its day than the port of Dublin, New Ross was a bustling town of fifteen thousand persons. Strangers filled the streets that fall, as emigrants carrying their possessions in bundles and wheelbarrows tramped to the quays and their ships. Patrick Kennedy undoubtedly paid the going price, the equivalent of about twenty dollars, and took steerage passage on a packet ship bound for Boston. His destination was a matter of indifference; the one hundred and fifty thousand Irish who sailed for America in 1848 were pursuing the glimmer of hope contained in the words often heard around the peat fire: "the States."

Payment of the passage money, a fortune in impoverished Ireland, permitted Patrick Kennedy to stake his life in a lottery that tens of thousands lost. Most of the vessels in the emigrant traffic were pitifully small, generally in the three-hundred-ton class.[10] The necessity for low fares ensured that the least seaworthy craft would be used, while the greed of the shipowners and the negligence of the British authorities ensured that the ships would be dangerously overcrowded. As the emigrant walked up the gangplank in New Ross, there was roughly one chance in three that he would not live to become an American citizen. The year before, more than thirty-eight thousand of the one hundred thousand Irish emigrants sailing in British bottoms to Canada had died before reaching their destination or soon afterward.[11] Rightly, the vessels hauling the outcasts of Ireland were called "coffin ships."

Spared the worst misfortunes in Dunganstown, Patrick Kennedy shared the frightful common lot during the slow voyage westward. Only in good weather were the emigrants allowed on deck, and then briefly. Most of the voyage was spent in the cramped space belowdecks, where a man could not stand without stooping. The law required shipowners to provide passengers with food, but the law was not enforced. Each emigrant carefully husbanded his own rations, aware that appeal to the captain in the event of shortage almost certainly would mean the surrender of all money and possessions. Water turned rank on the long passage, and could be gagged down only by adding steadily larger doses of vinegar to kill the odor. Unscrupulous shipowners sometimes saved a shilling or two by storing water in old wine casks, which made it undrinkable and condemned shiploads of parched men, women, and children to days and nights of torture. Sanitation was primitive; the reeking privies turned the atmosphere foul and choking. Disease dogged the fleeing Irish; the hasty medical examinations on the quay allowed the sick to slip aboard with the healthy and sent fever raging through the tight-packed holds. During rough weather, the passengers were imprisoned in the dark steerage for days on end; nerves rubbed raw, men erupted in murderous fights while women and children watched wide-eyed with terror. Worst of all was the plight of young, single women, denied all privacy and the prey of rapacious sailors.[12]

On their passage to the New World, requiring six weeks or longer, the Irish suffered a subhuman existence equaling in horror the dread middle passage of the African slave trade. Indeed, the Negro, as valuable property, probably fared better than the Irishman, who was looked upon as worthless chaff.

The circumstances of the first mass emigration to America cannot be drawn too starkly. In contrast to the adventurers, traders, religious dissenters, and land-seeking yeomen who preceded them across the Atlantic, the Irish for the most part were an uprooted peasantry, most of whom came from the poorest regions of the poorhouse of Europe. They were not drawn by visions of an exclusive tabernacle in the wilderness, or hopes of great riches, or the desire to possess vast empty prairies. They were driven by the elemental force of hunger. "There is a great many ill conveniences here," wrote a new arrival, "but no empty bellies."[13]

Rare was the Irishman who could describe the well-fed glory of America in his own hand. Seeking docility, the British had enforced illiteracy. Under the oppressive Penal Laws, dating from the seventeenth century, the Catholics of Ireland had been stripped of civil and religious rights, including the right to keep and attend schools. While these laws remained in force, generations of Irish, clinging to their faith, snatched what learning they could from schoolmasters who taught secretly in the fields and hedgerows. Although Patrick Kennedy possessed the skills of a farm laborer, he was as ill-prepared as the poorest wretch from the west of Ireland for entry into an advanced society. All the ordinary Irishman brought, really, was the strength of his back. Fortunately, it was enough. A young and expanding country, digging canals, building railroads, laying roads, and raising cities, needed the brute push of the Irish.

Kennedy toughness can be traced back to Patrick, who survived the crossing and stepped ashore on Noddle's Island, in East Boston, well enough to work. A small strip of land lying across a narrow arm of Boston Harbor, the island, until some fifteen years before Patrick's arrival, was probably the easternmost limit of the American frontier. Named for an early colonial settler, the island once had been the stamping ground of a notorious ne'er-do-well, Samuel Maverick, who mounted four large cannons to ward off Indians and hung a sign welcoming travelers. Riotous excesses in his public house and hospitality to escaped felons offended Puritan decorum. But Maverick was the first of the island's line of resourceful politicians: he calmed the elders' wrath, kept his wine-selling license, and even won the island for himself and his heirs, forever, in return for annual payment of a fat hog or forty shillings.[14] A skirmish during the Revolution won the island a measure of local fame, but it remained farmland, with only a tenant's dwelling, until 1833. The Cunard Line then fixed East Boston as the western terminus of its Liverpool run, and a syndicate of Boston land speculators, organized as the East Boston Company, began laying out streets and lots.

Wharf space, at a premium on the old Boston waterfront, attracted shipping and ship builders to the island. In 1845, Donald McKay arrived to build sleek clipper ships for the China and California trade; his yard became the most active in the country. An informal census of the island in 1849 counted more than nine thousand inhabitants, whose occupations ran chiefly to trades connected with the sea and ships.[15] Other industries sprang up, including a small sugar refinery and an iron foundry. With work available for the able-bodied, many emigrants ended their journey where they disembarked. Among those who stayed on the island and squeezed into the cheap boardinghouses huddled near the docks was Patrick Kennedy.

He found work as a cooper, a thriving trade, for most of the barrels held whiskey, and saloons multiplied with the influx of Irish. Accused, not unjustly, of being a drunken lot, the newcomers had cause to seek escape in cheap whiskey. As they emerged from the steerage, blinking in the sunlight, they were met by boardinghouse runners and contract labor bosses, who spoke disarmingly of the dear, old country as they herded the greenhorns to their downfall. Cheated by conniving countrymen, sweated by native employers who paid a laborer a dollar for a fourteen-hour day, the Irish were stupefied with exhaustion and constantly bewildered. Unaccustomed to buying food, they found the prices at the store incredibly high, and here there was no place to cultivate the potato or keep a pig. As numbers pressed against inadequate space, rents jumped and crowding worsened; one small, damp cellar sheltered thirty-nine souls each night.[16] Space to lie down in a stifling attic cost at least a dollar a week, in advance. A single noisome outhouse served scores of people, and filth and garbage rotted where it fell in the narrow alleys. Boston, a clean, healthy city that had not experienced a major epidemic of smallpox since 1792, suddenly found that it contained slums where the pox flourished, along with cholera, typhus, and tuberculosis.

Visiting the teeming Irish warrens in 1849, the Committee of Internal Health found horrifying conditions. "This whole district," the committee reported, "is a perfect hive of human beings, without comforts and mostly without common necessaries; in many cases, huddled together like brutes, without regard to sex or age, or sense of decency; grown men and women sleeping together in the same apartment, and sometimes wife and husband, brothers and sisters in the same bed. Under such circumstances, self-respect, forethought, all high and noble virtues soon die out, and sullen indifference and despair, or disorder, intemperance and utter degradation reign supreme."[17]

Clearly mingled in this account were compassion for the fellow creatures thus degraded and fear for the consequences of their being loosed upon a civilized society. Before the coming of the Irish, Boston was a city with little industry, a community of tradesmen, artisans, and merchants. Now it harbored a seemingly inexhaustible supply of men and women who accepted wages and working conditions that native labor scorned. They were a boon to capital, as witness the mills and factories rising on every hand. Yet the great alien mass dumped on the city's doorstep gave no sign of ever being ready to adopt the native's ways and enter the life of the community without wrecking it. Three hundred miles south, even larger numbers of Irish were being absorbed into rough and ready New York. There, newspaper editorials still complained of stray pigs attacking passersby on Broadway. But Boston was no melting-pot; its Anglo-Saxon culture was old and hard.

Still, for all its aloofness and pride of heritage, Boston was a seafaring city, whose ships were unlocking the riches of China, and foreigners who sought common ground with the natives were welcome. French, English, and German immigrants of this period, for instance, had little difficulty making a place for themselves. True, they trickled into Boston while the Irish came wave upon wave. Of the city's population of 136,881 in 1850, an estimated 35,000 were Irish, most of them recently landed.[18] But the difficulty did not lie in numbers only. What the other immigrants and the Bostonians held in common was an attitude toward the world, combining belief in the power of reason with acceptance of progress as both desirable and inevitable. Among the Irish, nothing in the experience of centuries gave cause for optimism concerning a man's chances on this mortal coil; he was subject to the mysterious forces of nature and the cruel whims of his overlords. Neither venturesome pioneers nor instinctive democrats, but stolidly conservative and superstitious after the timeless manner of peasants cut off from the world in which change occurs, the Irish clustered in their slums and turned inward, rejected by the native, to be sure, yet also rejecting a strange environment. Much of their antipathy arose from religious conviction, which the Catholic clergy bolstered with warnings against the wiles and wickedness of the Protestant. Concluded an editorial of the period in *The Pilot*, the voice of the hierarchy: "... cooperation for any length of time between *true* Catholics and *real* Protestants is morally impossible."*[19]

And so there came to exist in narrow Boston, as Oscar Handlin has written, "two distinct cultures ... with no more contact than if 3,000 miles of ocean rather than a wall of ideas stood between them."[20]

The clash of the native and the newcomer was bitter in such neighborhoods as the historic North End, a section of stately residences rapidly transformed into a slum. Conditions were better on the island where Patrick Kennedy had settled. An Irish contractor, Daniel Crowley, was one of the oldest residents, having built the third private

*Time produced a quite different spirit of tolerance. Commenting on the so-called "Catholic question" on April 9, 1960, *The Pilot* declared: "To proclaim the existence of a 'Catholic vote' readily stimulates the formation of a 'Protestant vote' —and all at once the community is divided strictly on religious lines.... This separation is a most unhappy one and does not in fact now exist."

dwelling. The mainspring of the development syndicate, William H. Sumner, paid tribute to the immigrants in a history of East Boston, praising the "adopted citizens . . . who, with strong arms and willing hearts, came to level the hills, fill up the lowlands, drain the marshes, erect docks and map the island with its pleasant wide and spacious streets and squares."[21] Promoter Sumner's idyllic rhetoric aside, life on the island was hard but tolerable. The Irish, finding reasonably steady work, scraped together the means to put down roots. Needing a church, they raised the considerable sum of five thousand dollars and bought the meetinghouse of the Maverick Congregational Society. When these quarters were outgrown, plans were made for a fine Gothic structure on the corner of Maverick and London streets, with a steeple nearly two hundred feet tall that would soar above the masts of the ships at the nearby wharves.

Meanwhile, the common ache of loneliness drew the Irish together, usually in the bright refuge of the corner saloon where they assembled of an evening to sing a song, dance a jig, tell a story, start a brawl, or quietly remember the indescribable shade of blue in the lakes of the sorely missed homeland. Raised in isolated villages and strangers on the voyage, they now shed mistrust in the forced intimacy of the city rookeries. They organized societies named for the counties they had come from, and transplanted the politics of Ireland, some of the political organizations being open and peaceful, others cloaked in secrecy and embracing physical force. A common consciousness began to evolve. A man from Mayo still would knock down anyone who disputed his boast that Mayo was best, but the neighbors across the way from Cork and Galway weren't really such a bad sort. They toiled as he did, lived in equally poor quarters, spoke with a reassuring brogue, went to the same church, and echoed his resentment of the Yankee who had succeeded the landlord as exploiter. Drawn to "their own kind" out of homesickness and shared affliction, the Irish became, self-consciously, the clannish "foreign element" of whom native Americans talked with mounting alarm.

These foreigners, taking a step fully as bold as their emigration, soon bound themselves to the new country. On small and uncertain wages, they married and raised large families. Among his friends, Patrick Kennedy met Bridget Murphy, a girl two years older than himself, whom he married. Three daughters were born to the Kennedys:

Mary, Margaret, and Johanna; and on January 8, 1858, a son, christened Patrick Joseph.

Children in the Irish slums, a Boston census taker sadly noted, seemed "literally born to die." More than 60 percent died before their fifth birthday in these years.[22] Neglect was rarely the cause, for Irish love of children was as strong as family loyalty. They died in spite of everything that overworked, impoverished parents could do. The Kennedy children survived, but Patrick Kennedy, worn out at thirty-five, succumbed to cholera less than a year after his son was born. He died as poor as when he landed in East Boston.

Left to support the family as best she could, Bridget Kennedy worked first in a small notions shop at the foot of Border Street, near the ferry landing; later she took a job as a hairdresser at Jordan Marsh in downtown Boston. Young Patrick, raised by his sisters, attended the neighborhood parochial school taught by the Sisters of Notre Dame. Irish efforts to organize parochial schools angered the natives, but the demand for separation was justified. The public-school curriculum reflected a powerful Protestant bias, teaching the youngster distrust of the Pope and the designs of Catholic Spain. The devoutly Catholic Irish kept their children away from the public schools as occasions of sin, a practice that lost its force spectacularly in succeeding generations. As a boy, Patrick helped his mother at the store each afternoon and on Saturdays. In his early teens, with money scarce at home, he left grammar school and went to work as a stevedore on East Boston's busy waterfront.[23]

Fair-skinned, blue-eyed, and well-muscled, Patrick Joseph Kennedy, or "P.J." as his friends called him, had the strength for heavy work, but not the disposition. The hard-drinking, brawling crew around him lived carelessly from day to day, but he rebelled at slipping into his father's life of aimless drudgery. Even after putting money into his mother's hand each week, he managed to save part of his wages. His deep, instinctive urge to get ahead was practically his only resource. A poor Irish youth with scant education, entering the Yankee-dominated commerce of Boston, could expect to begin and end sweeping floors, assuming he was hired at all. Newspaper advertisements often specified that only native Americans and Protestants need apply. Even the Negro, with an accepted place as a skilled laborer, faced less discrimination than the Irishman. Patrick Kennedy's opportunity to rise could come only within the immigrant community. As he worked and saved, he watched his chance.

Probably from his father's acquaintances in the whiskey trade, he learned of a saloon for sale in East Boston's Haymarket Square, and took it over on a shoestring. The quiet, self-possessed young man, working hard, made it a success. Year by year, he plowed back the profits, expanding into retail and wholesale whiskey distribution, eventually opening an office on High Street. He became a partner in two other saloons, one in the Maverick House, East Boston's finest hostelry since its opening in 1835, and the other opposite a shipyard, where the workers streamed in morning and evening for a drink and a bit of gossip.

Talk was the cheapest diversion known to the Irish poor. They babbled incessantly in the shops, on street corners, outside the church, around the kitchen stove—everywhere, but mainly and most animatedly where a man need not fear perishing of thirst. In the saloon, the club of the laboring class, the Irish, energetic organizers and joiners, caught up on the goings-on of the county societies, the religious and social clubs, the lodges and brotherhoods, the fire and militia companies. Always there was news from Ireland, and it was common to hear that the sums faithfully sent were at last enough for a younger brother's or sister's passage. An active Elk and a regular correspondent with his father's people in Wexford, Patrick Kennedy was unlike his neighbors in one respect: he preferred to listen. Though rarely seen lifting a glass containing anything stronger than lemonade, he stood behind the bar drinking in the endless conversation, absorbing names, occupations, and relationships, nodding at the liars and laughing with the jokers, becoming privy to the secrets, sorrows, and aspirations of the entire neighborhood.

Soon or late, the talk of the Irish turned to politics. During the generation after the great famine, their interest shifted from the remembered grievances of Ireland to more urgent concerns close at hand. Old arguments for repeal of the hated Act of Union joining Ireland with England drew respectful applause, but men won loud cheers when they declaimed on such issues as the necessity for free ferries to link East Boston with the mainland. Citizens now, many of them veterans who had fought with distinction under the emerald banner in the Civil War, the Irish saw the gaslit streets of Boston, and their own situation, through wiser eyes. Politics, promising a frolic, a fight, and perhaps a steady job, drew spirited Irishmen like the skirl of bagpipes; they flocked into the Democratic party, a tough band full of blarney and bold as brass. And Patrick Kennedy, sensing opportunity, led the way.

With his wide circle of acquaintances, the saloonkeeper came naturally to political influence. He knew the office seekers and their supporters, the conspirators and their intended victims, because caucuses were held and plots hatched on his premises. His advice was sought and carried weight, particularly because it was not lightly given. Reserved, even austere, an elegantly curled moustache completing the picture of dignity, Kennedy commanded respect. Just as he ran an orderly pub, so he kept at arm's length the ward heelers in derby hats and loud vests. A man who seldom raised his voice, he was not cast in the iron-fisted mold of Martin Lomasney, an orphan bootblack and onetime city lamplighter dubbed "the Mahatma" for his uncanny ability to marshal the electorate of Boston's Ward Eight. In shirt sleeves and battered straw hat, Lomasney received petitioners in his office—"the throne room"—each morning at nine o'clock, dispensing favors to the faithful and retribution to the strayed. Kennedy's style was less direct, but he and every other Irish boss of the period built their power on Lomasney's formula. "The great mass of the people," Lomasney used to say, "are interested in only three things—food, clothing and shelter."[24]

Kennedy strengthened his grip on the precincts of East Boston by running a pocket-sized welfare state. The Irish, suspicious of the charity of outsiders, expected and honored help from their own kind. The Irish worker was at most two weeks away from starvation; the man who found him a job, or helped him keep one, had the gratitude —and votes—of his family and friends. A round or two of free drinks, the loan of a few dollars before payday, a bucket of coal for the family whose breadwinner was laid off—such small gestures brought Kennedy a large and loyal following. He was elected to office by landslide majorities, first to the Massachusetts House of Representatives in 1886, then to the state Senate six years later.[25] But he disliked campaigning, could not make a speech, and had no appetite for office holding and public posturing. Why stammer through a speech when a word to his lieutenants could elect or defeat a candidate? With the clarity of the practical man, he saw that there was only one issue at stake in politics: who shall get what? His concern was with the substance of power.

Through the seventies and eighties, the Irish mass on Boston's doorstep stirred and groped upward. As prescient natives had feared, the weight of numbers was beginning to tell; the Irish, their birthrate high and their mortality rate declining, were fast approaching the point where they would make up half the city's population. The democratic doctrine of mass suffrage, and their control of the Democratic city machine, ensured ultimate success. Some Irishmen, notably the distinguished Patrick Collins, whom President Cleveland had appointed consul general in London, and who later became Mayor of Boston, tried to ward off a vengeful and discreditable Irish conquest of the city. "I love the land of my birth," said Collins in 1876, "but in American politics I know neither race, color nor creed. Let me say now that there are no Irish voters among us. There are Irish-born citizens like myself and there will be many more of us, but the moment the seal of the court was impressed upon our papers we ceased to be foreigners and became Americans."[26]

An admirer of Collins and a man disposed to reconciliation where it was possible, Patrick Kennedy was preeminently a realist: he cast his lot on the side of conquest. A member of the inner circle of power, popularly known as the Board of Strategy, he sat with like-minded men who doled out offices, jobs, and favors, wielding the Irish vote as a tool of their ambitions. Other bosses who gathered for the luncheon sessions of the Board of Strategy in Room 8 of the Quincy House, on Brattle Street near Scollay Square, included Joseph J. Corbett of Charlestown, James (Smiling Jim) Donovan of the South End, and a bantam rooster of a man, John F. (Honey Fitz) Fitzgerald, the dapper darling of the North End. Fitzgerald had been born in a tenement near the Old North Church in 1863, had gone to school under Lomasney (whom he called "my political godfather"),[27] and was unlike Patrick Kennedy in every way, except for a fierce will to succeed.

With the fortunes of many improving, the Irish were inspired to invent such classifications for themselves as "shanty," for the luckless, and "lace curtain," for the up and coming. Close questions of precedence were decided by the year (and even the month) of a parent's arrival, the "older" the family, the higher the rank.[28]

Patrick Kennedy had been courting pretty Mary Hickey, whose

family stood a rung or two above the Kennedys; but Kennedy, a state representative at twenty-eight, had only begun to climb. They were married in 1887, and on September 6 of the following year, their first child was born. He was named Joseph Patrick.

The first Irish Mayor of Boston, Hugh O'Brien, had been elected only three years before, and the Irish were whooping across the threshold to political power. But it soon was clear that the Yankee would not be easily overcome. He had, as it were, simply retired from the antechamber and double-locked the doors beyond, which, by reason of their peculiar construction, could not be forced. For Joseph Patrick Kennedy, life would center on the search for the key.

CHAPTER 2

P. J.'s Boy

A DOZEN YEARS before the turn of the century, East Boston was a quiet backwater of the city, which was itself slipping from the mainstream. The streets laid out with military precision by the engineers of the East Boston Company were built up with row upon dreary row of wooden houses, and echoed to the clatter of horse-drawn wagons and the high-pitched cries of pushcart peddlers. The street names had a quality of excitement that the drab scene lacked, for the Yankee speculators had not been unimaginative. Some names recalled stirring battles, such as Saratoga Street, site of the Atlantic Iron Works; others honored heroes, including, of course, New England's fierce-browed Daniel Webster. Along the waterfront were streets bearing seafaring names: Bremen, Havre, Hamburg, and Liverpool, remote and appropriate, for here foreign tongues predominated. The Irish still were in the majority in East Boston, but numbers of Italians, Slavs, Portuguese, and Jews were arriving and jostling for a place to set down their burdens.

The birth of Joseph Patrick Kennedy, in a modest frame house at

151 Meridian Street, not far from one of his father's saloons, doubtless caused a small ripple in the placid daily round. The Kennedys were a prominent family by now, and their newborn furnished a bit of neighborhood gossip to go with the news of the Law and Order League's crackdown on bootleggers, the opening of the new cyclorama, "The Battle of Bunker Hill," at the Tremont Street theater, and the latest development following the highly successful outing of Chelsea's Saint Rose parish: the Boston and Maine Rail Road had presented a bill for $31.27, covering seventeen broken windows and two couplings pulled loose when someone playfully set the brakes.[1]

Meridian Street, a busy thoroughfare, could not have appeared dull to a small boy: too many people and wagons passed; too many parades came tooting and drumming by, marking holidays and heralding elections. Enough Protestants remained on the island to muster a splendid Masonic procession, sending the Knights of Columbus into a flurry of activity, fluffing plumes and polishing swords in preparation for *their* next march in full regalia. And there were dark, cool shops up and down the street, with sawdust underfoot and tantalizing smells in the air—the clean fragrance of leather, the sweet aroma of fresh-baked bread.

Joe was the first of four children born to the Kennedys. Another son died in infancy, and there were two daughters, Loretta and Margaret. In the insular community, family ties were strong. A great event was a visit by Uncle Jim Hickey, a police captain in a neighborhood precinct, who was trailed up the street at a respectful distance by a gaggle of awestruck boys. He and uncles John Hickey, a doctor in nearby Winthrop, and Charles Hickey, mayor of Brockton, did a good job of spoiling their favorite nephew.[2]

Patrick Kennedy believed in tempering indulgence with firmness. A severe look from him was sufficient to quiet the children and enforce his absolute authority in the household. He was a family man who enjoyed simple pleasures, such as boating with a few friends on a Sunday afternoon. He rarely went out in the evening, except to an unavoidable political meeting or a fraternal gathering, and liked to sit reading, his spectacles pushed high on his forehead. After he finished the newspaper, he often reached for a book, usually about American history.[3]

By the depressed standard of East Boston, the Kennedys were affluent. But the absence of nagging concern with money, in the midst of poverty, only served to underscore for a perceptive youngster the *usefulness* of money, the lever by which a man, with better than average effort, could lift himself and his family. Within the fields of enterprise open to the son of immigrants, Patrick Kennedy moved astutely, investing the profits of saloon-keeping and whiskey-selling in such ventures as the Suffolk Coal Company and neighborhood banking. He helped organize the Columbia Trust Company in 1895 and the Sumner Savings Bank two years later.[4] Over the years he invested in a small way in local real estate, mainly vacant land, and took an occasional speculative flier in the stock of mining companies.[5] In steady, unspectacular fashion, Patrick Kennedy prospered. While Joe was a boy, the Kennedys left Meridian Street and moved up the hill to a four-story house at 165 Webster Street, overlooking the harbor.

Through his boyhood, Joe had before him the example of a determined man's ability to take the world as he found it and turn it to his own ends. A successful politician in an era of flagrant corruption, his father kept himself free of taint and was appointed to municipal office by Irish and Yankee mayors alike, serving as election, fire, and wire commissioners.[6] In contrast to "Honey Fitz," Pat Kennedy stayed in the background, aloof from the brazen fraud and vote-stealing, yet well-informed of the work of his lieutenants. One of Joe's earliest memories was the visit of a pair of ward heelers who reported proudly: "Pat, we voted one hundred and twenty-eight times today."[7] His father, then an election commissioner, was not displeased.

When civil war broke out among the Irish bosses, as it frequently did, the elder Kennedy first sought compromise, then waded into the fray. In 1898, Kennedy and the Board of Strategy battled Martin Lomasney for control of the city's Democratic nominating convention, which Kennedy packed up and removed to the Maverick House in his East Boston stronghold. Sharp-eyed sentries were posted at the approaches to East Boston to keep out Lomasney's delegates, but "the Mahatma" ordered his henchmen to dress in black, hired a hearse, and slipped through Kennedy's lines at the head of a "funeral" procession.[8]

Joe's boyhood was untroubled and uneventful. He came through a bout with diphtheria and grew tall and solidly muscled, with a temper to match his red hair. His father tried, unsuccessfully, to curb the youngster's pugnacity, while at the same time encouraging his powerful competitive urge. Most of Joe's friends came from poor families, and the pennies they could earn with odd jobs were needed at home. Patrick Kennedy watched with satisfaction as his son joined in the moneymaking scramble, not out of necessity, but out of a desire to excel in competition with his peers. Joe sold newspapers, worked in a haberdasher's, ran errands at the Columbia Trust, and even pocketed a few cents for lighting stoves and gaslights in the homes of Orthodox Jews on the Sabbath and holy days. When Dewey's fleet visited Boston Harbor after the Spanish-American War, friends of his father, who owned a sightseeing boat called *Excelsior*, hired Joe as a ticket taker. About all he gained from the job was a close-up look at the battleships; the way home on payday led past an irresistible candy counter at Lewis' store and he invariably arrived home filled with sweets, but penniless.[9]

Even so, a streak of shrewdness showed up early. Roast squab was a delicacy much admired in East Boston, and a chum, Ronan Grady, kept a coop. Pigeon-raising was slow work with a small flock; besides, the birds ate up most of the profits. Then young Grady took into partnership young Kennedy, who had a scheme to speed up matters. On a summer day, the boys would take birds from the coop, hide them under their shirts, and set off for Boston Common. With the birds struggling and tickling, the boys found transportation in the form of the slow-moving coal pungs, wagons drawn by two straining horses, which rumbled through the streets from the docks on Chelsea Creek toward the Boston ferry. Hopping on the rear of a long, flat coal pung, the free riders usually went undetected by the drowsing driver; in any event, they were well out of reach of his whip, a hazard on smaller, faster wagons. When they reached the Common, the boys released their birds among the wild pigeons and let nature take over. If all went well, at the coop that evening would be the two returning birds, plus two or more guests. Thus established on one of Boston's neglected resources, the boys' pigeon traffic thrived.[10]

When he was fifteen, Joe gave further evidence of moneymaking skill. In the pickup games on the mud flats, his ownership of the best baseball and bat had long upheld his claim to the captaincy. Now he organized a neighborhood team called The Assumptions, after the church the boys attended, and led a money-raising drive to buy smart white uniforms with a blue English-script *A* on the shirt and matching stockings. The Assumptions played a good game of baseball and drew surprisingly large crowds—so large that the freckled teen-ager at first base saw the possibility of making a good thing pay. He called on the owner of an enclosed ball park on Locust Street and boldly hired it. Thereafter, The Assumptions sold enough tickets to show a profit on the season.[11]

"The measure of a man's success in life," Joe Kennedy once remarked, "is not the money he's made. It's the kind of family he has raised. In that I've been mighty lucky."[12] Luck had little to do with Kennedy's success as a parent, which commanded the respect and admiration of even his bitter enemies. A decisive influence, probably, was the example of his own father. Pat Kennedy, like every good parent, showed keen interest in his son's development; in addition, he managed the rarer feat of conveying his interest to his son. Joe sensed his father's support and involvement in everything he did. Life, he came to understand, was a joint venture between one generation and the next.

Just as he moved his family away from the mud flats to the fine house on Webster Street, so Patrick Kennedy decided early to set his son apart from the run of fellow Irishmen. After having attended Assumption School and then Xaverian School, both Catholic institutions, Joe deliberately was thrown into the company of the Protestants of the West Side and the regions of the Back Bay. He was enrolled at Boston Latin School, where the sons of New England's leading families had been educated since 1635. The school's illustrious alumni included Cotton Mather, five signers of the Declaration of Independence (Adams, Franklin, Hancock, Hooper, Paine), Ralph Waldo Emerson, Charles Sumner, Henry Adams, Charles Francis Adams, and George Santayana. The school did not close its doors to the humbly born; John F. Fitzgerald had graduated with the Class of 1884. Though difficult, Boston Latin offered an avenue to acceptance. Early each morning, Joe ran to catch the North Ferry, which carried him across the ship canal for a penny, then dashed to the old Warren Avenue building, where the boy knew he was expected to compete hard for a place in the society that had been closed to his father.[13]

Then as now one of the best preparatory schools in the country, Boston Latin rigorously upheld its tradition of scholarship. Joe entered the school in 1901, one of seventy-one members of the sixth class. He was a poor student, frequently reprimanded for his indifferent performance in the classroom by Headmaster Arthur Irving Fiske, a frail, scholarly classicist who was hailed in his day as the greatest teacher of Greek in New England.[14] But Joe's winning smile and earnest promises usually enabled him to get around Mr. Fiske. The single bright spot in his academic record was in mathematics, a subject that came alive for him under the inspired instruction of Patrick T. Campbell, who patiently disciplined the boy's natural aptitude. (Campbell later became superintendent of Boston's schools, and Kennedy, embarked on a career requiring skill with large sums, occasionally sought the advice of his old teacher and friend.)[15]

An engaging personality was no substitute for passing grades, however, and Kennedy was forced to remain behind at Boston Latin for a year after his original class was graduated, making up his deficiencies.[16] Still, it was no small accomplishment, as he later saw it, to stay in this fast intellectual company at all. At the school's Tercentenary Dinner in 1935, Kennedy said in a nostalgic, self-revealing speech: "To strangers I could not possibly convey the reasons for the powerful and sweet hold which the School has upon my affections. It would be like trying to explain to strangers why I love my family.... The Latin School as we know it was a shrine that somehow seemed to make us all feel that if we could stick it out at the Latin School, we were made of just a little better stuff than the rest of the fellows of our own age who were attending what we always thought were easier schools.... Headmaster Fiske was not the strict disciplinarian and the dry-as-dust scholar we have always pictured him; he had a human side as well."[17]

From the first, the tall, slim, red-haired Kennedy made friends easily and was one of the most popular boys in his class. When he became colonel of the Latin School's cadet regiment and led it to victory in city-wide drill competition, he was the hero of the school's six-hundred-odd student body. As a senior, he was elected president of the class. He plunged into athletics, playing on the basketball team three years and managing the football team. But baseball was his consuming passion. Curiously, during a lifetime of high achievement marked by many honors, Kennedy always remained inordinately proud of his schoolboy baseball exploits, as though the role he loved best was captain of the nine. Decades later, he recalled games in perfect detail and would replay the highlights at the slightest hint of a listener's interest. He was a member of the Latin School team for four years and was the captain for two, a distinction that caused as much comment in East Boston as the cadet trophy and the class presidency.

A contemporary remembered Kennedy as a whole-souled competitor and a poor loser. "The first time I saw Joe was in 1907, when he was playing first base for Boston Latin against Salem High on the Bridge Street grounds in Salem. Boston Latin was losing and the game was almost spoiled by Joe's constant bickering with the umpire. I can still see him, glaring at the umpire and slamming his fist in his glove."[18]

He was a savage line-drive hitter. With an assist or two from the home-bench scorer, he made two hits in every three appearances at the plate in his senior year for a phenomenal .667 average, winning the Mayor's Cup for batting in the city high school league. The mayor was John F. Fitzgerald, who kept a closet stocked with trophies to award on any occasion likely to be attended by a newspaper photographer. This penchant for self-advertisement was one of several qualities about Fitzgerald that annoyed Pat Kennedy, who privately characterized his sometime ally as insufferable. But, on the day of the award to his son, the beaming elder Kennedy forgave "Honey Fitz" his camera smile.

The editors of the 1908 yearbook at Boston Latin tactfully predicted that Joe Kennedy, a good fellow with a mediocre academic record, would make his fortune "in a very roundabout way."[19] The twists and turns would come later. Now his first steps were as direct as the ambitions of Patrick and Mary Kennedy could devise. Joe would surely go on to college. Once again, however, his path would be different. Few Irishmen could afford to attend college in those days, and most of those who did went to the Jesuits of Boston College or Holy Cross, for the Church frowned on secular education. While the Kennedys were devout Catholics, they wanted something for their son that the Jesuits could not provide. Let the Church frown and the neighbors gossip: Joe would enroll at Harvard.

Although physically outside the city in neighboring Cambridge, Harvard stood at the center of the small world of Boston, as much a part of the inheritance of the leading families as the trust funds established by their grandfathers. Harvard, if one was so disposed, could provide an education; but the true function of the college on the Charles was to serve as the vestibule through which young gentlemen entered Society. Generation after generation of prominent Bostonians attended Harvard, as Henry Adams wrote, "because their friends went there, and the College was their ideal of social self-respect."[20]

Until the early years of the nineteenth century, as Cleveland Amory recounted in *The Proper Bostonians,* there was no nonsense about what Harvard was intended to do. Upon enrolling, each student was ranked by the president according to his family's social standing; in this scrupulously observed order, the undergraduates for the next four years marched in procession, sat in chapel, recited in the classroom, and served themselves at the table.[21] This official caste system, permitted to lapse mainly because of bothersome complaints from parents who felt undervalued, was succeeded by equally rigid, if less obvious, means of sorting young men according to who their grandfathers were.

For the grandson of an immigrant and the heir of a saloonkeeper, Harvard could be a hard experience. There would be no crude discrimination of the bullying sort, but a subtle, cruel exclusion, to remind one that he was an intruder in a place to which others were born. While a few liberal spirits did press for a democracy of talent at Harvard, the sprinkling of Irish and the few Jews in Kennedy's Class of 1912 were grudging concessions to the weight of numbers. In the matters that intimately concerned old Bostonians, change came slowly, and some things never changed. Also slow to change was the old Irish attitude of suspicion and enmity carried over from the days of the immigration. His Eminence William Cardinal O'Connell, Archbishop of Boston, sternly discouraged Catholic young men from straying into the groves of Protestant Harvard. Thus Kennedy was doubly an outsider at Harvard, by choice and by circumstance. But a tough-fibered young man with a streak of cynicism might console himself with the thought that Harvard and the Irish wards of Boston, in a sense, were not so different after all. Each was controlled by a self-perpetuating oligarchy.

Kennedy, by his own later account, did "all right" at Harvard,[22] receiving passable grades as he concentrated in history and economics. His main interest, as at Boston Latin, was in making the grade socially. Unlike others in the Irish minority, who commuted to Cambridge each day by trolley and took little part in college life, Kennedy lived in the Harvard Yard and made it a point to meet the leading undergraduates. He did not depend on his personality to attract them but instead determinedly sought out and cultivated such popular classmates as Bob Fisher, the widely admired football All-American, and Bob Potter, the scion of an old Philadelphia family, a varsity athlete, and a member of Porcellian. Fisher was particularly helpful to Kennedy. They roomed together at Hollis House in his senior year. ("I think right there that we had an indication that Joe was ambitious," said a classmate long afterward, "because when he picked his roommates he was satisfied with nothing less than the best.")[23] Fisher gave him a model of self-respecting behavior in the company of young Brahmins. He reminded Kennedy, who was not always comfortable, that he was always being watched for any lapse that would justify the anti-Irish prejudice of snobbish classmates.[24]

Kennedy was, of course, ineligible for the "best" undergraduate clubs, such as Porcellian, A.D., and Fly, but then so were all but a relative handful of his classmates, those who had attended the "right" Episcopal prep schools. Club spotters, surveying the freshman crop, considered not only a young man's religion, but also his family's wealth, which must have been amassed in the right way, at the right time. While Kennedy was in Cambridge, one of the wealthiest young men in New York entered Harvard, established himself and his valet in an apartment at a fashionable address, and confidently awaited the emissaries of "Porc" and Fly. Still waiting almost a year later, he withdrew from Harvard and beat a retreat to New York, where new money meant something socially.[25] A Brahmin would have adjudged Kennedy a social success for an Irishman—although Kennedy would have resented the condescension. He was elected to Hasty Pudding–Institute of 1770, and had the distinction of being "Dickey," that is, one of the first forty-five sophomores chosen. The Pudding, although it had a clubhouse and staged a musical comedy each year at Easter, was mainly a proving ground for the "final" clubs. Kennedy's final club was DU, which he made unfashionably late, in his senior year, but in interesting company: his pledge class included humorist Robert Benchley and industrialist Clarence B. Randall.[26]

While he held his own socially at Harvard, he took fun where he found it. He became friendly with other Irish youths in his class, including the witty Tom Campbell and the varsity baseball player Arthur Kelly. He went with his cronies to parties and to enjoy Harry Lauder from the balcony at the Keith. "They were great for musical comedies," Joe's sister, Margaret, later recalled. "They used to go into Boston to see shows like 'The Pink Lady,' with Hazel Dawn, and then they'd pick up the sheet music and come over to our house. Usually, my sister Loretta would play the piano, and they would all gather 'round and sing all the tunes."[27]

With his good looks and grace on the dance floor, Joe made a hit among the Irish young ladies. When it was especially necessary to make a good impression, he hired a stylish rig from Fitzgerald's livery stable. During these years, Kennedy discovered an unsuspected love of good music when a classmate from New York initiated him into the old Boston ritual of the symphony concert on Friday afternoon. Later on, only a few intimate friends would know he liked to relax with his large collection of classical records. It was as though he feared that an admission of refined taste would endanger his reputation for toughness.

Ironically, the hardest blow of Kennedy's Harvard years came on the baseball diamond, where the democracy of talent was strongest. The former Boston Latin star made the freshman team with little difficulty, but in his sophomore and junior years, he could not win a place on the varsity. By way of explanation years later, Kennedy said he threw out his arm in a game against Navy;[28] he also left the impression that a big-league career had beckoned until his mishap. Other players and classmates have a somewhat different recollection. Actually, they recall, Kennedy was slow afoot and his batting eye deserted him. He was bested at first base by "Chick" McLaughlin, who later became a pitcher and, of course, captain of the team. His pride smarting, Kennedy took the setback badly and showed open resentment toward McLaughlin.[29]

Surprisingly, however, McLaughlin asked the coach to put Kennedy in the 1911 Yale game for the final play, thus assuring him of a varsity letter he had done nothing to earn. About a year after the puzzling incident, a teammate asked McLaughlin why he had treated his sworn enemy so generously. Shamefacedly, McLaughlin said perhaps he had done the wrong thing. A few days before the game, he said, some friends of Joe's father had come to see him. They knew he intended to apply for a license to operate a movie theater when he was graduated from Harvard that June. If McLaughlin wanted the license, they clearly implied, he had better see that young Kennedy won his letter.

Said the former Harvard player to whom McLaughlin related the story: "Joe was the kind of guy who, if he wanted something bad enough, would get it, and he didn't much care how he got it. He'd run right over anybody."[30]

The summer of 1911 promised to be a lonely one for Kennedy. Mayor Fitzgerald was making a grand tour of Europe; more important, he had taken along his daughter Rose. Joe and Rose met as children when "Honey Fitz" brought his daughter along on his visits to East Boston. But the friendship between Pat Kennedy and "Honey Fitz" was motivated by political rather than social considerations. When Joe, while at Boston Latin, dated the mayor's daughter, who attended Dorchester High, both kept the fact quiet. A romance slowly blossomed, which Rose's father suspected and disapproved of.

"Honey Fitz's" distaste for the idea of having Joe Kennedy as a son-in-law was explained by the rising prestige of the Fitzgeralds in the Irish community. In the mayoralty contest of 1910, the beleagured Yankees had rallied around formidable James Jackson Storrow, a millionaire investment banker; whereupon the Irish bosses, accepting the challenge to a showdown, shelved their quarrels and united behind Fitzgerald. His victory over Storrow, the best the Yankees could offer, gave "Honey Fitz" new stature.[31] In January, 1911, slim, vivacious Rose, exquisitely gowned, made her debut at a glittering party attended by more than four hundred guests. She was the belle of Irish Boston. With an eye to fortifying his family's social position, Fitzgerald had selected a suitable European convent school for Rose and her sister, Agnes. When the time came, he expected to be consulted on the subject of a suitable husband. Joe Kennedy was not in the running, so far as "Honey Fitz" was concerned, but the mayor was seen to smile with fatherly affection on another of Rose's suitors: Hugh Nawn, the son of Harry Nawn, a wealthy contractor and treasurer of the Democratic City Committee. The Nawns lived in a mansion in Dorchester, not far from the Fitzgeralds. After a night of campaigning, "Honey Fitz" liked to sit in their kitchen talking and eating peanut butter sandwiches.[32] By the happiest of coincidences, young Nawn, a Harvard man, was planning to be in Europe that summer; the mayor would see that the paths of the young people crossed.

Meanwhile, Joe Kennedy, moping around his family's new home in Winthrop, received an invitation to play for the Bethlehem, New Hampshire, baseball team in the White Mountain League, composed of college players representing hotels in Maine and New Hampshire. After a bit of coaxing, he signed up for the ten-week season, along with a Harvard classmate, John Conley. They arranged to meet the manager, a young Bostonian named Henry J. (Harry) O'Meara, on the night boat to Portland. To protect their status as amateurs, the collegians received only room and board, as well as the chance for a little social life. On the boat, Kennedy asked O'Meara if there might not be some way to make money in the mountains. There was indeed: the *Boston Globe* wanted a "stringer" to report social news and baseball, golf, and tennis scores. An enterprising stringer, O'Meara added, could make as much as thirty dollars a week. Kennedy's eyes lighted up. Was the job taken?

"You've got it," said O'Meara.

Kennedy found Conley standing at the rail and reported his new sideline. Conley was impressed, not so much by the money as by the thought of writing for a newspaper.

"Gee, I love to write," he said. "I wish I had that job."

"You've got it," replied Kennedy. "All I'm interested in is the money."[33]

During the summer, Conley filed dispatches to the *Globe,* signed with Kennedy's name, while his friend pocketed the money. Conley did such an acceptable job that O'Meara received a letter from an editor on the *Globe,* inquiring if that able correspondent "Kennedy" would be interested in joining the staff.[34]

The players on the Bethlehem team were put up at the hotels in town, with the manager assigned to the Uplands, the most expensive place, and so on down through the squad. Kennedy stood high in the pecking order and his hotel was comfortable, but it wasn't the Uplands. Unhappy with less than the best, he waited a week or so, then persuaded O'Meara to lay this argument before the management of the Uplands: if each hotel boarded a player, how was the best hotel to distinguish itself, except by taking *two* members of the team? The gambit succeeded, and Kennedy moved in. Through the summer, he spent his free time mingling with the socially prominent guests, meeting people whose friendship could be useful.[35] When he teamed up with a well-known doctor to win a tennis doubles championship, Kennedy became an item in his ghost-writer's roundup for the *Globe.*

Unfailingly intent on his chances, Kennedy did not charm everyone he encountered. Some recoiled: a young man could have too much push. Among his teammates, Kennedy was wisecracking, profane, a rough competitor. But friends were surprised—and attracted—by what they saw when he let his guard down. He took his religious duties seriously. Attendance at Mass, particularly on a holy day, was difficult because the Catholic church was several miles from Bethlehem, a fact some of the boys on the team were willing to use as an excuse for staying in bed. On August 15, Feast of the Assumption, Kennedy rose early, routed out his sleepy and complaining friends, and packed them aboard a buggy he had hired for the ride to church.[36]

In his final year at Harvard, Kennedy briefly enjoyed club life, landed a paying job as coach of the freshman baseball team, and did little to redeem his academic record. Great teachers such as Bliss Perry and Charles Copeland won his admiration; he was flattered when "Copey" came by his room and invited him to attend his famous readings. But theory held little fascination for Kennedy. As a financier, he would one day penetrate the mysteries of a balance sheet in a moment's study; but as an undergraduate he could not cope with a course in accounting and was forced to drop out before he failed.[37] His interest ran to tangible, practical things, like money. In this department, his extracurricular performance was superlative.

While riding on a bus one day, he learned from the driver that the vehicle was for sale, cheap. Kennedy and Joe Donovan, a friend from Boston Latin and Harvard, bought the bus for six hundred dollars and went into the tourist business. Decked out in black-visored caps, Donovan sat at the wheel and Kennedy, barking through a megaphone, rounded up sightseers and reeled off a glib spiel on the historic landmarks of Boston, Concord, and Lexington. Business was good, but the partners knew it would be even better if they could operate from the choice location outside South Station.

A Cambridge bus owner held the license there. After much wire-pulling, Kennedy was granted a license permitting him to share South Station, on terms to be arranged with his competitor. When they met, Kennedy flashed a broad smile, thanked him warmly for being such a good fellow, and said he would settle for only four hours a day at South Station. Which hours? Kennedy replied that he wanted only 10 A.M. to noon, and 2 P.M. to 4 P.M. This request for a near monopoly sent the other fellow scurrying to the authorities. A compromise was worked out giving the rival buses alternate hours. It wasn't all Kennedy wanted, but he was satisfied to have more than he started with.[38] Over several summers as bus operators, he and Donovan each cleared a profit of five thousand dollars.

Regardless of what had been withheld, Kennedy, on his graduation from Harvard, realized he had gained something of value. The importance of being a Harvard man was summed up in the comment of a nineteenth-century Yankee, Edmund Quincy, whose father had been president of the college. "If a man's in there," Quincy used to say, tapping his Harvard Triennial Catalogue, containing a complete list of Harvard graduates, "that's who he is. If he's not, who is he?"[39]

Though still a trespasser in unyielding Yankee Boston, Kennedy could no longer be dismissed as a stranger.

CHAPTER 3

Young Man in a Hurry

Emerging from Harvard in June, 1912, Joe Kennedy entered an awesomely self-satisfied city, hardened in a mold the first families found perfect and meant to preserve against all change. To the Proper Bostonian, one's great-grandfather was more interesting than oneself. And the Hub, as the popular name implied, was unquestionably the center of the universe. ("Why should I travel?" demanded the Boston matron. "I'm already here.")[1] Little heed was paid to the dissenters, even to Charles Francis Adams, the leading Bostonian of his day, who sadly observed there was "no current of fresh outside life everlastingly flowing in and passing out."[2] In the mansions on the water side of Beacon Street and the brownstones along broad Commonwealth Avenue, the tall windows were shut tight and the heavy drapes drawn. In the banks and counting rooms downtown, the creak of old leather chairs had its echo in minds stuffed with old ideas.

Visiting in 1906, H. G. Wells found the city as beautiful, and as barren, as the Common at daybreak. "There broods over the real Boston an immense effect of finality,"[3] he wrote. "The capacity of Boston, it would seem, was just sufficient but no more than sufficient, to comprehend the whole achievement of the human intellect up, let us say, to the year 1875 A.D. Then an equilibrium was established. At or about that year Boston filled up."[4]

The English visitor chose his date well. Sometime in the final quarter of the nineteenth century Boston knew with chill certainty that its reign as the nation's financial center was ended, that it had been dethroned by the rising money power of New York. Its intellectual genius, culminating in the generation of Emerson and lingering through the long twilight of Holmes, had sprung from the less noble but indispensable genius for finding new ways of making money. When that genius waned, the city declined. It became the preserve of decent, unimaginative men who ate their oatmeal every morning though they hated it, who carried their umbrellas if a single cloud appeared in the sky, and who walked firmly in the footsteps of their fathers to oversee the wealth accumulated by their grandfathers.

From the Revolutionary War to the Civil War, Boston was quick with life, the period of greatest vitality coming just at mid-century. Stern, hard-fisted Down East men streamed into the city, each intent on gaining and getting. From their ranks rose the adventurous sea captains and daring merchant princes who founded great fortunes and families. The archetype of this breed was Colonel Thomas Handasyd Perkins. The son of a wine merchant, he grew so rich and powerful that he declined to be Secretary of the Navy under President Washington, explaining that his merchant fleet was larger than the infant Republic's navy and required his attention.[5] A number of ultra-respectable Boston families owed their lofty station to ancestors who had prospered in the triangular trade, shipping rum to Africa, slaves to the West Indies, and molasses back to Boston for the manufacture of more rum. In 1784, the full-rigged *Empress of China,* loaded with ginseng root, sailed from New York to Canton and opened the "China trade."[6] Ships from Boston followed, winning riches for men with bristling side-whiskers and gold buttons on their frock coats whose counting rooms overlooked India Wharf and Commercial Wharf. Between 1810 and 1840, nearly half of America's commerce with China was handled by the Boston firm of Bryant and Sturgis.

At the same time, the sons of farmers and small merchants were deserting to the crude factories that sprang up along New England's streams and rivers. In a generation of prodigious effort, they became lords of the loom, their realm extending from Maine to Rhode Island. These textile barons, who made their homes and kept their money in Boston, left their names on such towns as Lawrence and Lowell. By the 1850's, they had brought within their grasp one-quarter of the nation's cotton spindleage. From the banks of Boston, controlled by perhaps twenty families, came the capital for canals and railroads.[7] Later, as the yeomanry of New England pushed the frontier westward, money from Boston followed, opening mines, laying rails, building towns.

The vigorous fortune builders, distrusting the abilities of their heirs, habitually locked up their wealth through stern wills and spendthrift-proof trusts. Enterprise was succeeded by guardianship. Boston's best brains and energies gradually shifted from commerce, manufacturing, and speculation to banking, insurance, and conservative investment. The descendants of men like John Murray Forbes, the youngest ship's master in the China trade, the agent for the fabulous Canton merchant Houqua, and nearly a millionaire by his twentieth birthday, passed in sober file on the well-worn path from Harvard to State Street, along with generations of Lowells, Cabots, Peabodys, Perkinses, Lodges, Higginsons, and, albeit under protest, Adamses. From portraits over polished mantels the family founders, aglow with the creator's instinct, looked down on a cold, sterile, finished society.

For an aspiring Yankee who arrived in Boston much after the Civil War, the upper reaches of society were virtually closed. For an Irishman who came on the scene a generation or two later, the situation was hopeless. Money might be made, but money in itself meant little. Everyone's place had been decided long ago.

"Coming of age in Boston," said a thoughtful friend, "Joe Kennedy saw early what made the power and gentility he wanted. It wasn't talent; it was ancient riches. Power came from money. Joe had a keen mind, and it was honed against the great cynicisms underlying rank and station in Brahmin Boston."[8]

"You have plenty of Irish depositors," remarked Mayor Fitzgerald to a Boston bank president one day. "Why don't you have some Irishmen on your board of directors?"

"Well," said the banker, "a couple of the tellers are Irish."

"Yes," replied the Mayor, "and I suppose the charwomen are, too."[9]

The leading profession in a city of trust-encrusted wealth, banking was the predestined career of many of Kennedy's Harvard classmates. He decided to make it his career, too, but realized a direct approach would fail against minds closed as firmly as great steel bank shutters. His first step was an indirect, carefully measured one. Using the influence of his father and others to hasten his appointment, he passed a qualifying examination and became a state bank examiner at a salary of fifteen hundred dollars a year. The salary was unattractive and the hours were long, but the year and a half he spent traveling throughout eastern Massachusetts, poring over other people's ledgers, was richly rewarding. One who passed easily from Harvard into banking, Ralph Lowell, chairman of the Boston Safe Deposit and Trust Company, later reflected on what his classmate gained along his harder road. "That bank examiner's job laid bare to Joe the condition of every bank he visited, and what he learned about the structure and securities of state banks was valuable to himself—and to others."[10]

Life wasn't all toil in the counting room. Taking his close friends from among the up-and-coming Irish, as he would throughout his career, Kennedy pursued the pleasures available to a young bachelor with money in his pocket. In the summer of 1913, he made his first trip to Europe, sailing aboard a new German liner with a group of friends including Joseph L. Merrill and John L. Hannon from Harvard. Kennedy was a born organizer. Anxious not to appear unknowing, he talked with friends and acquaintances who had been to Europe, learning the ropes of ocean travel, noting the places to go and the people to meet, filling his pockets with letters of introduction. From the moment he stepped aboard the ship, his companions were kept jumping with a stream of confident instructions.

The first day out, he told them to get on deck early and see to the deck chairs, adding that he would be along later. When Kennedy failed to appear, his friends went in search of him. Passing an open door, they heard his voice. There he sat, feet propped on a desk, cracking jokes with the purser. Kennedy spotted his friends, excused himself, and told them: "I've got us a great deal." It seemed the ship's Imperial Suite was empty, and he had cajoled the purser into letting them have it for only fifty dollars each above their first-class passage.

But Merrill and Hannon, budgeting for a big splash in Europe, didn't care especially how they got there, and they turned down the bargain. Kennedy's face fell, and he stalked off. His friends returned to their deck chairs. A few minutes later, however, they looked up to see Kennedy striding along the deck, his smile restored, with the purser in tow. Now, he told them, the Imperial Suite could be enjoyed for one hundred dollars, only thirty-three dollars apiece—and he would toss in the odd dollar. That settled it; there was nothing to do but travel to Europe like kings.[11]

Kennedy and his friends toured Germany and France, and found use for his introductory letters, but an incident in Paris showed Kennedy's talent for managing his own introductions. The three Harvard men ran into friends from Yale, one of whom knew Nili Devi, a leading dancer at the Folies Bergere. Joining forces, the college boys were her guests at the Folies, and later escorted her to the Dead Rat, a Left Bank nightclub and haunt of celebrities. The proprietor begged her to dance; she agreed on the condition that other notables in the audience also would entertain. John (Jack) Johnson, the heavyweight boxing champion, followed her into the spotlight and took a turn at the bass fiddle. As the party picked up, waiters passed out small Celluloid balls and the guests happily pelted each other. Seated at a nearby table, the strapping Johnson offered a tempting target, and Kennedy playfully bounced a ball off the Negro fighter's head. Johnson turned around, stared for a moment, then broke into a grin. Kennedy went over and introduced himself. A few minutes later, while his companions watched enviously, he was gliding across the dance floor with Mrs. Johnson, the beautiful white actress Lucille Cameron. When he returned to his table, he casually displayed the champion's card, inscribed: "To Joe Kennedy, a fine fellow."[12]

The day before his departure from Boston, Kennedy had invested one thousand dollars for a one-third interest in the Old Colony Realty Associates, Inc., an investment company organized by Harry O'Meara, the former manager of the Bethlehem baseball team. Because he had a knack for laying his hands on money, the fledgling banker was elected treasurer of the company. On his return from his month-long European vacation, he walked in on O'Meara and asked if Old Colony had made any money while he was away.

"Yes," O'Meara said curtly. "Just about enough to pay for your trip."[13]

Taking the hint, Kennedy became a working partner and helped make Old Colony a success. The company profited by nimbly capitalizing on the mistakes and misfortunes of others. It took over defaulted mortgages on two- and three-family houses with a small amount of cash, repaired and painted the houses, and quickly resold them. The company also speculated in land and did some building, always with as little cash as possible. It was a hectic operation, and Kennedy and O'Meara often worked on Sundays in Old Colony's small office at 30 State Street. (He might as well work, Kennedy told his partner; Sunday was the only day Rose's father spent with his family, and he was not welcome.)

A full page advertisement in the *Boston American* for Sunday, May 21, 1916, described the one- and two-family houses Old Colony was building on lots in suburban Brookline, Newton, Chestnut Hill, and Winchester, at prices ranging from eighty-five hundred dollars to fifteen thousand dollars. The latter figure would buy a ten-room, three-bath stucco house with a red Spanish tile roof on fashionable Commonwealth Avenue. To the expanding middle class, made prosperous by the war boom, Old Colony promised carefully selected home sites providing "protection against the encroachment of undesirable elements," an assurance that comforted the grandchildren of the Irish famine immigrants.

By the time the company was dissolved during World War I, Kennedy's original one-thousand-dollar investment entitled him to one-third of some seventy-five thousand dollars in assets held by Old Colony.[14]

During these years, O'Meara saw Kennedy as few others did. One day, O'Meara was at work in the State Street office when a friend, Henry J. Siegal, came in with a sheet of paper in his hand. Siegal said he had volunteered to solicit pledges of help for a young man who was in a terrible plight. He was unemployed, his rent was long overdue, and he was to be evicted; worst of all, his child had died the day before. The man could not afford to bury the child and was too proud to approach the city or Church for charity. For a day and a night, the body, wrapped in a sheet, had lain in the front room of his flat, while he frantically sought work and a loan. Without asking for the man's name or any details, O'Meara wrote a check for fifty dollars and handed it to Siegal. Just then, Kennedy entered the office. He quickly heard the story, scowled at O'Meara, and told him to tear up the check. "Harry," he said impatiently, "what the hell good is fifty dollars to that fellow with the trouble he has? Don't do things halfway. Either do nothing or do the whole job."

Kennedy told Siegal to bring the man to the office. An hour later he appeared, gaunt, unshaven, looking much older than his twenty-odd years. As he came in, O'Meara recognized him: they had been altar boys together. Kennedy talked with him for a few moments, then handed him a check for $150 and told him to get decent clothes and see a barber. While he was gone, Kennedy arranged for burial of the dead child and telephoned the landlord to promise the rent would be paid. When the man returned, he was offered—and he accepted—a job as a salesman with Old Colony. Later he attended law school at night, was admitted to the bar, and became a successful trial lawyer.[15]

In the fall of 1913, Kennedy's apprenticeship in banking ended abruptly when a wave of bank mergers threatened to engulf his family's financial and sentimental interest in the Columbia Trust Company in East Boston. Columbia Trust was small, with capital of two hundred thousand dollars and a surplus of thirty-seven thousand dollars, but First Ward National wanted it and was on the verge of taking it over.[16] Patrick Kennedy scraped up what cash he could, enlisting the support of relatives and neighbors, and turned the counterattack over to Joe.

Striving for a majority at the approaching stockholders' meeting, Kennedy rallied proxies throughout East Boston and borrowed heavily to buy additional stock. Here, his ability to meet the right people paid off. While at Harvard, Kennedy, as the roommate of football star Bob Fisher, was well-supplied with tickets to the big games; once, he had been able to accommodate an old grad, Eugene V. Thayer, president of the Merchants National Bank. He now visited Thayer, who was more than willing to thwart First Ward National, and borrowed the remainder of the necessary forty-five thousand dollars. Pleased with his success, Kennedy realized too late that Thayer, following the customary practice, had discounted the loan, leaving him twelve hundred dollars short of the amount needed to assure control of Columbia Trust.[17]

With the showdown meeting two days away, Kennedy retraced his steps among his supporters. After a few disappointing calls, he burst in early Sunday morning on O'Meara, who was on his way to the golf course. O'Meara had already bought a few shares of Columbia Trust stock, but he now dug deeper and loaned Kennedy the twelve hundred dollars. O'Meara assumed that Kennedy, once he controlled the bank, would take over the key office of treasurer. He asked if this was his intention.

"Hell, no," said Kennedy. "I'm going to be president of the bank."[18]

Aware it had been outmaneuvered, First Ward National retired from the field without offering battle, and the directors of Columbia Trust dutifully elected Kennedy president. At twenty-five, he was the youngest bank president in Massachusetts; the Boston *Post,* the city's Democratic newspaper, immediately hailed him as the youngest banker in the country. True, the bank was small and obscure, but the title of president was impressive. In the massive granite money fortresses and gentlemen's clubs, Yankees asked one another who this Irish upstart was, and were somewhat reassured to discover he was a recent graduate of Harvard. Mayor Fitzgerald, as Kennedy had hoped, was dazzled. A bank president, and the youngest one at that, was an eminently eligible suitor for his daughter. Not long after, the society columns of the *Post* burst forth with the announcement of Rose Fitzgerald's engagement to Joseph Patrick Kennedy.

Kennedy could not pass up a chance for a bit of fun with his future father-in-law—literally at his expense. Dining one evening at Young's Hotel, where he and a friend ate regularly and took turns picking up the check, Kennedy saw "Honey Fitz" and a few cronies come sailing across the room with big hellos. The mayor, who enjoyed a well-deserved reputation as Boston's leading uninvited guest, sat down with his companions and all ordered dinner. During the meal, Kennedy drew the waiter aside and whispered that the mayor insisted on paying for the party. As "Honey Fitz" pushed away from the table and folded his napkin, the waiter handed him the check, adding brightly that he was looking forward to serving at his daughter's wedding reception. Fitzgerald looked at the check in disbelief, then glared across the table at Kennedy, who was gazing at the ceiling. As he fumbled for his wallet, "Honey Fitz" muttered peevishly to the waiter that there just might not be any reception or wedding.[19]

But the mayor, a tireless booster of "Bigger, Better, Busier Boston," quickly forgave the young go-getter who proved what he had been saying about the need for new Irish blood in the city's sluggish commerce. Besides, what Fitzgerald thought was academic; his daughter Rose, a determined young woman, had made up her mind.

Rose, one of six children and the eldest of three daughters, was

Fitzgerald's favorite. She resembled her mother, a slim country girl from South Acton, who had met "Honey Fitz" when he led a North End political club on a berry-picking excursion. Thereafter, the politician appeared without his berry pail to court Josephine Mary Hannon. A shy, retiring woman, Mrs. Fitzgerald was nonetheless the mainstay of the Fitzgerald family, the parent who shaped her children's character and instilled deep religious conviction. Rose inherited her mother's serenity and her father's curiosity. She was graduated at fifteen from Dorchester High—the youngest graduate in the school's history—and was voted Boston's prettiest high school senior by her classmates. Later, she attended the Convent of the Sacred Heart on Commonwealth Avenue in Boston and also studied at Manhattanville, New York. Her mother, who disliked the limelight as much as "Honey Fitz" craved it, gladly yielded place to Rose. While still in her teens, the mayor's daughter took on a full round of political and social duties, smiling through banquets and rallies, appearing at her father's side at wakes and funerals, launching ships and dedicating public buildings, and acting as hostess for the distinguished visitors who turned up at city hall.

Rose took celebrities in stride; she had been meeting them almost from the time she learned to walk. When she was seven, her father, then Congressman Fitzgerald, while traveling to Palm Beach one winter, stopped at the White House to show off Rose and her five-year-old sister Agnes to President McKinley. The President complimented Fitzgerald on his handsome children, adding that little Agnes undoubtedly was the prettiest girl ever to visit the White House. (When Rose told the story to her own children years later, she was brought up sharp by Jack's question: "Why didn't he say it to you, Mother?")[20]

As Rose grew into young womanhood, a delicious bit of gossip made the rounds of the Irish community to the effect that she would marry the Irish-born, multimillionaire tea trader and yachtsman, Sir Thomas Lipton, a good friend of her father. The rumor sprang from a garbled account of an exchange between Rose and Sir Thomas during a party at the Copley-Plaza Hotel. Pressed hard to declare when he would forsake bachelorhood, the middle-aged Sir Thomas finally said: "If you want to know who Lady Lipton is going to be, she is right in this room. Stand up, Rose!" To which Rose, in the spirit of the jest, quickly answered: "I won't accept you, Sir Thomas. I think you are altogether too fickle."[21]

She accompanied her father on his travels, joining him one year on a cruise aboard a United Fruit Company boat sailing to Latin America, where he inspected the Panama Canal and promoted the Port of Boston. On a tour of Europe, she shared one of her father's finest hours. Wishing to visit Sir Thomas' yacht *Erin,* lying at anchor at Cowes, Fitzgerald boldly marched aboard the King's launch and ordered the crew to take him. As the royal launch approached the *Erin,* it appeared to Sir Thomas and his guests, including a number of American socialites, that the King and Queen were paying a call. The women aboard, aflutter with excitement, practiced deep curtsies. Their jaws dropped as Fitzgerald's head appeared on the ladder, and Sir Thomas boomed out: "My heavens, it's my friend John Fitzgerald of Boston."[22]

Because strained relations between Church and state had led to the closing of convent schools in France, Rose and her sister were forced to change their plans to study there. Instead they went to the Convent of the Sacred Heart in Blumenthal, Prussia. Rose spent a year in this richly spiritual Old World atmosphere among the titled young ladies of Prussia, studying German, French, and music. She won a gold medal for her proficiency at the piano.

In the view of an Irish matron,[23] the Fitzgeralds, with their acquired taste for culture, travel, and study abroad, were "high Irish," well ahead of their own kind, but following the long-established Yankee custom. There was only one Society in Boston. Just as the upper ranks at Harvard were closed to Joe Kennedy, so the Yankee grand dames could not be thawed by the warm smile of "Honey Fitz's" daughter. On her return to Boston, she joined the Cecilian Guild, the Irish counterpart of the exclusive Junior League, and organized the Ace of Clubs, a circle open to Irish young ladies who spoke textbook French and had studied abroad. (The Irish, too, drew sharp social lines.) Attempts to conduct the meetings in French were unsuccessful, and the club soon became known mainly for the annual ball staged at the Somerset Hotel, at which Rose and her escort usually led the grand march. But the thinness of the imitative Irish society did not escape Rose. "Pink teas," she declared, "bore me."[24]

She had a serious, probing turn of mind. At twenty, she was the youngest member of the Boston Public Library examining committee, which selected reading material for children. And she found satisfaction as a Sunday School teacher in Dorchester and the North End, her father's birthplace, where the tenements were being emptied of Irish and filled by newly arrived Italians. Former pupils remember her as a painstaking catechism instructor, who prodded and encouraged her youngsters to one prize after another in annual competitions. Life with father had taught her to take winning very seriously.

The wedding of Rose Fitzgerald and Joe Kennedy, in October, 1914, was the talk of Irish Boston. They were married at a nuptial Mass celebrated by Cardinal O'Connell in the private chapel of his residence. Agnes preceded her sister down the aisle, and Joe Donovan stood up for his former tourist-bus partner. At the reception, "Honey Fitz," for once, did not try to outshine the bride, nor was "Sweet Adeline" sung. On their honeymoon, the newlyweds went to the Greenbrier at White Sulphur Springs.

Two weeks later, they moved into a gray frame house at 83 Beals Street in a middle-class neighborhood in Brookline. The house had cost sixty-five hundred dollars and the bridegroom, already deep in debt as the result of buying Columbia Trust stock, went two thousand dollars deeper to make the down payment.[25] Within a year, the first Kennedy child would be born. Success, formerly a matter of pride with Kennedy, now was an urgent necessity.

The banking prodigy at the Columbia Trust Company continued to fascinate the Boston *Post*, which covered Kennedy through the years, in the words of a former *Post* editor, "almost the way we covered City Hospital and the courts." A glowing feature article described Kennedy as "a direct action man who works in rolled-up sleeves, lunching on milk and crackers," and quoted him as saying, "The tango is my favorite vice. I love it." (A notable admission that, since Mayor Fitzgerald not long before had taken steps to ban the licentious dance in public places.)[26] Kennedy at length grew weary of the "youngest banker" tag and cut short one interview with a rather priggish quip: "Youth is neither a crime nor a novelty."[27] Present-day public-relations experts would diagnose his testiness as arising from concern with the Kennedy "image." Striving for an effect of dignity and for acceptance among financial leaders who did not dance the tango, Kennedy draped his athletic frame in ultraconservative clothes and affected an austere scowl.

It wasn't all window dressing. He was as quick to call a loan and foreclose a mortgage as the next moneylender. He learned a disagreeable lesson soon after he took the president's chair.

An acquaintance named Eddie Welch, who was about to be married, came to ask for a loan of five hundred dollars to finance his wedding trip. Kennedy, in businesslike fashion, asked for collateral. Welch said he owned a fine new automobile. Automobiles then were fairly novel, and Kennedy didn't own one, although he wanted to. When Kennedy accepted the car as collateral, Welch suggested that, since this was a friendly transaction, Kennedy could use it for a month in lieu of interest on the loan. A moment's calculation convinced Kennedy he should accept the offer rather than the small amount of interest. He and Welch shook hands on the deal. Within a few days, Welch had been married and was off on his honeymoon. Meanwhile, Kennedy drove proudly around town in the gleaming automobile, honking at his friends and boasting about the bargain he'd struck.

One evening, he drove to the theater and parked the automobile at the curb on a downtown street. When he returned a few hours later, it was missing. He telephoned the police to report the theft, all the while anxious about what he would tell Welch. The police solved that problem. After checking, they informed him the automobile had not been stolen; it had been repossessed. Kennedy, furious, pounced on Welch when he arrived home, demanding the principal of the loan plus interest. Welch repaid the five hundred dollars and told Kennedy with a laugh that he had received all the interest to which he legally was entitled. The red-faced banker dropped the matter.[28]

In spite of an unpromising start, Kennedy boosted deposits and landed new business for Columbia Trust. His relationship with Mayor Fitzgerald did him no harm; some favors owed Fitzgerald were assigned to his son-in-law. The mayor also took a hand directly in Kennedy's career. He appointed him the director for the city of the Collateral Loan Company, an institution originally set up to protect the city's poor against loan sharks, which had on its board a representative of the city and of the state.[29] This position, he hoped, would gain attention for his son-in-law in banking circles.

But the well-intentioned gesture backfired. Almost the moment Kennedy came on the board, scandal rocked the Collateral Loan Company, which was rent by long-standing internal dissensions and charges of embezzlement. It seemed that some twenty-six thousand dollars had been removed quietly from the company while the officers were not speaking to each other or watching the till. The company's president resigned under fire, and the city's newly appointed watchdog attempted to straighten out the mess. Kennedy found he had walked into a raking political cross fire. After five months of wild charges and counter-charges, ending in a general shake-up of the company, he resigned.[30]

Beneath the surface of this episode was a touch of irony. When "Honey Fitz" bestowed a city job on his son-in-law, he performed a ritual sacred to his class. Patronage had been the objective of the Irish bosses in their take-over of the municipal government. Starting at a time when steady work was scarce and the Irish lacked influence in business, men like Fitzgerald and Pat Kennedy looked to the city payroll as a bonanza. But by the time Joe Kennedy reached manhood, a job with the city was no longer the summit of an Irishman's ambitions, merely a springboard to better things. In his case, however, it was a setback, and the experience left Kennedy leery of political jobs for the next twenty years.

If an Irishman could not wrest social acceptance from the unbending Yankees, who were tightfisted with that commodity even among themselves, Kennedy decided he could earn respect in the marketplace. After resigning from the Collateral Loan Company, he began trying for a seat on the board of trustees of the Massachusetts Electric Company; in spite of rebuffs, he kept on trying for months until he finally was elected. Gordon Abbot, chairman of the utility company's board and also chairman of the powerful Old Colony Trust Company, apologized to Kennedy for the anti-Irish bias that had delayed his election, a large-spirited gesture Kennedy never forgot. "He was the only one who gave me a fair shake," he once said of the Yankee businessman.[31]

Some friends wondered why Kennedy was so determined to force his way onto the board of a moribund company. One who asked him recalled Kennedy's reply: "Joe said: 'Do you know a better way to meet people like the Saltonstalls?' I didn't, and I blushed for missing the point of what he was up to."[32]

CHAPTER 4

The Speculator's Apprentice

YOUNG Kennedy had no difficulty meeting one Yankee, a lawyer named Guy Currier, whose business it was to know everyone. His acquaintanceship extended from the elegant drawing rooms of the Back Bay to the shabby watering places of Irish politicians, and his skill at matching up individual interests in distant worlds made him an influential force in Boston and a millionaire many times over. A rural Yankee from the town of Methuen near the New Hampshire border, Currier arrived in Boston too late to share in the golden era of fortune building and family founding, but was resourceful enough to make the most of his chances. He had set out with the vague ambition of becoming an engineer. After being graduated from the Massachusetts Institute of Technology, he was attracted to the law and attended the Boston Law School. Just before the turn of the century, the young country lawyer, whose family was old and well-connected, entered politics as a Democrat, and was elected to the state House of Representatives and the state Senate. Early in the 1900's, he left the Legislature and opened a law office in Boston.[1]

Far from retiring from politics, he now capitalized on his experience and social standing. His Democratic party ties were so unobtrusive, yet so useful, that he won the confidence of many rockribbed Republican businessmen, who retained him to look after their interests in the legislature. Men from Wall Street particularly were drawn to the suave, darkly handsome lawyer, whom C. S. Mellen, president of the New Haven Railroad, described as "the shrewdest lobbyist on Beacon Hill."[2] After chatting with Mellen one day in 1913, Clarence W. Barron, publisher of *The Wall Street Journal* and the Pepys of high finance, jotted in his diary: "He [Mellen] says he [Currier] is a man who perhaps may not impress you as you talk with him as possessing any striking qualifications, but that he lays a deep plot, and in his particular line of service has worked with great success."[3]

With J. Otis (Jakey) Wardwell, the servant of various insurance, utility, and railroad interests, Arthur P. Russell, vice-president of the New Haven Railroad, and Charles Hiller (Charlie) Innes, Boston's gruff Republican boss, Currier was a member of the so-called Big Four, who adroitly stage-managed the legislature, controlling the men who controlled the voters. Almost never in the public eye and rarely met in the corridors and cloakrooms of the Capitol, Currier was an unseen ruler of the ruling class. He operated by means of affable telephone calls from his Hancock Street office, intimate dinners in private rooms at his clubs, casual but deliberately calculated introductions of importance to socially aspiring lawmakers (and their wives), and, of course, well-timed contributions to officeholders who were accommodating.[4]

As he grew comfortably rich, Currier displayed the taste of a Renaissance prince. Women admired him and fondly recalled his impulsive gifts of jewels and furs. His Beacon Hill mansion, at 65 Mount Vernon Street, was a gay showplace, with a ballroom on the top floor. He married a well-known Shakespearean actress, Marie Burroughs, and built for her a palatial estate in New Hampshire. Depressed by New England's harsh winters, he retreated to a villa in sunny Florence, where he collected paintings and illuminated manuscripts. Wherever they were, the Curriers were surrounded by a brilliant, sophisticated circle, uniting finance, politics, and the arts. So captivated was William Howard Taft that he seriously considered appointing his friend Currier to the Supreme Court.

Currier, at ease with the famous and powerful, never forgot he had molded his fortune and influence from common clay. When a young Yankee senator from Northhampton hesitantly confessed his desire to pursue politics "seriously," Currier measured the man and his ambitions, and agreed to assist him.[5] Years later, the climax of this serious career almost came, not in a symbolically apt rural parlor, but amid the luxurious trappings of the Currier estate at Peterboro, New Hampshire. For Vice-President Calvin Coolidge was a day's journey away from the home of his benefactor when Harding's death intervened, and Coolidge's father, a country notary public, administered the oath of office by the light of an oil lamp. One of Coolidge's first letters on White House stationery, addressed to Mrs. Currier, regretted that he had been unable to see the performance of *Romeo and Juliet* by a company of actors the Curriers had engaged for the entertainment of their guest.[6]

The princely Currier was the friend and confidant of James Michael Curley, who achieved a kind of greatness by outdistancing a host of rivals to emerge as the symbol of Boston's political rascality. Hard pressed for funds in the midst of a campaign, Curley knew a call to Currier would not go unanswered. In return, he passed on useful information. Once, he forewarned Currier of the city's plan to widen Cambridge Street. Currier allied himself with Martin Lomasney, the boss into whose neighborhood the plum had fallen. They arranged to buy cheaply the land which the city soon would buy dearly, agreeing to divide the profits evenly. At the last minute, however, Currier told Lomasney the deal was in jeopardy: another politician somehow had learned of the scheme and was threatening sabotage unless he received a share. Lomasney reluctantly consented to a three-way split. The following week and every week thereafter until all the land had been taken, the stranger appeared, always keeping silent and departing as soon as the money was divided. His unsociability rankled Lomasney almost as much as his piracy; the "Mahatma" prided himself on knowing every practicing politician in Boston, yet he could not place this fellow. Months later, he discovered the stranger's identity: he was a saloon lounger hired by Currier, who had been pocketing two shares to Lomasney's one.

Himself an accomplished trickster, Lomasney related the episode one evening as he strolled with a friend. The "Mahatma" spoke of Currier and his deception with new-found respect, as one craftsman might discuss the surprisingly good work of another.[7]

A close friend of Currier's was Gordon Abbot, with whom he served on the board of trustees of the Boston Public Library. Those who knew both men remember Abbot's deference to Currier's political experience, and suggest it would have been surprising if he had not spoken to Currier about the ticklish problem raised by Kennedy's bid for a seat on the board of the Massachusetts Electric Company.[8] Kennedy enjoyed impressive political backing, of the sort which utility companies are bound to respect. Whether or not Currier advised that Kennedy be seated, he took an interest in the younger man who seemed to know what he wanted. An introduction was arranged.

So far as Kennedy was concerned, Currier was a man well worth knowing. He had money and knew how to make it, and money was uppermost in Kennedy's mind. On assuming control of Columbia Trust, he had vowed to make a million dollars by his thirty-fifth birthday.[9] This was not a solemn oath, as some legend makers would have it, but the goal set by a self-confident youth of twenty-five who saw no reason why he could not accomplish anything he pleased within a decade. Although ten years seemed a long time, two years without much progress had made him impatient. Clearly, suburban banking and modest real estate operations would not enable him to amass important money. As it was, much of what he made went to retire his debts. Then, too, his family was growing rapidly. In July, 1915, Joseph Patrick, Jr., had been born at the Fitzgeralds' summer home, and Rose was expecting another child.* Currier found Kennedy an attentive listener.

One day in 1917, over lunch at Young's Hotel, Currier advanced a proposition.[10] He was the lobbyist for Bethlehem Steel, which recently had launched a shipbuilding subsidiary at the Fore River Shipyard in nearby Quincy, Massachusetts. With war raging in Europe and the United States almost certain to enter the conflict, the shipbuilding industry was undergoing breakneck expansion. Joseph W. Powell, the general manager of Bethlehem Ship, needed an assistant at Fore River. Would Kennedy be interested?

He accepted on the spot. Turning the management of Columbia Trust over to his father, Kennedy entered wartime shipbuilding, one

*Joe Kennedy's mother, Mary Hickey Kennedy, had an entirely different idea about naming a son "Junior." The *Boston Record American* (January 8, 1964) noted that when he was born, his mother didn't want her son known as "Junior" or "Little P.J.," but she did want him to bear his father's name. To accomplish both ends, she switched around the father's names and called their son Joseph Patrick.

of the dizziest whirlwinds in the history of American industry. When he arrived, Fore River looked like a chaotic boom camp in the California gold fields. Streaming into the yards from all over the country was a work force which reached twenty-two thousand persons. The assistant general manager's first assignment was to put roofs over the workers' heads, which required swift construction of a good-sized town.[11] In spite of the confusion and the pace of his work, Kennedy did not miss a moneymaking opportunity: he saw that eating facilities were as scarce as housing. As a profitable sideline, he opened a cafeteria, the Victory Lunchroom, which fed thousands daily.[12]

Following the United States' entry into the war, Fore River smashed one production record after another. Thirty-six destroyers were launched in twenty-seven months; one was delivered to the Navy only forty-six days after the keel had been laid. Bethlehem took on contracts from Electric Boat, and scores of submarines slid down the ways.[13] But production could not catch up with the inrushing orders.

As a harassed executive, Kennedy fought a running feud with an equally harassed official at the government end of the pipeline, Assistant Secretary of the Navy Franklin Delano Roosevelt. The patrician New Yorker, then thirty-five, had come to the Navy post with a reputation for diffidence. But he became a different man under the stress of wartime emergency. As in later years, Roosevelt usually had the last word in his dealings with Kennedy. "Roosevelt was the hardest trader I'd ever run up against," said Kennedy, recalling an arm-twisting bargaining session. "When I left his office, I was so disappointed and angry that I broke down and cried."[14]

Emotions ran high during the disagreement that arose over a pair of battleships built for the Argentine government and completed before the outbreak of the war but still lying in the Fore River yard. Kennedy, defending the rights of property, was under orders not to deliver the vessels until payment was received. Wishing to avoid an international row, Roosevelt came up with several conciliatory formulas, but Kennedy refused to compromise. Finally, the Assistant Secretary announced he would dispatch Navy tugs to tow away the battleships, which he did, leaving Kennedy fuming but impressed.[15]

For assuming big responsibilities, Kennedy received what was then big money: twenty thousand dollars a year in salary[16] and bonuses, plus the profits of his cafeteria. Bethlehem's dynamic chairman, Charles

M. Schwab, believed in nominal salaries and large incentive bonuses; men produced best, he knew, under self-imposed pressure. Under his philosophy, the earnings of the shipbuilding subsidiary soared, until fully half of Bethlehem Steel's profits came from Bethlehem Ship. Men silently cursed Schwab, but they slaved day and night for him. Schwab had forged a legendary career. As a groom in Andrew Carnegie's stable, he had caught the old man's eye; at twenty-four, he was president of a steelworks employing ten thousand persons and before he was thirty, he had built the giant Homestead Works. During the bitter, bloody Homestead strike, he remained in the besieged plant from early July through Christmas, curling up at night in a blanket on his office floor. Schwab's forceful presence hovered over Fore River, but Kennedy had never met him.

As he came to the yard one morning, Kennedy heard another executive say Schwab was expected to make a tour of inspection that week. Entering his office, he said to his secretary:

"I suppose you've heard the news. Schwab is coming. You know, someday I'd like to meet him."

Alice Fitzpatrick, a marvel of efficiency hired away from a Boston law office at double her former salary, said:

"You will—tomorrow."

Early that morning, she explained, Schwab's secretary had telephoned from Pittsburgh, trying to reach the general manager's office to relay a change in plans. Miss Fitzpatrick took the call, and learned Schwab would arrive from New York at noon the following day. He had no hotel reservation in Boston and no luncheon arrangements had been made. As she ended her report, Miss Fitzpatrick added: "Oh, yes, Mr. Schwab's favorite lunch is chicken livers." Kennedy nodded; he was already on the telephone.

Next day, he greeted Schwab at the Back Bay Station and whisked him to a suite at the Copley-Plaza. Later, Kennedy led the way into the dining room for a lunch of chicken livers, meticulously prepared by a chef who had been alerted twenty-four hours earlier. Afterward, Kennedy drove Schwab to Fore River and stuck close to his side during the tour of the yard. His invitation to dinner and the theater was accepted. That evening, the men talked for more than two hours.[17] When Schwab swung aboard an early train the next morning, he must have made a mental note to keep tabs on the able young man he had discovered.

Kennedy soon had an opportunity to show his gratitude to Miss Fitzpatrick. Her health impaired by overwork, she was forced to leave the shipyard. At his own expense, Kennedy sent her on a cruise to Europe.[18] He could be generous toward those who gave him wholehearted loyalty. A pair of young men he met at the yard, Edward B. Derr and C. J. (Pat) Scollard, showed the same capacity for hard work and self-effacement, and they joined Kennedy in a series of enterprises over the years. But he was unrelenting toward enemies, his own or his family's. Mayor Curley, for instance, badly wanted draft-exempt jobs at the shipyard for some of his protégés, but the son-in-law of his bitter foe, "Honey Fitz," blocked him at every turn.[19]

As soon as America entered the war, many members of Harvard's Class of 1912 hastened to volunteer for military service. Kennedy did not, a fact noted and resented by some classmates. "They took pride in not being drafted," Ralph Lowell remembered, "and they didn't appreciate a man not going into the war, as, for instance, in the case of Joe."[20]

With the armistice and the homecoming of Harvard classmates and friends in khaki, Kennedy confessed to a twinge of regret at having remained a civilian. But his work at Fore River had been useful to the war effort—and even more useful to himself as a liberating personal experience. The shipyard was only eight miles from Boston, but it was an entirely different world. There, place depended on daily performance; a name was just that and nothing more. Kennedy worked himself into a stomach ulcer striving to meet his job's demands, passing the only tests that men like Schwab imposed. Did the ex-stableman care that Kennedy's grandfather had not been a gentleman? Schwab would have blinked in amazement at businessmen who took ancestry into account when they judged a man's worth.

The return of peace caused a sudden collapse in the demand for shipbuilding. The huge emergency fleet would glut the ship market for years to come; soon, there would be scarcely a ship under construction in the yards of either of the American coasts. Well before the war's end, Kennedy was sent to solicit civilian orders, but there were none. He persisted, and during the spring of 1919 laid siege to the Boston office of broker Galen Stone, chairman of the Atlantic, Gulf and West Indies Steamship Line. Finally, he was granted a fifteen-minute interview. Arriving at Stone's office, he was informed by a secretary that the appointment had been canceled: Mr. Stone had been called unexpectedly to New York. Kennedy asked which train he was taking, raced in a cab to South Station, and slipped into the seat next to Stone. He proceeded to turn a fifteen-minute interview into a four-hour conversation, using all the persuasiveness at his command, but Stone wasn't interested in ships.[21] As they talked, Stone did become interested in the salesman who had cornered him so neatly.

The oft-told story of this train ride usually ends with the Yankee financier assigning the aggressive young Irishman a desk in his office, but Kennedy's rise was not a pat Horatio Alger tale. He was aware his job at the shipyard could disappear any day because of the slump; and he needed only the flicker of interest shown by Galen Stone to start a campaign to win a place in his firm. Guy Currier, of course, knew Stone, and he recommended Kennedy. So did Frederick C. (Buck) Dumaine, treasurer of the giant Amoskeag cotton mills in Manchester, New Hampshire, and a man who owed a large favor to former Mayor Fitzgerald.[22] Within two weeks, Kennedy was offered, and accepted, the managership of the stock department in the Boston office of Hayden, Stone and Company.

By the standards of the war boom, his ten thousand dollar salary[23] was unexciting, but he now sat at the right hand of one of the shrewdest speculators in Boston. Like his friend Currier, quiet, precise Galen Stone was a rural Yankee, from Leominster, Massachusetts. He had come to the city in the eighties to be a reporter on the *Commercial Bulletin* and later went to the *Boston Advertiser*, for which he wrote a column of respected financial comment under the pen name Rialto. From the *Advertiser*, he entered a broker's office, where he met an energetic young Bostonian, Charles Hayden. In 1892, they went into business for themselves, forming the firm of Hayden, Stone. The partnership was a success, Stone's calm solidity balancing Hayden's nervous dynamism, and the house financed copper mines, sugar refining, shipping, and railroads. Stone was a director of a score of companies,[24] but the restless Hayden went on to hold a record eighty directorships. Both became multimillionaires.

Stone made his headquarters in Boston, and Hayden operated from New York. According to a member of the firm, the gentle Stone and the short-tempered Hayden, after getting along for many years, gradually fell out on a number of issues, one of which was Stone's hiring of Kennedy. Hayden opposed him on the grounds of inexperience, but Stone would not be moved. A coolness developed between the partners, and they kept their distance except for essential business.[25]

Kennedy remained permanently in awe of Stone. A portly, balding man with a twinkling eye and a carefully trimmed white moustache, he never lost the journalist's appetite for facts. The chairman of the Atlantic, Gulf and West Indies line distrusted the view from a lofty office window, and regularly walked the docks, asking questions of seamen, clerks, and stevedores. When he was appointed a public trustee of the Boston Elevated, he rode downtown each morning on the trolley, ignoring the company rule against talking to the motorman and storing up information unavailable to those too important to ride trolleys.[26] Unfailingly courteous, he addressed even the office boys as "Mister." It was the practice for a young man eligible for promotion to be summoned to Stone's office, faced with a balance sheet, and subjected to searching examination. But Stone made the test somewhat easier by pointedly asking the candidate about the fortunes of a particular company a day or two before. Kennedy, whose responsibilities far exceeded his experience, was forced to rely heavily on Stone's patient instruction.[27]

The tricky postwar stock market baffled the most experienced speculators. As the guns ceased firing, the economy slowed down, a natural and expected reaction, but the oft-predicted recovery failed to materialize. "Industry in the United States is worth nothing," the once supremely optimistic Schwab told a friend, adding a bit of advice: "Don't buy a thing."[28] Galen Stone suffered sharp reverses. His income in 1919 had been so enormous that his tax bill was $1,500,000; in 1920, his losses were so huge that he had no taxable income. As Kennedy watched and learned, Stone guided the firm, carefully choosing solid investments and holding them for the rise which eventually must come. "Whatever money I have made," Stone was heard to remark, "has been in staying with a property and not regarding fluctuations."[29] This strategy became Kennedy's own, but only after he had acquired property to stay with.

His first moves in the market were clumsy. Like every novice, he fell prey to tips and rumors. Acting on information said to come from an impeccable source, Kennedy plunged hard on a stock selling at 160, then watched, heartsick, as it bumped down to 80.[30] He heard one day that the stock of Amoskeag Mills would split four shares for one, which would surely boost its price, and so he bought five thousand shares. A couple of days later, he saw "Buck" Dumaine on the street and asked about the rumor concerning his company. Dumaine said it was only gossip and laughed at Kennedy for buying heavily. Convinced there was nothing to the report, Kennedy sold the stock. Not long after, Amoskeag did split its stock, and he realized Dumaine had duped him, "just for the hell of it."[31]

After he became wealthy, Kennedy pooh-poohed "inside information," declaring that with enough of it and unlimited credit, "you are sure to go broke."[32] Applied to the gossip an ordinary market player might pick up, the stricture was sound enough. But Kennedy knew the value of information available only to a privileged few. An associate at Hayden, Stone and Company recalled a killing Kennedy made in Pond Creek Coal Company. Galen Stone, the major stockholder in Pond Creek, privately sold his interest to Henry Ford, who intended to integrate the coal company with his steel mills. Stone, who knew Kennedy had taken hard losses, privately told him of his transaction with Ford. Kennedy borrowed to the limit and bought some fifteen thousand shares of Pond Creek, then selling at about sixteen dollars a share. When a customer's man in the office also bought a few hundred shares on the basis of an outside tip, Kennedy, who had confided in no one, called the man aside and discreetly asked the reason. He listened, horrified, as his associate freely shared the sure thing. Kennedy swore him to secrecy. When the news of Ford's plans broke, Pond Creek jumped. Kennedy sold his stock at around forty-five dollars a share.[33]

Important money was to be made among the insiders, and Kennedy made every effort to break into their circle. "It wasn't too unusual for young Irishmen to go into the banks and brokerage houses," said Kennedy's Harvard classmate Ralph Lowell, "but it *was* unusual for them to rise. Joe obviously wanted to rise as far and as fast as he could. It was hard to ignore him." Said another who watched Kennedy on the way up: "Joe was born mature. He would meet powerful, socially prominent men in passing, and later they would say to each other, 'That fellow has something.' "[34]

Kennedy attracted attention with his instinct for new, moneymaking ideas. In 1919, an event occurred which sent a thrill of excitement through the ranks of Boston's capitalists, particularly small capitalists.

Max Mitchell of the Cosmopolitan Trust Company,[35] a small bank much like Kennedy's Columbia Trust, backed a suburban retail merchant who had taken it into his head to produce a movie. In these pre-Hollywood days, movies were being made, on shoestring budgets, in more than a dozen cities around the country. It was like wildcatting for oil, and the excitement came when banker Mitchell struck a gusher. His investment of $120,000 produced *The Miracle Man,* which went on to gross three million dollars.[36]

While others rushed to imitate Mitchell, Kennedy watched the banker pour his winnings into an effort to repeat. Inevitably, he failed. Kennedy, impressed by the hazards of movie-making, declined an offer to take over Mitchell's bankrupt production company.[37] He saw other opportunities, involving more acceptable risks. Enlisting Guy Currier and several other Bostonians, he headed a group that bought control of a chain of thirty-one small theaters in New England.[38] The chain acquired the regional franchise for Universal Pictures and proved a consistent money-maker—so profitable, in fact, that Kennedy downed his misgivings and took a brief flier in production.[39] In this first major investment Kennedy showed staying power that Galen Stone would have applauded. Although Maine-New Hampshire Theatres, Inc., dwindled to eight theaters, the chain remained in Kennedy's hands more than forty years, longer than any other property he owns.[40]

His well-known father-in-law was an asset to Kennedy, at least in the beginning. Between campaigns, Fitzgerald, a man of many parts, liked to dabble in the stock market from a desk in the office of Laidlaw and Company.[41] He thought nothing of calling upon important men throughout the country for information and advice. One day, while Kennedy looked on, Fitzgerald placed a telephone call to Bernard Baruch in New York, talked with him for several minutes about an investment he was considering, and then asked "Bernie" to hold the line while he put on a young man he ought to know. With that, "Honey Fitz" handed the receiver to his surprised son-in-law.[42]

Unfortunately, Fitzgerald's acumen as a speculator was on a par with his off-key singing, and Kennedy in later years disclaimed responsibility for his father-in-law's market operations. As his own reputation grew in Boston's financial community, Kennedy tried to ease out of the shadow of "Honey Fitz." It was clear to him that Fitzgerald's influence would last only so long as he held power or might conceivably regain it. He would always be the irrepressible "Honey Fitz," whose political stock-in-trade was his role of unassimilated outsider.

The Kennedys soon were sufficiently prosperous, and numerous, to have outgrown the house at 83 Beals Street. Before Joe, Jr., was two years old, John Fitzgerald was born, on May 29, 1917. In September of the next year, Rosemary arrived; and in 1920, Kathleen was born. The Kennedys moved to a twelve-room house on Naples Road, with high ceilings and a formal parlor, in a more fashionable section of Brookline. Rose was grateful for the large front porch, which she used as a playroom, separating the children with folding partitions so they wouldn't "knock each other down or gouge each other in the eyes with toys." In July, 1921, Eunice arrived. Fortunately, Rose did not have to cope with her growing family single-handed. In addition to domestic servants, she had a nurse and a governess to care for the children. Joe, in his infrequent free moments, willingly pushed a baby carriage.

Every prominent Boston family has a rich store of "grandfather stories," handed down from generation to generation to preserve the memory of the founder. In the Kennedy family, the stories are about Joe. According to a favorite tale of these early child-rearing years, he set out for a walk one frosty morning, pulling Joe, Jr., behind him on a homemade box sled, and became so absorbed in dreams of financial conquest that he failed to notice when the sled tipped rounding a corner, dumping the baby in a snowbank.[43] Legend has it that he trudged home pulling the empty sled, while a passerby retrieved Joe, Jr., from the snow. At a loss to explain Kennedy's moneymaking ability, writers have seized upon the empty sled as a symbol of superhuman concentration. It is true, he pursued wealth single-mindedly, but never as an end in itself. He made money as a means of uplifting his family; the true story of his morning walk, and how it came to be related, make the point.

In *As We Remember Joe,* the memorial volume assembled by Jack Kennedy after his brother's death in World War II, Eddie Moore, the family's close friend, recalled that he and his wife and Joe Kennedy went walking in the snow near Poland Springs with Joe, Jr., in the box sled. They fell into conversation, did not see him tumble off, and hurried back to find him smiling angelically in the snow.[44] The simple story was about the recollection of a smile. The tragic loss of the smile and so much else so affected Kennedy that he could never bring himself to read the tributes to his dead son. Not the empty sled pulled by a forgetful father, but the book unread by one who remembered too well, is the pertinent symbol.

The Kennedy household centered on the mother. Domestic servants freed Rose to enjoy her children. She was devoted, conscientious. Said a friend: "She would leave any party early to be home in time for a baby's feeding."[45] She kept a card index on the children, recording when each child had measles and mumps (one side or both), whether their vaccinations "took," the results of each physical examination and visit to the dentist. "On pleasant days," Rose has said, "I took the children for walks. I wheeled one in a baby carriage and two or three toddled along with me. I made it a point each day to take them into church for a visit. I wanted them to form a habit of making God and religion a part of their daily lives, not something to be reserved for Sundays."[46] Rose favored direct, old-fashioned discipline. "I used to have a ruler around, and paddled them occasionally, because when they're young that's all they understand."[47]

While Rose saw to the children's catechism and paddling, Joe enforced a different kind of discipline, strongly reminiscent of his father's. The new Brookline neighborhood of large, tree-shaded residences was distinctly Yankee and Protestant. But the Kennedys were determined not to be outsiders. When the boys were old enough, they were enrolled at the Dexter Academy, six blocks away, where they may have been at the time the only Catholic students.

If Joe and Jack were without Irish neighbors and schoolmates, they always had "Honey Fitz." A frequent visitor, he took the boys to ride on the swan boats in the Public Garden or to the zoo at Franklin Park or to see the Red Sox play.[48] "Grandpa Fitz" continued to campaign hard, sometimes practicing his speeches on his grandsons, but success eluded him in his comeback attempts. In 1916, he had fought a pitched battle against the Brahmin elder statesman, Senator Henry Cabot Lodge, only to lose by a scant thirty-three thousand votes.[49] Two years later, in a brass-knuckles campaign against Peter (Weeping Peter) Tague, Fitzgerald won the congressional seat for the Tenth District; but an investigating committee upheld Tague's charges of illegal registration and voting fraud, and "Honey Fitz" was unseated.[50] He felt neither remorse nor embarrassment. As a parting shot, Fitzgerald accused Tague of stirring anti-Irish prejudice in Congress in order to oust him.[51]

In 1922, Fitzgerald, yearning for any office, first announced he would take on Lodge in a return match, then decided to exploit a bitter Republican split and switched his candidacy to the governorship. Kennedy dutifully appeared at rallies in his new chauffeur-driven Locomobile. One of Jack Kennedy's earliest memories was touring the wards with his grandfather, who sang the inevitable "Sweet Adeline" and expertly executed "the Irish switch," which saw "Honey Fitz" pump the hand of one supporter, talk eagerly with a second, and meanwhile gaze affectionately at a third. But Fitzgerald committed a grave tactical error in the closing days of the campaign, hurling a patently false charge at his opponent and being forced to apologize publicly.[52] The election was an anticlimax: Fitzgerald was swamped, losing by more than sixty thousand votes.[53] Unknown to his grandsons, this defeat marked the end of "Honey Fitz's" active political career, a development which his son-in-law would accept with silent satisfaction.

Before the campaign, Kennedy slipped away for a few days to attend his tenth Harvard reunion at the Pilgrim Hotel in Plymouth. "Joe loved fun," said a classmate. "He was a leader at the reunions."[54] The theater operator entertained the gathering by showing the newly released films of the Jack Dempsey-Jess Willard and Dempsey-Georges Carpentier heavyweight bouts. He also saw that Prohibition didn't put a damper on the party. "Joe was our chief bootlegger," said another Harvard '12. "Of course, he didn't touch a drop himself, but he arranged with his agents to have the stuff sent in right on the beach at Plymouth. It came ashore the way the Pilgrims did."[55]

The wisecracking host and bootlegger stood out in the crowd of men in their middle-thirties as they took part in the good-natured horseplay and mutual appraisal that are equally part of a college reunion. In the ten years since graduation, he had done as well as any of them, yet he wore his success lightly. There, a classmate could have reflected as he sipped Kennedy's Scotch whiskey, was a fellow for whom things had gone very well indeed.

Another man would have shrugged off the setbacks Kennedy had experienced. They would have seemed so unimportant in the overall pattern of success as to be forgotten immediately. Kennedy allowed himself no such compromise. The smallest injury to his pride never healed. And because success was bound up with his sense of self-esteem, each failure, each disappointment was a wound.

There was one which hurt terribly. After spending a few summers with the Fitzgeralds, in heavily Catholic Nantasket, the Kennedys rented a large frame house overlooking a rock-studded beach at Cohasset. It was perfect for the children, but less congenial for the parents. Many of Boston's old families passed the summer in Cohasset and were resentful of newcomers, particularly Irish newcomers. When Kennedy sought membership in the Cohasset Country Club, he was blackballed.

"It was petty and cruel," said Ralph Lowell. "The women in Cohasset looked down on the daughter of "Honey Fitz"; and who was Joe Kennedy but the son of Pat, the barkeeper?"[56]

BOOK II
THE OPERATOR

"Boston is a good city to come from; but not a good city to go to. If you want to make money, go where the money is."

—*Joe Kennedy*

CHAPTER 5

Out of The Small, Clear Puddle

AFTER thirty years in which he amassed almost as many millions, Galen Stone gave up his partnership and retired at the end of 1922.[1] His protégé decided to strike out on his own. He stayed at Hayden, Stone and Company's 87 Milk Street address, but moved into a separate office behind a door lettered *Joseph P. Kennedy, Banker*. At thirty-four, Kennedy was now in business for himself, free to move as he pleased toward his own ends. The rising breeze from Wall Street bore the unmistakable smell of big money, so he followed his nose.

Although the big Bull Market was still far in the future, the economy was reviving from the postwar slump. True, the farmers were suffering, as they would throughout the decade; and Boston knew better than most cities that shipbuilding, textiles, and the shoe industries remained in the doldrums. But the young automobile industry was racing ahead, over newly paved roads, pulling to prosperity a whole group of related industries. And the popularity of the radio, introduced in the fall of 1920, was attested by the sale of sixty million dollars worth of radio sets, parts, and accessories in 1922.[2] Markets were expanding for telephones, electric refrigerators, phonographs, and other appliances. Women were taking up smoking, and production of cigarettes would more than double between 1918 and 1928.[3] Sales of cosmetics jumped; more often than not, the lipstick and powder were plucked from the counter of the "five-and-ten," the standardized, high-volume chain store that was revolutionizing retailing. Confidence in "conditions" grew daily. Urged on by businessmen who dreaded inventory pileups, consumers were beginning to regard cash as old-fashioned; they took eager steps on the primrose path of "easy credit." With the arrival of Coolidge, businessmen, long haunted by the bugaboo of a return to wartime government interference, were reassured by the President's fondness for long afternoon naps. Its style cramped by war and recession, the country was poised to kick up its heels and take off on the headlong pursuit of happiness.

Wall Street reflected the changing economy and popular mood, but it was far removed from Main Street. The unwary had no business in the canyons off Lower Broadway; the stock market was the closed preserve of tipsters, insiders, and manipulators. Sunday-supplement writers tended to overplay the romantic aspects of the Street, which they likened to the vanished frontier and identified as the refuge of rugged individualism in an increasingly organized economy. To be sure, there were colorful speculators with fat bankrolls, fast roadsters, and coveys of chorus girls, proof that the quickly turned dollar always would draw men of the stripe of Jim Fisk and Jay Gould. But the average man who made money in Wall Street was a conservatively dressed professional of regular habits. Like the frontiersman who died in bed at a ripe age, he was remarkable chiefly for his adaptation to a harsh environment. He survived and prospered because he possessed uncommonly strong nerves and a cool, appraising mind—as did Joe Kennedy.

Luxuriant legends have sprung up about Kennedy's exploits in the stock market. In truth, he was a clever lone wolf operator, but not one to rival, say, Jesse L. Livermore, another product of a Boston brokerage house who emerged from the Panic of 1907 with short-selling profits of three million dollars and the title of the "Boy Plunger."[4] Livermore operated from hidden offices near Wall Street equipped with a standard-size quotation board, thirty telephones, and a staff of twenty discreet assistants and statisticians. On a single deal, his profits could exceed a million dollars, as when he took an option on a block of Computing Tabulator (the forerunner of IBM) at forty dollars a share and engaged the canny floor trader Frank Bliss (known as "the Silver Fox") to run it up to eighty dollars before he unloaded.[5] Every dip in the market during the postwar years sent the whisper running from boardroom to boardroom: "Livermore's on a raid!"

Big operators like Livermore scarcely knew Kennedy existed, for he traded on a more modest scale. He also went about his operations with closemouthed secrecy. He was not a reckless gambler like tall, craggy Colonel William C. (Bill) Danforth, whose buying and selling in lots of as many as fifty thousand shares was the talk of Boston brokerage houses. Almost no one knew what Kennedy was up to, except faithful Eddie Moore, his confidential secretary, who had joined him in the real estate business and would remain by his side for the next forty years. Kennedy sometimes played golf with the expansive Danforth and others in the Boston trading fraternity, and kept his ears open for tips and indiscretions, but said nothing of his own market activity. "You didn't ask him any questions unless you had a darned good reason," said one who played in his foursome. "Joe confided in very, very few people."[6]

Thus, while Kennedy made friends easily and cultivated those who could be useful to him in this deal or that market "play," he withheld a part of himself, wherein were kept locked his interests. Instinctively, he heeded the rule laid down by George Whelan, a skillful market operator and co-founder of United Cigar Stores: "The stock market game does not make for personal friendships. Every man has to be independent."[7]

As part of his apprenticeship at Hayden, Stone and Company, he learned the moves and counter-moves of market manipulation. One technique used to deceive outsiders was the stock pool. According to an associate, Kennedy, while at Hayden, Stone, managed a pool in the stock of Todd Shipyards.[8] In a typical pool, a few traders would take options on, say, one hundred thousand shares of an idle stock at a price of twenty dollars a share. Acting through one or more brokers on the floor of the Stock Exchange, the pool would "advertise" the stock by trading shares back and forth across the tape until the public, seeing this activity, leaped at a seeming good thing. At the likely top price, perhaps thirty or forty dollars, the pool would "pull the plug," selling the gullible public all it wanted of the overvalued stock and pocketing the profits above the option price of twenty dollars a share. A refinement of this technique added the step (and profits) of short selling in the stock on its way down.

In addition to his market operations, Kennedy reentered the field of real estate speculation, through the Fenway Building Trust, and became a director of the New England Fuel and Transportation Company.[9] Brimming with self-confidence, he toyed with the idea of setting up a brokerage house in New York.[10] "It's easy to make money in this market," he told a friend. "We'd better get in before they pass a law against it."[11] With his Harvard roommate Bob Fisher acting as emissary, Kennedy invited classmates Tom Campbell and Ralph Lowell to go to New York with him.[12] But the idea died for lack of enthusiasm and capital.

Kennedy had good reason for self-confidence. A confidant believed he had the "ideal" temperament for speculation—"a passion for facts, a complete lack of sentiment, a marvelous sense of timing"—and outlined his strategy, which owed much to the tutelage of Galen Stone: "Joe wasn't interested in the day-to-day shifts of the market and the chance to make a few points here or there. He was interested in situations, in values. There's all the difference in the world between being a speculator and a gambler."[13] Kennedy himself once pinpointed the "fine distinction" between gambling and speculation. "I think the primary motive back of most gambling is the excitement of it. While gamblers naturally want to win, the majority of them derive pleasure even if they lose. The desire to win, rather than the excitement involved, seems to me to be the compelling force behind speculation."[14]

To satisfy his obsession for wealth, Kennedy went to extraordinary lengths. One evening in April, 1924, the doorbell of the Kennedy home on Naples Road rang insistently. Joe, suffering from an attack of neuritis, had retired early. He threw on a robe, came downstairs, and opened the front door to Walter Howey, a burly newspaperman who had come to Boston two years before as Hearst's manager. The colorful, hard-bitten Howey, after whom Ben Hecht and Charles MacArthur modeled the city editor in their Broadway play *The Front Page,* had met Kennedy during Fitzgerald's campaign for the governorship. Inexplicably, Howey had banned political news in his paper, which, its Irish readers believed, was like publishing blank pages. Kennedy persuaded Howey to lift the embargo, a break for "Honey Fitz," and added casually that Howey might call upon him should he ever need advice on financial matters. Kennedy's midnight caller, wearing a worried look, had come to take up the offer.[15]

Before coming to Boston, Howey had worked on Chicago newspapers, and had invested in the stock of the Chicago-based Yellow Cab Company, founded by John D. Hertz, sometime newspaperman, prizefight manager, and horse fancier. Yellow Cab, Howey explained to Kennedy, was in serious trouble. In March, the stock had been listed on the New York Stock Exchange, and had sold around 85; but by mid-April it had slid to 75, and the quotation after Good Friday was 50. This precipitous drop bore the earmarks of a bear raid; heavy sales, originating, it was believed, in the offices of the brokers, Block, Maloney and Company, were driving down Yellow Cab. Hertz was on his way to New York to rally support for the stock, said Howey. Would Kennedy be willing to meet him there?[16]

Disregarding his neuritis and the imminent birth of his sixth child, Kennedy summoned Eddie Moore and took a train to New York that night. He met Hertz and Charles McCulloch, Yellow Cab's vice-president, at the Waldorf, arranged terms for accepting the generalship of their campaign, and outlined his plan of defense. Money was needed, and Hertz returned to Chicago to raise five million dollars from such friends as chewing gum magnate William Wrigley and advertising man Albert Lasker. Kennedy then moved into a room at the Waldorf, equipped with a battery of telephones and a ticker.[17]

His job was to wrest control of the stock from the raiders, then stabilize it at the best possible price. Getting on the telephones, he placed buy and sell orders with brokers scattered across the country; his object was to cause Yellow Cab's movements to become so erratic the raiders would be confused. To keep *his* position clear in his mind, Kennedy jotted down the seemingly illogical buy and sell orders on a pad of paper. With Eddie Moore hovering to take calls, admit visitors and receive meals, Kennedy grappled with the bears. In the first hours of the battle, Yellow Cab dipped to 48. During the last week in April, the price ranged between 50 and 57, with ten thousand shares being traded on the last day of the month. The first Monday in May, the day before Kennedy's daughter Patricia was born, the stock opened at 62. Later that week it fell back to 50. On May 9, a whopping twenty thousand shares were traded at prices ranging from 46 to 51. But the bears had been beaten off; the stock did not fall under 50 again. Moreover, the raid had been halted with Hertz's five million dollars intact.[18] Worn by the battle, Kennedy left the Waldorf and caught a train to Boston to see his month-old daughter.

Months after he had put a seemingly solid floor under Yellow Cab, the stock fell. The break may have been touched off by a poor earnings report: the company's profits for the third quarter of 1924 were off 52 percent from the previous year. But Hertz suspected Kennedy of pulling away the props he had erected and selling the stock short; he threatened to punch him in the nose the next time they met.[19] To those who knew Kennedy, it would not have been unthinkable for him to switch sides and take advantage of Yellow Cab's weakness. His mind always detected the remote gains in immediate tasks. His politics worked that way, too.

In the summer of 1924, the Progressive party nominated a pair of popular senators—Wisconsin's Robert M. La Follette and Montana's Burton K. Wheeler—for the Presidency and Vice-Presidency on a platform of reforms that made businessmen apprehensive. Hopeful of support from Eastern labor and liberals, La Follette asked his running mate to visit his native Massachusetts and take soundings of opinion. Wheeler, vacationing on Cape Cod, became friendly with Kennedy, who took him to see Galen Stone. At Stone's summer home, the foe of rapacious finance was received with unexpected cordiality by the financiers, and Kennedy even hinted he would support the Progressive ticket. "We can't take much more of Cal Coolidge," said Kennedy.[20]

On Labor Day, Wheeler arrived in Boston to launch a New England campaign swing with a speech on the Common. Immediately afterward, Eddie Moore came to the senator's hotel room and presented Kennedy's check for one thousand dollars with the request that the contribution remain anonymous. Learning Wheeler was without transportation, Kennedy also provided a chauffeur-driven Stevens-Duryea to carry the candidate on a tour of towns as far north as Portland, Maine; and when Wheeler passed through Boston again on his way south, Kennedy turned over to him his own Rolls-Royce.[21] ". . . in swanky Newport, Rhode Island, and in all the principal towns from there to New York," Wheeler wrote in his autobiography, "I denounced Wall Street often from the back seat of a Rolls-Royce owned by a Wall Street operator. It occurred to me later on that Kennedy actually might have been trying to undermine me in this fashion."[22]

Wheeler's suspicions were aroused when he encountered Kennedy in Washington shortly before the election. Kennedy said he was worried: the large, enthusiastic crowds drawn by Wheeler indicated

La Follette might carry Massachusetts. Wheeler was surprised; what was worrisome about such signs to a man who had given financial support to the Progressive cause? Before Wheeler could ask, Kennedy went on to describe how normally Democratic Irish voters, who were unimpressed with their party's standard-bearer, John W. Davis, were being discouraged from bolting to La Follette. "We scared hell out of them," said Kennedy, laughing. "We told them that a Progressive party victory would close all the mills and factories. And in South Boston we told the Irish that the La Follette program would destroy their Church."[23]

Wheeler never did discover which side Kennedy actually favored, but the election returns from Massachusetts showed the boss-driven Democratic voters solidly behind Republican Coolidge. For all his shortcomings, "Cal" appealed to the cynical Democratic professionals and contributors; he would leave things as they were.

More than three decades later came an echo of Kennedy's "support" of the Progressives. Wheeler, after he left the Senate in 1946, practiced law in Washington; he heard nothing from Kennedy until one day early in 1960. Kennedy telephoned to ask whether Wheeler possibly had newspaper clippings mentioning Kennedy's role in the 1924 campaign. Wheeler reminded him that he had chosen to keep his contribution secret. Why should he want to have it made public now? "Jack was running in the Wisconsin primary," said Wheeler, "and Joe thought it might do some good to tie the Kennedy name to La Follette."[24]

Playing golf at the Woodland Country Club in the spring of 1925, Kennedy spotted his former real estate partner Harry O'Meara on the next fairway and called him over. "What are you doing up here?" asked Kennedy. "I should think you'd be down in Florida making money."[25]

The most delirious land grab in America in a century, the Florida boom was the warm-up for the speculative circus of the twenties. With money plentiful and credit easy, thousands rushed for a place in the sun. Miami, transformed into the "Fair White Goddess of Cities" by publicity men, was swarming with an army of fast-talking real estate salesmen—twenty-five thousand by one count.[26] Hucksters crooned of soft Caribbean nights, promoters sold swampland "estates" from bogus maps, and moonstruck bankers stuffed their vaults with paper of dubious worth. Men frantically bid to pay hundreds of thousands of dollars for business lots that had sold for a few hundred dollars only five years earlier. Stories of quick riches spread the land fever. Visiting in Palm Beach, Clarence Barron, of *The Wall Street Journal*, noted in his diary the sudden affluence of a man who had bought three miles of oceanfront for ten thousand dollars in 1909; in the midst of the boom he sold a mere five thousand feet of his land for $1,100,000.[27] If countless people were going to become rich as the result of the country's onrushing prosperity, it seemed smart to stake out a piece of the tropical paradise clearly destined to be the playground of the well-to-do.

That was Kennedy's plan. O'Meara was skeptical—why was godforsaken swamp worth more than choice property in the Boston suburbs? —but Kennedy persuaded him to go to Florida, saying he would back something good to the extent of one million dollars. O'Meara asked where the money would come from. "Why," said Kennedy, "we'll sell bonds. The bond salesmen are sitting on their backsides; they haven't got enough to sell. Florida will sell."

The day before he was to leave, O'Meara dropped by Kennedy's office, and found to his surprise that the sun had set on the scheme. Kennedy had discussed his plans with Galen Stone, who advised against the venture. Shaken but unconvinced, he then telephoned Matt Brush, another older financier who had taken a liking to Kennedy. Brush reported the doubts he heard expressed by leading New York bankers and businessmen. He told Kennedy: "Forget about Florida."

"Harry, any man can be wrong," said Kennedy, "but Galen Stone and Matt Brush can't both be wrong at the same time. Let's wait and see what happens."[28]

Kennedy thus showed his lifelong talent for picking the best brains before committing himself. Knowing the value of good advice saved him from disaster when the speculative bubble burst. Wholesale mortgage defaults sent Florida land prices tumbling, and hurricanes in the fall of 1926 flattened what was left of the dream. At his leisure, Kennedy plucked bargains from the wreckage.

In the phrase of one fascinated observer, Kennedy was "an angle-shooter who liked to move around the table."[29] His short, crowded career in the movies consisted of adroitly executed carom shots. A few years after investing in the chain of New England theaters, he saw an angle. He had been buying the American rights to English pictures for his theaters, and had gradually built up contacts among British film makers, some of whom used him as their agent in the U.S.[30] The British owners of a U.S. film-producing company and its distribution affiliate, Robertson-Cole Pictures Corporation, Inc., and Film Booking Office of America, Inc., respectively, were caught in a credit squeeze far from home. Learning of their plight, Kennedy decided that they might be persuaded to sell. "From the theater side of the business," said an associate, "Kennedy learned Hollywood could wring you dry. He wanted to get to where the wringing was done."[31]

With his lawyer, Bartholemew Brickley, he went to London in August, 1925, to try to swing a deal with Lloyd's and Graham's Trading Company, which controlled the movie properties. But key British bankers were elusive. As Brickley later told the story, he and Kennedy were at breakfast one morning, wondering what to do next, when Kennedy read aloud a newspaper dispatch, reporting that the Prince of Wales was enjoying a brief vacation in Paris.

"Let's go to Paris and see the Prince of Wales," said Kennedy.

"Why?" asked Brickley. "And how?"

"Leave it to me," replied Kennedy.

At the Prince's favorite restaurant in Paris, Kennedy bribed a waiter to seat him at a table near the royal visitor. When the Prince appeared, Kennedy approached him with a smile and outstretched hand. Introducing himself, he added: "But perhaps you remember me. We met at Bayard Tuckerman's reception. Wasn't that a grand party?"

This was sheer bluff. During the Prince's visit to the United States not long before, Tuckerman, a Yankee socialite, had given a reception at the exclusive Myopia Hunt Club. The Prince, who had shaken so many hands and smiled into so many faces that day on the North Shore, now shook hands and smiled again. He asked politely what brought Kennedy to Europe. Hearing of his difficulty, the Prince offered to write a letter of introduction for his American acquaintance. The letter arrived at Kennedy's hotel the following day, and thereafter the necessary doors in London opened.[32]

But this transatlantic transaction, the biggest thing Kennedy had tackled, involved seemingly endless questions, and the negotiations dragged on. His business unfinished, Kennedy returned to Boston and literally worried himself sick. Pat Kennedy told one of his son's friends:

"I'm concerned about Joe. His ulcers are giving him trouble. I'm afraid he's bitten off more than he can chew."[33]

To raise capital, Kennedy sold part of his interest in the theater chain, but the deal was too large for him to handle by himself. Guy Currier stepped into the picture, investing $125,000[34] and rounding up other backers to form a syndicate that included "Buck" Dumaine, of the Amoskeag Mills, and Louis E. Kirstein, head of Filene's Department Store.[35] Crucial support also came from one of Currier's clients, Frederick H. Prince, the testy, flamboyant railroad manipulator and multimillionaire.[36]

Freddie Prince, born in Winchester, Massachusetts, before the Civil War, was the son of Frederick O. Prince, a Yankee Democrat twice elected mayor of Boston before the Irish tide engulfed city hall. Young Prince quit Harvard to take a job in a State Street brokerage house, where, according to legend, he got his start in a fabulous railroad career quite by accident. Sent to Maine to inspect a small branch railroad on behalf of a customer, he was so impressed he agreed to buy it. On his return, he reported the purchase, but the customer meanwhile had lost interest, and the young man's employer coldly declared: "Mr. Prince, it appears that you own a railroad." Undismayed, Prince raised the necessary money and bought the first of forty-four railroads he would own. He also built four railroads and won control of the Chicago Union Stock Yards and the Armour Company.

Prince was the last of the handful of Yankees who helped Kennedy on his way. A short, powerful man with a massive head and hooded, deep-set eyes, he spoke with deceptive softness, almost distracting listeners from the grim lines around his mouth. At once bold and cunning, he had clashed head-on with Morgan the Elder in a railroad war and lived to tell the tale. ("I shook Mr. Morgan's hand and thanked him warmly for the great interest he was taking in me as a younger man and said I should never forget his advice. I knew at this time that he was doing everything he could to ruin me. . . .")[37] Prince lived in baronial splendor on a one-thousand-acre North Shore estate, Princemere, which boasted three mansions, the largest with seventy rooms. By his order, champagne was served at every meal and at teatime. His stables were filled with eighty polo ponies, and the best players in the country rode on the teams he fielded. With a few other wealthy men, he founded the Myopia Hunt Club, so named because the founders were both nearsighted and whimsical. A man with a quick, murderous temper, Prince, at the age of seventy, assaulted another player with a polo mallet during a match. The incident, for which he refused to apologize, led to a lawsuit, and Prince, with a farewell curse upon his "social enemies," withdrew from Myopia and retired in good order to Newport, Rhode Island.

Like the early nineteenth-century Yankee entrepreneurs, Prince had a fertile imagination and a zest for new ideas: he once sent a promoter to Czarist Russia with the idea of setting up a mail-order house. The fast-growing movie industry looked exciting and profitable; he agreed to Currier's request that he back Kennedy.

With Prince's support assured, Kennedy broke the logjam in the negotiations with the British. Years afterward, "Honey Fitz" gave a newspaperman an account of how his son-in-law clinched the deal:

"Joe and some friends were about to start for Florida on a trip they had been planning for weeks. While they were at the New York Harvard Club waiting for their train, Joe received a message.

"It informed him that Lord Inverforth, agent for a group of British bankers, was at a nearby hotel. Kennedy dashed out. Half an hour later, he was back.

" 'Sorry, fellows,' he said, 'Guess you'll have to go to Florida without me. I've just bought a motion picture company.' "[38]

Oddly enough, the announcement in February, 1926, of Kennedy's acquisition was made by "Honey Fitz," who telephoned his favorite editor at the Boston *Post* and gave him a story that ran on page one under this banner headline:

FITZGERALD A FILM MAGNATE

Down below the lead, the *Post*, as usual, identified Kennedy as the former mayor's son-in-law, adding that the thirty-seven-year-old businessman was "the marvel of the Boston financial world." The story said Fitzgerald would be "actively interested" in the movie venture, and included his promise that the names of the members of the syndicate would be made public "within a few days."[39] The names were not disclosed, and this story apparently marked the beginning and end of "Honey Fitz's" public involvement in his son-in-law's enterprise.

Deeply committed in the stock market and now the movies, Kennedy found Boston remote from his scene of operations. He also found its leading citizens stubbornly reluctant to recognize the rising millionaire in their midst as anyone but the son-in-law of "Honey Fitz"—an identity, as witness the *Post* story, which Fitzgerald insisted upon with equal stubbornness.

The Kennedys, Joe believed, had earned recognition as something more than moneyed Irish. As in the leading Yankee families, the Kennedy wealth was intended to serve as the foundation of a secure social position. A trust fund—the first of three—was established, with Rose as trustee. Each of the seven youngsters, including the infant Robert, born in November, 1925, shared equally, and would receive an income at the age of twenty-one. At the age of forty-five, each child would receive a share of one-half the principal of the trust fund. Eventually, additions to this fund, and the creation of two others in 1936 and 1949, would earmark upwards of ten million dollars for each of Kennedy's children.[40]

His purpose was to protect his wealth and his children's future. Admiring publicists of the younger Kennedys later suggested he had another motive. "It's been made into a myth, and I'd like to see the record set straight," said Jack Kennedy in 1959. "The story goes that he put a million dollars in trust for each of us to be self-sufficient so that we could devote ourselves to public life, and that he did this when we were very young. Well . . . he was speculating. It was a very risky business. He was speculating pretty hard and his health was not too good at the time, and that was the reason he did it. There was no other reason for it."[41]

But what good was money in Boston if it could not be translated into social prestige? His daughters, for instance, would not be invited to join the debutante clubs—"not that our girls would have joined anyway; they never gave two cents for that society stuff," Kennedy once told a reporter. "But the point is they wouldn't have been asked in Boston."[42]

In the spring of 1926, Kennedy packed his family and servants aboard a private railroad car and left Boston in grandly defiant style, bound for a new home in Riverdale, a suburb of New York City. Boston was "no place to bring up Catholic children," Kennedy later declared.[43] Perhaps not, but neither was it a promising place to pursue his vaulting financial ambitions. "This city was a small, clear puddle," recalled banker Ralph Lowell. "New York was a big muddy one, and that's what Joe wanted."[44]

CHAPTER 6

Hollywood Banker

FLANKED by assistants, the new president and chairman of the board of Film Booking Office of America, Inc., stepped across the threshold of his office in the Manhattan skyscraper and seated himself at the large polished desk. After testing his cushioned chair, he reached forward and pulled open the drawers of the desk one by one. He failed to find whatever he was looking for, but flashed a grin. "What this corporation needs first and most of all," declared Joe Kennedy, "is a box of Havana cigars."[1]

That was nonsmoker Kennedy's way of expressing his self-satisfaction. He had long been itching to get into the immensely profitable picture business. "Look at that bunch of pants pressers in Hollywood making themselves millionaires," he had remarked to a friend at Hayden, Stone. "I could take the whole business away from them."[2] Now he had his chance; and over the next three years, he almost would make good his boast.

During the booming twenties, Kennedy might have piled up millions in almost any fast buck enterprise, but the movies perfectly suited his talents and temperament. In Hollywood, with its pink stucco and palm-studded vistas, and its furriers transmogrified into moguls, he discovered the speculator's paradise: a land without substance and system, offering an endless variety of situations capable of being organized to his advantage.

The situation in the New York headquarters of Film Booking Office of America, or FBO, appeared worse than it actually was. The company's production and distribution operations were established moneymakers. The former British owners had been forced to sell for a fraction of their seven-million-dollar investment because they could not avoid short-term borrowing at high rates, up to a ruinous 18 percent.[3] A banker such as Kennedy could do considerably better. He knew, for instance, how easily stock certificates were swapped for cash in these years of prosperity and optimism. He set up an affiliate, Cinema Credit Corporation, which raised capital by issuing preferred stock. A large block of Cinema Credit preferred was purchased by Frederick H. Prince, who also lent FBO half a million dollars through his Chicago Union Stock Yards Company.[4] Next, Kennedy used his contacts and established a half-million-dollar line of credit at four banks. With these resources at his command, the credit squeeze was ended. FBO now had enough working capital, at moderate interest charges, to finance an entire year's production of films.

To run the company, Kennedy kept a few professionals from the former management, and brought in a flock of personally loyal lieutenants, Eddie Moore, John Ford, Frank Sullivan, Pat Scollard, and E. B. (Ed) Derr, who knew little about movie making, but a great deal about Kennedy's way of doing business. Throughout his career, it was Kennedy's standard operating procedure to move from job to job behind a protective cordon of cronies. Tight-lipped men with loud ties, they watched over the organizations to which they were temporarily attached with the sharp-eyed diligence of private detectives guarding the silver at a splashy Irish wedding.

With finances and personnel in order, Kennedy turned to where the money was made—production. He took the three-day train ride west to FBO's Hollywood studio. In 1926, his newly acquired company would produce some fifty films,[5] but its operations were dwarfed by such giants as Paramount, Metro-Goldwyn-Mayer, and First National, the pacesetters of an industry with a fantastic record of growth. Thirty years before, there had not been a movie business; now it represented a total capital investment of more than one and a half billion dollars, enough to give the upstart movies fourth place among the largest U.S. industries.[6]

The movies could be compared with other industries only in terms of abstract aggregates such as invested capital. In daily practice, there was no business remotely like the picture business; within the movie world and outside, many doubted that it was a business at all. Each film involved fresh problems and different risks. Individual and organizational fortunes swung dizzily from year to year. Kennedy caught on quickly. "When you make a steel rail," he soon told an interviewer, "you make something that is so long and so heavy and of such a quality. But when you make a foot of film, it is subject to the judgment of millions of people, each with his own standards of measurement."[7]

Sixty million Americans went to the movies each week in twenty-one thousand theaters across the country. Statistics of this sort supported the claim that the movies were Big Business. But the men at the corporate heights who guessed the whims of millions of moviegoers were an odd assortment of risen petty entrepreneurs. They included the former furriers Adolph Zukor and Marcus Loew, the ex-ragman Louis B. Mayer, the onetime glove salesman Samuel Goldwyn (Goldfish). Some of them were immigrants; Zukor had arrived from Hungary as a young man with forty dollars sewed in the lining of his coat.[8] Only a few, like vaudeville producer Jesse L. Lasky, had been established showmen before entering the movies. A typical route was taken by the four Warner brothers, who hung a sheet in a dingy hall in the wilds of Pennsylvania and attracted novelty-starved crowds with crude "chase" pictures cranked out on vacant lots. When the local undertaker needed his chairs, the Warners' audiences were content to stand. The enchantment that glowed in the faces before flickering screens in hundreds of makeshift nickelodeons was no small part of the secret of the pioneers' amazing success: the movies enthralled the masses and fit their meager pocketbooks. Beyond the popularity of what they were peddling, the early movie men owed their rise to shrewdness, boldness, and ruthlessness—in a word, *chutzpah.* What Zukor learned making novelty furs in a Chicago loft was perhaps the best possible training for the cutthroat, fast-changing movie game.

Haphazard, intuitive, uninhibited, the founders of the movie business were a new breed of self-made mogul. And their city, Hollywood, bore the stamp of their bizarre personalities. The "Dream Capital," as the sycophant press was coming to call it in the mid-twenties, had been a sleepy town a few years before. When Kennedy arrived in 1926, it was only thirteen years since a fledgling director named Cecil B. DeMille, working from a barn at Selma and Vine streets, which the company shared with the owner's horse, had made *The Squaw Man*, one of the first feature-length films.[9] That landmark picture, produced for peanuts, had played in legitimate theaters willing to tolerate a suspect novelty. But DeMille's 1923 epic, *The Ten Commandments*, had a budget that would beggar a prince and was booked into the most ornate palaces this side of Byzantium.

So accustomed to swift change were the moviemakers that they scarcely noticed a deep but gradual transformation occurring in the industry. Unique in every other respect, the movies were like any rapidly expanding business in the crucial need for large infusions of outside capital. It took money to make money, the moviemakers realized; and the more grandiose their designs, the more money it took to fulfill them. Inevitably, capital came accompanied by bankers, who first made suggestions, later imposed restrictions, and finally gave outright commands.

In a moment of reverie, the shaken mogul could trace the stages of the industry's rise and his unexpected decline. When the brilliant D. W. Griffith shot the works on *The Birth of a Nation*, exhausting relays of backers, and went on to gross eighteen million dollars in fifteen years, the sky became the limit for film budgets.[10] When the promoters of Mary Pickford introduced the "star system," they unwittingly breathed life into a Frankenstein monster. Acting jumped from a miserably underpaid to an outrageously overpaid profession. It was possible for an obscure English clown with baggy pants, Charlie Chaplin, to boost his salary overnight from $150 to $10,000 weekly; sweet little Mary Pickford demanded—and got—$10,000 weekly plus half the profits of her pictures. (Zukor told his star: "Mary, sweetheart, I don't have to diet. Every time I talk over a new contract with you and your mother, I lose ten pounds.")[11] But inflated budgets and salaries were only partly to blame; the moviemakers had caused their own comeuppance. Imperial ambitions had driven them to build and buy theaters frantically, needlessly, until they were property-rich and cash-poor. There had been nothing to do but go hat in hand to the bankers. The first supplicant to receive important help from Wall Street was Zukor, who, in 1919, talked Jacob Schiff into having his banking house, Kuhn, Loeb and Company, underwrite a ten-million-dollar issue of preferred stock.[12] A revolution followed. The movies, once financed from many sources of small capital, none of which exercised absolute authority, soon became entirely dependent on a few sources of big money.

Movie men naturally resented the intruders who had the final word, which was often no. Their resentment in time would build up to such outbursts as DeMille's indictment: "When banks came into pictures, trouble came in with them. When we operated on picture money, there was joy in the industry; when we operated on Wall Street money, there was grief in the industry."[13] But such bitterness lay in the future. As happened often in his career, Kennedy came on the scene at the right time, arriving on a flood tide of prosperity that swept men along in the easy assumption that everything could be worked out. Some moviemakers even acknowledged a measure of truth in the criticism of their unbusinesslike ways; and they looked hopefully for newcomers who would bring order without imposing suffocating regimentation.

At first, Kennedy was widely mistaken for a kinsman of Jeremiah J. Kennedy, the hardfisted, camera-smashing monopolist of the old Motion Picture Patents Company, with whom the pioneers had fought a death struggle more than a decade before. When it was clear who he was and why he had come, men like Marcus Loew were mildly incredulous but not unfriendly. "A banker! A banker? I thought this business was just for furriers," said Loew.[14] Kennedy was more than another mere guardian of money; he was a banker, to be sure, but he was also president of a studio, with direct operating responsibility. And with his quick grin, open manner, and direct speech laced with slang and profanity, he was refreshingly unlike the aloof, cold-eyed gentlemen who usually appeared from Wall Street. He looked and behaved for all the world like a picture man.

Writing in *Photoplay*, Terry Ramsaye, one of Hollywood's knowing chroniclers, expressed the general reaction to the new boss of FBO: "Now comes this banking person Kennedy and a very young person with freckles on his face and nonchalance in his manner. And he comes not as an angel hopefully backing a star-to-be nor by any of the other many sidedoor entrances but bolting in the main gate, acting as though he knows just what he is doing. Apparently he does."[15]

Kennedy knew better than to tamper with a going concern. FBO held a secure position in the industry as a low-budget producer specializing in "second features" aimed chiefly at action-hungry, small-town audiences.[16] Occasionally the company released a memorable picture, such as Mrs. Wally Reid's *Broken Laws*, but a staple product at a price was the successful formula.[17] The onetime shipbuilder set to work mass-producing movies. In 1926, while the major studios were releasing extravagant features like *Ben Hur, What Price Glory*, and *The Big Parade*, he turned out Westerns and melodramas at the rate of one a week for thirty thousand dollars apiece[18]—less than one-twentieth the cost of *The Big Parade*. Kennedy, who had taken to heart his comparison of a steel rail and a foot of film, knew his audiences wanted horse opera and derring-do, so he left the big, risky pictures to the artists and plungers.

FBO's roster of stars included Richard Talmadge, Evelyn Brent, and "Lefty" Flynn, the ex-Yale football hero, but the big box office attractions were boots-and-saddle types—Tom Mix, Bob Custer, and the enormously popular Fred Thomson, who owed his career to the love of a determined woman. He earned a Ph.D. from Princeton with the intention of becoming a college instructor, but while serving in the army during World War I, he met and stirred Frances Marion, a beautiful movie scenarist turned war correspondent. She allowed Thomson to pursue her until she caught him. Married in 1919, they set off on an eight-month European honeymoon. In Ireland, Thomson saw a spirited gray stallion, which he bought, patiently gentled, and named "Silver King." Seeing what a handsome pair her man and his horse made, Frances Thomson exclaimed: "Fred, you were born to be a Western star." She wrote a scenario and Thomson's career was off at a gallop. He set a precedent among Western stars, giving his horse top billing. "Silver King" lived in a twenty-five-thousand-dollar stable with mahogany floors and went on location in a custom-built Packard van.[19] The economy-minded Kennedy did not quarrel with well-earned extravagance, nor balk at Thomson's contract for 1927, which called for fifteen thousand dollars a week. In theaters outside the large cities,

Fred Thomson had the widest distribution of any actor, averaging ten thousand exhibitor contracts a year for every picture he made.[20]

A star of FBO's melodramas was gridiron hero Harold Edward (Red) Grange, whose screen popularity Kennedy pretested in unusual fashion. When Grange and his manager called at his New York office one day in 1926, Kennedy knew they had been turned down by other studios. Grange looked like a good bet, but did he possess audience appeal? Kennedy stalled a decision. That evening, he took up the question at home with a pair of experts. He asked his sons, Joe, Jr., eleven, and Jack, nine, if they would like to see "Red" Grange in the movies. "Yes, we would," they shouted. His doubts resolved, he hired Grange.[21]

Kennedy liked to tell this appealing little story, for it put the picture business in the sweet light of respectability. On the darker side of Hollywood were movies unfit for small boys. Because sex and crime sold, the moguls, unencumbered by any sense of public responsibility, had served up an increasingly gamy diet. At the same time, some stars gained ill fame by making lurid headlines with suicides, divorces, and sexual escapades, which provided grist for the nation's editorial pages and pulpits. Murmurs of public disapproval rose to an angry outcry when the tabloid press accused comedian Roscoe (Fatty) Arbuckle of starring after hours in a bacchanalian orgy which resulted in the death of a young actress.[22] Fearing boycott and disaster at the box office, the moviemakers belatedly organized a vice squad. Some half a million dollars' worth of Arbuckle negatives were scuttled, and the Motion Picture Producers and Distributors of America, Inc., was established, with Will H. Hays, postmaster general in the Harding administration, installed as morals czar at $150,000 a year.[23] Hays expelled some notorious undesirables from the film colony, but the industry that trafficked in images knew how badly its own needed polishing.

The personable Kennedy was a godsend to Hollywood's puff writers. What could be more presentable than a photogenic family man? Will Hays and Kennedy became good friends, a connection that was helpful in the latter's rapid rise to prominence.

Early in 1927, Kennedy assisted the movie industry's rehabilitation. Quietly mustering the support of alumni and friends on the faculty of his alma mater, he gained the sounding board of prestigious Harvard. Dean Wallace B. Donham, of the Harvard Graduate School of Business Administration, accepted Kennedy's proposal of a series of lectures on the movies, and when crusty President A. Lawrence Lowell skeptically said "all right," invitations were sent to a dozen top moviemakers.[24] Assembling them in Cambridge was no mean feat; many were suing one another, and they had to be assured that process servers would not confront them at the lectern. But every objection was overcome, as Kennedy had foreseen, by the flattery of a bid to speak at Harvard. The unlettered tycoons of Hollywood came swelled with pride. Facing the audience in Baker Memorial Library, Marcus Loew almost choked with emotion. "I cannot begin to tell you how it impresses me, coming to a great college such as this to deliver a lecture, when I have never even seen the inside of one before."[25] Another speaker self-consciously cracked a joke, saying he had come into the industry when movie men were reputed to know only one two-syllable word—"fillum."[26] Given weekly beginning in March, the lectures were a great success, drawing capacity crowds and sixty job applications from Harvard gentlemen who liked the prosperous looks of Loew and Company.

Kennedy himself, enjoying the role of the alumnus who had made good, spoke informally to the students, then answered questions. Asked about the future of the movies, his offhand reply foreshadowed the maneuvers that were to make him several million dollars richer. "We are on the eve now of big consolidations," he said. "They have become practically necessary.... Ours is an industry that lends itself very easily to consolidation..."[27]

A Marcus Loew did not need a college education to grasp the advantages of combining the interdependent elements of film production, distribution, and exhibition. There had been repeated attempts to unite and conquer during the industry's history, but independent operators died hard, mergers brought counter-mergers, and the shadow of the antitrust laws fell across the would-be monopolist's path. The largest obstacle was the nature of the business: it lived by selling novelty, and competition was murderous. However, the large, complex film organizations were geared to accustomed forms of competition; their leaders yearned for the security of routine and were hostile to unsettling new ideas. Hollywood, startled by the squawking birth of radio, could have taken the infant medium under its wing. Instead, it scoffed: was that noise to be taken seriously? Radio proved to be a very serious competitor. As soaring costs of film production sent box office prices as high as two dollars, people stayed home to enjoy the free entertainment on the airwaves. But the supercolossal mistake of the moviemakers was to turn away disdainfully when the screen learned to talk.

Sound did not take the movie industry by surprise. The idea had been around ever since Edison invented the phonograph; he was actually trying to expand the possibilities of his phonograph when he hit upon a workable device for making pictures appear to move.[28] The Vitaphone and Movietone sound systems that emerged in 1925 were not unexpected, but rather overdue.[29] Nevertheless, only William Fox and the Warner brothers decided to gamble on the talkies, the former mainly because he desired a musical accompaniment for his films less expensive than theater orchestras, the latter because their studio teetered on the brink of bankruptcy and might be rescued by a gimmick. The other leading moviemakers hung back, as Benjamin B. Hampton wrote in *A History of the Movies,* because they believed that "talkies were not good enough to satisfy the masses.... Blinded by their own vast empire, by the bricks and mortar of their temple-theaters, by the power of wealth and the adulation of sycophants, they [the pioneers of yesterday] had grown cautious, fearful of endangering the solid position they so comfortably enjoyed. And thus they missed their opportunity..."[30]

Their loss was Kennedy's gain. The round of mergers he predicted at Harvard was inspired by the industry's panicky discovery of its mistake. Audiences that sat on their hands before lavish silent films were wildly enthusiastic about the thin, scratchy voice of Al Jolson in *The Jazz Singer.* Now every studio, in self-defense, had to make the transition to sound. It would be costly, requiring new favors from Wall Street; and the difficulties would be magnified by the accumulated mistakes of the easygoing past. Kennedy, with his banking background and reputation for cost-cutting efficiency, soon found himself receiving more propositions than a flirtatious starlet.

One came from a cagey Scot, John J. Murdock, the longtime general manager of the Keith-Albee vaudeville circuit.[31] Early in 1927, Keith-Albee merged with Pathé-DeMille Pictures, landing Murdock in the presidency of Pathé.[32] A theater man, he squirmed uncomfortably in his new post; the coming of sound reinforced his determination to turn the job over to a moviemaker, preferably one who would "make 'em cheap."[33]

Meanwhile, an offer came to Kennedy from another quarter, one which at first glance looked like an invitation to back a loser. Western Electric, though the first to market sound systems, was not without competition. General Electric, Westinghouse Electric, and Radio Corporation of America had teamed up to perfect the Photophone.[34] As their entry came on the market, Radio's President David Sarnoff saw Western Electric, with a head start of several months, signing studios to long-term contracts and converting theaters to a sound system that was incompatible with his own. He decided the way to make up ground was to combine a film-producing company with a chain of theaters, thus forming an initial market for the Photophone system.[35] FBO, Sarnoff further decided, would do nicely as an entering wedge. Kennedy liked the sound of Sarnoff's idea, and they entered into negotiations. In a deal concluded in the fall of 1927, RCA bought an interest in FBO for nearly half a million dollars, Kennedy sealing the bargain with Sarnoff as they stood one noon at a Manhattan oyster bar.[36]

As rumors of Kennedy's alliance with the powerful radio and electrical interests circulated, Murdock pursued him more eagerly. *Variety*, seeing the pair with their heads together, speculated on the possibility of a merger of FBO and Pathé. However, the Sarnoff-Kennedy strategy called for a take-over of a chain of theaters. Forgetting Pathé for the moment, Murdock switched hats and dealt with Kennedy from the theater side of his interests, recently expanded through a merger of the Keith-Albee and Orpheum chains, producing Keith-Albee-Orpheum, or KAO.[37]

Murdock stood second on the corporate ladder at KAO. The nominal boss was president Edward F. Albee, who, with advancing age, had come to depend more and more on his faithful general manager. An impulsive, unshakable bestowal of trust on a chosen few was Albee's only really endearing quality, and the one which ultimately was his undoing. A hard-bitten veteran who had begun as a circus shill, Albee ruthlessly sought to become the absolute ruler of vaudeville. He thought nothing of tapping the telephones of his associates and planting stool pigeons backstage to report the grumblings of his performers, who were mercilessly punished with the blacklist.[38] They also despised him for imposing the flogging five-a-day schedule that eventually ruined vaudeville. Late in life, he responded to intimations of mortality and became an Episcopalian; he then fell into the habit of opening bargaining sessions with a mild injunction: "Let us do as the Nazarene would."[39] After which he proceeded as usual to crucify his adversary. Though he had a number of rivals, Albee probably was the most hated man in show business.[40]

In the twenty years since he had come from a Chicago theater to serve as Albee's right-hand man, Murdock had quietly piled up a fortune of twelve million dollars. In 1927, *Variety* ranked him fourteenth among the twenty wealthiest showmen.[41] Occasionally, he resisted his mulishly conservative superior, as when Albee fought the encroachment of the movies in his theaters. For the most part, however, Murdock kept silent or confined himself to bucolic rhapsodies about his gentleman farming. It was rumored that he once had conspired with Zukor to overthrow Albee, but if the boss heard the gossip, he gave no sign of distrust.[42]

After lengthy planning, Kennedy, in May, 1928, approached Albee with an offer to buy two hundred thousand shares of KAO stock for $4,200,000, the financial backing coming from Wall Street banking firms.[43] Albee at first declined, then talked with friends, probably including Murdock. It was pointed out to Albee that he would receive twenty-one dollars a share for his stock, compared with sixteen dollars quoted on the market; such an opportunity might not come again.[44] Now proud of his sharp trading as only a State of Maine Yankee could be, Albee told Kennedy he had changed his mind: he would sell. (Three months after Albee sold his stock to Kennedy and the Wall Street syndicate, the price soared to fifty dollars a share.)[45]

His sale of stock inspired hopeful rumors that he would resign, but Albee denied them, announcing that he and Kennedy had agreed on plans to expand the company's motion picture activities. As Kennedy took over the newly created chairmanship of the KAO board, it was clear he had won the trust and respect of Albee, who declared: "Mr. Kennedy has shown in a brief but colorful career in the picture business such constructive and organization genius that we consider him a tremendous asset to our business. He is energetic, dynamic and a straight-shooter."[46]

Albee was a poor judge of people. He did not realize how well-founded were the rumors of his retirement. Although he continued as president, his organization was taken over by Murdock and Kennedy, who launched a purge. Scores of Albee's favorites were fired and even his son, Reed Albee, was forced to resign. Kennedy called in his man, John Ford, and put him in charge of the Keith theaters. Albee's foes on *Variety* gleefully reported: "The Kennedy-Ford machine gun squadron in Keith's has turned its attention to agents and bookers this week, executing many of each, with more to follow."[47]

Soon, Albee himself fell. His illusion that he was still the boss lasted until he entered Kennedy's office one day to make a suggestion. The conversation, according to associates, was short and dagger-pointed: "Didn't you know, Ed? You're washed up," Kennedy said, "you're through."[48]

Albee understood, retired, and died shortly afterward, convinced he had been betrayed. The funeral was poorly attended.[49]

CHAPTER 7

The Big Money

For five frenzied months, from May through October, 1928, Kennedy darted about like a figure in an absurdly sped-up movie, starring in a success story no script writer could have devised. For the unimaginative movie folk believed that finance involved only money.

He now made more money routinely than ever before in his life, drawing a salary of two thousand dollars weekly from FBO and the same amount from Keith-Albee-Orpheum. When he made the long-expected move to Pathé as "special adviser" on production, another two-thousand-dollar paycheck arrived each week.[1] (Kennedy learned at least one trick from the "pants pressers" he scorned: the annual salary, a symbol of executive status in other industries, was foolishly vain in the highly paid picture business; the weekly salary meant two more pay days a year.) Even his princely salary shrank beside the profits Kennedy reaped from stock market operations. He demanded part of his compensation from each company in the form of options to buy its stock at favorable prices, a practice defended to the stockholders with the argument that it provided an incentive to better management.

Less was said about the fact that options permitted insiders to speculate with attractively limited risks.

In mid-June, however, even some insiders were hurt as wholesale dumping sent theater stocks crashing. Two surprising exceptions were Keith and Pathé. Reported *Variety*: "The spectacle of the issues always held in the least esteem holding up a bold front and the stocks which have been the subject of bullish enthusiasm for months back retreating in confusion made some of the ticker players who know the theater stocks lift an eyebrow... The behavior of the Keith issues gave color to several pretty well substantiated stories. One was that Mike Meehan, one of the shrewdest pool managers in the whole financial district, had been put in charge of the Joseph P. Kennedy shares' fortunes, and he was well fortified to make a stand that would attract attention to Keith and Pathé."[2]

The behavior of the stocks in which Kennedy was vitally interested was truly remarkable. Keith and Pathé stood as unlikely rocks against a tidal wave of liquidation. As selling orders on the Exchange sent volume above the then incredible five-million-share mark, the market was thrown into near panic. The break affected almost the entire list, and the stock ticker fell hours behind floor trading. Red-haired Mike Meehan, the Radio specialist and a hero of the Bull Market, was feverishly busy: Radio slid more than 23 points in a single day. The remarkably long-lived Bull Market, now almost six years old, seemed to have sunk to its knees. Throwing caution aside, a conservative New York newspaper announced without qualification on page one: "Wall Street's bull market collapsed yesterday with a detonation heard round the world."[3]

Kennedy, his ear attuned to the market, heard nothing of the sort. When omens of a real explosion appeared, he would be among the first to take cover. But this was only a passing fright. There was too much money and optimism around in mid-1928 for speculative enthusiasm to disappear at a stroke. Snapping the leash on his own bearish disposition, he bought while others sold. His coolness was quickly rewarded. Within a few days, the stampede halted, the public plucked up its courage, and the market resumed its advance as though nothing had happened.

Making money and movies cut deeply into Kennedy's time with

his family. Off on prolonged trips to California, where he lived in a large rented house on Rodeo Drive in Beverly Hills, he went weeks at a stretch without seeing Rose and the children, now numbering eight with the birth of Jean in February. Even the chore of house hunting for the perennially moving Kennedys fell to his aide-of-all-work, Eddie Moore, who was dispatched to scout suburban Westchester. A real estate agent listened patiently as Moore outlined the needs and desires of the Kennedys. "Hell," he said reaching for another stack of floor plans, "Kennedy can't use a residence. He wants a hotel."[4]

At length something suitable was found, and the family moved from Riverdale to an imposing brick Georgian mansion on Pondfield Road in Bronxville, surrounded by five acres of clipped lawns and well-tended gardens. This small estate, which cost close to a quarter of a million dollars,[5] offered not only elegance but elbowroom for the children. In the afternoon, Joe, Jr., and Jack brought friends from the Riverdale School to play baseball and football on the broad lawns. Sometimes a few schoolmates were invited to stay for a special treat: the latest movies in the Kennedys' basement projection room. Joe himself established a personal P.T.A., occasionally inviting his sons' teachers to the house for a chat and a movie show. The reports he heard on such evenings were generally good: Joe, Jr., was bright and willing; Jack, who did well in history, would one day learn to spell.

Life without father threw heavy responsibility on Rose. Quietly strong and self-sufficient, she bore up as her mother had during "Honey Fitz's" frequent absences. Joe's influence on the children grew as they grew older; in the early years Rose was the vivid, immediate presence in their lives. A friend detected her all-pervasive influence even in the inflection of their voices: "When Jack spoke, I could hear his mother's voice."[6] Said this friend simply: "She's the one who put the family spirit in them."[7] In her son Jack's eyes, Rose was the "glue" that held the Kennedys together.[8] Although a nurse and a governess helped with the smaller children, Rose took her meals with the youngsters, read to them by the hour, led shopping and sightseeing excursions, and faithfully heard their nightly prayers and their catechism lessons every Friday afternoon. Each morning, she rose early to attend Mass, returning to eat breakfast with the older boys and see them off to school. Comforter and confidante, she was, of necessity, also the disciplinarian. Bobby Kennedy, who was spanked with fair regularity, cannot remember ever being turned across his father's knee. "Hot water was my department," said Rose. "Business was Joe's department."[9]

The life of the Kennedys was more than departmentalized; it was divided into separate, airtight compartments. What her husband's business was, Rose could not have said. Not until almost two years after he acquired FBO did Rose discover her husband was in the movie business; and she was never clear on which companies he was connected with.[10] The strictest taboo forbade discussion of money at the dinner table; in Joe's view, there was no need for such talk. There was enough money, and that was all that mattered. Still, as a matter of discipline, Rose kept the children's allowances small. Jack, the impoverished beneficiary of a large and growing trust fund, chafed under such character-building restrictions and addressed a solemn appeal to his father.

"My recent allowance is 40¢," he wrote. "This I used for aeroplanes and other playthings of childhood but now I am a scout and I put away my childish things. Before I would spend 20¢ of my 40¢ allowance and in five minutes I would have empty pockets and nothing to gain and 20¢ to lose. When I am a scout I have to buy canteens, haversacks, blankets, searchlicgs [sic] poncho things that will last for years and I can always use it while I can't use chocolate marshmallow sunday ice cream and so I put in my plea for a raise of thirty cents for me to buy schut [sic] things and pay my own way around. . . ."[11]

There is no record that this proposal moved Joe to interfere in his wife's department. For young Jack, empty pockets was only one concern; an ever-present and formidable problem was his domineering older brother. Rose believed firmly in raising the first child well and setting him up as a model for the others. She may also have felt the need of an extra hand with discipline. In any event, Joe, Jr., early assumed a major role in the upbringing of his brothers and sisters. He was patient and gentle with the small ones, a good athlete who became their hero as he taught them to throw a ball, ride a bicycle, and sail a boat. But with the slight, willowy Jack, the only rival for his throne, he was a severe taskmaster and a taunting bully. They fought frequently, the younger children scattering and cowering in terror upstairs as their brothers wrestled on the first floor. The fights usually ended with Jack pinned and humiliated.

Joe Kennedy was aware of these one-sided contests, but he did nothing. His firstborn and namesake mirrored many of his own qualities; the quieter, introspective Jack was more like his mother. Joe decided the stronger should teach the weaker. He said he would not step between the boys when they fought, so long as they fought together against outsiders.[12]

Much moved in these years, the Kennedys did not set down real roots until 1928, when Joe bought a rambling white frame house with green shutters in the Cape Cod village of Hyannis Port. The spacious house, built around the turn of the century, contained fifteen rooms and nine baths, and proved easy to live in. They planned to call it "Happy Holiday," until they learned there was another house in the village with that name. It remained unnamed, but it came to be the place the Kennedys meant when they spoke of "home."

The house in Hyannis Port sat on a bluff overlooking Nantucket Sound; two and one-half acres of lawn sloped gently to a wide stretch of beach and a breakwater where the summer residents kept their boats. That first year, Kennedy was too busy elsewhere to enjoy his new home, but thereafter, it became his special domain, the place where family rather than business preoccupied him. During days filled with ceaseless activity, he shaped his children. Long before the much publicized mass gambols on the playing fields of Hyannis, the Fourth of July softball games and the bruising touch football scrimmages, he thrust each child into individual sports, such as swimming and sailing, believing these would best develop initiative and self-reliance. Firmly he implanted his conviction that playing the game was not as important as winning. Obediently, Jack named his first sailboat *Victura,* explaining that it was a Latin word "meaning something about winning."[13]

As they came of age, the girls were urged on as relentlessly as the boys. "Even when we were six and seven years old," Eunice recalled, "Daddy always entered us in public swimming races, in the different age categories so we didn't have to swim against each other. And he did the same thing with us in sailing races. And if we won, he got terribly enthusiastic. Daddy was always very competitive. The thing he always kept telling us was that coming in second was just no good. The important thing was to win—don't come in second or third—that doesn't count—but win, win, win."[14]

Winning, as a way of life, was of course an illusion. No one knew this better than Joe Kennedy, as the result of personal heartbreak. His eldest daughter, Rosemary, a sweet, attractive girl who resembled her mother, could not compete with her aggressive brothers and sisters. Shouts of win-win-win could not change what was tragically unalterable. She had been slower to crawl, slower to walk and speak than her two brothers. Concerned, Rose had taken her to several doctors, all of whom at first were reassuring: Rosemary would catch up later. But the truth soon wounded her parents in a way only a helpless mother and father can be hurt. Rosemary was mentally retarded; she would never be like other children.

To the suggestion that she be sent away to an institution, Joe reacted with fierce loyalty: "What can they do for her that her family can't do better? We will keep her at home."[15] And so Rosemary stayed with the family. At Hyannis Port, she was taken as crew in the sailboat races and glowed with happiness when she was in the winning boat. She sat, entranced, as Rose played the piano and sang to her in the evening. At the table, she could not manage a knife, so her meat was served already cut. Everything that love born of anguish could do, was done for Rosemary. Yet nothing helped.

Joe Kennedy spoke proudly of his children to casual acquaintances, yet even close friends of the family did not know about Rosemary. Over the years, the family devised all manner of stories and excuses to conceal her condition. When Kennedy finally disclosed the truth to a reporter in 1960, it was with a pathetic air of apology. "I used to think it was something to hide, something not to talk about," he said. "But then I learned that almost everyone I know has a relative or good friend who has the problem of a mentally retarded child somewhere in the family. You have no idea how widespread it is. I've won more hats and neckties betting people that they have that problem somewhere among their relatives or good friends."[16]

Against the constant preachment of victory and the appearance of unbroken success so embedded in the legend of Joe Kennedy should be set those hats and neckties, sad tokens of human self-doubt.

As Kennedy whirled through the hectic summer of 1928, overseeing three show business organizations, attentive to the chattering stock ticker, and sought after as a matchmaker for corporations, his working day was seldom less than fourteen hours. But the drive for wealth and position did not exhaust his restless energy. He sought ventures promising a different excitement and satisfaction. Somehow, he made time in his busy round for a demanding sideline, guiding the fortunes of glamorous Gloria Swanson.

To the movie audiences of the twenties, Gloria Swanson was the embodiment of the American dream of beauty, wealth, and sophistication. Petite, chic, her teeth dazzling white, her coiffure flawless and gleaming like patent leather, she was the queen of Hollywood. Her appeal to men was obvious, yet women, too, were attracted. As they watched her sweep through luxurious settings in sumptuous costumes, she reflected their daydreams. This was what it was like to be rich and beautiful. They studied every detail and imitated what they could. If she dabbed perfume behind her ear, and the label was visible on the screen, the sales of that brand leaped. It was well-known that she encased her tiny feet in size 2½ shoes; salesmen across the land struggled to satisfy women whose request was as bootless as that of Cinderella's stepsisters.

Off the screen, her life might have been a scenario. She introduced Hollywood to Society, and was the first movie actress to acquire a title.[17] When she returned from France as the Marquise de la Falaise de la Coudraye, Paramount's top star cabled an imperious command to Zukor: "Am arriving with the Marquis tomorrow. Please arrange ovation." Zukor humbly did as he was bid, issuing an executive order requiring every stenographer, stock player, and technician to make merry. On the day she arrived, production ceased, the streets were lined with Paramount employees, and extras dressed as flower girls curtsied and threw bouquets as Gloria drove triumphantly through the studio gates. In the darkness of a deserted stage, defying the edict to rejoice, sat mournful Wallace Beery, Gloria's first husband, who would be damned if he would cheer number three.[18]

Shortly after her return, Kennedy met the marquise and instantly fell under her spell. The queen of the films exerted an attraction that went beyond commonplace physical beauty. There were more beautiful women in the movies, but none possessed her silken grace and regal self-assurance. She also commanded attention by living on a scale befitting a queen: her black marble bathroom contained a gold tub and sink; an elevator was installed in her home to save walking up one flight of stairs; four secretaries fluttered about her on the lot. Adored by so many, she was accessible only to a select few. Dazzled and drawn by this radiant presence, Kennedy won entry to her circle, becoming banker, adviser, and close friend. They were seen together frequently at parties and dinners in New York and California, their mutual admiration apparent to everyone. So attached to Kennedy was Miss Swanson that she paid him the compliment of naming her adopted son, a French war orphan, Joseph.[19]

Kennedy appeared at a critical moment in the star's career, and encouraged her in a step that later proved mistaken. She was not yet thirty, but already so well established that she now determined to produce her own pictures independently. Behind her was the slapstick of the Mack Sennett comedies, in which she began as a teen-ager from Chicago, and years of growth with D. W. Griffith and DeMille, who directed her in such pictures as *Every Woman's Husband* and *Male and Female*. Her appeal was more durable than that of Clara Bow and Mary Pickford, stars who waned as they outgrew ingenue roles, and her salary at Paramount had risen steadily. Finally, Zukor, his hand trembling, proffered a contract calling for twenty thousand dollars a week.[20] But she decided she was worth more to herself. She joined United Artists, the company formed by Douglas Fairbanks, Charlie Chaplin, and other high-priced stars, which distributed films produced by the stars with their own or borrowed money.[21]

Although Kennedy loaned money to Gloria Productions, Inc., he did not allow friendship to stand in the way of sound business: he charged the going rate of interest and kept the negatives of her pictures until the loans were repaid.[22] The attentive friend saw to a great many matters. When the marquis, better known to Hollywood as Hank Falaise, grew bored hanging around the set, Kennedy packed him off to Europe in a vaguely defined capacity for FBO and Pathé. Miss Swanson did not lack for helpful admirers. When she was making *Sadie Thompson*, William Wrigley loaned her his Catalina Island, which for a month of location shooting became exotic Pago Pago.[23] But independent production was much more expensive than she had imagined, and her resources were eaten up at an appalling rate.

The first Swanson film that Kennedy financed was *Queen Kelly*, a legendary flop. Chosen to direct was the inspired but erratic Erich von Stroheim, famed for his finicky attention to detail and impulsive remaking of plots while the cameras rolled. The script of *Queen Kelly*, approved by Kennedy and cleared with the Hays Office, dissatisfied Von Stroheim, who proceeded to improvise a wildly different story.[24] Kennedy's investment stood at around six hundred thousand dollars when the star excused herself one day, walked off the set, and called her banker, who was relaxing in Palm Beach. "There's a mad man in charge here," she cried. "The scenes he's shooting will never get past Will Hays."[25]

Kennedy hurried to the Hollywood studio and viewed the rushes with shocked amazement. The film contained a scene of an admiring young priest administering the Last Sacrament to the dying madam of a bordello in Dar es Salaam; another vividly depicted the seduction of a convent girl. All this and more would appear under "Joseph P. Kennedy Presents." Kennedy recognized Von Stroheim's artistry, and he prided himself on being as open-minded as the next fellow, particularly where a large investment stood in jeopardy, but this was too much. He fired Von Stroheim and, on the advice of Sam Goldwyn and Irving Thalberg, brought in Edmund Goulding to try to domesticate *Queen Kelly*. However, neither Goulding nor anyone else could undo the excesses scattered through the twenty thousand feet of film Von Stroheim had shot.[26] After sinking more than eight hundred thousand dollars into *Queen Kelly*, Kennedy released the film unfinished in Europe, but dared not show it in the United States.*

The story of how Kennedy shelved *Queen Kelly* and wrote off a huge investment has been told and retold. It is the stuff that legends are made of. Making a million dollars is not nearly as impressive as losing almost that much money without breaking one's stride.

In fact, Kennedy lost little on the film. Under his contract with Miss Swanson, she was responsible for the money committed to the venture; and Kennedy's investment was repaid from her share of subsequent films. Yet Kennedy went ahead spreading the story of his awesome "failure," until Miss Swanson privately expressed her objection to subsidizing his self-flattery.[27]

Sound rushed in during the filming of *Queen Kelly*. A voice test, which meant sudden retirement for many stars of the silent era, showed Gloria Swanson could bring a new charm to the screen. Kennedy invested in her first "talkie," *The Trespasser*, hiring a dramatic coach, Laura Hope Crews, to guide the nervous star through every syllable of Goulding's script. *The Trespasser* was a smash hit. Kennedy put some of his winnings into a second "talkie," the last Swanson film he

*In 1950, American movie-goers caught a glimpse of *Queen Kelly* within the film *Sunset Boulevard*, starring Gloria Swanson. The script called for Miss Swanson, playing the role of Norma Desmond, a faded movie queen, to review her past screen glories; whereupon someone remembered a dusty print and a piece of Hollywood history.

backed, *What a Widow!* Reviewers sniffed ("a comedy of sorts," said *The New York Times*), but the public came, as usual, to see the gorgeously costumed star, and Kennedy profitably closed his career as a Hollywood angel. The end of his relationship with Miss Swanson was abrupt. "I questioned his judgment," she recalled. "He did not like to be questioned."[28]

In the movies as elsewhere, Kennedy patiently constructed a network of well-connected friends. His entry into Pathé, in early 1928, was sponsored not only by Murdock, his newfound ally, but also by Elisha Walker, an acquaintance from Wall Street who was to have an important influence on Kennedy's career over the next few years. Walker, president of the blue-ribbon banking firm of Blair and Company, entered the movie business as the representative of Pathé's major stockholder, Jeremiah Milbank.[29] Quiet-spoken and unassuming, Milbank had made millions in African copper mines[30] before he met Cecil B. DeMille in early 1925 and decided to make a most unusual movie. It was to be spectacular, even by DeMille's standards, in keeping with the extraordinary theme he had chosen. Skeptics in the industry doubted his idea could be executed, but DeMille, with Milbank's steadfast backing, went ahead. From its release in the spring of 1927, *King of Kings,* the first great religious epic, won universal acclaim; over the next four decades, as DeMille and Milbank reinvested their profits in new prints, the film played to worldwide audiences of more than 800,000,000.[31]

By mid-1928, Milbank had accomplished his purpose, and wished to extricate his capital from the movie business. He instructed Walker to improve the operations of Pathé and see if he could arrange "something in the way of a merger." Walker proposed Kennedy for the job; Milbank, who knew him by reputation, approved.[32]

In addition to the industry-wide difficulty of switching to sound, Pathé faced the inescapable problem of the independent studio: it was forced to compete with the large, integrated companies for theater outlets. At FBO, Kennedy had had almost unprecedented success as an independent; he lived up to his notices at Pathé. "He was clever and quick," said Milbank.[33] Kennedy boosted the company's sales seventy thousand dollars monthly. Simultaneously, he chopped Pathé's weekly overhead costs from $110,000 to $80,000.[34] Explaining his success, he later said: "Employees in moving picture companies were vastly overpaid. I found that an accountant, for example, whose pay in any other industry would range from $5,000 to $10,000, was getting $20,000 in Hollywood. I changed that."[35]

There were many changes. He dropped the title of "adviser" and became chairman of the board of Pathé, a bad omen to movie-maker DeMille. Personally friendly with Kennedy but hostile to the banker's breed, he sold his stock (at a tidy profit), and beat a symbolic retreat from the powers of Wall Street into the desert.

As if to test his endurance and ingenuity, Kennedy, now head of FBO, Keith-Albee-Orpheum, and Pathé, was approached with an invitation to lead a fourth company, and a large one at that. It was First National Pictures, then undergoing a major reorganization directed by Kennedy's old firm, Hayden, Stone and Company. Word of the offer got out and *Variety* attempted to read Kennedy's mind: "Kennedy may have concluded it is best for him not to tackle too much work in the show business. Other than his own company, FBO, which is running smoothly, he has undertaken to readjust Pathé, not so easy, and also to rehabilitate the Keith circuit, the latter a stupendous job for anyone at present."[36]

Kennedy came to a different conclusion. Approaching his fortieth birthday, he was in good physical condition, except for an occasionally troublesome ulcer, and thrived on work. He also had learned how to manage the work of others to his satisfaction, conserving his time and strength. His staff, Moore, Derr, Ford, Scollard, and the rest, acted independently within the broad guidelines he laid down; they had been given power and were expected to produce results. Kennedy himself concentrated on the large questions that answered many lesser ones. Barking orders, snatching telephones, and driving a flock of secretaries to distraction, he liked to work furiously when it counted most, then lapse into a state of relaxation so complete it resembled hibernation. Said an associate: "Joe always gave a deceptive impression because he wore dark suits, a homburg, and horn-rimmed glasses. But he was a physically big, rugged guy with a powerful torso and solid, muscular legs. Along with financial finesse, he had the sheer animal vitality to bull through a tough situation."[37]

Variety's solicitude was misplaced. Presented with additional power and wider opportunity, an irresistible combination, Kennedy became "special adviser" to First National, at an annual salary of $150,000,[38] receiving in addition his customary stock options. His move stirred an air of expectancy in the industry. Widely predicted was a combination of FBO, Pathé, and First National, creating a breath-takingly efficient giant.[39] It was calculated that a merger of the three companies could cut their combined overhead in half. The bankers involved were reported enthusiastic, and understandably so; a three-cornered alliance would mean a profitable recapitalization. When Ed Derr, treasurer of FBO, followed Kennedy to First National, as chief of operations, industry observers exchanged knowing smiles.

The pieces of the big deal appeared to be falling into place. On taking over First National in June, Kennedy had demanded absolute authority over production and distribution. The contract laid before him in early August formally met this stipulation.[40] With a stroke of his pen, Kennedy would be armed with power to push through the merger, thrusting himself to the pinnacle of the picture business. There was truth in the ballyhoo hailing him as "the coming Napoleon of the movies."[41]

Then, with stunning swiftness, everything collapsed. After six days of deliberation, First National's board of directors reconsidered Kennedy's contract and refused to ratify it.[42] Some directors expressed dissatisfaction with his production plans; others had second thoughts about the sweeping grant of power to a man bent on a merger they might not care to live with. The president said the company was not sick enough to need such strong medicine.[43] Kennedy had no choice but to resign.

This reversal threw him off stride only momentarily. Other deals were spinning. After his resignation from First National, Kennedy telephoned his wife at Hyannis Port and told her to join him in New York; they were sailing for Europe in a few days aboard the *Ile de France*. To reporters at the dock, Kennedy jovially explained that he and his companion, J. J. Murdock, needed the peace and quiet of a cruise to confer at length about the future of their enterprises.[44] Just before they sailed, a clue to their conversations emerged with the announcement that Murdock and Kennedy had signed contracts for RCA Photophone licenses for Pathé and FBO respectively.[45] Kept under wraps was a further agreement: RCA now had an option to buy control of FBO. As they lounged on the deck of the *Ile de France*, the subject that absorbed Kennedy and Murdock was the approaching fulfillment of David Sarnoff's grand design.

The elements of the biggest prize of Kennedy's movie career came together in October, 1928. It was announced that FBO and Keith-Albee-Orpheum had been merged with RCA Photophone to create Radio-Keith-Orpheum, a holding company with assets of eighty million dollars. Management control of the new RKO went to RCA,[46] which gained a market of some two hundred theaters for its Photophone sound equipment.

As the Sarnoff regime came in, Kennedy, who received $150,000 for arranging the merger,[47] bowed out and cashed in his stock. He and his partner, Guy Currier, sold their remaining interest in FBO for some five million dollars[48] and parted as men glad to be rid of each other. Currier's once warm regard for Kennedy had turned to cold distrust. In 1927, Currier had asked Stuart Webb, a Boston banker, to go into FBO to keep an eye on his interests, telling him with a smile: "Joe's all right until he gets to believing his own publicity."[49] Despite this precaution, Currier, at his villa in Florence that winter, learned of Kennedy's dickering with Sarnoff only after an agreement had been reached, a move he described as "betrayal."[50]

What Kennedy gained from the sale of FBO represented only part of his profits. He held an option on seventy-five thousand shares of Keith-Albee-Orpheum stock, which he exchanged for an option on a like number of shares of RKO "A" stock, at a price of twenty-one dollars[51] a share. First traded on the Curb Exchange, RKO common was admitted to the New York Stock Exchange in December. Mike Meehan, exploiting the magic name of Radio, immediately pushed it up.[52] Few market operators could match his muscle: RKO "A" stock rose to around fifty dollars a share. Kennedy rode the stock up, selling as he exercised his options and clearing a profit of some two million dollars.[53]

He was now out of the picture business, except for loose ties with Pathé and Gloria Productions. After thirty-two months in the movies, he was more than thirty pounds underweight—and perhaps five million dollars richer.[54]

CHAPTER 8

Crash!

As he relaxed in Palm Beach during the winter of 1928–29, Kennedy, like many others in that season, thought long and hard about what was happening to the stock market. His forethought saved perhaps all he had recently gained. For he decided to get out.

Kennedy, with cool professional detachment, was betting against the crowd and the weight of informed opinion. Hoover's resounding victory over Smith in 1928 had sent the Bull Market surging ahead, its supporters rejoicing at the prospect of "four more years of prosperity." Actually, the bulls' slogan was modest. Business leaders spoke earnestly of a "New Era," during which America would banish poverty and achieve permanent prosperity. Thousands of men and women, sober wage earners and pillars of the middle class, scarcely needed the goad of such propaganda to plunge into the stock market. Having watched others win fortunes during the market's upward march, they came to believe they could buy almost any common stock at almost any price and sell when its price had doubled or tripled, depending on how patient they were and how wealthy they wished to become. Everyone knew someone who had made a killing and now was set for life. Newcomers snapped up the stock of Seaboard Air Line, eager to get in on the ground floor of the aviation boom, and later were surprised to learn they were shareholders in a railroad. But that mistake, like every other in those happy times, cost little; rails were rising too.

The surge of public interest in the stock market was amazing: an estimated one person in a hundred in the population was playing stocks on margin at the peak of the boom in the fall of '29.[1] But it was not the amateur speculating on a shoestring who propelled the market on its dizziest spree; it was the experienced professional who presumably knew what he was doing. The rampaging Bull Market had trampled the old rules and smashed the old yardsticks. Once-wary veterans, fooled by setbacks that proved only breathing spells before new advances, abandoned skepticism and bought at prices that formerly had seemed impossibly high. Radio, for instance, had looked steep at 150 in 1927; a year later, buyers clamored to get it at 400. Why couldn't it go to 500? Radio would, and men would buy for the rise to 600.

The big bull operators rivaled movie stars as popular heroes. One of the biggest was William Crapo Durant, who founded General Motors, lost control to the bankers,[2] and now was staging a spectacular comeback at the head of a syndicate of multimillionaires jocularly known as "the Prosperity Boys." Durant, it was said, could muster enough buying power to nudge the market where he pleased; in 1928, he handled a fantastic eleven million shares. The seven Fisher brothers, made rich by the auto boom, organized a family investing company and were playing the market with a reported bankroll of twenty-five million dollars. Scores of stock pools were operating on the Exchange. Mike Meehan, at his accustomed place in the thick of intrigue, was rigging Radio and other favorites on a gigantic scale. Arthur W. Cutten, dubbed "the novice with a bag of tricks" by an admiring press, pushed up Sinclair Consolidated Oil as the manager of a pool rumored to have taken profits of nearly thirteen million dollars.[3] It was all wondrously easy, so long as the market rose. New York's leading bankers, Charles E. Mitchell of the National City and Albert H. Wiggin of the Chase National, from whom a counsel of caution might have been expected, exuded optimism, their reassurances echoing the popular conviction: the market was sound and sure to go higher.[4]

The businessman held the attention of a near-worshipful public;

he was the arbiter of taste and morals; his ideals were the nation's. For two successive years, Bruce Barton's *The Man Nobody Knows* topped the nonfiction best-seller list, proclaiming the gospel that Jesus was a go-getter, the first modern executive, who "picked up twelve men from the bottom ranks of business and forged them into an organization that conquered the world."[5] Millions avidly read the tales of enterprise fashioned by *American Magazine*. Included among its heroes was Joseph P. Kennedy, but he was merely one of many climbing the golden ladder. He was not identified in the popular mind with the "mission" of capitalism, as was, say, John J. Raskob, chairman of the finance committee of General Motors. Raskob, a lifelong Republican who deserted the G.O.P. to serve as Al Smith's campaign manager, thereby giving the Bull Market bipartisan blessing, signed an article for the *Ladies Home Journal* in the summer of 1929 with the eye-catching title, "Everybody Ought to Be Rich." He promised results if housewives faithfully invested as little as fifteen dollars a month in the stock market.

It was the age of the booster, and the philosophy of boosterism found eloquent expression in a book entitled *New Levels in the Stock Market*, published in August, 1929. The author, Charles Amos Dice, professor of business organization at Ohio State University, recalled the freebooting capitalists of a former day, then held up for admiration the enlightened statesmen of the New Era. "Have we not heard their voices over the radio? Are we not familiar with their thoughts, ambitions and ideals as they have expressed them to us almost as a man talks to his friends? The secrecy and mystery that surrounded the leaders have disappeared. Openness, frankness, and directness have taken their places."[6] The foundation of the stock market and prosperity, wrote Professor Dice, was the public's trust—its "sublime faith"—in the leaders.[7]

In this atmosphere radiant with trust and unselfishness, Kennedy was neither a dupe nor a deceiver. He knew better than Professor Dice how much faith some of the leaders deserved. He knew, for instance, that Raskob, who encouraged the little woman to shake her pennies from the sugar bowl and play the market, was the largest individual participant in the big Radio pool of 1928, which fleeced the lambs of hundreds of thousands of dollars. He would not have criticized Raskob, as he did, for shearing the lambs, or for resorting to hypocrisy; that was the insider's timeless way with the gullible outsider. What appalled him was the fact that Raskob, and scores of men like him, actually believed every word spoken about the bountiful future. They were victims of their own propaganda, self-hypnotized spellbinders.

An emotional man, deeply pessimistic by nature, Kennedy as a businessman had the saving ability to suppress his emotions and coldly analyze the facts, as when he curbed his impulse and stood fast during the short-lived market retreat of June, 1928. Now the situation had changed; unmistakable danger signals were flashing. Yet the big bankers and industrialists, the stalwarts of the nation's business Establishment, were optimists almost to a man. They could not—would not—see the peril in the runaway market. So compulsively bullish were the leaders that they dismissed disagreeable evidence right up to the last moment. Only a week before the crash, Charles E. Mitchell would declare: "I know of nothing fundamentally wrong with the stock market. . . ."[8]

As 1929 opened, the newly rich Kennedy respected the position and power to which he aspired; he still went out of his way to meet and impress those who wielded influence. For instance, he sought to gain the attention of the most important financial name of all. One day he strolled over to the offices of J. P. Morgan and asked to see the financial titan. However, Morgan the Younger sent out word that he was too busy to see Kennedy.[9] By the end of tumultuous 1929, Kennedy had lost all trace of awe, and regarded himself as the peer of any Establishment figure. Later, when businessmen spoke of Kennedy in tones of injury as a "traitor" to the common interest, and asked perplexedly how a "conservative" like him could stomach the New Deal, he sometimes recalled how wrong such businessmen had been, and how he had saved himself by ignoring them. After the crash, he made no effort to conceal his contempt for the mighty whose blindness had brought them low. "Big businessmen are the most overrated men in the country," he told his sons. "Here I am, a boy from East Boston, and I took 'em. So don't be impressed."[10]

As early as Christmas, 1928, the stock market appeared nervous, edgy, overstimulated. Only a month after the rally sparked by Hoover's victory, the market broke more sharply than it had during the previous spring. Leading issues lost scores of points during a single day's trading. Precisely why the slump occurred, and why the market perked up after a few ragged weeks, was unclear; but the influence of small margin players could not be doubted. For they got into the market by borrowing to the limit from their brokers; faced with a price break and calls for more collateral which they could not supply, they were sold out. Their stock was thrown on the market by brokers recovering their loans, and had the effect of accelerating every price drop. One day, buying support might come into the market too late, and the result would be panic.

After a rough winter, the market seemed to right itself in the spring of 1929. As it frisked, optimism revived and the shaky pyramid of brokers' loans rose higher. Kennedy stuck to his decision. The profits he took from the sale of his RKO stock and other holdings were not reinvested, but kept in cash. To a friend who expressed surprise at his gradual withdrawal from the market, Kennedy declared: "Only a fool holds out for the top dollar."[11]

In May, 1929, Patrick J. Kennedy died in Boston at the age of seventy-one. Unlike his son, whose homes were scattered from Cape Cod to New York to Palm Beach, the elder Kennedy, as the *Transcript* noted, had remained "loyal to the island district and . . . active in all movements for community welfare."[12] The worlds of the father and son were not merely different, as would be expected, but entirely separate. Though proud of his only son's success in far-flung business ventures, Pat Kennedy had no desire to step beyond the small corner of the city in which the Kennedys had made their beginning. The list of his honorary pallbearers, led by John F. Fitzgerald, read like a who's who of Boston politics.[13] Aside from insurance, the bulk of his estate, valued at less than fifty-five thousand dollars, consisted of stocks in the East Boston banks and the coal company he had organized.[14] As a small reminder of older ties, there was included in the estate a twenty-five-dollar bond issued in 1920 by the short-lived Republic of Ireland.[15] Acting as executor of his father's estate, Joe Kennedy assigned the bond a realistic value of nothing.[16]

During the summer of 1929, it seemed that stocks would soar forever into the cloudless blue empyrean. Prices rose out of all proportion to the earnings of the companies they represented, indicating the market's willingness, in Max Winkler's phrase, to discount not only the future but the hereafter.

After the crash, skeptics would seem men miraculously preserved, like the few survivors of a great mine disaster. How had they caught the faint creak of sagging timbers? What prompted them to leave while so many stayed? In later years, Kennedy shrewdly recognized that the less fortunate would more readily forgive a lucky hunch than another's superior judgment. He liked to tell of having to elbow his way into crowded brokers' offices during the summer of '29, and of having his shoes shined in the financial district by a boy who called the turn on several stocks in that day's trading. Then and there, so ran his recollection, he decided that a market anyone could play, and a shoeshine boy could predict, was no market for him.[17] Friends and associates in Wall Street smiled at Kennedy's self-caricature. They knew he was no hunch player, prone to make a snap judgment and turn on his heel. At most, the jostling crowds and the clever bootblack speeded him on his deliberately chosen course: to get out from under.

He was standing at a safe distance when stock prices cracked in September. There followed weeks of uncertainty during which the market held together, giving rise to hopes that this was only another break before a new upturn. But no rally could make headway. Optimism returned during a brief upsurge on October 22, and was buried the next day under an avalanche of orders to sell. On October 24, as wave upon wave of selling pounded the market, thousands of insecurely margined traders saw themselves ruined. Prices dropped almost vertically and those who looked for the inrushing bargain hunters saw only others like themselves, selling frantically. Panic was in the air when the Establishment finally resolved to make a stand.

Led by the bankers Mitchell and Wiggin, the patrons of the stricken Bull Market quietly slipped into the offices of J. P. Morgan and Company, diagonally across Broad Street from the Stock Exchange, where stunned, silent crowds were gathering. "The Corner" at 23 Wall Street had proved a financial Gibraltar during past panics. Could it cope with an emergency of unprecedented scope? Within a few minutes, the half dozen bankers present had agreed to create a pool of $240,000,000 to support the market. Their plan was to shore up selected stocks, and so rally the rest. As the somber-faced bankers filed out, Thomas W. Lamont, the Morgan firm's polished diplomat, faced a roomful of hushed reporters. With majestic sangfroid, he cleared his throat and said: "There has been a little distress selling on the Stock Exchange." Early that afternoon, Richard Whitney, vice-president of the Exchange and broker for the Morgan interests, strode from post to post on the floor, raising his voice above the bedlam to place orders to buy ten thousand shares of Steel as well as other key stocks at the current prices. Word of the bankers' pool spread rapidly, and the market steadied. Although the last transaction before the three o'clock gong did not appear on the overworked ticker until after seven that evening, and the volume of trading set a new record, Wall Street breathed a little easier.[18]

Torrents of reassurance gushed from business leaders in the next two days. President Hoover issued a statement declaring that "the fundamental business of the country, that is, production and distribution of commodities, is on a sound and prosperous basis." But soothing words no longer cast a spell. On Tuesday, October 29, the Bull Market, that unshakable symbol of the American way, came crashing down with a terrifying roar that was to haunt the dreams of a generation. That day, an incredible sixteen-million-plus shares changed hands. Kennedy's Harvard classmate, social historian Frederick Lewis Allen, wrote in his classic *Only Yesterday*: "The big gong had hardly sounded in the great hall of the Exchange at ten o'clock Tuesday morning before the storm broke in full force. Huge blocks of stock were thrown upon the market for what they would bring. Five thousand shares, ten thousand shares appeared at a time on the laboring ticker at fearful recessions in price. Not only were innumerable small traders being sold out, but big ones, too, protagonists of the new economic era who a few weeks before had counted themselves millionaires. Again and again the specialist in a stock would find himself surrounded by brokers fighting to sell—and nobody at all even thinking of buying."[19]

At the height of the panic, speculator Bernard E. (Ben) Smith rushed into the office of W. E. Hutton and Company, where he had a desk, and pushed through the milling, confused throng. Over the din of the boardroom and the jangling telephones, Smith shouted: "Sell 'em all! They're not worth anything."[20]

It was the cry of the bear, whose turn it now was to rule Wall Street.

Billions of dollars of capital values had vanished into thin air. With the public wiped out and the big bulls dazed, the stock market sank into the abyss. A year after the crash, prices stood below the post-panic levels. During the long descent, Kennedy made important money by selling the market short.[21] Stories of his short-selling exploits put his profits anywhere from a plausible one million dollars to a wildly improbable fifteen million dollars. Whatever the figure, his method was familiar. He operated from a desk in the uptown branch of Halle and Stieglitz, on Madison Avenue and Fifty-second Street, but discreetly sent most of his short orders outside the firm, to friends in the offices of J. H. Oliphant and Company and Bache and Company.[22]

Members of the bear fraternity occasionally dropped by Kennedy's office. There was William Danforth, who was forced to the wall when he went short prematurely; he guessed correctly in late summer, plunged hard and amassed a rumored seven million dollars in the space of a few days.[23] Lean, sardonic Tom Bragg rode the Bull Market as a pool manager, but jumped clear in time to make big profits through short sales of American Telephone and Telegraph.[24] The best known of the bears, who won not only a Street nickname with his reaction to the "Black Tuesday" debacle, but also a reputed ten million dollars in a month of short selling, was "Sell 'em Ben" Smith.[25]

Superficially, Kennedy resembled Ben Smith. Both were Irish Catholics, born in the same year. Smith's birthplace, a shabby West Side Manhattan brownstone, had been as remote from wealth as the Kennedy home in East Boston. Both men had attracted attention early: as a fifteen-year-old, nine-dollar-a-week office boy, Smith, acting on customers' tips, snowballed a small stake into thirty-five thousand dollars in the stock market.[26] Neither of them smoked or drank, but both had a rough sense of humor and relished a good time. Market operators told the story of Smith's visit to the office of his fellow bear, Tom Bragg, during which he remembered a telephone call he should make. As Smith picked up the telephone, Bragg yelled: "Wait a minute. I'm short of Telephone. Don't give them any business just now." To which Smith replied: "Aw, you don't know me, Tom. I'm shorting Telephone myself. After I get done using that thing I pick it up and drag it after me, with the wire and all. See?" And with a sweep of his broad arm, Smith ripped the telephone from the wall.[27]

However, beneath the surface similarity—the zest for horseplay, the swearing, swaggering pose of tough guy, the outspoken allegiance to the Democratic party, and scorn for Wall Street's Republican blue bloods—lay the difference between a man of direct motives and one pursuing a complex ambition. Smith wanted wealth; and thanks to his superlative talent for sniffing the market, he had it. Who could say what Kennedy wanted? He probably wasn't sure himself. Wealth, yes; but something more. If Smith was recognizably a speculator, what was Kennedy? He mixed well in all kinds of company, against every background. He was equally at ease with hard-eyed manipulators like Smith and Wall Street patricians like Jeremiah Milbank, with corporation bosses as different as Paramount's Zukor and GE's Owen D. Young, with bantering newspapermen and press lords like William Randolph Hearst, Colonel Robert R. McCormick, and Joseph M. Patterson. He could enjoy the companionship of celebrities at the Ziegfield Roof and of roistering theatrical unknowns at Bertolotti's in Greenwich Village. Kennedy moved through many worlds, and only the keenest observer would detect the profound detachment of this gregarious man who belonged to no world but his own.

Where advantage was temporarily to be found, Kennedy made a place for himself. Years after the heyday of the short sellers, he drew upon his experience for a humorous illustration of their influence. He wrote:

> On a morning of one of those other days a famous and feared short walked down Broad Street. He was up to his neck in short orders in the stock of a well-known corporation that was holding a directors' meeting that morning.
>
> "Where are you going?" a friend asked him.
>
> "Oh," the notorious short grinned, "I'm going to the so-and-so board meeting."
>
> "Did they put you, of all people, on the board?" he was asked.
>
> "Sure," he grinned again. "To represent the shorts."[28]

While Kennedy got along with such bears as Smith, Danforth, and Bragg, he was not one of them. A confirmed loner, he was treated with polite distrust. In November, 1931, several market players, in Boston for the Harvard-Yale football game, gathered for a drink in Bragg's suite at the Ritz. Kennedy, also in town for the big game, came by to say hello. After an exchange of greetings, there was a lull in the conversation, which Kennedy finally broke. "I see where Steel is way down," he said casually. Everyone in the room knew that Bragg was driving down Steel, and that Kennedy wanted a clue to his plans. Bragg shook his head in mock solicitude. "That's too bad about Steel, Joe," he said affably. "What do you think we ought to do about it?" Another awkward pause followed, until someone changed the subject.[29]

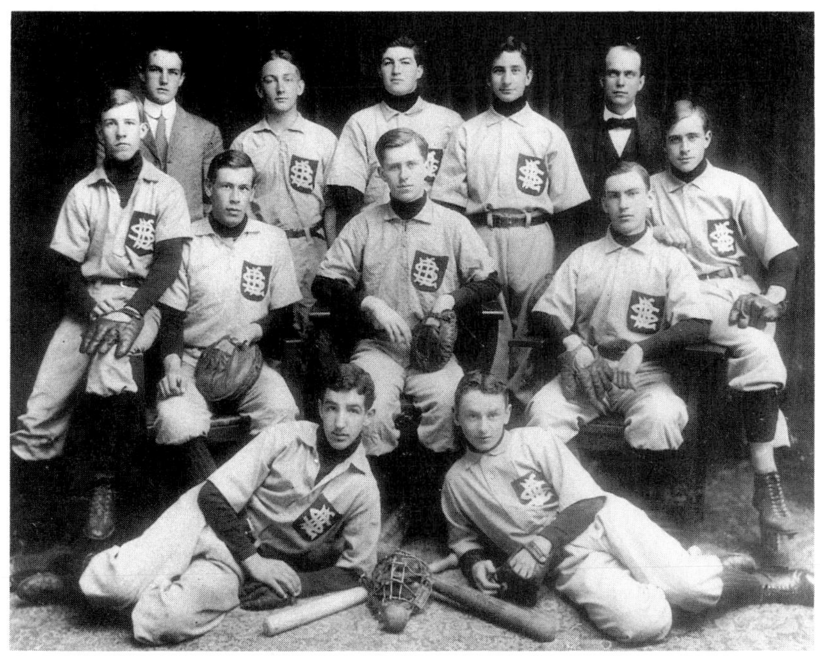

Kennedy as captain of his high school baseball team at Boston Latin School. He is seated third from left in middle row. (*UPI/Bettmann*)

Wedding photo of Mr. and Mrs. Joseph P. Kennedy on October 7, 1914. (*UPI/Bettmann*)

(RIGHT) Kennedy as President of the Columbia Trust Company after graduation from Harvard. (*UPI/Bettmann*)

(BELOW LEFT) Kennedy in the two-piece swimming attire of the period in 1917. (*UPI/Bettmann*)

(BELOW RIGHT) Kennedy shown with movie magnate Jesse Lasky in 1924. (*UPI/Bettmann*)

The Kennedys sail for Europe in the mid-twenties. (*Underwood & Underwood*)

Members of the Securities and Exchange Commission at their first meeting (SEATED, FROM LEFT) Ferdinand J. Pecora, Kennedy, James M. Landis; (STANDING, FROM LEFT) George R. Mathews, Robert F. Healy. (*Underwood & Underwood*)

Kennedy takes his oath as the new U.S. Ambassador to England, from Supreme Court Justice Stanley Reed (CENTER), as President Franklin D. Roosevelt (RIGHT) looks on, February 18, 1938. (*UPI/Bettmann*)

Ambassador and Mrs. Kennedy leave their London residence for a concert at Covent Garden in March, 1939. (*Wide World*)

Kennedy and Churchill outside 10 Downing Street in October, 1940. (*Wide World*)

Kennedy confers with Edward "Eddie" Moore, his longtime confidential secretary, for whom he named his youngest son. (*Life*)

Kennedy attends the 77th birthday party of his father-in-law, John F. Fitzgerald, former Mayor of Boston, on February 11, 1940. Honey Fitz is flanked by his wife and daughter. (*UPI/Bettmann*)

Former Ambassador Kennedy takes a break during his five-hour testimony on the Lend-Lease bill in January, 1941. (*Wide World*)

(ABOVE) Joseph P. Kennedy, Jr., as end on the Harvard freshman football team in 1934. (*Wide World*)

(LEFT) Kennedy and nine-year-old Teddy, sporting freckles and braces. (*Life*)

Ambassador Kennedy and his sons, Jack (LEFT) and Joseph P., Jr. (RIGHT) as they sailed for England in 1938. (*UPI/Bettmann*)

Kennedy is greeted by his son Jack, then twenty-three and a student at Stanford University, in San Francisco, in November, 1940. (*Boston Record-American*)

Robert Kennedy is sworn in as a Naval Aviation Cadet at First Naval District Headquarters by Comdr. Edward S. Brewer (RIGHT), as his father Joseph, Sr. (LEFT), looks on. (*UPI/Bettmann*)

Though he stood outside the bears' intensely secretive circle, Kennedy had ways of discovering what they were doing. One day Senator Burton K. Wheeler ran into him at the Harvard Club, and their conversation naturally turned to the stock market. The senator noted that Anaconda Copper, whose mining interests dominated his state of Montana, had slid to about twenty dollars a share. It looked like a bargain.

"If I find you buying Anaconda," said Kennedy, "I'll kick you in the pants. It will go to five dollars before we're through with it." To the puzzled Wheeler, Kennedy explained that Smith and Bragg had been double-crossed in a pool in Anaconda when other insiders dumped their stock without warning. Now the pair were determined to gain revenge by sabotaging a newly organized pool. Kennedy got wind of their scheme and quietly joined them. Before the disgruntled bears let up, Anaconda went even lower than Kennedy predicted.[30]

Absorbed with the stock market, Kennedy had little time for his role as chairman of the board of Pathé Exchange, Inc., and practically turned the management of the company over to such lieutenants as Ed Derr, Pat Scollard, and Frank Sullivan. (Derr somehow got the impression Kennedy had surrendered the reins, and proceeded to run Pathé as he pleased, a show of independence that angered his absentee boss and brought their relationship to an end.)[31] Pathé surely needed someone's firm hand. It was in serious trouble, caught up in the difficult transition to sound and saddled with a heavy load of debt assumed during the free and easy twenties. But Kennedy, in alliance with his friend and fellow Pathé director Elisha Walker, was preoccupied with turning a profit on his stock options.

Finally, the chairman was forced to act. His solution was to liquidate. Negotiating once again with David Sarnoff, Kennedy arranged the sale of Pathé's near-bankrupt production facilities to RKO, throwing into the bargain at Sarnoff's insistence the promise that Pathé would not resume film-making for a period of five years.[32] Kennedy would not be around to oversee that commitment. His movie career was about to end abruptly.

The Boston financier Stuart Webb, who had entered the picture business as Guy Currier's watchdog at FBO, was watching Kennedy from a new vantage point. Now a director of Pathé, he was unhappy with the do-nothing management. When Walker asked Webb, as a favor, not to sell any Pathé stock until Kennedy had a chance to unload, the latter's discontent turned to anger. Webb had no intention of selling his stock, and he questioned the propriety of Kennedy's maneuvers. The stock options had been given to him as an incentive to improve the company's performance. Webb decided to oust Kennedy and attempt to reorganize Pathé.[33]

Early in 1930, while Kennedy was in Palm Beach, Webb engineered a coup, rounding up enough preferred stock to win control of the board.[34] Before he realized what had happened, Kennedy found himself on the outside looking in. Within two months, he resigned the chairmanship, blandly announcing that Pathé was now strong enough to continue without his "executive aid."[35] He told reporters he would return to Wall Street and be associated with Elisha Walker.

Latest in the succession of influential men to whom Kennedy tied his fortunes, Walker was a native New Yorker, only nine years older than Kennedy but with almost two decades' longer experience in investment banking. He came into Wall Street in 1902, rising to a partnership in William Salomon and Company at thirty-one and the presidency of Blair and Company ten years later. As the banker for Sinclair Consolidated Oil, he gained a national reputation as the architect of some of the biggest oil deals of the twenties.[36] While overseeing the operations of Pathé for his friend, Jeremiah Milbank,[37] Walker caught the eye of a fabulous Californian, Amadeo Peter Giannini, a onetime San Francisco produce vendor and founder of a tiny immigrant bank, the Bank of Italy, which he built into the huge Bank of America.[38] Giannini, a dreamer with the will of a conqueror, wished to create a national bank, in spite of opposition from entrenched Eastern interests. Walker, sympathetic with the plan and wise in the ways of the East, seemed a useful partner; in 1929, Blair and Company merged with the Bank of America. In February of the following year, Giannini turned over to Walker the chairmanship and control of his billion dollar holding company, Transamerica Corporation. A few months later, Kennedy joined Walker, in an unofficial capacity, to help manage Transamerica's immense securities business.[39]

Unfortunately, the time was not propitious for an alliance of Giannini and Walker, whose temperaments were utterly opposite. With the grim onset of depression, Walker, showing himself to be every inch an orthodox Eastern banker, embarked on a program of retrenchment and liquidation. Although his delicately balanced financial pyramid was tottering, Giannini clung to his dream of a banking empire. Lashing out at Walker in furious disappointment, the aging Californian started a proxy fight to regain control of Transamerica.[40] It was one of the most dramatic corporate struggles of the thirties, with the opposing generals in San Francisco and New York sending armies of agents across the continent to woo stockholders and solicit proxies.

Caught in the middle, Kennedy declared his neutrality.[41] He privately agreed with Walker's policy of retrenchment—what else could be done?—and handled some transactions for Transamerica; but he was wary of incurring the wrath of the powerful Giannini, whom he knew from his Hollywood experience as a man possessed by implacable ambition. In the end, the founder of Transamerica routed the Walker forces and regained control. Only when the issue had been decided did Kennedy step into the picture. He helped Walker, who had been the largest single stockholder in Transamerica, dispose of his shares in private sales off the Exchange, a move which protected the price of the stock and in no way displeased the victorious Giannini.[42] Kennedy's hands-off attitude during the proxy fight soon made it possible for him to enlist Giannini as an ally in another contest—the 1932 presidential campaign.

Recovery, hopefully predicted in the months following the stock market crash, did not come. Instead, the economy sank in a remorselessly descending spiral of liquidation. Bank failures in 1930 numbered 1,345. Factories cut back production and finally shut down entirely. Month by month, unemployment rose; by the end of 1930, four million were jobless, and within twelve months the figure would be doubled. Agriculture, long depressed, was now prostrate. Foreclosures and evictions were stirring an ugly mood in the countryside. Two years before, the country had looked for the disappearance of poverty; now there were shocking signs of want and misery everywhere—the soup kitchen, the bread line, the corner apple seller.

At first men were drawn together in bewilderment at the enormity of what was occurring, then each took lonely account of his resources and prospects. In contrast to the jobless who trudged the streets and the homeless who huddled in the tar-paper shacks ("Hoovervilles") that sprang up outside the cities, Kennedy and his family experienced no physical discomfort or deprivation. His thirteen-year-old son, Jack, at the Canterbury School in New Milford, Connecticut, wrote in the fall of 1930: "Please send me the Litary [sic] Digest because I did not know about the Market Slump until a long time after, or a paper. Please send me some golf balls. . . ."[43] Yet Kennedy and other men of wealth shared the universal dread of what tomorrow might bring. While small depositors stood in disbelief before the shuttered windows of closed banks, rich men read with dismay the ticker report that United States government bonds, symbol of safety and security, were selling at a heavy discount. Rich and poor alike, men were afraid; and the more they had to lose, the greater their fear of a sudden fall into the disaster that had engulfed so many. They might even be pulled down by the people; a strong tide of resentment was running in the country. The bitter popular feeling of betrayal was expressed in the title of a book published in 1930, *People vs. Wall Street,* which arraigned the false prophets with statements from their own mouths.

Kennedy saw the future in the bleakest possible terms. Later, he wrote: "I am not ashamed to record that in those days I felt and said I would be willing to part with half of what I had if I could be sure of keeping, under law and order, the other half. Then it seemed that I should be able to hold nothing for the protection of my family."[44]

If law and order were indeed jeopardized by the breakdown of the economy, Kennedy was no better prepared than the next citizen to say what should be done. He had no political philosophy to speak of; his Democratic allegiance stemmed more from heredity than conviction. His father's professionalism, if anything, had helped drain politics of idealism, reducing it to an exciting but essentially cynical business in which office and advantage were all that mattered. As to the organization of society, the role of the individual and the place of the government, Kennedy's views were shapeless, little different from the shallow conservatism common to rich men. Perhaps his expressed wish to barter away half his wealth in return for security, an exchange impossible under a constitutional form of government, best illustrated the emotionalism of his approach to politics. With institutions long taken for granted now shaken, he would oppose no remedy that promised relief from fear, that spared the Kennedys.

Much could be lost without Kennedy being aware of it. His view of the economy was superficial and self-centered. He was a capitalist, yet one who stood apart from the *system* of finance, production, and distribution. He had no business, in the ordinary sense, and wanted none. He was adept at manipulating the externals—the price of a stock, the structure of a corporation; yet he had no deep understanding of the inner mechanism of the market economy, the interplay of individual decisions and actions that circulated goods and wealth through society. In his anxiety over the future, Kennedy could see only the flaws in the system, which he feared would provoke a radical redistribution of wealth. Anxious to forestall this, he would surrender the free economy to protect at least part of the wealth he had gained by exploiting it.

In 1930, he fastened his hopes on a man. At the invitation of Henry J. Morgenthau, Jr., he went to lunch at the Governor's Mansion in Albany, and renewed his association with Franklin D. Roosevelt.[45] His adversary from the World War I shipbuilding days could not have been more gracious, charming, eager to hear the views he poured out. Although Kennedy admired President Hoover personally, and always would regard him as an exceptionally able executive, he came away from a long afternoon in Albany prepared not only to contribute but also to campaign actively on Roosevelt's behalf.

"Roosevelt was a man of action," said Kennedy later. "He had the capacity to get things done.... Long before the campaign, long before his name was even seriously considered, I went out to work for him. I think I was the first man with more than $12 in the bank who openly supported him. I did this because I had seen him in action. I knew what he could do and how he did it, and I felt that after a long period of inactivity we needed a leader who would lead."[46]

In a more personal vein, Kennedy told a friendly journalist years later: "I wanted him [Roosevelt] in the White House for my own security and for the security of our kids, and I was ready to do anything to help elect him."[47]

Among his influential friends and acquaintances, Kennedy spread the name of his champion, not hesitating to proselytize even so staunch a Republican as Wall Street banker Jeremiah Milbank, Hoover's leading fund raiser. Recalled Milbank: "Joe called me one day in 1930 from California—I think he was staying at Hearst's ranch—and in the course of our conversation he asked me if I had a notebook. I said yes. 'Well,' he said, 'jot down the name of the next President. You're not hearing much about him now, but you will in 1932. It's Franklin D. Roosevelt. And don't forget who told you.'"[48]

BOOK III
THE NEW DEALER

"You can't tell the public to go to hell any more."
—*Joe Kennedy*

CHAPTER 9

The Man Who Called Hearst

EARLY IN 1931, Roosevelt's strategists, now more or less openly advancing his candidacy, set up headquarters in a small office on Madison Avenue in New York City.[1] Funds were chronically short. When the bills piled up, treasurer Frank C. Walker, a stolid, heavy-jowled lawyer, canvassed well-to-do Democrats, usually in company with another longtime Roosevelt backer, actor-producer Eddie Dowling.[2] On one such round in mid-Manhattan, Walker called on Kennedy, who asked what was going on in the Madison Avenue office. Walker invited him to come by and meet the man who ran it, Louis M. Howe.

Walker extended the invitation with some misgivings. It was one thing to introduce people to the organization's front man, James A. Farley, who grew heartier with each handshake. But Howe, the plotter in the back room, was a gnarled, waspish gnome of a man, wracked by an asthmatic cough, his clothes constantly rumpled (it was said on good authority that he *did* sleep in them) and sprinkled with ashes carelessly dropped from the cigarettes he chain-smoked. Roosevelt's veteran adviser kept his frail body going on the strength of his determination, now two decades old, to put "Franklin" in the White House. Beyond that, he gave not a damn for anybody or anything.

Keenly aware of Howe's rudeness to callers, Walker made a request several days before Kennedy's visit.

"Louis, as a special favor to me, please be nice to Mr. Kennedy when I bring him in, will you?"

"Oh, sure, sure, Walker," said Howe. "You needn't worry about me. Bring him right in."

Still uneasy, Walker repeated his plea a few hours before Kennedy was to arrive.

"Don't worry, don't worry," said Howe. "I'll put on my very best company manners for him."

That afternoon, Walker ushered Kennedy into Howe's dark, cluttered cell. Howe sat behind the desk with his arms folded and his head slumped forward, seemingly asleep. For a few moments of leaden silence, Walker and Kennedy contemplated the disheveled Buddha. Then Walker coughed politely, introduced Kennedy, and started a conversation. Howe did not lift his head, but merely opened one eye and fixed Kennedy with a baleful glare. At least five minutes passed before he sat up and took a desultory part in the conversation Walker had frantically kept going.[3] After a quarter hour, Kennedy was ready to explode. He left the office red-faced and angry.

Howe saw himself as Roosevelt's protector, and he disliked the risks he saw in accepting Kennedy's support. Having a notorious stock market operator close to the candidate might not go down well with voters who were thoroughly disillusioned with Wall Street. Howe also knew that Kennedy got along well with Roosevelt; the man who spoke often of "Franklin and I," as though referring to one person, was suspicious of anyone who might threaten his favored place. Deliberately, Howe had given Kennedy the "treatment," implicitly warning him to keep his distance.

However, Walker and others welcomed Kennedy. And Roosevelt, who gave no sign of knowing Howe's feelings, added his balm to the soft words that brought Kennedy around. His recovery from Howe's rebuff was speeded by his own dispassionate judgment: Roosevelt looked like a winner in '32 and he wanted to be with him. (He was not alone in his expectation; "Honey Fitz" and Jim Curley, though they were mortal enemies, jointly deserted their pro-Smith Irish colleagues in Massachusetts and shifted to the Roosevelt camp.)

Roosevelt could not afford to shut the door on anyone with money to contribute to his campaign. For he was following a strategy that affronted many customary Democratic contributors. Alone among the party's contenders, he indicted erring business leadership for the country's misfortunes, and urged drastic, if unspecified, reforms in the economy. It was a politics that was not so much radical as responsive to a clear emergency: since 1929, the national income had been cut in half; twelve million would be unemployed by 1932. He addressed his appeal not only to the anxious wage earners of the big cities, but also to the farmers and small businessmen of the stricken South and West. While distrustful of moneyed Easterners and devoted to the memory of William Jennings Bryan, they responded to Roosevelt's call for new government concern for "the forgotten man at the bottom of the economic pyramid."[4]

Such radical-sounding talk alarmed John J. Raskob, now chairman of the Democratic National Committee. He dropped all pretense of impartiality in the contest for the nomination and threw his weight behind the party's 1928 standard-bearer, Al Smith. Four years had worked a curious reversal of roles: Roosevelt, the Hudson River aristocrat, now frankly sought to arouse the multitude, while Smith, once the derby-wearing darling of the masses, was president of the Empire State Building, a resident of swank Fifth Avenue, and a man seldom seen in his old haunts, unless his chauffeur-driven limousine happened to flash by. Smith, the risen commoner, was the choice of the party's conservative wing. Not the least of his qualifications was his dislike of Roosevelt, who had nominated him in the "Happy Warrior" speech of 1924 and again in 1928, but who now wanted the prize for himself.

Roosevelt enjoyed the backing of a small band of wealthy men, including Jesse I. Straus of Macy's, Edward J. Flynn, Colonel Edward M. House, Judge Robert Worth Bingham of the Louisville *Courier-Journal,* William H. Woodin, president of the American Car and Foundry Company, and Herbert H. Lehman, Lieutenant Governor of New York. Kennedy's ready checkbook quickly gained him a place in this company. He gave twenty-five thousand dollars to Roosevelt's campaign and lent the Democratic party fifty thousand dollars more.[5] In addition, he raised one hundred thousand dollars among his friends and acquaintances, some of them Wall Street figures worried about the way the wind was blowing.[6] Bill Danforth, the big bear from Boston, occasionally put his personal pilot and plane at Kennedy's disposal for fund-raising forays around the country.[7] When contributions were given anonymously, Kennedy forwarded the money to the campaign treasury by means of his own personal checks, a practice which magnified his support and undercut the stubborn opposition of Howe.[8]

So far as Kennedy was concerned, the contest for the nomination had some of the aspects of a personal vendetta. His friend, Senator Wheeler, the former Progressive, had been the first Democrat of national reputation to announce his support of Roosevelt. In the spring of 1932, Wheeler and Kennedy were guests at a dinner in Boston. At the Harvard Club afterward, they discussed the campaign, and Kennedy asked if there was any chance Raskob would support Roosevelt. Through the smoke of a long Havana cigar, Wheeler said there was no chance at all; the lines were drawn for a fight to the finish. Roundly cursing the party chairman, whose hostility made fund-raising difficult, Kennedy said he would work hard for Roosevelt, if for no other reason than that "that son of a bitch Raskob" was against him.[9]

All was not zeal and enmity in Kennedy's politics. As Howe suspected, there was a cold, calculating streak of opportunism. Quite aside from anything else, there was a sufficient reason, from Kennedy's point of view, for putting himself ostentatiously on the side of reform: it appeared the reformers would run the show from now on. Utterly vanished was the popular faith in the country's business and financial leadership that had been evident prior to 1929. Rising in its place from the grass roots was an angry, vengeful spirit. Outcries for an investigation of the stock market fell on sympathetic ears in Washington. In April, 1932, the Senate Banking and Currency Committee opened public hearings.

For the better part of the next two years, men from Wall Street marched to the witness stand and described, with varying degrees of reluctance, their roles in the boom, the crash, and the bleak aftermath. It was doubtless true, as businessmen plaintively argued, that the politicians were seeking a scapegoat. But the hearings drew from the witnesses themselves admissions more shocking and damning than anything anti-business demagogues could contrive.

Appropriately, the first witness was the New York Stock Exchange's Richard Whitney. He parried the committee's questions about the stock pools and bear-raiding that flourished within his jurisdiction. Whitney vainly argued that such practices, if they existed, were not incompatible with free and fair markets.[10] Raskob appeared before the committee and took a mockingly defiant stance. Asked what his business was, he quipped: "Trying to make good Democrats out of a lot of misguided Republicans, I guess."[11] What did he think about pool operations? "Well . . ." he declared, "strange as it may seem, I really know almost nothing about the operations of the Stock Exchange."[12] This statement seemed very strange indeed when the committee unveiled evidence of Raskob's extensive pool trading and pointed to his name on Morgan's private list of influential men who received special favors in the market. There were other ghosts of the New Era, such as the bankers Charles E. Mitchell and Albert H. Wiggin, whose testimony revealed unconcern with the welfare of their depositors and stockholders, and ingenuity in their self-seeking. The hearings led through the labyrinth of holding-company finance, and the senators came away shaken at the discovery of how precarious had been the foundations of yesterday's imposing corporate edifices. There were moments of comic relief—a publicity-seeking midget hopped onto the ample lap of J. P. Morgan the Younger; "Sell 'em Ben" Smith, asked if he was known as a bear raider, roared: "No one has called me a bear-raider to my face . . ."[13] But the dramatic confrontation of the nation's money power and incensed public opinion could have only one outcome: it toppled into disrepute not only the men who had abused the free enterprise system, but the system itself.

Although he was as culpable as many of those called to Washington, Kennedy was not asked to testify, his strenuous efforts in Roosevelt's behalf having made him seem wholesomely unrepresentative of Wall Street. He took a certain satisfaction from the spectacle of the Establishment at bay. Recalling the investigation, he wrote in his 1936 campaign book, *I'm For Roosevelt:* "For month after month the country was treated to a series of amazing revelations which involved practically all the important names in the financial community in practices which, to say the least, were highly unethical. The belief that those in control of the corporate life of America were motivated by honesty and ideals of honorable conduct was completely shattered."[14]

Anyone who supposed that Kennedy's own motives and conduct had undergone a change through association with the reformers had a rude surprise in store.

By the spring of 1932, the balance of power at the approaching Democratic convention clearly rested with William Randolph Hearst

Allied with John Nance Garner and California's William G. McAdoo, the publisher controlled eighty-six convention delegates—forty-two from Texas, forty-four from California.[15] Pledged to Garner, who had no chance of winning, these votes could break a deadlock and throw the nomination to the man Hearst selected. Himself a frustrated office seeker, Hearst delighted in his potential power and cracked the whip over the heads of the front runners, Smith and Roosevelt, forcing them to kowtow to his pet dogmas. In a signed editorial in the New York *American* on April 24, he called down "A Plague o' Both Your Houses," describing Smith and Roosevelt as equally obnoxious internationalists. The previous year, two days after Hearst had announced for Garner, Roosevelt abjectly had repudiated the League of Nations, but had omitted mention of the League Court. "The unknown American man," wrote Hearst, "is not going to be benefited by Mr. Roosevelt's plan to put this country into foreign complications by the trap door of the League Court."

Faced with the necessity for another act of submission, Roosevelt sent Kennedy off to California on what was described as a "business trip." He chose his emissary well. While in the movie business, Kennedy had met and cultivated Hearst, the lavish patron of actress Marion Davies. Hearst grew to respect his financial acumen, all the more because he himself had a childlike concept of money. (When a friend once told him there was money in the movies, Hearst ruefully said: "Yes—mine.") Kennedy, an isolationist after Hearst's own heart, hurried to the publisher's castle at San Simeon and reassured him of Roosevelt's patriotism. He also tried to discover if there was any move afoot to deliver the Garner votes to the Smith forces, who now were anxious to stop Roosevelt at almost any price.

Early in May, Kennedy, accompanied by Eddie Moore, his father-in-law, and Jim Curley, reported back to Roosevelt, who was vacationing in Warm Springs, Georgia.[16] Hearst's "plague," it appeared, was not irrevocable; it might pass away if Roosevelt avoided giving offense. As for the Garner votes, there seemed little chance of Hearst and McAdoo joining the stop-Roosevelt drive, for McAdoo vividly remembered how his candidacy had been crushed by Smith and his rowdy Tammany followers at the bitter 1924 convention. Everything pointed to the likelihood of Texas and California acting independently.

As it happened, Chicago was the site of both party conventions, and the contrast in party spirit was striking. In mid-June, the Republicans listlessly went through the motions of renominating President Hoover. They did not dwell on the melancholy subject of the Depression; they had found nothing new to say about it. The liveliest debate came on the issue of Prohibition and ended with a straddle in the platform that dissatisfied wets and drys alike. Their cheerless business completed, the Republicans trailed out of the city.

In the vanguard of eager Democrats who arrived a week later was Kennedy, tagged after by faithful Eddie Moore. Roosevelt was well in front with close to a majority of the convention delegates, but he lacked some two hundred votes of the two-thirds necessary for the nomination. During the week before the convention opened, Jim Farley and Ed Flynn labored in the Roosevelt headquarters at the Congress Hotel, occasionally calling on Kennedy for help. He carried confidential messages, caught and spread high-level rumors, and buttonholed influential party figures. "Joe worked his fool head off," said one who was close to him in Chicago.[17] However, when Louis Howe arrived from New York, Kennedy discreetly faded into the background.

Farley and Flynn, inexperienced in national politics, failed to head off a foolhardy attempt on the part of Roosevelt supporters to dump the two-thirds rule. Finally, with defeat certain, the candidate himself had to call a humiliating halt to the effort.[18] Now the votes of Texas and California were indispensable, but the Garner supporters stayed aloof. Even before the first ballot was cast, delegates were telling each other that the convention could follow the pattern of 1924: deadlock, exhaustion, and a dark horse. Heard frequently in the hotel lobbies and corridors was the name of Newton D. Baker, who was rumored to have the backing of the utilities and of Bernard Baruch. (In truth, the prudent Baruch had private preferences, but would not publicly back a candidate until the convention nominated one. Like his friend Kennedy, he wanted to be with the winner.)

A Baker headquarters opened and telegrams urging his nomination bombarded the delegates. The boomlet was a blessing in disguise for the Roosevelt camp. For Baker, the Secretary of War in Wilson's Cabinet and a defender of the League of Nations, stood high up on Hearst's well-known blacklist. The possibility of so ardent an internationalist being nominated appalled the publisher. On the eve of the first ballot, the possibility seemed safely remote, but Roosevelt men in Chicago played up the danger in their repeated telephone calls to San Simeon. Kennedy called several times, warning Hearst to act before it was too late. Hearst, who had his own agents on the scene, was not to be stampeded. He said he would wait and see what the convention did on the first few ballots.[19]

What followed in the sweltering convention hall was a nightmare for Roosevelt's workers. Through three drawn-out ballots, their candidate gained little ground; they saw their prediction of deadlock and a dark horse coming true. Roosevelt was stalled only some eighty votes short of victory, but several states in the South, despite Huey Long's cajoling and bullying, were ready to bolt. The Roosevelt front could crack on the next ballot, and the way would be open for Smith or Baker. Now the switchboard at the Congress Hotel lighted up with calls to California. Farley tried in vain to get through. Curley sat in his room for hours awaiting a connection, finally turning the telephone over to an assistant who stayed at his post until four o'clock in the morning, when the operator told him Hearst had gone to bed and he might as well, too.[20] During that long, anxious day Hearst did accept a few calls. One came from an excited Kennedy.

Arthur Krock later recalled that he had been sitting in Kennedy's hotel room when he telephoned Hearst at San Simeon. Calling the publisher "W. R.," Kennedy put the matter bluntly: "Do you want Baker?" Hearst said he did not. Then, according to Krock, Kennedy said: "If you don't want Baker, you'd better take Roosevelt, because if you don't take Roosevelt, you're going to have Baker." Apparently unenthusiastic about this forced choice, Hearst asked if there was any chance that he could get the nomination for another dark horse, Maryland's Governor Albert Ritchie. "No, I don't think so," replied Kennedy. "I think if Roosevelt cracks on the next ballot, it'll be Baker."[21]

After talking with his representative in Chicago, Hearst decided his original plan to hold fast for at least seven ballots was impossible. Garner must deliver his delegates to Roosevelt. Informed of Hearst's decision, Garner concurred. Hours before the fourth ballot, he called his manager, Sam Rayburn, and told him it was time to break up the convention. Rayburn, for his part, had just about nailed down the vice-presidential nomination for Garner. That evening, as the clerk came to California in the roll call, the steaming, crowded hall fell silent. McAdoo rose proudly, aware that he was about to name a candidate and destroy an enemy. In a few moments, it was all over. Delegation after delegation, except for the Smith irreconcilables, swung aboard the Roosevelt bandwagon set rolling by California.

Over the pandemonium thundered the organ, playing the nominee's theme song—"Happy Days Are Here Again."

Many men had a hand in the decisive switch of the Hearst-controlled votes, but Kennedy later claimed full credit. Yes, he boasted long afterward, his telephone call had brought Hearst around, "but you don't find any mention of it in the history books."

Toward noon on the day after Roosevelt's nomination, following a night of wild celebration, Kennedy sat with two of Baruch's men, Hugh Johnson and Herbert Bayard Swope, in the latter's suite. Swope, clad in a gaudy robe, was consuming one of his celebrated late breakfasts while the others idly looked on. There was nothing to do until Roosevelt arrived that evening to accept the nomination. Baruch appeared, followed by Columbia University's Raymond Moley, the original "brain truster." Moley had come, at Baruch's request, to read one of the two versions of the candidate's acceptance speech. Under Roosevelt's direction, Moley had spent many weeks writing and rewriting an acceptance speech. But in the midst of last evening's jubilation, Howe, in a fit of jealousy, had gone off to draft a new speech, which he refused to show Moley. After Moley read what he hoped was the authorized text, Kennedy said enthusiastically: "I think it's a very bullish speech." The others agreed and Moley, with a grateful smile, went off to spend anxious hours awaiting the candidate. Before Roosevelt stepped into the spotlight that evening, he diplomatically inserted the introduction from Howe's labor of love into Moley's text.[22] Seated in the hall, Kennedy heard the phrase that would give a name to an era and a new identity to himself as Roosevelt intoned his peroration: "I pledge you, I pledge myself, to a new deal for the American people."

After his return to New York, Roosevelt embarked from Long Island on a restful week-long cruise up the New England coast aboard the yawl *Myth II*. Trailing the nominee's craft was the yacht *Ambassadress,* on which there was little relaxation. Kennedy, Jesse Straus, Ed Flynn, Robert Jackson, and Forbes Morgan conferred about campaign finances, for success in Chicago had not solved the candidate's money problems. "The great trouble with the Democrats," said Huey Long in the closing weeks of the campaign, "is that we have all the votes and no money. In the present situation I believe the best thing we could do is to sell President Hoover a million votes for half what he is going to pay to try to get them. We can spare the votes and we could use the money."[23]

Through the rest of the summer, Kennedy stepped up his calls on wealthy Democrats. Among those he now tapped was Hearst, who quietly contributed some thirty thousand dollars. Roosevelt was not unappreciative. In mid-August, he invited Kennedy to serve on the campaign executive committee, but the honor was declined.[24] Kennedy explained that he felt there should be no dissenting voice in Howe's office.

Even so, his voice was heard. At Roosevelt's request, he informally contributed ideas to the candidate's speeches on the economy. One speech incorporating some of his suggestions was delivered in Columbus, Ohio, on August 20. It was, in part, a strident partisan attack on "the new economics" of the Hoover era, described as "the heyday of promoters, sloganeers, mushroom millionaires, opportunists, adventurers of all kinds." Under the rhetoric, however, were some thoughtful proposals. Roosevelt urged measures to prevent "the issue of manufactured and unnecessary securities of all kinds which are brought out merely for the purpose of enriching those who handle their sale to the public . . . The sellers shall tell the uses to which the money is to be put. This truth telling requires that definite and accurate statements be made to the buyers. . . ." The candidate proposed a number of specific reforms in the nation's banking and financial system, including federal regulation of holding companies, and commodity and securities exchanges.[25]

Here was the blueprint for one of the New Deal's boldest innovations, the Securities and Exchange Commission. As he casually passed on his observations to speech writer Moley, Kennedy scarcely could have imagined that the responsibility for giving substance to the design ultimately would fall upon him.

In the fall, Kennedy accepted an invitation to accompany Roosevelt aboard his campaign train.[26] From mid-September until the eve of Election Day, the nominee was on the move, traveling some thirteen thousand miles and speaking at whistle stops, in town squares and big city arenas, at fairgrounds and race tracks, wherever crowds gathered to see the man who might be President. The long tour generated something of the excitement of a traveling circus; one could almost catch the smell of greasepaint in the air. Somehow the pat campaign routine always seemed new. Several times a day, Roosevelt drew a laugh from the crowds by introducing his lanky son Jimmy as "my little boy," and even the subject and the troupe grinned at the oft-repeated but effective touch. As the train sped along, there was ceaseless coming and going through the cars, hurried comparing of notes and redrafting of speeches, endless hand shaking and story telling with the stream of mayors, governors, congressmen, and senators who climbed aboard to appear before the voters with the candidate.

From early morning until late at night, Kennedy was caught up in the activity that so strongly resembled show business. He rode in the car ahead of the candidate, along with Farley, Moley, Senator Key Pittman, Breckinridge Long, an assistant Secretary of State under Wilson, and other advisers and convivial greeters. Newsmen identified Kennedy as one of Roosevelt's "silent six," his intimate counselors. When the train stopped for a spell, Kennedy usually separated himself from the official party, dropping in on local businessmen and bankers for a chat, gleaning information and impressions that he passed along to Farley and Moley. In blunt, pungent speech, he attacked the do-nothing Republicans and boosted Roosevelt. "Joe wasn't a sweet-talking salesman," said one who watched him campaign. "In fact, he was the antithesis of a salesman. He would hit you with the truth so suddenly it would be stunning."[27]

Kennedy's contacts proved invaluable. Early in September, he received a wire from A. P. Giannini. The Californian had turned Transamerica around since his proxy fight with Elisha Walker, but he feared Hoover was not leading the country toward recovery. Because Roosevelt was little known in the West, he asked Kennedy to answer some questions about him. Delighted by the inquiry, Kennedy arranged a meeting of Roosevelt, Farley, and himself with Giannini in San Francisco during the candidate's western swing. Although Giannini did not commit himself, the meeting confirmed his inclination. Top officers in his bank, loyal Republicans, tried to dissuade him, and even had Hoover make a personal telephone appeal ("You're a man of tremendous influence in California . . ."), but Giannini refused to endorse the President, declaring: "I'm not in politics at all."[28]

That, of course, was a polite fiction. To an associate in New York, Giannini sent a secret wire: "Please phone Joe Kennedy my congratulations on splendid way he and Farley are handling campaign. Also say if he will keep Carter Glass [the influential Virginia Senator with a strong conservative following] on radio between now and election he will roll up several more million votes . . . This is a confidential wire. Please destroy it after you have conveyed information to Joe."[29]

Kennedy frequently acted as Roosevelt's unseen eyes and ears. Just before the election, the Boston *Globe* reported: "Unrecognized in his home town and his presence here known only to a few close friends and relatives, Joseph P. Kennedy, New York financier, former motion picture magnate, and one of Gov. Roosevelt's confidential advisers in the presidential campaign, slipped into Boston on the eve of Al Smith's local appearance and departed Tuesday after the Roosevelt speech. . . . On his Boston visit of almost a week he lived up to his reputation as 'a man of mystery.' "[30]

Asked why the press had not spotted Kennedy, "Honey Fitz" said: "Joe is always in the background, you know. He keeps tabs on things independently of the official party."[31]

Among those on whom Kennedy secretly kept tabs was Father Charles E. Coughlin, the fiery Detroit priest who commanded a weekly radio audience of millions with his scathing attacks on the nation's "money changers."[32] Just as Kennedy could go in the garb of an isolationist to mollify Hearst, so he now might present himself as a leading Catholic layman and champion of social justice to keep Father Coughlin on the side of the New Deal. More than his money or his advice, Kennedy's easy access to many separate worlds was his greatest service to Roosevelt. The loner could be everyone's friend and sympathizer.

What Kennedy did for Roosevelt was done with an eye to the reward he wanted for himself. After the campaign ended, Eddie Dowling recalled many years later, "he [Kennedy] moved in close to those in power. He knew what he wanted and he fought for it, because he felt he had as much right to it as anyone else."[33]

On election night, Kennedy celebrated Roosevelt's victory as though it were a personal triumph, staging a lavish party that spilled through two floors of New York's Waldorf-Astoria. The endless playing of "Happy Days Are Here Again" matched his mood of exhilaration and anticipation. The excitement and stimulation he had enjoyed during the campaign were as nothing compared to what he thought was in store. He seemed assured of an important post in the new administration, and confidently expressed to friends the expectation that he would be tapped for Secretary of the Treasury.[34]

The merrymaking continued in Florida, as Roosevelt took a post-election cruise aboard Vincent Astor's yacht with his top backers and associates, including Kennedy. On shore, Henry Doherty, owner of the Miami Biltmore Hotel at Coral Gables, threw a big party. "Honey Fitz" and his wife were among the guests, and Eddie Dowling asked the stately Mrs. Fitzgerald to waltz. As they danced, she exclaimed brightly: "Isn't it wonderful! My son-in-law Joe Kennedy has made Franklin D. Roosevelt President!"[35]

Dowling's jaw dropped. What could be said? Evidently Mrs. Fitzgerald had the story straight from Joe.

CHAPTER 10

The Cop on Wall Street's Corner

ONE BY ONE, the men who had contributed to Roosevelt's victory were offered a share in it. Some advisers simply shifted familiar duties to new Washington offices. Louis Howe stayed close to "Franklin" as chief secretary at the White House. Ray Moley, appointed an Assistant Secretary of State, remained directly responsible to Roosevelt as taskmaster of the intellectuals. The new Secretary of State was the tall, courtly former senator from Tennessee, Cordell Hull, a Roosevelt stalwart in the South. The worsening economic crisis aroused intense speculation as to the new President's choice for Secretary of the Treasury. Roosevelt confounded the guessers by naming William H. Woodin, a businessman and an old friend who could be relied on to follow orders. There were embassies for several large contributors—Jesse Straus went to Paris, Breckenridge Long to Rome. Vincent Astor and Frank Walker gratefully declined similar invitations. Attempts were made to accommodate even the difficult Jim Curley, who wanted to be Secretary of the Navy or Ambassador to Italy, but was offered instead the U.S. Embassy in Warsaw. That, sniffed Curley, was a job fit for a Republican, and he returned to Boston.

Almost everyone who had played an important role in Roosevelt's election seemed to have been rewarded, with the exception of one man who had made no secret of his importance or expectations. Spending the winter in Palm Beach, Kennedy stayed close to the telephone, but the call from Washington did not come.

In March, Kennedy sent a telegram to the President, passing on praise he had heard of the new administration. Several weeks later, a polite but distant reply arrived, thanking him for his work during the campaign and closing with a vague invitation: "Do be sure to let us know when you are going through Washington and stop off and see us."[1] Evidently, Kennedy would see the New Deal only as a high-level tourist.

His pride wounded, his boasts deflated, he turned privately critical of Roosevelt. The burden of his complaints was that the President was guilty of the cardinal political sin—ingratitude. In his disappointment, Kennedy applied pressure to the Democratic party for prompt repayment of the fifty-thousand-dollar loan he had made during the campaign, even hinting he would take legal action.[2] His friends were sympathetic, but urged patience; when that no longer seemed appropriate, they advised him to bind up his bruised ego and go to see Roosevelt. After writing a highly complimentary letter to the President, Kennedy finally went to Washington.[3]

Ever the master of a difficult situation, Roosevelt invariably exerted a hypnotic charm over Kennedy in their face-to-face meetings. His greeting on this occasion was blandly disarming: "Hello, Joe, where have you been all these months? I thought you'd got lost."[4]

Roosevelt had not forgotten Kennedy's cash support and hard work. But there was opposition to him at the White House, chiefly from the implacable Howe.[5] This, combined with his own uncertainty about where to put this man of strong opinions, caused Roosevelt to defer the matter of Kennedy's reward. If he sensed that his former adviser was angry, he also knew Kennedy would come when he was called.

Unwelcome for the moment in the ranks of reform, Kennedy returned to Wall Street and his old ways. Even while campaigning for

Roosevelt, he had kept his speculative hand in, working through Elisha Walker.[6] In the summer of 1932, for instance, he had joined a group organized by Bernard Baruch that held 150,000 shares of Brooklyn-Manhattan Transit Corporation. Walker and Herbert Bayard Swope went on BMT's board of directors, and pressed for unification of the city's transit systems,[7] a move which would bring large profits to their syndicate. Eventually, the transit system was unified, but it came about through municipal ownership, and the Baruch-led group saw its plans collapse.[8]

It was through Walker that Kennedy reentered Wall Street. A friend of Walker's, Henry Mason Day, was senior partner of Redmond and Company, a long-established brokerage firm that had been reorganized in the fall of 1932. Walker introduced Kennedy to Day. In January, 1933, Kennedy invested in Redmond and Company, but concealed his interest by having Eddie Moore's name appear on the firm's records as a "special partner."[9]

His reluctance to associate openly with Day indicated Kennedy still had hopes of going to Washington. For the colorful, freewheeling Day was the sort of man of whom New Dealers violently disapproved. The taint of an old scandal clung to him. At the time of the Teapot Dome disclosures that rocked the Harding administration, he was an officer of the Sinclair Export Company and a lieutenant of Harry F. Sinclair, the central figure in the bold grab of government-controlled oil reserves. Day remained loyal to his embattled boss—so loyal, in fact, that he landed in jail with him. Anticipating a verdict of guilty in Sinclair's trial, Day hired private detectives to trail the jurors and seek evidence to sustain a motion for a mistrial. Discovery of this jury-shadowing put Day behind bars in 1928.[10] But he and Sinclair, sentenced to short terms in a Washington jail, resourcefully turned their punishment into a vacation, and even received passes which permitted them to come and go as they pleased. Day wound up marrying the hospitable jailer's daughter.

Day's talent for exploiting a situation was apparent in the spring of 1933. During the eventful first hundred days of his administration, Roosevelt relieved the somber mood of crisis by acting on the Democratic platform promise to bring back beer. It was an enormously popular move. As Congress and state legislatures hastened to rid the country of the ignoble experiment of Prohibition, small investors began returning to Wall Street, attracted by the prospect of a profitable rebirth of the liquor industry and a surge in related businesses. Public enthusiasm for the so-called "repeal stocks" gave Day an idea, which he outlined to Walker. Why not boost a stock that only *appeared* to be caught up in the coming "booze boom"?

They hit upon the idle, little-noticed stock of the Libbey-Owens-Ford Glass Company, which manufactured plate glass. It could easily be confused with Owens Illinois Glass Company, a bottle manufacturer and a legitimate entry in the repeal sweepstakes, especially if insiders deliberately set out to confuse amateur tape-watchers. Through his banking contracts, Walker learned LOF had a good-sized loan nearing maturity and could use cash. The first requirement of a pool was a large supply of the stock to be manipulated. As Walker hoped, the opportunity to unload a large block of stock at handsome prices, and thus gain cash to repay the loan, was attractive to LOF.[11] After some dickering, the Libbey-Owens Securities Corporation, a holding company, issued an option to the would-be operators, which covered sixty-five thousand shares at $26.50 a share (roughly the market price) and three additional blocks of twenty thousand shares each to be picked up monthly at prices of $27.50, $28.50, and $30.50 a share.[12]

Six investment banking firms and brokerage houses signed up for the pool, including Redmond and Company, Kuhn, Loeb and Company (which Walker recently had joined), Lehman Brothers, Bell and Beckworth, Wright and Sexton, and the Hyva Corporation, which was Harry Sinclair's private company.[13] There were only two individual participants: auto-maker Walter P. Chrysler and Joe Kennedy, whose share was twice as large as Chrysler's.[14]

Stock pools were planned and managed in brokerage offices, far from the Exchange, but a canny floor trader was needed to execute the complicated maneuvers. Day, the pool manager, chose as his floor general Charles Wright, who in turn enlisted the help of a veteran market rigger, Frank Bliss, whose nickname in the canyons downtown was the "Silver Fox."[15] Their job was to whip up outside interest in the stock by creating the appearance of great activity, buying and selling the stock themselves in a process known on the Street as "churning." It was pure sham, intended only to deceive the public. However, when the Senate Banking and Currency Committee later uncovered the LOF pool and called Wright to testify, he innocently described his function as much the same thing as distributing groceries or other consumer commodities.[16]

As the pool started operation, exciting rumors were spread concerning Libbey-Owens-Ford. And the stock promptly showed signs of life that appeared to bear out the glowing reports. The heady smell of legal alcohol permeated Wall Street that summer, intoxicating shoestring players who sent the volume of trading on the Stock Exchange to heights untouched since the panic of October, '29. In order to dispose profitably of the 125,000 shares covered by the option, the LOF pool bought and sold some one million shares from June to October.[17] The stock went as high as thirty-seven dollars a share, well above the highest price set forth in the option agreement.[18] As a result, the pool participants truly enjoyed something for nothing: not once during the four months were they required to put up a cent.

Records later produced before the Senate committee indicated that the LOF pool cleaned up profits of $395,238, of which Kennedy's share, deposited in one of six numbered accounts at Redmond and Company, was $60,805.[19] Years afterward, Kennedy hinted that the pool's (and his own) actual profits were considerably higher.[20] It is not known whether he used his inside information to trade independently of the pool, but he was a confirmed loner, as was demonstrated by an incident that occurred during the summer.

The enormous volume of trading in the "repeal stocks," combined with the operations of dozens of pools, caused unusual situations to arise on the floor of the Exchange. A floor trader who was not privy to the secrets of the pools sometimes found it difficult to execute normal buy and sell orders. Toward the close of the market one afternoon, a trader received an order to buy ten thousand shares of Libbey-Owens-Ford. Thinking he could pick up the stock at the market price, he confirmed the order at one-quarter of a point above the last quoted price. However, he was not able to buy the stock before the gong sounded, ending the day's trading.

Next morning, he went to buy the stock and was horrified to see that the opening price of Libbey-Owens-Ford was eight points higher than the previous day's closing price. To fulfill the order he had confirmed, he now would have to pay eighty thousand dollars out of his own pocket. On the verge of panic, he suddenly remembered that his friend, Charles Wright, was running a pool in LOF and would be sure to have a supply of stock on hand. The trader elbowed his way across the crowded floor, explained his predicament to Wright, and begged to buy ten thousand shares at the previous day's closing price.

Wright, who had been in many a tight spot himself, let his friend have the stock. As ruthless as they were with the public, the professionals were not without a certain empathy toward each other. The grateful trader told others of Wright's handsome gesture, and word got back to the members of the pool for whom Wright was working. None of them said anything—except Kennedy. He telephoned Wright and gave him a tongue-lashing.[21]

Still there was no word from Washington. Conscious of the enmity of some of those around Roosevelt, Kennedy had cultivated a friendship with the uniquely influential Jimmy Roosevelt. The President's son, after an undistinguished career at Harvard, had settled in Boston and was pursuing a dual ambition: to make as much money as possible, as quickly as possible, and to be Governor of Massachusetts.[22] During the 1932 campaign, Kennedy saw Jimmy almost daily; he also saw the wisdom of aiding his ambitions. When Jimmy went into the insurance business in Boston, lucrative accounts bypassed established firms and came flocking to him. His clients included the Boston Port Authority, National Distillers Products Corporation, Consolidated Oil, Hayden, Stone and Company, and two Boston banks—the National Shawmut and the First National.[23]

In September, 1933, Joe and Rose Kennedy took ship for Europe with Jimmy and Betsey Roosevelt, on a trip combining pleasure and profit. By midsummer, enough states had ratified the repeal amendment to ensure the end of Prohibition in 1933. Kennedy was turning his tidy profit in the Libbey-Owens-Ford pool, and he now wanted to be in on the liquor boom when it came. So did a great many others. Representatives of British distillers were already lining up American distributors. The competition for liquor franchises was intense, for they were virtually licenses to become rich. Instead of taking his chances in the scramble at home, Kennedy went to the top in London, taking along his friend, the son of the new President.

On their voyage to Europe, the Kennedys and the Roosevelts commanded the deference due Very Important Persons. Every attention was paid to their comfort and convenience, right down to reserving front row seats for them in the ship's movie theater while others were seated on a first-come, first-served basis. One evening, however, two of their seats were occupied by a pair of matronly women. Informed by the steward that they had taken the places intended for the son of the President and his party, they were unimpressed. Said one of the women, settling firmly in her chair: "We're American citizens, too."[24]

The British distillers, more conscious of rank and station, treated Kennedy royally. He was appointed the U.S. agent for Haig and Haig, Ltd., John Dewar and Sons, Ltd., and Gordon's Dry Gin Company, Ltd., which meant millions of Americans thirsting for good Scotch and honest gin would get it through Kennedy. "The British didn't select their agents haphazardly," said a knowledgeable U.S. liquor distributor. "They felt Jimmy Roosevelt was a good connection, so they gave their lines to Kennedy."[25]

Kennedy's connections also won him a head start in the liquor business. He arranged for his newly organized Somerset Importers to import and stockpile thousands of cases of liquor, the whiskey coming into the legally dry U.S. under "medicinal" licenses issued in Washington.[26] Thus, months before Prohibition officially ended, Kennedy's warehouses were filled to overflowing with Haig and Haig and John Dewar Scotch. This gambit was used by others, but not on the same scale. So huge were Kennedy's shipments that the federal liquor czar appointed by Roosevelt ordered Somerset's permits reduced, adding, however, that he found no impropriety in the way they had been issued.

What of Jimmy Roosevelt? He had a pleasant ocean voyage. In a 1938 magazine article chronicling Jimmy's meteoric rise, Alva Johnston said that Roosevelt's company wrote the insurance policies protecting Kennedy's whiskey on the high seas, an allegation the latter vehemently denied, protesting that "I've never purchased a cent's worth of insurance from James Roosevelt in the time we've known each other."[27] Some said Jimmy had foreseen a profitable whiskey partnership with Kennedy, and had been told by Joe: "You can't do that, it would embarrass your father." Said an old Washington hand who was close to Kennedy: "Jimmy wasn't in the same league; Joe could laugh him out of any schemes he may have had."[28] In any event, Kennedy, as usual, had no partners, and his reply to subsequent criticism of the deal was short and tart: "Kennedy was doing all right by himself before he ever met Jimmy Roosevelt."[29]

Kennedy had another nonpartner in the liquor business, according to a suit brought by one John A. McCarthy in November, 1934. Mc-

Carthy, a pre-Prohibition brewer in Boston, alleged in a complaint filed with Suffolk County Superior Court that he and Kennedy had had an agreement to go into the liquor-distribution business together, sharing equally in the profits. Kennedy had indeed gone into the liquor business in Massachusetts, forming a company with the regional distribution agency from National Distillers Products Corporation. According to the account in the Boston *Transcript*, McCarthy's suit claimed that "while Kennedy was allowing McCarthy to believe that he was doing everything for the benefit of McCarthy, he in reality was working secretly to get the agency . . ."[30] McCarthy's suit dragged on for two years and was headed for a jury trial when it was dropped.[31]

For many months after his post-inaugural visit to the White House, Kennedy heard nothing from President Roosevelt, except an indirect suggestion that he serve as New York director of the newly created National Recovery Administration.[32] Compared with Kennedy's known ambitions, the position was distinctly second-rate; and the absence of a follow-up to the offer made it almost insulting. However, Kennedy stayed on intimate terms with Jimmy Roosevelt, whom he entertained in Palm Beach during the winter of 1933–34,[33] and secretly hoped for a sudden, dramatic invitation to high office.

His sights still were fixed on the Treasury, particularly when it became apparent that Secretary Woodin, whose health was failing, would be forced to resign. Woodin left office in January, 1934, but Roosevelt then chose Henry Morgenthau, Jr., an old friend and Dutchess County neighbor, to succeed him.[34] Although there had been no outward sign that he was in the running, Kennedy greeted the news with cold fury.[35] In the years ahead, this disappointment contributed to his dislike of Morgenthau.

When it finally was bestowed, Kennedy's prize was a piquant surprise and clearly worth the frustrating wait. His was a new office, created as part of a fundamental change in the government's role in the economy. During the feverish Hundred Days in the spring of 1933, Congress had passed the Truth-in-Securities Act, requiring full disclosure of all pertinent facts in the issue of new securities. The Federal Trade Commission was charged with administering the act, which the President described as one which "at last translates some elementary standards of right and wrong into law." The act did more than that: it overwhelmed the last redoubt of laissez-faire in the generation-old struggle between the public interest and the nation's money power that had begun under another Roosevelt.

Early in 1934, Congress took up a companion piece of legislation, a bill to regulate the stock exchanges. The long Senate investigation of the stock market, with its succession of shocking disclosures, had built up impressive support for federal regulation. But Wall Street's old guard, led by Stock Exchange President Richard Whitney, was determined to stop the radicals in their tracks. Proud, arrogant, loftily self-confident, Whitney described the Exchange as "a perfect institution," rallying in defense of its accustomed ways what Sam Rayburn called "the most powerful lobby ever organized against any bill which ever came up in Congress."

Ultimately, the rigid defense of the Whitney forces cracked under the weight of past excesses and the defection of important Wall Street figures who were uncomfortable championing a sacred "right" to manipulate the stock market. The reformers, too, reluctantly gave ground, and the Securities Exchange Act of 1934 that emerged from Congress was less harsh than the draft originally proposed. Administration of the act, and of the 1933 securities law, was made the responsibility of a new Securities and Exchange Commission. And much of the authority over the exchanges, originally conceived as mandatory, was now left to the commission's discretion.[36] Plainly, the SEC would be what the first commissioners made it.

Competition for the chairmanship of the commission was keen, with the more ardent reformers arrayed behind a pair of candidates. Lean, taciturn James M. Landis, a former professor at Harvard Law School and a protégé of Felix Frankfurter, had helped draft both securities laws and had administered the 1933 act as a member of the Federal Trade Commission. Another man with a strong claim, or so he and his supporters believed, was Ferdinand J. Pecora, the able chief counsel of the Senate Banking and Currency Committee, whose determined probing and cross-examination had laid bare the secrets of Wall Street.[37]

At the President's request, Ray Moley, who had guided the bill to passage, recommended possible appointments to the commission. In a memorandum delivered to the President early in June, he suggested eight names for the five places, coolly assessing the likely interplay of their personalities and the direction in which they would exert influence. At the head of the list was Kennedy's name, next to which Moley wrote: "The best bet for Chairman because of executive ability, knowledge of habits and customs of business to be regulated and ability to moderate different points of view on the Commission." His estimate of Landis was shrewd: "Better as member than as Chairman because he is essentially a representative of strict control and operates best when defending that position against opposition from contrary view." Shortly after he submitted the list, Moley acknowledged Pecora's burning desire to be chairman of the commission, and added his name verbally.[38]

By one account, Roosevelt had doubts about naming Kennedy as chairman. According to Eddie Dowling, the President at first sent Frank Walker, his fund raiser and loyal lieutenant, to offer Kennedy only a place on the commission. Dowling and Walker then were sharing a room at Washington's Mayflower Hotel. Dowling recalled: "Each night Walker and Kennedy would tramp around the city for three or four hours and, when he returned to the room, Frank would say to me, 'Eddie, I just can't move him. He wants to be chairman and nothing else.' "[39]

Kennedy had his way. In mid-June, Roosevelt told Moley he had about decided to appoint Kennedy as chairman.[40] However, it was certain that there would be criticism. The previous February, Senate investigators looking into the manipulation of "repeal stocks" had brought to light Kennedy's participation in the Libbey-Owens-Ford pool. With the liberal friends of Landis and Pecora noisily beating the drums in their behalf, it would be awkward to appoint a Wall Street operator, guilty of the very practices the SEC was supposed to halt, over the heads of two popular watchdogs of the public interest. As word leaked out that Kennedy was being considered, there were angry protests.

On the morning of June 30, Moley flew from New York to Washington with Roy Howard of the Scripps-Howard newspapers. They spent most of the flight arguing over Kennedy. Moley said it would be unwise to reject him simply because he had professional experience in the field the commission would oversee. He said the appointment would reassure businessmen of the New Deal's friendly intentions. But Howard was flatly opposed to Kennedy's appointment. Finally, Moley said that, if he felt so strongly, he ought to go to the President and state his case.[41]

Later that day, Howard saw Roosevelt. It was a strained session, and the publisher stalked from the White House to dictate an editorial for the late edition of the Washington *News*. The President, declared the *News*, "cannot with impunity administer such a slap in the face to his most loyal and effective supporters as that reported to be contemplated in the appointment of Joseph P. Kennedy."[42]

When Moley entered the President's office that evening, he saw the *News* editorial lying on his desk. "Send for Kennedy," said Roosevelt. "I'll get Baruch in."[43]

Baruch happened to be visiting the White House; Kennedy was staying at the Shoreham Hotel. When Moley telephoned, Kennedy said he had been hurt by the *News* editorial. And it promised to be only the beginning. Howard, with whom he was personally friendly, had called after firing the broadside, warning him to decline the appointment before all of the Scripps-Howard papers were forced to attack him.[44]

At the White House later that evening, Moley, Baruch, and Kennedy met with the President. Roosevelt picked up Moley's memorandum and read it. "Kennedy," he said, without looking at the men seated before him, "is first on the list here. I propose to give him the five-year appointment and the Chairmanship."

Kennedy, half rising, objected. "Mr. President, I don't think you ought to do this," he said. "I think it will bring down injurious criticism."

Moley, familiar with the workings of Roosevelt's mind, interrupted, saying what he knew the President wanted said. "Joe, I know darned well you want this job. But if anything in your career in business could injure the President, this is the time to spill it. Let's forget the general criticism that you've made money in Wall Street."

In *After Seven Years*, Moley described the climax of the interview: "Kennedy reacted precisely as I thought he would. With a burst of profanity he defied anyone to question his devotion to the public interest or to point to a single shady act in his whole life. The President did not need to worry about that, he said. What was more, he would give his critics—and here again the profanity flowed freely—an administration of the SEC that would be a credit to the country, the President, himself, and his family—clear down to the ninth child."[45]

His pungent, all-embracing oaths satisfied Roosevelt. So far as the

President was concerned, Kennedy could be admitted to the administration as a New Dealer in good standing.

July 1, 1934, was a good newspaper day. In Germany, Hitler, whom many Americans dismissed as a ranting little man with a comical Charlie Chaplin moustache, had ruthlessly crushed a revolt by his rivals in the Nazi party. At home, the ten-month feud between NRA Administrator Hugh Johnson and Henry Ford was breaking up; the autocrat of Dearborn reportedly would accept the NRA code. In Newport, two of America's oldest families had been united in the glittering wedding of John Jacob Astor and Ellen French. And the notorious John Dillinger had struck again, taking twenty-eight thousand dollars from a South Bend, Indiana, bank.

But the story given the best "play" on page one of that morning's *New York Times* bore a Washington dateline and reported that the public career of Joseph P. Kennedy had been launched with his appointment to the Securities and Exchange Commission. The *Times* described the appointment as a "surprise," noting that it marked "the first emergence of this New Yorker from what seemed to be political eclipse since the campaign of 1932."

The decision to make the celebrated speculator the cop on Wall Street's corner seemed to some a typical Roosevelt stroke. But liberals were astonished—and angry—at the trust given one bearing such dubious credentials. Commented *The New Republic:* "Had Franklin Delano Roosevelt's dearest enemy accused him of an intention of making so grotesque an appointment as Joseph P. Kennedy to the chairmanship of his Stock Exchange Commission, the charge might have been laid to malice. Yet the President has exceeded the expectation of his more ardent ill wishers."[46] Columnist John T. Flynn, an impassioned critic of Wall Street's ways with other people's money, exploded in disbelief: "I say it isn't true. It is impossible. It could not happen."[47]

Secretary of the Interior Harold L. Ickes expressed the sentiment of many New Dealers, writing skeptically in his diary: "The President has great confidence in him [Kennedy] because he has made his pile, has invested all his money in Government securities, and knows all the tricks of the trade. Apparently he is going on the assumption that Kennedy would now like to make a name for himself for the sake of his family, but I have never known many of these cases to work out as expected."[48]

When Moley broke the news, Thomas G. Corcoran, the New Deal's premier cynic, at first was indignant, but he ended on a note of satisfaction. "Oh, well," he said, "we've got four out of five anyhow."

Moley asked what he meant, demanding to know if all five weren't satisfactory appointees.

"What I mean," said Corcoran, "is that four are for us and one is for business."[49]

Some businessmen weren't at all certain that they had a friend in Kennedy. One of his Harvard classmates was attending a railroad dinner the evening his appointment was announced. A banker received a wire bearing the news and, after showing it around, said: "I'll make a bet that Kennedy will be in the job no more than a year. You know why? Because the stock market is static just now, and Joe can't make money in a static market. He does well only when the market's moving up or down. And when the market moves, he'll move out."[50]

Confusion as to Joe Kennedy's true identity and interest was hardly new. Only a few months earlier, with Henry Mason Day in the witness chair, stock market investigator Ferdinand J. Pecora had paused in his scrutiny of the Libbey-Owens-Ford pool and had tried to find out something about this man of mystery.

Pecora: Who is Joseph P. Kennedy?
Day: Mr. Kennedy is a capitalist, or well-known private citizen.
Pecora: Do you know what his business is?
Day: I do not think he is in business. . . . My understanding of a capitalist is somebody who has considerable funds and does not have to work.

Except in the sense of routine drudgery, Kennedy was not free of toil; his greatest labor was just beginning. But he was remarkably free of entangling allegiances, and so could enlist without qualm in the New Deal that promised to "reform" capitalism and the business society. It was an alliance that probably would have amused Pat Kennedy. He and "Honey Fitz" and other ambitious Irishmen had honestly exploited the politics of underdoggery to escape the bottom and gain money and influence. Now his son, who had gone beyond his father's dreams, was caught up in a new politics ringing with old promises of social justice. Figuratively speaking, the rich son had picked up the coal scuttle and free turkey and continued to climb the stairs.

CHAPTER 11

Mr. Chairman

SHIMMERING WAVES of July heat danced above the Washington streets. Inside the Federal Trade Commission building, a gray stucco-and-lath structure erected as temporary quarters during World War I, the temperature in midafternoon was 93 degrees. The first meeting of the new Securities and Exchange Commission, at which President Roosevelt's five appointees would be sworn in, had been set for three o'clock. But the scheduled hour had come and gone, and the newspapermen assigned to cover the ceremony still were pacing the stifling corridors.[1]

Behind closed doors, the commissioners were locked in an argument over who should be chairman. By law, they were empowered to elect one of their number. Actually, Roosevelt, in appointing them for terms of from one to five years, had indicated his choice by naming Kennedy to the longest term. At the urging of Raymond Moley, who feared a slipup, he had gone further, scribbling a note addressed to James Landis, George Mathews, and Robert Healy, a majority of the commission, informing them that he wanted Kennedy. As he wrote it,

Roosevelt laughed at this seemingly excessive precaution, but Moley's suspicions were confirmed immediately. When he telephoned Landis to report the President's choice and ask that it be relayed to the others, Landis refused. Moley explained that the President had put it in writing. Did Landis wish to see the note? He did. All right, said Moley in exasperation, the note would be placed in Kennedy's hand and he would bring it to the first meeting of the commission.[2]

Kennedy arrived shortly before three o'clock at the Trade Commission building, affably fended off the press, and went to confer with Healy and Mathews in the latter's office. Pecora appeared a few minutes later, his round swarthy face grim and beaded with perspiration. Two days before, Jim Farley had broken the news of Kennedy's appointment to Pecora. ("Ferdie," Farley recalled, "took it pretty well.")[3] The chunky, crusading investigator, a $255-a-month government lawyer who had matched wits with the highest priced legal talent Wall Street could muster, understandably resented the interloper Kennedy, whose predatory stock-pool activity he had uncovered. But he also was embarrassed; a few days earlier, with the SEC appointments as yet unannounced, he confidently had wired the chairman of the Senate Stock Exchange Investigating Committee, announcing he would accept the chairmanship of the commission.[4] Now he came, humbled, to sit as the commission's junior member, appointed for one year only. As he headed for Landis' office and shut the door behind him, the rumor ran along the corridors that Pecora would refuse to serve and would issue a statement blasting the administration, a move that could destroy confidence in the commission before it began to function.

Landis, his gaunt face more solemn than usual, left his office several times during the next hour and hurried four doors east to Mathews' office. He brushed past the reporters and ignored their questions, but it was clear he was acting as go-between for Pecora and Kennedy. A little after four o'clock, he popped out of Mathews' office, this time accompanied by Kennedy, and the pair entered the office where Pecora waited.

Another hour dragged by. At five o'clock the building was emptied of its swarm of clerks and stenographers who poured out onto the steaming sidewalks, leaving halls and offices silent. The drowsy afternoon wore on.

Suddenly, the door of Landis' office swung open. Out stepped Landis, Pecora, and Kennedy, all grinning from ear to ear. Side by side and in perfect step, the three marched down the hall. Pecora and Kennedy, noted the reporter from *The New York Times,* appeared "as chipper as two long-parted and suddenly reunited brothers."[5] After a few moments of confusion as the commissioners and the press crowded into Mathews' office, it was discovered that Judge Healy was missing. Weary of waiting, he had slipped up to his office on the floor above to take a nap. A telephone call brought him hurrying back in his shirt sleeves. At last assembled in one place, the members of the Securities and Exchange Commission were sworn in as flashbulbs popped.

After a brief executive session, the commission faced the press, Kennedy sitting behind a large table flanked by Pecora and Landis. The chairman was asked the reason for the two-hour delay.

"We were simply discussing policies and matters like that," replied Kennedy. "We discussed a dozen different things." Had the discussion of the chairmanship taken as long as all the other subjects put together? Kennedy turned to the men seated beside him. Their reply to the press was a unanimous smile.

A man of charm when he wanted to be, Kennedy had won at least the temporary support of his distrustful colleagues. To each of them, he had said in effect: "Now, what do you have against me? I'm only trying to do this job right, and if we all work together, we'll get it done." He did not stop with his fellow commissioners. The next day, at the inexpensive, open-front Tally-Ho Tavern Coffee House, an unlikely party of four sat down to lunch. With Landis at his side, the former speculator Kennedy greeted Ben Cohen and Tommy Corcoran, who had helped draft the bill to curb speculation, and asked point-blank: "Why the hell do you fellows hate me?"[6] Put so directly, the question rather startled these men of subtle intelligence, and they spent the next several minutes assuring their host he was mistaken.

Meanwhile, Kennedy, who understood and respected the power of the press, launched a counterattack against his critics. Two of his friends, Bernard Baruch and Herbert Bayard Swope, called on their friend, Arthur Krock, of *The New York Times,* and asked his support for the SEC chairman.[7] The influential columnist promptly wrote a glowing account of Kennedy's career, referring to him as "a famous baseball player at Harvard," an astute young banker who had been "invited" to take over Columbia Trust, an able executive who "ran" the Fore River Shipyard, and a stock-market operator who "has never been in a bear pool in his life or participated in any inside move to trim the lambs." Krock concluded: "He is committed to the central idea of the securities legislation—that investors shall be protected from speculators and market-riggers. He is committed further to the President's plan that the laws shall be so administered as to revive the capital market and take relief burdens off the government. He may be counted on to make it easy for honest issues and very, very difficult for the other kind."[8]

Kennedy gratefully remembered this handsome introduction to public life, and mentioned it to Krock, with whom he was soon on intimate terms, many times over the years. His ability to befriend the "right" people in any environment soon was apparent. Not so noticeable, except to those who were involved, was his loosening of older ties that were no longer useful. Elisha Walker, for instance, now saw his once close friend infrequently. In a short while, Kennedy would declare privately but emphatically to a newfound friend in the capital: "I have yet to be indebted to anybody in Wall Street."[9]

Before leaving Hyannis Port to assume the SEC chairmanship, Kennedy told a reporter: "I have dropped everything for the next five years and will make my headquarters in Washington." The implication that he would serve his full term on the commission was misleading. He had taken the job on condition that Roosevelt would allow him to resign as soon as the SEC was organized and running smoothly, which he hoped would require no longer than a year. His approach was that of an impatient man, horrified at the prospect of routine and boredom. Hence he entered the new position with a likely departure date already in mind; it became the goal he pursued single-mindedly, like a pilot flying a radio beam to his destination.

The commission held an important place in the administration's plans for reviving the economy. But Kennedy received no formal instructions from Roosevelt on how to proceed. Very definite ideas were advanced by doctrinaire New Dealers, who knew little about business except that it should be brought to heel. The President wisely ignored these views; he badly needed results. He realized that the SEC, a radically new idea, was doomed to fail unless it won a measure of cooperation from the conservative business community, and he believed Kennedy should be left to move as his experience and common sense dictated. The chairman's relationship with the President was informal and personal, symbolized by the white telephone installed on his desk that connected him directly with the White House.

Kennedy's criticism of Roosevelt had ceased when he received his reward, but some would not let him forget the hard things he had said. Soon after taking over the SEC, he met an acquaintance and asked what he thought of Roosevelt.

"Well, Joe," came the needling reply, "for giving you that job, I think just about what you *used* to think of him."

Kennedy, unamused, cut the conversation short.[10]

Though he had badly wanted the Treasury post, Kennedy soon reconciled himself to the SEC. An associate who knew him well in Washington recalled: "Joe analyzed the increments of power and cut away the fuzz on the edge until the bare bones showed. He had the sense to recognize the opportunity offered by the SEC. While the Secretary of the Treasury *symbolized* power and prestige, here, in the new SEC, was the *real* power. The Treasury was the tent, hung with trappings, but the SEC was the sword of command, the power to purge. Joe could tell the moneymen in New York what they would do, and they damned well better do it, or he could sweep them into the sea."[11]

From Kennedy's first day in office, it was apparent that he was aware of the power he possessed. "The days of stock manipulation are in the past now," he told the reporters gathered around his desk. "There will be little, if any, of this 'buy today and out Thursday' business from this time on. Times have changed and things that seemed all right four or five years ago are now out of the picture."

Knowing Krock's column would appear the next morning, the chairman underscored the point that he was a man maligned and misunderstood. "Any success I ever achieved," he declared, "was in administrative work and not in market operations. Of course, I know something about the exchanges, and my experience is that money made in speculation is negligible in amount when compared to the returns received by those who invest their money in securities that have a future and hold on to them." To complete the appealing self-portrait, Kennedy said he was inclined to describe himself as a "liberal," and added that he had been one of the first men in the country to discuss stock-exchange regulation with Roosevelt.[12] As they came away from the interview, the reporters realized they were not the first newspapermen with whom this newcomer had talked.

The chairman's first lengthy public discussion of the commission came on July 25, in a speech before the National Press Club. He described the SEC's task as "one of the most difficult and one of the most delicate" ever given a governmental agency. Simultaneously, the financial community was to be regulated and revived. He proposed the terms for a new relationship between business and government. "Everybody says that what business needs is confidence. I agree. Confidence that if business does the right thing it will be protected and given a chance to live, make profits and grow, helping itself and helping the country." While the commissioners did not regard themselves as "coroners sitting on the corpse of financial enterprise," they did expect business to join in "the necessary and no longer escapable effort" to make finance more responsible to the public interest. "There are no grudges to satisfy, no venom which needs victims," said the chairman. "The rules are simple and honest. Only those who see things crookedly will find them harsh."[13]

His speech had the desired effect. New York Stock Exchange President Whitney, a bitter foe of the securities legislation, pronounced Kennedy's approach "sane and sound." Apprehensive businessmen everywhere tentatively lowered their guard. Was there really a New Dealer who was sympathetic to business? Meanwhile, in an entirely different quarter, Kennedy's unpublicized deeds were making an equally favorable impression. In his first weeks, he had shown the reformers a few tricks. Jim Landis, who had come to the SEC from the Federal Trade Commission, soon cast aside his misgivings about the chairman. "I'd been pounded for a year by the financial interests and I knew how difficult it was going to be to get the SEC off the ground," he recalled. "Kennedy was impressive. *They* would take things from him that they wouldn't take from us reformers. For instance, he could call up the president of Bethlehem Steel or Standard Oil and tell him to send his comptroller around for a little chat, and the fellow would come. At this stage, we didn't have that kind of power. We didn't know who was who."[14]

Within a fortnight of his arrival in Washington, Kennedy's new-won popularity was tested. The Senate Stock Exchange Committee issued a report, the first of six fat volumes, which cited the Libbey-Owens-Ford pool as an example of stratagems used to deceive the investing public. Here was a cue to renew criticism of the former pool operator heading the SEC, but not a word was said. The SEC commissioners, reported *The New York Times*, "are united in saying . . . that the disagreement now has been eliminated, and that Mr. Pecora and Mr. Kennedy are on the best of terms." Soon after its shaky beginning, the commission was said to be functioning in "perfect harmony."[15]

That it was functioning at all was a tribute to Kennedy's organizing techniques. These were the same he had used in business, beginning with the hardcore of Irish assistants who knew everything and said nothing. Eddie Moore took up his familiar position at the boss's right hand, becoming the guardian of his time and the smooth refuser of impossible favors. Unobtrusive and efficient, Moore won Kennedy's praise as "an artist in personal relations."[16] "Honey Fitz's" onetime secretary had a way with strangers, unquestionably, but the true measure of his artistry was his ability to survive close daily contact with the mercurial Kennedy personality over a span of more than thirty years. *Time* once wrote: "Eddie Moore, Irish as a clay pipe, was the first member of the family Kennedy founded, nurse, comforter, friend, stooge, package-bearer, advisor, who played games with Joe and the children, bought neckties and bonds for Joe, opened doors, wrote letters, investigated investments, saw to it Joe wore his rubbers."[17] Some derisively summed up Moore's functions in the word "valet," but the white-haired, self-effacing Moore was too busy trying to please to notice.

Because he was on Kennedy's personal payroll, Moore posed a bit of a problem to the government's lawyers, who questioned whether he could have access to confidential documents. To get around this technicality, he was made a federal employee at a salary of one dollar a year. When he received his check, it was for only eighty-eight cents, having been subjected to the cut uniformly applied to all federal salaries as an austerity measure. Moore wrote a tongue-in-cheek note of protest to Marguerite (Missy) LeHand, the President's secretary.

Roosevelt, enjoying the joke, replied in kind. "I am appalled at the treatment which you have received at the hands of an appointee of mine. I feel that you are entitled to the full compensation of one dollar without any deductions for going to sleep after lunch, getting to the office after 8:30 A.M., or going to your grandmother's funeral." The President directed Moore to show the letter to Kennedy, so that he might note an "Executive request" that Moore's salary be increased by 25 percent. "I realize," Roosevelt wrote, "that this increase is greater than that given to any other employee in the Government at one time since I first took office, but in your case I feel that this heavy expenditure on the part of the Treasury is fully justified."[18]

This exchange provided a welcome break in the drudgery at the commission. Although he had a lively sense of humor, Kennedy was a grimly exacting taskmaster. A Harvard classmate who once declined an invitation to join him summed up what it meant to be Joe's man: "You had to be sharp and alert, but not *too* sharp. Above all, you had to take orders. Joe had the habit of command."[19]

Among those who came to the SEC were Joe Sheehan, a baseball teammate of Kennedy's at Boston Latin School, and James A. Fayne, a former partner in the brokerage firm of Hornblower and Weeks. Ironically, although Fayne felt so strongly against the New Deal that he vowed to stay out of Wall Street until Roosevelt left the White House, he saw nothing inconsistent about helping Kennedy as a personal favor.[20] The chairman gave such personal loyalty top priority. In need of a general counsel for the commission, he asked his own attorney, Bart Brickley, to recommend a lawyer who was both smart and dependable, i.e., not a New Dealer. Brickley came up with the name of John J. Burns, the first Roman Catholic on the Harvard Law School faculty and a Massachusetts superior court judge at the age of thirty. Seated on the Bay State's highest bench only three years, Burns already was bored and envious of the young lawyers who paraded before him pleading all manner of interesting cases. Offered the SEC position, he threw off his robe without a moment's hesitation. Not long after, he wrote enthusiastically to another lawyer looking for a job: "Come on down to Washington. Every time you write a letter here, you're writing new law."[21]

The SEC rapidly grew to some seven hundred employees. Many were experienced professionals, drawn from banks, law firms, brokerage houses, and financial newspapers. Kennedy believed they could learn what they needed to know about working for the government in a week or two; it would take much longer than he could afford to tutor civil servants in the intricacies of finance. New Deal Washington was a mecca for eccentric job-seekers. One day, a young applicant turned up with a fistful of letters of recommendation from senators and congressmen. He was asked about his experience in securities trading.

"I'm the world's leading layman in finance," he answered brightly.

"I have the unique record of having taken every tip ever given me. That's why I need a job now."[22]

Some prospects simply weren't interested. Jim Fayne, assigned the task of setting up SEC field offices in key cities, found and recommended an able, well-connected lawyer to head the Chicago office. When Kennedy offered the job, however, he was turned down by Adlai E. Stevenson.[23]

The early months of the commission's life were hectic. In passing the Securities and Exchange Act, an optimistic Congress had set midnight of October 1 as the deadline for a massive undertaking: the registration of the twenty-four leading exchanges, their twenty-five hundred members, and some five thousand listed securities. The cumbersome registration procedures inherited from the Federal Trade Commission had to be scrapped, and streamlined procedures devised and introduced as swiftly as possible.[24]

However, the biggest obstacle to the commission's success was not procedural, but psychological. Not knowing what to expect from Washington, the financial community sat tight. Kennedy set out to allay the fears of Wall Street. Small groups of leading brokers and exchange officials were invited to his office for informal conversations. They were informed of what they knew but dreaded—the days of their autonomy were ended; yet they also were pleasantly surprised by their important role in the new scheme of things. Exuding sweet reasonableness, chairman Kennedy asked merely that they accept the SEC's rules and act as their own policemen. There was only the barest hint of disagreeable consequences if their cooperation was withheld, as when Kennedy, in mid-August remarked: "In a large measure, we would have the exchanges do their own policing. They are in much better shape to do this than to have the government send in a staff."[25]

Actually, there was no question that the exchanges would comply with the new law. They had to obey it or go out of business. The crucial question was whether the law would be administered in a spirit of cooperation or antagonism. Kennedy wisely allowed the exchanges considerable latitude in proposing the regulations under which they would live. The New York Stock Exchange, by far the largest and most important, conferred with the commission through the summer and early fall. In the end, the big board adopted as its own the trading rules set forth by the SEC. Smaller exchanges quickly fell into line. A few minor, notoriously rigged securities markets—the New York Mining Exchange, the Boston Curb Exchange, the California Stock Exchange—were closed by SEC order; others of similarly bad reputation took the warning and shut down voluntarily.[26]

When the deadline arrived, all but a few listed securities were within the fold, in spite of the fact that the Securities Act did not specifically require the registration of stocks. Kennedy overcame what he regarded as legislative oversight by applying indirect pressure. Any company that failed to register its stock, he strongly intimated, would find trading in that stock prohibited on the national exchanges by order of the commission.[27]

Chairman Kennedy was unfamiliar with the details of the law he administered; he did what seemed necessary and left the search for legal justification to John Burns and Jim Landis. His manner at meetings of the commission was dictatorial. If he felt there was too much debate around the table on what course to follow, he would suddenly interrupt to issue a stream of summary conclusions and terse orders, all the while impatiently stabbing the air with his finger. It was easier to bend the law than to disagree with him.[28]

A friendly newspaperman dropped in one day and found Kennedy in an expansive mood. "You know," he said, "when I took this job I told the boss I didn't want to tie myself down or take on work that would be more than temporary, but I must admit I get a kick out of it.... There's always something interesting turning up.... I had a prospectus submitted to me the other day by a company applying for a registration of a new issue of securities. Everything was as it should be, but when I read it I noticed that under the company's by-laws its policies could be controlled by a majority vote of the stockholders present at meetings and not by a majority of all stockholders. I threw it out. I wanted them to take me and the commission into court to decide whether we had jurisdiction. I thought it would be interesting to air the whole thing in public. They wouldn't do it. I won without a contest, but I was disappointed. I would have enjoyed the fight."[29]

Clearly within the commission's jurisdiction lay the emotionally charged question of short selling. The bears, widely blamed for the depressed stock market's inability to snap back, found a friend in

Kennedy, who would not outlaw the breed to which he belonged. The bears, he once remarked, perform "a useful function when they don't carry their policy to extremes. . . . Really, it takes more courage and cunning to be a bear than to be a bull. A bear is betting against the popular, optimistic side of business sentiment."[30]

Kennedy summoned the spokesmen of twenty exchanges to hear their views on short selling, and was dismayed to discover each wanted a different rule.[31] As a result, no rule was issued until the subject had been studied exhaustively. What finally emerged was a simple decree. The chief objection to short selling was its use to hammer down a stock, with each decline in price triggering new sales that forced the price lower. The new rule declared that a short sale could not take effect at a price lower than the last one quoted. This meant a bear could not bet that a given stock would fall until it first rose. As Kennedy claimed, the introduction of short selling only on the "uptick" curbed persistent evils, without impairing the usefulness of a necessary market device. Over the years he also created the impression that this ingenious rule was his personal handiwork, a claim unsupported by the recollections of others on the SEC staff.

In addition to regulating the legitimate investment business, the commission moved to combat fly-by-night con men and bucket shop operators. State blue-sky laws were ineffective against the fast-moving gyps. This was especially true of perhaps the most lucrative securities racket in the country at the time, the sale of bogus oil and gas royalties. Many states, including New York, did not legally recognize a royalty interest as a security. The racket struck embarrassingly close to home when the mother of an SEC staff member was fleeced of ten thousand dollars.[32] The new SEC regulations, defining an oil royalty as a security, became virtually the only safeguard against such fraud.

Kennedy did not hesitate to pursue the racketeers outside the law. "The Commission had a productive process which I call whitemail . . ." he later wrote. "Learning of old slickers up to new stunts or in new locations, the SEC would send an investigator or query the veterans as to their operations. I recall one old-timer who had been, in his way, one of the minor wolves of Wall Street. He said that SEC espionage gave him a temptation he could barely resist—to go honest."[33]

While he expressed the hope in a radio speech that the initials SEC "will come to stand for Securities Ex-Crookedness," Kennedy repeatedly warned that the government could not become "a judge of values."[34] There was no way for the government to guarantee anyone's success; the public could not be protected from itself.

There were few illusions on that score among the SEC staff. One day, Commissioner Healy, an able, rather staid Yankee Republican who had once been a judge, sat with an SEC lawyer, reviewing a questionnaire submitted by a company seeking approval of a stock issue. After reading each question aloud, he asked: "In your opinion, does this reply yield sufficient information to protect the average prudent investor?" The young lawyer dutifully answered "yes" a couple of times, then interrupted as Commissioner Healy began reading the next question. "Judge," he said wearily, "in my humble opinion, the average prudent investor is a greedy son of a bitch."[35]

In an article reviewing the first five years of the SEC, *Fortune* said: "The new Commission's most important job was to dynamite the capital log jam. . . . It was a job of bringing two parties together and it suited Joe Kennedy superbly."[36]

The parties in question, in the broadest sense, were U.S. business and the investing public. Between them stood the underwriters, the key middlemen who marketed securities—at least that was the function they were supposed to perform. New corporate financing was almost nonexistent. During the seventeen months before March, 1935, new issues, secured bonds, and debentures amounted to only eighty-nine million dollars. In January, for instance, there were no new issues of any consequence; and in February the total was less than two million dollars.

The common explanation of the sluggish capital market was "lack of confidence." But New Dealers detected a more sinister motive and arrived at a harsher judgment. They angrily accused Wall Street of waging a strike of capital. They believed the large underwriters were deliberately dragging their feet and holding back new financing in the hope of forcing the SEC to relax its regulations.

Admittedly, the registration requirements for new issues under the Federal Trade Commission had been onerous and prohibitively expensive. In order to float a bond issue, Republic Steel, for instance, found it necessary to file a statement running to some twenty thousand pages. But as the SEC simplified the registration forms, making it easier for seasoned companies to raise money, and still saw no pickup in new financing, Kennedy concluded business was "sulking." There seemed no valid economic reason for its behavior. The Depression had sent interest rates plummeting; financing was cheaper than it had been in a generation. An estimated three billion dollars' worth of corporate issues could be refinanced during 1935 at immense savings in carrying charges, yet business apparently would pass up the opportunity.[37]

Early in 1935, Swift and Company of Chicago asked SEC approval of a forty-three-million-dollar bond issue, a fat figure in those lean days. Indeed, it was the largest single issue ever registered under the Act. That the company was getting a bargain was obvious: it quoted a 3¾ percent rate on its bonds, the first important issue to be offered below 4 percent since before World War I. With the proceeds, Swift would redeem securities paying a rate of 5 percent, for an annual savings in interest of roughly half a million dollars.

But the crucial fact was that the underwriters in the deal, Salomon Brothers and Hutzler, had been persuaded—by whom, it was never revealed—to sell the bonds directly to the public rather than through a syndicate of other investment houses. The underwriters took as their commission only 4/10 of 1 percent, instead of the customary 2 or 3 percent.[38] This radical departure from the traditions (and profits) of investment banking caused eyebrows to leap along the Street.

"If we get a few big ones coming in," said Kennedy as he announced approval of the Swift issue, "others will feel that they can do the same thing." From the underwriters' point of view, there was cause for concern that others would follow the lead of Salomon Brothers and Hutzler. All at once, the logjam broke with a mighty rush of new financing. Pacific Gas and Electric came forward with a forty-five-million-dollar bond issue, and Southern California Edison followed with a seventy-three-million-dollar issue.

Pleased but not entirely satisfied, Kennedy appeared before a luncheon attended by one thousand businessmen in New York City and expressed alarm at "the low state to which courage and confidence" had fallen in the nation's financial capital. All but calling his listeners cowards, he went on to scold them for being slackers: "Don't dodge the duties of citizenship by blaming government . . . for the lack of business initiative and enterprise." Only toward the end of his speech did he temper his reprimand by sounding a note of optimism, declaring that the recent bond registrations were evidence of "a real upward trend."[39]

His forecast for the capital market proved accurate. By the end of 1935, corporate underwritings totaled $2.3 billion (versus $491 million in 1934). Capital had gone back to work.

Kennedy earned Roosevelt's confidence with prodigiously hard work. The SEC chairman lived a spare, uncluttered existence, arriving each day at his office before eight-thirty and staying until past six. In the evening, he and Eddie Moore repaired with packed briefcases to their bachelor quarters at Marwood, a rented estate deep in the Maryland countryside. The lavish, twenty-five-room house, built at a cost of half a million dollars by a playboy for his chorus-girl wife, boasted gold-plated bathroom fixtures in the master suite and a one-hundred-seat movie projection room in the basement. Kennedy called Marwood "the Hindenburg Palace,"[40] but it had a view of the Potomac and was the only house he could find large enough to accommodate all the Kennedys when Rose and the children came on an occasional visit.

Living at isolated Marwood suited Kennedy, for he was able to direct his energies as he chose. Safely remote from the social life of official Washington, he was at home only to those whom he wished to see. "Joe took good care of himself," said a friend. "He didn't smoke or drink. He ate well. He slept. He exercised. You have to admire the organized human material—not a bit of waste."[41] Kennedy rode for a half hour almost every morning, not because he loved horses, but because he loved physical activity. After dinner of a summer evening, he liked to relax by listening to classical records. As he sat on the terrace one evening, the strains of Beethoven's Fifth Symphony filling the air, a couple of his cronies begged for "a little hi-di-ho" as a change of pace. Joe scowled. "You dumb bastards don't appreciate culture,"[42] he said, dismissing their plea.

The lights often burned late at Marwood. On a given evening, the guests at dinner might include Jim Farley and Arthur Krock, the White House secretaries "Missy" LeHand and Grace Tully, and the affable Tommy Corcoran, who had brought along his accordion. Sometimes a special guest would show up at the hideaway. Roosevelt liked to slip away to Kennedy's retreat to sip double martinis and watch the latest movies in the basement. The President was "especially fond" of Kennedy, noted the insider Krock. "The two argue constantly over acts and policies, and the President hears more objections than assents from the chairman of the SEC. But he consults Mr. Kennedy on everything, and when the argument is over, President and adviser relax like two school boys."[43]

From the height of his wealth, which gave him independence and self-assurance, Kennedy was determined not to be awed by FDR. "He reached the point quite early," said an associate, "where he didn't give a damn for anybody. He would tell Roosevelt to his face what he thought in very blunt language."[44] This quality, rare among the sycophants surrounding the President, did not go unappreciated. Mrs. Roosevelt once remarked to Kennedy: "I want you to go right on telling Franklin exactly what you think."[45]

Still, there was something doggedly ingratiating about Kennedy whenever he saw the chance to extend his influence. Late one afternoon, a half dozen senators who had been invited to Marwood were about to leave the Capitol when one of the party, Senator Lynn J. Frazier of North Dakota, was called away. Just then, a clerk happened to wander into the office and asked what was going on. He found himself promoted on the spot to United States Senator and whisked off to Kennedy's stag dinner. Kennedy, who knew all his guests but Senator Frazier, fell for the trick and made quite a fuss over the stand-in. ("It was Senator Frazier this and Senator Frazier that," reported one of those present.) His guests stayed so late that the host invited them to spend the night. Kennedy assigned "Senator Frazier" the best guest room, saw that he was provided with a pair of silk pajamas, and bade him good-night with the comment that he was looking forward to hearing more about North Dakota the next morning. Somehow, the clerk and the senators managed to keep straight faces through breakfast and left Kennedy believing he had scored a triumph with the impressionable gentleman from Hoople, North Dakota.

It wasn't until a couple of days later that Kennedy discovered he had lavished his attention on a nobody. The climax of the jest came the next time he saw Roosevelt. "Say, Joe," the President said casually, "I hear you met Senator Frazier."[46]

Kennedy's success in winning over the suspicious liberals at the SEC owed much to the fact that he was, after all, the boss. In Roosevelt's official family he had no such advantage. Doubts about the sincerity of his conversion lingered, and jealousy was aroused by reports that he and the President were boon companions. The President, in self-protection, played off the men around him one against the other. He left each with the feeling that he privately agreed with his point of view and would support him openly, but for the necessity of keeping those of an opposite mind in line. As a result, the liberals blamed Kennedy, sometimes unfairly, for pushing the President toward a "pro-business" position.

Conscious of his vulnerability, he tried hard not to give his enemies an opening. But from the first, Secretary of the Interior Harold L. Ickes fixed his sharply critical gaze on the SEC chairman, ready to pounce at the first sign of reactionary backsliding. In October, three months after Kennedy's appointment, Ickes and Kennedy attended an evening conference at the White House, called by Roosevelt to discuss the possibility of dropping direct relief to the unemployed and substituting expanded public works. Kennedy, Ickes noted in his diary, "did not warm up to this proposition at all... [and] expressed the confident belief that we were on the very edge of a business revival, but it was remarked by others in the conference that that has been held out now from 1929 on."[47] At the end of the session, Roosevelt asked Ickes to consult with PWA engineers and return with their recommendations on works projects.

Evidently, Kennedy was convinced that he was wrong—or at least out of step. At the White House the following week, he reversed himself and urged a large public works program[48]—an action which caused Ickes and others to watch him all the more closely.

At this stage of his career, Kennedy was more an object of passing curiosity than of permanent concern to the New Deal's palace intriguers. It was assumed, from his own statements, that he shortly would return to Wall Street, thereby losing most of his presumed influence with the President. Certainly he was a self-conscious amateur in government, excited and more than a little impressed at being close to the center of great events. When the Supreme Court handed down its momentous decision in the Gold Clause cases, Kennedy felt himself a participant, however modest, in the unfolding of history.

The United States had abandoned the gold standard in June, 1933, under a joint resolution of Congress declaring that the right to require the payment of gold obligations in gold was against public policy. Debts incurred in gold were repayable in the paper, or "legal tender," which Congress arbitrarily decreed was money. This exercise in expediency immediately was assailed by holders of bonds bearing the promise of the U.S. government to redeem them in gold, the promise on which the same U.S. government now had reneged. As their suit moved to the Supreme Court, still dominated by men basically hostile to the New Deal, it was widely expected that the Court would rule against the government. In anticipation of such a decision, stock prices fell, gold-clause bonds rose to a premium, and foreign currencies fluctuated wildly. Amidst this uncertainty, the chairman of the SEC prepared for the possibility of chaos.

The Supreme Court decision was delivered on Monday, February 18, 1935. At intervals during the dramatic day, Kennedy dictated a memorandum, a copy of which he immediately forwarded to the President:

> From all indications, copies of newspapers attached, the Supreme Court of the United States will today announce the Gold Decision.
>
> I arrived at the office about 9 o'clock and called a meeting of the Commission to see if they had any ideas as to what action should be taken regarding the closing of the exchanges. They all agreed that there was certainly no purpose in closing the exchanges before the decision and that we would have to govern ourselves as to what action we can take when the decision is made. The meeting adjourned then until 12 o'clock, when the Supreme Court was to come in. At 10:30 I called up the President and got Mr. McIntyre, his secretary, on the line, who told me the President was shaving. I asked him if the President had any ideas or suggestions and he said that after talking with him the President would be available, with everything cleaned up, at 12:00, and I could get in touch with him from then on, if anything arose.
>
> The Secretary of the Treasury called me on the phone as to the status of the arrangements at the Supreme Court and I notified him that we had the only line out of the marshal's office, and Judge Burns and Ike Stokes of our legal department would be there. He said Mr. Laylin from the Treasury would go along with them, and he would be with the President at the White House.
>
> At 11:55 Miss LeHand called up, and in a very serious tone announced that since it was a very nice day the President had decided to take a nice, long automobile ride and would return sometime later in the afternoon or evening and was sure that everything would be well handled. I am citing this to show that while the whole world was on the verge of nervous prostration at the possibilities of the Gold Decision, the President of the United States, the one most vitally interested, was not so upset that

he couldn't have a little joke, thus demonstrating his capacity to take this along with everything else in stride and to relieve the tension that anyone might feel.

The newspapermen notified me that there was no question about the Decision, as special passes had been issued at 11:45. Judge Burns then called me from the Supreme Court, saying that the Marshal in charge of the Court had a little bun on and everything looked like it was getting started in the right direction. Promptly at 12:00 we opened our telephone lines to the Court and at 12:07 Judge Burns called me and notified me that upon the first case the Supreme Court had decided in favor of the Government. I immediately took up the private line to the White House, connected with line 33, which was the line direct to the President. The phone was answered by Secretary Morgenthau, to whom I delivered the first message. He turned the phone over to the President and I relayed the first message from the Supreme Court. About two minutes later Judge Burns notified me that on the second case the Court had decided also with the Government and I then announced this over the line to the President, who in turn relayed it to the group sitting with him at the White House.

The stock market started to rise very rapidly, some gains going as high as ten points. There were 1,000,000 shares dealt in between 12:00 and 1:00. The Chicago Board of Trade closed down because of the volume of orders. I called the President and advised him of all these facts. With a full victory in sight, I called the President to remark on the amazing similarity of the legal point he made in his speech that he had read to me a week ago Sunday, which would have been a classic in American history and which he would have delivered if the Supreme Court had decided against the Government in the Gold Case. He seemed to put his finger on the proper solution of the problem that the Supreme Court should have taken, and in spite of all the guesses that had been made as to how it would be decided, it was on the basis of his outline that the Supreme Court finally determined the fact. I suggested to him that when he wrote his memoirs this speech should find a place somewhere in it. He was in marvelous humor and his only regret was his inability to deliver the speech.

About 2 o'clock Judge Burns notified me from the Supreme Court that the vote was five to four, and that Mr. Justice McReynolds was sounding off in a Fourth of July campaign speech. I relayed that immediately to the President.

Later in the day I called Miss LeHand and assumed that since the victory was the President's, now was the good time to get that week's vacation. She said the President was then in swimming and due consideration would be given to my proposal.

I left the office about 8 o'clock, and the President tried to reach me on the phone. I went to keep an appointment, and called him about 9:45 at the White House from a drugstore. He told me to take the week off,

> after I had convinced myself that there were no jitters in the stock market . . .
>
> I am writing this memorandum because I feel the occasion is a historical one and I feel that the opportunity of being the person to relay this information to the President would be of value historically to my family.[49]

Roosevelt knew how much Kennedy missed his family. In a memorandum dated February 19, the President gave an order that Kennedy would be delighted to obey: ". . . in view of the sleepless nights and hectic days of the Chairman of the S.E.C., in view of his shrunken frame, sunken eyes, falling hair, and fallen arches, he is hereby directed to proceed to Palm Beach and return to Washington six hours after he gets there [and on a second sheet of paper] and AFTER TEN INTERVENING DAYS HAVE PASSED BY (FOOLED AGAIN)."[50]

Within the hour, Kennedy was in a chartered plane flying to Florida.

CHAPTER 12

A Private Occupation

SINCE 1933, the Kennedys had enjoyed three homes. In addition to the mansion in Bronxville and the rambling house in Hyannis Port, there were now comfortable winter quarters on North Ocean Boulevard in Palm Beach. The six-bedroom tile-and-stucco house, designed in pseudo-Spanish style by Addison Mizner and built for Rodman Wanamaker of Philadelphia in 1923, had cost Kennedy about one hundred thousand dollars. Although he spent another twenty-five thousand dollars altering the house to meet his large family's needs, it remained extremely modest by comparison with the showplaces along "Millionaire's Row." (Jealous of his reputation as a sharp trader, Kennedy liked to give visitors the impression that he had picked up a depression-forced bargain; one otherwise sober journalist came away to report the purchase price at a ridiculously low figure.) The house was set on two acres facing the ocean, and entrance was gained from the boulevard through an arched doorway. The gallery beyond opened onto a courtyard. When the returning Kennedy swung open the heavy oak door and his footsteps came echoing along the tiled gallery, the household snapped to attention.

Kennedy had no roots in a particular place; his roots were entirely in his family; and home was wherever they were. Home was a flashing ring of familiar smiles and a chorus of voices that for weeks of absence had come thinly over the long-distance telephone. Home also was where a blurred, vaguely mysterious figure came into focus.

To different people in different places, Kennedy in mid-career was known as a banker, a showman, a speculator, and a New Dealer. In the twentieth report of the Harvard Class of '12, published in 1932, he gave his occupation as "capitalist." This was a bare description for a man perpetually in motion, an entrepreneur who plunged into situations promising wealth and prestige and pulled out quickly when the possibilities were exhausted. Nowhere, it seemed, did he leave a clue to his underlying purpose. Within the tight circle of Kennedys, however, he came literally and figuratively to rest, revealing that the only occupation to which he ever committed himself was fatherhood.

"From the beginning, Joe knew what he wanted—money and status for his family," said one who knew him intimately in Washington. "He had the progenitor's sense. What he did, he did with his children always in mind. He played the game differently than if he had been after something entirely for himself."[1]

Of his children Kennedy once remarked: "No interest of mine is as great an interest as my interest in them." Even when he stood at the brink of a crisis such as the Supreme Court's gold-clause ruling, his impulse was to connect the event and his role to the Kennedys, as witness his memorandum to Roosevelt specifically written to preserve a small place in history for the Kennedy name.

He felt an extraordinary responsibility for, and participation in, the success of his children. Similarities exist between the Roosevelt and Kennedy families, but in this respect they were strikingly different. The sons of Franklin D. Roosevelt started with an old name and fortune, and rapidly gained immeasurably greater advantages. During the years of FDR's ascendancy, many anticipated the emergence of a Roosevelt "dynasty." But the young Roosevelts sometimes found it necessary to make an appointment to speak with their self-absorbed father. And although their mother, ubiquitous and forever embroiled, was much to the world, she was a mother only incidentally. The success of the Roosevelts was individual, not collective.

In contrast, the Kennedys consciously used one generation as the foundation for the next. Their rise reflects a will to power without precedent in American life—the will of Joe Kennedy, who shaped each child to the purpose he had conceived for the family as a whole. What the Roosevelts lacked, the Kennedys possessed in abundance. Because of these qualities, the Kennedys, ironically, could even press into their service the under-exploited Roosevelt fame. When the script of John F. Kennedy's carefully calculated drive for the Presidency called for a figure who could evoke nostalgia for the New Deal, as in the West Virginia primary of 1960, the son and namesake of FDR stepped forward to perform, eventually taking as his reward a second-rank appointment in the Kennedy administration.

"The joys of parents are secret; and so are their griefs and fears," wrote Bacon. "They cannot utter the one; nor will they utter the other."[2] Countless thousands of words have been written about the rearing of the Kennedy family; the small details of home life have been recited endlessly. Acutely conscious of their "image," even to the extent of mother Rose once suggesting that the press forget daughter-in-law Ethel's physical activity and play up "a more serious angle,"[3] the Kennedys have lavishly publicized themselves. But their truly illuminating joys, griefs, and fears are almost invariably obscured in the published recollections of an intensely private family life.

Even without relying on the retrospective exercises of the Kennedys, or on the implausible accounts of sycophants, it is evident that Joe Kennedy returned from distant points to a home filled with affection. Mutual love and respect are fundamental ingredients of the family's success. Until Kennedy's departure from Hollywood, the task of family-building was almost entirely Rose's, one which she accepted with a sense of vocation rooted in her religious conviction. A teacher by instinct, she implanted the seeds of faith and unity in her offspring. She taught them the pride their father tempered. Yet she was not consumed by motherhood. Affectionate yet tough-fibered, she always stood slightly aloof from the whirlwind activity, and so preserved her identity.

If there was a "secret" underlying the rearing of the Kennedys, it was probably this: the parents skillfully involved themselves in their children's lives, in direct and subtle ways, yet did not take over these lives or surrender their own.

"Years ago," Rose told an interviewer in the late thirties, "we decided that our children were going to be our best friends and that we never could see too much of them. Since we couldn't do both, it was better to bring up our family than to go out to dinners. The Kennedys are a self-contained unit. If any of us wants to sail or play golf or go walking or just talk, there's always a Kennedy eager to join in."[4]

The Kennedy "unit" was completed in February, 1932, with the birth of the ninth child, a boy. He was named for Eddie Moore, his father's confidential secretary and the family's close friend. The arrival of Teddy caused adjustments. During the four years since the birth of Jean, the Kennedys had acquired a Wianno class junior sailboat; there being eight children plus the parents, the craft was called *Tenovus*. Soon after Teddy's birth, Joe Kennedy bought another boat, which he christened *Onemore*.

"Little things are important," Kennedy told a reporter some years ago. "When Jack and Joe were just kids, when they were in a baseball or football game, or when the girls were in a school play, no matter where I was, Washington or the West Coast or wherever, and no matter how busy I was, I'd somehow get back to see them perform. That way they know you are interested, really interested, and when you tell them something it means something."

Kennedy may have exaggerated the details, there being no evidence that he ever took a train ride from California merely to please a child; but he certainly did not exaggerate the impact of his words on the children. When he spoke, they listened and obeyed.

As the thirties opened and the older boys rose into their teens, Kennedy assumed the major role in supervising their development, a welcome figure in what had long been Rose's lonely and demanding "department." As a rule, she instantly accepted his judgments and decisions; an exception was the question of the children's schooling. She believed they should attend Catholic schools. Joe, like his own father, firmly believed in secular education, especially for his sons.

In discussing the matter years later, he slid over the disagreement. "Their mother insisted that the girls go to Catholic schools," he said. "I had other ideas for the boys' schooling. There is nothing wrong with Catholic schools. They're fine. But I figured the boys could get all the religion they needed in Church, and that it would be broadening for them to attend Protestant schools."[5] A friend, himself a Catholic, reflected on Kennedy's course. "What Joe said, in effect, was: 'I'll send my girls to the Church to believe, my sons to the marketplace to know better.' "[6]

He also sent his sons to complete the transition from East Boston that he began, but never quite accomplished. Even after winning wealth and prominence, he remained sensitive to real and imagined slights. When a Boston newspaper in the thirties referred to him as an "Irish-American," he roared in protest: "I was born here. My children were born here. What the hell do I have to do to be an American?"[7] To suggest that Joe Kennedy was symbolic of the rise of newer Americans, an exemplar of democracy's upward march, would be to draw a caricature of the man. He found no inconsistency between his resentment of discrimination and his residence in Bronxville, a community notorious for the systematic exclusion of nonwhites and Jews.[8]

For his oldest boy and favorite, young Joe, he chose Choate, a rather select Episcopal preparatory school in Wallingford, Connecticut, attended by the sons of many upper-class Yankee families. But when Jack turned thirteen, he was enrolled at Canterbury, a Catholic prep school in New Milford, Connecticut, and the only parochial school he ever attended. Perhaps this was the result of insistent pleas by his mother, or of the boy's wish to escape his overbearing older brother, or of a combination of several motives. In any event, the sons were allowed to go their separate ways.

Canterbury required each student to write a weekly letter home. In his first letter, Jack wrote: "Its [sic] a pretty good place but I was pretty home sick the first night."[9] The atmosphere of the school was all that Rose could desire. ("We have chapel every morning and evening and I will be quite pius [sic] I guess when I get home.")[10] His spelling was poor, as were his grades. When his Latin marks fell below passing, the school told the Kennedys what they well knew: "He can do better than this."[11] Although Jack was lackadaisical and absent-minded, he enjoyed reading. "We are reading Ivanhoe in English," Jack wrote to his father, "and though I may not be able to remember material things such as tickets, gloves and so on I can remember things like Ivanhoe and the last time we had an exam on it I got a ninety eight."[12]

Young Joe had made a name for himself at Choate as an excellent student and varsity athlete. At Canterbury, the tall, slightly built Jack went out for several sports and tried hard to match his brother's exploits, but he could not make the first team. Even so, he told his father of the bruising lessons he was learning on the playing field. "One fellow was running for a touchdown and I made a flying tackle and landed him. . . . One of there [sic] fellow [sic] was seventeen and when he hit you you stayed hit. One time I got him out and what a pleasure it was to see him roll and writher [sic] on the ground."[13]

Just before the Easter recess in 1931, Jack woke in the middle of the night in severe pain; he was rushed from the dormitory for an emergency appendectomy that abruptly ended his stay at Canterbury. After a summer of convalescence, he looked forward to returning to the school, but his father wanted his sons together in the school he chose.[14] That fall, Jack was sent to Choate.

Once more within the shadow of Joe, Jr., who would win Choate's Harvard Trophy as the football player who best combined scholarship and sportsmanship, Jack had to be satisfied with reflected glory as a cheerleader. He seemed unwilling to apply himself to his schoolwork. ". . . he is casual and disorderly in almost all of his organization projects," his housefather wrote to the Kennedys. "Jack studies at the last minute, keeps appointments late, has little sense of material values, and can seldom locate his possessions."[15] In letters to his son, Kennedy kept up a drumfire of criticism.

But this pressure produced no results beyond a visible weakening of self-confidence. As Jack Kennedy's biographer, James MacGregor Burns, noted: "His letters home were full of defensive, self-belittling remarks about his grades and his athletic skills. He offered excuses for his poor showing, at the same time denying that these were alibis."[16] Under fire from his father, Jack looked to his mother for reassurance. "Maybe Dad thinks I am alibing but I am not," he wrote to her. "I have also been doing a little worrying about my studies because what he said about me starting of[f] great and then going down sunk in."[17]

If Rose was sympathetic, she also was scrupulous about upholding standards, particularly the ones her husband wished enforced. In her deceptively quiet-spoken way, she was an equally strict disciplinarian. A friend of the family recalled being at lunch with Rose and several of the children at Hyannis Port. One of the girls remarked that she had seen a pretty coat in a Boston shop and asked if she might buy it. Jack, then in his late teens, cut in to observe sarcastically that she had a closetful of coats; why did she need another one? Rose put down her fork and turned to her son. "Leave the table and go to your room," she said. "Say one hundred times, 'I must learn to mind my own business.' " Jack obeyed, and returned in a few minutes to finish the meal in silence.[18]

There were unequivocal rules in the Kennedy household, e.g., the smaller children were forbidden to ride their bicycles off the property and knew they must be in the house when the lights came on; all were expected to be seated at the table five minutes before mealtime. But the discipline imposed was not that of rote and lockstep. Beginning with Joe, Jr., whom Rose carefully trained as a "substitute father," the parents encouraged the older children to show example, and the younger ones to heed it. In spite of the nearly seventeen years separating the first child from the last, the young Kennedys grew with a sense of mutual responsibility. At their request, proudly granted by their mother and father, the older children served as godparents to the younger ones. The children learned to depend more on each other than on their parents. If Joe wished to correct the behavior of one of the girls, he sometimes would talk to her older sister, who would pass on his rebuke in the gentler form of a suggestion.

Joe Kennedy took the roundabout way only so long as it yielded results; he never hesitated to play the drill sergeant and issue blunt, direct commands. His children responded out of love tinged with an element of fear, the latter not so much dread of his tongue lashings, although these were colorful and memorable, but rather fear of failing to measure up to his expectations. He was the supreme arbiter whose approval the children constantly sought.

Kennedy dispassionately appraised the strengths and weaknesses of each of his children as though he were sizing up an all-important investment. Having gauged a child's potential, he relentlessly encouraged its fulfillment, keeping up a pressure for improved performance that stopped just short of each child's point of rebellion or dejection. As limited as it was, the time he spent with the children was exclusively theirs. While the SEC chairman showed Jack a fine point of sailing, or taught Bobby how to grip a football, or held little Jean in the pool while she practiced the scissors kick, his work was forgotten and nothing less than a call from the President could interrupt.

The theme he incessantly expounded was the importance of excelling. He saw life as a contest in which the winner took all. The runner-up was merely a loser. On the evidence of his own rise, he believed that the Kennedys were born to win, that they could do anything they were determined to do. Proud and implacable, he thrust his ideas and ambitions on his children. His exhortatory lectures lacked philosophical content, for he was not given to introspection. Instead, he spoke in the simple imperatives of the pep talk, giving fierce emphasis to banalities ("When the going gets tough, the tough get going"),[19] directing his children with the sheer force of his personality. He defined success narrowly: winning became an end in itself. And he pressed his point urgently, all but foreclosing the possibility of failure. He watched intently to see that his lessons took. When the boys raced on Nantucket Sound, he trailed them in his boat, noting every mistake for that evening's unsparing postmortem. Anyone whom he suspected of giving less than maximum effort was held up to scorn; the boy who slacked in a sailing race was sent in disgrace to eat in the kitchen.[20]

Just as Kennedy drove his children to realize his expectations, so he readily forgave the child who confessed a mistake and bowed to his will by trying again.

Shortly after he assumed the SEC chairmanship, Kennedy received a letter from Jack, then a senior at Choate. Jack wrote that he and his roommate Les Billings had been discussing their poor work, "and we have definitely decided to stop fooling around. I really do realize how important it is that I get a good job done this year, if I want to go to England. I really feel, now that I think it over, that I have been bluffing myself about how much real work I have been doing."[21]

In reply, Kennedy expressed "great satisfaction" over this "forthrightness and directness that you are usually lacking." After praising his son's improved penmanship, the chairman of the SEC pushed aside other business and addressed himself to the task that took priority—the molding of his child.

"Now, Jack," he wrote, "I don't want to give the impression that I am a nagger, for goodness knows I think that is the worst thing any parent can be. After long experience in sizing up people I definitely know you have the goods and you can go a long way. Now aren't you foolish not to get all there is out of what God has given you. . . . After all, I would be lacking even as a friend if I did not urge you to take advantage of the qualities you have. It is very difficult to make up fundamentals that you have neglected when you were very young and that is why I am always urging you to do the best you can. I am not expecting too much and I will not be disappointed if you don't turn out to be a real genius, but I think you can be a really worthwhile citizen with good judgment and good understanding. . . ."[22]

An extravagant legend would spring up about Joe Kennedy's autocratic manner at the family dinner table; he was supposed to have imposed a rigid protocol which permitted the boys to speak only in the order of their ages and the girls not at all. No such rule was necessary. He held forth before listeners who were attentive because he compelled their interest. His acquaintanceship ranged from the famous to the picaresque, and his vantage point was usually behind the scenes. The young Kennedys grew up in awe of the parent who spoke so knowingly of so many things.

"It's a natural thing to do, to talk about the people you know and the people you read about," Kennedy once observed. Jack recalled the family talks as "mostly monologues by my father . . . well, not exactly monologues. But we didn't have opinions in those days. Later, the discussions included us more, but mostly about personalities, not debates on issues and things. I never had any particular interest in political subjects in those days."[23] At Choate, his father gave him a subscription to *The New York Times*, which he scanned faithfully each morning, but the world of politics and government was still remote.

So was the world of business, and Joe Kennedy intended to keep it that way. As late as 1957, when *Fortune* published an article on America's great fortunes and placed Kennedy's above $250,000,000, his wife would ask: "Why didn't you tell me that we had all that money?" The subject of money was strictly taboo. "We never discussed money in the house, well, because money isn't important," he declared. "It's just not an important enough matter to discuss. No point in it."[24] Occasionally, his business cronies turned up at Hyannis Port and fell to swapping stories; one of them remembered how Jack, who wanted to listen, was shooed away by his father.[25] Kennedy believed he had closed the subject by making all the money his family would ever need. With the creation of the trust funds, he boasted to a friend, "I fixed it so that any of my children, financially speaking, could look me in the eye and tell me to go to hell."[26]

The young Kennedys reached maturity almost innocent of the meaning of money, as it is understood by those born without wealth. As a disciplinary measure, Rose kept the children's allowances small—so small that Bobby, when he was about ten, decided to sell magazines in Bronxville. He stayed at it for a few weeks, then began canvassing in the family's chauffeur-driven Rolls-Royce. Finally, the chauffeur delivered the magazines while Bobby stayed home in a room piled high with unsold copies.[27] Compared with their mother, the children found their father a "soft touch," prone to indulge them and reward their achievements in a material way. The childhood habit of dependence persisted in adult life. As grown men and women, the younger Kennedys still look to their father's staff of accountants to keep track of their expenditures and see to their personal finances.

This scant acquaintance with money, an exceedingly minor deprivation, would go unnoticed except for the necessity of the Kennedys, as politicians, to concern themselves with the ordering of other people's lives. Making money might be pointless for them, but it was a matter of sharp necessity for almost everyone else, and the Kennedys sometimes showed an unsatisfied curiosity. A bit surprised at first, journalists close to the late President grew accustomed to his questions about the salaries they earned, as though he were trying to correlate their work and their rewards. Having almost everything material that life can offer poses a special problem: how does one decide the value of anything?

As they came of age, the children were told repeatedly that they had been freed of commonplace cares and given "advantages" only to fulfill the obligation of success imposed by their father. His exciting involvement in the government, which had lifted himself and all the Kennedys to prominence, made a deep impression on his eldest son. While still in his teens, Joe, Jr., showed he was the proper grandson of "Honey Fitz" and Pat Kennedy by announcing that he would pursue a career in politics. He showed that he was Joe Kennedy's son by grandly declaring he would become the first Roman Catholic President of the United States.[28] In spite of the discouraging precedent of Al

Smith's defeat, his father took this high-flown ambition in stride. The idea of a Kennedy in the White House had crossed his own mind.

After young Joe's graduation from Choate in 1933, his father suggested that he go to England for a year of study under the Socialist Harold J. Laski, at the London School of Economics. It was unusual, to say the least, for a self-styled capitalist to send his son to sit at the feet of a notoriously seductive radical. Laski, Kennedy later remarked, was "a nut and a crank. I disagreed with everything he wrote. We were black and white. But I never taught the boys to disapprove of someone just because I didn't like him. They heard enough from me, and I decided they should be exposed to someone of intelligence and vitality on the other side."[29] Kennedy had unusual confidence both in his son and in himself. Moreover, he prided himself on being a realist. While he had no sympathy for the doctrines of socialism, neither did he have illusions about the leftward turn of politics in the world under the weight of the Depression. The "other side" looked like the winning side.

At the London School the youth attended daily lectures, wrote a weekly essay, and tried to follow the finely spun debates that often were over his head. His mind, Laski noted, "was only just beginning to discover the enchantment of thought." But the professor found Joe, Jr., eager and engaging, and took him on a trip to the Soviet Union in the summer of 1934. "He had his heart set on a political career," Laski wrote years afterward. "He has often sat in my study and submitted with that smile that was pure magic to relentless teasing about his determination to be nothing less than President of the United States."[30]

Young Joe returned to enroll at Harvard without a trace of Marxist infection, yet not altogether unchanged. Now the discussions at the dinner table became distinctly two-sided. His son's new independence and inquisitiveness pleased Kennedy; and they were not really far apart in their views. But both of them were hot-tempered, and their exchanges grew heated. During one debate, the son bolted from the table; another time, the father stalked away. Soon, Jack was drawn into the verbal battles. One evening, he and his brother joined forces in a highly emotional argument. Rose watched in alarm as the boys took sides against their father, and she later mentioned it to him.

"I can take care of myself," replied Joe. "The important thing is that they fight together."[31]

By the early spring of 1935, Kennedy believed the Securities and Exchange Commission was established solidly, and he began looking for an opportunity to resign. Roosevelt knew of Kennedy's restlessness, and was aware of the approach of his deadline for departure. But the President also was reluctant to lose an able administrator and a politically useful nonpolitician. Kennedy enjoyed extraordinary acceptance among businessmen; *The New York Times* reported that the business and financial community regarded him as "the most constructive and stabilizing influence for recovery in the Administration."[32] Seemingly more conservative than his New Deal colleagues, he was a persuasive salesman for liberal economic policies.

Roosevelt tried to involve Kennedy more deeply in the administration. The popular appeal of the New Deal was undiminished, but it could point to few concrete accomplishments. For one thing, unemployment stayed stubbornly above nine million. It had been decided to emphasize public works rather than direct federal relief, and a bill was pushed through Congress over strenuous opposition. With the works program beginning, Roosevelt asked Kennedy to head the advisory committee that would pass on the proposed projects. Kennedy at once saw that he would stand squarely between the antagonistic Harry Hopkins and Harold Ickes, and so he declined, explaining that he could not work with the cantankerous Ickes.[33] However, he did agree to serve on the committee, as the member responsible for reviewing the financing of self-liquidating projects under the four-billion-dollar works program.

Alert to such obvious dangers as standing in the Hopkins-Ickes cross fire, Kennedy still was a novice in Washington's sophisticated infighting. In potentially hazardous situations, he turned to Roosevelt for advice. In April, he dispatched an urgent note to the White House, one which disclosed more than a little naïveté. Wrote Kennedy:

> The Senate Committee on Audit and Control, headed by Jimmy Byrnes, has summoned me to appear before them on Monday at twelve-thirty to give my impressions of the Wheeler Resolution demanding the investigation of railroad financing in this country. The general impression is that the railroads do not want this investigation because nothing will be gained by it except to dig up old corpses. Wheeler wants to . . . start the ground work for his campaign for public ownership of railroads . . .
>
> I very definitely am on the spot . . . I am to be asked whether I think an investigation should be made—what can possibly be accomplished and what I think may happen to the value of securities in the stock

> market. In other words, it looks like I am on the spot. Have you any opinion? I can go on my own and do the best I can unless you have some angle—it occurs to me that there may be some political angle to this investigation. Shall I go or have you any suggestions?[34]

Roosevelt answered immediately. "If you can get out of going it would be best."[35] Failing that, he briefly outlined a number of evasive moves. Thus counseled, Kennedy managed to avoid an appearance before the Byrnes Committee. Roosevelt may have felt mild annoyance at Kennedy's frequent need of sympathy and reassurance. Equally inexperienced men in the administration made their way unaided through the political jungle. "The trouble with Kennedy," Roosevelt said privately, "is you always have to hold his hand."[36]

But this minor failing did not impair their close friendship: it was rumored that Kennedy made three or four unannounced evening visits to the White House each week.[37] But he was tugged by stronger ties. He disliked being away from his family. Beyond that, he estimated that he was losing one hundred thousand dollars a year because he could not play the stock market; his government salary, he once groused, scarcely paid the telephone bills.

Late in May, Kennedy resolved to leave the government. The emergency-inspired truce between government and business, which had made possible the swift establishment of the SEC, was disintegrating. Conservative Democrats in business and finance had launched the American Liberty League to oppose the New Deal. Reform, they believed, had been succeeded by radicalism; and in 1935 they were spending twice as much as the Republican party to warn the public of the danger from the Left. In April, the annual meeting of the United States Chamber of Commerce in Washington had condemned the administration. It was true, a number of influential Eastern bankers and businessmen sought an accommodation with the government, and Kennedy worked closely with them. But the rising hostility of business generally foreshadowed war, and Kennedy had no stomach for an extended stay in the trenches.

One afternoon in May, he later recalled, he left his office bound for the White House with a letter of resignation in his pocket. He passed a newsboy hawking an early edition of the *Washington Star*. Large, black headlines screamed the news that the conservative Supreme Court, determined to halt the march of government centralization, had overthrown the National Recovery Act. With the NRA literally put out of business, the administration's economic policy was in disarray. Kennedy returned to his office and tore up his letter of resignation.[38]

In July, he was routinely reelected to another one year term as chairman of the SEC. That same month, he was drawn into the bitter fight over proposed government regulation of public utility holding companies.

Lengthy investigations had brought to light shocking abuse of the holding-company device. Such empire builders as Samuel Insull of Chicago had stacked corporations one atop another in dizzyingly complex pyramids, siphoning off the profits of operating companies and pumping water into stock values.[39] Insull and others made their fortunes in the electric utility industry, which became the chief target of the would-be regulators. The New Deal's indefatigable draftsmen, Tom Corcoran and Ben Cohen, drew up a bill proposing that the SEC assume life and death power over utility company systems.[40] As the powerful utility lobby sprang to the defense, its complaints were echoed in part by none other than SEC chairman Kennedy. For he, too, believed the government was in danger of overstepping itself.

Kennedy stated his objections in a letter to chairman Wheeler of the Senate Interstate Commerce Committee. "I cannot be too vehement in urging upon you my feeling that this section [Section II of the proposed bill] . . . is most unfortunate," he wrote. He dissented on two grounds—"the limitations on human capacity to achieve results" and "my conception of what is wisdom in government." Nowhere in the bill, he pointed out, was there a definition of the "public interest" to guide the SEC in deciding which holding-company systems were to be broken up, and how. But "by far the more important" objection, he continued, "is my strong conviction that it is not a wise policy to vest in any one group of men the tremendous responsibility involved in this grant of power. Certainly, this is true unless such a grant is hedged with precise and defined standards set up by Congress itself."[41]

Thus, during a struggle that gripped the capital for weeks that summer, Kennedy sat in his newly air-conditioned office coolly stating the case for limited government. With the administration committed to sweeping legislation, Kennedy's show of independence carried weight in Congress. What better authority was there on a proposed law than the man who would administer it? In the end, Roosevelt suffered a rebuff: the Utility Holding Company Act that emerged from Congress was a watered-down compromise.[42]

But Kennedy's strictures against ill-defined government expansion had been entirely *ad hoc*. A year later, he authored a book vigorously defending the New Deal and all its works; his desire to see Roosevelt remain in power overwhelmed any doubts about how far the power of government might reach.

Kennedy postponed another attempt at resigning until the holding-company act took final shape and the scope of the SEC's responsibility was clear. The new law greatly enlarged the commission's functions, but important provisions would not take effect for a year. Kennedy saw no reason to delay further. He spent two weeks in August with his family at Hyannis Port, returning after Labor Day, and celebrated his forty-seventh birthday at his desk. To staff members and well-wishers, he handed out pieces of a cake sent by Rose and the children. Later that afternoon, before flying again to Cape Cod, he dictated a letter to the President.[43]

"To discontinue my official relations with you is not an easy task," he wrote. "Rather it is one involving genuine regret assuaged only by the privilege of your friendship.... You know how deeply devoted I am to you personally and to the success of your administration. Because of this devotion, after retiring from the post of Chairman of the Securities and Exchange Commission, I shall still deem myself a part of your administration...."[44]

Two weeks later, Roosevelt announced from Hyde Park his acceptance of Kennedy's resignation and made public a "Dear Joe" letter, praising his "skill, resourcefulness, good sense and devotion to the public interest...."[45] It was well-merited praise; many early critics had come to regard the SEC as the New Deal's most constructive reform. The previous spring, Kennedy had told a reporter: "I'd hate to go out of here thinking I had just made some changes in accounting practices."[46] His accomplishment was unmistakable. He had taken a law that seemed almost unworkable, and had administered it so as to reassure business, simplify corporate borrowing, and boost investor confidence. To his successor as SEC chairman, thirty-six-year-old James Landis, he turned over an experiment that had achieved the stature of an institution in the amazingly brief span of four hundred and thirty-one days.

On September 25, Joe, Rose, and Kathleen sailed for England aboard the *Normandie*. They planned to tour the British Isles, France, Italy, Switzerland, and Holland. In his office a few days earlier, Kennedy had outlined his plans to the press. "I am going to feel that I'm out of politics—if this is politics—for the rest of my natural life," he said, laughing. "I'm all through with public life."[47]

CHAPTER 13

I'm for Roosevelt

NOW AN unofficial New Dealer, Kennedy resumed his old relationship with Roosevelt, that of informal adviser and confidential emissary. By prearrangement with the President, his six-weeks' European tour took him to the nations of the gold bloc for a survey of the "nervous" money situation; in the key capital of London, he talked at length with such men as Montagu Norman, head of the Bank of England, and Neville Chamberlain, Chancellor of the Exchequer and widely mentioned as the next Tory Prime Minister. On his return in mid-November, he made an overnight visit to the White House and delivered a pessimistic report. European experts placed economic recovery ahead of monetary stabilization, but recovery was lagging as burdensome arms spending increased. No break was visible in the dark clouds, heavy with the threat of war, that had gathered over the Continent since Hitler's rise to power in Germany. About the only cheering news he brought was the general admiration of Roosevelt; important Europeans liked his "guts" and looked upon the New Deal as a success.[1]

This was in sharp contrast with the opinion of influential Americans, such as Kennedy's friend, William Randolph Hearst. The publisher, who had played a major role in winning the 1932 nomination for Roosevelt, subsequently had blasted the NRA, fought the administration's labor policy, and identified the New Deal as a hive of radicals and Communists.[2] At Kennedy's urging, the President had tried to charm his critic; in a cordial note to "W.R." in 1934, Roosevelt said he was "delighted to hear from Joe" that Hearst was coming to Washington, and invited him to stay at the White House.[3] But Hearst had refused the olive branch. When Kennedy now suggested another attempt at peacemaking, explaining that Hearst was in financial trouble and angry over higher taxes, the President curtly described his foe as a vicious influence, and Kennedy let the subject drop.[4]

He also carried a message for Roosevelt from a high official of the Catholic Church, who once had described Kennedy as "a genius."[5] This appreciative friend, the Most Reverend Francis J. Spellman, Auxiliary Bishop of Boston, was pleased with Kennedy's talents on this occasion, for he noted in his diary on November 15: "Wrote letter to Cardinal Pacelli that Joe Kennedy had conversation with President Roosevelt and the President had practically determined to recognize the Vatican."[6]

Affairs of Church and State now occupied Kennedy only in the time he could spare from his own enterprises. His tenure as overseer of the financial community had sent his prestige soaring. And his influence made him a sought-after corporate consultant.

His first client was David Sarnoff's Radio Corporation of America. Once the bellwether of the great Bull Market, Radio now was imprisoned by a capital structure that bore no relation to the company's earning power. Watching dividend arrears mount, two classes of preferred stockholders jealously warred with one another and with the common stockholders, who had never received a dividend.[7] The obvious solution was recapitalization, which would adjust the company's obligations to its income; but numerous plans had been drawn up, weighed, and rejected. All of them held out the prospect of offending one or another group of stockholders. Finally, Sarnoff decided to shift the onus of devising a plan from management to an impartial outsider, and called in Kennedy.[8]

Radio's future in mid-Depression was no less exciting than it had been in the exuberant twenties; for one thing, looming on the horizon were the limitless possibilities of television. Kennedy believed that Radio was a "growth company," and that its capital should consist solely of common stock.[9] In the space of six weeks, he and his staff drew up an ingenious plan with this objective. Delicately balancing one stockholder interest against another, the plan called for low interest bank loans to retire outright one class of preferred stock; another class of preferred was to be swapped for a new preferred issue, which could eventually be converted to common stock. The dilution of the latter was sweetened by the realistic prospect of dividends.[10]

At RCA's annual meeting in April, 1936, President Sarnoff announced that the plan had been approved by 98 percent of the stockholders' votes. Someone rose in the audience to ask what the Kennedy Compromise had cost. Sarnoff prudently turned the microphone over to the plan's architect.

"At the SEC we always demanded the truth, and I guess some of you will get a shock," said Kennedy. "My fee was $150,000, from which I paid $30,000 to accountants." The stockholders were either so shocked—or so well satisfied—that they asked no further questions.[11]

Impressive as that figure was, more impressive still was the way it was reached. According to RCA veterans, Kennedy originally agreed to draw up the plan for a fee of one hundred thousand dollars. When his proposal was well received by the company's board (and perhaps after he had totted up the thirty-thousand-dollar accountants' bill), Kennedy asked for an additional fifty thousand dollars—and got it from the grateful management. As a result of the costly Kennedy plan, RCA was free to move forward, and in 1937 paid the first common-stock dividend in its history, twenty cents a share. Modest by ordinary standards, the dividend delighted stockholders who had clung to their hopes during a nineteen-year drought.

Before tackling RCA's tangled finances, Kennedy had taken his customary Christmas holiday in Florida. On the way south he and Rose stayed overnight with the Roosevelts. In January, the President sent a note thanking Joe for a gift. "... I am sure I forgot to say to you while you were here how much I am enjoying the contents of the two trunks. I am saving some for you...."[12] The trunks contained Scotch, courtesy of Kennedy's Somerset Importers.

Enclosed with the President's note was a list of businessmen sympathetic to the administration, which had been prepared by Commerce Secretary Dan Roper. It was perhaps symptomatic of how business felt about the New Deal that the list contained only fifty names. With less than a year remaining before Roosevelt's bid for reelection, Kennedy had offered to try to rally business support, provided he could find an audience. He had in mind arranging dinners for businessmen at which the case for the New Deal could be presented as emotionlessly as the reading of a balance sheet. With the help of columnist Arthur Krock, he also had begun writing a small book upholding Roosevelt's policies.

But politics, for the moment, was a sideline. Following his success at RCA, Kennedy turned to a sick movie company, Paramount. Burdened with debt and chronically mismanaged, the company had emerged unsteadily from bankruptcy only months earlier. The danger of backsliding was apparent. Paramount was "a great sprawling business," Stanton Griffis, chairman of the executive committee, later wrote, "a Gulliver rapidly being made captive by its self-created Lilliputians."[13] Late in April, Kennedy joined the company as a special adviser and began preparation of a detailed report on its operations. He had assembled the usual task force of trusted associates—Joe Sheehan and Jim Fayne, from the SEC; Pat Scollard and John E. Ford, from the movie days; and Lucius Pond Ordway, an ex-partner in the brokerage firm of Redmond and Company.[14] For several weeks, they turned Paramount inside out. Kennedy paid a lengthy visit to the large West Coast studio where, he knew from experience, money was made or lost in the movies. His fifty-four page, fifteen-thousand-word report hit the Paramount boardroom like a bombshell.

The directors still were stunned from the document when Kennedy jolted them further by asking that his findings be made public, lest he mistakenly be assigned responsibility for the company's future decisions. The board refused. Whereupon Kennedy leaked to the press the gist of his report. He criticized the influence of Wall Street, declaring that Paramount had gone into eclipse while relying on the advice of "the best downtown business brains."[15] Bankruptcy and reorganization under "quality businessmen" had solved nothing, proving the futility of "calling in big business" when the problem was failure as a show business organization.[16]

He tore the studio apart, exposing colossal waste and extravagance. Negative costs were exceeding their budgets by seven million dollars annually; shooting schedules were being disregarded; one scenario (average cost: $14,500) was being junked for each one filmed; film writers, driven half mad trying to please inarticulate directors, sulked in their bungalows at fat salaries; costly stars were being alienated; and the planning of the 1936–37 program was hopelessly inchoate.[17] He said the mess in the studio showed the "cumulative effects of a chain of incompetent, unbusinesslike and wasteful practices," for which much of the fault lay with the equally incompetent New York headquarters.[18] Diagnosing the fundamental problem as "one of man-power and morale," he said competent executives would not come to Paramount, nor would morale improve, as long as directors responsible for "dissension and division in management policies" sat on the board.[19] Concluded Kennedy: "It would be little short of criminal if, on the threshold of a period of prosperity for the industry, this opportunity to eliminate waste and substitute profits were to be passed by without action."[20]

Action came swiftly. No sooner had the report been submitted than heads began rolling. Paramount's president, in office only a year at a salary of $150,000, was fired with four years of his contract unexpired.[21] The board was shaken up, ten changes occurring over the next several months. A "showman," Barney Balaban, head of Paramount's successful Midwestern theater affiliate, took over the presidency and launched a recovery program based on the report's recommendations.[22] Kennedy had left the amount of his compensation to the discretion of the board. After expressing "deep appreciation for his invaluable services," the board valued his services at fifty thousand dollars (plus five thousand dollars for expenses) and awarded twenty-four thousand dollars to his assistants.[23] One service Kennedy performed was indeed invaluable. He took time from his investigation to persuade the Sabath Congressional Committee on corporate reorganizations to postpone indefinitely its scheduled inquiry into Paramount,[24] thus sparing management the acute embarrassment of simultaneously trying to purge itself of incompetence and prove it was above reproach.

Kennedy's next call took him to the debt-ridden Hearst empire, where he helped work out a comprehensive plan of reorganization at a salary of ten thousand dollars a week. The difficulty with Hearst, as always, was trying to restrain his imperial whims. The man who looted castles of their treasures on his excursions abroad, and then left his purchases uncrated and gathering dust in America, perpetually was pursued by accountants and lawyers, clamoring to inform him of the cost of his excesses. He did not care, and with an income above fifteen million dollars a year, he long avoided caring.[25] But the reckoning had come, and was anguishing, for it cost him pride and property, including the New York *American*, his "love child," which was indulged to the point of a one-million-dollar-a-year loss and then suddenly put to death.[26] Advisers such as John Francis (Jack) Neylan toiled for Hearst as long as their strength lasted, and then left almost literally to save their lives. Kennedy, who wisely served only as an occasional consultant, could withdraw at will from the organization's unending struggle to keep up with Hearst and his creditors.

During the summer, Kennedy was able to spend several weeks with his family. At Hyannis Port, his gaze often fell on his son Jack, alert for signs of returning illness. Like his mother, the youth never would admit he was sick; his father could tell only by looking closely. An attack of jaundice had cut short Jack's stay at the London School during the summer of 1935. Still shaky, he had returned to the U.S. and enrolled several weeks after the beginning of the semester at Princeton, the college he insisted on attending with friends from Choate; but at Christmas the jaundice flared up again and he was forced to withdraw.

The choice of Princeton over his own alma mater had disappointed Joe Kennedy. During months of convalescence, Jack changed his plans. This fall, he would follow his father's and brother's footsteps, if not his own original desire, and enroll as a freshman at Harvard.

On the porch at Hyannis Port, Kennedy read the galley proofs of his campaign book, which would be published in late August, the timing suggested by the President. The manuscript had been completed in June, and he sent it to the White House asking approval. When he had no reply, he anxiously wrote again. Finally Roosevelt sent a reassuring note. "I thought you got my message sent more than ten days ago—that I thought the manuscript splendid and that it will be of real service . . ."[27]

The tempo of the campaign was rising slowly. Thus far, the Republican presidential nominee, Kansas Governor Alfred M. Landon, was saying, in effect, only that the G.O.P. would govern more efficiently and balance the budget. But resentment of Roosevelt ("That Man") went deep, particularly in business circles; the campaign inevitably would draw blood. This implacable hostility toward the New

Deal was much on Kennedy's mind as he discussed his book with a reporter at Hyannis Port late in July.

"If you shove your neck out, you're bound to get it slapped," he said. "Some of my friends in the business and financial world have told me that I might as well make up my mind I have had my last job from anyone in the business world once the book is published." He was tired of "hearing rich and powerful men express their hatred for the President..." As usual, he expressed his emotions in terms of his family. "I stand to lose as much as any of them... and I am just as concerned about what is to happen to my children as they are about theirs. And, because of my children, I am a stronger Roosevelt man than ever before."[28]

His contempt for the business Establishment was ill-concealed in this interview. "I'm afraid some people are laying up bad trouble for themselves the way they are acting.... You can't tell the public to go to hell any more. Fifty men have run America, and that's a high figure. The rest of America is demanding a share in the game, and they'll get it." Warnings against inflation were false, he said, pointing out that the large banks—"all of them anti-Administration"—were buying more and more government securities. "With their bitter feeling about the New Deal, they wouldn't load up with its paper if they really believed it was going to destroy them. It shows they don't mean what they say, or don't know what they mean."[29]

When Kennedy's book appeared, published by Reynal and Hitchcock, its whole meaning could be read in the title, *I'm for Roosevelt.* The author was for Roosevelt without significant reservation, contending that he had saved capitalism despite an ungrateful and uncomprehending capitalist community. He vaguely conceded "many mistakes" by the New Deal and renewed his criticism of the 1936 tax on undistributed corporate profits, but these caveats were swallowed up by the credit he bestowed on the administration for every improvement in the economy since 1933. Early in the book, he declared his purpose: "I have no political ambitions for myself or for my children and I put down these few thoughts about our President, conscious only of my concern as a father for the future of his family and my anxiety as a citizen that the facts about the President's philosophy be not lost in a fog of unworthy emotion."[30]

His examination of the President's "philosophy" actually shed light on his own lack of settled convictions. His emotional loyalty to Roosevelt caused him to embrace uncritically such dogmas as the absolute need of government planning. "An organized functioning society," Kennedy wrote, "requires a planned economy. The more complex the society the greater the demand for planning. Otherwise there results a haphazard and inefficient method of social control, and in the absence of planning the law of the jungle prevails."[31]

This passage illustrated the enthusiastic shallowness of the book as a whole. The author said nothing about the limits, if any, of government planning, ignoring such questions as who would regulate whom, and for whose benefit. He omitted a definition of "social control," a euphemism for state coercion. The implication that efficiency was the overriding social virtue was disquietingly glib, for it called to mind countries where efficiency flourished at the expense of freedom. In the end, Kennedy's attempt to dispel the fog around Roosevelt merely disclosed his own fuzzy perception. He seemed not to recognize that, prior to the vogue of planning, the scorned system that now appeared "haphazard and inefficient" was in fact the market economy, which had worked well enough to make his fortune. Moreover, he had found the "jungle" of competition hospitable and would again. If unawareness was the sin of Roosevelt's enemies, it was also Kennedy's.

The book was a curious product from the pen of an avowed realist. It took no account of Roosevelt's opportunism and ventured perilously far out on a limb to applaud its hero. Within two years the thesis of the book, in the judgment of collaborator Krock, would be destroyed by Roosevelt's slashing attack on business, in which he laid the recession that had wiped away the New Deal's gains to conspiracy on "the part of a selfish few."[32] Within five years, Kennedy's fundamental misjudgment of his subject would leave the taste of ashes in his mouth; and the title of his book would mock his true feelings toward the President.

The New York *Daily News,* then ardently pro-New Deal, hailed Kennedy's effort as "a masterpiece," and said it was "the best answer we have yet seen to those who blindly hate President Roosevelt for having saved their shirts and possibly their skins for them."[33] This extravagant praise possibly owed something to the fact that Kennedy, in addition to advising Hearst, was a consultant to the *News'* publisher, Joseph M. Patterson. Equally predictable was the criticism he encountered. *The New York Times,* then stanchly conservative, accused Kennedy of ducking "the argument that federal planning and economic control may be carried to the point where capitalism would surrender slowly to state socialism."[34] Through the President's secretary, "Missy" LeHand, Kennedy solicited a handwritten note of appreciation for the book, explaining that he wanted it for his children. On the margin of one of his letters, Miss LeHand wrote a reminder to her boss: "You must do this!"[35] Many months after publication of the book, the request finally was granted. "Dear Joe," wrote Roosevelt, "I'M FOR KENNEDY. The book is grand. I am delighted with it. . . ." The note was framed and displayed on the living room wall at Hyannis Port.[36]

The great success of Roosevelt's 1936 campaign lay in defining the shapeless, pragmatic New Deal in terms of its opposition. He made his own popularity the only real issue in the election, running against what he called the forces of "organized money." Opposition to the President was scarcely the monopoly of the wicked, reactionary rich, but the event proved the appeal of class politics.

Kennedy's mission was to divide the broad ranks of business, to drive a wedge between small and large entrepreneurs, exposing the world of difference between the corner grocer and the Du Ponts. In a nationwide radio speech in October, sponsored by the Progressive National Committee which he had helped organize, Kennedy addressed the "average businessman," advising him against being "jockeyed into a position of antagonism to the rest of the nation because a few stuffed shirts have lost their silk hats."[37]

Yet he did not neglect those who dressed for dinner; leading businessmen and financiers were invited to attend feasts of reason. However, in attempting to arrange a dinner in New York, he met an arctic rebuff. Some invitations went unanswered. Others who sent regrets gave flimsy excuses: one businessman declined because of his wife's fear of being left alone at night in their Manhattan apartment. A candid investment banker told Kennedy to forget the whole thing, claiming "Landon is in, anyway." He gladly would have forgotten the futile project, except for his promise to the President.[38]

In the closing weeks of the campaign, the unreasoning antagonism of Roosevelt's bitterest opponents burst forth in accusations of "dictatorship" and covert sympathy with communism.[39] The most unrestrained assaults on the President came from the demagogic Detroit radio priest, Father Charles E. Coughlin, whose newly formed Union Party had fielded a presidential candidate, Senator William Lemke, in a loosely knit coalition with the old-age pensioners mobilized behind Doctor Francis E. Townsend and the followers of the late Huey Long. In wild tirades, Coughlin publicly called Roosevelt a "scab," a "betrayer," and a "liar."[40]

These attacks ended Kennedy's persistent attempts to cement an alliance between the pair. The plump, bespectacled priest, who sprinkled his conversation with worldly "hells" and "damns," was a force to be reckoned with, receiving a weekly average of eighty thousand letters, and as many as a million after an especially spirited oration. *Fortune* called him "just about the biggest thing that ever happened to radio." An ultra-inflationist, he applauded the main thrust of the early New Deal. Roosevelt welcomed his support and actively sought it, pointedly quoting from the Papal Encyclicals in a speech on a visit to Detroit. Catholics around the President—including Kennedy—made frequent pilgrimages to the bell tower in Royal Oak to hold Coughlin in line.[41] Early in the 1936 campaign, Coughlin interrupted his criticism of the administration to praise Kennedy. Making a bad pun, he said the chairman of the SEC "was a shining star among the dim 'knights' of the present administration's activities."[42] Even after he parted with the President on major issues, attempts at peacemaking continued. By an odd coincidence, the news of Huey Long's assassination in September, 1935—a violent deliverance for the New Deal from a worrisome foe—had reached Roosevelt over lunch at Hyde Park, where he sat with Kennedy and Coughlin.[43]

Now the break was final and complete. Kennedy's prominence as a Catholic layman, which had helped win Coughlin's confidence, now made him an effective spearhead of the counterattack against Coughlin. Before an audience of businessmen in Boston, he lauded Roosevelt as "a God-fearing ruler, who has given his people an increased measure of social justice," a blow at Coughlin's National Union for Social Justice. To the charge of dictatorship, he answered that the threat had passed in the dark days of 1933, when "we could have had a dictatorship in the twinkling of an eye—President Roosevelt's eye." If there were any semblance of dictatorship, he concluded, driving home his point against an unmentioned but unmistakable enemy, "the words 'liar' and 'betrayer' would have been uttered only once."[44]

Kennedy wound up his campaigning on October 31 with a radio

speech from Boston echoing the theme that Roosevelt was blameless and that the abuse of him stemmed from "efforts to clean up the financial mess he inherited from the Republican administration." By this time, the high-minded public servant of Kennedy's fancy was spoiling for a fight. That same evening, at a rally in New York's jampacked Madison Square Garden, the beaming Roosevelt uplifted his face in the white spotlights, letting the applause of the frenzied crowd wash over him wave upon wave. "I should like to have it said of my first Administration that in it the forces of selfishness and of lust for power met their match," he declared. As he began to speak again, cheers welling up from thousands of throats drowned his words. "Wait a moment!" he shouted. Then, perspiring under the hot lights and possessed by the emotion of the moment, he cried: "I should like to have it said of my second Administration that in it these forces met their master."[45] At that flash of vengeful egotism, the throng came roaring to its feet.

Roosevelt had masterfully gauged the mood of America. On election day, November 3, the verdict was certain by early evening: FDR had swept the country, amassing the largest presidential vote and the largest presidential plurality in history. Only Maine and Vermont, with a scant eight electoral votes, had stood for Landon against the tidal wave. The mood of the victor's camp was magnanimous; at midnight, Postmaster General Farley issued a statement promising "no reprisals" against outspoken opponents of the administration. Relieved that a tense, emotion-draining campaign at last was over and the outcome known, Wall Street on the following day sent the stock market soaring to its highest levels in more than five years. Even usually slow-moving government bonds made surprising gains. "That Man" would rule for another four years and might yet ruin the country, but it was a disaster brightened by the assurance of uninterrupted government spending; and that meant "buy."

On November 5, the Kennedy mansion in Bronxville was scrubbed and polished to perfection to receive a very distinguished caller. Late the previous month, Kennedy had sent word to Bishop Spellman, now the channel of communication between the White House and the Vatican, that a luncheon at Hyde Park had been arranged for Eugenio Cardinal Pacelli, the Papal Secretary of State, at the end of his visit to the United States. After his talk with the President, the Vatican's chief diplomat boarded a special train for New York City. As a mark of his favor, he and his party stopped on the way to take tea with the Kennedys.[46] It was a signal honor for this Catholic family, who would next meet their guest in Rome.

Away from Washington for a little more than a year, Kennedy was discovering that he missed the thrill of being at the center of great events. He missed the proud satisfaction of being more than just another wealthy citizen. He once had remarked to the President: "I'll take any job you want me to and even work for nothing at it so long as it's interesting. I never want to be bored."[47] Increasingly bored by business, he looked toward a return to the government, perhaps in a Cabinet post such as the long-sought Treasury or the equally congenial Commerce. After all, he told friends, he deserved some excitement for the six hundred thousand dollars a year he paid in taxes.[48]

Roosevelt's reelection brought the offer of a job for Kennedy, but not in the Cabinet. It was a dirty task deep in the engine room of government. The President asked him to take over the recently established Maritime Commission and see if a respectable merchant marine could be created out of the high-cost, low-efficiency, strike-plagued shipping industry. At first reluctant, Kennedy went to the White House for a chat and swiftly capitulated. "I can say no to that fellow on the telephone," he said afterward, "but face to face he gets me."[49]

If Kennedy had not been drawn to public life, presidential suasion would have been unavailing, for he paid a large price for his ticket to Washington. Although he remained publicly optimistic, as early as February he began privately expressing misgivings about the economy, warning of the downturn that came the following fall. To hold office he forfeited the chance to trade profitably on his accurate prediction in the stock market.

Appointed to the chairmanship of the five-man commission in March, he wrote to the President raising the question of his eligibility, pointing to his ownership of twelve hundred shares of Todd Shipyards, Inc., worth about $60,500, which were included in his children's trust funds. Members of the commission were forbidden to have a financial stake in the shipping industry. Roosevelt forwarded the letter to the Senate, along with an opinion from the Solicitor General declaring no conflict of interest existed.[50] The stumbling block was removed quickly. So eager was Congress for Kennedy to have the job that it passed an unprecedented joint resolution waiving the requirement that he divest himself of the stock.

Congress set out the welcome mat for Kennedy because it was apparent that the Merchant Marine Act of 1936, setting up the commission, would fail under anything less than an inspired administrator. The act was the latest in a succession of government programs, dating back to World War I, intended to keep the U.S. flag flying on foreign trade routes. At the outbreak of World War I, the belligerent nations had called home their vessels from U.S. ports, leaving cargo piled on the docks and freight cars backed up for miles inland for lack of American ships to haul the goods. Since 1914, Congress had spent an estimated $3.5 billion to subsidize the building and operation of U.S. merchant ships. The government had even gone into the shipping business itself. But all efforts were without success: as of 1937, the shipping industry was declining rapidly, and with international tension rising, the U.S. faced the loss of an essential arm of its defenses.[51]

The government subsidy program had been rocked by disclosures of scandal. Under the old system, subsidies had been paid in the form of contracts to carry foreign mail. In practice, shipping companies received enormous sums of money, a total of twenty-six million dollars annually, for carrying a negligible amount of mail. Government regulation of the subsidies had been flagrantly corrupt and negligent; one company receiving bounty from the taxpayers because of its plight was found to be paying two top officers salaries and bonuses totaling $1.5 million. The Merchant Marine Act of 1936 was the outgrowth of a dogged Senate investigation led by Senator Hugo L. Black, and its provisions were so stringent as to raise doubts of the new law's practicality. The government mail contracts had been abrogated; in their place, shipping companies now were offered a choice: if a company wanted to build a new ship for foreign trade, the government would pay part of the cost and lend the company most of the rest; if a company planned to operate a ship, new or old, on a foreign trade route, the government would pay part of the cost of running it. To qualify for a subsidy, however, a company practically was required to turn itself over to the government. As a last resort, the government was empowered to build ships itself.[52]

Thus Kennedy was asked to undo damage that was largely the doing of the government itself. Once again, he enlisted under Roosevelt for the short term only, stipulating that he must be relieved as soon as the commission was functioning and the new operating contracts were established. Congress had allowed a year for settlement of the companies' claims arising from cancellation of the mail contracts, and for substitution of new subsidies calculated under the act's complicated criteria. A year had seemed barely long enough. By the time Kennedy walked into his office on April 19, however, only seventy-three days remained to complete this dual assignment before the July 1 deadline under the law. With twenty-nine shipping companies pressing astronomical claims, and with each line's subsidy involving separate problems and decisions, the commission faced a seemingly impossible task. Wrote Arthur Krock of the former SEC chairman's new trial: "Such is the penalty of having once performed a miracle."[53]

Kennedy again rented his old Maryland retreat, Marwood, and he and Eddie Moore moved in, picking up the early-rising, late-working regimen of their SEC stint. He also prevailed on the former SEC chief counsel, John Burns, to assist him. Burns had recently started a law firm with offices in Boston and New York, and could not afford another extended tour of government duty. Kennedy signed him aboard as a consultant to oversee the contract negotiations, and he, too, moved into Marwood. On Burns' arrival in Washington, after introducing him to a group of shipowners, Kennedy led the way to his office, where he threw up his hands in a gesture of impatience and said:

"Now you can see why the merchant marine is in such lousy shape."

Burns shook his head. "What's wrong?"

"Why," said Kennedy, "there wasn't a guy in that room who could write a check for a million dollars."[54]

If the shipowners were undercapitalized by Kennedy's standards, they were nonetheless resourceful bargainers. The time limit fixed by Congress was now patently impossible and could be extended, but Kennedy made no secret of his stubborn intention to wind up the talks by July 1. That being the case, many of the shipowners decided to stall, in the hope of winning fatter settlements as the deadline neared. But the chairman would not play the waiting game.

"Nobody could ever blackmail Joe," said an experienced Washington hand. "He would have you on your back and your head off in nothing flat."[55]

Kennedy refused to bargain over a new operating subsidy until a company had settled its mail contract at what he deemed a fair price. In one case, he decided not to bargain at all, rejecting a staff recommendation that a line be paid a nuisance settlement of twenty-five thousand dollars and offering instead precisely nothing. "I had a hunch," he said later, "that this boy was trying to razzle-dazzle us into giving him something for nothing. So I called him in, told him his claim wasn't worth a cent, and we'd fight any suit he brought for any amount; and when he swallowed that and settled for nothing, then I *knew* he'd been trying to razzle-dazzle us."[56]

Using such brass-knuckles tactics where necessary, and a rough but equitable rule of thumb in place of the clumsy new subsidy formula, the commission settled the $73,000,000 claims of twenty-three of the companies for less than $750,000. The government also won agreement to operating subsidies totaling $4,600,000, compared with the former bill of $7,600,000 under the mail contract system. All this, moreover, was accomplished within the allotted seventy-three days. Through the spring and early summer, under droning office fans that cut feeble gaps in the oppressive Washington heat, Kennedy drove himself and his staff mercilessly, his manner as crisp as the fresh white suits he wore in hot weather. He arose at six each morning, went for a short ride, ate a light breakfast, and set off for his office, arriving about nine o'clock. Lunch, taken at his desk, usually consisted of tea and toast.[57] His day often lengthened to fourteen hours or more, as staff members and shippers accompanied him to Marwood and continued their dickering well into the evening. But Kennedy knew how to relieve the pressure. During one particularly trying day, there was a sudden silence around the table. The chairman rose and told the astonished commissioners: "I'm going out to play with Teddy."[58]

Newly acclaimed as a legendary doer, Kennedy knew the first principle of getting a job done was *not* to do himself what others could do well enough. As much as possible, he delegated responsibility, narrowing his function to making the final decisions. In the flush of his victory over the calendar and the shippers, he acknowledged the debt he owed to the man who laid the groundwork, the unsung, exhausted chief negotiator, John Burns. If Kennedy moved in an aura of success, it was partly because he had an unusual ability to inspire prodigious effort from those who worked under him.

"It was the showman in Joe," said a former New Dealer. "You were riding with human destiny when this glamorous personality beckoned you to his side."[59]

Armed with the commission's godlike power of granting or withholding subsidies, Kennedy intended to weed out inefficient and superfluous shipping lines, consolidate the stronger ones, and eventually reduce the number of American companies to perhaps a dozen giants, able to compete route for route, and cargo for cargo, with the powerful foreign monopolies. At an industry dinner in New York he outlined this rigorous approach to one thousand steamship men. The chairman said that the commission would not "subsidize laziness, inefficiency and poor management." He warned that the days of running steamship companies from the offices of Washington lobbyists were ended. "The talent for getting money out of the Treasury is not the talent that makes a business go."[60] These sentiments won polite applause; the shippers welcomed reform, as long as it didn't affect them. They discovered Kennedy meant what he said. When the commission announced, for example, that no executive of a subsidized company could receive a salary of more than twenty-five thousand dollars, enthusiasm for industry-government cooperation virtually disappeared.

Yet such a partnership was essential to the commission's plans. The government's objective, in contrast to that of other maritime powers, notably Japan, was not breakneck expansion of the merchant fleet, but emergency replacement of obsolete tonnage. Toward this end, the government, again in contrast to other nations, did not want to run the shipping business. It did urgently want action on the situation summarized in a single fact: within five years, nearly 85 percent of American merchant vessels would be fit only for retirement and the scrap heap. In June, the President sent to Congress a bill providing for a $160,000,000 program of shipbuilding. As their share of the cost of fleet reconstruction, the shipping companies were required to commit only a fraction of that amount. But few shipowners, as Kennedy early recognized, could write million-dollar checks. And those who could, would not. They preferred to let the government bear the risks and costs of building ships, which the industry then would lease. It was cold economics: five vessels could be leased for the price of building one.[61]

Faced with industry inertia, Kennedy declined to take the course seemingly forced upon him. Instead, he soon went before the House Appropriations Committee and delivered what was, for the head of a federal agency, an unheard of request. *Don't* appropriate funds for building ships, he asked the startled congressmen. "Giving us cash might involve an obligation to spend it, and we're not going to do that until we know where we stand."[62]

The shipping industry's scarcity of capital was directly related to its vexing labor troubles. These, too, were dumped in the commission's lap under the Merchant Marine Act, which provided that subsidized vessels must obey government regulations pertaining to minimum wages, manning scales, and working conditions. As a rule, pay was poor and working conditions were squalid. The sailors, as hard as their environment, were, in the words of a contemporary *Fortune* account, "the true proletariat of the Western world, the homeless, rootless, and eternally unmoneyed."[63] Radical firebrands, like the hawk-beaked Australian longshoreman Harry Bridges, touched off wild demonstrations against the shipowners in particular and the "ruling classes" in general. A maritime walkout in San Francisco in 1934 led to the death of two pickets under police gunfire and ended in a general strike that immobilized the city. Faced with hundreds of "quickie" sit-down strikes aboard ships on the East Coast, the companies retaliated with lockouts. On the docks of every major port, crowds of sullen sailors and stevedores, hemmed in by mounted police, were a familiar and ugly sight. Adding to the chaos were free-swinging feuds and jurisdictional struggles among rival maritime unions. In 1937, labor strife cost the shipping industry more than one million man-hours of work, and threatened to scuttle the merchant marine before the commission could begin rebuilding it.

Kennedy tried to deal with labor firmly but fairly. Promising "a square deal," he pressed investigations into the sailor's lot, and was appalled by what was uncovered. For reasons of safety, he said, no member of his family would ever again be permitted to sail aboard an American vessel. In return for "the special treatment" of the unions envisaged under the act, he demanded responsibility. "You can have a merchant marine with first-class men even if they sail second-class ships," he said in a speech, "but second-class men can't be trusted on the finest ships that float."[64] Addressing the graduating class at the New London Coast Guard School, he deplored the slack discipline on American ships, a criticism followed by a proposal for training schools for seamen under Coast Guard supervision. The unions and their sympathizers were incensed; talk of "discipline" smacked of strikebreaking and union busting.

His plain speaking won the enmity of Miss Frances Perkins, Roosevelt's quixotic choice for Secretary of Labor, to whom the right to strike anywhere, anytime, was sacred. A native of Boston, the daughter of a Yankee twine manufacturer, she was a veteran social worker, an earnest, humorless alumna of Hull House. She knew with unshakable faith that there was no such thing, really, as a bad boy or an irresponsible labor leader. Among her favorites was Joe Curran, a lantern-jawed giant of a sailor who had led a well-publicized sit-down strike in 1936, and had gone on to become general organizer of the CIO National Maritime Union.

One day during the summer, Curran marched into Kennedy's office. A little later, the Secretary of Labor received a telephone call from the chairman of the Maritime Commission.

"Your sweetheart was just in here," said Kennedy.

"Oh," replied Miss Perkins, "Joe's a nice boy."

"Not in my book, he's not," snapped Kennedy, "and don't send any more bums like that in here trying to tell me what my authority is."[65]

Just how broad his authority was, Kennedy was never certain. As at the SEC, he dealt with each threat to his objectives with the power that came to hand. When the crew of the government-owned steamship *Algic* came near mutiny out of sympathy for striking dock workers in the port of Montevideo, he ordered the ship's master to put the ringleaders in irons unless they obeyed lawful orders. Fourteen seamen were arrested after the *Algic* docked in Baltimore, and a storm of protest broke. His union would "get the scalp" of the Maritime Commissioner, swore Curran, "and we're going to get it soon."[66] The embattled Kennedy took his troubles to the President. "I asked Roosevelt what he would do if I was in the wrong," he later recalled. "He said, 'I won't do anything. If you're wrong, you'll have to swing for it.' "[67] The outcry gradually subsided, and Kennedy kept both his scalp and the authority he had asserted.

Before many months had passed, the commission's study of the shipping industry convinced Kennedy there was little to choose between dealing with the unions and the shipowners. He flew to Seattle to mediate a paralyzing dock walkout and ended by giving an audience of striking longshoremen a lecture on the state of the industry in language they understood. "I don't know where the hell we are going to finish, if we keep up the way we are going. Everybody knows the shipping business is lousy.... The American merchant marine is a mess today—it's either got to get in more capital or be turned over to government ownership.... Everybody would be a lot happier if we could get together."[68]

In early summer, Kennedy stole time from the frustrations of keeping the merchant marine afloat to attend the twenty-fifth reunion of his Harvard class. It was a four-day gathering, and the whole family accompanied him; Kennedy received special permission to bring the children's governess. The paterfamilias encountered a continual seating problem. At a dinner in Symphony Hall, he could not find an adequate table; rather than split up the family, he led the way to a restaurant two blocks away. When the class secretary heard the Kennedys had left, he ordered a special table, and went to escort them back to the hall.[69]

The highlight of the reunion was a musical revue, with book by humorist Robert Benchley, Kennedy's fellow DU, and lyrics by Ray Wilkins, who became chief justice of the Massachusetts Supreme Court. The revue included a skit spoofing Kennedy, "In the Good Old Maritime." The curtain rose on a secretary frantically answering a battery of telephones. "No, it can't be nine o'clock because Mr. Kennedy isn't here yet." "No, sir, your clock must be fast; it can't be nine o'clock...." At this point, the Maritime Commissioner, played by Edward Gallagher, once treasurer of the Boston and Maine Railroad, strolled in sporting a bowler, gloves, and spats, jauntily twirling a cane. He told the secretary: "Get me Franklin at the White House." Feet propped on the desk, he picked up the telephone. "I'm here, Franklin. It's nine o'clock. You can start the country."[70] Horns blew, whistles shrieked, bells clanged. Seated in the front row of the audience, their accommodations having been given special attention, the Kennedys laughed and applauded.

Kennedy's sense of humor came under heavy strain as his classmates, mostly dyed-in-the-wool Republicans, gleefully needled the prominent New Dealer in their midst. In the report, one correspondent suggested that the troubles of the Class of '12 would be over as soon as Kennedy put every classmate on the federal payroll at a minimum annual salary of ten thousand dollars.[71] The climax of the reunion was a dinner at Boston's Harvard Club, addressed by such notable members of the class as industrialist Clarence B. Randall and Ambassador to Canada Richard Wigglesworth. When it came Kennedy's turn, he misjudged the lighthearted mood of the occasion and gave a fairly serious, mildly New Deal talk. A chorus of boos greeted him. "The razzing was all in fun," said a member of the class. "They'd do that to anybody."[72]

The class had failed to note the change in Kennedy. The congenial bootlegger of the tenth reunion and the freewheeling "capitalist" of the twentieth now was jealously conscious of his public dignity. Instead of the grin and wisecrack his classmates expected, Kennedy's cheeks flushed crimson and he sat down unsmiling. This was the last class reunion he attended.[73] In years to come, for a number of reasons he found sufficient, Kennedy adopted an attitude toward Harvard that friends and classmates sadly described as hatred.

Kennedy was powerless to work a miracle with the merchant marine, and he knew it. In spite of the authority he enjoyed on paper, years of decay had produced an obstinate reality that could not be changed overnight. Indeed, the damage could not be repaired at all with the tools at hand. Early in December, he testified before the House Merchant Marine Committee and dejectedly called the Merchant Marine Act unworkable—"about the worst thing of its kind I have ever seen." He proposed a number of amendments, but the spark of optimism was absent from his presentation. Only one new ship had been laid down during his eight months as chairman of the commission, he told the congressmen. Asked if others would be built, he replied: "I have no assurance under the act as it stands that any ships will be built." Shipping, he concluded, was "a very sick industry."[74]

And he was heartily sick of it. In September, the resignation of his indispensable aide, John Burns, had aroused speculation concerning Kennedy's next move. Jim Farley planned to leave the government for a job with Pierce-Arrow; rumors spread that Kennedy, as a favor to the President, would replace Farley as Postmaster General, a rumor to which Kennedy testily shot: "Perfectly ridiculous." Only one job in the

Cabinet excited his interest and could keep him in the government. And if there were favors to be granted by anyone, past and present service had put the President deeply in *his* debt.

As frequently as ever, Roosevelt sought Kennedy's advice. The stock market, true to his prediction, plunged in the fall, and he and the President discussed the ramifications of the break over lunch at Hyde Park. He emerged from the mansion to tell reporters the President was "trying hard to balance the budget" and had a "very, very good chance." Strong emphasis concealed weak conviction and long-standing doubts. The previous spring, with business improving and the relief rolls declining, Roosevelt had brushed aside Kennedy's bearishness and joked about his anxiety over the budget. "Now, Joe," he had said, "just go away and stop worrying. Henry and I have another white rabbit to pull out of our hats." "Mr. President," he had answered skeptically, "if you have got it, I am going to get drunk. . . ."[75]

Roosevelt never quite dashed Kennedy's hopes of taking over the Treasury, but he had no intention of putting an opinionated and stubbornly independent man in this sensitive post. "I think Henry Morgenthau has tried to carry out my plans in every respect," the President told Jim Farley around this time. "I couldn't put Joe Kennedy in his place, for example, because Joe would want to run the Treasury in his own way, contrary to my plans and views."[76]

An asset to Kennedy's ambitions was his close friendship with the President's son, Jimmy, who had moved into the White House, filling the vacuum left by the death of Louis Howe. Jimmy now served as the "clearing house" for his father with the independent government agencies. His powerful position stirred jealousy and distrust, as did Kennedy's favored access to the inner circle. In March, 1938, Harold Ickes wrote in his diary: "Jimmy has his father's ear at all times. When the President is tired or discouraged, Jimmy is at hand to say what may be influential. Jimmy has no political ideals, he is not a liberal, and he is trying to make a place for himself in public life. Joe Kennedy's influence has been bad too. It was Kennedy who dissuaded the President from appointing Lowell Mellett as Kennedy's successor on the Maritime Commission. Kennedy was afraid that Mellett would settle the labor difficulty which he had not been able to settle, and so he persuaded the President to appoint a stooge of his own. . . ."[77]

Another mark against Kennedy, in the peevish Ickes' book, was his cultivation of Harry Hopkins, the WPA administrator and Roosevelt's confidant. Hopkins underwent surgery for cancer in the winter of 1937–38, only months after losing his wife to the same disease. His daughter moved into the White House while he gratefully accepted Kennedy's invitation to recuperate in Palm Beach, which the President described as an "ideal spot."[78] Midwinter hospitality in sunny Florida was a source of Kennedy's influence. His guests the previous year had included Bishop Spellman, "Missy" LeHand, Krock, and Mrs. Jimmy Roosevelt.[79]

During the fall of 1937, Kennedy's gaze shifted from the Treasury to a remote but no less glittering office. Robert Worth Bingham, the U.S. Ambassador to the Court of St. James's since 1933, fell ill in London and returned home. From a bed in the Johns Hopkins hospital the dying Louisville publisher submitted his resignation. When Kennedy heard it had been quietly accepted, he told his friend Jimmy Roosevelt that he was interested in the vacancy, a message taken promptly to the President's ear.[80]

Many considerations were before Roosevelt as he weighed the choice of Bingham's successor. The man, of course, must be a Democrat of proved loyalty to the party and, more important, to the President, whose personal representative he would be. That he must also be a man of wealth was obvious: the American Ambassador in London was compelled to entertain on a lavish scale, yet received an annual salary of only $17,500, plus a piddling allowance of $4,800, the whole sum scarcely enough to cover a few suitably elaborate receptions. Kennedy clearly passed the tests of loyalty and means, but could he cope with the unforeseeable tests of diplomacy? A fact in his favor was his acquaintance with Great Britain's leading economic and financial figures, whose intimate views he had reported following his 1935 tour. (The President was inclined to take their opinions less seriously than did Kennedy; FDR privately called Montagu Norman of the Bank of England "old pink whiskers.") Kennedy was an exceptionally skillful negotiator, a major qualification in view of the looming necessity to bargain hard with the British on trade and maritime interests. His lack of diplomatic experience was no unique handicap in an ambassadorial corps heavily staffed with political appointees. An ambassador, after all, did not make foreign policy; he served as the eyes, ears, and voice of his government in a foreign land. Kennedy would be a trustworthy eavesdropper on the mounting rumors of war, and a candid reporter of what he saw and heard. Any doubts that had existed in Roosevelt's mind were slowly overwhelmed by the advantages. Kennedy deserved a handsome reward for his cash support and hard work.

Because Secretary of State Cordell Hull knew Kennedy only slightly, Roosevelt arranged a get-acquainted meeting between them at the White House. As they chatted, Kennedy mentioned a conversation with Krock over luncheon a few days earlier. They had discussed the appointment of Hugo Black to the Supreme Court, which had been followed by the sensational disclosure of Black's onetime membership in the Ku Klux Klan. Krock had expressed shock that Black accepted the appointment without informing Roosevelt of his embarrassing past.

The President asked: "Joe, when Krock said that, what did you say to Krock?"

Kennedy grinned. "I said to him if Marlene Dietrich asked you to make love to her, would you tell her you weren't much good at making love?"

Roosevelt laughed, but Hull's mouth fell open. The Secretary stared at Kennedy in silent amazement.

Afterward, Kennedy told a friend: "Hull must have been saying to himself, 'My God, is this the kind of guy we're going to send to the Court of St. James's?' "[81]

Regardless of what Hull thought, Roosevelt, prior to announcing Kennedy's appointment, experienced second thoughts. The President was trying to ease out Commerce Secretary Roper.[82] Kennedy, in view of his talents and experience, seemed a likely replacement, especially with business so shaky. Although he had already given the promise of London to Kennedy, Roosevelt sent his son to Marwood one evening to propose an exchange: Commerce instead of the Court of St. James's.[83] If Jimmy had been able to offer the Treasury, Kennedy probably would have taken it on the spot. As it was, he merely asked for time to think over the proposition. He talked with friends, who unanimously advised against the swap. When one said, "Joe, you'll be the most important American in Europe," Kennedy decided to hold out for the Ambassadorship.

The news that he would succeed Bingham broke in the *Times* on December 9. Since it was still unofficial, he sparred with the press: "It sounds like just one of those things." By coincidence, that evening he played host at dinner for the White House correspondents and their wives; to ward off their questions and ribbing about wearing knee breeches and silk stockings to Court, he stationed a waiter behind each guest, with instructions to keep the wine glasses brimful. Meanwhile, he drank water. Next morning, the correspondents groggily exchanged notes on a grand party at Marwood, but knew nothing of Kennedy's plans.[84]

He wound up his work at the Maritime Commission with a flourish, submitting to the President a forty-thousand-word report describing in ruthless detail the shortcomings of the shipping industry and existing maritime legislation. "A more hard-boiled document has never come out of official Washington," commented *Time*. He urged federal mediation of labor difficulties, and when Miss Perkins and the unions opposed this step as "premature," he went before the Senate Commerce and Labor Committees to fire a parting shot at his foes. "I submit that if the maritime industry is not 'ripe' for conciliation and mediation of its labor disputes, then it is overripe for ruin." At the close of the hearing, Senator Royal S. Copeland, chairman of the committee, leaned toward the witness chair and told Kennedy sincerely: "We wish you would stay here."[85]

The senator's wish was widely echoed, and not merely because Kennedy was a capable administrator. The original New Dealers, men like Ray Moley and Jim Farley, were becoming estranged from the President and soon would be critics of his administration. Stepping into their places were men like Hopkins and Corcoran, self-conscious agents of the revolution that Roosevelt had wrought in the government, the economy, and the Democratic party. They were concerned, not with reform of an older political and economic system, but with the construction of a new order around centralized authority. By temperament and experience, Kennedy belonged to the group of earlier New Dealers, whose influence was waning. Lamented the *New York Herald Tribune:* "If only his departure did not leave such a void of practical wisdom behind him."

In a letter accepting Kennedy's resignation in February, the President praised him for upholding his "justly earned reputation of being a two-fisted, hard-hitting executive."[86] For his part, the retiring chairman of the Maritime Commission passed a sober judgment on his ten-month tenure. "This is the toughest job I have ever handled in my life, without any reservations whatever."[87]

His new post would be demanding, Kennedy admitted to friends, but he was determined to justify to the President his insistence on having it. He also had been led to believe that he might yet have the

Treasury if he performed creditably in London. There was talk that he and Morgenthau would trade jobs within a year.[88] For the present, he agreed with "Honey Fitz," that lifelong connoisseur of patronage, who pronounced his son-in-law's assignment "the most important job the administration has to give out."[89] More than its importance accounted for Kennedy's pride and sense of gratitude toward Roosevelt. The President had conferred on him the distinction of being the first Irish Catholic named ambassador to Great Britain. Tradition had dictated that distinguished men of Anglo-Scotch ancestry and Protestant faith should represent the U.S. in London. The President's piquant decision to confront His Majesty's Government with a Boston Irishman—with nine children, to boot—brought sniffs of displeasure from some Boston Yankees and disapproving headshakes from some professionals in the State Department, but elsewhere it won applause. Wrote FDR's good friend, Ambassador to Mexico Josephus Daniels: "As a constructive iconoclast, I am happy to see you breaking archaic precedents."[90] The British press unrolled the red carpet and poised itself for the coming of the colorful Kennedy and his photogenic family. Noting the close relationship between the President and his appointee, the London *Daily Telegraph* called the choice "the highest compliment Roosevelt could pay to Great Britain."

Almost a year before he received it, Kennedy gave a clue to what his new title would mean to him. In a speech before the American Society of Newspaper Editors, he had said that getting good men to work in Washington was more than a matter of paying higher salaries. Until American public servants were given the prestige accorded British civil servants through knighthood, and lawyers through elevation to the bench, the slow parade of competent government officials back to private life could not be halted. He analyzed the historic attractiveness of judgeships to Americans of talent and great earning capacity in private law practice, and concluded that "they made the exchange gladly, because in their new position their families were honored." Their readiness to work hard for small pay was "due almost entirely to that psychological element of honor and prestige. To most men that quality alone cannot be translated into money."[91] It was precisely this "psychological element" that had driven Kennedy to enlist and reenlist in the government. Now and for as long as he lived, he would be "the Ambassador," and the Kennedys "the Ambassador's family."

He made his purpose explicit in a farewell conversation with a friend. "I've got nine children," he said, "and the only thing I can leave them that will mean anything is my good name and reputation."[92]

That legacy seemed as secure as the trust funds he had provided for the rising generation of Kennedys. And it promised to be enhanced by the prize awaiting him at the end of his triumphal passage across the Atlantic. He could not know, for there was no premonitory sign, that he was embarked on the darkest episode of his life, which would end in humiliation, defeat, and eclipse for the name of Kennedy.

BOOK IV
THE AMBASSADOR

"Well, Rose . . . this is a helluva long way from East Boston, isn't it?"

—Joe Kennedy, as he dressed for dinner with the King and Queen in the suite at Windsor Castle that once had been occupied by Queen Victoria

CHAPTER 14

The Nine-Child Envoy

FROM BEHIND their broad ocean moats Americans in the thirties looked on distant wars and threats of war with resolute indifference. They were preoccupied with the small daily struggle to stay fed, housed, and solvent. Of what concern to them was Japan's thrust into China, Italy's rape of Ethiopia, rearmed Germany's march into the Rhineland, Spain's cruel Civil War? The enfeebled condition of the League of Nations attested the foresight of American statesmanship in steering clear of foreign intrigue. As most citizens conceived it, the purpose of U.S. foreign policy was simply to ensure that America would be left alone.

A generation earlier, the tradition of isolation from the Old World's quarrels had been overthrown in a burst of fervent patriotism and idealism. Americans looked back on the crusade in bitter disillusionment. At a terrible price, the Great War had purchased, not the just and lasting peace of Wilson's eloquent high-mindedness, but the cynical Treaty of Versailles and a sullen truce. With the laconic Coolidge, Americans also had thought that their allies "hired" the more than ten billion dollars in U.S. war loans and were bound to repay the money. Now they knew better, for only little Finland was living up to the bargain. Year by year, the will of the victors to enforce the terms of Versailles had weakened visibly; it seemed only a matter of time before great armies clashed once again on the Western Front. But America had turned inward. This time, what happened over there was none of America's business.

During Roosevelt's first administration, Congress enacted a series of laws on neutrality which in effect established a new policy toward foreign wars. This legislation was influenced by the sensational Nye Committee investigation of war profiteering by the so-called "merchants of death," those international bankers and munitions tycoons who were believed to have lied and tricked the U.S. into war. The Johnson Act, passed in 1934, prohibited loans to any foreign government in default of its war debts. The Neutrality Acts of 1935 and 1936 called for an embargo on all shipments of arms to belligerents whenever the President should proclaim "a state of war," and denied American citizens the right to make loans to governments engaged in war. In January, 1938, the House of Representatives, under White House pressure, narrowly defeated a proposed amendment to the Constitution providing that, except in the case of invasion, the U.S. could not wage war unless a majority approved in a national referendum.[1]

Policy makers at the highest levels of government were extremely sensitive to this popular feeling. The President barely had entered the White House when he torpedoed the London Economic Conference of 1933 by his refusal to subordinate the domestic crisis to a program of international cooperation. To be sure, he was free of the xenophobia represented by the *Chicago Tribune* and the isolationist bloc in Congress, but he thought twice before offending this body of opinion and would challenge it only as a last resort.[2] There was in the President's makeup a recognizable trace of the same suspicion of England that fired Colonel McCormick and his sympathizers. In 1933, as the administration tried to nudge commodity prices upward by purchases of gold, Roosevelt hesitated to consult London. "Every time we have taken the British into our confidence," he said ruefully, "they have given us a trimming."[3]

This distrust of the British stood in ironic contrast to earlier trust, and was in part a defensive reaction to past gullibility. American Ambassadors to the Court of St. James's sometimes had fallen so completely under the sway of their hosts that the London Embassy became practically an annex of Whitehall. Probably the classic diplomatic anglophile was the man of letters, Walter Hines Page. One day in 1914, Ambassador Page appeared at the Foreign Office with a long dispatch from Washington contesting Britain's authority to halt contraband going to neutral ports in U.S. ships. "I am instructed to read this dispatch to you," he told Sir Edward Grey. Page read and the Foreign Secretary listened. "I have now read the dispatch," said the American, "but I do not agree with it; let us consider how it should be answered!"[4]

In the Depression, the England of empire, ancient titles, and rigid class distinctions no longer inspired awe as the cultural and political motherland. To many Americans it seemed old, cunning, and narrow. Not only the levelers and anti-imperialists of the political Left, but the mass of ordinary citizens, harbored a distrust of the British. The old American attitude of deference, the long habit of dependence, had been dropped in favor of a new posture of self-assertion.

Roosevelt had recognized this mood in choosing the new Ambassador. Kennedy, a man of uncommon shrewdness and ability, held a commonplace attitude toward England. His feelings were those of the average American. He could be counted on to deal unsentimentally with the British, taking them as a nation of shopkeepers and not of literary gentlemen.

For the peaceful U.S., the pace of diplomacy in early 1938 could be unhurried. Almost six weeks elapsed between Kennedy's appointment and his departure for England. He originally planned to travel with his wife and children, but Rose suffered an attack of appendicitis and was forced to enter the hospital for an operation. While awaiting her recovery, Kennedy carefully avoided comment on the duties he had not yet taken up. ("I've heard too many people blab about things they were ignorant of and make fools of themselves," he said.)[5] By late February, he could not wait any longer and reluctantly decided to precede his family. On the eve of his sailing, he made an unscheduled visit to Hyde Park, staying several hours. Next day, he blandly told reporters he had received no instructions from the President. As waves of well-wishers spilled into his crowded stateroom on the liner *Manhattan*, the Ambassador shrugged before the press and said: "I'm just a babe being thrown into—" A voice suggested: "The lion's mouth?" Kennedy flashed a noncommittal smile.[6]

Not the mouth of Britannia's lion, but its outstretched paw, gave

Kennedy pause. The coolness of Americans had had a noticeably warming effect on the British. "Their new anxiety to please Americans and approve everything American would be amusing," wrote *The New York Times'* correspondent in London, "if it were not pathetic proof of their bewildered sense of insecurity and need of friends."[7] To Kennedy's extreme annoyance, it was whispered that the sly British would beguile the self-made American with their dazzling pomp, titles, and socializing. He left the U.S. determined to remain American in thought, word and deed.

The palatial, thirty-six room London Embassy, the gift of J. P. Morgan, stood at Prince's Gate in Grosvenor Square. Most previous occupants, taking their cue from the surroundings, had tended to affect the manners of English gentlemen. Kennedy, choosing to be himself, received British reporters with his feet cocked up on his polished desk. "You can't expect me to develop into a statesman overnight," he said engagingly. "Right now," he said, "the average American isn't as interested in foreign affairs as he is in how he's going to eat and whether his insurance is good. Some, maybe, even are more interested in how Casey Stengel's Boston Bees are going to do next season."[8] His callers from Fleet Street hurried off to write admiring introductions of an American who was at once unconventional and refreshingly authentic.

A stroke of luck gave Kennedy's popularity a boost with the sports-loving British. Playing his first round of golf in England, on the Stokes Poges course in Buckinghamshire, he lofted an iron shot into the cup on the 128-yard second hole. Within hours, the feat was front-page news all over the British Isles; when the publicity persisted, the Sunday *Observer* even making it the subject of a verse competition, Kennedy fashioned a quip which he used regularly in afterdinner speeches: "I am much happier being the father of nine children and making a hole in one than I would be as the father of one child making a hole in nine."[9] Back in the States at Harvard, Joe, Jr., and Jack, who almost never beat their father at golf, sent a deflating wire: "Dubious about the hole in one."[10]

A week after his arrival in London, Kennedy, dressed in white tie and tailcoat, stepped into an ornate British state carriage driven by a top-hatted coachman and attended by footmen and outriders in flowing scarlet cloaks. In a half-hour ceremony at Buckingham Palace, King George VI, resplendent in the uniform of an admiral of the fleet, received the Ambassador's credentials.[11] Back at the embassy, Kennedy encountered a pair of wire-service reporters, told them of his visit to the palace, and repeated the King's remark that he would like to see the Kennedy children when they arrived. A secretary who had been listening to the interview jumped up as the reporters left and caught them by their coat sleeves in the hall. "Of course," he said anxiously, "you won't publish anything the Ambassador has just said." They agreed, for they realized, as the Ambassador obviously did not, that he was speaking out of turn. Court protocol treated the presentation of credentials as a personal matter between the King and a foreign envoy, which became official only after a brief announcement appeared in the Court Circular. And while visitors sometimes told the press how well the King looked, they refrained from quoting what he said.

The alert secretary's sense of relief was short-lived. What he did not know was that the Ambassador had spoken earlier to the *Daily Telegraph,* which prominently displayed the embarrassing story.[12]

With the arrival in mid-March of Rose, accompanied by Teddy, Jean, Bobby, Patricia, and Kathleen (Rosemary and Eunice followed shortly), Kennedy rode the crest of a tidal wave of publicity. A tabloid dubbed him "The U.S.A.'s Nine-Child Envoy." In a radio program comedy routine he displaced George Washington as "the father of his country." The *Evening News'* cartoon "Sights of London" depicted a motor bus outside the embassy, with the caption: "Mr. Kennedy takes his family to the theatre." It was reported that the Ambassador had purchased seven horses so that the family might ride together. The *Daily Mail* noted six-year-old Teddy's wide-eyed wonder at hearing his father called "Your Excellency" ("Is that your new name, Daddy?") and his fascination with the lift in the three-story mansion.[13] Bobby, Jean, and Teddy were enrolled in London schools; Eunice and Patricia transferred from the Sacred Heart convent school in Noroton, Connecticut, to the Sacred Heart convent school in Roehampton, England. Kathleen, nicknamed "Kick," a poised young lady of eighteen, had completed her studies and now assisted her mother as hostess at the embassy. Smiling out of the pages of London newspapers and magazines back home (American editors were as susceptible as their British colleagues), the Kennedys seemed a uniquely handsome, happy family, to whom only good things happened.

The parents kept up that appearance by keeping their sorrows, such as Rosemary's mental retardation, in the farthest corner of their hearts. She was now nineteen and gave no sign of improving, but her father insisted that she stay with the family. Years afterward, Eunice wrote: "Mother was worried about Rosemary in London. Would she accidentally do something dangerous while Mother was occupied with some unavoidable official function? Would she get confused taking a bus and get lost among London's intricate streets? Would someone attack her? Could she protect herself if she were out of the eye of the governess? No one could watch out for Rose all the time. . . ."[14] Yet the Kennedys watched attentively enough that no one outside the family was aware of her condition; so determinedly did they push her along that Rosemary, with her mother and Kathleen, was presented at Court.

The British Court, one of the world's perfected things, followed the ritual of centuries down to the smallest detail. The women wore three feathers in their hair and twenty-one buttons on their gloves—no more, no less. The invitation prescribed the men's attire: knee breeches, white waistcoats, decorations, riband and star, and miniature medals.[15] From the moment his appointment became known, Kennedy was mercilessly kidded about the necessity of wearing knee breeches. Roosevelt advised him not to worry, adding playfully that he'd be a knockout.[16] On landing in Plymouth, the new Ambassador was asked at once whether or not he would bend a silk-stockinged knee to English custom. "Not Mrs. Kennedy's little boy," he retorted. As the day drew near, he apologetically explained to Lord Halifax, the Foreign Secretary, that he simply could not be photographed in knee breeches: it would "ruin" him in America. And so, on the evening of the season's first Court, while his staff wore the prescribed garb, Kennedy appeared at the palace wearing a tailcoat and long trousers. As he came forward, Queen Mother Mary was said to frown. Commented the London *Evening Standard's* diarist: "Mr. Kennedy's desire to shield himself from the charge of flunkeyism achieved the somewhat paradoxical result that the only trousers at last night's Court were those worn by himself and some of the less important waiters."[17]

If the Ambassador caused comment, so did the Kennedy women. Hundreds of bejeweled and titled guests were ignored as newspaper photographers swarmed around the Americans. Mrs. Kennedy wore a sumptuous Molyneaux gown of gold and silver embroidered lace over a white satin foundation. She carried a white ostrich fan and wore a tiara of diamonds and rubies. The girls also wore Molyneaux gowns. "There were pictures other than those of the Kennedys," reported the Associated Press, "but for sheer photographic space they beat the field ten to one."[18] Upper-class Britons, whose Court photographs were posed in studios, peered distastefully at the candid shots of the Kennedys on the front, back, and middle pages of London's papers. An Ambassador and his family, they tut-tutted, ought not to behave like celebrities.

Kennedy had very definite ideas about what an Ambassador should not do. For one thing, there was the bothersome practice of annually choosing some thirty American debutantes, from among at least ten times that number of applicants, for presentation to the King and Queen. Since the Ambassador rarely knew any of the young women, the selection was bound to be arbitrary, largely determined by endorsements from socialites and public officials. After checking with the President, the State Department, and the British authorities, who were all of a like mind, Kennedy decided to abandon the whole business of boosting social climbers.[19]

He arranged with his friend, Massachusetts' Republican Senator Henry Cabot Lodge, to use a letter from Lodge, forwarding a debutante's application, as the occasion for announcing the new policy.[20] In a "Dear Cabot" reply, Kennedy turned down the application, said the presentations served no useful purpose, and declared that henceforth only the families of American officials and permanent American residents would be presented at Court.[21] It had been Lodge's understanding that he would make Kennedy's letter public, expressing warm approval of his decision. Somehow, a mix-up occurred, the letter was released in London, and newspapermen not unreasonably assumed that Kennedy had administered a democratic rebuke to a stuffy Brahmin.[22] Quickly, Lodge issued a "Dear Joe" letter, reading in part: "As I said when we talked this over before you sailed, I think this is a good decision. . . ."[23] The Court, then cracking down on British presentations but wary of offending important Americans, privately added its compliments.

A politically appointed Ambassador to a friendly capital could, if he chose, confine himself to the social and ceremonial functions of his office, leaving serious diplomacy to the professionals. But Kennedy realized that these duties, while well-publicized and agreeable, were merely incidental. When the veteran counselor, Ray Atherton, one of the State Department's outstanding career men, explained how efficiently the embassy was organized, intimating that the Ambassador could easily devote himself to "contacts," Kennedy rejected the idea. The staff could handle routine business, provided he was informed of it. He intended to be a working diplomat.[24]

Pride would not allow Kennedy to take the title and not the job, but the craft of diplomacy was unlike anything he ever had undertaken. He had entered with great fanfare a world in which men moved circumspectly, a world in which words of carefully shaded nuances were chosen more often to conceal than to convey the speaker's intentions, for the diplomat was aware that his words would be noted down the moment he left the room. The diplomat surrendered the right to express personal opinions except in absolute privacy; no matter how strong or well-grounded his views, he was only the spokesman of those in his homeland who held the power of decision and commitment. And as chiefs of state more and more spoke directly to one another outside regular channels, it was entirely possible that an Ambassador would not perform even this traditional function.

In Kennedy's previous government experience, he had enjoyed executive power, considerable autonomy, and direct access to the President. Now he was an agent responsible for gathering and reporting information which would be used as the policy makers in Washington saw fit. Although he was Roosevelt's appointee, he received orders from and reported to the bureaucracy headed by the Secretary of State. His new position called for self-discipline, unfailing discretion, and submersion of egotism.

Kennedy's ingrained pessimism showed itself in an off-the-record luncheon with American correspondents only a few days after his arrival in London. The Ambassador said he "temporarily" enjoyed Roosevelt's confidence and flattered his guests by observing that they would "make or break" him in the way they reported his activities. He went on to say that England, in the average American's view, was "the bad boy" of foreign affairs, not in the sense of being an enemy, but because "England will expect America to pull her chestnuts out of the fire." Kennedy gave the impression that he would go home rather than get his fingers burned. His parting shot underscored his bearishness: "I hope all you boys will be down to see me off when I am recalled."[25]

Kennedy's pessimism always had a theatrical quality. It was in the nature of this hot-tempered, cold-blooded speculator one moment to persuade associates everything was going to ruin, and the next to startle them by behaving like the soul of bullish optimism. What Kennedy did, friends discovered, provided a more reliable clue to his thoughts than what he said. He would not have come to London if his chances of success were as slim as he led the press to believe. If, as a result of heightening his honest doubts, the correspondents' dispatches were a bit more sympathetic to him, his performance at lunch would not have been in vain.

The Ambassador was sharply reminded of the importance of his "image" in America when a prominent Englishman shook his hand at a reception, congratulated him on a splendid beginning, and confessed that he had received a curious letter from Harry Hopkins. The President's adviser had written to his English acquaintance to warn him that Kennedy, while a great fellow, was also a sharp operator who would bear watching. The Ambassador laughed, but he must have felt cold steel between his shoulder blades.[26]

Anxious that it be well-received in the States, Kennedy worked for several days on his first speech before an English audience. It was intended to demonstrate beyond a doubt that he had not been taken into camp. (Roosevelt still needled him, as in this postscript to a note in March: "When you feel that British accent creeping up on you and your trousers riding up to the knee, take the first steamer home for a couple of weeks holiday.")[27] Beyond its personal purpose, he intended the speech as an important statement of U.S. foreign policy—so important that he called Washington on the transatlantic telephone and asked Secretary of State Hull to postpone a scheduled speech so that Kennedy's would receive due attention. Hull turned down the unusual request.[28]

Kennedy's forum was the dinner traditionally given by the Pilgrims Club to every new American Ambassador; his audience was nearly four hundred British political, diplomatic, and business leaders. After a few minutes, they were straining forward on the edge of their chairs, intent on catching every word. The speech was not the customary obeisance to the unity of the English-speaking peoples, but an astonishingly frank lecture on national self-interest in American diplomacy.

It was his duty, Kennedy said, to tell the British, as accurately as he possibly could, what was in the minds and hearts of Americans. They were afraid of losing their jobs and of getting into war. They would support every effort to preserve peace. Their government, faithful to the tradition of no entangling alliances, was "careful and wary" in dealing with foreign countries, refusing to bind itself to an automatic course of action in the future. This American attitude, said Kennedy, was often dangerously misunderstood. "In some quarters, it has been interpreted to mean that our country would not fight under any circumstances short of actual invasion." He called this "a dangerous sort of misunderstanding to be current just now." Here the audience applauded, only to fall back into thoughtful silence at the next sentence. "Others seem to imagine that the United States could never remain neutral in the event a general war should unhappily break out." This, too, said the Ambassador, was a dangerous misapprehension. "My country has decided that it must stand on its own feet. . . ."[29] The implication was plain to his somber-faced listeners.

Kennedy's speech pleased one of the leading U.S. isolationists, Idaho's Senator William E. Borah, who singled out the Ambassador for praise as the administration's most sensible foreign-policy spokesman. Borah, a powerful Republican member of the Foreign Relations Committee, was a supporter worth having, and Kennedy wrote to him, making a promise. "The more I see of things here, the more convinced I am that we must exert all of our intelligence and effort toward keeping clear of any involvement. As long as I hold my present job, I shall never lose sight of this guiding principle." British officials privately had assured him that they understood public opinion in America. ". . . they are going ahead with their plans without counting on the United States to be either for or against them. They have never given me the slightest impression that they want or expect anything special from us. Having had this clearly understood from the beginning, I have been able to deal with them in a frank and business-like manner. . . ."[30]

In the spring of 1938, the curtain was rising on the final act of the tragedy of appeasement. It had been in progress almost five years, and the denouement was approaching. Winston Churchill warned repeatedly that the end of it all was likely to be another war, but Churchill, branded an office-hungry Cassandra, was forced to deliver his warnings from among the spectators. On the great stage of power was a cast of well-intentioned, muddle-minded men raised to high office at the wrong time and kept there for the wrong reason. To their words, dress, and manner clung a whiff of the Victorian age; their old-fashioned minds were crammed with thoughts of pounds sterling and empire; they were incapable of comprehending Nazi ideology. Through the thirties, the British yearned for tranquillity and the appeasers, unwilling to enforce peace, bought it at the price demanded.

Versailles lay heavily on the conscience of many Britons; when Hitler arose to proclaim Germany's grievances, he struck a response in the British sense of fair play. It was but a short mental hop from recognizing the merit of some German complaints to embracing a policy of making amends—of appeasement. The sense of doing justice overwhelmed twinges of self-doubt. Generally speaking, the appeasers felt an affinity toward Germany, a strong aversion toward Communist Russia. They distrusted the France of Léon Blum and the Popular Front. Many considerations conspired to justify the policy of allowing Germany to grow stronger.

Hitler's 1935 denunciation of the disarmament clauses of the Treaty of Versailles, and the speedup of German rearmament begun earlier in secrecy, brought only remonstrations from the League of Nations. When, a year later, Hitler brazenly occupied the Rhineland, again violating the treaty, he again met only verbal resistance. (Later, France and England learned the German troops would have been ordered to retreat if they faced opposition.) At the time, the move appeared no more menacing to the British government, as one official remarked, than a householder's stroll into his back garden. There was no official disposition to curb Italy when Mussolini's legions ravaged Ethiopia; the weak-kneed and ineffective sanctions imposed only angered the dictator and hastened the political collapse of the League. When the totalitarian powers intervened in Spain, England and France stood aside. When the Berlin-Rome Axis was created, and extended across the Pacific to Tokyo, Britain's imperturbable leaders did not respond.

The policy of appeasement that sprang from Prime Minister Stanley Baldwin's concern with winning British elections on the unbeatable issue of peace entailed little more than passively swallowing lies and looking the other way. Under Baldwin's successor, Neville Chamberlain, self-deception was advanced by active diplomacy. Chamberlain, who rose from the Chancellorship of the Exchequer in May, 1937, saw Europe from the perspective of industrial Birmingham.[31] "Although I cannot boast of the blueness in my veins or of the fame of my forebears," he once said, "I am yet prouder of being descended from these respectable tradesmen than if my ancestors had worn shining armor and carried great swords." He plunged into foreign affairs with the boundless goodwill and ignorance of a banker who believed that two parties always could be reconciled, if only the terms of trade were made sufficiently attractive.

The motives inspiring the vengeful fanatic who had gained mastery of Germany were inconceivable to Chamberlain. It was true, as Alfred Duff Cooper angrily said, that "Chamberlain had never met anybody in Birmingham who in the least resembled Adolf Hitler." Following his first interview with the Führer, the Prime Minister confided in a letter: "I had established a certain confidence, which was my aim, and on my side, in spite of the hardness and ruthlessness I thought I saw in his face, I got the impression that here was a man who could be relied upon when he had given his word."[32] It was characteristic of the empty hopefulness of the appeasers that their feathery impressions weighed heavier in the scales than the accumulated evidence of deceit and treachery.

By early 1938, observers in America were growing apprehensive about the trend of events in Europe. In January, President Roosevelt sent a secret message to the British Prime Minister, proposing to take the initiative by inviting the democracies and the dictatorships to a conference in Washington to discuss the underlying causes of unrest. Roosevelt thought the conference could serve a useful purpose by making known the dictators' demands and thereby demonstrating their unreasonableness before the world. More important, the alignment of the U.S. on the side of the democracies in seeking peace would give the aggressors an implied warning of common interests that might produce a like alliance in the event of war. Roosevelt told Chamberlain he would approach France, Germany, and Italy only if his plan met with "the cordial approval and wholehearted support of His Majesty's Government."[33]

Astonishingly, it did not. Fearing that a lineup of the democracies would arouse Hitler's suspicions and resentment, Chamberlain politely declined the offer, explaining that he was pursuing his own promising plans for conciliating Italy and Germany. Up to now, there had been, in Churchill's phrase, "one strong young figure standing up against long, dismal, drawling tides of drift and surrender"[34]—the handsome, dashing Foreign Secretary Anthony Eden. Eden did not share the Prime Minister's delusion of British self-sufficiency, but was not informed of Roosevelt's proposal until Chamberlain had rejected it. Cumulative discouragement came to a head, and in mid-February Eden left the Cabinet.

"I do not believe we can make progress in European appeasement," he said in his resignation speech, ". . . if we allow the impression to gain currency abroad that we yield to constant pressure. I am certain in my own mind that progress depends above all on the temper of the nation, and that temper must find expression in a firm spirit. That spirit, I am confident, is there."[35]

Confidence was well-placed in the spirit of the British people, who would show themselves to be braver than the men who had misled them. But real leadership would emerge only from the disaster toward which Chamberlain's policy blindly steered.

Kennedy landed in England on March 1, scarcely a week after Eden's resignation and only eleven days before Chamberlain's next submission to Hitler's design in Europe. This was the annexation of Austria, foreshadowed as early as the Nazi murder of Austrian Chancellor Dollfuss in July, 1934. Hitler's unbroken string of successes had given the *Anschluss* the appearance of inevitability. When the day finally came that the swastika snapped in the breeze over Vienna, His Majesty's Government resignedly accepted the *fait accompli.* And it also accepted the fact that beyond Vienna lay Prague, now isolated and exposed. It was certain that Hitler would not pass up the prize of Czechoslovakia.

The drama unfolding in Central Europe did not alarm the newly arrived American Ambassador. He found the professional diplomats "semi-hysterical" in their anxiety. His talks with members of the British Cabinet and acquaintances in the City, London's banking and financial district, convinced him no war was in the immediate offing. If and when war did break out in Europe, Kennedy wrote to friends in America, it would be time enough for the U.S. to weigh the situation and decide on a course. He quickly came to the conclusion that Europe's most urgent problems were economic and that the endless round of diplomatic maneuver was play-acting which failed to come to grips with the root evil of unemployment. To the jobless European worker, he declared in early letters to the States, it made little difference which flag flew over his hungry family.

The men with whom Kennedy was soon on the friendliest terms inclined naturally to the belief that economics could redeem politics. They were the men who manipulated money in the City and those who gave that powerful interest political voice. After he moved to 10 Downing Street, Chamberlain remained essentially a brilliant Chancellor of the Exchequer, who cherished a dream of economic cooperation with Germany as the foundation of peace. He impressed Kennedy as tough and able. He had not been in London long when he told a friend with disarming candor: "I'm just like that with Chamberlain. Why, Franklin himself isn't as confidential with me."[36]

Before the first month of his ambassadorship was out, Kennedy entertained twenty-two leading British bankers, including three directors of the Bank of England. The dinner was something of a reunion, for these men had been Kennedy's hosts and informants during his 1935 trip. Chairs pushed back and brandy and cigars within easy reach, the company talked informally at the table well into the evening. Although hopes of appeasing Hitler were still high, Britain had belatedly embarked on a large-scale rearmament program. It was extremely costly; the government, through taxation and borrowing, now took fully one-fifth of the national income. Kennedy, anticipating a like program in the U.S., questioned his guests closely to draw out the lessons of Britain's experience. He doubted that Britain's economy could sustain the heavy burden, but the financiers of the City were somewhat more sanguine. They expressed the hope that arms spending would stimulate heavy industry and ward off recession. As in the past, they expected to make the best of the worst and go on with business as usual.

By late spring, however, these hopes had vanished, and Kennedy noted an attitude of fatalism, as though the power to shape Britain's future was slipping from British hands. More and more, Britain would look to America for help.[37]

The appeasers were not confined to one British party or class. "Right or Left," wrote an opponent of Chamberlain, "everybody was for a quiet life."[38] But the Left, especially after the outbreak of the Spanish Civil War, sniffed Fascist sympathizers everywhere. Wealthy Tories seen in the company of German diplomats were prime suspects. In 1936, *The Week*, a mimeographed left-wing newsletter edited by Claud Cockburn, noted the Anglo-German weekend parties at the estate of Lord and Lady Astor, and coined a phrase which the newspapers picked up—"The Cliveden Set."[39] Soon, it was firmly established in the public mind that Cliveden, the Astors' splendid country estate on the Thames in Buckinghamshire, was the seat of pro-appeasement influence in England. In the fancy of the press, a "second Foreign Office" functioned under the Astors' roof, with Cabinet ministers in tweeds deciding policy over whiskey and soda. It was taken for granted that the views expressed at Cliveden inspired the leaders of the *Times* and the *Observer*, which were controlled by Lord Astor's brother.

Appeasement, of course, was not foisted on England by Tory conspirators. It grew out of a state of mind detectable at every level of British society. It held sway, not because of what transpired in country houses, but because of what was said and done in Parliament and the Foreign Office, with the support of public opinion. Moreover, the "Set" was not a formal clique, but a highly miscellaneous collection of Tory and Liberal politicians, Oxford dons, editors and writers, diplomats, men of affairs, and titled hangers-on, all of whom were brought together by Cliveden's hostess, the vivacious, American-born Nancy Astor. When her husband succeeded to his title, she stood for his seat in Commons, becoming the first woman member of the House. Her gaze was direct, her tongue formidably edged and given to such causes as temperance and women's rights. A confirmed do-gooder, she sailed into situations that would have frightened the most intrepid angel. Once, at a diplomatic gathering in Moscow, she found herself standing next to Stalin. "When are you going to stop killing people?" she coolly demanded. But Lady Astor had the defect common to the appeasers: her decent impulse was poorly directed by a humbug-cluttered mind. Worthy of general application to the "Set" was an observer's comment: "For her, a declaration of good will is equivalent to a realization of justice."

During the spring of 1938, a newcomer appeared among the guests at Cliveden and danced in the ballroom of the Astors' London mansion on St. James's Square.[40] It was the gregarious new American Ambassador.

Press reports of Kennedy's social life did not pass unnoticed in Washington. The Ambassador, wrote Harold Ickes in his diary, "appears to have been taken in hand by Lady Astor and the Cliveden set."[41] In April, Ickes had a firsthand impression of Ambassador Kennedy from a liberal English friend, Colonel Josiah Wedgwood, an MP for three decades and a foe of appeasement. Ickes later summarized Wedgwood's appraisal: ". . . at a time when we should be sending the best that we have to Great Britain, we have not done so. We have sent a rich man, untrained in diplomacy, unlearned in history and politics, who is a great publicity-seeker and who is apparently ambitious to be the first Catholic President of the United States."[42]

The gossip that Kennedy had White House ambitions was hardly new. With tradition apparently barring Roosevelt from a third term, Kennedy, uniquely esteemed by both FDR and business, was among those often mentioned in speculation over the 1940 Democratic nomination. Now, curiously, Kennedy was engaged in long-distance wooing of the Washington press corps, which revived the rumors. He was known to be sending letters containing his views on England and Europe to several correspondents in the U.S. capital; at least one of them had never met Kennedy. Much of this "confidential" information was turning up in the newspapers; some of it was indeed news to the uninformed White House and the State Department. So shocked was one correspondent by the sensitive nature of Kennedy's confidences that he bundled up the letters he had received and took them to the President.[43]

Administration insiders could not agree on what Kennedy was up to. Some pundits, not knowing the Ambassadorship had been his idea, suggested that his appointment to London amounted to banishment at the hands of the liberals. One theory held that Kennedy certainly did not wish to fade away, that his letters were intended to keep his name before the newspapermen who made and unmade public reputations. Another theory started from the fact that the war debts and trade talks were going badly; perhaps the Ambassador had decided to make his case in advance, preparing the press for failure and clearing himself of responsibility.

The evidence of high political ambitions was entirely circumstantial. Friends who talked with him at the time, hinting they would be pleased to work on his behalf, received no encouragement. A good part of the Kennedy-for-President talk was the echo of the press talking to itself. In May, Ernest K. Lindley headed an article in *Liberty* magazine, "Will Kennedy Run for President?" and left the question unanswered, except to report that Kennedy was obviously a long shot. Some of the whispering was surely malicious, intended to fire jealousy. Harry Hopkins, for one, believed he had Roosevelt's blessing for 1940, and would resent any challenger.

Not to be overlooked was the fact that the administration's left wing had a new reason for hating Kennedy. When it had been reported that the administration was preparing to lift the embargo on arms shipments to Spain, a ban which worked to the disadvantage of the embattled leftist government, Kennedy protested in cables to the President and the Secretary of State.[44] Pressure from the Catholic hierarchy and press finally forced Roosevelt, who had not been enthusiastic, to abandon the idea. To the committed liberal, one's position on the embargo was the supreme test of friendship or enmity. The Spanish Civil War, as William V. Shannon has written, "was the first major issue on which most Irish Catholics divided from other groups in the liberal coalition. For Catholics, Franco's war was the opening round in the great struggle against world communism; for liberals, the Spanish Loyalists were defending freedom and democracy in the opening round of the war against fascism."[45] Kennedy, more than ever, was identified as the enemy.

At the same time, the Ambassador's freewheeling behavior, so popular with the British, was causing increasing friction with the State Department. Kennedy made no attempt to conceal his feelings. In June, Ickes, a widower who had just remarried, stopped in London with his bride on their honeymoon trip. They were wined and dined royally at the embassy, appearing just in time for the big dinner of the season honoring the Duke and Duchess of Kent. Afterward, Kennedy, although he neither liked nor trusted Ickes, spoke with his usual blunt candor, and diarist Ickes took it all down:

> Joe Kennedy was full of the European situation. He was greatly afraid that hell might break loose at any time over Czechoslovakia. He inveighed eloquently against "the career boys" in the State Department. He insisted that the State Department did not know what was going on in Europe and that there was no use trying to keep the State Department informed. He complained that everything leaked through the State Department and that nothing got to the President straight unless he sent it to the President direct. . . ."[46]

Ickes and others passed on to Secretary Hull Kennedy's criticism of "the career boys." The ranking officers of the department, initially neutral toward Kennedy, began turning hostile.

Ironically, the most popular Ambassador to Great Britain in living memory had, in the space of three months, become markedly unpopular in certain quarters in America. A trip to the States was urgently in order. In June, Joe, Jr., was being graduated from Harvard; the Ambassador announced he would return briefly to the U.S. to attend his son's commencement. The British press burst forth with "inside" stories, declaring Kennedy would see almost everyone, settle almost everything, and practically reshape U.S. foreign policy during his nine-day visit. It was a flattering testimonial, but the Ambassador's business at home was personal.

CHAPTER 15

Munich

I'M JUST THE SAME—you won't find me changed a bit," Kennedy assured a welcoming newspaperman over the ship-to-shore telephone as the *Queen Mary* neared New York.[1] Other reporters rode down the harbor in a cutter with Jimmy Roosevelt to greet the Ambassador. He met them with a flat denial of the rumors that he was angling for the Presidency. "If I had my eye on another job," he declared, "it would be a complete breach of faith with President Roosevelt."[2] In the bantering give-and-take, the inevitable knee breeches question popped up. Had he worn long trousers to hide something? Kennedy spotted a pretty girl reporter in the crowd. With a broad grin, he offered to show her, privately, that he was neither knock-kneed nor bowlegged.[3]

His Excellency, the Ambassador to the Court of St. James's was clearly the same wisecracking Joe Kennedy who had left the U.S. four months earlier, and his spirits were high at the prospect of a reunion with his sons.

Now that they were grown, he saw little of his older boys for months at a time, but he remained as confident of their trust and affection as when they were youngsters. The wall of reserve that commonly separated the generations did not exist between the Kennedys. One evening in 1937, the chairman of the Maritime Commission had come to Harvard to give a talk at his sons' residence, Winthrop House. Joe, Jr., and Jack arrived late, after everyone had begun eating, and they hesitated on entering the dining room. The housemaster saw them and said, "Go on, boys, say hello to your father." Without a trace of embarrassment, they stepped forward and embraced and kissed their father.[4]

The gulf of two years between young Joe and Jack, impassable in boyhood, seemed to narrow at Harvard. While each had his own friends and interests, the brothers ate at least one meal together daily, usually dinner, at which they exchanged news for the telephone call or letter their parents expected.[5] Yet Jack remained sharply aware of being outdone by his older brother and yearned to win distinction; but sickness and misfortune continued to hamper him. When his father sailed for England, he lay ill with the flu in the Harvard infirmary. The illness intervened as he was attempting to gain a backstroke position on the varsity swimming team. A friend smuggled steaks and chocolate milk shakes into the infirmary, and Jack slipped out the back door late each afternoon to swim in the deserted pool, training for the trials in which the squad would be picked to oppose Yale. Still weak, he swam hard in the trials, but lost out to classmate Richard Tregaskis, who later gained prominence as author of *Guadalcanal Diary*. Afterward, he wrote dejectedly to his mother: "It means a whole season has gone to waste."[6]

His luck was no better on the football field. A lithe, agile end on the junior varsity, he had the will but lacked the weight to excel in the pounding sport. During a scrimmage one day, he hit the frozen turf hard and was slow to rise. Although he waved away helping hands, he had suffered a severe back injury that would plague him throughout his adult life.

During his first two years at Harvard, Jack tried so single-mindedly to prove himself in athletics that he neglected his academic work. He read a great deal, mostly history and biography, but his grades consistently fell short of his father's expectations and kept him on the defensive. His attitude began to mature during the summer of 1937, when he and his old Choate classmate, Les Billings, toured war-shadowed France, Italy, and Spain. Because of Billings' tight budget, they traveled on a shoestring. At the Vatican, Cardinal Pacelli cordially received the son of Joseph P. Kennedy, but this was an exceptional encounter with a person of lofty rank. For the most part, Jack met and talked with the people who rode railway coaches and stayed at side-street hotels. He listened and observed. All at once, a world he had only read about came into focus. In a letter to his father from war-torn Spain, he wrote that he was impressed by "the almost complete ignorance 95% of the people in the U.S. have about situations as a whole here."[7]

At Harvard that fall, Jack, who had decided to major in government, gave promise of an awakened scholarly enthusiasm by writing a creditable thesis on the career of Congressman Bertrand H. Snell. This minor New York politician, the House Republican leader and an outspoken foe of the New Deal, was an odd choice for the son of a leading New Dealer. But Jack could not have written *I'm for Roosevelt.* He neither shared nor dissented from his father's commitment; the New Deal simply did not touch him. He explored Snell's career with the detached curiosity of a biologist dissecting a mildly unusual specimen. Politics engaged only his cool, analytical mind. Never would he lose himself in an emotional allegiance to a hero or a cause.

Emotionally as well as physically, young Joe was entirely different. "Little Joe" was his father's son, on whose broad shoulders the elder Kennedy rested his highest hopes for the family. The youth had an intense loyalty to his kin. Once, when a Harvard chum made an innocent wisecrack about "Honey Fitz," young Joe leaped from his chair and took a swing at him.[8] But his violent temper subsided as quickly as it flared. Warm and outgoing, Joe, Jr., prepared for his career in politics by serving on the student council three years, winning the chairmanship in his senior year. Without seeming to be absorbed in his books, he did well enough in his prelaw courses to graduate *cum laude.* He also won the place on the varsity football team that his younger brother badly wanted. Yet the handsome, personable star of the Kennedy family was not immune to an occasional disappointment. During his three seasons on the team, he did not play against Yale and thus failed to win his letter.

His last chance came in 1937. That afternoon, the elder Kennedy sat in the grandstand with an old friend and classmate, Tommy Campbell. In the closing minutes of the game, the Harvard coach, Richard (Dick) Harlow, used several reserves, but young Joe remained on the bench. Kennedy was incensed. His son's *H* was just as important to him as his own varsity letter had been to Pat Kennedy a quarter of a century earlier. As the gun sounded, Kennedy exploded in anger. He kept up a stream of oaths as he stalked from his seat to the field, where he cornered Harlow and berated him. By one account, the coach had intended to send in the senior for his letter, but misread the time remaining on the field clock.[9] By another account, from no less reliable sources, Harlow resented having received a number of unusual messages from alumni urging him to play young Kennedy against Yale, and so purposely kept him on the bench. In any event, Joe Kennedy reacted as though he and his son had been struck a blow.

The Ambassador's return to Harvard in the spring of 1938 was clouded by another disappointment. Early that year, friends had sought for him an honorary degree, which would be awarded at his son's commencement. Their request was turned down. The sting of this rejection was especially sharp, for it aggravated an earlier injury to Kennedy's pride. In 1936, he had been nominated for the Harvard Board of Overseers, one of a dozen candidates from whom the alumni would elect five.[10] Kennedy ran tenth.[11] Among those ahead of him in the balloting were several older men long associated with the university and alumni activities—a well-known federal judge, the editor of the *Atlantic Monthly,* the director of the Boston Museum of Fine Arts. Behind him in the voting were the senior Maryland district court judge and the vice-president of New York's First National Bank. Even to be nominated to stand with such distinguished men was no small honor. And eminently eligible men often ran at least twice before being elected, as would be the case with the New York banker. But Kennedy refused to be comforted in defeat. A Kennedy ran, not for the honor of running, but to win. Privately he expressed the suspicion that he had been passed over because of anti-Catholic bias.[12]

So badly did he take the setback that classmates hit upon the honorary degree as a means of restoring his good humor and affection for Harvard. In May, *The New York Times,* quoting "authoritative sources" in Boston, reported that the degree would be conferred.[13] But the degree committee, headed by Charles Francis Adams, found appointment to an ambassadorship an insufficient mark of distinction.[14] As a result, Kennedy felt compelled to save face and publicly "declined" what had not been offered to him. The spectacle provoked mirth at the White House. When a Cabinet member called the newspaper story to the attention of the President, Roosevelt asked in disbelief, "Can you imagine Joe Kennedy declining an honorary degree from Harvard?"*[15]

During Class Week, the Ambassador went to Wianno, Massachusetts, with his sons, where they competed as members of Harvard's seven-man sailing team against several other Eastern colleges for the MacMillan Cup, symbol of the collegiate championship. A surprisingly strong Williams College boat jumped into the lead and entered the final race five points ahead of Harvard. A brisk wind blew across Nantucket Sound, raising dancing whitecaps on the blue-green water and billowing the sails of the sleek boats. These were the home waters of the young Kennedys, and they now sailed, as they had for fully half their lives, under the exacting eye of their father. As he watched from the shore, the boat flying the Crimson pennant edged away, opened a lead as it slid gracefully around the course, and came flashing past the final buoy ahead of the field.[17] Shouts for Harvard's victory rose from the spectators. A proud father cheered two of the young men in the winning boat.

Kennedy came to Harvard directly from Hyde Park, and reporters asked about his conference with the President. The meeting, he said, was not important. "If it had been, the President would have given it out."[18] The visit did not produce the break that self-interested bystanders had done their best to encourage. Liberals in the administration wanted an end to Kennedy's influence; conservatives wanted a row that would embarrass the President. White House press secretary Steve Early had played razor-edged politics by informing the *Chicago Tribune*, the leading anti-administration paper, of Kennedy's

*Over his lifetime, Kennedy collected honorary degrees from ten colleges and universities—six of them in Ireland and Great Britain—but never one from Harvard. However, in small things as well as large, the aspirations of the father were realized by the son. Jack Kennedy won election to the Harvard Board of Overseers and also received an honorary LL.D. degree from his alma mater. "Of all the boys Jack likes Harvard best," Joe Kennedy once remarked. "Bobby and Teddy don't care for it much and I guess I have the old Boston prejudice against it."[16]

out-of-channels correspondence. After the Hyde Park meeting, the *Tribune* reported the conversation had been conducted "in a frigid atmosphere because Mr. Roosevelt had received positive evidence that Kennedy hopes to use the Court of St. James [sic] as a stepping stone to the White House in 1940." This bit of wishful thinking was off by several degrees.

Roosevelt was too astute a politician to give the *Tribune* and other ill-wishers the ammunition they wanted. He did not mistake the nature of the potential threat Kennedy represented. If, despite his plausible denials, Kennedy did dream of entering the White House, he stood far down the list of claimants to the throne. He had never held an elective office and lacked an established political base. His access to the nominating and vote-getting machinery of the Democratic party was blocked by the bulky figure of Jim Farley, a fellow Catholic who, it was suspected, wanted the nomination in 1940. Roosevelt could afford to indulge and even gently lift Kennedy's hopes, as he did with others to ensure their tractability.

The President's real concern was that the Ambassador would become, not a rival, but a critic. The faltering New Deal was vulnerable to the business-oriented opposition that a disaffected Kennedy could mobilize. With his impressive credentials, he might do great damage if he attacked the sluggish recovery program. Whatever chill existed at Hyde Park was calculated to convey the President's displeasure at the indiscretions that impaired the Ambassador's usefulness. But Roosevelt saw to it that they parted amicably.

Afterward, the President discussed Kennedy's visit with Harold Ickes. "I was interested both in the substance and the point of view of the President's remarks . . . ," Ickes wrote in his diary. "I do not think Joe is fooling him very much. He said . . . that he did not expect Joe to last more than a couple of years in London because he was the kind of man who liked to go from one job to another and drop it just when the going became heavy. . . . He knows that Joe is enjoying his job in London, where he is having the time of his life although he cries 'wolf.' "[19]

Here was a hint of the fundamental difference between Roosevelt and Kennedy. It was a clash of personalities, an innate temperamental divergence that would widen under stress. At bottom, Roosevelt was a dauntless optimist, Kennedy a confirmed pessimist. Coming crises would lay bare the innermost nature of each man.

With Kennedy and his sons aboard the *Normandie* for the voyage back to England was a friend, financier Bernard M. Baruch. Ostensibly making his annual vacation trip to Europe, Baruch actually had undertaken a confidential mission for the President, who asked him to verify the reports of growing Nazi military strength received from Kennedy and intelligence sources.[20] Baruch disagreed completely with Chamberlain's foreign policy. He was the oldest and best American friend of Winston Churchill, whose views he echoed in Washington.[21] Before he sailed, the New York *Post* speculated prematurely that Baruch intended to throw his weight behind Churchill. The shrewd South Carolinian's immediate task was to provide the President with an independent judgment of the situation in Europe.

A few days after his return from America, Kennedy was awarded an honorary degree by the National University in Dublin. Young Joe accompanied him on what proved to be a sentimental journey to Ireland. Following rutted dirt roads and narrow country lanes, they visited the ancestral homes of the Kennedys, in Wexford Field, and the Hickeys, in Clonakilty. Kennedy's first glimpse of the little-changed land and humble cottages his grandparents had left stirred him deeply. Unlike his father, he had not kept up with the relatives in Ireland; nor had he thought to visit them, as had Pat Kennedy just before World War I. In Boston, he ignored the Irish-American societies and bristled at the newspapers' attempt to make him a hyphenated American. But now that he walked the "ould sod," his Irishness came welling up.

Just before a state dinner in his honor at Dublin Castle, Kennedy said he was afraid to speak: he might burst into tears of joyful homecoming.[22] He did not weep, and spoke with unusual eloquence of the lasting peace that had succeeded enmity between England and his native land and the land of his fathers. Kennedy's emotions betrayed the racial pride that influenced his thinking and behavior. When a friend once asked him why he did not get along with certain Englishmen, Kennedy offered a revealing preface to his reply. He could not forgive those who had been responsible for sending the infamous Black and Tans into rebellious Ireland.

At this stage of his ambassadorship, Kennedy was open to criticism in Washington chiefly on the matter of style. The results he achieved could hardly be faulted. His administrative skill was evident in the efficiency with which he organized the work of the embassy staff of close to two hundred persons. He introduced changes in procedure, unafraid of treading on sensitive toes in the process. For instance, it took him only a short while to discover that some of the younger attachés habitually passed on to Washington the gossip they gleaned over luncheon tables and in club lounges. Rumors and unverified information seemed to him a shaky foundation for policy making. Kennedy ordered all reports submitted to him for review before transmission to the U.S. If he came upon a rumor concerning Chamberlain, he simply picked up the telephone and asked "Neville" for the facts. This method dramatically swelled the flow of reliable information from London.

The State Department appreciated the Ambassador's excellent personal relationship with the Prime Minister, but had its own ideas about how it should be exploited. Negotiations between the U.S. and Great Britain on the trade treaty bogged down in late July. Secretary of State Hull, exasperated with British horse-trading, fired off a long cable to Kennedy, asking him to remind Chamberlain that the U.S. desired the agreement, "not primarily for the dollars and cents immediately involved," as important as that was, but "as a powerful initiative" for stability and peace. Hull noted that Germany, Italy, and Japan were watching the fruitless talks, "and I think that it would greatly harm not only our two countries but also the whole outlook for peace . . . if we, after months of haggling, should turn out a little, narrow, picayunish trade agreement."[23]

Bringing parties together at the bargaining table was Kennedy's special talent, and he took up the assignment enthusiastically. He sent word that Britain's reluctance stemmed from an unfavorable trade balance with the U.S., which officials in London felt could only be worsened by yielding further concessions. Members of the Cabinet told Kennedy they already feared criticism in Parliament of their overgenerosity. Then, too, the government was increasingly preoccupied with restive Germany, which pushed considerations of trade into the background. Still, Kennedy patiently sounded out officials, searched for areas of compromise, and chipped away at British resistance. He reported to Hull that only Chamberlain among the Cabinet ministers seemed interested in reaching a worthwhile agreement. When a letter appeared in the *Times*, from the economist John M. Keynes, asserting that England should buy overseas only where she could sell advantageously, Kennedy promptly wired Hull. The dispatch showed the way his mind worked in touch-and-go trading: "If you can give me some inside advice as to what you will take to settle I will go to work on it. I cannot find out yet whether Keynes' letter is a plant and whether it is the beginning of propaganda against the agreement, but I think we must be very alert here."[24]

Instead of "inside advice," he received a formal rehearsal of the arguments already laid before the Foreign Office. Denied anything with which to entice the British, he felt a bit foolish and altogether useless, and told the Secretary so in a cable edged with sarcasm.

"It strikes me that the tone of the last document you handed the British was definitely in the nature of an ultimatum and the British so regard it. Far be it from me to make any suggestions as to how those handling the trade agreements should avail themselves of the Ambassador's services, but it does seem to me that if they really want a trade agreement it might be well to have the man on the spot find out just how much further we could go without kicking the thing over."[25]

Nor was this undiplomatic admonition the sum of his lecture to the Secretary. Later that day, he added a postscript: "As I have said to you over the telephone I am not in a position to judge the value of the agreement or the terms of it. I merely know what some people are likely to do in a game of cards when they are called."[26]

To this advice Hull curtly replied: "I appreciate your interest." Kennedy's brass-tacks approach—to say nothing of his profane running commentary on the telephone—unsettled the staid State Department. In this instance, however, he was right and the professionals were wrong. The U.S. soon settled on essentially the British terms, and Secretary Hull gracefully acknowledged his debt to Kennedy. "In reaching this decision, I have been influenced by your excellent telegraphic reports, particularly your comments about opposition to the agreement within the British Cabinet."[27]

Kennedy's intimacy with leading British officials, while useful, caused some misgivings in the State Department. Washington was concerned that he was becoming too closely identified with Chamberlain and too ready to defend his policies under the guise of reporting them. (Some Americans in London acidly noted that the Ambassador had "gone British," even to the extent of peppering his speech with the adjective "bloody.")[28] Certainly Kennedy had achieved a rare rapport with his hosts. He was one of the few men to whom the austere Prime Minister granted the privilege of first-name informality. And no other foreigner was favored with so many confidences. This was not, as some suspected, a guileful attempt to lure the American and his government into Britain's diplomatic web. Chamberlain sincerely preferred to go it alone. ("It is always best and safest to count on nothing from the Americans but words," he had remarked after rejecting Roosevelt's plan for a peace conference.)[29] Nor was Kennedy a trusting anglophile. He and Chamberlain were drawn together in genuine friendship by the near identity of their views on the large issues, of which the most urgent was the question of war or peace. On the necessity of avoiding war, they were of one mind.

The thought of war horrified Kennedy. He was extremely anxious for the safety of his children. A colleague at the SEC recalled a conversation with him in 1936 about the darkening situation in Europe. "I have four boys," said Kennedy with visible emotion, "and I don't want them to be killed in a foreign war."[30] As the threat of war drew closer, Kennedy's desire to shield his family grew stronger.

He also dreaded the economic and political consequences of war. "Joe thought war was irrational and debasing," said a friend with whom he often talked. "War destroyed capital. What could be worse than that?"[31]

Chamberlain, the Birmingham entrepreneur, and Kennedy, the Wall Street speculator, had been shaped by their experience as capitalists. Their conception of European civilization was bound up with the accustomed economic system; nothing must be permitted to disturb the network of commerce and finance extending from the City of London to the markets and trade centers of the Continent. War would reduce Europe to rubble and make a shambles of capitalism, almost certainly preparing the triumph of communism. In the unhappy choice of evils, nazism, despite its objectionable features, was clearly preferable. Hitler's professed anti-bolshevism had the ring of truth; the logical path of his expansionist dreams lay to the East, which would inevitably bring him into conflict with the Soviet Union. Chamberlain closed his eyes to much in the Reich out of blind distrust of Russia, and clung to the hope of forging a Western anti-Communist alliance that would include Germany.

Chamberlain and Kennedy also feared involvement in war because of the radical social, economic, and political changes it would produce in their countries. In order to wage modern war effectively against a totally mobilized dictatorship, capitalism as they knew it would almost certainly have to be sacrificed in favor of some form of collectivism. Thus war could usher in a peacetime reign of socialism. Why fight to hand the system over to the Socialists?

Kennedy was a thoroughgoing isolationist. So, in a real sense, was the Prime Minister charged with leading an island people and safeguarding a far-flung empire. Chamberlain consciously turned his back on the tradition of British intervention on the Continent to preserve a balance of power. Britain had long taken the side of the weaker European states against the more powerful out of awareness that her immutable interest lay in keeping potential enemies divided. Always implicit in the balance-of-power strategy was the risk of war. Now that risk appeared unacceptable, and the most likely enemy appeared to be Russia. Therefore Chamberlain befriended powerful Germany at the expense of the latter's weak neighbors, in the hope that a satiated and grateful Germany ultimately would befriend England. It was an ill-conceived and dishonorable policy, yet one which won the sympathy and endorsement of Kennedy.

Since Germany's annexation of Austria, Czechoslovakia had trembled in expectation. This small, highly industrialized state contained a large German-speaking population in the Sudetenland, led by swaggering Nazi bullies and rabble-rousers who owed their allegiance to Hitler. The Führer's declared objective was to bring all the German minorities of Central Europe under the protection of the Reich. From Berlin through the spring and summer of 1938 resounded propaganda on the complaints of the Sudeten Germans and the necessity of their incorporation into the Fatherland.

This heightened the danger of war. France was bound to Czechoslovakia in a treaty of military alliance, and Russia was committed to go to Czechoslovakia's assistance if France did. Britain, of course, was allied with France. Anxiously Paris and Moscow looked to London for a sign of Britain's intentions.

Britain did not intend to fight. While Czechoslovakia, with its liberal democratic government, had many friends in the press and Opposition circles, it struck key decision makers within the government as an artificial, racially unstable country, the troublesome heir to the perpetually boiling minority conflicts of Middle Europe. One vexed diplomat in Prague had gone so far as to begin a dispatch to London with the flat statement: "There is no such thing as Czechoslovakia."[32] Chamberlain concluded that the situation was fundamentally unsound and not worth a war to maintain. To preserve peace, the Czechs must make every sacrifice, even to the point of dismembering their country.

Berlin, too, watched London closely. Seizure of Czechoslovakia would establish German hegemony over Central Europe. It would deny the democracies a well-equipped military force and a highly developed munitions industry. Surely Britain was not blind to the implications of such a loss. Hitler prepared to fight.[33] As early as June, 1937, the German General Staff began to prepare for the invasion of Czechoslovakia. It was inconceivable to Hitler that Britain wanted only to do his dirty work. And so, while the British anxiously awaited a precise statement of German demands, which they would force the Czechs to accept, the Führer kept up a barrage of purposely vague threats.

The war of nerves upset Kennedy. On August 30, during an hour-long conference, he told Chamberlain that if Hitler seized Czechoslovakia, "it will be Hell!"[34] He saw the danger of a general European war, which could involve America. But he told the Prime Minister that President Roosevelt had decided to "go in with" Chamberlain, and that whatever course he chose to follow, the President would approve.[35]

This sweeping assurance of U.S. support for a renewed attempt at appeasement conveyed a false impression of enthusiasm on Roosevelt's part. Treasury Secretary Morgenthau interpreted the President's thinking quite differently. "The President's mood in the last days before Munich was one of discouragement," Morgenthau wrote in his diary. "He became increasingly irritated at Kennedy. 'Who would have thought that the English (the Cliveden Set) could take into camp a red-headed Irishman?' he demanded at Hull and me in an anxious conference on September 1 . . . As for Chamberlain, the President called him 'slippery' and added, with some bitterness, that he was 'interested in peace at any price if he could get away with it and save his face.' "[36]

Even allowing for Morgenthau's antipathy toward Kennedy and Chamberlain, the President's irritation at his envoy cannot be doubted. On August 31, Kennedy angered Roosevelt by giving an "exclusive" interview to the Hearst-owned Boston *American*. Over the transatlantic telephone, the Ambassador told the newspaper he had just returned from a midmorning conference with Halifax, the Foreign Secretary. "Keep cool—things aren't as bad as they seem," said Kennedy. "The thing to do here and in the United States is not to lose our heads." He said the mounting crisis had united the British public "very strongly" behind the Cabinet.[37] Apparently given an inkling of Chamberlain's dramatic plans for a settlement, he ventured a prediction: "No war is going to break out during the rest of 1938."[38]

Several days after the interview appeared, the President reprimanded Kennedy in a letter.

> As you know, we were all greatly disturbed by the appearance of an "exclusive" message of advice from you which was published as having been given to the Boston American and then passed on to the other Hearst papers.
>
> I know that the Secretary [of State] wired you about it and the other day I saw what you sent to the Secretary. It is not a question of "getting along reasonably well with the agencies"—for, of course, you do that but it does involve the use by an American newspaper or a single news agency of a "special interview" or "special message of advice" to people back here.
>
> I know you will understand.[39]

Meanwhile, Kennedy became embroiled with the State Department over the text of a speech he proposed to deliver at Aberdeen, Scotland. He would not consent to censorship of the draft he submitted until the department appealed over his head to the President, who overruled him. At Roosevelt's order, Kennedy struck the following sentence from his speech: "I can't for the life of me understand why anybody would want to go to war to save the Czechs."[40] Referring to Kennedy, the President told Morgenthau: "The young man needs his wrists slapped rather hard."[41]

The occasion of the Ambassador's remarks was the laying of the cornerstone of a memorial in Aberdeen Cathedral to Samuel Seabury, first Episcopal Bishop of the United States. Appropriately, the speech dealt with religious freedom and indirectly assailed the persecution of the Jews in Germany and Italy. "In certain parts of the world," said Kennedy, "the profession and practice of religion is being called a political offense." Because of their religion, "men and women are being deprived of their natural born citizenship and they are being thrown out of the land of their nativity . . ." In contrast, he said, the U.S. and Great Britain were "imbued with certain old-fashioned but still useful qualities—respect for the rights of others and for the sanctity of engagements as well as a genuine love of freedom for the individual."[42]

If such talk pleased the anti-appeasers, at a luncheon that same day Kennedy's words tended to comfort the supporters of Chamberlain. The Ambassador professed to see a parallel between the European crisis and a recent Anglo-American dispute over several tiny Pacific islands, resolved by an agreement providing for joint administration. This arrangement seemed to Kennedy "a cameo of what world settlement might be if the same intelligent good-neighborliness were always exhibited by different nations.... After all, the issues over which governments make such a fuss are generally small ones or, at least, they start as small issues."[43]

In the tense days that followed, Chamberlain would publicly bemoan the imminence of war "because of a quarrel in a far-away country between people of whom we know nothing."

On the evening of September 12, all Europe bent close to the radio set. From Nuremberg came the voice of Hitler, haranguing a rally of thousands of fanatical Nazi followers enflamed by a week-long orgy of drumbeating pageantry and violent speechmaking. The Führer was expected to disclose his final decision for war or peace with Czechoslovakia.

In the embassy in London, Kennedy spent the last minutes before Hitler's speech writing to a friend in America. Despite Chamberlain's unshakable faith and his own prophecy of peace through the year's end, he was sunk in gloom. War had never seemed closer. Kennedy wrote that he was thinking of sending Rose and the children home—perhaps never to see them again. The stillness in the room was broken as an assistant tuned in Nuremberg and the radio gave forth a frenzied chant rising higher and higher: *Sieg Heil! Sieg Heil! Sieg Heil!*

Hitler decided to toy with his prey a while longer. Though brutal in his denunciation of the Czech leaders, he contented himself with the familiar demand for "justice" for the Sudetenland. The "Big Four" of the British Cabinet—Chamberlain, Halifax, Chancellor of the Exchequer Sir John Simon, and Home Secretary Sir Samuel Hoare—had been meeting in almost constant session. Following Hitler's speech, the Prime Minister completed preparations for a bold mission. He would go to Germany and personally save the peace.

It was not merely that Chamberlain would not fight; he did not see how ill-prepared England could go to war. The whole aim of appeasement had been to remove the causes of war, rather than, as Churchill, Eden, and others insisted, to deal with the dictators from a position of imposing strength that made war unappealing. In stripping Germany of weapons, the Versailles Treaty ironically had worked to Hitler's advantage, for he had rebuilt the Reich's war machine from scratch and made it the most modern in Europe. Britain had begun rearming more than two years after Germany, at the grudging, self-indulgent pace of a democracy led by men who refused to accept the possibility of war. As a result, Britain's defenses, particularly her defenses against air attack, were pitifully inadequate.

On the morning of September 15, Chamberlain, accompanied by a pair of aides, flew to Berchtesgaden. The rough, seven-hour flight was the first the sixty-nine-year-old Prime Minister had made. Two more would follow in the next crowded fortnight. Chamberlain left behind a Cabinet in which faith in appeasement had been shaken by the prospect of humiliation. Foreign Secretary Halifax began edging toward a stronger stand even though it meant risking war. If Britain fought, the odds would be heavily against her unless the U.S. provided support in the form of prompt shipments of arms and supplies, which could be purchased only if Congress revised the neutrality law. In view of the vaunted Nazi *Blitzkrieg* tactics, a delay of even a few weeks in altering the law could prove fatal. The U.S. might be reluctant to help a country whose leader was less interested in defending democracy than in dickering with Hitler. Then again, it might not impose any penalty for further attempts at appeasement. Intent on discovering the U.S. attitude, Halifax arranged a meeting with Kennedy.

The Foreign Secretary asked the Ambassador what the U.S. would do about the neutrality law if Britain were involved in war. Here was a subtly proffered opportunity for Kennedy to support a policy of firmness by saying that the U.S. attitude would depend upon the energy and sincerity of Britain's effort to play a full role in the democratic front against the aggressors. But Kennedy did not exploit the opening; he was wholeheartedly committed to Chamberlain's approach.[44]

The Prime Minister received a cold reception from Hitler. He told Chamberlain the fate of the Sudetenland must be determined by the inhabitants. Chamberlain agreed "in principle" to self-determination, which would surely mean turning the territory over to Germany. In effect, he thus assured Hitler in advance of Britain's unwillingness to oppose the breakup of Czechoslovakia.

After his return to London, Chamberlain, in consultation with the French, drew up a set of stark proposals, calling for either a plebiscite or a direct transfer of the Sudetenland, which the Czechs would be forced to accept if they did not wish to fight Germany alone. With consent wrung from the victim, Chamberlain on September 22 flew east once again, this time meeting Hitler at Godesberg.[45] But the Führer cynically dismissed the Anglo-French proposals as no longer adequate. His new terms were set forth in an ultimatum calling for the occupation of the Sudetenland by October 1, the date he had set for the long-planned invasion of Czechoslovakia.

Chamberlain came home persuaded he had no choice but to submit—that is, to compel the Czechs to submit. To quell the murmurs against further appeasement, he painted a frightful alternative for the Cabinet. Wrote the Secretary of State for War, Leslie Hore-Belisha: "The P.M. yesterday spoke to us of the horrors of war, of German bombers over London and of his horror in allowing our people to suffer all the miseries of war in our present state. . . . Chiefs of Staff view—to take offensive against Germany now would be like 'a man attacking a tiger before he has loaded his gun.' "[46]

Kennedy buttressed this belief with the opinion of an expert he summoned, Colonel Charles A. Lindbergh. More than a decade had passed since the "Lone Eagle" had conquered the Atlantic, but America's foremost aviator remained the lanky, boyish-looking world symbol of the hero. In 1936, at the invitation of the American military attaché in Berlin, he had exploited his enormous popularity in Germany to gain a close-up look at the infant *Luftwaffe*. After that disquieting visit, he tried to warn British leaders of the coming peril. Prime Minister Baldwin placidly nodded and sucked his pipe. Lindbergh returned to Germany in 1937 and 1938, following up the most recent visit with a brief inspection of air power in Russia and Czechoslovakia. Anxious diplomats and military men awaited him in the Western capitals. In Paris, he briefed American Ambassador William C. Bullitt and the French Under-Secretary for Air. Then, at the invitation of Kennedy, he went on to London, arriving on September 21.[47]

Lindbergh's oral report on Nazi air power was so alarming—indeed, terrifying—that Kennedy asked him to submit his views in writing, which he did in a long letter to the Ambassador dated September 22.[48] While Lindbergh conferred with an official of the British Air Ministry whom Kennedy had alerted, the Ambassador cabled the substance of the letter to the Secretary of State. Lindbergh expressed the opinion that Germany's air force now was the most powerful in the world, the result of rapid strides during the years while the democracies were asleep. One day, even the long U.S. lead in aviation might be closed by Germany. From his firsthand observations, he believed the *Luftwaffe* was stronger than all other European air forces combined, and could level at will the capitals of Europe. Perhaps never in history had European civilization stood in greater peril. Kennedy omitted Lindbergh's strongly expressed belief that Europe should avoid a general war in the near future at almost any cost,[49] but this advice was implicit in the extremely pessimistic appraisal. Interestingly, although Kennedy requested that the cable containing Lindbergh's views be forwarded to the President and the Navy and War Departments, it apparently circulated only within the State Department.[50]

But the bad news reported in the dispatch from London was no secret to the U.S. government. Within a few months, the military intelligence division of the U.S. General Staff revealed an estimate of European air strength similar to Lindbergh's. Germany was said to command five bombers to Britain's one, and eleven to America's one. German fighter superiority was as marked. Hitler had virtually won mastery of the skies over Europe by default.[51]

Even Baruch, who wished mightily it were otherwise, concluded that Germany held the upper hand over the laggard and divided democracies. On the basis of searching talks on both sides of the Channel, he cabled Roosevelt a warning that Britain and France would not be able to fight.[52]

Yet, so swiftly were events moving, it appeared the unwilling Western allies would have to fight. On September 23, after straining on a British leash for several days, the Czech government ordered general mobilization. The split within the Cabinet became sharper, Halifax trying to stiffen Chamberlain's backbone and Duff Cooper, First Lord of the Admiralty, pleading for permission to mobilize the fleet. While the Cabinet debated on the evening of September 24, Kennedy telephoned Hull, reporting a division between those who wanted "peace at any price" and those who did not "want to take any more back talk from Hitler," in the belief that they "would have to fight anyhow."[53]

As a last resort, Chamberlain wrote a personal letter to Hitler, asking that the details of the transfer of Czech territory be settled by an international commission of Czechs, Germans, and English. The letter was carried to Germany in the briefcase of Sir Horace Wilson, the soft-spoken, deferential civil servant who occupied a room at 10 Downing Street and was a tireless intriguer for appeasement. Hitler shrieked and ranted, reviling Chamberlain and his emissary. In a gesture of contempt, he refused the Prime Minister's plea and demanded an affirmative answer to his ultimatum to the Czechs by the afternoon of September 28.[54]

The same day, the Cabinet at last overcame Chamberlain's reluctance and declared a state of emergency. The fleet prepared for action. Antiaircraft gunners were called up and the coast defenses were manned. Frightened civilians awkwardly tried on gas masks. War seemed only hours away.

The tension that had been building over the summer now became almost unbearable. Britain had tried to escape by frantically pursuing the pleasures of a vanishing peace. Shops were crowded with people off on what might be a final buying spree. Never were the trains to the seashore more heavily freighted with eager vacationers. The parties in the great country houses glittered with a fragile brilliance, as though the guests feared that the sounds of music and laughter might be stilled in a moment by the heart-piercing whistle of falling bombs. "You had the feeling," Jack Kennedy recalled, "of an era ending, and everyone had a very good time at the end."[55] The long weekend between the remembered last war and the dreaded next seemed to be drawing to a close.

In Washington, Roosevelt received frequent telephone calls from Kennedy, passing on what he learned on his trips to Downing Street and the Foreign Office. Chamberlain kept his friend informed of the government's every move, and grateful Britons detected the Ambassador's hand in a message which the President addressed to the heads of Europe's governments, asking for continued negotiations and proposing a peace conference in a neutral European capital.[56] "It can't do any harm," Roosevelt told Hull as the statement was issued. "It's safe to urge peace until the last moment."[57]

The deliverance for which Europe prayed came almost literally at the last moment. Chamberlain sent a new plan to Hitler, suggesting another conference. On the afternoon of September 28, the date set by Hitler for surrender or war, the House of Commons was filled to overflowing. Kennedy sat in the tight-packed gallery near the ambassadors of France, Italy, and Czechoslovakia. Also present were Queen Mary and the Duke and Duchess of Kent. The atmosphere in the stuffy chamber crackled with pent-up anxiety and excitement. Subdued applause greeted Chamberlain's appearance. In the middle of the Prime Minister's speech on the crisis, a messenger arrived from the Foreign Office and handed a note to Halifax, who quickly had it passed to Chamberlain. Forgetting the microphone set up to carry his words to an overflow crowd in another room, the Prime Minister leaned over and whispered to Sir John Simon. "Shall I tell now?" Simon nodded.[58]

Chamberlain announced that Hitler had agreed to receive him for a third time. He would fly to Munich the next morning. Cheers rose from the Tory benches, and were echoed by the Opposition as Clement Attlee gave his blessing to the plan. Papers were flung in the air. In the gallery Kennedy beamed his approval.

Amidst the hysterical rejoicing, Churchill kept his seat near the gangway.[59] Eden walked out of the room.

At Munich on September 29, in a meeting that lasted thirteen hours, the fate of Czechoslovakia was decided. No Czech representative was permitted to be present. Hitler exacted a merciless tribute, gaining almost all his demands. His enemies within the German Army, who believed him to be an insane warmonger, had been poised to challenge him if the British and French stood firm. Now they were confounded by another bloodless victory.

Early on the morning of September 30, Chamberlain delivered the tragic terms of the agreement to the waiting Czechs. Included in the territory ceded were the Czech border fortresses, which left her defenseless. Chamberlain, fatigued by his labors, yawned continuously during the brief conversation.[60]

At Heston Airport, a huge, lustily cheering crowd welcomed the returning Prime Minister. The thin figure in black, his smile more self-satisfied than usual, alighted from the plane carrying that ever-present symbol of British prudence, the rolled umbrella. Later, as crowds spilled into Downing Street, he looked down from a window and held aloft a piece of paper, telling the jubilant throng: "I believe it is peace in our time."[61] Britain heaved a sigh of relief. At Lloyds the odds jumped to 32 to 1 against war within a year. *The Spectator* nominated the Prime Minister for the Nobel Prize. Some expressed gratitude, in so many words, that the sacrifice of Czechoslovakia had saved their skins. "Thanks to Chamberlain," wrote the middle-aged *Express* columnist Lord Castlerosse, "thousands of young men will live. I shall live."[62]

Kennedy added his congratulations. During Chamberlain's fortnight of one-sided parleying with Hitler, his American friend had lent more than moral support to the cause of appeasement. On September 22, as the Prime Minister flew to Godesberg, the Foreign Office called to Kennedy's attention several disturbing scenes in a Paramount newsreel released that week. The film included an interview with A. J. Cummings, political editor of *The News Chronicle,* in which he said: "The fact is that our statesmen have been guilty of what I think is a piece of yellow diplomacy."[63] Fearful of offending Hitler and upsetting the public, Whitehall asked the Ambassador to use his influence with the London representative of the Hays Office to have the newsreel censored. Kennedy complied and the scenes were suppressed.[64] When this episode came to light several weeks later, Opposition members of Parliament questioned the propriety of a foreigner lending assistance to the government's propaganda efforts. A government spokesman defended Kennedy, saying the Ambassador "considered he was rendering a service to peace."[65]

Peace had been purchased at a shameful price, as Kennedy indirectly acknowledged many years afterward. Recalling the Munich period, he said President Roosevelt had cabled him a congratulatory message for Chamberlain. "I went over to 10 Downing Street the day I received the cable," said Kennedy. "But instead of handing the cable to Chamberlain, as is customary, I read it to him. I had a feeling that cable would haunt Roosevelt some day, so I kept it."[66]

CHAPTER 16

"The End of Everything"

UNTIL Kennedy became Ambassador to the Court of St. James's, the key factor in his success probably had been his superb sense of timing. He had the rare knack of harnessing his fortunes to the momentum of events before other men realized what was happening and how it could be exploited, as when he jumped clear of the crashing stock market and swung aboard the emerging New Deal. Experience, shrewdness, and ruthless detachment, plus a bit of Irish luck, enabled him to detect warning tremors and shift his ground before it was too late. But the mission to London took Kennedy onto unfamiliar terrain; the acuity shown in business and politics deserted him in diplomacy.

He was one of the last important figures to enlist in the cause of appeasement. While Chamberlain flew to Munich to meet Hitler, Kennedy declared to Lord Halifax, whose faith in appeasement was waning, that "he himself was entirely in sympathy with, and a warm admirer of, everything the Prime Minister had done."[1] He said the dangers and difficulties of the European situation had to be faced "in a spirit of realism."[2] As he defined it, realism consisted of doing whatever was necessary to preserve peace. There was no alternative; war was suicidal insanity. Despite his red hair, flaming temper, and rough tongue, which gave an impression of Celtic pugnacity, the dominant side of Kennedy's personality was extremely cautious and virtually pacifist. As he told reporters in December, 1938, expressing his constant motive during a year of crisis, "I am pro-peace. I pray, hope and work for peace."[3]

On the surface, such a commitment was beyond reproach. Was not peace a universally popular ideal, and its pursuit the height of statesmanship? But Kennedy resisted the use of U.S. influence to discourage war, which reduced the pursuit of peace to an ineffectual rhetorical exercise. An uncomprehending witness to the rise of new revolutionary forces, he could conceive of no conflict abroad that would affect vital American interests,[4] no issue worth risking the lives of his or anyone else's sons. Although he lined up ostentatiously with Chamberlain during the Czech crisis and approved the belated British show of firmness, he had earlier informed the counselor of the Germany Embassy in London that he intended using all his influence to keep the U.S. out of war.[5] Kennedy believed his country could live with any settlement of European differences short of war, even with a Continent dominated by an aggressively expanding Third Reich.

So astute in other speculations, Kennedy in this instance misjudged the market. There was a limit to the price the democracies would pay to avoid war. And that limit had been reached in the brutal transaction at Munich.

As the initial wave of relief ebbed in Britain, it was evident that the psychological props of appeasement had been undermined. The long-simmering quarrel within the Cabinet boiled into public debate as Duff Cooper resigned in protest from the Admiralty. Angry dissenters rose up in Parliament to assail Chamberlain and echo Churchill's indictment of Munich: "We have sustained a total and unmitigated defeat." There were troubled second thoughts voiced in the press. Most significant yet least visible was the change occurring in the temper of the British people. During the helter-skelter mobilization, a previously complacent population had been shaken awake and faced with alarming evidence of ill-preparedness. Britain could not stand up for herself without trembling. That she must resist or be bullied was clear from Hitler's performance; he had behaved like a common blackmailer and therefore could be expected to call again with a more humiliating set of demands. Much as the average Briton dreaded war, he would stand and fight rather than be pushed too far. An ironic effect of Chamberlain's promise of peace was to stir in an awakened populace new and vocal support for England's swift rearmament.[6]

Later, this speed-up of the arms program would lend plausibility to the myth, propagated by Kennedy among others, that surrender at Munich had "bought" a precious year in which England could prepare for war. Actually, the outbreak of war in September, 1939, found England relatively weaker vis-à-vis Germany than had been the case when Czechoslovakia was abandoned.[7] In the fall of 1938, Germany's mobilization was incomplete. Hitler succeeded in a gigantic bluff, afterward telling his generals he had faced only a collection of "little worms." Chamberlain returned home, not to rearm, but to restore if he could a climate favorable to striking a far-reaching bargain with Hitler. The Prime Minister thought a cloud had passed from Anglo-German relations. Hitler had said that the take-over of the Sudetenland satisfied Germany's last territorial claim in Europe; he had emphasized that he wanted no Czechs, only Germans, within the Reich. Of course, this was another soothing lie; plans were being laid by the German General Staff to seize the remainder of Czechoslovakia at the first opportunity. But the appeasers and their sympathizers could not very well distrust Hitler without questioning their own assumptions.

Through the fall and winter of 1938, the disillusioned defected from the camp of the appeasers. Among those who left were many veterans, appalled at their error of judgment. But Chamberlain found a steadfast ally in the newcomer Kennedy.

The first ambassador ever so honored, Kennedy was invited to address the Trafalgar Day dinner of the Navy League, held annually in tribute to Lord Nelson's historic victory. He spoke on the evening of October 19, barely three weeks after Munich and in the midst of the rising national debate on the results. Kennedy had spent most of the three weeks working on his speech, in which he intended, as the American spokesman on the scene, to give a vote of confidence to the British government for having spared Europe a catastrophe. Washington's reaction had been one of approval. On the radio following the Munich conference, Under Secretary of State Sumner Welles had gone so far as to claim a lion's share of the credit for Roosevelt and his last-minute appeal for a peaceful solution.[8] And Kennedy, of course, had in his possession the message of congratulations Roosevelt had cabled to Chamberlain.

Still, the Ambassador anticipated criticism and tried to answer it in advance. At the outset of his speech he sounded an unusually personal note, remarking that his wife had become nervous when she learned what he was planning to say. "Have you thought how this would sound back home?" he quoted Rose as saying. "You don't want folks to get the idea you are seeing things through English eyes." With this preliminary, Kennedy launched into a plea for coexistence with the dictatorships.

In introducing the key passages, he again inserted a personal reference:

> It has long been a theory of mine that it is unproductive for both the democratic and dictator countries to widen the division now existing between them by emphasizing their differences, which are now self-apparent. Instead of hammering away at what are regarded as irreconcilables, they could advantageously bend their energies toward solving their common problems by an attempt to re-establish good relations on a world basis.[9]
>
> It is true that the democratic and dictator countries have important and fundamental divergencies of outlook, which in certain areas go deeper than politics. But there is simply no sense, common or otherwise, in letting these differences grow into unrelenting antagonisms. After all, we have to live together in the same world, whether we like it or not.[10]

A year or two earlier, the counsel of "live and let live" had seemed ordinary common sense. Now it was critically received. From the uproar he provoked on both sides of the Atlantic it was at once clear that Kennedy had committed a personal and diplomatic blunder.

His attempt to disarm his likely critics backfired, for by admitting much forethought, he made the error of what he proposed all the more egregious. He had even quoted Rose as saying, "If you want to talk about that idea in any useful way . . . you will find yourself discussing issues which a diplomat should not raise."[11] It mattered little whether she had actually said that or whether the Ambassador merely attributed to her the reservations he himself had overcome. The fact remained that his judgment stood doubly indicted: not only were his opinions wrong; his decision to speak them publicly compounded the folly.

The speech offended British foes of appeasement, for it was, as the correspondent of *The New York Times* noted, "an excellent summary of the attitude repeatedly stated here by Prime Minister Neville Chamberlain and his Cabinet colleagues."[12] The pro-appeasement London *Times* praised the speech for encouraging "an atmosphere in which the policy of the Munich declarations can work itself out toward its proper consummation. . . ."[13] In the U.S., the speech, with its echo of British policy, distressed stalwart isolationists in Congress. Until now Kennedy's supporters, they began to suspect he had perhaps been taken into camp after all. To opponents of a "soft" line toward Hitler, Kennedy's disclaimer of British influence sounded like a hint of a dubious turn in U.S. foreign policy. The *New York Post* blazed away: "If this precious specimen of diplomatic expedience had been written by the British Foreign Office it could not have served better to bolster the propaganda of Prime Minister Chamberlain."[14]

Young Jack, who had just returned to Harvard, wrote in a letter to his parents that the speech, "while it seemed to be unpopular with the Jews etc. was considered to be very good by everyone who wasn't bitterly anti-fascist . . ."[15] A Jewish friend of the Ambassador, reluctant until now to foreclose the possibility of a Kennedy presidential candidacy in 1940, read the Trafalgar Day speech and ceased his efforts on Kennedy's behalf.[16]

Washington pundits tried to discover the underlying significance of the speech. Arthur Krock called at the State Department and was informed that U.S. policy had not changed. Nor would any change be signaled by a mere ambassador. What, precisely, was this unchanged policy? A long and unsatisfying answer followed, on the basis of which Krock wrote a column noting "the difficulty faced these days by a government with an idealistic foreign policy that cannot be applied or very clearly explained."[17]

The decision to grapple with this difficulty was Kennedy's own, and his speech had been cleared by the State Department, but not even the policy makers were certain what U.S. policy actually was. Only after the speech was criticized did the department realize Kennedy had gone too far. Predictably, there was a round of official buck-passing, recorded in the diary of Jay Pierrepont Moffat, chief of the Department's Division of European Affairs. He wrote:

> The Secretary is very upset over the effect of Kennedy's recent speech. . . . He thinks we should have definitely called Kennedy off in advance, despite his claim that he was advancing "a pet theory of his own."

> The Secretary asked Sumner [Welles] why he did not see the danger of the speech. Sumner replied that he had been thinking of Mexico and had assumed that the Secretary himself had given attention to the matter and had initialed blind. The Secretary then said that I had not appeared unduly perturbed when I discussed the matter with him. This is not strictly accurate as I told him there would undoubtedly be repercussions, but that I thought the phrase "a pet theory of my own" would keep the Department and the Secretary out of the range of editorial attack. The truth of the matter is that the Secretary dislikes calling down Kennedy and Bullitt as they have a way of appealing to the White House over his head. . . . However, a "goat" is needed and I shall have to be the goat. In the long run, however, no one is going to be hurt unless it be Mr. Kennedy himself . . .[18]

A new strain developed between Kennedy and Roosevelt. The President was fully aware of the ambiguity and outright contradictions in U.S. foreign policy, but such a policy seemed the only feasible one in terms of domestic politics. It mirrored the ambivalence of Roosevelt and Americans generally. America yearned for isolation but felt a growing distaste for the dictatorships; she was sympathetic to her sister democracies, England and France, but distrusted self-serving European diplomacy. Events blew U.S. policy to and fro. As early as October, 1937, in a much-quoted speech in the isolationist stronghold of Chicago, Roosevelt had urged a "quarantine" of the aggressor nations. Yet the pragmatist in the White House was equally capable of declaring in a letter after Munich that "I am not a bit upset over the final result."[19]

By speaking out of turn, Kennedy had created the impression that the U.S. now meant to follow a clear course, if only in the wake of British policy. This was not Roosevelt's intention. He and Hull decided a flourish of militant rhetoric was in order. The State Department prepared a speech sharply critical of the dictatorships, which the President delivered within a week of Kennedy's indiscretion. Speaking over the radio, Roosevelt hammered home his point. "There can be no peace if the reign of law is to be replaced by a recurrent sanctification of sheer force. There can be no peace if national policy adopts as a deliberate instrument the threat of war. There can be no peace . . ."[20]

Roosevelt's "hard" speech amounted to public repudiation of his Ambassador, and Kennedy privately described it as a stab in the back. But he refused to stand corrected. Nor would he keep to himself his caustic personal opinions of Roosevelt. The Ambassador's "confidential" memos continued to flow to friendly U.S. newsmen. In a "dope" story in the Hearst-owned New York *Mirror*, columnist Boake Carter wrote that "the White House has on its hands a fighting Irishman, with blazing eyes and a determination to strip the bandages of deceit, innuendo and misrepresentation bound around the eyes of American citizens." He predicted that there soon would be a showdown between the Ambassador and his enemies in the White House and the State Department.[21]

Before Kennedy could renew the arguments raised in his controversial speech, an act of barbarity occurred in Nazi Germany that threw the appeasers into stunned, embarrassed silence.

A seventeen-year-old German Jewish refugee, whose father had been among ten thousand Jews deported to Poland in boxcars, took revenge by shooting and mortally wounding the third secretary of the German Embassy in Paris. The murder furnished the Nazi high command with a pretext for "spontaneous" reprisals against the six hundred thousand Jews in Germany. On the night of November 9–10, in a scene of horror unmatched in Europe since the Middle Ages, Nazi gangs rampaged through the ghettos of Germany, burning, looting, raping, and murdering. Almost a thousand Jewish shops and homes were destroyed, some two hundred synagogues wrecked, and twenty thousand Jews arrested. There could be no doubt of official inspiration of this latest and worst outbreak of anti-Semitism. The German government confiscated the insurance money due the Jews for their destroyed property and imposed on them a staggering one-billion-mark fine for, as Goering put it, "their abominable crimes, etc."[22]

The civilized world recoiled in shocked disbelief. Roosevelt denounced the Nazi regime in unprecedentedly strong language, expressing amazement that "such things could occur in a twentieth century civilization."[23] He recalled the American Ambassador from Berlin. From Washington the German Ambassador warned his superiors: "A hurricane is raging here." This furious storm of protest blew U.S. policy still further away from the course Kennedy had proposed. Revealed with terribly clarity by the Nazi plunge into barbarism was a "difference" between dictatorship and democracy that could not be talked away or ignored. Nothing more was heard publicly from Kennedy about the "theory" he had expounded only weeks before.

Until the November outrage, the British appeasers by and large had averted their gaze from the evil being done inside Germany. In some cases, the reverse side of their pro-Germanism was anti-Semitism. Even when their sympathies were aroused, the appeasers chose to remain silent rather than risk offending Hitler and upsetting their hopes of an Anglo-German accommodation. Intent on this goal, Chamberlain said and did as little as possible concerning the touchy Jewish question.[24]

Kennedy, too, avoided the subject publicly. But he discussed the Jews privately and at some length with the German Ambassador in London, Herbert von Dirksen, whose dispatches were among the German diplomatic papers captured during World War II and published by the State Department in 1949. On June 13, 1938, Von Dirksen relayed to Berlin the substance of recent conversations with his American colleague. He found Kennedy sympathetic toward Nazi Germany. "Although he did not know Germany, he had learned from the most varied sources that the present Government had done great things for Germany and that the Germans were satisfied and enjoying good living conditions."[25]

Later in the same dispatch Von Dirksen reported: "The Ambassador then touched upon the Jewish question and stated that it was naturally of great importance to German-American relations. In this connection it was not so much the fact that we wanted to get rid of the Jews that was so harmful to us, but rather the loud clamor with which we accompanied this purpose. He himself understood our Jewish policy completely; he was from Boston and there, in one golf club, and in other clubs, no Jews had been admitted for the past 50 years. His father had not been elected Mayor because he was a Catholic; in the U.S., therefore, such pronounced attitudes were quite common, but people avoided making so much outward fuss about it."[26]

In another dispatch, Von Dirksen said: "Today, too, as during former conversations, Kennedy mentioned that very strong anti-Semitic tendencies existed in the United States and that a large portion of the population had an understanding of the German attitude toward the Jews. . . . From his [Kennedy's] whole personality I believe he would get on well with the Führer."[27]*

*In sharp contrast, a Jewish friend of Kennedy's recalled that the Ambassador

While Kennedy believed the refugees were a minor concern of the U.S. government, his personal response to their plight was humane. He was instrumental in getting a number of individual Jews out of Germany. The Jews, of course, were not alone in suffering religious persecution in strife-torn Europe. On his first visit to the convent of the Sacred Heart at Roehampton, where his daughters Eunice, Patricia, and Jean were studying, Kennedy learned of twenty-eight Spanish nuns of the order who were trapped in the Sacred Heart convent in Barcelona, the only nuns left in the Loyalist-held city. Acting unofficially, he spent four months cutting through red tape and finally won the Spanish government's consent for the departure of the nuns. They were taken aboard a British destroyer, ordered to the scene by Chamberlain as a favor to his American friend.[28]

No such rescue could be arranged for the mass of German Jews. Indeed, much as the free world pitied them, no clear idea of how they might be helped or by whom had emerged. In the summer of 1938, thirty-two nations had set up a permanent Inter-governmental Refugee Committee, which opened headquarters in London in August. This elaborate gesture satisfied a humanitarian impulse but left the crucial questions unanswered. However, the chairman of the committee, George Rublee, an energetic seventy-year-old Washington lawyer and former diplomat, intended to make the organization effective. He wished to go to Germany and win permission for large-scale Jewish emigration, and hoped for support from the American Ambassador.

But Kennedy would not commit himself. Through the anxious weeks before the September crisis and the hopeful ones following Munich, he politely but persistently fended off Rublee, making it clear that he would lend only moral support to the refugee committee. Official moves on behalf of the Jews might snap the thread of personal access to Hitler, which Chamberlain prized so highly. "I soon found that there was not much interest in British Government circles or

said he wished to see Hitler, a visit Roosevelt and Hull would never permit, "in order to tell him off." When Von Dirksen's dispatches were published, Kennedy described the views attributed to him as "complete poppycock," said he could recall no such conversations, and suggested that Von Dirksen "must have been trying very hard to set himself right in Germany by telling the German Foreign Office the things he thought they'd like to hear." Certainly the reference to Pat Kennedy was ludicrously garbled, but the German clearly had talked to someone who was well acquainted with the religious bias of Boston clubs.

generally in the diplomatic corps in my work," Rublee later recalled. "The United States Ambassador, Joseph P. Kennedy, did not seem interested and never gave me any real support or assistance. . . . I think the Ambassador . . . thought that my mission was not to be taken seriously because it was impossible for it to succeed."[29]

Finally, in October, Rublee telephoned Washington, and the President reportedly indicated his personal concern in messages to Kennedy.[30] Even so, Rublee got the impression that Roosevelt, too, felt the cause was hopeless, and merely was going through the motions.[31] It was not until the pogrom of November 9–10 had touched off a worldwide protest that the Ambassador finally swung into action. As the London correspondent of the *Nation* reported, "it required sharp prodding, along with Hitler's latest tornado of anti-Semitic terror, to persuade Mr. Kennedy to bestir himself."[32]

Mid-November saw Kennedy beat a path from the embassy to 10 Downing Street for conferences on the refugee problem with members of the Cabinet. Not only the enormity of events in Germany accounted for this sudden official interest in assisting the Jews. Nazi excesses also shook the world's confidence in "the spirit of Munich" and endangered the prospects of appeasement. The rescue of the Jews would remove an annoying stumbling block to British policy.[33]

Even assuming that the Nazis would permit mass emigration, the problem now was enormously complicated by the one-billion-mark fine that had been imposed on the Jews, which left them penniless and in debt to the German government. Nations reluctant to admit Jewish immigrants who could pay their own way certainly would not welcome an influx of paupers. Yet the clamor for their assistance grew louder. Kennedy, between conferences with the British, impatiently told the press that emotion and sympathy were useless. The need was not for words but for deeds.[34]

It soon leaked out that a bold plan of action, breathtaking in its scope, was being devised. The scheme, quickly dubbed the "Kennedy Plan," called for snatching tens of thousands of Jews from Hitler's grasp and transporting them to sparsely populated regions in Africa and to North and South America. The British had ruled out unrestricted immigration to Palestine, but felt sufficient empty space could be found elsewhere in the empire. There was talk of sending thousands of refugees to Tanganyika. History offered no exact parallel for the vast undertaking now hastily being planned. It would require a huge fleet of ships. It would be necessary to erect refugee camps and provide rehabilitation for the transplanted Jews. And it would take an enormous sum of money, vaguely estimated at from $150 million to $600 million,[35] which, hopefully, would be forthcoming from sympathetic governments and individuals, particularly Jews in America. Everything was up in the air, but raising the necessary money seemed to Kennedy the only real obstacle to rescuing the Jews. "Now we will see how sorry the world is for them," he observed.[36]

The dramatic simplicity of his plan excited widespread enthusiasm. "What Mr. Kennedy has managed to do," reported *The New York Times,* "is the talk of diplomatic circles in London at the moment." Said an amazed British diplomat: "That man has Chamberlain eating out of his hand."[37] Commented *Life:* "Kennedy is rated the most influential U.S. Ambassador to England in many years. If his plan for settling the German Jews, already widely known as the 'Kennedy Plan,' succeeds, it will add new luster to a reputation that may well carry Joseph Patrick Kennedy into the White House."[38]

Despite such boosts, the "Kennedy Plan" never got off the ground. In later years Kennedy described the refugee problem as "essentially a simple one" and attributed the failure of his scheme mainly to British red tape and bureaucratic foot dragging.[39] It might be said with equal justice that the so-called "Plan" was little more than a spur-of-the-moment response to popular demands that something be done. Washington watched the performance skeptically. When a reporter mentioned the plan to Secretary Hull, he said he knew nothing about it.[40] "Hull came as near to being tart as he ever does in his comments on Kennedy's reported activities," wrote an observer. Roosevelt, too, professed ignorance of what his Ambassador was doing.[41]

In fact, the real work was being done, without fanfare, by Rublee. Following the November pogrom, German officials at last responded to his pleas. Evidently, he later recalled, "it was decided in Germany that some restraint on the [anti-Semitic] radicals . . . was necessary and that a negotiation with me should go forward."[42] Early in January, 1939, Rublee and a pair of assistants went to Germany and patiently worked out an agreement under which the Nazis ultimately would permit four hundred thousand Jews to emigrate. The property of the refugees still would be confiscated, but their expenses would be paid as far as the German border and they would be allowed to purchase supplies. A corporation was to be formed in London which would send agents to Germany to arrange orderly emigration.[43]

On his return to the British capital in February, Rublee was greeted with expressions of disbelief at his success. As he later recalled, "There was great surprise in London when they learned what had happened. They could hardly believe it and the attitude toward me was entirely changed." The change in Kennedy's attitude was striking. "He called me up," Rublee remembered, "and in an entirely new tone expressed great surprise, 'How could it have happened? Why hadn't they done something like this before if they were willing to do such things?' He thought it was very extraordinary."[44]

However, before the Rublee agreement could be implemented, war intervened and the Jews in Europe were doomed.

During the closing months of 1938, criticism of Kennedy increased in liberal circles in America; the critics also grew bolder, turning from sniping to frontal attack. Sharp accusations came from journalists known to receive confidences from the White House inner circle. Since the Trafalgar Day speech, anti-appeasers in Britain had stepped up their complaints against Kennedy, finding receptive listeners in Ickes and Morgenthau. In columns and articles appearing in the U.S., it was charged that the Ambassador was a pawn of Chamberlain, more interested in bolstering British policy than in advancing America's; that he was a dazzled captive of the Cliveden Set; that he secretly sympathized with the dictators and turned a deaf ear to their victims until ordered to help them; and, finally, that he was a disloyal intriguer against Roosevelt, pursuing a deep-laid plot to capture either the presidential or vice-presidential nomination in 1940.

Warmed-over gossip could safely be ignored by Kennedy, but he could not dismiss the constant theme of the hostile press: that he had fallen out of step with shifting American opinion. If this were true, he would be a failure by his own standard, which was to represent faithfully his country's point of view. Prolonged absence from America caused self-doubt. Only by going to the U.S. could he reassure himself. Early in December, Kennedy sailed alone for the U.S., telling reporters: "I am just going home to rest and do some thinking about America."[45]

His thoughts about Europe had become darker. Appeasement was not succeeding. The menace of nazism could no longer be doubted; Hitler wanted war and would eventually get it. On his arrival in New York, Kennedy said the European situation "appears to change every day, and not for the better." Only once did he flash his old bantering form with the press, and then to underscore his pessimism. Reminded that on his last visit he had predicted there would be no war and the stock market would rise, he said: "I had a couple of bad days with those predictions on my mind and I'm going out of the prophecy business."[46] He flew to Washington and went directly to the White House. During a lengthy conference, he warned Roosevelt of the very great possibility of war by spring.[47]

This forecast of rising tensions was entirely accurate, but it did not alter Kennedy's basic assumption: that the U.S. could escape the consequences of whatever occurred in Europe. The President was less optimistic. It was decided to press Congress for revision of the neutrality legislation, a move favoring France and Britain. Roosevelt also was beginning a drive to build up U.S. military strength, and sent Kennedy to testify before the hesitant military committees of Congress. The Ambassador endorsed rearmament, arguing that America should arm to preserve the Western Hemisphere as an island of peace and prosperity in a sea of troubles.

From Washington Kennedy flew to Florida, where he spent days in the sun talking over the telephone at poolside to friends across the country. He saw his Palm Beach neighbor, Colonel McCormick, of the *Chicago Tribune*, and others who assured him the U.S. was 100 percent in favor of isolation. He detected no groundswell against appeasement and saw no reason to apologize for his sympathy with the appeasers. Chatting with Damon Runyon and Walter Winchell in Florida, he gave the latter a "scoop" by acknowledging that he, Kennedy, had brought Colonel Lindbergh and the British together at the peak of the Czech crisis. It was implied that Lindbergh's estimate of the *Luftwaffe*'s awesome strength had influenced Chamberlain to yield at Munich.[48] This ill-timed story furnished new ammunition to Kennedy's critics.

Jack, the only member of the family left in America, joined his father for Christmas in the house on North Ocean Boulevard. Rose and the other children had gone to the Swiss resort of St. Moritz for the holidays. On Christmas Day, the ten Kennedys were reunited via the transatlantic telephone, as the father talked in turn to each of the children. A few days later, the London *Express* called Rose in Switzerland to check a report from Washington, to the effect that the Ambassador would resign shortly and bring his family back to America. The rumor, spread hopefully by Kennedy's enemies, was half-true: Kennedy, believing his assignment in London completed, had begun toying with the idea of resigning; but he had made no definite plans. Nor had he said anything about the rumor to Rose, who spoke emphatically. "We hope to stay in England for a long time, perhaps years. We like England and we just love the English. I've had some of the happiest times of my life in England. All the children like it too."[49]

This glowing testimonial was at once diplomatic and sincere. Of all the Kennedys, Rose probably liked England best. Indeed, she wrote to the President from St. Moritz, wishing him a happy new year and thanking him, on behalf of herself and the children, for having made possible the exciting and stimulating experiences they had enjoyed in 1938.[50] The Ambassador's lady lived a richly satisfying life in London. She commanded attention wherever she went and moved among the lofty social circles toward which she had been pointed since girlhood. No longer was it necessary, as during the trip abroad with her father long ago, to bluff one's way aboard the royal launch. Royalty now anticipated Rose Kennedy's pleasure. A trim and handsome matron, she went regularly to the exclusive salons of Paris to purchase dresses and gowns in the latest styles for herself and her daughters. To her secret delight, she was told frequently (and truthfully) that she looked like the older sister of Rosemary and Kathleen. A well-remembered compliment had been extended by Roosevelt's son-in-law, John Boettiger, just before the Kennedys left for England. On being introduced to the svelte mother of nine, he exclaimed: "At last I believe in the stork!"[51]

Kathleen, or "Kick," the second eldest daughter, was the belle of the American community in London. A gay, quick-witted girl of eighteen, she was escorted about town by a number of titled young Englishmen. One of them, whom she met at a garden party, was handsome William (Billy) Cavendish, the heir of the Duke of Devonshire. The younger girls were with the Sisters of the Sacred Heart; Bobby, too, was away at school. All had adjusted more or less smoothly to the family's status and the ways of a strange country. All except six-year-old Teddy, who came to his mother one day with a solemn request. Could he please punch a schoolmate named Cecil? Asked why, he explained: "Well, he's been hitting me every day and you tell me I can't get into fights because Dad is the Ambassador." The request was taken up at the dinner table, and after some discussion the Ambassador gave Teddy permission to fight back without fear of causing an international incident.[52]

"Obviously," said Rose, years after the Kennedys left London, "we had a superior entry to nearly everything. If we went to the races we watched from the owners' boxes. We all had tea with the Queen. The children got a great deal out of it."

It was reported that the family, as befitted the representatives of a democracy, did much of their sight-seeing by bus. "They're out to see the world, and to enjoy it," wrote a correspondent of *The New York Times*. "If they meet interesting people on their bus travels, they talk, and if they meet shy people, they overcome their shyness with gifts of chewing gum. They are natural 'mixers.' "[53] All the older Kennedys, it was noted, were keeping travel diaries.

Young Joe, taking a year off to see something of the world before entering Harvard Law School, roamed widely over Europe, having a succession of adventures that made him more than ever the hero of his younger brothers and sisters. His father arranged a temporary post for him at the U.S. Embassy in Paris. Immediately after the Munich pact was signed, Joe, Jr., went to Czechoslovakia, carrying dispatches across the sealed border to the legation at Prague. He watched the final agonies of the betrayed Czech government, then moved on to Warsaw, Leningrad, Stockholm, Copenhagen, and Berlin before returning to Paris.

When the elder Kennedy arrived in London from his winter vacation in America, cut short partly because the Spanish Civil War was entering a climactic phase, he learned that young Joe already had gone to Spain. A cable was waiting: "Sorry I missed you. Arrived safely Valencia. Going Madrid tonight." ("And that," the Ambassador told reporters, "is the reception I get after being away for two months.")[54] In Madrid, Joe, Jr., shared the Loyalists' skimpy siege diet of sardines and rice for seven grim weeks, and finally saw the city fall to Franco. The letters he wrote to his father from Spain were so detailed, the Ambassador boasted to friends, that Chamberlain asked to read them.[55]

With his eldest son performing so creditably, Kennedy decided Jack also should have a taste of diplomatic life. He had not yet settled on a career and might wish to enter the foreign service. A junior at Harvard, Jack readily agreed to his father's suggestion that he take a semester's leave of absence and make himself useful around the London and Paris embassies. The youth told classmates he would be "a glorified office boy," but, of course, he enjoyed what his mother called "superior entry." During the spring and summer of 1939, the Ambassador's son traveled through Europe, the Soviet Union, the Balkans, and Palestine. From each capital, he faithfully mailed to his father a report of all he had seen and heard. For a twenty-two-year-old American, it was a unique opportunity to look behind the scenes as the stage was set for the Second World War.

The Ambassador and his son Jack sailed for England in early February, 1939. Also aboard the *Queen Mary* was an acquaintance of Kennedy's, Lord Lothian. His country houses had long rivaled Cliveden as gathering places of the British appeasers, but the past year had produced mounting disillusionment. Soon to be named Ambassador to the United States, Lothian had just completed an introductory visit, during which he had told President Roosevelt, with all the authority of a former ranking appeaser, that appeasement was a dying policy.[56]

An American liberal journalist, Louis Fischer, also happened to be aboard the ocean liner, traveling on an arms-buying mission for Loyalist Spain. One day he and Lothian fell into conversation. Like many Englishmen who were changing their minds, Lothian was uncomfortable under the burden of responsibility for his past error, a humanly agonizing position that put him on the defensive. When Fischer touched a sensitive nerve, Lothian testily said that the only people in the U.S. who disliked Chamberlain and his policies were "radicals, Jews and lecturers."[57] This peevish observation went straight into Fischer's notebook as a nicely shocking example of upper-class English attitudes. The journalist also noted, disapprovingly, the congeniality between Lothian and Ambassador Kennedy.[58] From many such small incidents slowly was built the new, unflattering reputation of Joseph P. Kennedy.

It was his misfortune to be judged harshly by the company he kept. Throughout 1939, the year of reckoning, Chamberlain and other appeasers humanly sought a self-exculpating excuse for the coming disaster of war. And many of them found it, not surprisingly, in the Jews, of whom it could fairly be said that they wanted nazism destroyed. What the appeasers said, of course, was quite different: Jewish "pressure" was pushing the world into an unnecessary war. This sort of "anti-Semitism" had nothing to do with race and religion, everything to do with responsibility. Partly because of his association with the appeasers, Kennedy became the target of persistent whispers of "anti-Semitism," which followed him for the rest of his life.

Less than a month after his return from America, Kennedy was ordered to Rome by President Roosevelt to attend a ceremony more meaningful to the Ambassador than any other he had witnessed officially. A new Pope of the Roman Catholic Church was to be crowned, and the entire civilized world, anxious under the shadow of war, turned toward the Eternal City and an ancient ritual affirming the promise of peace on earth. For the first time, the U.S. was to be represented at a papal coronation. Kennedy's pride at being selected was magnified by his personal acquaintance with the new Pope Pius XII, who as Cardinal Pacelli had visited the Kennedy home in Bronxville in 1936.

The entire family went to Rome, with the exception of young Joe, who was in besieged Madrid. The Kennedys traveled in relays: Rose went on ahead by herself; next came the children and their nurse and governess, occupying an entire sleeping car on the Golden Arrow Express from London; last to arrive were the Ambassador and Jack. More than forty nations were represented in Rome, and the importance attached to the Papacy at this uncertain moment in history was reflected in the high rank of the emissaries. On the train with Kennedy was the Duke of Norfolk, a Catholic and the leading member of the English aristocracy, representing the King and the British government. France sent the distinguished Catholic poet, writer, and statesman, Paul Claudel. Small Ireland paid the highest compliment, sending Prime Minister Eamon De Valera.

A minor crisis arose when Kennedy discovered there were no small American flags to decorate the fenders of his limousine. Aides were sent scurrying to correct the oversight, and spent several hours searching shops and imploring American residents of the city to ransack their closets, all to no avail. The displeased U.S. representative was forced to ride through the streets of Rome in gleaming black anonymity.[59]

The majestic pageantry and spiritual grandeur of the coronation moved Kennedy deeply. He told the *New York Herald-Tribune* afterward that he had experienced "a day overwhelming in its memory, in its magnificence, in its universal appeal."[60] On the following day, the newly crowned Pope received him in a private audience, coming forward to clasp Kennedy's hands as he appeared. They conversed in English for twenty minutes; then Mrs. Kennedy was summoned from an antechamber and presented to the Holy Father. Finally, the children, their governess and nurse (Misses Elizabeth Dunn and Luella Hennessey, respectively), and members of Kennedy's staff, including Eddie Moore, were permitted to enter the room. Abandoning customary protocol, the Pope rose, walked to a table and distributed rosaries as gifts. He recalled his earlier meeting with the family; Teddy, then four, had climbed on his knee and asked about the cross and ring he wore. The youngster still seemed to be his favorite. "I told my sister Patricia I wasn't frightened at all," said Teddy after the audience. "He [the Pope] patted my hand and told me I was a smart little fellow. He gave me the first rosary beads from the table before he gave my sister any."[61] The next morning, the boy received his first Communion from the Pope, perhaps the first non-Italian so honored.

Pius XII held the Kennedy family in special esteem and affection throughout his reign. He named only one Papal Countess, Rose Kennedy, during his reign and to Kennedy himself he awarded the Order of Pius the Ninth, an honor usually reserved for heads of states and the highest ranking officials. Such recognition sealed Kennedy's unswerving loyalty to the Church and her interests. His elation on returning from the coronation was recorded in the diary of the then Bishop Francis J. Spellman: "Joe Kennedy phoned me from London expressing his joy at all that has taken place and the honors he has received from the Holy Father."[62]

Less than six months of peace remained to Europe. A perceptive student of diplomatic history, William W. Kaufmann, has written that Kennedy's reports during this period "had something of the frantic inconsistency that one associates with accounts of mysterious natural phenomena. The omens were uniformly ominous, yet he hoped that events would take a turn for the better, and he grasped at every straw in the wind."[63]

In Fascist Italy, Kennedy found cause for optimism. The democracies had been apprehensive that Mussolini, goaded by envy of Hitler's gains, would press territorial claims of his own and thereby provoke a crisis. But it appeared that the Italians sincerely wanted to avoid war and were, in fact, unprepared for it.[64] After meeting the Italian Foreign Minister, Count Ciano, Kennedy reported to Hull: "I also met Ciano. . . . I have no idea how able he is in his office, but I have never met a more pompous ass in my life. He spent most of his time rushing girls into a corner for conversation, and at the dinner he would not talk seriously for five minutes for fear that two or three of the girls who were invited in order to get him to come, might get out of sight. . . . I came away with the belief that we could accomplish much more by sending a dozen beautiful chorus girls to Rome than a flock of diplomats and a fleet of airplanes. . . . Every time the President says anything, nobody in the Cabinet or Government in Rome is fit to talk with for the rest of the day."[65] Whether this was a sure sign of receptivity to U.S. opinion concerned Kennedy not at all; it was a straw and he grasped it.

Only weeks after warning the President of the grave possibility of war by spring, the Ambassador cabled from London:

> My observations, and I have talked with Chatfield, Simon, Hoare, Halifax and Chamberlain, in addition to many other people, are that they thoroughly believe that England is on its way; that Germany will not attack; that the problem of last fall when they were obliged to do things that perhaps they would rather have done otherwise, is gone . . .[66]

The assumption that Hitler had been halted was rudely upset in mid-March. At a signal from Berlin, the Nazi war machine rolled forward and Czechoslovakia ceased to exist. As the Führer entered weeping Prague in triumph, Chamberlain at first tried to hold together the pieces of his grand design. But within forty-eight hours he recognized that it had been utterly destroyed. In a speech at Birmingham, he reacted like an upright businessman who had been flagrantly cheated. "I am convinced," said the Prime Minister, "that after Munich the great majority of the British people shared my honest desire that that policy should be carried farther, but today I share their disappointment, their indignation, that these hopes have been so wantonly shattered."[67]

Here was the long-postponed, much-evaded end of appeasement. If Germany went further, Britain would be forced to fight for her life. The British people, many of whom were ahead of their leaders, took the radical change in official position calmly. So calmly, in fact, that Kennedy told American friends with whom he spoke on the telephone not to be misled. Compared with the Czech crisis of the previous September, he said, "the danger may be as great or greater."[68] Churchill, in conversation with the Ambassador, saw a fifty-fifty chance of war.

On March 31, 1939, Britain reversed the course of her foreign policy over the previous five years and announced a guarantee of the independence of Poland, Hitler's next intended victim. For months, the theme of German propaganda had been the need to recover the port of Danzig. From Poland Jack wrote to his father: "The Polish people will not give up Danzig to Hitler, not without fighting for it."[69] Realizing this fact and its implications, Chamberlain had given the guarantee to Poland with the utmost reluctance. He had given it because he had no choice; his bridges had been set ablaze by the arsonist in Berlin. The British public would not stand for further truckling before the dictators.

In Washington, Secretary Hull privately questioned whether the notoriously sympathetic Kennedy was adequately representing the U.S. viewpoint to Chamberlain.[70] The substance of this viewpoint did not emerge candidly until many years later. In December, 1945, Kennedy had a conversation with James V. Forrestal. Later Forrestal wrote in his diary:

> Played golf today with Joe Kennedy. I asked him about his conversations with Roosevelt and Neville Chamberlain from 1938 on. He said Chamberlain's position in 1938 was that England had nothing with which to fight and that she could not risk going to war with Hitler. Kennedy's view: That Hitler would have fought Russia without any later conflict with England if it had not been for [William C.] Bullitt's urging on Roosevelt in the summer of 1939 that the Germans must be faced down about Poland; neither the French nor the British would have made Poland a cause of war if it had not been for the constant needling from Washington. Bullitt, he said, kept telling Roosevelt that the Germans wouldn't fight, Kennedy that they would, and that they would overrun Europe.
>
> Chamberlain, he says, stated that America and the world Jews had forced England into war. In his telephone conversation[s] with Roosevelt in the summer of 1939 the President kept telling him to put some iron up Chamberlain's backside. Kennedy's response always was that putting iron up his backside did no good unless the British had some iron with which to fight and they did not.[71]

More important than England's military weakness was her strategic blunder. Chamberlain disdained an alliance with the Soviet Union,[72] the only power whose armies actually could get to Poland in the event of a Nazi attack. The price of Russia's partnership was a free hand with the small states of Eastern Europe, an ugly bargain to be sure, but no uglier than the one Chamberlain had made earlier with Hitler. However, the Prime Minister could not overcome his loathing of the Kremlin, and so lost the only chance of success for his policy. It seemed to Kennedy, who shared Chamberlain's anti-Soviet prejudice and penchant for wishful thinking, that Hitler might obligingly march eastward and attack Russia, making a formal Anglo-Russian alliance unnecessary. As he told Joseph E. Davies, U.S. Ambassador to Moscow, "Russia would have to fight for Poland and Rumania anyway . . . because it was vital to Russia's self-interest."[73] A collision of the totalitarian powers, resulting in their mutual destruction, would free the West of worry.

However, the wily former Prime Minister, Lloyd George, saw more clearly the shape of things to come, and declared: "If we go in without the help of Russia, we shall be walking into a trap."[74]

Even after Chamberlain's admission of fateful miscalculations, Kennedy's judgment of his friend never wavered. Indeed, he often remarked that the British should erect a bust in honor of the Prime Minister for the great service he had rendered at Munich by gaining a breathing space for unprepared England.[75] Once an American friend of the Ambassador's said Chamberlain probably would go down in history as England's worst Prime Minister. Kennedy stoutly defended Chamberlain, saying he might very well be remembered as the best.[76]

During the tense summer of 1939, Kennedy stood by Chamberlain and urged limited U.S. financial aid to England,[77] confident the British leader understood that America remained determined not to go to war in Europe. The Ambassador went so far as to encourage President Roosevelt to consider outright repeal of the Neutrality Act.[78] Both countries benefited from a barter agreement Kennedy negotiated, the U.S. swapping surplus cotton for British rubber.[79] One of Kennedy's important services to the British was little publicized. He persuaded the hesitant King and his ministers that America would cordially receive royal guests, and handled many of the arrangements for the early summer visit. It was a triumph, one which stored up valuable goodwill for an embattled Britain.

The closer Kennedy appeared to be to the British, the more criticism he encountered in America. During hearings on a bill to revise the Neutrality Act, General Hugh S. Johnson, the former NRA Administrator and a firm isolationist, told the Senate Foreign Relations Committee: "Walter Hines Page was a British Ambassador to Washington. It would be a good idea to inquire whether we have not got another of those things at the Court of St. James's now. The dowagers and the duchesses—not to mention the debs—are a potent pill."[80] A gibe by Mrs. Harold Ickes, which Ickes mischievously attributed to the isolationist Senator Borah, made the rounds of the Washington cocktail party circuit: "Chamberlain has decided to increase his Cabinet so that he can give Joe Kennedy a place in it." When Roosevelt heard this crack, he threw back his head and roared with laughter.[81]

Men who were poles apart from General Johnson and Senator Borah agreed emphatically that the U.S. should avoid involvement with Chamberlain's government. Philip La Follette, former Governor of Wisconsin and a left-wing liberal, returned from a tour of Europe to demand that the President recall Kennedy immediately. It was essential, he told the Economic Club of New York, "that our representatives abroad really believe in democracy, and that they think first, last and all the time of the interests of the American people."[82]

Such criticism encouraged Kennedy in a decision that had been taking shape in his mind since returning from America. Once the royal visit to the U.S. was concluded, he would resign. He reserved a seat on one of the first flights of the new Pan-American transatlantic clipper, and told friends in New York and Washington to expect him shortly. He could muster an impressive array of reasons for quitting: his business interests were suffering from neglect; the out-of-pocket costs of the ambassadorship were staggering; the younger children were picking up British ways and ought to be taken home.[83] This last concern was a projection of Kennedy's own uneasy awareness of being out of touch. He was, in a word, homesick.

Several friends wrote, begging him to reconsider. He answered in the tone of a thoroughly disenchanted officeholder, saying he was weary of attacks that took no account of his service and sacrifice. He wrote that he would gladly let some other patriot have such dubious glory. In May, as he received an honorary degree at Manchester

University, Kennedy departed from his speech and gave a hint of his impending resignation. "I still insist that, whenever I leave England, whatever my record is, I shall still be known as the father of nine children."[84] To the coolly appraising James Reston, then an Associated Press correspondent, the Ambassador, during an interview a month later, appeared to be chafing under the orders and restrictions that were inescapably part of his job. Also evident in his remarks was a new impatience with the British. "A lot of people tell me that Britain is relying on two things today: One is God and the other is the United States, and recently you don't seem to have been counting too much on the Deity."[85]

Meanwhile, in Washington, Ickes brought to the President's ear every scrap of anti-Kennedy gossip, such as an issue of the British left-wing newsletter, *The Week* which said: "Carried away by his pro-Franco sentiments, Mr. Kennedy, an ardent Catholic, who wrongly believes that in this way he is serving the interests of his church, goes so far as to insinuate that the democratic policy of the United States is a Jewish production."[86] Ickes thought that if Kennedy actually had said this, it should mean his immediate recall.[87] Roosevelt read the item and did nothing.

Undiscouraged, Ickes continued to gather information against Kennedy. After a conversation with John Cudahy, U.S. Minister to Eire, he wrote in his diary: "I discussed Joe Kennedy fully with John. He admits that Joe . . . does some pretty loud and inappropriate talking about the President. He does this before English servants, who are likely to spread the news. According to John, Kennedy is vulgar and coarse and highly critical in what he says about the President. And when John cautioned him on one occasion not to talk as he was doing before the servants, Joe said that he didn't give a damn."[88]

Roosevelt hardly needed Ickes to tell him that Kennedy didn't give a damn; he had known this, and much more besides, when he sent him to London. But the President, unlike the tale-bearing Ickes, was disposed always to give useful people the benefit of the doubt. Kennedy, an accurate and bluntly realistic reporter, served Roosevelt's purposes, even if he was something less than a loyal servant.

As had happened before and would again, when Kennedy informed the President of his firm decision to leave London, Roosevelt exercised his persuasive charm and the decision crumbled. The Ambassador was told he could not think of resigning until the fall at the earliest. Nothing could be permitted to give the impression of division within the administration over foreign policy. By early July, Kennedy had canceled his reservation on the clipper and promised to remain on the job through September.[89] Soon after, in a speech before the Pilgrims Club, he sounded almost sorry for himself. London, he said, was the most difficult place for an American Ambassador to succeed because "here you make good by what you prevent from happening rather than by what you cause to happen."[90]

Late in July, Kennedy left anxious London for a vacation with his family at a beautiful estate famous for its roses, Domain de Ranguin, five miles from Cannes, on the French Riviera. For a lazy month, he swam from a rented yacht, played golf every afternoon, and coddled his stomach ulcer. It was well that he took this needed rest, for unbelievably bad news came as he returned to England.

The mortal enemies, Nazi Germany and Soviet Russia, had signed a nonaggression treaty. On August 23, amid toasts and handshakes in Moscow, the incredible and hypocritical deed was done. The trap foreseen by Lloyd George had been sprung on the West. A visitor at this time, broadcaster H. V. Kaltenborn, found Kennedy in an extremely dramatic mood. "You have come to me in one of the most important moments in world history," exclaimed the Ambassador. "We are engaged in a fight for time." Admittedly, the chances of working out a settlement with Hitler were slim, but he added: "Anything that keeps Britain at peace is in the interest of the United States. . . ."

The British government earnestly hoped that this was true; a strategy that had saved Britain's skin once might be revived if the U.S. would go along. Sir Horace Wilson, acting on Chamberlain's behalf, came to Kennedy with a highly secret proposal,[91] which the Ambassador promptly relayed to Washington. "He [Kennedy] said that the British wanted one thing of us and one thing only, namely that we put pressure on the Poles. They felt that they could not, given their obligations, do anything of the sort but that we could," wrote Jay Pierrepont Moffat. Roosevelt, Hull, and ranking State Department members unanimously scorned the proposal. "As we saw it here, it merely meant that they wanted us to assume the responsibility of a new Munich and to do their dirty work for them," commented Moffat.[92]

The Kennedys attend the 1946 dedication of a chapel in memory of young Joe. Seated next to their parents are (LEFT TO RIGHT) Patricia, Jean, and Teddy. (*Boston Record-American*)

The Kennedys attend the opening of the Hialeah race track in Florida in January, 1950. (*UPI/Bettmann*)

Mr. and Mrs. Kennedy and their daughter-in-law Jacqueline arrive at a Bronxville church for the marriage of their son Edward and Miss Joan Bennett in November, 1958. (*Wide World*)

The triumphant first family at Hyannis Port on the morning after the 1960 election. (*Life*)

Joseph P. Kennedy and John F. Kennedy together on Inaugural day 1961.

Reviewing the Inaugural parade (LEFT TO RIGHT) Eunice Kennedy Shriver, Ann Gargan, Joseph P. Kennedy, President John F. Kennedy, Vice President Lyndon B. Johnson. (*Life*)

The parents of the President in Palm Beach, Florida. (*Life*)

Assisted by a dozen grandchildren, Kennedy blows out the candles marking his seventy-second birthday in 1960. (*Wide World*)

As her father wound up his campaign for the Presidency, Caroline and her grandfather went horseback riding on Cape Cod. (*Wide World*)

Joseph P. Kennedy and the President, accompanied by Secret Service men, drive to the Palm Beach airport. (*Life*)

This long-range photograph shows one of the last meetings of father and son before the President's assassination. (*Life*)

The bereaved parents and brother of slain Sen. Robert Kennedy, are shown at the family home at Hyannis Port as they express their gratitude to the nation in a brief national television message, June 15, 1968. (*UPI/Bettmann*)

Rebuffed, Chamberlain lost all hope. After a gloomy session with him, Kennedy reported: "He says the futility of it all is the thing that is frightful; after all, they cannot save the Poles; they can merely carry on a war of revenge that will mean the destruction of all Europe."[93]

Jack, who had been in Berlin, returned to his father with a message from the U.S. Charge d'Affairs, Alex Kirk: war would break out within one week.[94] Kennedy's mood now came to resemble Chamberlain's. The Ambassador had difficulty controlling his emotions, and in his frequent calls to Washington was prone to excited exaggeration. In a cryptic telephone conversation on August 27, he told Hull that "the jig was up," and added that he had sent a long cable—"the most serious one he had ever sent in his life."[95] It was a hot Sunday afternoon in the U.S. capital. Hull hastily assembled several aides and they waited for Kennedy's telegram. When it came, Moffat wrote later, it "did not bear out the sensational forecast." Kennedy recounted the British Cabinet's attempt to enmesh Germany in negotiations, "which struck all of us as a mere play for time and completely unrealistic..." The message aroused the suspicion that "the British were not above a dicker leaving Poland to pay the price."[96]

But the days of dickering were ended. At dawn on September 1, Germany attacked Poland. The "party is on," Kennedy told Hull that morning. Asked if there was any question of Britain's going to war, he answered: "Oh, unquestionably none."[97]

For almost two days, however, there was suspicious questioning of Britain's intentions toward her ally. While Poland fought alone, the French debated and the British feverishly sought a way out. There was none. Few Englishmen really wanted to fight for Poland, a state that had helped herself to a piece of Czechoslovakia under cover of Nazi aggression; but the line had been drawn, and crossed, and now there must be war.

Early on the morning of September 3, Chamberlain summoned his American friend and showed him the speech he would deliver in a few hours. Profoundly moved, unashamed tears filling his eyes, Kennedy read the words Chamberlain would speak: "Everything that I have worked for, everything that I have hoped for, everything that I have believed in during my public life has crashed in ruins."[98]

Hurrying back to the embassy, Kennedy sent off a triple-priority cable to Hull, informing him that there would be a British declaration of war at eleven A.M. Then he put through a call to the White House. It was a few minutes after four A.M. in Washington when the telephone at the President's bedside rang and awakened him. His voice quavering, Kennedy recited to Roosevelt the substance of Chamberlain's speech. Then, almost overcome with despair, the Ambassador said a new Dark Age was descending on Europe and predicted that the war, regardless of which side won, would have only one result —chaos. Urgent thoughts were racing through Roosevelt's mind, but he spent several moments trying unsuccessfully to steady Kennedy. The half-choked voice from London kept repeating: "It's the end of the world, the end of everything."[99]

CHAPTER 17

"This Is Not Our Fight"

WAR came to England on a clear, bright Sunday. Whether they prayed or swore, Britons were ready in spirit. Evacuation of schoolchildren from London to the relative safety of the countryside proceeded smoothly; within weeks, more than a million persons, young and old, would be moved from the metropolis. Those who stayed, including housewives, pitched in to dig trenches and fill sandbags. Taxis were scarce; many had left the streets to be fitted out for fire-fighting duty.[1] The government, on the basis of grim guesswork, had given orders to prepare a quarter of a million hospital beds for the expected casualties of early bombing attacks.[2] Less than an hour after war had been declared, the warning sirens wailed and barrage balloons rose above the spires of London. People calmly descended to the shelters and braced for the first raid. They traded small jokes ("Jerry's right on time"), as though hiding underground from high explosives and incendiary terror were already a bothersome routine. Several minutes later, the "all clear" sounded. It had been a false alarm.[3]

Since his early morning call to Washington, Kennedy had regained his self-possession under the discipline of absorbing tasks. His personal preparations for war were completed. The week before, he had hastily moved his family to a country house near the capital. The location of this refuge would be kept secret until Rose and the children were safely out of England. That morning, as usual, the Ambassador had been driven into the city in a Chrysler sedan, waved on by bobbies who spotted the CD (*Corps Diplomatique*) disk on the radiator grill. The embassy now was housed in a seven-story, red-brick former apartment building at No. 1 Grosvenor Square. After repeated requests from Kennedy, the State Department finally had authorized construction of an air-raid shelter. Until it was completed, the Ambassador and his staff would have to dash for the shelter at Claridge's Hotel, several hundred yards away.[4]

On the first day of the war, Kennedy's most urgent concern was the safety of nine thousand Americans in England. They had been urged to go home, and were leaving as fast as ships could carry them. To speed the exodus, young Joe was negotiating for berths aboard tramp steamers headed for the States. In peacetime, Sunday afternoon usually found Kennedy on the Addington golf course with three regular partners. One of them was his number two personal secretary, James Seymour, a veteran of the movie days, who, like Eddie Moore, was on Kennedy's personal payroll. On this hectic Sunday, antiaircraft batteries studded the golf courses. Kennedy ordered Seymour to select a small night staff and begin around-the-clock operation of the embassy. An optimist, Seymour had a folding cot brought into the office, on the chance that after nightfall, the jangling telephones would be silent and he could steal a nap.

There was no sleep that night or for several nights thereafter. At three o'clock on the morning of September 4, Seymour telephoned Kennedy with stunning news. The British liner *Athenia,* bound for Canada with three hundred Americans among her 1,400 passengers, had been torpedoed by a German submarine.[5] The unarmed, 13,500-ton vessel, ripped by explosions, was sinking in the Atlantic west of the Hebrides. Jolted awake, the Ambassador clung to the telephone. As further reports arrived, he dictated a cable to the President: "All on *Athenia* rescued except those killed by explosion. The Admiralty advises me survivors picked up by other ships. List of casualties later. Thank God."[6] Kennedy called the U.S. consulates in Belfast, Dublin, and Liverpool, where most Americans had embarked, and ordered the names of passengers forwarded to London at once. Then he went down the hall to Jack's room and awakened him. As pale streaks of dawn tinged the sky, the youth and Eddie Moore hurried to Scotland, where the rescued passengers of the *Athenia* were being brought.

From his father, twenty-two-year-old Jack had received a two-fold assignment: to assist the Americans who had lost everything in the disaster; and to get the facts of what had happened.[7] The Berlin radio was already accusing the British of having sunk the liner themselves to arouse American sympathy. That falsehood would have to be refuted in the U.S. protest note to Germany. In Glasgow, Jack for the first time saw the grief and misery of war in the haggard faces of Americans who had spent up to twelve hours adrift in lifeboats. One hundred and twelve men, women, and children had gone down with the *Athenia*.[8] Twelve Americans were dead or missing. The eyewitness accounts he received from the passengers established beyond doubt that the ship had been attacked without warning by a German submarine. Jack faced an angry, insistent clamor for the protection of the American flag. "We want a convoy," cried the passengers. "We've got six billion dollars worth of United States Navy and they won't do this for us?" shouted a man from New Jersey. A college girl shook her fist at the embassy representative, who was himself only a college student.[9] Jack telephoned his father and received a definite reply: there would be no convoy. Just that week, in a move to safeguard America's neutral status, President Roosevelt had ruled out Navy convoys of refugee ships in European waters. Gently but firmly, Jack told the passengers they would be picked up by an American liner, the *Orizaba,* and carried safely to New York, without a convoy. Unimpressed, they continued to berate the only available symbol of U.S. officialdom. It was a trying experience, but Jack handled it well. After attending to the needs of the passengers, he wired a full report to London.[10]

The embassy was humming with activity. A steady flow of cables reported developments on the Continent, and Washington kept up a stream of queries and instructions. To this flood of official messages were added telegrams from the anxious relatives of Americans in England. Such inquiries had no standing and government funds could not be spent answering them. With a parent's compassion, Kennedy not only saw that replies were sent promptly, but also paid for as many as one hundred and fifty personal telegrams daily. When Seymour, frowning, reminded him that he was already paying dearly for the privilege of working too hard, Kennedy smiled. "It has to be done," he said.[11]

From wartime London, the pace of peacetime Washington appeared impossibly slow, and Kennedy lost patience with standard operating procedures. The State Department had announced that ships bound for South America would be diverted to the refugee-packed ports of Europe. When the promised ships were slow arriving in England, Kennedy complained profanely to the department, then went defiantly out of channels, telephoning a demand for action directly to an old friend on the Maritime Commission.[12] This free-wheeling gesture did not improve Kennedy's relations with the embarrassed department.

War had affected everything in England, including the status of the American Ambassador. If Kennedy impatiently kicked over the traces, it was because his independence was steadily being reduced. "My days as a diplomat ended Sunday morning at eleven o'clock," he confided to a friend during the first week in September. "Now I'm just running a business—an officer of a company. I'm back where I was ten years ago. Instead of going up I've gone down."[13] He smiled as he spoke, but the smile masked serious doubts about the future.

On the third day of the war, Kennedy celebrated his fifty-first birthday working at his desk. The weather was sweltering for London, and the Ambassador tossed his coat on the back of a chair, tugged loose his tie, and rolled his shirt sleeves above muscular, freckled forearms. The windows behind him were flung open. In the modestly furnished, blue-walled office, the only evidences of rank were two radio sets and two vases of freshly cut flowers. The August page still had not been torn from the desk calendar.[14] That evening, only Jack was missing from the circle of Kennedys around the birthday cake. Afterward, they watched a new movie. Kennedy was easily pleased; he liked almost any film he had not seen before. This one, a comedy entitled "Bachelor Mother," may have caused Rose wry amusement. At the end of the month, she would return to America with the children and reopen the house in Bronxville. In the past decade, she, too, would have come full circle, the only difference being that her absent husband now would be across the ocean.

The issue of *Time* for September 18, 1939 contained a cover story on the Ambassador ("London Legman"), the inspiration of his friend, Editor-in-Chief Henry R. Luce. *Time* sized up Kennedy as a dual personality: on the one hand, an unusually representative American ("a common denominator of the U.S. businessman—'safe,' 'middle-of-the road,' a horse-trader at heart"); on the other, a singular individual ("a super common denominator, uncommonly common-sensible, stiletto-shrewd"). He was portrayed as a wary observer of England's war, acting on the basis of coldly defined American interests. "As Ambassador Kennedy," wrote *Time*, "his attitude is the same as that of Businessman Kennedy: Where do we get off?"

To Kennedy, England's war looked like a losing proposition even if she "won."[15] Chamberlain and Simon had opened the secret balance sheets to Kennedy, and he knew that England, already in shaky financial condition, faced the danger of bankruptcy within a relatively short time. His worried friends at Downing Street and Whitehall saw the same specter. Everybody in Britain hated Hitler, Kennedy wrote to Roosevelt, but they did not "want to be finished economically, financially, politically and socially, which they are beginning to suspect will be their fate if the war goes on very long."[16]

If the British were to wage a drawn-out, losing fight, Kennedy feared, the pressure for U.S. intervention might become irresistible. He could foresee a gallant but foolhardy America rushing to Britain's rescue, her commitment leading by inevitable stages to sending American boys to spill their blood in Europe. He shuddered when he thought of the impact of war on America. ("Joe's usually a bear," said a friend after a gloomy lecture, "but this time he is a whole den.")[17] But the U.S. could be spared, and the best interests of England and the world served, the Ambassador persuaded himself, if the war were to end quickly through negotiations.

On September 10, with the war just a week old, the Ambassador held a confidential conversation with two high-ranking friends in the British government. The defeat of Poland was certain, all agreed. What would be Hitler's next move? The Britons feared that he would halt his armies and propose peace, hoping to divide the Allies. It would not take much, they suspected, to get disunited and demoralized France out of the war. But no matter how attractive the terms Germany offered, Britain would be compelled to refuse; it would be politically impossible for the British government to deal with Hitler. Very soon, then, Britain might be isolated, anxious for peace but waging a war she could not win.[18]

Kennedy agreed this would be a tragedy. Thoughtfully he observed: "It seems to me that this situation may crystallize to a point where the President can be the savior of the world. The British government as such certainly cannot accept any agreement with Hitler, but there may be a point when the President himself may work out plans for world peace." In a cable to Washington on September 11, he raised the possibility of Roosevelt playing the role of peacemaker.[19]

The reaction was swift. Said Secretary Hull in a wire the same day:

> The President desires me to inform you, for your strictly confidential information and so that you may be guided thereby without divulging this message to any one, that this Government, so long as present European conditions continue, sees no opportunity nor occasion for any peace move to be initiated by the President of the United States. The people of the United States would not support any move for peace initiated by this Government that would consolidate or make possible a survival of a regime of force and aggression.[20]

The explicit distrust of Kennedy's ability to keep secrets from his British friends was not the only jarring note in this chilly message, only slightly warmer than a reprimand. Also revealed was the great and growing divergence in the thinking of Kennedy and Roosevelt. The Ambassador was transfixed by the terrible consequences of the war, actual and potential. Nazism seemed to him a dreadful nuisance, yet one which, unfortunately, could be eliminated only by means of a catastrophic conflict. The President, in contrast, was inclined to view the war from the opposite perspective of the necessary end, namely, the destruction of an intolerable "regime of force and aggression." Far from dwelling on the consequences, he seemed almost to disregard them.

However, Kennedy and leading British officials were apprehensive that, even if Britain defeated Germany, nazism might be succeeded by communism.[21] But when the Ambassador brought up this fear in a letter to the President, Roosevelt complacently dismissed it. "I do not think people in England should worry about Germany going Communist in the Russian manner," wrote FDR. "They might blow up and have chaos for a while but the German upbringing for centuries, their insistence on independence of family life, and the right to hold property in a small way, would not, in my judgment, permit the Russian form of brutality for any length of time."[22]

Roosevelt regularly had thrust into his hand by Harold Ickes British leftist propaganda, such as the September 13 issue of *The Week*, which reported: "There are those in 'high places' in London who regard it as axiomatic that the war must not be conducted in such a manner as to lead to a total breakdown of the German regime and the emergence of some kind of 'radical' government in Germany. These circles are certainly in indirect touch with certain German military circles—and the intermediary is the American Embassy in London (after all, nobody can suspect Mr. Kennedy of being unduly prejudiced against fascist regimes and it is through Mr. Kennedy that the German Government hopes to maintain 'contacts.')"[23]

After reading this bit of gossip, framed in malevolent recollection of Kennedy's pro-Franco position on Spain, Roosevelt, according to Ickes, observed: "There is a lot of truth to that."[24]

The truth was that Kennedy, who came close to rejecting war as an instrument of national policy, rejected absolutely the concept of "total war," which later would lead to the blindly righteous folly of "unconditional surrender." The notion of a democratic "crusade" went against his ingrained skepticism. When he heard British friends privately echo their patriotic slogans, he bristled, telling them: "For Christ's sake, stop trying to make this a holy war, because no one will believe you; you're fighting for your life as an Empire, and that's good enough."[25]

Adolf Hitler probably had greater respect for the British Empire, likening it to the Roman Catholic Church as a stabilizing institution, than did Franklin Roosevelt. On September 13, the President had a conversation at the White House with Jim Farley, who had just returned from a vacation trip to Europe. He had been unable to visit England, and asked the President how Kennedy was getting along in London.

"I want to tell you something," Roosevelt confided, "and don't pass it on to a living soul. Some weeks ago Joe had tea with the King and Queen, who were terribly disturbed about the situation. Afterwards he saw Sir Samuel Hoare and several others connected with the British government, and they, too, were quite worried. After his talks Joe sat down and wrote the silliest message to me I have ever received. It urged me to do this, that, and the other thing in a frantic sort of way."[26]

Kennedy, the President continued, had been "taken in" by his acquaintances in the British government and the royal family. He was more pro-British than Walter Hines Page had been. Warming to his subject, the Hudson River patrician declared that "the trouble with the British is that they have for several hundred years been controlled by the upper classes." The policies of the government were designed to serve the interests of these classes, to preserve their control of England's economy.[27] Roosevelt left little doubt that he would welcome a sweeping change.

Whether or not he had been "taken in," Kennedy sympathized with the traditional rulers of England, who now watched apprehensively as pent-up forces of social and economic change were released by the war. Talking one day with Sir John Simon, Chancellor of the Exchequer, Kennedy asked, point-blank, what the British were fighting for. They could not restore Poland. Even if Hitler were deposed, Germany would be thrown into chaos and might go Communist. The war would exhaust England and France, leaving them vulnerable to radicalism. What, Kennedy demanded, was the sense of fighting?[28] Simon glumly shook his head and said there was no way of getting around the British people. They were making themselves heard as never before. "If they [the government] were to advocate any type of peace," Kennedy wrote to Roosevelt, "they would be yelled down by their own people, who are determined to go on."[29]

This popular resolve, which was shaking the old Tory power structure, won Roosevelt's great admiration. But it saddened Kennedy. In the same letter to the President, he wrote: "I have yet to talk to any military or naval expert of any nationality this week who thinks that, with the present and prospective set-up of England and France on one side and Germany and Russia and their potential allies on the other, England has a Chinaman's chance. . . . England and France can't quit, whether they would like to or not and I am convinced, because I live here, that England will go down fighting. Unfortunately, I am one who does not believe that is going to do the slightest bit of good in this case."[30]

At this early stage of the war, to be well informed on England's weaknesses was to be pessimistic. But few Britons went as far as Kennedy in the direction of defeatism. Such a man as Winston

Churchill soberly acknowledged the long odds against England and the possibility of defeat, but he was inspired to fight the harder. The declaration of war had been an unwanted but resounding vindication of his unheeded warnings from the political wilderness. Now the shunned Cassandra wore a prophet's mantle and had a Cabinet minister's portfolio. Urgently needing the support Churchill could rally, Chamberlain had invited him to sit in the newly formed War Cabinet and also had given him command of the Admiralty, the same post he had occupied during World War I. Just before his arrival, an affectionate signal went out to the Fleet: "Winston is back."[31] In nine short months, Churchill, the has-been, would succeed to the Prime Ministership.

Churchill's rise to power hastened Kennedy's decline. The Englishman distrusted the Ambassador, whom he regarded as a prominent member of the appeasement clique. Just as he had opposed their past errors, so he now opposed their quiet campaign for peace on Germany's terms. He was resentfully aware of the Ambassador's bleak reports to Washington, which filtered back to him through friends at the White House, including the President. Little common ground existed between Kennedy and Churchill. They could not meet, as Kennedy did with Chamberlain, in the easy fellowship of high finance. Churchill was neither a businessman nor a capitalist. He was an aristocrat, and therefore something of an anachronism in a Tory party whose leadership was no longer dominated by the landed gentry, but by spokesmen for capitalism and big business. In his years out of office, Churchill, a comparatively poor man, had not taken the usual directorships in the City; he had supported himself with his facile pen and had taken up painting.[32]

The new figure at the helm of the Admiralty was an extraordinarily skillful politician, who combined subtle intelligence, dazzling eloquence, and soaring ambition. His mother was an American gentlewoman, and he felt a special affinity for Americans; but he was, first and last, an English patriot, resourceful, and if need be, ruthless, in getting what was essential for his country's survival. He regarded Kennedy as an obstacle to be circumvented. Early in 1941, after the Ambassador had left London, Harry Hopkins, an advocate of all-out aid to England, visited Churchill and reported to Roosevelt: "... I told him there was a feeling in some quarters that he, Churchill, did not like America, Americans or Roosevelt. This set him off on a bitter tho fairly constrained attack on Ambassador Kennedy who he believes is responsible for this impression. . . ."[33]

In Churchill, Kennedy faced a bargainer whose instinct for advantage, honed by England's peril, gave new meaning to the phrase "sharp trading." From their first encounter, Churchill complained about the U.S. neutrality legislation that hampered Britain's war effort. But he did not rely on sympathy alone to move the Ambassador to action. He coupled his complaint with a stark appeal to American self-interest, telling Kennedy: "If Germany bombs Great Britain into a state of subjection, one of their terms would certainly be to hand over the Fleet. . . . If they got the British Fleet, they would have immediate superiority over the United States and then your troubles would begin."[34]

Kennedy urged that the neutrality laws be changed, and supported other forms of assistance to Britain, but he was intent on keeping British and American interests neatly separate, a necessary condition, he believed, of keeping America out of the war. Churchill worked ceaselessly to merge the vital interests of the two democracies, creating a broadly defined common interest that would be the foundation of the grand alliance that was his dream. In this contest of conflicting purposes, Kennedy was by far the weaker protagonist, not only because he was a novice pitted against a master, but also because he dueled at an unusual disadvantage.

Churchill enjoyed the privilege, unique among foreigners, of confidential access to President Roosevelt, which enabled the Englishman to wield influence on Anglo-American relations rivaling that of the American Ambassador in London. The arrangement was Roosevelt's idea. On September 11, by coincidence the same day on which he rejected Kennedy's proposal of a U.S. peace initiative, the President sent a cordial note to the new First Lord of the Admiralty. "What I want you and the Prime Minister to know," he wrote to Churchill, "is that I shall at all times welcome it, if you will keep me in touch personally with anything you want me to know about. You can always send sealed letters through your pouch or my pouch."[35] Churchill responded gratefully, keenly aware of the advantage he had been granted, and signed himself "Naval Person." (When he became Prime Minister, he would sign "Former Naval Person.")

Thus began a correspondence unprecedented in American diplomatic history. The President of the United States, speaking in the name of a neutral power, opened a confidential line of communication with a subordinate official of a foreign country engaged in war. Most of the messages exchanged before and during the Second World War, upwards of seventeen hundred by Churchill's count, remain secret almost two decades after the end of the war. No period in Kennedy's life is wrapped in greater mystery than the one during which he served as the intermediary for the two most powerful men in the English-speaking world.

Crushed by Hitler's *Blitzkrieg*, Poland fell on September 27, 1939. Then the war abruptly stopped. Instead of hurling his panzer divisions and dive bombers at the West, Hitler paused before the Maginot Line and launched a psychological and political offensive. German troops displayed signs informing the French they had orders not to fire unless fired upon. As an unreal quiet fell on the Continent, armchair strategists talked of the "phony war" and people joked nervously about the *Sitzkrieg*. Chamberlain found the war "boring" and predicted peace would come by the spring of 1940.

Kennedy, too, experienced an emotional letdown. "I was amused and delighted," Roosevelt wrote to him, "to hear you say over the telephone that it is actually boring in London now that you have got rid of most of the returning Americans."[36] The Ambassador sought escape from boredom at the movies, and even turned movie critic. When he saw the new comedy, *Mr. Smith Goes to Washington,* he was shocked and fired off an angry telegram to Will Hays, with a copy to the White House. It was nothing short of "criminal," he declared, for Hollywood to give foreigners the impression that such outrageous things could occur in the U.S. Senate. Panic-stricken by this bombshell, everyone connected with *Mr. Smith,* led by director Frank Capra, sprang to the defense of the film.[37] The panic subsided when someone remembered that the wrathful Kennedy, Ambassador or not, was just another patron who didn't like a movie.

With Rose and the children gone, the country house was lonely and silent. The blackout depressed Kennedy, and behind the heavy curtains, he liked to keep the lights blazing. He wrote home often, sending letters to each of the children. The painstakingly copied and recopied replies from the younger ones showed the wisdom of treating all equally. Jack's letters from Harvard revealed new interests (he enclosed an occasional editorial written for the *Crimson*), as well as a familiar undergraduate concern: "Was wondering what my allowance would be? Could you let me know as I want to arrange my budget?"[38] Rose cheered and encouraged her husband, and sometimes admonished him. "I am praying that I shall see you soon," she wrote. "Do pray too, and go to church, as it is very important in my life that you do just that."[39]

Prolonged separation from his family affected Kennedy more intensely than ever before. Past sacrifice had been outweighed by a sense of accomplishment, by the certainty that what he was doing was important and rewarding. But now the influence Kennedy had enjoyed was disappearing. All power and responsibility were concentrated in Washington. One day, Montagu Norman, Governor of the Bank of England, stopped by the embassy for a chat. "I see that you folks in the United States are contemplating industrial mobilization," he snorted. "Who's going to run it? God Almighty?"[40]

This was but one of several powerful government posts for which Kennedy felt he was qualified. Since his arrival in London, he had compiled voluminous, detailed memoranda on England's mobilization, and he believed he was well equipped to apply the lessons of British experience to American industry. He also wished to return to U.S. politics. In 1940, the biggest job of all, the Presidency, would be contested in a campaign that was certain to be marked by a debate on U.S. policy toward the war. If England suffered reverses before the election, he feared a cry would go up for America to get into the fight. On the basis of his experience, Kennedy believed he had the hard, factual answers to rebut the war hawks.

In late November, it was announced that the Ambassador had been summoned to Washington for "consultations" and would return sometime after Christmas. This assurance met with some skepticism in London. It was generally believed, wrote the correspondent of *The New York Times,* that "Mr. Kennedy will have to be persuaded to continue his mission at the Court of St. James's."[41]

He was impatient to get away. "I haven't been back in almost a year," he told a farewell caller. "I'll bet anything that within an hour after I land I'll be in all sorts of arguments."[42]

Kennedy flew home by way of Lisbon aboard the Dixie Clipper, the four-engine flying boat swooping down on Long Island Sound off Port Washington like a great silver duck. The press formed the usual gauntlet and pelted him with questions. What did the British think of America's reaction to the war? The British, said Kennedy, were puzzled by expressions of sympathy for their cause, which invariably were followed by affirmations of America's neutrality. "It's like a fellow sticking out his tongue at a man and not being ready to punch him in the jaw." But, he quickly added, there was "not the slightest expectation" on the part of the British government that the U.S. would enter the war.[43]

Although a Gallup poll showed 84 percent of those responding wanted an Allied victory, with 14 percent undecided and only 2 percent favoring the Axis, no significant body of Americans questioned the merits of neutrality. After a six weeks' fight in Congress, Roosevelt had succeeded in getting the arms embargo repealed; the Allies now could purchase war supplies in the U.S., provided they paid cash and hauled the goods in their own ships. Except for this concession, however, the Neutrality Act of 1939 reasserted the validity of isolationism.[44]

But a truly tumultous national debate was brewing on the question of a third term for Roosevelt. No President had dared defy the precedent established by Washington when he stepped down after two terms, and Roosevelt was saying privately that he would not seek another term. But he was saying nothing publicly. This eloquent silence, combined with his unwillingness to groom a successor, had convinced many that FDR would run again. Younger New Dealers like Tom Corcoran ridiculed the two-term tradition. Conservative Democrats like Jim Farley felt they had gone far enough with Roosevelt; it was time for a change and Farley, for one, was willing to move into the White House. So was Cordell Hull. A bitter intraparty split was in the making.

Before Kennedy broke away from the press, he was drawn aside by a friendly newspaperman who had known him in Boston. He once had boosted Kennedy for the Presidency and knew what the Ambassador said privately of Roosevelt.

"How do you stand on the third term, Joe?" he asked.

Kennedy had time for only the barest explanation of his intentions. Even so, his answer, spoken as one Boston Irishman to another, left nothing essential unsaid.

"I can't go against the guy," said Kennedy. "He's done more for me than my own kind. If he wants it, I'll be with him."[45]

Two days later, the Ambassador made it official, talking to reporters on the steps of the White House before a conference with the President. He stressed Roosevelt's invaluable experience. "The problems that are going to affect the people of the United States—political, social and economic—are already so great and becoming greater by the war that they should be handled by a man it won't take two years to educate." But it was Roosevelt's sworn devotion to peace that won Kennedy's endorsement. "First and foremost, we know from what we have seen and heard that President Roosevelt's policy is to keep us out of war, and war at this time would bring to this country chaos beyond anybody's dreams. This, in my opinion, overshadows any possible objection to a third term."[46]

This statement, which newsmen described as "strong," took the political world by surprise. It "contributed importantly to the doctrine of indispensability" promulgated by New Dealers since the outbreak of war, wrote Arthur Krock, who called Kennedy "almost the last man in the Administration from whom anti-New Dealers and New Dealers alike expected such a statement."[47] There was no mistaking Kennedy's motive. "To any one who comes within hailing distance," wrote Joseph Alsop and Robert Kintner in their newspaper column, "our Ambassador to England freely predicts the collapse of capitalism, the destruction of democracy and the onset of the dark ages. He says that only an early peace, at almost any price, can save the world."[48]

Conservative Democrats, who had counted Kennedy in their camp, were sorely disappointed. They grumbled that Joe was suffering from "shell shock," brought on by overexposure to Europe's troubles. A third term for FDR could destroy the system of checks and balances; surely Kennedy saw that. His differences with Roosevelt were well known too. Why, then, had he lined up with Corcoran and Ickes and Morgenthau, Hopkins and Wallace and Perkins, and deserted his friends?

Kennedy was in the grip of black, blinding pessimism. Not even in the dark trough of the Depression had he been so shaken. In Washington he told a group of Army and Navy officers that morale in England and France was very low; the people yearned for peace. Economic conditions were so bad in both countries that Germany, despite the British blockade, might outlast the Allies. Nazi submarines were being launched faster than the British could sink them. He doubted that England could stand the terrible strain of war beyond another year. By the end of 1940, if not sooner, he feared that the people of England and France, and all Europe for that matter, would be desperate and ready for communism.[49]

In Boston for a visit, he made his first public speech since the start of the war. He spoke extemporaneously in East Boston before a reunion of parishioners of Our Lady of the Assumption Church, where he once had been an altar boy. His message appealed to the Boston Irish, with their strong strain of anglophobia. But the Ambassador either forgot or did not care that newspapermen also were present, their pencils flying over notebooks.

"As you love America," said Kennedy, "don't let anything that comes out of any country in the world make you believe you can make a situation one whit better by getting into the war. There is no place in this fight for us. It's going to be bad enough as it is." He could see "no reason—economic, financial or social—to justify the United States entering the war." He warned against being misled by a "sporting spirit," by the desire not to see "an unfair or immoral thing done." Such sentimentality must be cast aside. "This is not our fight."[50]

When his words were printed in England, Britons were shocked by the Ambassador's outspoken isolationism. Commented the weekly *Spectator:* "Not, of course, that we ever expected America to come in unless the situation changes catastrophically. But it would seem there are plenty of eminent persons in the United States to give isolationist advice without the Ambassador to the Court of St. James's, who knows all our anxieties, all our ordeals, finding it necessary to join himself in that number."[51]

As usual, Kennedy spent Christmas in Palm Beach with his family. But this year, his mid-winter vacation lengthened into late February, 1940, arousing speculation that he did not plan to return to England at all. In view of his early support of the third term, the press thought he might play a key role in Roosevelt's predictably tough fight for reelection. Kennedy was indeed waiting for a new assignment, but the President merely encouraged him to stay on in London.

Early in the year, a surprising Kennedy-for-President boomlet sprang up in Massachusetts. Without his consent, a campaign was started to elect candidates pledged to him in the March Democratic primary. This show of pride in a celebrated native son came as Bay State Democrats brawled over the third term. Jim Farley, who was to break with the President on this issue, enjoyed strong support in the heavily Irish Catholic state, but the organization faithful were prepared to back Roosevelt if he ran again. One of the most active Farley men was young Joe Kennedy, taking his first political steps by running for a delegate's seat at the Democratic National Convention. After a conference at the White House in February, the elder Kennedy formally withdrew his name from consideration in Massachusetts. "Appreciating as I must the great honor implied in this step," he declared, "nevertheless I must with positiveness state that I am not a candidate."[52]

Despite his endorsement of Roosevelt, Kennedy had not changed his extremely critical opinion of the President. At the State Department one day in February, Kennedy walked into the office of William C. Bullitt, Ambassador to France, who was being interviewed by Joseph M. Patterson, publisher of the New York *Daily News*, and Doris Fleeson, a *Daily News* Washington correspondent. What followed was related afterward by Bullitt to Harold Ickes, who wrote in his diary:

> He [Kennedy] cheerfully entered into the conversation and before long he was saying that Germany would win, that everything in France and England would go to hell, and that his one interest was in saving his money for his children. He began to criticize the President very sharply, whereupon Bill took issue with him. The altercation became so violent that Patterson finally remarked that he suspected he was intruding, and he and Doris Fleeson left, but Joe continued to berate the President. Bill told him that he was disloyal and that he had no right to say what he had before Patterson and Fleeson. Joe said that he would say what he Goddamned pleased before whom he Goddamned pleased—or words to that effect. Joe's language is very lurid when it is unrestrained, as it was on this occasion. Bill told him that he was abysmally ignorant on foreign affairs and hadn't any basis for expressing an opinion. He emphasized that so long as Joe was a member of the Administration he ought to be loyal—or at least keep his mouth shut. They parted in anger.[53]

Bullitt, a talented and opinionated diplomat, rightly called "the soul of indiscretion," was more anti-Kennedy than pro-Roosevelt. Their feud, springing largely from mutual jealousy, was of long standing. Soon after this latest flare-up, however, the antagonists were complaining in unison that the President had forgotten *his* loyalty to *them*.

Roosevelt functioned as his own Secretary of State, telling Hull only what he deemed too important to withhold. Late in February, without consulting Hull, Kennedy, or Bullitt, the President decided to send a personal emissary on a tour of Rome, Berlin, Paris, and London, for the purpose of testing the possibility of a peaceful settlement in Europe.[54] Roosevelt had conceived no dramatic "peace plan," and his representative would offer only the old blandishments of disarmament and trade expansion. But the lull in the war provided an opportunity for a formal, noncommittal exploration, which just might turn up an honorable basis of negotiations. He chose for the mission perhaps the most polished American diplomat, Under Secretary of State Sumner Welles.

When Kennedy learned Welles would bypass the London Embassy and deal directly with the British, he protested vehemently to the President, who may have reminded him that he himself showed scant respect for established diplomatic procedures. In any event, his trip to the White House changed nothing. Late in February, the Ambassador left for Europe.

He landed at Genoa, passed through Switzerland, and stopped briefly in Paris, where he had a conversation with Robert Murphy, counselor of the U.S. Embassy. Kennedy, Murphy later wrote, "told me of his bad health, his discontent over returning to London, his belief that everything he could do there could just as well be done by a $50-a-month clerk, that he wanted to quit but didn't see how he gracefully could before the elections. He said the United States would be crazy to go into the war, and that he didn't mind telling the British that they were kidding themselves if they believed otherwise."[55]

In London, Kennedy was asked by the press if isolationist sentiment was growing in America. "If you mean by isolation a desire to keep out of the war," he said, "I should say it is definitely stronger." He then added: "I think it is stronger because the people understand the war less and less as they go along."[56]

These ill-considered words incensed the British press. The *Daily Express,* England's largest newspaper, suggested that Kennedy, on the basis of his firsthand experience, could very well have explained the war to Americans. The once gushingly friendly columnist, A. Beverley Baxter, of the *Sunday Graphic,* asked sharply, "My Dear Ambassador, Why Didn't You Tell Them?" Writing in *The Spectator,* Harold Nicolson, a Member of Parliament, noted that Kennedy had given his countrymen a black view of Allied prospects, and continued: "Were I to frequent only those circles in which Mr. Kennedy is so welcome a guest, I also should have long periods of gloom."

The young, dramatic-voiced London correspondent of the Columbia Broadcasting System, Edward R. Murrow, commented: "There is no doubt that a considerable number of people over here have resented

Mr. Kennedy's utterances concerning the war. The British aren't accustomed to ambassadors expressing their frank opinions on international affairs in public—it isn't in the British tradition."[57]

Suddenly Kennedy found London chilly. Having drawn a line of national self-interest, he discovered that many Britons whom he had considered good friends intended to stay on their side. Later that spring, an American correspondent wrote: "The British had come to think of him [Kennedy] as one of their own. They expected him to plead the British cause when he went home. Joe was shocked by the changed atmosphere. He spent more time with Embassy people and American friends since the British social invitations were not as numerous as in pre-war times."[58]

Stubbornly the Ambassador defended his position. His much-criticized Boston speech, he told a British newspaperman, "was not an iota different from what I had said here." It should not have surprised Britons, because it reflected American opinion. Of the war, he declared: "I have very little idea what it's really all about, and nobody else seems to have much more."[59]

When Under Secretary Welles and his assistant, Jay Pierrepont Moffat, arrived in London in March, Kennedy warned them that anti-American feeling was rising rapidly. The British were not grateful for the relaxation of the U.S. arms embargo; on the contrary, they chided "Uncle Shylock" for waxing fat on Britain's misery. American complaints against British infringement of her neutral rights, through tight censorship of the mails (even Kennedy's letters were opened) and interception of merchant vessels by the blockade, brought only curt replies and new questions as to why the U.S. was not fighting alongside Britain. "The press is becoming full of gibes, and our friends are growing sarcastic," noted Moffat in his diary.[60]

During Welles' stay in London, Chamberlain gave a small stag dinner at Downing Street. Among the ten men present were Churchill and Kennedy. Moffat, a professional diplomat, long had had doubts about the Ambassador's capacity for statecraft, but he was moved to frank admiration by his performance in this intimate setting. Noting that conversation at the table had stayed off war topics, Moffat wrote:

> Toward the end of the evening, Joe Kennedy brought the talk around to actualities, and under the cloak of horseplay was able to get across many unpalatable home-truths regarding Anglo-American relations. It was superlatively done. He made it very clear that certain things, such as taking our ships into the combat area, could not be done without risking a

serious flare-up. Churchill protested, but in the end agreed. . . .

Churchill kept doing more and more of the talking. He thought that no one understood better than he the mentality of the ordinary Britisher. "Take the workman, for instance. His back is up. He will stand for no pulling of punches against Germany. He's tough." "Well," replied Joe Kennedy, "if you can show me one Englishman that's tougher than you are, Winston, I'll eat my hat." And on this sally, the party broke up.[61]

Nothing came of the Welles mission; the Axis had no interest in any peace settlement but the one they would impose. At dawn on April 9, 1940, the ominous pause in the war ended as the Nazis launched a lightning invasion of Denmark and Norway. The Danes surrendered within a matter of hours. In desperation, neutral Norway turned to England. Attempting a counterattack, British forces landed along the Norwegian coast, but were beaten back and forced to retire by sea. The amphibious operation, botched from start to finish, deepened Kennedy's pessimism about England's chances. In a cable to Roosevelt and Hull on April 26, the Ambassador delivered a long indictment of the British government's unpreparedness and inefficiency.[62] On May 3, as Norway begged an armistice from Germany, the President, in a letter revealing his own agitation, tried to lift his envoy's spirits. "These are bad days for all of us who remember always that when real world forces come into conflict, the final result is never as dark as we mortals guess it in very difficult days."[63]

Kennedy's indigo dispatches reflected his increasing dejection. To a friend in America, he wrote confessing utter discouragement. His usefulness had ended; he was accomplishing nothing, merely wasting time. Nothing in the past year had altered his ideas. As firmly as ever, he believed that, if war came to America, it would be the end for everybody. He was convinced that he must resign—but how? He dreaded the thought of winding up years of government service by being suddenly out of a job and open to criticism for leaving his post. Perhaps Roosevelt could be persuaded to offer him another position.

His friend soon replied that Kennedy might arrange to exit gracefully by taking over the chairmanship of the Democratic National Committee. By this time, however, the Ambassador had reconsidered, and he vetoed the suggestion. The war had entered a crucial and perhaps decisive phase. To leave London now "would be too much like walking out in the pinches."[64]

CHAPTER 18

The Secret War

CRITICISM of the government's conduct of the war had been rising steadily before the Scandinavian disaster. Even at Lady Astor's Cliveden there was grumbling, as a frequent weekend guest noted: "No one is satisfied that Neville C. is directing the war with the necessary energy and imagination." After the fall of Norway, the debate in Parliament was acrimonious as former allies deserted Chamberlain and joined with the Opposition. Easily the cruelest blow came from the Prime Minister's longtime colleague, Leo Amery, who rose from the Tory benches and quoted Oliver Cromwell's words to the Long Parliament: "You have sat too long for any good you have been doing. Depart, I say, and let us have done with you. In the name of God, go!"[1]

In the division of the House, the government retained a majority, but one much reduced by Tory defections and abstentions. England was wobbling; neither the shaken Chamberlain nor his clamorous critics had a plan to infuse the war effort with vigorous purpose. "Everybody is mad and all wanting to do something and go places," Kennedy reported to Washington, "but no one has the slightest idea of what should be done."[2] Literally overnight, this state of indecision was forcibly changed.

Early on May 10, 1940, without pretext or warning, the Nazis unleashed their long-awaited Western offensive, thrusting deep into the Low Countries and on toward France. The vaunted fortifications of the Maginot Line were outflanked as the Nazi armored divisions overran neutral Holland and Belgium at terrifying speed. Recognizing the need for national unity, Chamberlain invited Clement Attlee and other leaders of the Opposition to join a coalition government. They declined to serve under him. Just short of his third anniversary in office, the Prime Minister was forced to step down. His personal choice of a successor was Lord Halifax, but a Peer of the Realm had a poor chance of leading the Commons. The inescapable choice was a galling one. Chamberlain turned to the man who had attacked him longer and harder than any other critic; he turned to Churchill.

Churchill, after the ceremonial summons to Buckingham Palace, quickly formed a national coalition government, assuming both the Prime Ministership and the Ministry of Defense. On his first appearance in Commons, he received a unanimous vote of confidence. This, the crowning moment of a life of high adventure, called for eloquence equal to the occasion. "I have nothing to offer but blood, toil, tears and sweat," he told the hushed House. "You ask, what is our policy? I will say: It is to wage war, by sea, land, and air . . ."[3]

England now had a leader of whose spirit and purpose there could be no doubt.

On the evening of May 14, the day Dutch forces capitulated to Germany, Kennedy had an interview with the new Prime Minister, and sent the following telegram to Roosevelt:

> I just left Churchill at one o'clock. He is sending you a message tomorrow morning saying he considers with the [likely] entrance of Italy, the chances of the Allies winning is slight. He said the German push is showing great power and although the French are holding tonight they are definitely worried. They are asking for more British troops at once, but Churchill is unwilling to send more from England at this time because he is convinced within a month England will be vigorously attacked. The reason for his message to you is that he needs help badly. I asked him what the United States could do to help that would not leave the United States holding the bag for a war in which the Allies expected to be

beaten. It seems to me that if we had to fight to protect our lives we would do better fighting in our own backyard. I said you know our strength. What could we do if we wanted to help you all we can. You do not need money or credit now. The bulk of our Navy is in the Pacific and we have not enough airplanes for our own use and our Army is not up to requirements. So if this is going to be a quick war all over in a few months what could we do. He said it was his intention to ask for the loan of 30 or 40 of our old destroyers and also whatever airplanes we could spare right now.

He said regardless of what Germany does to England and France, England will never give up as long as he remains a power in public life even if England is burnt to the ground. Why, said he, the Government will move to Canada and take the fleet and fight on. I think this is something I should follow up. . . .[4]

On May 16, Kennedy cabled an account of a conversation with an "absolutely reliable" informant. Churchill had flown to Paris to bolster the sagging French. "Assuming the French do not stiffen up, the President might start considering what he can do to save an Allied debacle. . . . My friend thinks nothing can save them from absolute defeat unless the President with some touch of genius and God's blessing can do it. . . ."[5]

Repeatedly, Kennedy urged American readiness to sue for peace on behalf of the beaten Allies. "I saw Halifax last night," the Ambassador cabled on May 24. "The situation according to the people who know is very, very grim. The mass of the people just never seem to realize that England can be beaten or that the worst can happen to them. . . . I do not underestimate the courage or guts of these people but . . . it is going to take more than guts to hold off the systematic air attacks of the Germans coupled with terrific air superiority in numbers. . . . Halifax . . . is definitely of the opinion that if anybody is able to save a debacle on the part of the Allies if it arrives at that point it is the President. . . ."[6]

On May 27, with the British Army on the Continent retreating to the port of Dunkirk, Kennedy expressed black forebodings. "My impression of the situation here now is that it could not be worse. Only a miracle can save the British expeditionary force from being wiped out or as I said yesterday, surrender. . . . I think the possibility of the French considering a peace move is not beyond the realm of reason and I suspect that the Germans would be willing to make peace with both the French and British now—of course on their own terms, but on terms that would be a great deal better than they would be if the war continues. . . ." Kennedy foresaw aerial blackmail: the *Luftwaffe* would devastate one French city after another until the French government capitulated.

"I realize this is a terrific telegram," the Ambassador continued, "but there is no question that it's in the air here. The result of that will be a row amongst certain elements in the Cabinet here; Churchill, Attlee and others will want to fight to the death, but there will be other numbers who realize that physical destruction of men and property in England will not be a proper offset to a loss of pride. In addition to that, the English people, while they suspect a terrible situation, really do not realize how bad it is. When they do, I don't know which group they will follow—the do or die, or the group that want a settlement. . . ."[7]

Resolutely facing a terrible situation, Britons supplied the "miracle" that Kennedy rightly said was required to rescue the trapped British Army. A seafaring people, piloting hundreds of small craft (Churchill dubbed them the "Mosquito Armada"), went to the blood-stained beaches of Dunkirk, helped evacuate more than three hundred thousand British and French troops, and ferried them across the channel to fight again.

The evacuation ended, Churchill on June 4 hurled defiance at the enemy and rallied his followers. "We shall go on to the end . . . we shall defend our island, whatever the cost may be, we shall fight on the beaches, we shall fight on the landing-grounds, we shall fight in the fields and in the streets, we shall fight in the hills; we shall never surrender. . . ."[8]

The stunning succession of Allied reverses during the spring and early summer of 1940 aroused sympathy and apprehension in America. "The USA is at last profoundly moved and frightened," wrote Lord Lothian, the British Ambassador, to Lady Astor. "We shall doubtless get what help we want, short of war."[9] In late April, William Allen White, a well-known Republican newspaper editor from Kansas, was the guiding spirit in organizing the Committee to Defend America by Aiding the Allies. The lines were forming for a great national debate on the war.[10]

Emotions ran high at Harvard, yet none of the vociferous anti-fascism around him seemed to rub off on Jack Kennedy. He took a detached view, strongly influenced by his father's isolationism. "Everyone here is still ready to fight till the last Englishman," he wrote to his father, "but most people have a fatalist attitude about America getting in before it is over—which is quite dangerous."[11]

Now in his senior year, Jack was working harder than ever, doubling up on credits to recover the semester lost while he worked abroad. He wished to graduate with honors, and therefore applied himself to his senior thesis. With impressions of Europe fresh in mind, he chose to write on "Appeasement at Munich." Through the winter and spring, he spent long hours in Widener Library, tackling with rising self-confidence his first piece of disciplined intellectual work. He drew on books, newspapers, and magazines, as would any undergraduate; being the Ambassador's son, he also received a stream of the latest statistical data from London. Along with this research material came paternal advice and encouragement.

"Finished my thesis," Jack wrote exultantly in early spring. "It was only going to run about the average length, 70 pages, but finally ran to 150. Am sending you a copy. . . . It was finally titled 'Appeasement at Munich: The Inevitable Result of the Slowness of the British Democracy to Change from a Disarmament Policy.' Thanks a lot for your wire. Worked it in. I'll be interested to see what you think of it, as it represents more work than I've ever done in my life."[12] There was some question as to who had inspired the thesis. The Ambassador took a large share of the credit, telling a friend in London: "When I was in the States with Jack, and heard some professors talking about Munich, I realized they knew nothing about it. I said to Jack: 'You get down to it and tell them all about it.' "[13] Many years afterward, however, Jack said the thesis had been his idea. "I wouldn't say my father got me interested in it. They were things that I saw for myself."[14]

Actually, it made little difference; the son's thesis was almost a carbon copy of his father's position. The young man excused Munich as inevitable because of Britain's delay in rearming and defended the submission to Germany as a desirable means of buying time. He fixed the blame for Britain's unpreparedness on "underlying factors"—on foolish pacifism, on blind faith in the feeble League of Nations, on false economizing, on self-seeking by business and labor, on petty political partisanship, on almost everyone and everything, it seemed, except the men responsible for leading England. Explaining this apparent omission, he contended that "leaders are responsible for their failures only in the governing sector and cannot be held responsible for the failure of a nation as a whole."[15] He chided Americans for their emotionalism over Munich and challenged the belief that Chamberlain had been badly duped. The Prime Minister, he wrote, "could not have fought, even if he had wanted to. . . . I believe that English public opinion was not sufficiently aroused to back him in a war."[16]

Awarding his thesis a grade of *magna cum laude,* Jack's professors suggested that he try to have it published. He wrote to London: "I thought I could work on rewriting it and make it somewhat more complete and maybe more interesting for the average reader—as it stands now—it is not anywhere polished enough although the ideas etc. are O.K."[17]

The Ambassador heartily approved these plans. He had shown the thesis to several people, he wrote, all of whom agreed it was "a swell job." However, he added: "I suggest that when you are going over the material again . . . check your references. I have found several instances where you have misspelled names and got your dates wrong."[18] A more basic criticism was expressed in a long letter on May 20. Granted that the responsibility for England's plight lay ultimately with the apathetic people, he thought Jack ought not to be overly generous in exonerating Baldwin and Chamberlain. A politician should not only discover the people's wishes, wrote Kennedy, "he is also supposed to look after the national welfare, and to attempt to educate the people." Jack obediently replied: "Will stop white washing Baldwin." Sentences from his father's letter were incorporated almost verbatim into the book's concluding pages.[19]

His well-received thesis enabled Jack to graduate *cum laude.* Unable to attend the commencement with Rose and the rest of the family, his father wired congratulations. "Two things I always knew about you one that you are smart two that you are a swell guy Love Dad."[20] He also sent a check. ("Thanks for the wonderful graduation present," wrote Jack. "It was nice of you to think of it and it will enable me to remain solvent.")[21] Proudly Kennedy telephoned a friend in New York to pass on word of Jack's academic honors to Walter Winchell.

At the Ambassador's request, Arthur Krock helped Jack get his book published. Krock advised him on the rewriting of the manuscript and recommended a title, *Why England Slept,* playing deliberately on the title of an earlier Churchill book, *While England Slept.* (Jack wrote to his father that he hoped Churchill wouldn't mind.) Krock also steered the youth to an agent. Grateful for his assistance, Jack asked the columnist to write the foreword, but was overruled by his father. The Ambassador insisted on obtaining a well-known "name" and enlisted Henry R. Luce, of Time, Inc. The manuscript was accepted by Wilfred Funk, Inc., which hurriedly brought the book out in July.

Why England Slept sold surprisingly well: eighty thousand copies in the U.S. and England. The Ambassador sent the book to the Queen, Churchill, and Harold Laski. Selection by the Book-of-the-Month Club also was arranged. Reviewers generally praised the timely book; it hardly seemed possible that a twenty-three-year-old undergraduate could have written such a measured, dispassionate study of such an emotionally charged subject. *The London Times Literary Supplement* declared, "A young man's book, it contains much wisdom for older men." American reviews highlighted the author's argument for rapid U.S. rearmament. In addition to winning a certain fame, Jack earned about forty thousand dollars in royalties—the first important money he had ever earned. He bought a Buick with his American royalties and donated the English royalties to the bombed town of Plymouth.

His father appreciated the intangible benefits of successful authorship, and wrote approvingly: "You would be surprised how a book that really makes the grade with high-class people stands you in good stead for years to come."[22]

When the Ambassador admonished his son not to let the appeasers off too lightly, it was because each day brought fresh evidence of their costly errors. A note of doom sounded in Kennedy's dispatches. England was "appallingly weak"; her state of preparedness was "pitiful."[23] Yet Kennedy did not regard England as a stock that had suddenly dipped and now should be dumped; she was a decent and comfortable land, containing good friends and happy memories, exerting a powerful emotional attraction. Without changing his somber estimate of her chances, Kennedy supported aid to England. When the BEF was forced to abandon its weapons at Dunkirk, he endorsed the quick release and sale of rifles and ammunition, machine guns, and field guns from U.S. military stockpiles. He also softened the stand he had taken in mid-May, and backed Churchill's request for "overage" U.S. destroyers, asserting that the "psychological effect would be of even more value than the actual help."[24]

As this argument indicated, the Ambassador was closely attuned to, and increasingly anxious about, British public opinion. He cabled Washington:

> There is constant agitation here in the newspapers alleging that the Allies have asked for help from the United States; planes are mentioned most often and destroyers occasionally. I think it is important that some kind of statement should be made over there by some important person or over here after the policy has been decided explaining just why the United States is limited as to what she can give the Allies. I suggest this in order to save a great deal of ill-will that will arise towards the United States if nothing is done because refusal to give them destroyers or planes will unfortunately appear to the British public as American unwillingness to help them in their battle of death. . . . There is no point in having the Allies expect what there is no physical possibility of their getting . . . [particularly] if at some later date we might want the British to take action on the Navy, that might be of service to us. We do not want a united hostile people in England.[25]

Hull replied that the suggestion was "admirable," said the British purchasing agent in Washington would make a statement with full publicity in England, and added that the quantity of planes, weapons, and supplies flowing to the Allies was "considerable" and in all probability could be increased still further.[26] However, the statement issued in Washington disappointed Kennedy. He promptly urged Hull to give the matter "much more serious attention and thought." Of course, he said in a dispatch on June 10, "it is impossible for me in London to judge what is the best action to take from the American point of view in America. My only knowledge of what is going on in the United States is taken from press clippings. . . . [But] the feeling of the people of Great Britain towards the United States is going to be a matter of major importance, not only in this crisis but for many years to come. Regardless of what appears on the surface there is very definite anti-American feeling. . . . The majority of the English people feel America should be in this fight with the Allies. . . .

"If things go badly for Great Britain," he continued, "everyone here is going to look for somebody to blame. As it stands today they have the Baldwin and Chamberlain governments, but the attack on them is going to pale into insignificance when they have someone like the United States to blame. . . . We are well on our way to becoming the 'patsys' when Great Britain looks for somebody to blame. . . . I can visualize their possible eventual acceptance of a German victory, but they will never forgive us for not having come to their aid. . . ."[27]

With his British friends, Kennedy was defensive and anxious to justify himself. It was no use, he told a newspaperman on June 11, for him to say the hopeful things people wanted to hear. "From the start," he said, "I told them they could expect zero help. We had none to offer and I knew we could not give it, and, in the way of any material, we could not spare it. I could have easily said the usual blah and poppycock, but, what's the bloody good of being so foolish as that? An Ambassador's duty is to be frank, not to mislead. I considered that my duty and I discharged it. What the hell are you worth if you just mislead them?"[28]

Implicit in the Ambassador's agonizing over where the blame would fall for Britain's inevitable defeat was his assumption that the U.S. was justified in *not* going to extraordinary lengths to aid the British. Their cause was lost. America should concentrate her resources and energies on strengthening the Western Hemisphere against the Axis threat.[29] This was a powerful point of view in America, with a host of champions in Congress. And the events of the next few weeks appeared to sustain it. But a contrary assessment of England's fight and its implications for America was gaining influence.

On the same day that Kennedy cabled a warning against incipient anti-Americanism, President Roosevelt was to deliver a speech to the graduating class at the University of Virginia, which he hoped would prepare American opinion for expanded aid to Britain. Just before leaving the White House, he received the news that Italy was about to declare war on France. He seethed with anger on the train to Charlottesville. Only days before, he had tried once more to woo Mussolini from Hitler, offering to act as mediator between Italy and the Allies, and promising to assume personal responsibility for the execution of their agreements. But Mussolini wanted war and a seat at the conference table when the spoils were divided. In his speech, Roosevelt pledged that America not only would speed her own rearmament, but also would "extend to the opponents of force the material resources of this nation." His address ended, he added a spontaneous sentence white-hot with indignation. "On this tenth day of June, 1940," cried the President, "the hand that held the dagger has struck it into the back of its neighbor."[30]

In London that evening, Kennedy visited Churchill, whom he found roundly cursing Mussolini and anticipating the trouble Italy would make. Reported the Ambassador: "He is still pleading for destroyers, and I should judge from his conversation that he believes that with the bombing of well-known places in England the United States will come in."[31]

Well past midnight, the weary Prime Minister and a group of officers listened to Roosevelt's speech on the shortwave radio in the Admiralty War Room. At the remark on Italy's treachery, Churchill later recalled, "there was a deep growl of satisfaction." The words from across the sea moved him to write to the President before retiring. He complimented Roosevelt on his speech, asked once again for the destroyers ("they will bridge the gap of six months before our wartime new construction comes into play"), and closed by thanking him warmly "for all you are doing and seeking to do for what we may now, indeed, call the Common Cause."[32]

The Churchillian flourish was premature, but not mistaken. By the middle of the summer, Roosevelt would move decisively, if deviously, to England's side.

In a letter from Washington on June 12, Lord Lothian wrote to Lady Astor that the change in America's attitude toward the war in the past fortnight had been "staggering." It was the British Ambassador's optimistic view of the Americans that "it would take very little to carry them in now—any kind of challenge by Hitler or Mussolini to their own vital interests would do it."[33]

By coincidence, in a dispatch from London that day, Kennedy took note of the same assumption among the British, namely, that it required only an incident and America would be at war. "If that were all that were needed," he observed darkly, "desperate people will do desperate things."[34]

In his judgment, the British were indeed desperate—and with good reason. "I am of the opinion that outside of some air defence, the real defence of England will be with courage and not with arms. . . . it is only fair to say that short of a miracle this country after, and if and when, France stops fighting will hold on in the hope that the United States will come in. Churchill said quite definitely to me [that] he expects the United States will be in right after the election; that when the people in the United States see the towns and cities of England, after which so many American cities and towns have been named, bombed and destroyed, they will line up and want war. . . ."[35]

Hour by hour, the situation on the Continent deteriorated. The dispirited French Army flew like chaff before the Nazi whirlwind. On June 14, Paris fell. Two days later, the Reynaud government resigned and the new Pétain regime sought terms from Germany. On June 22, in the same railway car in the Compiègne forest in which Germany had signed the 1918 armistice, the French bowed to Hitler. Now the swastika flew over Europe from the North Cape to the Pyrenees. England looked and felt very much alone.

The U.S. Embassy in London told the four thousand Americans remaining in the country to return home immediately by way of neutral Eire, warning that this might be their last chance to leave for the duration of the war. In London, some seventy Americans not only chose to stay, but to fight as well. As the island mobilized to meet the apparently imminent Nazi invasion, they formed the 1st American Squadron of the Home Guard, wearing the British Home Guard uniform and a red eagle shoulder patch. Kennedy strongly disapproved of this display of militant Anglo-American solidarity. He told an officer of the squadron that "it might lead to all United States citizens being shot as *francs-tireurs* when the Germans occupied London."[36]

The Ambassador was unsparing even with his old friend, Neville Chamberlain, who was in the early stages of a fatal illness. Chamberlain wrote in his diary for July 1: "Saw Joe Kennedy who says everyone in the U.S.A. thinks we shall be beaten before the end of the month."[37]

This chilling statement was very nearly true. Polls showed that only 30 percent of the American people still believed England could win. However, Churchill realized all that really mattered was what one American in particular believed. He had to convince President Roosevelt that, not only was England's fight far from lost, but also that it could be won, to America's great advantage, if help was forthcoming. The Prime Minister used the only effective means of persuasion at his disposal, the British Fleet.

A few days after his ringing June 4 speech ("We shall never surrender"), Churchill instructed Lord Lothian to see the President and explain that the speech, while cheering to America, was intended chiefly for German and Italian ears, and therefore ought not to be taken too literally. The promise never to yield the fleet could not, of course, bind a future British government. If England were defeated and a pro-German regime installed, Roosevelt must expect that desperate Englishmen, striving for the best possible bargain with Hitler, would hand over the fleet. "You should talk to him in this sense," Churchill directed his Ambassador, "and thus discourage any complacent assumption on the United States' part that they will pick up the débris of the British Empire by their present policy. On the contrary, they run the terrible risk that their sea-power will be completely overmatched. . . . If we go down, Hitler has a very good chance of conquering the world."[38]

Lothian made his representations at the White House on the night of June 16, shortly after news had arrived that the French had begun armistice negotiations with Germany. After commending Churchill's appeal to the French fleet to regroup in British harbors and carry on the fight overseas, the President expressed the hope that, if a similar crisis were to arise in England, the British fleet would sail to the far corners of the empire and continue the war. Should British bases become useless, he went on, the fleet could certainly use American facilities. And the U.S. Navy would join in patrolling the Atlantic and protecting Canada and other British possessions. The U.S. might not formally declare war on Germany because of constitutional difficulties, he concluded, but it would become in effect a belligerent, "assisting the Empire in every way and enforcing the blockade on Germany."[39]

This far-reaching commitment, hinging on England's defeat, moved the U.S. closer to a policy of attempting, by all means short of war, to stave off that defeat. The next phase, extending through July, saw Roosevelt come to the momentous decision that England's cause was not hopeless, and that American assistance could make all the difference—provided he was willing to flout the neutrality America claimed under international law and proclaimed in domestic legislation.

On June 19, Roosevelt took a step that he had been weighing for six months, one now justified by the European crisis. He introduced bipartisanship to the Cabinet, easing out the Secretary of the Navy and dismissing the Secretary of War, whom he replaced with Republicans Frank Knox and Henry L. Stimson, respectively. Of crucial significance was the fact that the ousted Democrats had been isolationists, while the newcomers were ardently pro-British and strong advocates of American intervention in Europe. The President briefly considered appointing still another Republican with similar views to the important War Department post, but decided that the man he had in mind would be more useful in unofficial roles.

The man was Colonel William J. (Wild Bill) Donovan, the World War I commander of the famous "Fighting 69th" Regiment, a winner of the Congressional Medal of Honor, and in civilian life a prominent New York attorney. He and Roosevelt, classmates at Columbia Law School, had never allowed politics to interfere with their friendship. During the Second World War, Donovan would serve as director of the super-secret Office of Strategic Services, and would credit William Stephenson, an old friend from England, with having taught him all he knew about foreign intelligence.

In June, 1940, Stephenson, a quiet-spoken, Canadian-born inventor and self-made millionaire, was moving adroitly to further his country's vital interests. Acting on orders from Churchill himself, he came to New York to establish headquarters for the British intelligence service. On his arrival, he looked up his friend Donovan, who immediately arranged a meeting for both of them with the new Republican Cabinet members, Knox and Stimson. Before his departure from England, Stephenson had been lectured by the Prime Minister on the urgent necessity of the British getting the U.S. destroyers. Ways and means of overcoming the legal obstacles to the transfer were the chief subject of the conversation in Washington. Almost as formidable as U.S. neutrality laws was the widespread assumption that the British were beaten, causing even sympathetic American officials to balk at sending warships to a navy that soon might fall into German hands. Stephenson realized that the bleakly pessimistic reporting of Ambassador Kennedy from London worked to England's disadvantage. He now proposed that Donovan go over and size up the situation himself. Knox warmly approved the idea, as did Roosevelt. In mid-July, Donovan left for London, traveling as the President's personal representative.[40]

Alerted by Stephenson, the British rolled out the red carpet for the visiting American. Donovan was received in audience by the King and held long, candid conversations with Churchill and members of the Cabinet. He inspected training centers, war factories, and coastal defenses. He spoke with military officers, industrial leaders, and ordinary Britons, measuring the nation's strength and morale. He spoke with American military officers attached to the U.S. Embassy. But he conspicuously avoided Ambassador Kennedy, who was not informed by the White House of Donovan's tour. Roosevelt's oversight was deliberate, Donovan's snub calculated.[41] Kennedy protested to Washington, declaring that the mission was superfluous and contrary to sound organization, but his complaints were ignored.[42]

"Donovan greatly impressed by visit," Stephenson cabled London. In sessions with the President and Cabinet officials after his return, the Colonel gave as his informed opinion that England had a very good chance of pulling through. Her morale was excellent; defense preparations were making rapid progress. The army and navy were in shape to fight. RAF bases and radar stations were well dispersed, increasing the difficulty of a concentrated Nazi attack. Indeed, the British were confident they could not only maintain air superiority over England, but also mount punishing bomber attacks against Germany. On Roosevelt's orders, a member of the U.S. Army's General Staff went to England and retraced Donovan's steps. He rendered a concurring judgment: England could resist an invasion that fall unless Hitler was willing to pay a staggering toll.[43]

Meanwhile, Kennedy, though wounded in his pride, tenaciously defended his viewpoint. In a dispatch sent while Donovan was in London, the Ambassador said: "Don't let anybody make any mistakes; this war, from Great Britain's point of view, is being conducted from now on with their eyes only on one place and that is the United States. Unless there is a miracle, they realize they haven't a chance in the long run."[44]

While Kennedy was suffering the embarrassment of the Donovan mission, his eldest son, a member of the Massachusetts delegation to the Democratic National Convention in Chicago, was undergoing a political ordeal. Young Joe, only a few days shy of his twenty-fifth birthday and a student at Harvard Law School, had won a delegate's seat from the West End district of Boston. In the poor, solidly Democratic neighborhood, the son of Joe Kennedy and the grandson of "Honey Fitz" could have coasted to victory. But he campaigned hard, pumping hands and knocking on doors as though his family were unknown. Like his candidate, Farley, he was unalterably opposed to a third term for President Roosevelt.

The Massachusetts delegation went to the convention pledged to vote for Farley. Another avowed candidate was John Garner, twice elected Vice-President but unwilling to run with Roosevelt again. Maryland's Senator Millard Tydings also had announced his candidacy as a protest against the third term. Montana's Senator Burton K. Wheeler, the onetime Progressive, had entered the race, but his chief concern was getting a strong antiwar plank in the platform. Although he was not a candidate, Cordell Hull had a small, devoted following. However, as the delegates streamed into Chicago Stadium on July 15, they quickly learned what most of them had long suspected: no one had a chance of winning the nomination except FDR, who had planned it that way.

In order to gain an unprecedented third term, the President had fanned a spurious "draft Roosevelt" movement. Whipping up support for him in Chicago was Harry Hopkins, Roosevelt's confidant and a resident of the White House. His command post in suite 308–309 of the Blackstone Hotel, equipped with a direct line to the noncandidate in Washington, was shared with the suave Senate operator, Jimmy Byrnes of South Carolina. The two, in alliance with such big-city bosses as Mayor Kelly of Chicago and Mayor Hague of Jersey City, were intent on creating the appearance of overwhelming popular demand for Roosevelt; their aim was a unanimous convention vote. They even toyed with the idea of dropping the roll call of the states and having Alabama move the nomination of the indispensable leader by acclamation.

But some of the old-line Democrats resisted the New Dealers' high-handed tactics. Their opposition stemmed from many sources: the liberal take-over of the party since 1936; FDR's Supreme Court "packing" scheme and his abortive "purge" of dissident Democrats in Congress; the administration's abandonment of orthodox economic doctrine and the rise of radical labor influences; the conviction that Roosevelt's egotism, fed by ambitious sycophants, would wreck the party. For such reasons and more, the powerful "draft" blowing down the corridors of the Blackstone stirred little genuine enthusiasm.

Every conceivable pressure was brought to bear on the anti-Roosevelt forces. At a caucus of the Massachusetts delegation, chairman William H. Burke announced that he had switched from Farley to Roosevelt, blandly explaining that his pledge to the former had always been subject to change if and when the latter became available. Earlier loyalty to FDR had brought Burke the plum of appointment as Boston's customs collector. To the hard-boiled "pols," jobholders and favor-seekers who represented the Bay State Democracy,

Burke was simply behaving sensibly, and many of the delegates followed suit. A few did not, including delegate Kennedy.[45]

Now the New Dealers went to work in earnest on the stubborn holdouts. They pounded young Joe, reminding him of the honors his father owed to Roosevelt, professing dismay at his ingratitude, hinting heavy-handedly that his political career would be over before it began if he bucked the organization. Again and again, he faced the question: Why back a loser? Be smart, was the advice; go along. Harassed, the young delegate sought out the family's friend, Arthur Krock. He explained that there were no hidden strings on his pledge to Farley; that he had given his word. Sympathetically, Krock listened, then told him that Farley would understand and release him from the pledge if he wished. Young Joe said he would not ask. Instead he returned to the Massachusetts caucus, and each time the delegation was polled a resolute young voice continued to call out "James A. Farley."[46]

Unable to crack the son, the Roosevelt backers turned to the father. A telephone call was put through to London. Couldn't the Ambassador talk some sense into his boy?

"No," said Kennedy firmly. "I wouldn't think of telling him what to do."[47]

Mechanically the convention ground on to its predetermined conclusion. Taking no chances on the delegates' spontaneous support of Roosevelt, Mayor Kelly sent a swarm of hired "demonstrators" onto the convention floor. They grabbed state standards and shoved aside delegates, bearing aloft banners reading "Roosevelt and Humanity." Deep in the bowels of the arena, in a basement room containing the amplifier equipment, the leather-lunged Chicago superintendent of sewers sat gleefully shouting into a microphone. His voice, booming over the loudspeakers, filled the hall. "The party wants Roosevelt!" "The world wants Roosevelt!" "Everybody wants Roosevelt!"

Not quite everybody, as the roll call revealed. Despite the efforts of Hopkins, Byrnes and Company, the nominating vote was well short of unanimous, Roosevelt receiving 946½ votes, Farley 72½, Garner 61, and Tydings 9½.[48] Young Joe had stuck by his candidate to the bitter end. As the convention broke up, he received a note from Krock: "You'll feel all right with yourself and your father tonight."[49]

Following Dunkirk and the fall of France, England lived in daily anticipation of the Nazi invasion that would never come. Holidays at the seashore were curtailed as the military fortified the beaches. Church bells were strangely silent; orders had been given to ring them only to warn of invading parachutists. But Hitler seemed to be marking time, as though waiting for England to realize that further fighting was pointless and ask for peace terms. Only as a last resort did he intend to carry out Operation Sea Lion, the invasion scheduled for late September, 1940.

Thus England gained a breathing space on the land, while she waged a desperate struggle on the sea. Nazi submarines and dive bombers were inflicting heavy losses on the shipping that kept the island alive. The precious British destroyer force was dwindling: of the one hundred available to patrol the home waters, nearly half had been sunk by the end of July. It was then that Churchill, who had been silent on the subject for some weeks, again addressed a plea to President Roosevelt. "It has now become most urgent for you to let us have the destroyers, motor-boats, and flying-boats for which we have asked. . . . Mr. President, with great respect I must tell you that in the long history of the world this is a thing to do *now*."[50]

At a White House Cabinet meeting on August 2, as the President noted afterward, "it was the general opinion, without any dissenting voice, that the survival of the British Isles under German attack might very possibly depend upon their getting these destroyers."[51] Roosevelt had long been weighing the question of how the vessels could be sent. He dared not ask a generally isolationist Congress for special legislation; and the route of a formal treaty not only was too lengthy, but also might come suddenly to a dead end in the Senate. Others had been thinking about the problem, notably a group of influential lawyers in New York, including Dean Acheson. They now offered to the President an ingenious solution. He could move to England's aid secretly, through an executive agreement, yet so enhance U.S. security by what he did that criticism of the means would be silenced. Proposed was a new twist to the old isolationist argument, which held that Britain, in payment of her defaulted World War I debts, should make base sites available to the U.S. in her Western Hemisphere possessions. Now a *quid pro quo* might be arranged; the U.S. would swap fifty World War I "four-stacker" destroyers for ninety-nine-year leases on military and naval bases on British soil.

Roosevelt forwarded such a proposal to Churchill, who immediately accepted. Negotiations began in London, with Kennedy playing a role, but soon were shifted to Washington, where the leaders dickered through Lord Lothian. Kennedy, uninformed of the progress of the talks, became increasingly upset. "It would be helpful to me here if I could know the gist of Lothian's message of August 8," he cabled rather plaintively to Washington almost a week later.[52] There were differences to be resolved between the two governments. For one thing, Churchill was reluctant to make the requested promise that the fleet would not be surrendered, for he feared the demoralizing effect on public opinion of a pledge based on the possibility of England's defeat. The Prime Minister also wished to avoid offending the imperial pride of his followers by seeming to trade away historic British possessions for a few dozen obsolete vessels. He proposed that the bases in Bermuda and Newfoundland be considered outright gifts freely given to a trusted friend. No less intent on keeping up political appearances in America, Roosevelt insisted on receiving the remaining bases in return for the destroyers, a bargain which even the *Chicago Tribune* would approve.

The outsider in most of this, Kennedy resented the fact that the British knew what was going on in Washington and he did not. He protested to the White House, receiving this reply from the President on August 28:

> The destroyer and base matter was handled in part through you and in part through Lothian but the situation developed into a mapping proposition where the Army and Navy are in constant consultation with me here and the daily developments have had to be explained verbally to Lothian.
>
> There is no thought of embarrassing you and only a practical necessity for personal conversations makes it easier to handle details here. . . .
>
> Don't forget that you are not only not a dummy but are essential to all of us both in the Government and in the Nation.[53]

This transatlantic pat on the back failed to remove the cause of Kennedy's complaints, namely his ignorance of events in Washington, as he pointed out several times in a cable to Hull: "The Cabinet is advising Lothian to tell the President that while they accept his proposition they want the right to announce that . . . they are making the deal this way because of legal and constitutional difficulties in the United States. Now, of course, as I told you, I know nothing about the background in the United States for all these negotiations but I am sure that there is a complete misunderstanding on the part of the British Cabinet as to the situation in the United States." The Ambassador reported that some British officials wanted any sort of agreement that united the U.S. and Britain, while others thought that if it was to take the form of a bargain, it should not be a bad one.

"Don't misunderstand me," Kennedy went on, "England never gets the impression that they are licked and therefore they never can understand why they should not get the best of a trade. I have seen these undercurrents growing here and realize that delays have taken place but because I had no background I have not been able to do anything about it." Twice more in the dispatch Kennedy called attention to his lack of information, before ending on this note: "I may be completely out of tune because I am not familiar with the background."[54]

By the evening of August 29, the final details of the destroyer–bases agreement had been ironed out. After seeing Churchill and Halifax, Kennedy told Washington it had been decided that "England will handle her politics in the manner which she thinks best and the United States will of course handle hers in her own way. . . ."[55] Of the British, the Ambassador said: "I think they are inordinately happy about the result. . . ."[56] It seemed to him that Roosevelt had driven a splendid bargain, including Churchill's personal promise to send the fleet to Canada in the event England was defeated. Kennedy ventured the opinion that "no matter what criticism may be leveled at the giving of a few destroyers, the President can very properly say: 'At least I have conducted the affairs of this country in such a manner that it has been possible to obtain these important bases for 99 years with no real loss of anything worth while to America.' "[57]

In his satisfaction at a seemingly one-sided trade, Kennedy failed to see that America had surrendered something that he himself highly prized—neutrality. The President had bound the U.S. to Britain in a tacit military alliance. Churchill, of course, appreciated the significance of the agreement. He wrote years afterward: "The transfer to Great Britain of fifty American warships was a decidedly unneutral act by the United States. It would, according to all the standards of history, have justified the German Government in declaring war upon them. . . . [It] was an event which brought the United States definitely nearer to us and to the war. . . ."[58]

The Anglo-American exchange was announced on September 3, the first anniversary of the war. By this time, Hitler, his patience exhausted, was trying to terrorize England and destroy the RAF as a preliminary to invasion. That day the *Luftwaffe* struck in force three times. "It was a day of fierce air battles, fought at great height in blue and silvery sky all over Southeast England," reported correspondent James Reston.[59] In London that afternoon, Kennedy attended a commemorative service in Westminster Abbey with Churchill and other high government officials. When the air raid siren sounded, all eyes turned toward the Prime Minister's pew. Churchill rose and walked to the cloister, spoke with the Dean, and then returned to his place. It was announced, over the muffled sounds of the raid and the ack-ack batteries, that the service would go on.[60] This was a day on which England had special reason for prayer.

The disclosure of the destroyer–bases agreement electrified America. The staid *New York Times* splashed an eight-column streamer headline across page one, as though war had been declared. In the eyes of some angry Americans, it had. Isolationists raised an outcry against the "dictator" in the White House. But as Roosevelt had shrewdly foreseen, the clear advantages of the bargain, which he likened to the Louisiana Purchase, tended to mute criticism of his methods. As their surprise subsided, the people generally approved. The Republican presidential candidate, Wendell Willkie, who had been forewarned of the deal, was himself a strong supporter of aid to England and expressed only perfunctory regret over the bypassing of Congress.[61]

The popular and political reaction might have been much different if it had been disclosed that the agreement was the climax of almost a year of secret diplomacy. Had the President's patently unneutral correspondence with Churchill come to light, the resulting public uproar could have destroyed his hopes for a third term. Just such a disclosure nearly occurred; but the administration, acting through Kennedy, took extraordinary measures to ensure silence.

The Roosevelt-Churchill correspondence, it will be recalled, began with the latter's entry into the British Cabinet as First Lord of the Admiralty in September, 1939. Thereafter, messages from Churchill, under the pseudonym "Naval Person," passed through the London Embassy to Washington, outside the usual Foreign Office channel and without British censorship. Usually Ambassador Kennedy read the messages before they were transmitted, although occasionally he did not see what had been sent until the following morning. This was due to Churchill's habit of taking a nap during the day and working until the small hours of the morning. Frequently his letter came to the embassy late at night, carried from the Admiralty by a naval aide. The sealed envelope was turned over to the senior embassy official on duty, then forwarded to the code room, which had begun around-the-clock operations with the outbreak of war. The U.S. used several codes, designated by colors, ranging from simple ones that facilitated rapid handling to more complicated and therefore slower ones. The Gray Code, a fast, nonconfidential code, was used regularly for the Churchill cables.[62] The coding was done by clerks, whose work, while highly sensitive, was fairly routine and mechanical. There was one young clerk, however, who read and reread the messages exchanged by Churchill and Roosevelt. In the solitude of the code room, he brooded about their meaning. His name was Tyler Gatewood Kent.

At about ten o'clock on the morning of May 20, 1940, Kent was in his London flat, a bedroom-sitting room, at 47 Gloucester Place. He had come off duty at midnight and was to return to the embassy that afternoon. Suddenly there was a knock at his door. A man, identifying himself as a police officer, demanded entry. "No," shouted Kent, "you can't come in." With that, the door was forced and four men burst into the room—two Scotland Yard detectives, an officer of British Military Intelligence, and the embassy's second secretary. Kent offered no resistance as they produced a warrant and searched the flat.[63]

What they found astonished them. Copies of confidential official documents were stacked in an unlocked cupboard and stuffed in a brown leather bag. By the embassy's count, there were fifteen hundred pieces of paper;[64] by Kent's later estimate, roughly five hundred pertained to political matters.[65] Also discovered were two photographic plates of embassy documents, a pair of duplicate keys to the embassy's code room and index bureau, and a package containing gummed stickers ("sticky-backs") printed with antiwar and anti-Semitic propaganda. Kent was arrested, taken to the embassy, and brought before the Ambassador.

In a sensational newspaper interview four years later, Kennedy recalled the confrontation. "When Kent was arrested I asked him how on earth he could break trust with his country and what he must be thinking about in its effects on his parents. Kent never batted an eye. He played up and down the scale of an intense anti-Semitic feeling, showed no remorse whatever except in respect to his parents and told me to 'just forget about him.' It was a tragic scene."[66] Years later, Kent flatly disputed Kennedy's recollection, declaring that there was no mention of Jews during the interview.[67] When Kennedy demanded to know why he had taken the papers, Kent replied that he considered them "important historical documents."[68] The confrontation between Kennedy and Kent lasted about fifteen minutes, whereupon the Scotland Yard men led Kent to another room, where he sat waiting until mid-afternoon. He then was taken to Brixton Prison and locked in a cell.

Who and what was Tyler Kent? Kennedy, and those who accepted his version of the episode, afterward said that Kent had sent U.S. secrets to Germany, implying that he was a traitor to his country.[69] Kent himself steadfastly maintained his loyalty, insisting that he had defended the right of Congress and the American people to know of secret commitments illegally made by the President and his ambassadors. The whole truth about Tyler Kent is inseparable from the documents he took, the most revealing of which, after almost a quarter of a century, still are hidden from public view in the Roosevelt Library at Hyde Park, New York.

The Kent case, unquestionably one of the strangest episodes in U.S. diplomatic history, throws a revealing light on the character of Joseph P. Kennedy. For both he and Kent professed a determination to keep the U.S. out of Europe's war. Eventually Kennedy's attitude toward the war would cause his embittered estrangement from Roosevelt. Yet in 1940 the Ambassador served as an accomplice in maneuvers designed to deceive the American people as to the ramifications of Roosevelt's foreign policy. Moreover, he persisted in this duplicity long after any apparent purpose of state was to be served. Throughout the Kent episode, Kennedy was faced with a choice between acting on his professed beliefs or on his immediate personal interests. Unfailingly he chose the latter.

Tyler Kent was of average height, had clean-cut handsome features, and was quiet and reserved in manner. At the time of his arrest he was twenty-nine years old. Born in Newchang, Manchuria, he was the son of William Patton Kent, a career official in the U.S. Consular Service. The Kents, an old Virginia family, traced their ancestry to Scotch-English settlers in the seventeenth century and claimed kinship to the frontiersman and hero of the Alamo, Davy

Crockett.[70] Young Kent lived at his father's various posts—China, Germany, Switzerland, England, and Bermuda—and was well educated, attending Princeton, the Sorbonne, the University of Madrid, and George Washington University. He studied history and English and learned several languages, preparing for a diplomatic career. Just prior to his twenty-third birthday, in February, 1934, he entered the U.S. Foreign Service. Two years later, he was sent to the Moscow Embassy, where he was employed as a code and cipher clerk. He remained there until his transfer to London in October, 1939.

Kennedy vaguely knew Kent as one name and face among his staff of two hundred until May 18, 1940, when a representative of Scotland Yard called on the Ambassador and told him that the code clerk "had become the object of attention by Scotland Yard through his association with a group of persons suspected of conducting pro-German activities . . ."[71] One of them, he said, was a White Russian woman, a naturalized British subject, named Anna Wolkoff, who was believed to be in communication with Germany.[72] "The Scotland Yard man told me," Kennedy said afterward, "that they had been on Kent's trail a long time. I was upset that they had not notified me of their suspicions earlier, but the British said they wanted to get the whole picture before saying anything. This was unfortunate, because it raised the question of whether Kent had been giving the Germans copies of our embassy's secret cables to the President and the State Department ever since October, 1939 . . ."[73]

A delicate problem faced the British. Kent was an American citizen, entitled to the privilege of diplomatic immunity; the documents in question and the embassy were, of course, U.S. government property. The man from Scotland Yard asked the Ambassador what course he wished the British to follow. According to testimony given at Kent's trial, Kennedy decided to take an unusual step, in unusual haste. He elected to waive Kent's immunity,[74] thereby giving the British authorities jurisdiction over him. That evening, the Foreign Office was informed of the Ambassador's decision. Curiously, Kent, despite these grave suspicions, was permitted to continue at his post, and was not arrested until two days later.[75]

It should be noted here that England in mid-May was caught up in a severe crisis. Only a week before, Chamberlain had stepped down in favor of Churchill. The dismal news from the Continent raised the specter of imminent Nazi invasion. At the start of the war, Parliament had adopted sweeping emergency defense regulations; now it finished the job of taking away the freedoms Englishmen had won over the preceding thousand years. In order to fight for survival, England transformed herself into a rigidly authoritarian state. A roundup was ordered of all persons who conceivably might hamper the war effort. Caught up in the dragnet and jailed were a number of unlikely persons, including a member of Parliament and retired military officers.[76] Informed that Anna Wolkoff would be picked up on May 20, Kennedy authorized a search of Kent's flat on the same day. That morning, a "very secret cable" approving the waiver of Kent's immunity arrived from Washington.[77]

Three days after his arrest, Kent, in his cell, was handed a letter dismissing him from the embassy, as of May 20. Only a small item appeared in U.S. newspapers, reporting the June 1 announcement of the Home Office that he had been detained "in consequence of action taken by the American Ambassador in cooperation with British authorities."[78] The State Department refused comment "for the protection of this Government."[79] Kent's widowed mother, who lived in Washington, besieged the department for news and finally was received by Assistant Secretary of State Breckinridge Long. According to Mrs. Kent, he gave her little information, but kept repeating in extreme agitation: "Nothing like this has ever happened in American history."[80]

Whatever had happened in England, Mrs. Anne H. P. Kent, stout, pleasant-faced and determined, whom Kennedy once described as "a really wonderful woman,"[81] knew from a lifetime of experience in the Consular Service that the decision to try her son under British law was highly unusual. She immediately launched a tireless, five-year campaign for his return home, so that his guilt or innocence could be determined under U.S. law. It was two months after his arrest before Kent was formally charged.

Of this long interval Kent himself said afterward: "I don't think there was any intention originally of pressing any charges against me. I believe it was done as a result of pressure from officials of the United States."[82] Tending to support his belief was a deportation order issued by the Home Office on May 23, indicating that the British were prepared to expel him from the country just three days after his arrest.[83] If the U.S. government was willing, even eager, to have the British deal with Kent, it probably was because England, under her emergency wartime laws, was a much better place than America in which to keep a secret. At the discretion of the bench in England, judicial proceedings could be held *in camera*. It was in a closed session of Bow Street Police Court, in August, that Kent was charged with offenses under the Official Secrets Act of 1911.[84]*

On October 23, 1940, in Central Criminal Court, London's famed Old Bailey, began the trial of Rex v. Tyler Gatewood Kent. It no sooner had opened than the judge decreed that the case be heard *in camera*. Bailiffs thereupon pasted brown paper over the glass of the courtroom doors. England's Solicitor General, Sir William Jowitt, appeared for the prosecution; a London barrister, Maurice Healy, for the defense. Immediately, Healy challenged the right of a British court to try Kent, contending that it would be "entirely contrary to the general principles of international law and the comity of nations that an ambassador should hand over one of his own subjects out of his own protection into the hands of the country in which he was arrested."[86] It was, he declared, "a monstrous thing."[87] Sir William retorted that the privilege belonged to the Ambassador and not to the individual, and therefore could be waived by the former. The court avoided a direct ruling on the question, and merely held that the privilege no longer protected Kent at the time of his indictment.[88] Thus he could be tried under English law.

The issue of jurisdiction settled, the trial of Tyler Kent unfolded in four days of secret testimony.

There was little dispute about the facts of the case, and the prosecution briskly marshaled evidence in support of charges against Kent under the Larcency Act, for stealing documents, and the Official Secrets Act. The all-important question was his purpose in taking the embassy papers and disclosing their contents. In the defense's turn, Kent was the only witness called. Beginning his story in Russia, he told a tale of disaffection leading to a fateful decision.

"While in Moscow," he testified, "I was not satisfied with American foreign policy. I thought Roosevelt's policy contrary to the interests

*The Act provides that "if any person for any purpose prejudicial to the safety or interests of the State obtains or communicates to any other person any document or information which might be directly or indirectly useful to an enemy, he shall be guilty of felony." Mindful of the difficulties of proving a suspect's purpose, i.e., his thoughts, the framers of the Act further provided: "On a prosecution under this section it shall *not* be necessary to show that the accused person was guilty of any particular act tending to show a purpose prejudicial to the safety or interests of the State, and notwithstanding that no such act is proved against him he may be convicted if from the circumstances of the case or his conduct or his known character as proved it *appears* that his purpose was a purpose prejudicial to the safety or interests of the State."[85] (Emphasis added.)

of the United States."[89] Kent favored a policy of isolationism and wished the U.S. to avoid involvement with all countries outside the Western Hemisphere. He believed that the administration had been less than forthright with the American people. They "were not being adequately informed, they were . . . being told half-truths, instead of the strict truth."[90] He was alarmed by what he read in the dispatches of his superior in Moscow, Ambassador William C. Bullitt, who later moved to the Paris Embassy, and in the cables sent on from Warsaw by the U.S. Ambassador to Poland, Anthony Drexel Biddle. Kent said he "began to acquire evidence of American diplomats . . . who were . . . actively taking part in the formation of hostile coalitions in Europe . . . which they had no mandate to do."[91] Bullitt especially, through his advice to foreign governments, seemed to be exceeding his authority and threatening to involve the U.S. in the "catastrophe" of war.[92] The idea slowly formed in Kent's mind that he must reveal what he had learned to the U.S. Senate or the press. Because he would need evidence to support his allegations, he decided to remove copies of secret documents from the embassy. After accumulating much material, however, he realized that he might not be able to get the documents out of Russia undetected. Just before his departure for London, he destroyed the papers.[93]

On his arrival there, he testified, "I saw more documents . . . than I had seen before; they confirmed my views."[94] London, acting as a clearinghouse, received copies of cables sent by U.S. embassies throughout Europe. Within ten days of taking up his new post in October, 1939, he resumed his former practice. On the witness stand, Kent conceded that he owed a duty to his employer, the Ambassador, but felt that this was not the sum of his duty.

Q. To whom did you consider you had another duty?
A. Well, putting it in a dramatic way, to the American people.
Q. Which duty did you consider the higher of the two?
A. Naturally, the one to the people of America.[95]

Kent dipped into the stream of embassy secrets with little fear of discovery. He either made his own copies of documents, or took copies that were routinely discarded and therefore would not be missed from the files. He admitted having duplicate keys made so that he would have access to the index bureau and the code room if he were shifted to other duties. All sorts of documents came into his possession, ranging from relatively unimportant consular reports to the most confidential high-level messages. At his leisure, he began to sort and classify the mass of papers.

Early in 1940, a friend introduced Kent to Anna Wolkoff, the proprietress of a fashionable London dress shop. Born in Russia in 1902, she was the daughter of Nicholas Wolkoff, a former admiral in the Imperial Russian Navy, who had been naval attaché at the Czarist Embassy in London at the time of the 1917 Revolution. Unable to return to Bolshevik Russia, the Wolkoffs lost everything and the former admiral opened a restaurant, The Russian Tea Rooms, frequented by emigrés who said it served the best caviar in London. Anna Wolkoff violently hated Communists, Jews, and Freemasons, whom she weirdly lumped together as the architects of the Russian Revolution and the agents of her family's downfall.[96] For his part, Kent testified that he had had "anti-Semitic tendencies for many years." He spoke fluent Russian.[97] Miss Wolkoff, though physically unattractive, was vivacious and witty, and made an easy conquest of the impressionable young American, frequently coming around to his rooms.

Because of her father's background, Miss Wolkoff was acquainted in diplomatic and political circles. She soon took her new American friend to the Onslow Square home of Captain A. H. M. Ramsay. A graduate of Sandhurst, a wounded and decorated officer of the Coldstream Guards during World War I, and a Tory Member of Parliament,[98] Ramsay was a sincere but thoroughly muddled English patriot. He believed the war could have been avoided, but had no sympathy for nazism. However, he ranked its threat on a par with a vast Jewish conspiracy which he imagined had taken over England from within. From his anti-Semitic obsession had sprung an organization called the Right Club, which engaged in anti-Jewish propaganda.[99] (The anti-Semitic "sticky-backs" found by the police in Kent's flat belonged to Miss Wolkoff, who, with friends from the Right Club, slapped the stickers on buildings in the dark of night.) Captain Ramsay recruited Kent, who testified later that he had no idea what the Right Club was and never attended a meeting.[100]

As he grew friendlier with Captain Ramsay, Kent found him "misinformed" on the origins of the war, and helpfully undertook to "enlighten" him by inviting him to inspect embassy documents at his flat.[101] The judge, shocked by Kent's casual breach of confidence, directed a question to the witness:

Q. Would you agree that the revealing of the contents of the documents was a big step, going a great deal further than merely taking them for the purpose you have described . . . ?

A. Yes, but it did not strike me so at the time, although it does now.[102]

As Captain Ramsay browsed through the papers, his interest was aroused by a pair of messages addressed to the President and signed "Naval Person." He easily guessed the latter's identity, and questioned the propriety of this correspondence, especially the manner in which it was being conducted outside censored channels.[103] He mentioned the possibility of making it the subject of a question in Parliament. The question, of course, would be whether Chamberlain was aware of his subordinate's unusual intimacy with the head of a foreign power.*

On a visit to Kent's flat in March, Miss Wolkoff accompanied Captain Ramsay and noted his particular interest in the "Naval Person" messages. Shortly afterward, she asked Kent, apparently without Captain Ramsay's knowledge, if she might borrow these documents. Kent testified that he *thought* she intended to take them to their mutual friend, and therefore consented.[105] Instead, Miss Wolkoff went to a photographer, Nicholas Eugenovitch Smirnoff, who once had worked with her father at the Russian Embassy. While he photographed the papers, she took tea with his wife. About a week later, Miss Wolkoff gave Kent a cardboard box containing two negative plates. Kent said he asked: "Why has this been done?" Miss Wolkoff simply said he would be told later, Kent testified, and he let the matter drop.[106] Smirnoff later told the British authorities he had made three prints of each document, but these vanished without a trace. He swore that he had never seen Kent.[107]

The indiscretions admitted by Kent were staggering, and easily explained why gossip in political circles of mysterious high-level messages was quickly traced to him at the embassy. But he could be convicted under the Official Secrets Act only if it were proved to the jury's satisfaction that he had acted with a purpose "prejudicial to the safety or interests of the State." And this question depended on

*Churchill, in his memoirs, asserted that Chamberlain was fully informed, and historians generally unhold this assertion. However, Kent later declared that "a part of the correspondence was devoted to questions as to how to have Churchill replace Chamberlain as Prime Minister." According to Kent, Roosevelt was in touch with the "war party" in England, including Churchill, Eden, Duff Cooper, and others, who were opposed to the compromise peace with Germany favored by Chamberlain and his supporters.[104]

the prosecution's success in affixing to Anna Wolkoff the label of "foreign agent."[108]

It was a label with a very special definition, contained in the Official Secrets Act of 1920. A "foreign agent" was defined so as to include anyone who was reasonably suspected of having committed an act prejudicial to the safety or interests of the state. At Kent's trial, evidence was introduced to show that Anna Wolkoff had attempted to send a letter to William Joyce, the Brooklyn-born "Lord Haw-Haw" who broadcast virulent anti-British propaganda over the German radio. In the letter, intercepted by British Intelligence, she advised stronger attacks on the Jews. The prosecution also established that she was most friendly with a military attaché at the Italian Embassy, before Italy entered the war, "though there was no evidence," Sir William later acknowledged, "that she had passed any secret information to such attaché."[109] In a book entitled *Some Were Spies*, published in England in 1954, the then Earl Jowitt wrote: "Anna Wolkoff was not a 'foreign agent' within any ordinary accepted meaning of the term; she was not employed by any foreign Power, nor did she ever receive any payment from any foreign Power."[110]

There was no charge of conspiracy between Kent and Miss Wolkoff; and a letter from the Public Prosecutor, produced at Kent's trial, said that the prosecution had no intention of claiming that he participated in, or had any knowledge of, her attempt to communicate with Germany."[111] But once her legal status as a "foreign agent" had been established, Kent's fate was sealed.

In his charge to the jury, the judge noted Kent's "very exceptional position" before the bar of English justice and observed that it was "only under exceptional circumstances that such a case as this could possibly arise in the Criminal Courts of this country."[112] It took the Englishmen sitting on the jury only twenty-five minutes to decide that Kent, regardless of his citizenship, had jeopardized the safety and interests of *their* State. In a statement before he was sentenced, Kent affirmed his loyalty to the United States.[113]

He was sentenced to seven years' imprisonment. Anna Wolkoff, also found guilty at her subsequent trial, was sentenced to ten years. Kent served most of his sentence at Camp Hill, an internment camp for political prisoners built around an old monastery on the wind-swept Isle of Wight.

The Kent case gained attention in America only by accident. In

1944, a member of Parliament asked a question about Captain Ramsay, imprisoned for four years without charge, and suggested that he was being held because Kent had passed on to him the explosive secret of the Roosevelt-Churchill messages.[114] An American correspondent reported the question and his dispatch miraculously cleared British censorship.[115] In response to the resulting congressional outcry for further information, the State Department issued a long statement on the case, conceding in opaque language that Kent's immunity had been waived in 1940 because the interest of Britain, then fighting for her existence, was "preeminent."[116] A few days later, a Scripps-Howard reporter, Henry J. Taylor, gained an exclusive interview on the case with Kennedy, who had resigned as ambassador four years earlier.

Week by week during late 1939 and early 1940, Kennedy recalled, British officials had given him detailed reports on the country's strength. "We had to assume that week by week this same data went to Berlin by way of Kent . . . ," said Kennedy. How and why had the code clerk sent the data? "Kent's reported friendliness with the Russian girl, Anna Wolkoff, had its place in his attitude," Kennedy replied, "but apparently she didn't have safe and regular channels into Germany, although both their trails lead to a small London photographic studio where Anna Wolkoff had left two of Kent's decoded messages and where British agents found these reduced to microfilm by an employe proven to be in the German spy ring."[117]

As Taylor scribbled down the uncheckable "inside story," Kennedy improved on the case made by the British prosecutor. Kent, he said, "used the Italian Embassy to reach Berlin. For the most part he passed our secrets out of England in the Italian diplomatic pouch. Italy, you recall, didn't enter the war until after Kent was arrested." At this point, Kennedy was moved to pass a harsh judgment on his former subordinate. "If we had been at war I wouldn't have favored turning Kent over to Scotland Yard or have sanctioned his imprisonment in England. I would have recommended that he be brought back to the United States and been shot."[118]

Kennedy went on to describe events of which the trial record made no mention. While the British were searching Kent's flat, he asserted, "a telephone call to Kent from the Italian Embassy put us on the trail of his Italian outlet to Germany."[119] Kennedy also alleged that Kent had crippled the U.S. government's confidential communications system. On the night of May 20, he said, "America's diplomatic blackout started all over the world. I telephoned the President in Washington saying our most secret code was no good any place.... The result was that for weeks, right at the time of the fall of France, the United States Government closed its confidential communicating system and was blacked out from private contact with American embassies and legations everywhere.... no private message could be sent or received. ... This lasted from two weeks to a month and a half—until a new unbreakable code could be devised in Washington and carried by special couriers to our diplomatic representatives throughout the world."[120]

By this account, it would have been impossible for Kennedy to communicate privately with Washington on May 24 and May 27, 1940, six and nine days, respectively, after he learned of the suspicions against Kent. Yet he *did* send very confidential cables on these days, both of which have been quoted earlier in this chapter. Furthermore, it will be recalled that he described the May 27 dispatch as "terrific" in its implications, for it raised the possibility of England's capitulation. This information could have been of incalculable strategic and propaganda benefit to Germany. It would, that is, *if* the code system had actually been breached. The Gray Code was not secret. Indeed, according to Kent, the papers in his possession were not in code at all. Following standard security practice, the messages were paraphrased before being placed in the embassy files.[121]

A clipping of the 1944 newspaper interview, sent to Kent by his mother, brought this reply: "Kennedy's statements are arrant lies."[122] Just before Christmas, 1945, Kent was released and returned to America. In view of Kennedy's assertions, the State Department took a remarkably indifferent attitude as Kent reentered U.S. jurisdiction, announcing that it had no further interest in the case. As Kent's ship docked, an official of the department told the *New York Post:* "We do not give a damn what happens to him."[123]

For years prior to her son's release, Mrs. Kent tried to enlist Kennedy's assistance, but he returned her letters unopened.[124] One day they met by chance in a Washington hotel lobby, and Mrs. Kent made a personal plea. He told her pleasantly there was nothing he could do, but she persisted. "This might strike one of my sons," said Kennedy, closing the conversation.[125]

CHAPTER 19

Homecoming

On the afternoon of September 7, 1940, *Reichsmarschall* Hermann Goering stood on the cliffs of Pas de Calais and watched as the bombers and fighters of *Luftflotte* 2 roared out over the gray waters of the Channel and on toward their target. At bases near Paris another powerful force was preparing to take off for the same objective. The Battle of Britain, which had begun over the Channel ports and moved on to assaults on RAF bases and radar stations, was entering a new phase. Now the target was London. Through mass bombing attacks on the great metropolis, pressed relentlessly around the clock, the Nazi high command hoped to break the spirit of the British people and force Churchill's government to capitulate.[1]

This first large-scale attack caught the British off guard and was a complete success. Wave upon wave of German bombers flew up the Thames estuary and pounded the sprawling London waterfront. The attack continued intermittently for twelve hours; the huge fires set by the daylight raids lighted the night skies and guided the bombers that came ghosting through the thin, sweeping fingers of the searchlights.[2]

On each of the next fifty-six nights, an average of two hundred German planes rained death and destruction on the world's largest city.[3] This was the cruel siege called the Blitz.

Anyone living through the bombardment of the British capital, Kennedy wrote to a friend that fall, could hold up his head proudly whenever tales of war experiences were swapped. He almost had been looking forward to the attacks as an antidote to incurable British optimism. "Perhaps," he told a friend in early summer, "when the bombing begins in earnest, there will be a little less of this wishful thinking and they will come down to brass tacks. I think I'll have my baptism of fire here, go through one good raid, before I quit and go back."[4] The baptism lasted longer than he expected.

The Ambassador kept track of the number of raids he went through, later coming up with the impressive total of two hundred and forty-four.[5] During one raid, the automobile carrying him was thrown up on the sidewalk by an exploding bomb, but he escaped unhurt. The embassy had advised Americans to live outside the city, and Kennedy himself left London nightly for his country house at Windsor Great Park. In the country, bombs destroyed several nearby cottages. A German ME-109, shot down during a dog fight, narrowly missed Kennedy's house; he remarked afterward that he "could see the fuzz on the pilot's face and almost count his buttons."[6] Inspecting burnt-out shells following another raid, an embassy colleague picked up one that bore, by an odd coincidence, the initials JPK. "That one had your name on it," he told the Ambassador. "Initials don't count," replied Kennedy.[7] The day after a particularly heavy raid, he told an English newspaperman: "You know, George, I'm not going to be killed by a bomb. I wrote to my wife last night and told her that."[8]

Before the war, it had been axiomatic among politicians and military men that aerial bombardment would cause panic among civilian populations. Kennedy had great respect for the power of the *Luftwaffe;* its mass raids had swiftly demoralized Warsaw, Rotterdam, and Paris. Could London stand up under attacks of unprecedented size and ferocity? Day after day, the city took punishing blows without flinching. Her seven million inhabitants proved amazingly tough and resilient; they emerged from the shelters after each raid, picked their way through the rubble, and stoically went on about their business. The prewar forecasts of their behavior under fire were upset by the calm conviction of Londoners that they were combatants, as surely as the RAF fighter pilots who flew to meet the invader. "I've seen some horrible sights in this city during these days and nights," CBS correspondent Edward R. Murrow reported to America, "but not once have I heard man, woman or child suggest that Britain should throw in her hand."[9]

In letters home, Kennedy wrote compassionately of the suffering of Londoners, forced to live under the strain of constant alert, bombed out of their homes and made destitute, cramped night after sleepless night in damp, chilly shelters. He saw them standing on the streets, gray-faced and weary, waiting for trams that were always late and sometimes did not come at all. He admired their "guts," but doubted their cause. In the scales of his realism, qualities of the human spirit were intangibles, without weight alongside the physical destruction the country was suffering. Brave men could not bring down bombers and hurl back an invasion with their bare hands. Where would the planes, tanks, and guns come from if the bombing knocked out the factories, railroads, and communications? Would the people be pushed beyond their endurance? The "great problem" facing England, he remarked, was lack of sleep. As late as September 19, he doubted that the air war had really begun, and gloomily guessed that the *Luftwaffe,* then actually hard pressed, had committed thus far only a twentieth or a thirtieth of its bomber strength against Britain.[10] Although he was aware that the British routinely monitored the calls, Kennedy told friends over the transatlantic telephone that London simply would not be able to take it.[11]

"Joe was a supreme realist who wanted the facts, not his own or somebody else's feelings, to shape his decisions," recalled a friend. "During the Blitz, he looked at Britain's situation in cold, hard terms of pounds sterling. When Britain's reserves ran out, he thought the country would be finished."[12]

In his dispatches, Kennedy warned that the damage caused by the bombing of industrial targets was worse than the British, for obvious reasons, were willing to admit. He cabled on September 27: "Production is definitely falling, regardless of what reports you may be getting, and with transportation being smashed up the way it is, the present production output will continue to fall." It was his feeling that the British were "in a bad way."[13]

This was well-founded skepticism, and the judgment he passed was one that knowledgeable Britons privately echoed. But Kennedy, a diligent gatherer of facts, regularly yielded to his innate pessimism and pushed the facts to extreme—and erroneous—conclusions. The State Department came to discount his warnings, especially when Kennedy himself, having second thoughts, telephoned to ask that a particularly gloomy cable be disregarded or read in the light of another message he was sending.[14] For the most part, however, the Ambassador stuck by his stark prophecies; and he was tortured by the humiliating realization that his words were being ignored. In his hurt pride, he seized every opportunity to restate his conclusions in terms calculated to jolt Washington out of its indifference.

Such an opportunity arose in late September. Churchill, needing a victory to bolster morale, gambled heavily on a politico-military move in French West Africa—and lost. The Royal Navy attempted to land Free French forces under General de Gaulle in the port of Dakar, but a series of blunders and the superior firepower of the Vichy French defenders forced retreat.[15] In his cable on September 27, Kennedy described Dakar as "a bitter pill" for England, one that had produced "the first real break in the Churchill popularity."[16] With the departure of Chamberlain, the Ambassador now looked on the government with cold detachment. He left little doubt that he approved the downgrading of Churchill, reporting "a definite feeling" among the British that "they have not a Prime Minister but a Generalissimo."[17] That said, he launched into a savage critique of the country's war effort that ended by condemning England to her fate.

> I cannot impress upon you strongly enough my complete lack of confidence in the entire conduct of this war. I was delighted to see that the President said he was not going to enter the war, because to enter this war, imagining for a minute that the English have anything to offer in the line of leadership or productive capacity in industry that could be of the slightest value to us, would be a complete misapprehension. . . . It breaks my heart to draw these conclusions about a people that I sincerely hoped might be victorious, but I cannot get myself to the point where I believe they can be of any assistance to the cause in which they are involved.[18]

Before it was published years later by the State Department, this telegram apparently underwent considerable editing. What was deleted can be guessed from the fragments contained in captured German diplomatic documents, for an informant in Washington passed on to the German Embassy the substance of Kennedy's dispatch. Charge d'Affaires Hans Thomsen reported to Berlin that Kennedy had "warned the President urgently not to take irreparable steps. England was finished (completely through) and the U.S.A. would have to pay the bill."[19] According to Thomsen, Kennedy had gone on to caution that "the English will try very hard to bring the U.S.A. into the war as soon as possible."[20] Concluded the German diplomat: "In contrast to the optimism exhibited here on the score of England's ability to resist, Kennedy nevertheless perseveres consistently in his opinion that the defeat of England is unavoidable."[21]

Thomsen's analysis was sound. Since early summer, the consensus had been building within the administration that England's survival was indispensable to America's security and that her defeat therefore must be avoided by extending all necessary assistance. This premise generated a dauntless optimism about England's chances. Reverses such as Dakar, which Churchill hastened to explain to Roosevelt before Kennedy did, caused only passing disappointment at the White House. The formalities (and the legalities) of alliance had been omitted, but the U.S. was firmly committed, beyond any possibility of backing away. Popular support for aid to England had grown steadily, and had been endorsed by the conventions of both political parties. Newspapers and newsreels vividly portrayed the ordeal of London, which became a symbol of democracy at bay. British refugee children were warmly welcomed and "bundles for Britain" flowed from sympathetic America.

Still, the sentimental impulse to assist England was restrained by America's profound desire to stay out of war. As a result, the Roosevelt foreign policy was purposely wrapped in ambiguities, the policy makers not daring to alarm public opinion. Intent on winning reelection, the President did not so much lead the people as encourage them to stumble along blindly and trustfully at his heels. The basic contradiction in the popular mood and prevailing policy stood unresolved in the widely accepted slogan urging all aid to England "short of war." No one in authority had defined exactly how far the U.S. safely could go, and many suspected that the crucial line had already secretly been crossed.

Suspicions of Roosevelt were strong within the Midwestern orbit of the influential *Chicago Tribune;* it was there that the isolationists raised their standard, organized as the America First Committee. Speaking in Chicago in early October, the committee's acting chairman, General Robert E. Wood, of Sears, Roebuck and Company, demanded an end to the dangerous muddle of policy and opinion. "We have the anomalous situation of the polls showing a majority of the people favoring a course [increased aid to Britain] that is bound to get us into the war, while the same polls show 86 per cent of the same people oppose actual entry into the war."[22] Prominent citizens such as Colonel Lindbergh joined America First and sounded the call for an unequivocal stand against U.S. military involvement in Europe.

Representing the opposite tendency in the divided nation was the Committee to Defend America by Aiding the Allies, which boasted some six hundred local chapters by the fall of 1940. A vocal faction of the committee desired immediate intervention and abandoned all pretense of nonpartisanship to work for the defeat of isolationist Republican Congressmen. As this group gained the upper hand, the organization was torn by dissension and chairman William Allen White resigned, declaring that, if he were making a motto for the committee, "it would be 'The Yanks Are Not Coming.' "

The heated presidential campaign discouraged forthright debate on U.S. foreign policy. At the Democratic convention, Roosevelt had promised to stand on his record and refrain from personal campaigning. He said he would intervene only to correct "deliberate or unwitting falsification of fact."[23] This tactic relieved him of the necessity of justifying his foreign policy before the electorate until the moment of his own choosing, and then in the language of an injured rebuttal to unfair criticism. The Republican candidate, a utility executive and newcomer to politics, Wendell Willkie, whom Ickes labeled "a barefoot boy from Wall Street," proved an effective campaigner and soon gave the President cause to mount the stump. As the campaign entered the closing weeks, Willkie ignored other issues and concentrated on presenting himself as the sincere guardian of peace. Capitalizing on the President's silence, Willkie played on the popular fear of secret Anglo-American agreements. Speaking in New York on October 8, he scornfully asked if there was anyone in the audience "who really thinks that the President is sincerely trying to keep us out of war?" He demanded that the President state publicly whether there were any "international understandings to put America into the war that we citizens do not know about."[24]

In London sat an unhappy Kennedy, privy to the deepest secrets of Roosevelt's policy, yet more and more an opponent within the administration's ranks. Temperamentally, he belonged in the camp of the noninterventionists. Politically, he was bound to the President and his policies, which had taken America halfway into the war. Kennedy's awkward straddle would end in a fall, but not until he had played a dramatic and possibly decisive role in the presidential campaign.

"I think Londoners felt that London now really was the center of the world, that it was good to be there, and still alive in the morning." So wrote a visitor to the city in late September, 1940.[25] Kennedy felt quite differently. His thoughts were of a small, private world far away, one from which he had been absent too long. As usual, Rose and the children had spent the summer in the house in Hyannis Port. At the annual Labor Day awards night of the yacht club, the Kennedys had scored a spectacular triumph, walking off with an even dozen silver cups, trays, and clocks won in sailing competition.[26] It was a special moment, one of many he had missed. The Ambassador had had his fill of diplomacy and London and the Blitz. Weary of being chained to his post by an unending succession of crises, he had given up looking for an excuse to resign. He would simply go.

Something more than homesickness prompted his decision to leave. He wished to return before America went to the polls, for he felt he had much to say that was urgently important. The indifference he encountered at the State Department had built up a determination to take his views directly to the people. Rejection inflated, rather than crushed, his sense of the unique value of his counsel. As he would confide to a reporter soon after his arrival in America, "Everybody is always asking if Joe Kennedy is going back home when I'm over there, and if he's going back over when I'm home. Nobody wants to know his ideas or to find out if he's got any. I know more about Europe than anybody else in this country because I've been closer to it longer. I'm going to make it a point to educate America to the situation."[27]

Roosevelt, of course, disagreed with the Ambassador's self-estimate, and ignored his repeated pleas for permission to leave London. The only way past this obstacle, Kennedy had decided, was to bowl it over. Consequently he gave out the story to the newspapers that he definitely would go home and resign before year's end. "For months," reported the correspondent of *The New York Times*, "he has been planning to get home in time to vote in November."[28]

Well-informed observers believed this was precisely the plan the President was trying to thwart. Joseph Alsop and Robert M. Kintner, whose information often came from the White House, wrote in their newspaper column that the leaked story of Kennedy's resignation was perhaps "the last move in an obscure but exciting little game." Noting that it baffled many why Roosevelt insisted on Kennedy staying in London, they advanced "a striking and highly vouched-for theory," namely, that he was being kept there in order to keep him quiet. Kennedy, they wrote, "has strong convictions and less than no remaining fondness for his chief. He will certainly express his opinions to every available American listener the instant he gets through customs. . . . The President is represented as fearing he will reduce large numbers of leaders of opinion to such a state of hopeless blue funk that our foreign policy will be half-immobilized by fear."[29]

Columnist Arthur Krock also found support for the theory that Kennedy was deliberately being kept abroad. "After the election, it will be different," he quoted a top-ranking Democrat as saying. "But if Joe is publicly pessimistic [about Britain] now, the impression might be spread that the President is backing the wrong horse, which won't be helpful in November."[30]

Roosevelt understood Kennedy and his moods very well. In his present temper, he was best kept at a distance until he had calmed down. Roosevelt, a superbly gifted manipulator, knew what the Ambassador's casual acquaintances did not: that Kennedy habitually called his friends unfriendly names; and that should he be challenged afterward by one of them, he would say with beguiling sincerity that he had said nothing of the sort and didn't mean it even if he had said it. Those who did not know Kennedy intimately saw only the tempestuous surface and missed the cool depths below. They read into his mercurial shifts of temper an unwarranted conviction. To be sure, he passionately believed the hard words he spoke, *at the moment he said them,* just as Irish politicians of the era of "Honey Fitz" meant every syllable of their campaign abuse of an opponent with whom they later took a friendly private supper. Kennedy derived a malicious delight from letting his shockingly frank opinions fly.

His favorite target long had been the White House. In conversation, Kennedy spoke caustically of the President and the liberal clique around him. He denounced the forces within the administration that were trying to bring America into the war by stealth. The cumulative effect of his criticism had been to convince a number of people that a break between Kennedy and Roosevelt was imminent. After the story of the Ambassador's coming resignation appeared, rumors flew that he would return home to denounce Roosevelt's foreign policy and proclaim his support of Willkie. Kennedy himself encouraged friends who were Willkie backers to believe that he would hurl a sensational bombshell that just might decide the election. It seemed to many that the "obscure but exciting" game being played between London and Washington involved the highest stakes.

As Kennedy related the sequence of moves afterward to a close friend, his game with Roosevelt entered a climactic phase in early October.[31] Once again he cabled the State Department for permission to leave London, pointing out that other ambassadors were being rotated home while he had been kept cooling his heels for three months. When Secretary Hull failed to reply, Kennedy sent a message to Under Secretary Welles, announcing that he was coming home, with or without permission. According to his later account, he told Welles that he had prepared a memorandum, which had been forwarded to Eddie Moore in New York. Moore, he continued, had been instructed to release the memorandum to the press unless Kennedy arrived in the U.S. before the election.[32] The Ambassador implied that the memorandum contained his views on the war and U.S. foreign policy. This thinly veiled threat had the desired effect; the White House relented and granted the permission he sought. It was important that he have it, for if he took unauthorized leave, he could expect his enemies to accuse him of fleeing the Blitz.

Taking no chances on Washington changing its mind, Kennedy immediately informed the newspapers that he would begin his homeward journey one week hence, on October 23. "It is doubted that he will return as Ambassador—and it is certain he will not if he has his way about it," reported *The New York Times*. "He has made it no secret among intimate circles that he feels he has done his bit and that he is entitled to a long, peaceful holiday and to pick up his life with his family after a long separation."[33]

In Washington that day, Roosevelt told reporters emphatically that Kennedy was *not* coming home to resign.[34]

During the next week, the Ambassador coyly evaded reporters' questions. "I tank I go home," he jovially quipped, borrowing actress Greta Garbo's line. "I'm in the same boat with Garbo."[35] He made a round of farewell visits, calling on the King and Queen, Churchill, and the dying Chamberlain. British newspapers were uniformly generous in summing up his tenure as ambassador. It was a time when the spirit of "hands across the sea" was urgently desired by England, and some of the tributes to Kennedy were rather transparently self-serving. "Forever, in deeds if not in written words, we are Allies. Largely, that is Joseph Kennedy's work," gushed the *Daily Herald*. "Good-by Joe! Heaven bless you! Your job is done."[36] Such words soon would read strangely. More judicious was the compliment bestowed on him by the *Times*. "Whether he comes back to us or not, he has earned the respect due to a great *American* ambassador who never for a moment mistook the country to which he was accredited for the country of his birth."[37]

London still was holding up bravely under the deadly shadow of the *Luftwaffe*. Before leaving, Kennedy confessed that he had changed his mind about the city's endurance. "I did not know London could take it," he said. "I did not think any city could take it. I am bowed in reverence."[38]

A British journalist who spoke with Kennedy two days before his departure noted in his diary: "Looks mentally exhausted; physically tired, lacks interest."[39] But a confidential embassy aide, who knew the agitation boiling beneath the listless surface, advised his superior: "For Heaven's sake do not say anything before you see Roosevelt . . ."[40]

Early on the morning of October 23, 1940, after two years and nine months of service, Kennedy left London aboard a plane provided by the British government and flew to Portugal, where he would catch the New York bound clipper. He said nothing to the newspapermen who flocked around him in Lisbon. Roosevelt had made a countermove. Waiting for Kennedy was a letter from the President, directing him to keep silent until he came to Washington. After a lengthy delay, the clipper took off on the next leg of the westward flight, to Bermuda. And there, too, a similar message from the President was handed to the Ambassador.[41]

The clipper landed at New York's La Guardia Airport on the afternoon of Sunday, October 27. In his hurry to avoid the press, Kennedy also eluded Rose and four of the girls. When they caught up with him in the terminal building, all embraced tearfully. A newspaperman observed that the Ambassador "looked for all the world like a man bursting with things to say."[42] The country, fed a diet of dramatic rumors, was eagerly attentive. Kennedy's comment only heightened the suspense. "I'm going right to the White House," he said, "and I'll talk a lot when I'm finished with that."[43]

The invitation to Washington had been extended in a wire from Roosevelt. Another telegram, from Senator James F. Byrnes, one of Roosevelt's chief lieutenants, again urged Kennedy to remain silent. Byrnes had been alerted to Kennedy's arrival in a telephone call from the President earlier that day.[44] Rose sent the children home to Bronxville with the family chauffeur and accompanied her husband to Washington. The silver and blue plane carrying them touched down in the capital at about half-past six that evening. As Kennedy came down the steps, he smiled and obligingly doffed his homburg for the newsreel photographers. Rose, wrapped in a fur coat, followed him. They entered a waiting limousine and drove away toward one of the most important appointments of Joe Kennedy's life.

Waiting to greet them at the White House were Senator and Mrs. Byrnes and FDR's personal secretary, "Missy" LeHand.[45] (Their presence, Kennedy later told a friend, was clear evidence that Roosevelt was unwilling to face him alone.)[46] Almost immediately, Byrnes asked Kennedy if he would make a radio speech endorsing the President.[47] Network time had been purchased by the Democratic National Committee for the following Tuesday evening. Kennedy declined, explaining that he did not have it in his heart to make such a speech.[48] The Kennedys then were welcomed by the President and the party went in to dinner.

Afterward, Roosevelt turned the floor over to his disgruntled Ambassador. Kennedy needed no prompting, and proceeded to unburden himself, using, as Byrnes drily noted afterward, "many words not found in dictionaries."[49] He denounced the State Department in blistering language, citing chapter and verse of the shabby treatment he had received.[50] Especially galling, he said, were the special envoys, such as Welles and Donovan, who came to London to negotiate over his head.[51] He complained of being ignored and kept on the shelf, uninformed on vital matters.[52] The President listened closely. It was his habit on such occasions to nod his head and say, "yes, yes," which greatly encouraged those who poured out their hearts to him, but actually signified nothing more than that he had heard what was said.

When Roosevelt at last spoke, he took Kennedy by surprise. For he offered no defense of the State Department, but instead echoed and improved upon the Ambassador's indictment. He blamed officious "desk men" for the deplorable state of affairs described by Kennedy, and said that he had tolerated it only because he was so engrossed in the European crisis. Bill Bullitt had made much the same complaint, he said. "They" could not treat his good friends and valued ambassadors so outrageously, declared the President. After the election, he promised there would be a thorough housecleaning at the State Department.[53]

"As the President went on," Byrnes later wrote, "I thought Kennedy was even beginning to feel a touch of sympathy for the State Department boys. In any event, once his complaint had been made and approved, Kennedy became more cordial and the President asked him to make a radio speech advocating his reelection. The moment Kennedy agreed, Miss Le Hand telephoned the National Committee and arranged for radio time . . ."[54]

Roosevelt sacrificed the State Department to appease Kennedy's wrath without a moment's hesitation, for he regarded it as little more than an annoyance to be circumvented as he personally conducted the country's foreign policy. The swiftness with which Miss Le Hand sprang to the telephone when Kennedy said "yes" suggests that he was duped by a smooth, prearranged performance. But the joke, in the light of Byrnes' account, actually was on the hopeful Willkie supporters who believed that Kennedy had come home to lead a crusade against America's drift into war.

Undeniably, this version of the Kennedy-Roosevelt meeting suffers from a nagging sense of incompleteness. Kennedy's dramatic flight to Washington and his speech soon thereafter seem to demand an intervening *quid pro quo*. Certainly, the Ambassador thought he was in the running to be named chairman of the newly created Advisory Defense Commission, a very important post and an eminently desirable springboard for a man of Kennedy's ambitions. Stewart Alsop has written that Kennedy left Roosevelt that evening believing he had been promised the Democratic presidential nomination in 1944.[55] It is a plausible theory; Roosevelt, for all his charm, relied heavily on the bribery of promises. But if there were any promises made or imagined on this October evening, nothing ever came of them.

The search for a "deal" overlooks more subtle factors influencing Kennedy's behavior. The first was Roosevelt's sheer artistry as a manager of men, which had given him the advantage in every encounter with Kennedy since their World War I test of strength at the Fore River Shipyard. Kennedy simply could not say no. On this latest occasion, he yielded to the President's suasion even though he was not wholly convinced. Afterward he confided to a friend that the State Department really wasn't to blame for the treatment he had received; it was the fault of Harry Hopkins, with Roosevelt's tacit consent.[56]

Another factor was Kennedy's belief that Roosevelt, in a real sense, was as indispensable as the ardent third-termers insisted. His original motive for backing FDR, in the dark days of the Depression, had been fear of social and economic upheaval. The wealthy speculator had seen the specter of revolution among the hungry men on the street corners. Much as he might disagree with specific New Deal measures, Kennedy's original motive had never lost its force. Soon after his speech for Roosevelt in 1940, the Ambassador was asked whether he had spoken with private misgivings. He said he had not, and then explained: "I supported Roosevelt because I feel he's the only man who can control the groups who have got to be brought along in what's ahead of us." He said he did not mean the men who ran the nation's industry. "They have a stake that they've got to defend. I mean the have-nots. They haven't any stake of ownership. They've got to take it in whatever faces us."[57]

Finally, there was the factor that, by Kennedy's own admission, carried the greatest weight. This was his wife's advice.[58] The poised and gracious Ambassador's lady was, and always would remain, the firm-jawed favorite daughter of "Honey Fitz." The years in London had displayed the European finishing school side of her girlhood; but the ward-politicking side existed too. This submerged side came into play as Rose greeted her husband on his arrival in New York. His abrupt resignation in the midst of a campaign would violate the unwritten rules of their political upbringing. She urged him to remember what the President had done for him, a Roman Catholic, in appointing him

Ambassador to the Court of St. James's. She pleaded with him not to do anything that would make him appear ungrateful or disloyal. Her words, he confided afterward, had enabled Roosevelt to disarm him.[59]

Of the drama within the White House the world, of course, knew nothing. Outsiders were forced to judge by appearances. During dinner, word had been sent to the waiting reporters that Kennedy had been invited to ride aboard the special train leaving that night to take Roosevelt on his final campaign swing. Washington protocol dictated that such presidential invitations never were declined. Assuming that Kennedy would board the train, most of the reporters drifted away. Only a corporal's guard kept watch.

Their vigil was rewarded. Shortly after ten o'clock, Kennedy emerged from the White House. He explained that he was flying back to New York; his wife would spend the night in Washington. He admitted that the President had mentioned riding the campaign train, but it had been agreed he would not. Nor did he plan to attend the Madison Square Garden rally at which Roosevelt would speak the next evening. Before getting into a limousine, Kennedy said he probably would make a statement to the press the next morning at the Waldorf Towers.[60] As he drove away, the circumstantial evidence of a break with the President seemed conclusive, and the reporters hurried to telephone stories for the late editions.

The next morning, the leading Republican newspaper, the *New York Herald Tribune*, gave page one display to a story on the apparent rift between Roosevelt and Kennedy. The wire services carried the news over the country. There was knowing gossip of the terrific behind-the-scenes pressure being exerted to silence the Ambassador, but smiling Willkie supporters confidently predicted that Joe Kennedy would speak his mind.

A score of reporters waited at the Waldorf at eleven o'clock, but Kennedy failed to appear. Instead, a secretary distributed a release announcing that the Ambassador would speak on the radio the next evening. It was stated that the time had been made available by the Democratic National Committee, which led the press to assume that, if Kennedy had strayed, he was now safely in the fold. Then came "clarification" of the arrangement: Kennedy would speak under the auspices of his family and would pay for the time, upwards of twenty thousand dollars, out of his own pocket.[61] Now the hopes of the Willkie supporters revived. For the next twenty-four hours, friends who were backing Willkie frantically telephoned the Waldorf, but Kennedy could not be reached.

Some discerned the hand of a master showman behind the buildup for the broadcast. "There's no mystery as far as Wall Street is concerned over Ambassador Kennedy's radio talk tomorrow night," wrote Leslie Gould, astute financial editor of Hearst's *Journal-American.* "He'll ride with his party, even though the dope for some time has been that he is not in full sympathy with the New Deal war-mindedness."[62] When that appeared in print, Gould was told by die-hard Willkie men on the Street that he just didn't know Joe Kennedy.

The skeptics knew him well enough. As Jimmy Byrnes later revealed, it was Kennedy who had conceived the political melodrama during the Sunday evening session at the White House. He decided to pay for the radio time himself so that suspense would be sustained right up to the moment he stepped before the microphone.[63]

On Tuesday evening, October 29, Kennedy spoke to a nationwide audience over a special hookup of one hundred and fourteen C.B.S. stations.[64] He began by saying he had returned to the U.S. renewed in his conviction that "this country must and will stay out of war." Doubtless some would "look askance" when an Ambassador spoke on the radio in the closing week of a presidential campaign, he observed. But it was because of his special position and experience that he had come home to give the American people "an accurate report and my estimate of the future on the eve of this, probably the most critical election year of our existence."

After affirming America's dedication to peace, he argued that only by rearming rapidly could the country be certain of staying out of war. He vigorously defended Roosevelt. "Unfortunately, during this political campaign there has arisen the charge that the President of the United States is trying to involve this country in the world war. Such a charge is false. . . ." Actually, he went on, a U.S. declaration of war would be harmful to England; the flow of aid would be reduced drastically by the need to give priority to the buildup of American military strength. "England's valiant fight is giving us time to prepare."

Early in his speech it became evident that the Ambassador was appearing primarily as a character witness for the President. "If President Roosevelt were as wicked as his opponents charge, which he is not, and even if he had undisclosed commitments, which he has not, the facts are against our participation in the war." Kennedy told of receiving a letter from a former colleague, reminding him of his duty, regardless of his friendship with the President, to inform the American people if there was "a secret commitment . . . by Roosevelt to Great Britain to lead us into war." The President, said Kennedy, "has already denied that, and I, as the Ambassador of the American people in London, who would certainly become aware of this fact in one way or another, can assure you now with absolute sincerity and honesty that there has been no such commitment."

Coincidentally, Kennedy had departed from London on the opening day of the trial of Tyler Kent. The American people and Congress would know nothing of the Roosevelt-Churchill correspondence for almost four years.

Before endorsing Roosevelt, Kennedy conceded they did not always see eye to eye. "It is true that there have been disagreements between the President and me—I have disagreed with him on methods employed in carrying out objectives on which we were agreed. . . . However, there are times, as you all know, which clamor for national unity—times when national teamwork is vital and when only fundamental disagreements should be considered. Happily, on these great, momentous questions of foreign policy, trade, commerce and the future of our American way of life I find little basis for disagreement with the President."

Kennedy dismissed the third term issue ("the least of the many considerations which the American people should take into account"), contending that the two years needed to train a new President could be fatal with the world "on the move at a speed never before witnessed." He made his final appeal as the head of the Kennedy family. "My wife and I have given nine hostages to fortune. Our children and your children are more important than anything else in the world. The kind of America that they and their children will inherit is of grave concern to us all. In the light of these considerations, I believe that Franklin D. Roosevelt should be re-elected President of the United States."

Kennedy's testimonial delighted the President, who wired: "I have just listened to a great speech. Congratulations."[65] High praise was merited; the Ambassador's well-known position on the war lent special persuasiveness to his endorsement of Roosevelt. "As a vote-getting speech, it was probably the most effective of the campaign," commented *Life*. "For more than anything else it allayed fear that Mr. Roosevelt would 'take this country into war.'"[66]

It was a measure of the impact of the speech that Willkie, in his counterattack the next day, chose not to attack the speaker directly. While he deplored ambassadors "making cheap political speeches," the Republican candidate offered no rebuttal but suggested that Kennedy, too, had been duped by the infamous deceiver in the White House.[67] Before a wildly cheering throng in Baltimore, he recalled how Virginia's Senator Carter Glass had risen dramatically from a sickbed eight years before to assure the electorate that Roosevelt would keep the platform promise to preserve sound money. "Mr. Third-Term Candidate," Willkie shouted hoarsely, "is your pledge about peace and the acceptance of the Democratic platform in 1940 more or less sacred than the pledge you made about sound money in 1932? Are you kidding Joe Kennedy the way you kidded Carter Glass?"[68] As the crowd roared, Willkie cried out: "On the basis of his past performances with pledges to the people, if you re-elect him you may expect war in April, 1941!"[69]

Meanwhile, Roosevelt had gone to Boston for a major address, in which he planned to announce his decision to permit the British government to place billions of dollars' worth of new munitions orders in America.[70] That meant jobs and prosperity for a nation still suffering the lingering woes of the Depression. But it also was a commitment so immense as to cast doubt on his promises to stay out of war. And peace was the constant theme of his appeals.

No celebrity, and certainly no President, visited Boston without shaking the hand of "Honey Fitz." Jack Kennedy, who favored FDR but took no active part in the campaign, accompanied "Grampa" to the railroad station. Ever the master of the adroit compliment, Roosevelt greeted Fitzgerald warmly: "Everywhere I went on my South American trip they were asking after you. They all remember your singing 'Sweet Adeline' when you were down there." As Fitzgerald glowed, the President told him the natives had gone wild over "Adelina Dulce."[71]

At the Boston Garden that evening, Roosevelt made a gesture to the city's Irish and his own recent benefactor, remarking that he had been pleased to "welcome back to the shores of America that Boston boy, beloved by all of Boston and a lot of other places, my Ambassador to the Court of St. James's, Joe Kennedy."[72] He had chosen this formulation, "*my* Ambassador," over the protests of his speechwriters, and was technically correct, but the Republicans jumped on the personal pronoun as evidence of Roosevelt's colossal egotism. Kennedy, they asserted, was everybody's ambassador.

In this same speech, Roosevelt committed a far greater and more memorable transgression of which the Republicans would remind the voters often in coming years. The President, warned by the Democratic bosses that peace was all the people cared about, now outdid himself in expressing a categorical assurance. The words he chose, Roosevelt later said privately, were so obscure as to be meaningless,[73] but as he delivered them, they were clear enough to the nation. "And while I am talking to you mothers and fathers," said the President in his resonant, convincing voice, "I give you one more assurance. I have said this before, but I shall say it again and again and again: Your boys are not going to be sent into any foreign wars."[74]

Among the many parents who bitterly would remember that promise was Joe Kennedy.

On November 5, the American electorate went to the polls and gave Roosevelt a third term. His margin was uncomfortably thin; despite a lopsided Electoral College vote, Willkie succeeded in cutting Roosevelt's plurality to the smallest of any winner since 1916.[75] Kennedy, who had helped tip the scales, celebrated by submitting his resignation. It was customary for leading appointees to offer their resignations at the start of a new presidential term, but Kennedy visited the White House during the week following the election and made it clear that his letter was no formality. When he suggested that his resignation be announced immediately, Roosevelt asked that he keep the title of Ambassador until his successor could be chosen. Kennedy agreed.

Thus he remained a member of the administration as he prepared to embark on his personal campaign to mobilize public opinion against America's entry into the war. In the first phase, he planned to spread the message over his personal network among leaders of business and finance, publishing, and entertainment. He also was in touch with prominent isolationists in Congress, and with the organizers of the America First Committee, who had considered him for the national chairmanship, an honor he declined.[76] His itinerary called for a trip to California to talk to William Randolph Hearst and others who were opposed to war. But first he took time over a weekend to go to the Lahey Clinic in Boston for a physical checkup. While in his home town, he agreed to talk with three newspapermen, a casual appointment that was to have unforeseen consequences.

The three came to Kennedy's suite in the Ritz-Carlton Hotel on the afternoon of Saturday, November 9. Leading the way was Louis Lyons, of the *Boston Globe*, who had interviewed the Ambassador in the past. A reporter on the *Globe* since 1919, Lyons had covered many of the top stories of the era, and had been one of the first nine recipients of the Nieman journalism fellowships at Harvard.[77] At this time, he was playing the dual role of reporter and Curator of the Nieman Foundation. Accompanying him was a Nieman fellow, Charles K. Edmondson, an editorial writer on the *St. Louis Post-Dispatch*, and the latter's boss, *Post-Dispatch* editor Ralph Coghlan, who was visiting Boston. Kennedy liked the strong isolationist editorial policy of the St. Louis newspaper, and had consented to give Edmondson and Coglan a background briefing on England, the war, and his views on U.S. foreign policy. However, Lyons had been assigned to write a feature story based on the interview for Sunday's *Globe*, and it was his understanding that Kennedy's conversation would be on the record.

The newspapermen found Kennedy relaxed and in an expansive mood. He was sitting in his shirt sleeves eating apple pie with American cheese, his suspenders hanging loosely around his hips. The Lahey Clinic had never found him healthier. A steady stream of callers, old friends and Harvard classmates, had come by to welcome him home, and the Ambassador had talked freely to one and all. This was his usual practice with newspapermen, too. Early in his career, Kennedy had recognized what other wealthy and powerful men hired "public relations" experts to learn. Newspapermen were humanly susceptible to the flattery of good fellowship and friendly confidences from important personages. The small but effective device of calling a reporter by his first name as soon as they met had probably won Kennedy as much favorable publicity as an expensive press agent could have connived. Essentially, Kennedy's technique for handling the press was to appear guileless and without technique. He spoke with startling candor, saying outrageous things, confident that his friends of the Fourth Estate would assume the responsibility of self-censorship and see to it that he said only respectable things in print.

Kennedy spoke to the newspapermen for an hour and a half. Midway in the story that Lyons later wrote, under the subhead "Reporter's Dilemma," was this revealing passage:

> Coglan and I rushed for a cab to get to an office where we could compare notes and save every crumb we could of Kennedy's talk. Coglan, an editorial writer, wanted it only for background. He didn't have a story to write.
>
> "I wouldn't be in your shoes," said Coglan. "How do you know what you can write? He just puts it up to you to follow your own conscience and judgment and protect him in his diplomatic capacity."
>
> "Well, last time I interviewed him, in 1936, he poured himself out just like this, without laying any restrictions on me, and I wrote every bit of it, and it went all over the country—the interview in which he said why he was for Roosevelt. And he said it was the best interview he'd ever had. But he wasn't an Ambassador then."
>
> "It all depends on how you handle it," advised Coglan. "Any story can be told if it's told right."[78]

The way the *Globe* presented Lyons' story showed a curious standard of journalistic judgment, as though the editors questioned whether telling so much was "right" and tried to play it safe. The story was placed on page one under this black headline:

Pinch Coming In
U.S. Trade Loss

The "news" proclaimed by this headline was not reported until the *forty-first* paragraph, which consisted of the following quote from Kennedy: "It's the loss of our foreign trade that's going to threaten to change our form of government. We haven't felt the pinch of it yet. It's ahead of us." Nor was the second deck of the headline much more indicative of the story's true contents:

Ambassador Asks Aid To England
Be Viewed As "Insurance";
Begs America Wake Up,
Give More Power to Mobilize Industry

Interestingly, the *St. Louis Post-Dispatch,* which used the Associated Press rewrite of the Lyons story, ran this more sensational but accurate headline:

**"Democracy
All Done In England,"
Kennedy Says**

**"If We Get Into War
It Will Be In This Country, Too,"
Boston Paper Quotes Him.**[79]

Under Lyons' byline in the *Globe* appeared the first clue to the story's sensational nature—a copyright line. Evidently the *Globe* was aware it had something, but uncertain what to do with it. For the story beneath the misleading "news" headline began in rambling, slow-paced "feature" style, describing Kennedy's shirt-sleeve informality and the rapport he had achieved with the admiring Coglan. Then, without warning, the fireworks started in the sixth paragraph.

"I'm willing to spend all I've got left to keep us out of the war," Lyons quoted Kennedy as saying. "There's no sense in our getting in. We'd just be holding the bag." The reporter briefly mentioned Kennedy's opinion-molding "crusade," then quoted his subject directly. "I know more about the European situation than anybody else, and it's up to me to see that the country gets it."

Thereafter Lyons laid bare the private opinions of Joe Kennedy. It was a stunning revelation; ambassadors simply did not say such things publicly. Lyons quoted Kennedy's lavish praise of the Queen. ("She's got more brains than the Cabinet.") Then the story continued:

> "What do you say about Eleanor Roosevelt?"
>
> "She's another wonderful woman. And marvelously helpful and full of sympathy. Jim will tell you," as he turned to Dean James M. Landis of the Harvard Law School, coming in as we were going out, "that she bothered us more on our jobs in Washington to take care of the poor little nobodies who hadn't any influence, than all the rest of the people down there together. She's always sending me a note to have some little Susie Glotz to tea at the Embassy."

In books and magazine articles afterward, the quote pertaining to Mrs. Roosevelt appeared in foreshortened form, omitting Kennedy's praise of her kindness and sympathy and making it seem that he had stated baldly: "She bothered us more on our jobs . . ." Similarly, the remark that was fatal to his popularity in England usually appeared out of context, so that he was quoted as saying flatly: "Democracy is finished in England." But this was only part of what he had told Lyons:

> "People call me a pessimist," [said Kennedy.] "I say, 'What is there to be gay about? Democracy is all done.' "
>
> "You mean in England or this country, too?" [asked one of the newsmen].
>
> "Well, I don't know. If we get into war it will be in this country, too. A bureaucracy would take over right off. Everything we hold dear will be gone. They tell me that after 1918 we got it all back again. But this is different. There's a different pattern in the world."

Later in the interview he said:

> "Democracy is finished in England. It may be here. Because it comes to a question of feeding people. It's all an economic question."

In his radio speech for Roosevelt, Kennedy had referred to the Emergency Powers Act, passed by the British Parliament in May, 1940, which he said gave the government "the power to take over every person and all property . . . to go totalitarian."[80] He predicted to Lyons that "national socialism" was coming in England. As it turned out, England's postwar socialist government clung to the rigidly planned wartime economy. However, in 1940, the stark but prescient judgment —"Democracy is finished in England"—stood by itself to infuriate Englishmen of all persuasions.

Equally offensive were some of Kennedy's other observations. "It isn't that she's fighting for democracy," he said of England. "That's the bunk. She's fighting for self-preservation, just as we will if it comes to us." Kennedy boasted that he and the outspoken noninterventionist, Senator Burton K. Wheeler, were "buddies." And, he told his guests, "Lindbergh's not so crazy either." Consistently he portrayed himself as a man with a mission ("I say we aren't going in. Only over my dead body").

To close his article, Lyons quoted Kennedy's unconsciously ironic parting words—"Well, I'm afraid you didn't get much of a story."

It was quite enough to demolish Kennedy's reputation.

On Sunday, November 10, 1940, Neville Chamberlain died, almost six months to the day after his fall from power. In the office of the *Boston Globe*, Joseph Dinneen, a reporter filling in as city editor, put through a telephone call to Bronxville and asked for Ambassador

Kennedy, whom he had known for many years. Overnight, Kennedy had returned to New York from Boston. He was impatient on the telephone; Rose was waiting to go to Mass with him. He told Dinneen to call back in an hour; by then, he would have prepared a statement on Chamberlain's death. Before hanging up, Dinneen remarked casually:

"That's quite an interview you gave Louis Lyons for this morning's paper."

"Why? What did he say?" asked Kennedy.

"What did he say? He wrote everything you told him. I've got it here." Dinneen skimmed down the long story, reading the quotes aloud. There was dead silence on the other end of the line. Dinneen thought for a moment he had been disconnected. Then Kennedy asked incredulously:

"He wrote all that?"

"All that and a lot more," said Dinneen. "Anything wrong with it? You said it, didn't you?"

"I said it," replied Kennedy.[81]

After getting Dinneen's promise to call again and read the entire story, Kennedy went off to church. Meanwhile, queries from newspapers and wire services were pouring into the *Globe*, asking whether the Ambassador had been quoted accurately. Dinneen passed on Kennedy's admission that he had. When he tried to call Bronxville again, the line was jammed with calls from overseas, from the London newspapers. Finally, Dinneen got through and spent a half hour reading the story. At the end, Kennedy said quietly:

"He didn't miss a thing."[82]*

It has often been written, incorrectly, that the *Globe* interview "cost" Kennedy the ambassadorship. And the story persists that he subsequently tried desperately to redeem himself and hold onto his position. Actually, he had already resigned and was relieved to be free of the job. What the story did cost Kennedy was his hope of a graceful exit from the administration, in which he would leave behind a grateful President, indebted to him for his eleventh-hour help in

*Despite the clamor over his interview, Kennedy did not miss paying tribute to Chamberlain. On their parting three weeks earlier, he said Chamberlain had known that "he would not live long." Kennedy said the former Prime Minister was "misunderstood in America," and recalled that he had been closer to Chamberlain than any other English friend. "He really gave his life that England might live."[83]

the campaign. After the story appeared, Kennedy fought to overcome the disadvantage at which he had placed himself through his own indiscretion.

Although his words were imprisoned inside quotation marks and he had admitted saying them, Kennedy issued a statement the next day blandly repudiating the interview. He said that he had cautioned Lyons that their conversation was to be off-the-record. He asserted that Lyons had made no notes and had written entirely from memory. "Many statements in the article show this to be true because they create a different impression entirely than I would want to set forth. Many of them were inaccurate."[84]

Having vouched for the story to the world press, the *Globe* had no choice but to stick by its reporter. The paper published a statement regretting that the Ambassador took exception to publication of the interview. When Kennedy demanded Lyons state publicly that the interview had been off-the-record, the latter refused.[85] Kennedy next demanded a retraction, and one was written for his approval, but the *Globe's* managing editor, Lawrence Winship, reportedly threatened to resign if the paper yielded to pressure.[86] The *Globe* killed the editorial. Kennedy, in a gesture of retaliation, withdrew from the newspaper the liquor advertising controlled by his Someset Importers.[87]

It was an episode that reflected little credit on all concerned. Kennedy, the avid publicity-seeker, had run the risk inherent in his hail-fellow technique once too often; the wonder was that it had not tripped him up long before. ("Unguarded talk was always one of the defects of his qualities in London," commented *The New York Times.*)[88] Lyons insisted then, as he does to this day, that he came by his story fairly.[89] Not long after it appeared, he resigned from the *Globe* to become full-time Nieman curator. The bystander from St. Louis, Ralph Coglan, later wrote to a friend that Kennedy had erred by *not* stating specifically that he was talking off-the-record, but that Lyons should have protected him anyway.[90] James M. Landis, who heard a good part of the conversation, believed that Lyons sincerely misunderstood the terms of the interview and later could not retract what he had written in good faith.[91] The Boston *Globe* would prefer to forget the whole episode.*

*The clipping of the Lyons article is kept safe from prying eyes in a special envelope in the *Globe* morgue, and may be inspected only by permission of the managing editor. Permission at first was granted to the author and then was withdrawn without explanation. A copy of the article was obtained from another source.

"Apparently Joe Kennedy is out to do whatever damage he can," wrote Ickes in his diary early in December. "The President said that in his opinion the interview obtained with Kennedy in Boston a couple of weeks ago was authentic, despite its subsequent denial by Kennedy."[92]

The ambassadorship to the Court of St. James's, the crowning achievement of Kennedy's public career, which had begun with pomp and dignity, now ended ingloriously. Any debts and promises that might have been outstanding between him and Roosevelt were canceled. And the open break between them, postponed by the campaign speech, drew closer.

On the morning of December 1, Kennedy flew to the capital and went to the White House for an unscheduled conference with the President, which reportedly was "amicable." That evening, Kennedy announced to the press that he had submitted his resignation on November 6.

"Today," he said, "the President was good enough to express regret over my decision, but to say that, not yet being prepared to appoint my successor, he wishes me to retain my designation as Ambassador until he is. But I shall not return to London in that capacity. My plan is, after a short holiday, to devote my efforts to what seems to me the greatest cause in the world today, and means, if successful, the preservation of the American form of democracy. That cause is to help the President keep the United States out of war."[93]

If Roosevelt welcomed Kennedy's assistance, he gave no outward sign. This time, there was no "Dear Joe" letter of public praise, no invitation to consider himself still a member of the administration after his return to private life. Those days, and that friendship, were past. After saying his farewells at the State Department, Kennedy remarked, "Well, I'm out of a job now and off the payroll here."[94] Influential persons within the administration were resolved that his unemployment would be permanent. When a reporter asked whether the former ambassador might be recalled to another government post, the President's press secretary, Steve Early, answered with authority: "I don't see anything like that in the picture right now."[95]

Citizen Joe Kennedy found a host of enemies waiting as he entered the raging debate over the U.S. stand on the war. There was no longer a need for the restraint formerly dictated by his identification with the administration. Joseph Alsop, deep in the interventionist intrigues of New York's Century Club, lashed out at Kennedy in the Alsop-Kintner column on December 4:

> Let there be no mistake about it. When Joseph P. Kennedy grandiloquently announced he was laying down his office to fight for the cause of peace he really meant he was going to peddle appeasement all across the United States. . . . To date Kennedy's great "peace crusade" has been an indirect effort to sway public opinion by off-the-record talks with influential individuals. Thus it is almost impossible for the Administration to deal with him. . . .[96]

In a signed editorial in the left-wing *Nation*, editor Freda Kirchwey linked Kennedy and the United Mine Workers' John L. Lewis as prime movers of appeasement. "Both are strong and determined and devious, and they know what they want," warned Miss Kirchwey. Kennedy's "passion for peace," she charged, "is rooted in a contempt for democracy . . . his desire to appease the dictators is linked with a strong fear of socialism and the power of labor."[97]

Kenneth G. Crawford, in his column in *PM*, wrote of the former ambassador with heavy sarcasm: "I am happy that he and all the little Kennedys are back home safe for the holidays and that they will stay here. Our Ambassador to Great Britain should be somebody with a heart to fight for the kind of democracy Mr. Kennedy doesn't understand."[98]

Kennedy's foes made much of his visit to California, where he saw Hearst and considered a proposal by banking interests that he rejoin the Hearst enterprises. While in Hollywood, Kennedy spoke to about fifty leading moviemakers at a private meeting in one of their homes. According to Drew Pearson and Robert S. Allen, who reported the meeting in their widely syndicated newspaper column, Kennedy had his listeners "almost pop-eyed with his confidential views on the outcome of the war and appeasement." These views, as reported by Pearson and Allen, were:

> 1.—That England, although fighting heroically, faced overwhelming odds, and the United States might as well realize that England was virtually defeated.
>
> 2.—That the United States should carefully limit its aid to Britain so as to gain time to become fully armed, in order to be in a better position to do business with the Axis victors.
>
> 3.—That Hollywood producers should stop making films offensive to the dictators.[99]

On this last point, film writer Ben Hecht later added a footnote. In 1940, he was attempting to whip up anti-Fascist protests among his fellow Jews in Hollywood, but he ran into Kennedy-inspired opposition.

> Hollywood . . . movie chieftains, nearly all Jews, protested that I was on the wrong track . . . They told me that Ambassador Joseph Kennedy, lately returned from beleagured London, had spoken to fifty of Hollywood's leading Jewish movie makers in a secret meeting in one of their homes. He told them sternly that they must not protest as Jews, and that they must keep their Jewish rage against the Germans out of print.
>
> Any Jewish outcries, Kennedy explained, would impede victory over the Germans. It would make the world feel that a "Jewish War" was going on.[100]

Meanwhile, the Boston *Globe* interview and reports of similar statements by Kennedy had produced angry resentment in England. Like their American colleagues, some British newspapermen took the opportunity to settle old scores. Just before Munich, A. J. Cummings, of the London *News Chronicle*, had had his anti-appeasement opinions censored from a newsreel at Kennedy's instigation. Wrote Cummings in a slashing attack: "While he was here his suave, monotonous style, his nine over-photographed children and his hail-fellow-well-met manner concealed a hard-boiled business man's eagerness to do a profitable business deal with the dictators, and he deceived many decent English people."[101] In a scathing open letter, George Murray of the London *Daily Mail* told Kennedy: "You have said things about us that we regret to hear. They are things which in time, I think, you will regret having said. . . . Perhaps you were always a defeatist and never owned to it in public. . . . We can forgive wrongheadedness, but not bad faith."[102]

More in sorrow than in anger, Murray rebuked Kennedy: "How little you know us, after all. Your three years as Ambassador have given you no insight into the character and traditions of the British people."[103]

This criticism forms part of the explanation of Kennedy's diplomatic failure. Although temperamentally unsuited for statecraft and lacking the broad political knowledge and understanding to excel at his post in a critical moment in history, Kennedy might have come through—"muddled through," in the British manner—except for one failing. He identified himself with the "top people" in England and moved to embrace their views. But these men and women of lofty rank and distinguished lineage belonged to a dying England. Dazzled, charmed, delighting in his acceptance, Kennedy spent little time at other levels of society, in the company of men holding radically different (though not necessarily "radical") opinions, who would lead England's struggle and revive her spirit in days of supreme trial. The intimate of those who first lost their function, then their faith in themselves and in their country, Kennedy rode high and handsome at their side, and shared their fall.

So far as could be judged, he had learned little from the experience and had changed not at all. In a letter to a friend in London, he expressed "amazement... that the English would use that [the *Globe* interview] as an excuse to write attacks on me, and when that was followed up the other day by ——— [Cummings?] on the children, why then, I can't understand it. To be attacked here by columnists, and bitter partisans, that's understandable, but to have England jump into the fray is beyond me...."[104]

Responding to the newspaper attacks, he issued a statement. The British had sorely disappointed the Ambassador. "If an interview, which was repudiated by me, and a story in a gossip column are going to be sufficient to wipe out... my two years and nine months in London," Kennedy concluded sadly, "then I begin to wonder if I ever had very much standing in London."[105]

BOOK V

THE PATRIARCH

"I have a strong idea that there is no other success for a father and a mother except to feel that they have made some contributions to the development of their children. . . ."

—Joe Kennedy, in a letter following his son's election to the Presidency

CHAPTER 20

The Dark Years

THE fabric of the friendship between Roosevelt and Kennedy was not slashed cleanly in a moment's anger; the knife of their antagonism was too dull for that. Rather, the fabric frayed, slowly but irreparably. A sharp, sudden break merely would have hurt Kennedy; the drawn-out tearing away left him embittered.

Once safely past the hurdle of reelection, the President moved openly to commit America to England's side. On December 29, 1940, he took to the radio for perhaps his most famous and effective "fireside chat." If England lost the war, he said, America would live at the point of a pistol. Although he reaffirmed that his "whole purpose" was to keep out of war, the President insisted that all-out aid to England was the safest course for America in the long run. For the first time he conceded that there was risk in "any course we take." This departure from his emphatic campaign assurances was followed by the declaration of a new national purpose: "We must be the great arsenal of democracy."[1]

Taking shape within the administration was a scheme to aid England that would signal the abandonment of America's neutrality. The plan was being drawn up to offset the imminent exhaustion of England's dollar credits for the purchase of war supplies. Popularly called "Lend-Lease," it would permit the President to assist any country whose defense he deemed vital to that of the U.S. by the sale, transfer, lease, or exchange of everything from bullets to Flying Fortresses. In his State of the Union message to the new Seventy-seventh Congress on January 6, 1941, the President virtually declared economic warfare on the Axis. Regardless of the risk, he asserted that "the happiness of future generations of Americans" might well depend on how swiftly U.S. aid was given to the foes of aggression. "The Nation's hands must not be tied," Roosevelt declared, "when the Nation's life is in danger."[2]

The actual danger, some Americans believed, lay in the hasty action urged by Roosevelt, who showed a disturbing tendency to confuse his will with the nation's. Roosevelt replied to his critics in his State of the Union speech, warning against those who "with sounding brass and a tinkling cymbal preach the ism of appeasement."

In this atmosphere of passionate commitment, Kennedy's stand was noncommittal. Clearly he wished to keep a foot in both camps, but his wish was futile. Even if he would not commit himself, others were only too willing to label him. Thus, *Life* ran his picture as part of a two-page spread under the caption, "Roosevelt Brands Foes of His Foreign Policy." The "foes" arrayed by the editors of *Life* included Lawrence Dennis ("America's No. 1 Intellectual Fascist"); several ladies from America First; Anne Morrow Lindbergh and Colonel Charles Lindbergh; General Hugh S. Johnson; William Rhodes Davis, international oil (and mystery) man; and Kennedy, who was described as "defeatist about Britain, in favor of a quick peace."[3]

As the President moved with new clarity of purpose, his former ambassador tried to maintain the fiction that they were essentially in agreement. Kennedy professed to see no inconsistency in giving all-out aid to England and staying out of the war. He insisted that both policies could be applied "without confusion and without risk of contradiction." The most effective rebuttal of this argument was his own unsatisfying explanation of where he stood.

Goaded by criticism, Kennedy spoke on the radio on the evening of January 18, 1941. "Mr. Kennedy evidently felt himself to be virtually on trial, charged with disloyalty to the President . . . ," the *Chris-*

tian Century commented afterward. ". . . [His] resort to the radio constituted an appeal to the court of public opinion."[4]

He based his appeal on the claim that his views had been consistently misrepresented. "The saddest feature of recent months is the growth of intolerance," he said.[5] "Honest men's motives are being attacked. Many Americans, including myself, have been subjected to deliberate smear campaigns merely because we differed from an articulate minority. A few ruthless and irresponsible Washington columnists have claimed for themselves the right to speak for the nation." He rejected the label of "defeatist," denying he had ever predicted the defeat of England. The true defeatists, he said, were those "who have lost hope for peace in America." He denied the charge that he was an "appeaser." Finally, he went so far as to disavow any sympathy with the group he called "Isolationists."

The position outlined in his speech was singular—and shaky. He favored giving the "utmost aid" to England, for America thereby would gain the "most precious commodity we need—time—time to rearm." He implied that England's quick defeat, and the loss of her fleet to the Germans, would imperil an unprepared America. Almost in the next breath, however, he indicated that the danger to America had been exaggerated. "For the life of me, I cannot understand why the tale of a great military machine 3,000 miles away should make us fear for our security."

The former ambassador said that England's war aims—beyond self-preservation—were so unclear that they should not be underwritten. "Are we to sign a blank check?" He debunked the notion of a common democratic cause: "England is not fighting our battle. This is not our war. We were not consulted when it began. We had no veto power over its continuance. It does happen that England's spirited defense is greatly to our advantage. Therefore we ought to arm to the teeth and give as much help as we can. But let us do it on the basis of preserving American ideals and interests."

The question, of course, was how this could be accomplished. Kennedy's counsel was so self-contradictory as to be almost meaningless. Noting that the Lend-Lease bill would "confer upon the President authority unheard of in our history," he seemed to approve, declaring that he was "a great believer in centralized responsibility." But, he quickly added, "I am unable to agree with the proponents of this bill that it has yet been shown that we face such immediate danger as to justify this surrender of the authority and responsibility of the Congress."

Hearings on the proposed Lend-Lease legislation, which had been assigned the provocative number H.R. 1776, began in mid-January before the House Foreign Affairs Committee. Kennedy, invited to appear as the first opposition witness, came to Washington two days after his radio address. The night before he was to testify, he sat up talking with a small group of newspapermen, including Joe Patterson, of the *New York Daily News,* and condemned the bill as certain to involve America in the war. His listeners came away convinced that Kennedy would sharply attack Lend-Lease the next day.[6]

Several hundred persons, the largest crowd to attend the hearings thus far, filled the Ways and Means Committee auditorium to overflowing. At ten o'clock, Kennedy strode into the room, trim and sunburned, his light sandy hair untouched by gray. The arch foe of H.R. 1776, New York's Republican Congressman Hamilton Fish, came forward to shake the witness's hand before a circle of press and newsreel photographers.

Kennedy testified for five hours, but the expected attack on Lend-Lease never came.[7] Echoing the views stated in his radio talk, he became so thoroughly entangled in ambiguities that not even his friends on the committee could extricate him. He was visibly torn between lingering allegiance to the President and grave doubts as to the wisdom of so broad a grant of power to him. He repeated his endorsement of centralized authority, yet insisted that Congress should not be reduced to a mere rubber stamp. At one moment, he emphasized that this was not America's war, and in the next spoke of her large stake in England's victory. Yet when asked whether he knew any method of ascertaining the war aims of England, he replied: "I certainly do not."

The main theme of his testimony was a dread that America would be drawn into a war for which she was not prepared. "I am primarily interested in the proposition that I do not want to see this country go to war under any conditions whatever unless we are attacked. And I would like to see the Congress of the United States still have a hand so that they can represent the feeling of the people in the legislation."

Repeatedly he stated his opposition to the bill in its current form, but was unclear as to how it might be amended. This led to an amusing exchange between Kennedy and a woman member of the committee, Mrs. Edith N. Rogers of Massachusetts. When Mrs. Rogers inquired whether Kennedy would prepare an alternative bill, he replied:

"That request is only beaten by the one of the Senator who asked me if I thought I could prepare the peace terms on which England and Germany could get together. I am afraid I would not attempt to do so. Mrs. Rogers, I cannot express an opinion on that. I am not an expert on that at all. I have no experience drafting bills. I am afraid I am one of those critics that only becomes constructive after he sees what the other fellow has done."

"You are a lawyer?" persisted Mrs. Rogers.

"No, I am not," replied Kennedy.

"But you've had a great deal of experience with lawyers?" asked the flustered Congresswoman.

"Who has not?" shot Kennedy.[8]

Other members of the committee tried to pin down the witness's specific objections to the bill, but he tossed the responsibility back in their laps. At one point, he said candidly: "I do not want to make any suggestions, because I do not know what I am talking about."[9]

Despite his inconclusive performance, at the close of the day's hearings Kennedy was praised by Congressman Fish as "the one man, who more than any other, is trying to keep the United States out of this war." The audience burst into sustained applause, and the ladies from the peace societies stepped up to congratulate the Ambassador.

Congressman Fish's compliment notwithstanding, Kennedy was an ineffective opponent of intervention compared to his outspoken friend, Senator Burton K. Wheeler. On the popular radio show *American Forum of the Air,* Wheeler called the Lend-Lease program "the New Deal's triple-A foreign policy," charging it would "plow under every fourth American boy." Roosevelt was incensed by the remark, which he branded "the most untruthful, the most dastardly, unpatriotic thing that has been said in public life in my generation." Under the rules then prevailing at the White House, reporters could not quote the President directly. But Roosevelt ended his denunciation of Wheeler by ordering: "Quote me on that!"[10]

Afterward, Kennedy told Wheeler that "if the President hadn't criticized that speech of yours, there wouldn't be five thousand people who remembered it. Now five million people will remember it." He said that he had made the same comment to White House aides.[11] In his desire to stay safely in the middle, Kennedy almost didn't talk to Wheeler at all.

On his arrival in Washington to testify on Lend-Lease, he had telephoned the senator and invited him to his suite at the Hotel Carlton. Evidently Kennedy later thought better of seeing, even in the privacy of his suite, the man whom FDR had declared to be anathema. When Wheeler knocked on Kennedy's door, there was no answer. After knocking for several moments, he saw a maid in the hallway. Identifying himself, Wheeler said he had an appointment with his friend, the Ambassador, who probably had fallen asleep. Would she open the door for him? She would indeed. As Wheeler walked into the room, Kennedy sheepishly emerged from behind the door. "I thought you were somebody else," he mumbled.[12]

In a lifetime of rough-and-tumble Western politics, Wheeler had learned to take everything in stride, and he quickly forgave Kennedy his timidity. Some time later, in Palm Beach, Kennedy confessed to him: "I can't take criticism; I don't see how you can."[13]

Kennedy remained the target of constant liberal criticism. The *New York Post,* which had praised his campaign speech for Roosevelt, now identified him as a leader of "America's Cliveden Set."[14] When Kennedy's sometime Wall Street associate, speculator Ben Smith, paid a mysterious visit to Vichy and conferred with high officials of the French collaborationist government, the hotly interventionist Alsop-Kintner column linked Smith and Kennedy in an alleged campaign by international financiers to push a dubious negotiated peace with the Axis.[15] There were continuing echoes of resentment from England. Taking as his text Kennedy's much-quoted statement that British democracy was "finished," Professor Harold J. Laski, who had been young Joe Kennedy's tutor at the London School of Economics, wrote in *Harper's* magazine: "It is possible—since the study of doctrine has never been one of Mr. Kennedy's major activities—that he means no more than a prophecy that British democracy after the war will be compelled to plan its economic life in more wholesome fashion than in the past; and his judgment may involve an identity in his mind between democracy and those rights of the economic adventurer in the period before 1933 which the New Deal, at its best, has been seeking to destroy."[16]

More painful than such predictable criticism must have been Kennedy's awareness that his cause was faltering. Since the election, opinion in the country had moved steadily in the direction pointed by the President. In mid-January, polls showed that about 70 percent of those responding favored all-out assistance to England even at the risk of involvement in the war. The Gallup poll reported that 62 percent of Republican voters and 74 percent of Democrats approved the principle of Lend-Lease.[17] This reading of the nation's mood was confirmed when the bill easily passed both houses of Congress in early March. Still, the American people were opposed to entering the war. The U.S. had moved from neutrality to intervention to nonbelligerency, but balked at the final, irrevocable step.

Resolved that America should not budge beyond this already risky position, Kennedy continued to sound his familiar warnings. In May, at Atlanta's Oglethorpe University, he delivered a blunt-spoken commencement address, maintaining that the U.S. should not go to war "just because we hate Hitler and love Churchill." His arguments by now were well rehearsed, but his words were less ambiguous. He no longer shrank from a position of thorough-going isolationism. "From 90 to 95 percent of our trade is internal," he said. "If worse came to worst we could gear ourselves to an intelligent self-contained national economy and still enjoy a fair degree of prosperity."[18]

Clearly he had adjusted to his new vantage point as a private citizen. In his January testimony on Lend-Lease, he expressed faith in President Roosevelt's peaceful intentions, refused categorically to discuss the Anglo-American negotiations leading to the destroyer–bases deal, and professed doubt that the State Department was withholding from the public "any very great secrets." But now a strong note of suspicion could be heard in his public statements. He told the Oglethorpe students:

> Facts are what the country needs, not slogans. . . . The people who must suffer and give up their lives are entitled to know all the facts before their judgment can be won to the interventionist cause. It is a mockery of liberty to withhold from a democratic people the essential facts upon which this, the most awful decision of our times, must be based. We must have the completest candor; we must have the fullest disclosure; we must have the freest debate.[19]

Then he launched into an attack on leaders who were "professional liberals," including by plain implication, President Roosevelt.

The word "liberal," he told the students, "has become entirely suspect because of the grossest sins committed in its name. Today many so-called leaders are professional liberals. They would rather be known as liberals than to be right. They have tortured a great word to cover a false philosophy, to wit, that the end justifies the means. Liberalism ... has never meant a slavish devotion to a program, but rather did liberalism connote a state of the spirit, a tolerance for the views of others, an attitude of respect for others...."[20]

Kennedy had become one of the "others," a mere witness to the drama on the remote stage of power. He had lost his place among the small company who made the decisions that shaped the lives of men and nations. All that he had won was gone or slipping away. But there was some compensation: Kennedy, having lost so much, at last could afford to drop the mask of pretense and be himself.

The end of Kennedy's public career freed him to concentrate on the vocation of fatherhood. Not that he ever had forgotten the order of priority. During the decade since his original enlistment under Roosevelt, official and political business never had been allowed to absorb him entirely. As much of himself as could be withheld from his duties remained with his family, for this uncommonly ambitious man did not regard his children as ambitious men often did, as an engaging distraction, for whom time might be stolen from the central activities of life. *They* were the center of Kennedy's life; and his time, though lent to other interests, belonged to them as surely as the name he had given them.

While the family lived in Bronxville, Kennedy organized and led the younger children on Saturday excursions to New York City for a roast beef lunch at Longchamps and such movies as "Pinocchio" and "Huckleberry Finn" at the Radio City Music Hall. The children were kept on small allowances, with the result that the pleas Kennedy had heard from Jack were echoed by young Bobby and Teddy. "If you wanted something special," Teddy later recalled, "you had to make a pretty good case for it." Once, eight-year-old Teddy wanted a very special boat, a kayak which a Hyannis Port workman was willing to sell for three dollars. The boy begged and pleaded for the money, but

Kennedy refused, explaining to his son that he soon would lose interest in the boat. When Teddy persisted in his pleas, Kennedy reluctantly advanced the three dollars from his son's quarter-a-week allowance. For a few days the boy spent every waking moment in the kayak; then he forgot it. But he was forcefully reminded of his father's words by the deductions made from his allowance each week until close to Christmas.[21]

One of Teddy's jobs at Hyannis Port each summer was to be at the dock early to rig the sailboats used by his older brothers, just as each of the others had performed this chore for the boy ahead of him. The pyramid of sibling precedence, established by Kennedy, had at its apex his eldest son, "Little Joe." The vital, handsome, argumentative young man always was closest to his father's heart, and it was taken for granted that he would succeed him as the family's standard-bearer.

"I think a lot depends on the oldest one, and how he turns out," the elder Kennedy once reflected. "The younger ones follow his example. If the oldest one is a playboy and spends all of his time at El Morocco, the other ones who come along are apt to follow his example and do the same thing. If the oldest one tries to set a good example, the other ones try to live up to it."[22]

Young Joe, in turn, walked in his father's footsteps. In 1941, his opinions on Roosevelt and the war were almost identical with his father's. Now in his second year at Harvard Law School, he helped organize noninterventionist sentiment on the campus, arguing that America would be better off for economic reasons engaging in barter trade with a Nazi-dominated Europe than waging total war on the side of England. "Honey Fitz" once noted that his grandson, when forced to the wall in a hot argument, invariably fell back on his final incontestable authority, saying, "Ask my father."[23]

The young man had a zest for life and a powerful urge to win at everything. He loved to bet on a horse race, on a golf match, on the time it would take to hike a given distance—on anything. If his father ever disapproved of young Joe, it probably was in small matters, such as his grown son's liking for strong, black cigars. According to a friend, the elder Kennedy had practical, rather than moral, objections to smoking. "He couldn't understand why a man would spend money for something that wasn't going to do him any good."[24] Promising a reward, Kennedy asked his children not to drink or smoke before they reached the age of twenty-one. The honor system prevailed, and he handed each of them a check for one thousand dollars on their twenty-first birthday. Two of the boys refused the checks. One of them was Jack, who afterward confessed that he drank some beer at Harvard.[25]

Following his graduation in June, 1940, Jack had informed his parents that he would attend Yale Law School—not Harvard, for he had had enough direct competition with young Joe. During the summer, however, he changed his mind about law and began to think about following his father into business. That fall, he went to California and enrolled at Stanford University, taking graduate courses in business administration. But he soon discovered that business would not provide the fulfillment he was restlessly seeking. In February, 1941, he left Stanford after only a semester, and set out on a long, aimless tour through Latin America.[26] When he returned home late that spring, he learned that his older brother had made a decision, and in his drifting state, Jack was drawn to follow his example.

Like his father, young Joe combined isolationist beliefs with staunch advocacy of a powerful U.S. military establishment. Since October, 1940, America's youth had been registering for the draft under the new Selective Service Act. Although he was only a year away from graduation at Harvard Law School, Joe, Jr., chose not to wait and be drafted; he volunteered for Navy aviation training. In mid-July, 1941, only days before his twenty-sixth birthday, he said good-bye to the family at Hyannis Port and reported for primary training to the Squantum Naval Air Station, just outside Boston. After he was sworn in, reporters asked how the family—particularly his father—felt about him entering the service. "My father, especially, approves of what I am doing," he replied. "He thinks I'm doing what I should be doing and he's glad for it."[27]

Meanwhile, Jack, just turned twenty-four, also decided to enlist—in the Army. However, the back injury he had suffered in the college football scrimmage three years before disqualified him. Next he tried the Navy recruiting office. Again he was rejected. Disappointed but too proud to admit inadequacy, he resolved to strengthen his back. For the next five months he exercised daily, as though the prize were a place on the varsity. In September, he again took the Navy fitness test, and this time passed.

Much as he was concerned for their safety, Kennedy proudly watched his older boys strike out on their own. He also was proud of Kathleen, now twenty-one and independent; she was working as a reporter on the *Washington Times-Herald,* owned by his friend, Colonel McCormick. But there was another leave-taking in 1941, one which caused him great anguish and left a permanent gap in the family circle.

In her twenty-third year, Rosemary was retrogressing, becoming more withdrawn, irritable, and difficult to manage. Her memory and concentration and judgment were failing. Throughout her teens, her parents, especially Rose, had had their hearts broken daily, for they had no satisfactory answers to her innocent questions. Why couldn't she take out a boat alone? Why did the boys at dancing school dance with her sisters and not with her? Why was she different? "My mother took Rose to psychologists and to dozens of doctors," Eunice Kennedy Shriver wrote years afterward. "All of them said her condition would not get better and that she would be far happier in an institution, where competition was far less and where our numerous activities would not endanger her health. . . ."[28]

Competition was the central fact of life within the Kennedy family. At last, her parents accepted the insurmountable fact that Rosemary could not compete. After much searching, they selected St. Coletta's School, a well-run Catholic institution in Jefferson, Wisconsin, and sent their daughter there. For almost two decades thereafter, the family could not bear to speak the truth publicly about Rosemary, with the result that pathetic untruths found their way into print. In his book, *The Kennedy Family,* which a member of the family read before it was published in 1959, Joseph Dinneen wrote:

> In large Catholic families, it is a commonplace that at least one child shall have a "vocation," a divine call to the priesthood, the Christian Brothers or a woman's religious order. All of the Kennedy children loved rough and tumble sports except Rosemary. She cringed and shuddered at violence of any kind; she was a spectator, but never a participant. Unlike her siblings, she shunned the limelight and was shy and retiring. It was inevitable, perhaps, that she should study at the Merrymount [sic] Convent in Tarrytown, New York, and devote her life to the sick and afflicted and particularly to backward and handicapped children.
>
> She is the least publicized of all the Kennedys. She prefers it that way and her wishes are respected. . . .[29]

On December 7, 1941, Kennedy was at his winter home in Palm Beach. Like other Americans, he was stunned when the calm of that

Sunday afternoon was shattered by the flash from Hawaii on the radio. Japanese planes had bombed the U.S. Pacific fleet at anchor in Pearl Harbor. America was at war.

Angry patriotism swept aside all other emotions as Kennedy immediately sent a telegram to President Roosevelt: "In this great crisis all Americans are with you. Name the battle front. I'm yours to command."[30]

But no command came from the White House. A few days later, Kennedy received a letter of acknowledgment from Steve Early, the President's aide. It was a form letter, such as thousands of other citizens received, thanking him for his splendid assurance of support. As several days went by, it seemed that his offer to serve had been ignored and thus tacitly rejected.

Perhaps hoping to recall his message to the busy President's mind, Kennedy sent Roosevelt a modest Christmas present of a few bottles of champagne; but he received only a perfunctory note of thanks.[31] Then, early in January, Representative John W. McCormack, the House Majority Leader, told Kennedy that Roosevelt privately had expressed surprise that his former Ambassador had not volunteered when war broke out. McCormack said he had told the President that Kennedy *had* sent a wire; Roosevelt had said he would look it up.[32] But weeks slipped by and still there was no response. Late in February, Kennedy heard indirectly from Senator Alben Barkley that Roosevelt once again had remarked on Kennedy's failure to come forward.[33] Tortured by this misunderstanding, Kennedy telephoned the White House. The President, he was informed, was unavailable; would he care to leave his number? Kennedy did, but his call was not returned.[34]

Finally, he wrote a letter to the President and sent it to Grace Tully with a note asking that she personally deliver it to her boss. He also enclosed copies of his telegram and of Early's reply.[35] It was a difficult letter for a proud man to write, and Kennedy was painfully aware that he might seem to be begging for a government appointment, but he wanted his position understood. His experience ought to be worth something in the crisis.

Roosevelt answered on March 7:

> It is mighty good to get your letter and I am very certain I did not get your telegram of December seventh. This was probably because several thousand came in at the same time and were handled in the office without my ever seeing them.

> I was, of course, sure that you wanted to do everything possible to help and I have had the suggestion from the Maritime Commission that you, knowing its earlier work and having had former experience with Fore River people, could be of real service in stepping up the great increase in our shipbuilding—especially in getting some of the new production under way.
>
> I know, for example, that you do not want to be merely a member of one of the many Commissions—that you do want actual, practical and effective responsibility in turning out ships.
>
> Land and Vickery are keen to have you do this. Will you? I do hope to see you soon.[36]

The nation's emergency shipping coordinator was Rear Admiral Emory S. (Jerry) Land, Kennedy's former colleague on the Maritime Commission. The U.S. was launching a fantastic shipbuilding program, calling for the construction of eight million deadweight tons by the end of 1942 and twenty-three million tons by the end of 1943.[37]

Kennedy met with Admiral Land in Washington and then wrote to Roosevelt. "I think you know that if I am given a job clearly and concisely I will work hard to get you the results you want, but running around without a definite assignment and authority, I'd just be a hindrance to the program."[38] Privately, Kennedy said he had been crossed up so many times by the White House, he would not take the job unless it was clearly defined.

In a letter to the President, he expressed the hope that the ship construction effort would be divorced from the rest of the shipping program, and that a full-time shipbuilding administrator would be appointed. Roosevelt passed on Kennedy's letter to Admiral Land, scribbling on the routing slip: "What do I do about this? My personal slant is that you offer him a specific, definite job: (a) To run a shipyard; (b) To head a small hurry-up inspecting organization under Vickery to iron out kinks and speed up production in all yards doing Maritime Commission work."[38a]

By this time, however, Admiral Land already had set in motion his own plans and was satisfied with their progress. The best he could offer was the tentative suggestion that Kennedy might strengthen the organization and management of a pair of shipyards at Portland, Maine.

There was intense open and behind-the-scenes opposition to Kennedy's return to the government. His old foe, Joe Curran, of the CIO's maritime union, protested: "If you want to win the war you don't put in a key spot, like shipping, a man who wants to make peace with

Hitler."[39] A well-known businessman and Harvard classmate wrote to the White House and lodged a similar complaint against Kennedy's possible appointment. The chief hostility to him came from within the administration. During the summer, Bill Cunningham, of the *Boston Herald,* wrote a column headed, "Kennedy Sidelined by New Deal Clique," in which he reviewed his friend's career and said, presumably on the best authority, that it was not the President who was keeping Kennedy out of Washington. "It's the bureaucrats, the Perkinses, Frankfurters, Hopkinses and other on and off the record advisers who want no part of him, and mostly because he never wanted any part of them and was unpolitic enough to say so."[40]

Kennedy discussed the shipping post with Roosevelt, but nothing came of their conversation or of subsequent rumors of assignments that reportedly would be offered to the New Deal's former ranking troubleshooter. When, in April, 1943, there was renewed talk of a job for him, the *New York Post* published a violent attack in the guise of a news story from Washington, reporting "considerable alarm . . . inside and outside the Roosevelt administration," that Kennedy might hamper the war effort. "Because of his record," said the *Post,* "members of the Administration and friends of it who have always been uncompromisingly opposed to Nazism and wholeheartedly for the war against it, believe that Kennedy's appointment would have a disastrous effect upon the nation and are fighting his return."[41]

The unrelenting liberal vendetta succeeded, forcing Kennedy to remain on the sidelines for the duration.

Whenever an opportunity arose, he repaid his enemies. In 1942, Massachusetts' Republican Senator Henry Cabot Lodge, Jr., came up for reelection, and a New Deal Democrat, Congressman Joseph E. Casey, of Clinton, announced he would oppose Lodge. Kennedy, talking one day with his cousin, Joe Kane, said it was too bad there wasn't some good anti-New Deal Democrat around who could defeat Casey for the nomination in the primary.

"Well, your father-in-law isn't too busy at the moment," said Kane, a hard-boiled, lifelong pol. "Why don't you get him to run?"

Fitzgerald, though nearly eighty, thought it was a grand idea. He eagerly mounted the stump, describing Casey as Roosevelt's "rubber stamp." A few days before the primary, Kane led Kennedy to the offices of a Boston advertising agency and showed him a spread prepared for their candidate's campaign.

"This will give 'Honey Fitz' the nomination," said Kane.

"I agree," Kennedy replied. "But can he lick Lodge?"

Kane shook his head.

"And the campaign would cost between two and three hundred thousand?"

"Right," answered Kane.

Kennedy buttoned up his overcoat. "Isn't that nice," he said. "I don't know where you're going, but I'm going back to the Ritz."[42]

Fitzgerald ran a respectable race against Casey, polling 80,000 votes to the latter's 108,000. Campaign records disclosed that Kennedy contributed only one thousand dollars to his father-in-law's losing cause. Even for that modest sum, he bought a fair amount of trouble for the administration: the Lodge forces used tape recordings of Fitzgerald's speeches to help defeat Casey in the general election.[43]

Despite the coolness between them, Roosevelt did not hesitate to turn to Kennedy when it was expedient; and the latter still had wary respect for the President's powers of persuasion. Two weeks before the primary, Representative McCormack telephoned from Washington to ask Kennedy to make a speech for Casey. Kennedy refused. Twenty minutes later, the telephone rang again. This time it was the White House calling. Kennedy, who was with Joe Kane, put his hand over the receiver and asked anxiously: "What shall I say, Joe?" After a quick discussion, they decided on an answer. Kennedy told the President he didn't consider it proper for him to make a speech against his father-in-law. "I quite agree," said Roosevelt, letting the matter drop.[44]

Inevitably Kennedy became an outspoken critic of Roosevelt's conduct of the war. As in England, he opposed the concept of total war and the doctrine of "unconditional surrender." In a casual, fifteen-minute news conference following the Casablanca conference on January 24, 1943, the President had informed the press that he and Churchill were determined to accept nothing less than the unconditional surrender of Germany, Japan, and Italy. Kennedy was among those who believed that this policy, which denied a beaten foe all hope of a negotiated peace, would needlessly prolong the war.

Just before leaving for Casablanca, the President had made special arrangements to accommodate Archbishop Francis J. Spellman, the Catholic military vicar, who was anxious to tour the European front.

He would be permitted to pass through belligerent territory and visit the neutral Vatican City in Rome. Early in February, 1943, the Archbishop left New York on the first leg of a twenty-four week, 46,000-mile journey. At the Vatican, the Archbishop talked for several hours with Pope Pius XII; the substance of their conversations never has been disclosed. At the time, enthusiasm for a negotiated peace was growing inside Germany. Franz von Papen, the German Ambassador in Ankara, attempted to arrange a meeting with the American prelate during his stay in Turkey, but Berlin squelched the plan. Archbishop Spellman returned to America in early August; a month later, he was an overnight guest at the White House.

In their conversations, the President proclaimed himself a "realist," causing Archbishop Spellman to prepare a memorandum afterward setting forth Roosevelt's disturbing thoughts: "He hoped, 'although it might be wishful thinking,' that the Russian intervention in Europe would not be too harsh.... It is natural that the European countries will have to undergo tremendous changes in order to adapt to Russia, but he hopes that in ten or twenty years the European influences would bring the Russians to become less barbarian.... The European people will simply have to endure the Russian domination...."[45] The Archbishop went on to sketch the plans being laid for postwar Germany. The Reich would be dismembered and denied a central government. There would be no peace treaty; the Big Four would rule by decree. The Germans would be disarmed for forty years.[46] This, in rough outline, was the Draconian "peace" envisaged in the so-called Morgenthau Plan, then being drawn up for the Treasury Secretary by his chief assistant, Harry Dexter White, who was at the very least a Communist sympathizer.[47] The Archbishop returned to New York thoroughly chilled by the President's "realism."

In October, 1943, Lawrence Dennis received a telephone call from his friend Paul Palmer, then as now a senior editor of *The Reader's Digest*. Before the war, Dennis had contributed to the *Digest*, but the author of *The Coming American Fascism* since had become too controversial for his byline to appear in the nation's largest magazine. Now he received a $500-a-month retainer as an editorial consultant. One of his recent efforts had been a memorandum sharply critical of unconditional surrender and the rumored plans to break up Germany. Palmer invited Dennis to lunch in his suite in Manhattan's St. Regis

Hotel, saying he would meet someone there who was thinking along similar lines.[48]

It turned out to be Joe Kennedy. Over lunch, Kennedy said he had been seeing Archbishop Spellman almost daily. He said the Archbishop had returned from Rome with word that Hitler's generals might attempt to overthrow him if they were offered terms less hopeless than unconditional surrender. Kennedy grew emotional and castigated Roosevelt. He talked of his two sons in the service, and declared that the war could be ended within two weeks if the German generals were given encouragement.[49]

Of course, no Church official could speak out against the folly of Roosevelt's policy, but Kennedy could, and this had been Palmer's purpose in arranging the luncheon. The editor asked whether the former Ambassador would write, or at least sign, an article condemning unconditional surrender. The impact of such an article, given Kennedy's former standing in the administration, could be enormous. But he did not accept the invitation,[50] and the war being fought by his sons and so many other young men raged on.

After Jack Kennedy was commissioned, the Navy assigned him to a job it deemed appropriate for a best-selling author. He was put to work in Intelligence helping to prepare a news digest for the Navy Chief of Staff in Washington. After Pearl Harbor he applied for sea duty, but as the months passed it appeared he would spend the war behind a desk. Finally, he asked his father's help.[51] The elder Kennedy knew Under Secretary of the Navy James Forrestal, who formerly had been president of the Wall Street investment banking firm of Dillon, Read and Company. With a push from the top, Jack at last was headed toward the sea. He was assigned to a Motor Torpedo Boat squadron, and spent six months training to handle the fast, tough little boats at Portsmouth and Newport. Early in 1943, he shipped out of San Francisco for the South Pacific.

For the young men who fought, the war was the decisive event of their lives. This was especially true of Jack Kennedy, who had not yet undergone a formative experience. The Depression was something he had asked his father about in a letter from prep school; the New Deal had gone by almost unnoticed; the war in Europe was the subject of an academic exercise. Never had he been thrown entirely on his own resources in an exacting situation. Indeed, the Kennedys, because of their wealth and mutual affection, were unusually well protected against personal crises. Realizing this, Joe Kennedy had simulated "crises" by encouraging the incessant family competition, and had tirelessly preached independence and self-reliance. But the test of his lessons would be how each of his children reacted alone to a real challenge.

On the night of August 2, 1943, as PT-109 patrolled the dark waters of Blackett Strait west of New Georgia in the Solomons, Jack Kennedy's ordeal of self-discovery began. Afterward, the tale would be told and retold in magazines, books, and a film: his boat was rammed and shattered by the Japanese destroyer *Amagiri;* he and the ten other survivors escaped the flaming hulk and, after fifteen hours in the water, took refuge on a tiny island in enemy-held territory. The young skipper heroically led his men through four days and nights, until, as hope was ebbing, a message he carved on a coconut shell and gave to friendly natives brought rescue for all hands.[52] With this harrowing adventure, Jack Kennedy, for the first time in his life, performed a deed of supreme importance unaided by his father or his family.

When Joe Kennedy received the wire from the Navy Department informing him that Lieutenant (j.g.) John F. Kennedy was missing in action, he put it into his pocket and said nothing to Rose and the children. He clung to the small ray of hope in the word "missing." Four days later, his prayers were answered. Rose heard the news on the radio and came running to her husband. "They say Jack's been saved," she said. "Saved from what?" He shrugged and said: "Oh, nothing."[53] To his son in the South Pacific, he sent a simple message: "Thank God for your deliverance!"[54]

Jack, who always had been forced into second place, for once took precedence over his older brother and saw action first. Young Joe went through flight training at the Naval Air Station in Jacksonville, Florida, where he was named the outstanding cadet in his class. In 1942, he received his ensign's commission and pilot's wings from his father in a special ceremony. But it was not until September, 1943, that he left for England and the U.S. Fairwing Seven Squadron, the first U.S. outfit to be attached to the R.A.F. Coastal Command. During the winter of 1943, he flew radar-equipped Liberator bombers on around-the-clock antisubmarine patrols over the Channel and the North Sea.[55]

On his furloughs, Joe often visited his sister, Kathleen. Earlier that year, she had given up her newspaper job in Washington and had come to London as an American Red Cross worker. "Kick" provided coffee and doughnuts and morale-boosting conversation to service men at the Hans Crescent Club in Knightsbridge. It was there that she again met William John Robert Cavendish, the Marquess of Hartington, the handsome "Billy" Hartington who had been one of her favorite escorts in prewar days. Now he wore the uniform of an officer of the Coldstream Guards. A romance quickly blossomed, and they became engaged.[56]

It was a star-crossed match, made in the face of strong disapproval from both families. For the Cavendishes, one of England's oldest titled families, were militantly Protestant. Billy's father, the tenth Duke of Devonshire, was head of the Freemasons. The Kennedys were no less staunchly Catholic, and Kathleen, who had been educated by the Sisters of the Sacred Heart, was devoutly religious. She could not be married in the Church of England, for that would mean her excommunication. Nor would Hartington consent to raise their children as Catholics, an agreement which would have enabled her to obtain a dispensation permitting their marriage before a Catholic priest. In the end, tormented by doubt and guilt, she reluctantly agreed to a civil ceremony, which in the eyes of her Church was not a valid marriage. It was not, however, in itself ground for excommunication.[57]

Early in May, 1944, Kathleen became the Marchioness of Hartington in a brief ceremony in the Chelsea Registry Office. The bride wore a dress of pink crepe, a short mink jacket and a little hat of bright pink and blue ostrich feathers, a gaily defiant touch of color against the drab background of wartime austerity. Instead of rice, the well-wishers at the door threw flower petals. At the reception, the guests, an oddly mixed company including Lady Astor and American soldiers, ate plain fruit cake without icing. Young Joe gave his sister away and his smile in the wedding picture reflected her happiness. The young couple received the blessing of Billy's parents, but there was no word from the Kennedys.

"Never did anyone have such a pillar of strength as I had in Joe in those difficult days before my marriage," Kathleen wrote afterward.

> From the beginning, he gave me wise, helpful advice. When he felt that I had made up my mind, he stood by me always. He constantly reassured me and gave me renewed confidence in my own decision. Moral courage he had in abundance and once he felt that a step was right for

me, he never faltered, although he might be held largely responsible for my decision. He could not have been more helpful and in every way he was the perfect brother, doing, according to his own light, the best for his sister with the hope that in the end it would be the best for the family. How right he was![58]

The marriage caused a crisis within the family. Kennedy of course was pained by his daughter's decision to marry outside the Church, but he never thought of forbidding it. He respected "Kick's" right to live her life as the individual he had reared her to be. Among the children, however, strong objections came from Bobby and Eunice, both of whom had considered entering the religious life. Rose Kennedy was desolate. She was ill at the time and bedridden in Boston's St. Elizabeth Hospital. At her request, the nuns in several convents offered special prayers. It was indicative of the strained relations between Kathleen and her family that Rose learned of her daughter's wedding from a friend who telephoned after hearing the news on the radio. To the reporters who gathered at the hospital, Rose sent word that she was "too sick to discuss the marriage."

The newlyweds moved into an apartment in the Westminster section of London, but they had only a little more than a month together before Hartington joined his Guards regiment for the invasion of France. Kathleen returned to America, planning to stay with her family for the duration of the war.

So it was that Joe Kennedy had his family around him in July, 1944, except for young Joe, who had completed two tours of duty and had received orders to return home. Instead he volunteered for an extremely dangerous mission. A PB4Y Liberator was to be loaded with twenty-two thousand pounds of high explosives and flown to within striking distance of the heavily fortified Nazi submarine pens on the Belgian coast; then the two pilots would parachute into the Channel and escorting planes would guide the flying bomb by remote control to its target. It was a desperate plan, but the pens were seemingly invulnerable to ordinary attack.

Young Joe, who had just celebrated his twenty-ninth birthday, and his co-pilot, Lieutenant Wilford J. Willy, of Fort Worth, Texas, a thirty-five-year-old Navy regular with three children, succeeded in getting their explosive-laden plane off the ground and on course above the Channel. Just before they were to parachute, the plane disintegrated under the force of two explosions. Neither of the bodies was recovered.

On August 2, the anniversary of the sinking of PT-109, the Kennedys were together at Hyannis Port. The war was over for Jack. Gaunt and weak, he was a patient at the Chelsea Naval Hospital, but was able to come home on weekends. Kathleen had returned. And the rest of the children, Eunice and Pat and Jean and Bobby and Teddy, were around and about the house, coming and going in the familiar summer routine. When young Joe returned to the States, the war that Joe Kennedy had so feared would indeed seem far away.

He was with Rose and the children when word came that two priests wished to speak with him. Such callers may have caused a shadow of foreboding to fall across his mind. But he could not have anticipated the blow he was to receive, a blow so terrible in its impact that he never would be quite the same person. For in the few moments it took the priests to deliver their sad message, Joe Kennedy was a man suddenly diminished, bereft of the portion of life he had lived in and for his beloved first son. When he returned to the family, his face was ashen. He spoke only a few words, then went upstairs to his room and locked the door.

CHAPTER 21

The Road Back

FEW outside the family ever would know Joe Kennedy's grief. For several months after his son's death, he spent hours each day sitting alone and listening to recordings of symphony music. He withdrew into himself and avoided people; those who were admitted behind the wall he erected came away saddened. Late in 1944, a Harvard classmate saw Kennedy for the first time in years, and was shocked by his emotional state. He remembered him as a tough-fibered fatalist, prepared to accept what he was powerless to change. (A sign on Kennedy's desk in Washington had read: *After you've done your best, the hell with it.*) Now he met a different man. "Joe was in wretched shape; he could not reconcile himself to the loss."[1]

Nor would the passage of time ease his anguish. Thirteen years later, Hearst columnist Bob Considine, then preparing a series of articles on the family, asked Kennedy over lunch in Palm Beach to give him thumbnail sketches of his children. Sitting in the sunshine on the terrace of his seafront home, the host happily complied, ticking off the children, their attributes and their accomplishments. All but one of them. When Considine prompted him on the one he had omitted, Kennedy's composure shattered. At the mention of his dead son's name, he dropped his head and tears rolled down his cheeks. Finally he gestured toward Rose. "Ask her about that one," said Kennedy. "She can talk about him. I can't." Quickly and quietly, she described her son for the embarrassed guest.[2]

Young Joe had been the embodiment of his father's highest ambitions and unattainable dreams. Jack Kennedy captured the feelings of his father and the entire family when he later wrote: "It is the realization that the future held the promise of great accomplishments for Joe that has made his death so particularly hard for those who knew him. His worldly success was so assured and inevitable that his death seems to have cut into the natural order of things."[3]

It was as though Joe Kennedy had mounted, with painstaking attention to the smallest detail, a drama intended to be long and triumphant, only to see the curtain rung down with cruel finality after the prologue.

Among the messages of sympathy that came to the inconsolable father was a handwritten "Dear Joe" note, dated August 20, 1944, from Navy Secretary Forrestal:

> I'm not very strong on letters of condolence—they always sound pretty hollow and inadequate to me. But your boy was so unusual in every respect that I can't help writing to say I'm sorry about his death.
>
> All hands in England were devoted to him; he was a splendid officer and a fine pilot. In short, he had those qualities that have built this country of ours—guts and character—and in addition an extraordinary personality. I hope you won't mind me sending you this when, I know, letters don't mean much.[4]*

Young Joe was posthumously awarded the Navy Cross "for extraordinary heroism and courage," and Destroyer 850, launched in the

*This letter, of course, meant a great deal to Kennedy. The implicit praise of his success as a parent came from a man with singular ideas about parenthood. It was Forrestal's conviction that most people he knew were failures as parents. A tough, hard-driving man from Wall Street, a self-made millionaire who resembled Kennedy in some respects, Forrestal explicitly rejected the role of "full-time father" because, he said, he could not be "bothered" by children as he pursued his career.[5] Yet he revealed in this note an appreciation of the fruits of the devoted fatherhood of which he himself was incapable. More men envied Kennedy's paternal success than envied his millions.

fall of 1945, was named in his honor. Following his brother's death, nineteen-year-old Bobby took his place by enlisting in the Navy; he left Officer's Training School to serve as an able-bodied seaman aboard the *USS Joseph P. Kennedy, Jr.* After the war, the family established a lasting memorial, the Joseph P. Kennedy, Jr., Foundation, which, because of Rosemary's misfortune, has concentrated its philanthropy in the field of mental retardation, donating about a million and a half dollars annually to homes, hospitals, and research institutions.

Now Jack, as the eldest surviving son, assumed the family responsibilities that position entailed. Lying in the Chelsea Naval Hospital, awaiting an operation on his back, he had long, solitary days in which to remember and meditate. He conceived the idea of assembling a book dedicated to his brother's memory, containing tributes and reminiscences drawn from members of the family, friends, classmates, and comrades-in-arms. The result of his work over the next several months was a slim, maroon-bound volume, entitled *As We Remember Joe,* of which five hundred copies were privately printed.

In the Introduction, Jack passed an arresting judgment. "I think that if the Kennedy children amount to anything now or ever amount to anything, it will be due more to Joe's behavior and his constant example than to any other factor. He made the task of bringing up a large family immeasurably easier for my father and mother, for what they taught him, he passed on to us and their teachings were not diluted through him, but rather strengthened. . . ."[6]

The special place Joe had held in the family was defined by Kathleen, who gratefully remembered his strength during the days when she stood alone. "In a large, united family," she wrote, "the eldest brother is often looked upon with something closely akin to awe. Younger brothers and sisters regard him as the foundation stone of the family, and that is the way we all unconsciously regarded Joe. . . ."[7] Their father had looked upon his first-born as the foundation stone of what he was building; now there was only an overwhelming sense of emptiness.

Only a fortnight after young Joe's death, another blow fell. Kathleen received word that her husband had been killed in action. In a plane provided by the British government, she flew at once to be with the parents of the husband she had scarcely known; they embraced her as a daughter. Thereafter, Kathleen remained in England, and made a long spiritual retreat. In a letter to a friend some time after her husband's death, she expressed the resignation born of the faith that had sustained her. "I guess God has taken care of the problem in His own way, hasn't He?"

In 1944, the Duchess of Devonshire wrote a letter to Rose Kennedy that began: "I want to tell you of the joy that Kathleen brought into my son's life. . . ." For four years, Kathleen separated herself from her family, becoming more a Cavendish than a Kennedy. Then, early in May, 1948, Kathleen and her father, who was in Paris, made plans to vacation together on the Riviera. A friend in London, Earl Fitzwilliam, a wealthy thirty-eight-year-old peer, was flying to Cannes and invited her to join him aboard his small chartered plane. Flying at night in rain and fog, the plane smashed into the side of a peak in the mountains of the Ardèche. Kathleen, Fitzwilliam, and the two crew members were killed instantly.

Joe Kennedy flew from Paris to Lyon, then hurried to the small village of Privas, in the Rhone Valley. Informed that his daughter's passport had been found in the wreckage, he said he would not give up hope that there was some mistake. Grief-stricken, he watched as his beloved "Kick's" body was brought down from the mountainside in a peasant's cart. The twenty-eight-year-old Kathleen was buried, next to her husband, in the cemetery at Chatsworth, Derbyshire.

Legend has it that the sorrowing Kennedy turned to real estate speculation in an attempt to take his mind off his son's death. "I thought I'd get a kick out of such trading," he was heard to say, "but I didn't."[8] Actually, he began his operations in March, 1943, more than a year before young Joe's death. And he acted on the basis of a coldly unemotional economic judgment. Throughout the 1940's, his mood was extremely bearish; he was convinced, as were many economists, that the U.S. faced a difficult postwar adjustment, perhaps another depression. He had lost both the desire and the incentive for the nerve-racking business of large-scale stock market speculation, although he preferred to give another explanation. "I wish I hadn't acquired respectability," he remarked in a speech before the Economic Club of Chicago in 1945. "I'd be out selling the market short."[9]

His fantastic real estate career had a commonplace beginning: he owned a house that he wanted to sell. Early in 1941, he transferred his permanent legal residence from New York to Florida, which had no income or inheritance taxes, and decided to dispose of the twenty-room mansion in Bronxville. Archbishop Spellman suggested the broker who handled the Archdiocese's extensive holdings, John J. Reynolds. Reynolds, a dapper, aggressive Bronx Irishman, had risen to become one of Manhattan's leading brokers, largely as the result of the patronage of the Church. After the mansion had been sold, he was eager to do additional business with Kennedy.

"Do you think I could make some money in real estate?" Kennedy asked him.

"We both could," replied Reynolds.[10]

During and immediately after World War II, Kennedy made more money than he had in the previous three decades—by Reynolds' estimate, one hundred million dollars.

Expecting hard times, Kennedy knew from profitable experience that hard cash would have many uses. He built up a cash reserve and looked for investments in "safe places." Reynolds, naturally, could think of nothing safer than real estate, particularly Manhattan real estate, which had fallen to what looked like bedrock prices in the fifteen years since the last building boom. Thus, it might be said that Kennedy grew enormously richer in spite of himself. The bust he expected never came, but his operations left him ideally situated to profit from the postwar inflationary boom.

In contrast to his lone wolf exploits in Wall Street and Hollywood, Kennedy's new moneymaking ventures were not marked by feverish activity. Now he moved through his broker and agents, buying and selling properties in the names of trustees, or through two private holding companies, Park Agency, Inc., and Ken Industries. Yet the appearance of inactivity was deceptive, as knowing observers realized. A colleague from the movie days recalled meeting Kennedy in a New York nightclub during this period. "I asked Joe what he was doing. He said, 'Absolutely nothing.' I knew that was a damned lie."[11]

Where a dollar of his money was involved, Kennedy, as usual, made the final decisions. "You'd approach Joe with a proposition and even if you thought you knew all the details, he'd break it into fundamentals and make you wish you'd studied harder before going to him," said Jim Landis, former chairman of the SEC, who became one of Kennedy's financial advisers after the war.[12] Recalled another associate: "Joe went quickly, *surgically,* to the heart of the matter, without wasted time or motion."[13]

A Harvard classmate, himself a highly successful speculator, described Kennedy as "a natural in business, the way Caruso was a natural in singing." Kennedy had no permanent business "because he had the real banker's instinct—like old J. P. Morgan. He preferred to pick winners, to find somebody who had a good thing going, and then back him. He wanted to be in a lot of things, not have his time and money tied up in one place."[14]

To another friend, whose fortunes were bound up with the giant corporation he had founded, Kennedy seemed "a pure capitalist," committed single-mindedly to gaining the maximum return on his invested capital, unattached to any institution or organization. When Kennedy warned in the early postwar years that "things are going to hell in a handbasket," this businessman replied that he could not get out even if he agreed. He recalled that Kennedy looked at him almost pityingly.[15]

Under Reynolds' astute guidance, Kennedy moved into promising situations, exploited them, and quickly moved out. Although he invested in several areas of the city, he decided the most undervalued real estate in Manhattan lay in midtown, between Forty-second and Fifty-ninth streets and east from Sixth Avenue, with Lexington Avenue identified as a street with an especially bright future. His transactions were routinely spectacular and brilliantly confirmed his judgment. He bought a property at Fifty-first Street and Lexington Avenue for $600,000 and later sold it for $3,970,000; another at Forty-sixth Street and Lexington Aveneue cost $1,700,000 and sold for $4,975,000; still another at Fifty-ninth and Lexington cost $1,900,000 (only $100,000 in cash was needed) and sold for $6,000,000. He bought the Fahnestock mansion, a familiar landmark on Madison Avenue and Fifty-first Street, just behind St. Patrick's Cathedral, for $200,000, although it was assessed at five times that amount, and later sold it for $450,000. He did equally well in the suburbs outside Manhattan; in one deal, he bought land on Pelham Parkway in the Bronx for $1,000,000 and later sold the parcel for $2,000,000.[16] He also invested in office buildings in White Plains and Albany, New York, and in shopping centers around the country.

In his real estate operations, according to an associate,[17] Kennedy used the strategy of "leverage on equity." It worked this way: Kennedy would buy a commercial building for, say, $2,000,000; being Joe Kennedy, he could borrow as much as $1,800,000 at close to the prime bank rate, around 4 percent. Annual interest on the loan would come to $72,000. Assuming a rental income on the building of 6 percent of the purchase price, or $120,000, Kennedy would net $48,000 over interest charges on his original $200,000 cash outlay, a return of 24 percent on his investment.

In September, 1944, the general welfare committee of New York's City Council heard complaints against Kennedy from tenants in the Siegel-Cooper Building, a West Side loft building he had bought the previous year. A garment manufacturer testified that his rent had been raised from $42,500 a year to $73,000, under a compulsory five-year lease which the landlord alone could cancel after two years. Another small businessman said he had been informed his rent would be boosted from $15,000 to $30,000 on a ten-year lease; when he balked, he said, a lease on his premises had been given to another concern.[18]

Reynolds appeared before the committee and confirmed the tenants' reports of sudden, steep rent hikes. However, his sole concern seemed to be the unfavorable publicity his client was receiving, and he jumped to his defense: "Why spread the name of Mr. Kennedy all over this case? Mr. Kennedy didn't buy the property and he never saw it. It was bought by John J. Ford of Boston, in trust for the children of Joseph P. Kennedy, and I operate it for him."[19] No absentee British landlord in nineteenth-century Ireland ever had a more loyal and diligent agent than Kennedy had in Reynolds.

In response to the outcry of tenants against such tactics, New York imposed controls on commercial rents, and the freeze remained in effect for two decades. But Kennedy was not caught in this punitive situation. After holding the Siegel-Cooper Building only a year, he sold it for a million-dollar profit.[20]

Bricks and mortar turned to gold under Kennedy's touch. In 1957, after he had sold or mortgaged himself out of most of his Manhattan properties, Kennedy stood athwart the path of the bulldozers preparing the way for the slum clearance project that included Lincoln Center for the Performing Arts. His building at 70 Columbus Avenue occupied only a small part of the project's plot, but the city was unable to take up the property in blanket condemnation proceedings. Instead, the city was forced to make a special deal to buy the building, assessed at $1,750,000, for $2,500,000. According to a survey prepared for the city planning commission, this meant the land under the buildings adjacent to Kennedy's was worth $9.58 a square foot, but his was worth $62.88. When pressed by reporters, a spokesman for the city slum clearance committee conceded that 70 Columbus Avenue was "an expensive building to acquire."[21] Ironically, only a year before, Kennedy's lawyers had insisted that a municipal valuation of the building for tax purposes was too high. The actual value of the building, it was maintained, was only $1,100,000. In upholding the higher price paid by the city, State Supreme Court Justice William C. Hecht, Jr., said that Kennedy's figure had not represented the true value of the property and the court "cannot constitutionally deprive the owner of just compensation because the latter was greedy enough to try to pay less than its fair share of taxes. . . ."[22] Kennedy thus succeeded in having it both ways.

Though spectacular, his transactions in Manhattan shrank beside his biggest acquisition—Chicago's Merchandise Mart. Real estate men still marvel over the deal that made Kennedy owner of the world's largest commercial building.

Opened by Marshall Field in 1930, the twenty-four-story Mart boasted ninety-three acres of rentable space. It had been built at a cost of some $30,000,000, and in 1945 was valued on the books of Marshall Field and Company at more than $21,000,000. But the company saw compelling reasons for selling: the Mart no longer was needed for the company's operations, and more than one-third of the office space was occupied by federal and state government agencies paying low rentals. Cash from the sale of the building could be used to retire some of the company's funded debt; and any loss suffered on the transaction could be applied against wartime excess-profits taxes.[23]

Not since his days in Hollywood had Kennedy come upon such a situation. In a boldly conceived and executed deal, he bought the Mart for $12,956,516,[24] borrowing $12,500,000 on a mortgage from the Equitable Life Assurance Society. Figuring Reynolds' commission and legal expenses, Kennedy's cash outlay was approximately $1,000,000, which he got back rapidly. Just four years after the purchase, in 1949, he replaced the Equitable mortgage with one for $17,000,000 from the Prudential Life Insurance Company of America, thus enhancing his equity in the property by about $4,000,000.[25]

When he bought the building in 1945, some real estate men believed that Kennedy had become the owner of the world's largest white elephant. Well in advance of the purchase, however, his agents had made discreet inquiries in Washington and had received assurances that the federal tenants would move out as their leases expired. On taking over, Kennedy launched a promotion campaign that attracted private tenants at higher rentals. The Field company, in contrast, had been worried that the government tenants *would* move out, leaving behind unrentable space.

"Seven months before the building changed hands, we had it, provided the government approved the tax deal devised by the Fields," Reynolds chortled long afterward. "In the meantime another syndicate offered more money, but we had it sewn up."[26]

Now valued at $75,000,000 and producing annual rentals in excess of $13,000,000 (more than the original purchase price), the Mart is the biggest single part of the Kennedy fortune.[27]

In 1946, the year Jack entered politics, Kennedy decided to get out of the liquor business. He had enjoyed thirteen profitable years, but the whiskey trade was vaguely embarrassing and not at all in keeping with the public effect of dignity that Kennedy wished to achieve. Countless people who knew nothing else about him somehow knew, as though it were part of the folk wisdom, that he controlled the importation of popular brands of whiskey. And they never tired of telling one another that he had wangled the liquor franchises when he was Ambassador to England, unaware that his franchises antedated his ambassadorship by almost five years. Alva Johnston, writing in *The Saturday Evening Post,* dubbed Kennedy "our Ambassador to the Court of Haig and Haig."[28]

Kennedy rarely visited the Manhattan offices of his Somerset Importers, leaving the day-to-day operations of the company to a pair of cronies, Ted O'Leary and Tom Delahanty. But he was alert to unusual opportunities. When war broke out in 1939, he directed that orders be placed for two hundred thousand cases of Scotch whiskey above Somerset's usual quota. Most of this extra supply was kept in U.S. warehouses for the duration.[29] An importer could not guarantee the transfer of his franchises to a prospective buyer; this was the prerogative of the English distiller. Hence, when Kennedy offered his business for sale, his only solid asset was the huge inventory of Scotch that he had shrewdly stockpiled. In the period of postwar shortages, it was liquid gold. He sold out to Renfield Importers for $8,000,000 in cash.[30]

Kennedy realized immense profits on his original investment of $100,000 in setting up Somerset. In addition to the millions of dollars he netted on the sale to Renfield, he had enjoyed, according to trade sources, an estimated average net income from the company of around a quarter of a million dollars annually. So profitable was whiskey selling that he included Somerset stock in the trust funds he had established for Rose and the children. Over the years, O'Leary and Delahanty became almost members of the family, and they hoped for a crack at the business or a share of the profits amassed. They discovered to their disappointment that blood was thicker than whiskey. The millions Kennedy received were channeled into investments for the benefit of the family trusts, while O'Leary and Delahanty each received a farewell bonus of about $25,000.[31]

As with many such stories, the tale of Kennedy's niggardly payoff to a pair of loyal associates soon circulated among his acquaintances. To some, it seemed ruthless. Others cited little-known instances of his help to needy persons. This, they said, was typical of the man they knew. Neither his detractors nor his supporters could speak the whole truth, for Kennedy showed different sides of his nature to different people. "Joe Kennedy had a hot heart and a cold head," said one intimate observer. "That's what made the steam in him."

As Kennedy walked down the street in Boston one day, accompanied by Francis X. (Frank) Morrissey, for whom he had arranged a municipal judgeship, he was hailed by a shabbily dressed elderly man. Kennedy recognized him as the doctor who had taken care of his children. After their brief conversation, Kennedy asked Morrissey to look into the man's evident plight. The report came back that the doctor's practice had faded away; he was virtually penniless. Soon after, the doctor received an invitation to join the staff of one of Boston's hospitals at a salary of $10,000 a year. He accepted the position and held it until his death, unaware that Kennedy had created the job and provided the money for his weekly paycheck.[32]

On another occasion, Kennedy met Al Mills, a onetime classmate at the Assumption School in East Boston. As they reminisced, Mills said he had recently visited the old school and had learned from the elderly Mother Superior who had taught them that the plumbing in the building was sixty years old and constantly in need of repair. New plumbing, she told him despairingly, would cost nearly three thousand dollars, a sum the parish could not afford. Mills offered to solicit funds among graduates of the school, but the nun objected, saying most of them were poor and any donation they gave would be a hardship. Kennedy told Mills to arrange to have the plumbing installed and the bill sent to him. But, he added, Mills must tell the Mother Superior he had approached a number of graduates, each of whom had contributed. Mills followed these instructions and the nun wept at this show of loyalty by her former students.[33]

An aging newspaperman in Boston, out of work and short of money, came to the attention of Kennedy, who, in remembrance of better days, sent him a check for one thousand dollars. The man proudly returned it, but Kennedy mailed it right back, enclosing a note explaining that he wished to retain the ex-reporter for some "public relations" work. Once again, the check was returned, but Kennedy had won a steadfast, unpaid public relations man.[34] In a city the size of Boston, stories of his many small, personal charities spread by word of mouth, creating a fund of goodwill and evoking the memory of days not long past when an Irishman in trouble had nowhere to turn for help but to his own kind.

Faithful to the code of Pat Kennedy and "Honey Fitz," he looked after many of his former employees and associates. At the Maritime Commission, he had worked with a Boston Latin School classmate. Before leaving the Commission, he appointed him president of the government-owned Dollar Steamship Line. This prompted Joe Kane to remark cynically that his cousin, Kennedy, took his old friend "out of the breadline and put him at the head of the Dollar Line."

When Kennedy's successor as chairman of the SEC, James M. Landis, left the government in 1937 to become dean of the Harvard Law School, William O. Douglas expected to replace him. But strong opposition developed in Wall Street, which had lost patience with reform. Discouraged, Douglas received an invitation to return to Yale Law School and decided to accept it. He was packed and ready to catch a train out of Washington one day when Kennedy telephoned. "Don't take that train," he told Douglas. "I think you'll get a call from the White House. Just sit tight." On the strength of that word from Roosevelt's intimate, Douglas postponed his departure. Later that day, the President called and asked him to become SEC chairman. Douglas went on to perform so impressively in the post that, just nineteen months later, Roosevelt appointed him to the Supreme Court. The Justice, who became a close friend of the Kennedy family, did not forget the thoughtful telephone call that changed his life.[35]

In 1948, Jim Landis, who had returned to government service, learned from President Truman that he would not be reappointed to another term on the Civil Aeronautics Board. Landis had about one thousand dollars in the bank and no prospects. Kennedy heard the news and telephoned from Palm Beach.

"Hell," he said, "come on down here and join the Kennedy enterprises."

Landis asked what they were.

"Well, dammit, I don't know," came the reply, "but come on down and we'll figure it out."

Landis went, lay in the Florida sun for three weeks, and joined Kennedy's legal staff.[36]

Kennedy was a devoted lifelong friend to his Harvard roommate, Bob Fisher. When Fisher died in the summer of 1942, he left unpaid a note for five thousand dollars which Kennedy had endorsed. He promptly told Fisher's widow not to worry, he would pay the debt.[37]

For years, Kennedy regularly sent money to the widow and children of Lieutenant Willy, the Navy pilot killed with young Joe.[38] Such acts of charity won Kennedy the gratitude and prayers of many individuals. Recalling his kindness and unpublicized philanthropies, a former Boston newspaperman believed Kennedy's generosity occasionally was abused, leaving him hurt and disappointed. "He would go out of his way for people, and sometimes he'd get their finger in his eye."[39]

Yet the hard, unforgiving side of Kennedy could not be denied. A once-close friend, speaking through the pain of a secret hurt, described Kennedy as "absolutely without sentiment." He challenged the belief that money caused many of Kennedy's falling-outs. "Not money, but poor judgment about people lay at the root of many episodes. With all his brilliance, there were definite flaws in Joe's judgment."[40]

Kennedy had boundless, often arrogant confidence in his judgment; if it was disputed, he reacted furiously, then lapsed into glacial coolness. John J. Burns, the former SEC counsel and perhaps the most valuable assistant Kennedy had during his government service, parted with him in the late nineteen forties. In a professed economy move, Kennedy cut the annual retainer for Burns' legal services from six thousand to three thousand dollars; but the dispute over this trivial sum formed only the surface of a deep personal clash. The break between the two men never could be repaired. Soon after Burns died in 1957, Landis approached Kennedy for a contribution to a memorial room honoring Burns at the Harvard Law School. Kennedy curtly refused.[41]

"If Joe liked you, you were tops—no matter what anybody else thought," said the family's financial adviser, Jim Fayne. "If he stopped liking you, you simply didn't exist any more. Some people were hurt, but not Joe. He'd seen so many come and go."[42]

Throughout his life, Kennedy always had around him a tight protective circle of retainers, agents and hangers-on. Eddie Moore, his confidential secretary, was for many years the leading member of this exclusive fraternity. Another was canny John Ford, a Bostonian almost unknown in Boston business circles, who managed Kennedy's New England movie theaters, served as trustee of the family trust funds, and invariably acted as treasurer and paymaster for the Kennedy political campaigns in Massachusetts. Long the court jester in Kennedy's retinue was Arthur Houghton, a retired New York theater manager, who appealed to the fun-loving showman in Kennedy. A witty, engaging companion, Houghton lived with Kennedy for some time in Palm Beach, and conspired with him to spring private jokes on outsiders. When financiers joined them on the golf course and the conversation turned to intricate deals, Houghton, although he had no idea what was being discussed, would interject: "What about the debentures?" He spoke so knowingly that the question never failed to draw solemn nods.

Others in the ever-changing constellation around Kennedy included Joseph (Joe) Timilty, Boston's former police commissioner, and Judge Frank Morrissey. Timilty, after years of intimacy, abruptly fell from favor; Morrissey, one of Jack Kennedy's early political mentors, managed to hold his place. This could be a difficult feat. Not only were the men around Kennedy blindly loyal, recalled a family friend; they also were extremely jealous. "If you got too close to Joe, they would shoulder you out of the way."[43]

Kennedy had a pessimistic view of human nature. One who had pulled many a sharp trade, he always was wary of having the tables turned on him. Even the smallest deception that might make him appear foolish would arouse violent anger. In January, 1961, he was being interviewed by Bob Considine while a *New York Journal-American* photographer took candid pictures.

"Would you mind adjusting your tie, Mr. Kennedy?" asked the photographer.

As Kennedy reached up, the photographer snapped a picture. Kennedy's face turned beet-red and he wheeled on the man.

"I don't like that," he snapped. "Don't try tricking me into anything like that. If you want a picture of me adjusting my tie you tell me you want a picture of me adjusting my tie. What you did was dishonest."

The photographer opened his camera and handed over the film.

"I don't want your film," said Kennedy. "I just don't want to be taken in by trickery."[44]

Intermittently during the war years, Kennedy worked on the memoirs he had started to write while in London. He told friends he intended to "set the record straight" on his relations with Roosevelt, and hinted that he would demonstrate the President's large degree of responsibility for America's involvement in the war. Kennedy was sympathetic to the "revisionist" historians, led by the eminent Charles A. Beard, whose thesis it was that America had been tricked into belligerency. Kennedy praised revisionist Harry Elmer Barnes for his spirited pamphleteering against the "historical blackout," and agreed with him that there existed a powerful clique of self-appointed censors —"the smearbund," he called it—intent on keeping the truth hidden and all opponents on the defensive.[45] Kennedy's manuscript, which might have proved illuminating to the revisionist scholars, was written and rewritten and put aside for long spells. As his sons entered politics, his enthusiasm for upsetting popular illusions, particularly those concerning Roosevelt, sharply waned.* When Charles Callan Tansill's massive and scholarly study, *Back Door to War,* appeared in 1952, Dr. Barnes wrote a letter asking Kennedy's help in distributing the book, but it came out in an election year. Kennedy replied that the proposal unfortunately would not fit into the family's plans.[47]

Oddly enough, Kennedy's only contribution to revisionist history dealt with a relatively unimportant incident of the war in which

*The manuscript finally was completed in 1961. It would be published, Kennedy then told friends "after Jack leaves the White House." Aides of the President, noting the political ambitions of Kennedy's other two sons, expressed doubt at the time that it would ever be published.[46]

Americans had scant interest. In 1950, in collaboration with Landis, he wrote a pamphlet defending the decision of Belgium's King Leopold III to surrender his army to the Germans in late May, 1940.[48] At that time, France's Paul Reynaud and, to a lesser degree, Churchill, had denounced the surrender as an act of treachery that exposed the allied left flank and endangered the retreat to Dunkirk. Kennedy and Landis analyzed allied troop dispositions and the instructions sent to the field, concluding that confusion in the British War Cabinet caused misunderstandings of the Belgian monarch's plans. They argued that his action had permitted the escape of a large portion of the allied forces from a hopeless situation. The pamphlet could be read as another installment in Kennedy's feud with Churchill. When the latter's memoirs began appearing, Kennedy, in a letter to *The New York Times,* challenged the accuracy of the former Prime Minister's presentation of historical material.[49] In 1959, Belgium's King Baudouin I, the son of Leopold, gratefully bestowed on Kennedy his country's third highest decoration, the Grand Cross of Leopold II.

Through the war and afterward, there had been no such honors for Kennedy from Washington. Rumors continued to crop up that he would be appointed to a high government post, reports which Kennedy himself may well have inspired. In February, 1944, the *Boston Herald,* quoting "a reliable authority," said Kennedy had been invited to succeed Jesse Jones as Secretary of Commerce, adding that he was weighing the idea at his winter home in Palm Beach. But this story, too, proved unfounded.

In the fall of the year, Kennedy's estrangement from Roosevelt seemed complete, and many credited the gossip that he would oppose the President's bid for a fourth term. Late in October, it was reported that Kennedy had contracted for radio time on the eve of the election, in order to announce his support of the Republican candidate, New York's racket-busting district attorney, Thomas E. Dewey. Soon afterward, Kennedy turned up at the White House for a surprise visit. There were many versions of what occurred, ranging from a rumor that Roosevelt had threatened to investigate Kennedy's income taxes to reported promises of unspecified favors if he would keep silent. When the visitor left the White House, he said that politics had not been discussed, denied having bought radio time, and declined to predict the outcome of the election.[50]

The last assignment Kennedy received from Roosevelt was to make an informal study of the "jobs for all" program of postwar industrial reconversion proposed by steelmaker Henry J. Kaiser. Kennedy, according to associates, was unimpressed with the plan and candidly told the President so. This was the last recorded contact between them before Roosevelt's death in April, 1945.

In paying tribute to the President, Kennedy echoed his own sentiments about the war that was coming to an end. "A greater love hath no man than he who gives his life for his country," he said. "As a member of President Roosevelt's official family for many years, I know that he felt that justice had been violated seriously by this war, and he had dedicated his life that the grave injuries to states and inhabitants should be rectified."[51]

The following August, the use of the first atomic bomb on the Japanese city of Hiroshima aroused Kennedy to an effort to avert what he considered a gross, senseless injustice. He and his friend Henry Luce called on Cardinal Spellman, who wrote in his diary on August 8: "Russia declares war on Japan. Harry Luce and Joe Kennedy came to see me to ask if I would ask President Truman for five or six days' truce to give Japan a chance to surrender."[52]

The press still kept alive Kennedy's controversial reputation. Irritated by the sniping of hostile journalists, he granted his old friend Joe Dinneen, of the *Boston Globe,* a private interview in May, 1944. Dinneen brought along a colleague, Lawrence Spivak, then editor of *The American Mercury.* The session, in Kennedy's suite in Boston's Ritz-Carlton Hotel, lasted two hours and covered a wide range of topics. Dinneen, a shorthand expert ("the only person who ever beat me was Billy Rose"), was able to take down Kennedy's remarks verbatim.[53] Spivak made no notes—and later would greatly regret his oversight.

During the interview, Dinneen repeated accusations frequently made against Kennedy. "They say you're a fascist," said Dinneen. Kennedy replied that "the word can mean anything today and it is applied to almost anybody." He went on to assert: "There nothing in my life or record that will support it."

The next question concerned an accusation that had plagued Kennedy for years, and one that would continue to trouble many Americans. "They say that you're a Jew hater and a Jew baiter," said Dinneen. "And that goes hand in glove today with modern fascism." Kennedy replied at length:

Who says it? And where do they get the idea? It is true that I have a low opinion of some Jews in public office and in private life. That does not mean that I hate all Jews; that I believe they should be wiped off the face of the earth; or that I favor pogroms or persecutions. I don't. It was inevitable that I should find myself in conflict at times with Jews. I do, and have done, business with them. I can show you the names of Jews on my own books; Jews whom I have carried for years. They're all right. They're good businessmen.

Anti-Semitism is their fight—just as anti-Irishism was my fight and the fight of my fathers in this country; and I'm sorry to say that many of them actually promote anti-Semitism in their very efforts to combat it. I'm sorry to say that there are, in my opinion, Jews who actually exploit anti-Semitism. I have never before discussed anti-Semitism in public, because I could never see how it would be helpful. Whenever I have been asked for a statement condemning anti-Semitism, I have answered: "What good would it do?" If the Jews themselves would pay less attention to advertising their racial problem, and more attention to solving it, the whole thing would recede into its proper perspective. It's entirely out of focus now, and that is chiefly their fault.

The cure of anti-Semitism is education. They know that as well as I do. And the Jews must be the educators. Other races have their own problems to solve. They're glad to give the Jews a lift and help them along the way toward tolerance, but they're not going to drop everything and solve the problems of the Jews for them. Jews who take an unfair advantage of the fact that theirs is a persecuted race do not help much.

If a Jew enters public life, he becomes a target for public criticism. That's the normal, American way. Too often, if he is criticized, he ascribes it to anti-Semitism, when the bald fact is that the person is being criticized and not the race. It is no secret that I have not a high opinion of Felix Frankfurter—or of Henry Morgenthau, Jr., or of a number of Jews in high places; but that doesn't mean that I condemn all Jews because of my personal feelings for some. There are more of them in high places than there ever have been before, and it naturally follows that there is more criticism of them. They've got to be able to take that criticism. They've got to be able to answer it. And the answer is not a charge of anti-Semitism against the critics.

Publicizing unjust attacks upon the Jews may help to cure the injustice, but continually publicizing the whole problem only serves to keep it alive in the public mind. A magazine piece with pictures, extolling the heroism of the Jews in this war, is all right, until it becomes an unexpected argument against anti-Semitism, and then a reader of Irish, Swedish or Italian descent, reacts immediately by saying: "True; but what about us?" Each race can make out a flattering record in this war. I happen to be proud of the record of the Irish. Pride in race is a poor weapon to use in fighting anti-Semitism. I try to see the whole problem in its proper perspective. If that's anti-Semitism, then I don't understand the word. That's the way I feel about it. At least, they can never call me a hypocrite.

On the testimony of friends, some of them Jews, Kennedy was neither a hypocrite nor an anti-Semite. Despite his antipathy toward Morgenthau, whose job he badly wanted, Kennedy often walked and chatted with him in the small park behind the Treasury Building in Washington. One summer during the thirties, Morgenthau was planning to vacation on Cape Cod and asked Kennedy's help in arranging a guest membership at the golf club in Wianno. Kennedy proposed him, but Morgenthau was turned down. Twenty years later, Kennedy would say: "I haven't been in the place since." Similarly, in Florida, he did not patronize the exclusive Everglades Club, "even though I got their real estate deal for them." Kennedy played instead at the golf club near his home, and boasted of being "the only Christian member."[54]

Still, Kennedy offended many because he habitually sprinkled his conversation with crude racial epithets—"sheeny," "kike," "wop," and, impartially, "mick" for his fellow Irishmen. He was a man of emphatic, rather than enlightened, opinions.

In 1944, the *Boston Globe* decided not to print Kennedy's remarks on his alleged anti-Semitism and Joe Dinneen filed this portion of his story away. In 1959, he used three paragraphs of the material in his book, *The Kennedy Family*. At the Copley-Plaza in Boston one evening in 1959, Dinneen, as a courtesy, gave a set of the galley proofs of his book to Jack Kennedy, who was about to leave on a campaign trip to the West Coast. Several days later, Dinneen received a telephone call from Oregon.

"You've got to take out those three paragraphs," Jack said.

Dinneen explained that, since he had seen him, the galleys had been returned to his publisher, Little, Brown and Company, and plates of the book had been prepared. It was too late to make any changes.

"I don't give a damn," said Jack, "I want those paragraphs out of there."[55]

Dinneen argued that the elder Kennedy didn't care whether his views were published. But the candidate did care and was adamant. Finally, Dinneen consented to the deletion. He asked his publisher to remove the offending paragraphs and substitute three that he wrote to fit the space.[56] (These appear on pages 104 and 105 of *The Kennedy Family,* as an aside in Dinneen's account of the 1944 interview.) After two decades, Joe Kennedy's answer to the whispers finally has been put on the record.

Just before the war ended in 1945, Kennedy emerged from exile and returned to public life, not in frantically busy Washington, but in drowsy, provincial Massachusetts. At the invitation of Governor Maurice J. Tobin, he agreed to serve as chairman of a commission to study the establishment of a state department of commerce. The Bay State, her industry long in decline, had reversed the trend during the war boom, but an agonizing reconversion loomed with the approach of peace. In announcing Kennedy's appointment, young Governor Tobin hailed him as "one of the country's shrewdest businessmen."[57] However, when Kennedy predicted Massachusetts had only five years in which to escape a yawning economic grave, the alarmed lieutenant governor labeled him a "Jeremiah."[58]

The return of the long-absent native inspired journalists to search for literary analogies. "In a midnight blue Chrysler," reported *Time,* "he rode like a Paul Revere through the textile, shoe and machinery producing towns in Middlesex, Essex and Berkshire counties."[59] On his whirlwind tour of inspection and exhortation, he gave some thirty speeches within ten days, telling businessmen: "I'm willing to come back to live because this is where my heart is. But I don't expect to come back to stay until I think there has been a change for the better."[60] Commented his friend Bill Cunningham, in the *Boston Herald:* "His story is that he had to leave Boston to make good. . . . Kennedy's preaching out of the past, but the strange part of it is that he's likely to find himself a Pied Piper of the future."[61]

Not everyone rushed to form ranks behind Kennedy. Skeptical Yankees pointed out that his heart might belong to Massachusetts, but his money recently had gone to Chicago for the purchase of the Merchandise Mart. Why hadn't he invested in his beloved Boston? "Because," Kennedy retorted, "the condition of real estate in Boston is scandalous and that of politics is worse. The only property offered to me in Boston was a building in bad condition that was 20 percent vacant."[62]

Kennedy had not come home merely to help lift Massachusetts by her bootstraps or to debate the merits of his investments. He had returned mainly to reintroduce the name of Kennedy. Henceforth his business would be politics.

In 1945, if anyone had dared ask his opinion, Kennedy probably would have conceded, sadly but with unsparing realism, that his name was not widely known in America. To be sure, he was known to most of the relatively few people in the country whom *he* thought were important, the leaders in government, business and industry, finance, and the press; they had a sophisticated respect for the influence he wielded through his fortune. But the public generally was unaware of Kennedy. Those who did recognize his name placed him as a wealthy former ambassador, a vague identification fitting a number of large contributors to the Democratic party. The distinction still conferred on him by the honorary title of "Ambassador" was not without drawbacks; for one thing, it served as a reminder of the unpopular opinions that had brought his public career to an end. An empty title and the notoriety bestowed by riches could not satisfy his hunger for prestige. On the contrary, he was gnawed by the realization that his name, already half-forgotten, was passing into obscurity.

Yet his name, Kennedy often said, was the greatest part of his legacy to his children. Despite his millions, he could not by himself restore their depleted inheritance. If the name of Kennedy was to regain prominence, it would be through the rising generation, for whom time and opportunity were plentiful.

For a man approaching sixty, usually an age of consolidation, the steep path toward the summit might have proved impossibly strenuous, except for a pair of factors. Few wealthy men ever approached Kennedy's mastery of the techniques of using money to satisfy personal ambition. Men who possessed the talent for piling up riches through aggressive investment often were hesitant about using their riches for self-aggrandizement. Kennedy knew the price of his social and political aspirations and never shrank from committing the sum required.

But money was the lesser factor in Kennedy's favor. It was evident to him that politics alone gave access to the power on which lasting fame could be founded. This was a demanding route; regardless of his determination and the thrust of his massed dollars, he himself could not make the journey. Beyond number were the tales of rich, strong-willed fathers who had failed pathetically in attempts to push their inadequate heirs to the heights. But Kennedy had reared sons who were capable of seizing the advantages he provided. His would be the driving will, theirs the legs that would go the distance.

Following his discharge from the Navy in March, 1945, Jack Kennedy gravitated toward the only occupation for which he had some training and credentials—writing. Through friends of his father, he joined Hearst's International News Service as a special correspondent. He covered the founding of the United Nations in San Francisco, reporting on the conference "from a GI viewpoint," and later went to England, where he saw Churchill rudely toppled by a war-weary British electorate. These were choice assignments for a neophyte journalist, but Jack found reporting too "passive" and his editors were unimpressed with his stilted copy. He soon drifted out of journalism and began thinking about a career as a college teacher, but that meant a return to academic discipline and years of additional study, an unpalatable prospect for a restless young man.

His entry into politics as young Joe's replacement probably was inevitable, although he and his father later would make it sound like the result of a dramatic command decision. "I got Jack into politics, I was the one," Joe Kennedy told an interviewer many years afterward. "I told him Joe was dead and that it was therefore his responsibility to run for Congress. He didn't want to. He felt he didn't have the ability and he still feels that way. But I told him he had to."[63] Jack himself told a friendly newspaperman: "It was like being drafted. My father wanted his eldest son in politics. 'Wanted' isn't the right word. He demanded it. You know my father."[64]

Political opponents would depict Jack Kennedy as a puppet dancing under the hands of a ruthless, dictatorial parent whose ambitions he had been forced to fulfill. But this "puppetmaster" theory said more about Joe Kennedy's egotism and his son's self-mocking quality than about what actually happened. By a gradual process that involved little self-denial, Jack came to agree with his father's wish that he enter politics. After all, there was no compelling reason why he should *not;* he had been taught since childhood that he must do something worthwhile with his life. Responding both to his father's urgings and to the promise of stimulation, he accepted the career held out to him. However narrow his choice, it was to prove a satisfying one. For he would discover in politics an animating purpose—to win.

CHAPTER 22

Home Base

WHEN Jack Kennedy came to Boston in mid-1945 to launch his political career, he was a stranger in the city of his birth. Almost the only person he knew there, he later would recall half seriously, was "Grampa Fitz," then eighty-three and living in retirement in the Hotel Bellvue, a politicians' hangout near the State House on Beacon Hill. Jack, too, moved into the Bellvue, but not to sit at the feet of "Honey Fitz" and his garrulous cronies. As usual, the elder to whom Jack listened most attentively was his father, who soon established himself in a suite at the Ritz-Carlton.

Though the Kennedys had been absent from Boston for two decades, their local fame had grown. The city's parochial press had chronicled every step of Joe Kennedy's career, particularly his giant stride to London. Indeed, the nonresident Kennedys sentimentally were regarded as the city's leading Irish family. To be sure, some members of the inbred political fraternity, when informed that "young John" would seek public office, spoke scornfully of the arrivals from Florida as "carpetbaggers." But the general response was one of hearty welcome, with an especially cordial greeting from the ranking office-holder of the commonwealth, Governor Tobin.

Facing a tough reelection fight, Tobin thought the Ambassador's handsome, war-hero son would make an attractive running mate. He flew to Palm Beach during the winter and proposed that Jack join the state Democratic ticket as the candidate for lieutenant governor. The office was an obvious steppingstone to the governorship, but Joe Kennedy at length decided to reject the proposal. Inflation, shortages, and unemployment were spreading discontent among the nation's voters, which spelled trouble for Democrats running for state offices in "swing" states like Massachusetts. His judgment was sound; on election day, Tobin went down to defeat.[1]

The question of which office Jack should seek was decided, ironically enough, by "Honey Fitz's" old archenemy, James Michael Curley.* Boston's most celebrated scoundrel had fallen on evil days. Found guilty of fraud, he was forced to repay the city forty-two thousand dollars, which left him broke. Several attempts at a comeback were thwarted by younger candidates with greater appeal to a new generation of voters. Finally, in 1942, he had managed to win a seat in Congress. But a life of obscurity as just another lawmaker in Washington was not to Curley's taste. The aging "Purple Shamrock" yearned to recapture the mayorship of Boston and resume his role of all-powerful municipal lawgiver. In the fall of 1945, the voters granted his wish and restored "himself" to his old throne at city hall.[3]

This created a vacancy in the office of U.S. Representative for the Eleventh Congressional District of Massachusetts. After careful study, Kennedy and his son agreed this was the opportunity they had been seeking. Misshapen by repeated gerrymandering, the Eleventh District

*In July, 1917, Curley, then Mayor of Boston, was hotly attacked by Fitzgerald, his challenger in the forthcoming election, for permitting an antiwar socialist parade and meeting. Replied the incomparable Curley in the next morning's newspaper: "... the frothing of a certain person on Boston Common last evening was not directed against me personally ... but was with a view to stifling free speech in general, as a measure of personal protection from the truth, which in its nakedness is sometimes hideous though necessary.

"I am preparing three addresses which, if necessary, I shall deliver in the fall, and which, if a certain individual had the right to restrict free speech, I would not be permitted to deliver.

"One of these addresses is entitled: 'Graft, Ancient and Modern,' another, 'Great Lovers: From Cleopatra to Toodles,' and last, but not least interesting, 'Libertines: From Henry VIII to the Present Day.' "

Fitzgerald, alarmed at the prospect of plain speaking on the subject of Miss "Toodles" Ryan, discreetly withdrew from the race.[2]

sprawled across East Boston, the North and West End, and then over the Charles River into Charlestown, Cambridge, and part of Somerville. The poor, slum-ridden district was unshakably Democratic, but the party consisted of warring Irish and Italian factions, ruled by petty satraps. There was no district-wide organization, no single boss who could mobilize the polyglot voting population. Thus, the Democratic primary in June, the only election that mattered, promised to be a wild free-for-all. By April, ten candidates had announced.

In addition to his family's matchless financial resources, Jack enjoyed the advantage of impersonal fame. While he was unknown to the voters, his grandfathers were well remembered in the district that embraced their old bailiwicks, and everyone had heard of Ambassador Kennedy. Informed that John Fitzgerald Kennedy had entered the race for his vacant seat, Mayor Curley remarked that a candidate blessed with such a double-barreled name could forget campaigning and proceed at once to Washington.

However, no matter how broad the coattails of preceding generations, Jack's election was not assured. It was by no means certain that the voters in the working-class district, accustomed to the derby-wearing, backslapping breed of "pol," would accept the wealthy young newcomer. His siege of malaria had left him drawn and emaciated, making him appear even younger than his twenty-eight years. With his air of diffidence and his Harvard *a*, he looked and sounded like a graduate student who had strayed absentmindedly from cloistered Harvard into the strange environment of the Boston slums. His world of exclusive schools, trips abroad, debutante parties, and weekends in the country was remote from this dreary world of monotonous drudgery, crowded tenements, and Saturday night drinking bouts. As he climbed rickety stairs and poked into dark, noisome corners, seeking out his prospective constituency, he encountered endless and not very pleasant surprises. It was a revelation to him, his guide later recalled, that the gas stove and the toilet actually could be in the same bleak room.

As Jack doggedly knocked on doors, shook hands and made small talk, he may have thought how effortlessly his dead brother would have performed these chores that he found so difficult and distasteful. Assailed by doubts and full of apologies, he often confided to campaign workers: "I'm just filling Joe's shoes. If he were alive, I'd never be in this."[4]

Yet he was more than the driven proxy for the ambitions of others. No less than his gregarious brother, shy, reserved Jack was the heir to the family's rich political tradition. And he was proud, as all Kennedys were proud. Whatever his sense of obligation, he wanted to win for himself. Beginning his campaign months before his opponents, he slowly gained poise and self-confidence. The process of self-discovery, begun in the South Pacific, continued to unfold in the daily round of campaigning.

One day that spring, Frank Morrissey and Joe Kennedy drove over to Maverick Square in East Boston, once the center of Pat Kennedy's Irish stronghold, but now at the heart of an Italian ghetto. Swarthy men congregated on the sidewalk, coat collars turned up, hands jammed in their pockets, wide-brimmed hats pulled low over expressionless faces. As Kennedy watched from across the street, his gangling, shock-haired son arrived and walked through the distrustful group, thrusting out his hand, introducing himself, and asking for their votes. In a few moments, he was winning smiles and friendly replies.

"I never thought Jack had it in him," said an astonished Joe Kennedy.[5]

No one, least of all the candidate, could forget for a moment the powerful figure in the background. A taunting opponent in the primary dubbed Jack "the poor little rich kid." Rumor had it that Joe Kennedy was boasting he could elect his chauffeur to Congress with all the money he was spending.[6] Asked years afterward what he had done to help his son, Kennedy replied: "I just called people. I got in touch with people I knew. I have a lot of contacts. I've been in politics in Massachusetts since I was ten."[7]

The telephone was the instrument and symbol of Kennedy's power. That a man of his enormous wealth enjoyed influence was not unusual; but the scope of his influence was extraordinary. Absorbed in national politics and diplomacy over the past decade, he had ignored Boston's inconsequential politics. But in that city, as everywhere he moved, he kept a mental inventory of people who had been, or could be, useful to him. On his return, he knew precisely whom to call to move the levers of local political power.

At the outset, it was necessary to correct an oversight. Someone discovered that Jack Kennedy was not an enrolled Democrat. While in the service, he had cast absentee ballots from various naval stations, but had never appeared in person, as Massachusetts law specifically required, to enroll in the party of his choice. The law said a candidate must be a certified party member for at least twenty days before the filing deadline for the primary, which in this case was April 30. Fortunately for Jack Kennedy, his oversight was caught in the final week in which he could satisfy the law's clear and inflexible requirement. On April 3, the would-be Democratic standard-bearer in the Eleventh District quietly slipped into City Hall and enrolled as a Democrat.[8]

Jack's campaign had two separate and distinct sides. On display before the voters was the candidate, surrounded by clean-cut, youthful volunteer workers, some of them college chums and Navy buddies, the total effect being one of wholesome amateurism. But the appealing contrast with the ward-heeling professionalism of much of the opposition was more apparent than real. At work on the hidden side of the campaign were the professional politicians whom Joe Kennedy quietly had recruited. In his hotel suite and other private meeting places, they sat with their hats on and cigars aglow, a hard-eyed, cynical band, brainstorming strategy. Kennedy's cousin, Joe Kane, a veteran of forty years of political warfare in Massachusetts, came up with a campaign slogan and theme: "The New Generation Offers a Leader."

This theme perfectly fitted the "image" of the campaign, but Joe Kennedy believed the new generation's leader also should know something of old-fashioned practical politics. He assigned Kane to tutor his son. During one session, "Honey Fitz," the intentionally neglected elder statesman, ambled into the room. Kane spotted him and shouted to a henchman:

"Get that son-of-a-bitch out of here!"

Young Jack looked startled. "Who? *Grampa?*"

Out went Grampa. Hearing of the incident later, Joe Kennedy smiled and told his son that he would not have lasted three hours in the campaign with "Honey Fitz" calling the signals.[9]

The command post of the campaign was Kennedy's suite at the Ritz. There, he personally interviewed key workers recruited by his son; no one was officially "in" until the Ambassador gave his approval. Even then, certain aspects of the campaign were off limits to all outsiders. A young Navy veteran and lawyer, Mark Dalton, whose family was well-known in the district, took up the duties of campaign manager. But neither Dalton nor any other stranger was permitted to handle Joe Kennedy's money. Campaign funds were doled out by Kennedy's business associate, John Ford. "Regardless of how many young guys were picked up by the Kennedys," a worker recalled, "Joe always saw to it that every cent of campaign money was in the hands of old-timers."[10]

Nothing seemed to escape the elder Kennedy's attention. Frank Morrissey dropped by headquarters daily, and was regarded by the younger workers as the Ambassador's "spy." Two or three times a week, Kennedy telephoned Dalton and demanded a detailed briefing on every facet of the campaign, interspersing his questions with terse commands. All plans and arrangements were subject to change at his order. Late one night, the candidate and his manager sat in Kennedy's suite, discussing the evening's speech-making. Dalton, an accomplished speaker, had given Jack a rousing introduction, a more striking performance, actually, than the halting speech that followed. Joe Kennedy complimented Dalton, then laid down the law: the two would not speak again on the same platform; the manager was taking the spotlight away from the candidate.[11]

Kennedy's concern would have amused the other candidates in the primary. So far as they could tell, the Kennedys appeared to own the spotlight of newspaper publicity. Partly, the blanket coverage Jack received was the natural result of having a name that made news. But partly, too, it was the result of having an influential father who spent hours on the telephone talking to political writers and editors. Kennedy not only expertly picked their brains ("What do you think?" "What do you hear?"); he also traded confidences and asked favors.[12]

The free newspaper publicity supplemented the most elaborate professional advertising effort ever seen in a Massachusetts congressional election. Once again, the son was the beneficiary of the father's shrewdness and foresight. While in the liquor business, Joe Kennedy had acquired the franchise for Riondo Rum, but instead of turning the account over to Somerset's large New York advertising agency, he chose a smaller Boston agency. Thereafter the John C. Dowd Agency became in effect Kennedy's personal public relations organization. Ambitious "Jack" Dowd had further cause to be grateful to the Ambassador when the latter helped him arrange a merger with a New York agency.[13] The Dowd agency wrote speeches and handled public relations for Kennedy's campaign to rehabilitate Massachusetts' industry. One day in 1945, Dowd came to Kennedy with a request for a speech, but the Ambassador declined. "No more speeches for me," he said. "Jack's going into politics."[14]

The voters of the district were saturated with Kennedy advertising—billboards, posters, car cards, leaflets, and radio "spots." The people, a campaign worker remembered, "saw Kennedy, heard Kennedy, ate Kennedy, drank Kennedy, slept Kennedy, and Kennedy talked and we talked Kennedy all day long. . . . He was well advertised."[15]

Opinion polling, a costly luxury at the level of a congressional primary, was used extensively, for Joe Kennedy had great respect for black, emotionless numbers. During the campaign, the *Boston Post* published a poll that showed Jack Kennedy receiving almost as many votes as his nine opponents combined. His father, skeptical of this statistical landslide, hurried down to the newspaper office and pored over the data. It seemed much too optimistic, so he decided to double check as only he could. He telephoned his friend, Joe Patterson, publisher of the *New York Daily News,* and borrowed the crew that conducted the newspaper's famous "straw polls." Flown to Boston, the *Daily News'* expert canvassers fanned out through the Eleventh District as though testing the fortunes of a presidential hopeful. Their findings confirmed those of the *Post:* Jack Kennedy was far out in front.[16]

What had put him there? "It takes three things to win," the preceptor, Joe Kane, liked to observe. "The first is money and the second is money and the third is money."[17] Joe Kennedy was rumored to be spending upward of a quarter of a million dollars on the campaign. An insider later estimated the actual outlay at perhaps one-fifth that amount, still far more than any opponent. A smoothly efficient organization planned and executed every phase of the Kennedy campaign—e.g., volunteer hostesses at Kennedy house parties were provided with cups and saucers, coffee and cookies, silver and flowers. Tight scheduling enabled the candidate to appear at as many as half a dozen such parties in an evening. The name of every person who attended was forwarded to headquarters, and volunteers wrote and telephoned to solicit their help.

But the money so freely spent and the work so flawlessly done were not decisive. In the final analysis, the candidate owed his long lead to himself. His injured back laced in a brace, his thoughts on the steaming bath at day's end that would ease his pain, Jack campaigned fourteen hours a day. And yet it was not really as a politician that he was sweeping the field. Although his speaking ability improved steadily, his message was predictable. He stuck to the staple topics of bread-and-butter liberalism—jobs, housing, lower rents and prices, veterans' benefits and social security. Even on this safe ground, he was cautious and noncommittal. At a meeting of the Harvard Liberal Union during the campaign, a Radcliffe girl asked the speaker, former Congressman Thomas H. Eliot, whether Kennedy would make "the kind of progressive representative we're working for." Replied Eliot: "I spoke with Jack for about three hours the other afternoon on some of the issues facing this country—and I don't really think I'm qualified to answer your question."[18]

The excitement Jack Kennedy kindled in bright-eyed volunteers and the enthusiasm he evoked in audiences had little to do with what he said, almost everything to do with who he was. He was a Kennedy and therefore a celebrity. Although they had heard of the famous family, few of the voters in the district, particularly among the younger generation, had ever seen a Kennedy at close range. To grant the small favor of a vote to the candidate who had everything was a rare satisfaction.

He was very young and perhaps overeducated, but his heroic war record marked him as a man among men. Wage earners who would have balked at backing a millionaire crossed jealously drawn class lines to support the skipper of PT-109. Early in the campaign, one of Joe Kennedy's polls disclosed keen popular interest in his son's war exploits. A standard nonpolitical speech was prepared for delivery before religious and fraternal organizations. In telling the story, Jack modestly referred to himself in the third person and emphasized the bravery of his crew.

Although the Kennedys were celebrities, they were engagingly democratic. Voters were startled (and flattered) to answer the doorbell and find one of the Kennedy girls, Eunice, Pat, or Jean, flashing a smile and holding out her brother's campaign brochure. Twenty-year-old Bobby, just out of the Navy, was assigned to run a campaign office deep behind enemy lines, in the tough neighborhood of East Cambridge. It was hoped that he might cut the expected vote against

Jack from five-to-one to four-to-one. Bobby ranged through the Italian neighborhood shaking hands and eating spaghetti, but his reputation as "a regular guy" was sealed when he deserted his office to play softball with the kids in a park across the street. The returns from Cambridge would show Jack Kennedy running neck and neck with the local favorite, Mayor Mike Neville.

This show of strength could be traced to a remarkable social event one evening at the Hotel Commander in Cambridge. The inspiration of a group of women volunteers at Kennedy headquarters, it amused the professionals no end. To every name on the voting list was sent a hand-addressed engraved invitation, requesting the pleasure of the recipient's presence at a formal reception and tea honoring the candidate and his family. Who, the pros demanded, had ever heard of asking the voters to dress up to be presented to a candidate as though he were royalty? With this high-hat gesture, the sages at the Bellvue agreed, the Kennedys had outsmarted themselves. The evening of the reception was unseasonably hot, but fifteen hundred voters, most of them women in their best gowns, showed up at the Hotel Commander. They formed a queue extending through the hotel lobby, across the street, and into a nearby park. At the head of the receiving line, dressed in white tie and tails, stood the former Ambassador to the Court of St. James's, making his first and last political appearance for his son.[19]

From that evening on, the formal reception became a standard feature of Kennedy campaigns, for the inspiration of the amateurs rested on brilliant political psychology. "That reception was the clincher," said William McMasters, the veteran Cambridge politician who managed Mayor Neville's campaign. "Everybody wanted to be in Society with the Kennedys."[20]

The irony was that the Kennedys themselves were still rejected by old Boston's Society, and still felt the rebuff keenly. One day when Jack was a student at Harvard, he had been picked up by his family for the ride home to New York, and had brought along a classmate who was from one of Boston's loftiest families. During the ride, Rose Kennedy turned to her son's friend and, with a note of desperation in her voice, said: "Tell me, when are the nice people of Boston going to accept us?"[21]

To the housewives of Cambridge in their wilted finery, meeting the Kennedys for tea seemed a sweet, if short-lived, arrival. To the parents of the candidate, arm-weary and determinedly smiling, it was but another step on their arduous climb toward eminence the "nice people" could not ignore.

True to the pollsters' predictions, Jack scored a smashing victory in the primary. Almost doubling the vote of runner-up Mike Neville, he took more than 40 percent of the ballots cast, an arresting feat in a ten-man race. Against his father's advice that he had "peaked" and should ease up, he campaigned right up to the last minute. As the returns came in, Joe Kennedy stood in a corner apart from the self-possessed candidate and his jubilant supporters, a proud, quietly happy onlooker. It remained for the irrepressible "Honey Fitz" to climb on a table and celebrate by dancing a stiff-legged jig and singing "Sweet Adeline." That was the swan song of an era in Boston politics. The tough, gaudy old pros had raised their last hurrah.

Campaigning in leisurely fashion, Jack beat his hapless Republican opponent in the November election by better than two-to-one. However, the trip to Washington to claim his seat in Congress was anticlimactic. Just as he had striven to win as a child mainly because he thereby won his father's esteem, so victory in the election had been an end in itself. Committed to no program and lacking a political philosophy, he easily became annoyed at attempts to label him "liberal" or "conservative," and finally insisted on being called simply a "Massachusetts Democrat." One interviewer, an earnest young liberal on the Harvard *Crimson,* afterward wrote: "Kennedy seems to feel honestly that he is not hedging . . . by refusing to offer a positive specific program. He feigns an ignorance of much in the affairs of government and tells you to look at his record in two years to see what he stands for."[22]

In two years (or four or six, for that matter), the only accurate label for Kennedy would remain the one he had chosen. He voted the interests of his working-class constituency in the Eleventh District of Massachusetts, siding with House liberals on Fair Deal measures appealing to low-income voters, switching to the conservative side on foreign policy issues. His was a voting record calculated to please his poor, predominantly Catholic, strongly anti-Communist electorate. Later, when a more consistently liberal "image" became necessary to fulfill wider ambitions, he offered various excuses and explanations for his early wobbling. One in particular had the ring of truth: "I'd just come out of my father's house at the time, and these were the things I knew."[23]

The opinions Jack heard from his father in the latter half of the 1940's were vociferously conservative. Vanished without a trace was the enlightened liberal capitalist, the admiring New Dealer who had written *I'm for Roosevelt.* Now Joe Kennedy outdid veteran opponents of the New Deal in condemning the overgrown federal government and the stealthy advance of socialism.

In October, 1945, addressing five hundred Boy Scout leaders on Long Island, he warned against a power-hungry state that was bent on "reducing men to mere ciphers and substituting state-disciplined loyalties for individual dignity." Attacking the "Santa Claus" concept of government, he declared: "The state means to most untrained minds some vast, nebulous institution which will somehow or other assume all the burdens of life and support the individual who lacks the ambition or energy to support himself."[24] Speaking the following month at a youth conference in New York's Madison Square Garden, Kennedy called attention to "the political enemies among us—the shock troops of European ideologists" who were invading Washington. He went on to express distress at "how often our schools and colleges have been the hotbeds of alien political ideas." "Don't listen to these sirens of state socialism," he exhorted his audience.[25]

The onetime critic of the big business Establishment now vigorously championed the free enterprise system against government intervention. "Whether we keep our free economy or trade it for something about which we know very little is the big political issue ahead," he told one thousand listeners at a dinner meeting of the Chicago Economic Club in December, 1945. "It is up to businessmen to sell our economic system to the public. They must do as good a job on that as they do on their own products. Unless the advantages of our system over others are brought home to everyone, there is no reason to believe that the trend toward more and more government will be checked."

His urgent admonition was prompted by the statement of Harold J. Laski, chairman of the British Labour Party, that capitalism was dead in America, and should be replaced with some form of socialism. Kennedy angrily denounced his sons' former tutor. "How can Laski have the gall to assert that capitalism is dead when the British empire has been twice saved in thirty years by the capitalistic United States. I know Laski and he is an arrogant apostle of anarchy who has spent his time shuttling between Moscow, London and New Haven peddling his particular brand of socialism." In his peroration, Kennedy said the public was "confused about the major issues today both in international and domestic fields," and gave businessmen the task of spreading enlightenment. "It is the last chance for those who believe in our system of constitutional government. We must win now or the cause is lost."[26]

Early in 1946, Kennedy attempted to define the fundamental tenets of America's postwar foreign policy in an article published in *Life* magazine. As he saw it, the cardinal objective was the prevention of World War III. Criticizing the hasty demobilization of the victorious U.S. armed forces, he urged the rapid rebuilding of a strong, permanent military establishment. He advocated close cooperation with Great Britain, support of Nationalist China, and encouragement of a Western European bloc. He cautioned against "minding other people's business on a global scale," and against wishful thinking about the peace-keeping effectiveness of the newly formed United Nations, which was all too clearly divided within itself. Finally, he called for a policy of "brutal realism" toward the Soviet Union. His "realism" consisted of drawing lines that the Communists would cross at increasing peril to themselves. War, they would be forewarned, was a certainty in the event of aggression against the U.S. sphere of the world.[27]

Considering the temper of the time, this counsel, amounting to a call for "containment," was sound and much needed. Many of America's opinion-molders were still living in the dream world created by the U.S.-Soviet wartime alliance. While the Kremlin cooed of "peace" and lulled the self-deceived, Communists everywhere were waging political warfare. In the flush of victory over the Axis, Americans had had enough of crusading, and craved peace, nylons, and new automobiles. Those in Washington who foresaw the coming struggle felt almost powerless against the weight of apathy and pro-Soviet propaganda. Chief among this lonely company was Kennedy's friend, James Forrestal, whose congratulatory wire ("THE NAVY IS PROUD OF YOU") hung prominently on Congressman Jack Kennedy's office wall.

Soon to become the first Secretary of Defense, Forrestal wrote in a letter during the spring of 1946: "In my opinion we are now facing a far more serious business than we ever faced in the thirties. I hope it is not too late to deal with it."[28] Trying to deal with it, while fighting a losing inner battle, eventually would drive Forrestal to suicide.

In the early postwar period, there were fresh reports that Kennedy would return to the government. In March, 1946, he was mentioned in the *Boston Globe* as a possible Under Secretary of the Navy. That June, after the presidency of the International Bank for Reconstruction and Development had been vacant for several months, Democratic National Chairman Robert E. Hannegan began boosting Kennedy for the post. But Roosevelt's old ally, Secretary of State Jimmy Byrnes, quickly deflated the boom, and Eugene Meyer, owner of the *Washington Post,* was chosen.[29]

Probably it was just as well that Kennedy remained a private citizen. As a public man, he might well have embarrassed his son. While it was true that he saw the Soviet threat early, this was because he had never lost sight of it. Before the war, he had feared Moscow more than Berlin; the world had changed, but his thinking was essentially unchanged. Some listeners had difficulty deciding precisely what his thinking was. Both supporters and opponents of the $3,750,000,000 U.S. credit to Great Britain claimed the former Ambassador as a sympathizer. Finally, Kennedy declared that he favored giving the aid as "an outright gift" and forgetting about repayment. "I agree, it is true, with virtually everything said by those in both countries who oppose a British loan as formulated by the United States Government," he said in a statement to *The New York Times.* "The United Kingdom fought from 1939 to 1942 to save its own skin. . . . So we owe the British nothing on that basis. But we have already spent about $200 billions in a war we were told would save civilization. And we had better give another $4 billions to that end, even though we can ill afford to do that. . . ."[30]

In May, 1947, Kennedy, in a long, discursive article in Hearst's *New York Journal-American,* argued in dead earnest that the U.S. could best assist countries threatened by communism by concentrating on its own prosperity. He was convinced, he wrote, that "America with its matchless resources, its skills and abilities, has merely to continue to be the land of free enterprise which our forefathers made it in order to attain a lasting prosperity inspiring to the dejected peoples of other nations who are striving to escape political serfdom and attain national independence." Although he sharply attacked "the so-called Truman Doctrine of aid to Greece and Turkey," he confessed that he was "not greatly concerned with the military or political aspects of [such] aid." Declared Kennedy: "The dangers at home are far more real to me. Concretely I regard as dangerous a public policy which rushes headlong into tax burdening expenditures abroad and does nothing to bring about tax relief at home. . . ."[31]

Toward the Marshall Plan of economic aid to war-ravaged Western Europe, Kennedy's attitude was one of critical skepticism and deepening pessimism. The U.S. could not sustain such massive outlays, he warned, and even if it could, the money would be better spent closer to home. On his return from a tour of the Continent in early 1948, his first visit to Europe since leaving London, he reported finding everywhere an "underlying feeling of hopelessness and discontent," the ideal foundation for communism. "To sink billions of dollars into countries which can produce nothing that matters to us, that in the end turn Communist," he said, "is merely to waste our strength." Instead, he would build up the economic strength and self-sufficiency of the Western Hemisphere.[32]

As Kennedy rephrased his prewar isolationist views, he drew the fire of liberal internationalists, notably the then youthful Harvard Hotspur, Professor Arthur M. Schlesinger, Jr. "Even in America, the capitalist fatherland," wrote Schlesinger in *Partisan Review*, "the death wish of the business community appears to go beyond the normal limits of political incompetence. . . . The foreign policy of the business community is characteristically one of cowardice rationalized in terms of high morality. The great refusal to take on the Russians today is perfectly typical. That *doyen* of American capitalists, Joseph P. Kennedy, recently argued that the United States should not seek to resist the spread of Communism. Indeed, it should 'permit Communism to have its trial outside the Soviet Union if that shall be the fate or the will of certain peoples. . . .' "[33]

Following the outbreak of the Korean War, Kennedy adopted an unequivocally isolationist stance. Clearly audible in his public remarks were echoes of his old defeatist opinions. Indeed, in a speech at the University of Virginia in December, 1950, he drew a tenuous parallel between the U.S. position and that of Britain at the time of Munich.[34] He spoke under the auspices of the Student Forum at the

Law School, and was introduced by his son Bobby, the Forum's president. Describing the foreign policy of the Truman administration as "suicidal," the elder Kennedy said the U.S., like Britain in 1938, was perilously overextended, saddled with commitments that could not be fulfilled even at the cost of the war that these reckless pledges invited. He depicted the U.S. as virtually friendless, the prey of grasping foreigners, all of whom were too indifferent to defend themselves. Americans were dying by the thousands in Korea "to accomplish some unknown objective," while communism was everywhere on the march. "Our policy," cried Kennedy, "is politically and morally a bankrupt policy."

What he proposed, with utter candor, was a policy of wholesale retreat. Dismissing the veto-ridden United Nations as "a hopeless instrumentality" for preserving peace, he said Americans must rely exclusively on their own strength and trim their commitments accordingly. The first step was "to get out of Korea—indeed, to get out of every point in Asia which we do not plan realistically to hold in our own defense." The same principle should be applied to Europe. "Today it is idle to talk of being able to hold the line of the Elbe or the line of the Rhine.... What have we gained by staying in Berlin? Everyone knows we can be pushed out the moment the Russians choose to push us out. Isn't it better to get out now and use the resources, that otherwise would be sacrificed, at a point that counts?"

As in the prewar period, the speaker recognized no vital American interest in the fate of the peoples and resources of Western Europe. By his curious logic, the best hope of defeating communism lay in surrendering Europe. "The truth is that our only real hope is to keep Russia, if she chooses to march, on the other side of the Atlantic, and make Communism much too costly for her to try and cross the seas. It may be that Europe for a decade or a generation or more will turn Communistic. But in doing so, it may break of itself as a united force. Communism still has to prove itself to its peoples as a government that will achieve for them a better way of living.... The more peoples that are under its yoke, the greater are the possibilities of revolt."

Conceding that the policy he had outlined might be attacked as "appeasement," Kennedy insisted that the word would be used mistakenly. "Is it appeasement to withdraw from unwise commitments, to arm yourself to the teeth and to make clear just exactly how and for what you will fight? If it is wise in our interest not to make commitments that endanger our security, and this is appeasement, then I am for appeasement." Yearning for a vanished security, he clung to the odd, self-justifying parallel he had drawn between Chamberlain's England and Truman's America. "I can recall only too well the precious time bought by Chamberlain at Munich. I applauded that purchase then; I would applaud it today. Today, however, while we have avoided a Munich we are coming perilously close to another Dunkirk."

Clearly the opportunity for reflection afforded Kennedy over the past decade had left him more convinced than ever of the rightness of the appeasement policies that his friend Chamberlain had acted upon. Commentators who had disagreed then opposed him now with undiminished ferocity. Wrote Joseph and Stewart Alsop in their syndicated newspaper column: "Back in 1940, Joseph P. Kennedy returned from the London embassy to advocate giving the world to Nazi Germany. He did not put it quite that way, but total triumph for Hitler would still have been the result of his program. In the same manner in 1950, Kennedy has just crawled out of his richly upholstered burrow to advocate giving the world to the Soviet Union. Again, he does not put it quite that way, but his program . . . insures total triumph for Stalin."[35]

The Russians, ever willing to profit by the blindly repeated mistakes of the West, paid the capitalist Kennedy the unusual compliment of reprinting the full text of his speech in *Pravda*.[36]

After helping his son establish a political base in Boston, Kennedy seldom returned to the city, preferring to divide his time between New York and Palm Beach. His life in Florida was pleasant and well ordered. On a typical day, he awoke about seven, ate breakfast in his room, and read his mail and several newspapers before going downstairs around nine-thirty. From mid-morning until noon, he basked in the sun beside the pool, conducting his far-flung business by long distance telephone. Lunch included a special dessert to appease his sweet tooth. Afterward he usually took a half-hour nap, then played a round of golf. In the long, tropical twilight, he might have a drink, but only one. Following an early, well-served dinner, which avoided all dishes that might inflame his ulcer, he watched television or a new movie, and retired well before ten o'clock. Each tranquil day he grew richer.

"I really began to make money," he once told a friend at poolside, "when I came down here to sit on my butt and think."[37]

Understandably, his thoughts often turned from making money to paying taxes. He complained to an acquaintance that taxes were eating up so much of his income that he was forced to dip into his capital to meet living expenses. "And," he added, jabbing an emphatic finger into his listener's shoulder, "there are goddamned few people in this whole world that have a bigger income than I've got."[38] With the assistance of such astute advisers as Jim Landis, Kennedy tried to make the most of opportunities created by the tax laws. "It would have been criminal if a man of his wealth had not taken advantage of the tax laws," said Jim Fayne, another adviser.[39]

As fast as Kennedy moved into real estate in the nineteen forties, he got his money out by mortgaging his properties heavily. Some of the cash generated went into oil ventures offering the tax benefits of depletion allowances. Like many another Eastern investor, he started by joining syndicates backing wildcatters. The famed Kennedy luck ran hot and cold. "Joe had eleven dry holes in a row, then a dozen that hit," recalled an associate.[40]

Kennedy never liked investing with a crowd. In the late forties, he found an arrangement he liked. Transwestern Oil Company, of San Antonio, Texas, had spun off Transwestern Royalty Company, which held producing and nonproducing oil royalties. Transwestern Royalty had been bought by Raymond F. Kravis, a Tulsa petroleum engineer, and the partners of the New York brokerage firm of Reynolds and Company, who promptly split the company between them—Kravis calling his half Roytex, the Reynolds partners naming their half Arctic. When their investment qualified for capital-gains tax treatment, the Reynolds partners put it up for sale. At first they approached a Baptist charitable institution, but when the Baptists dickered too hard, Kravis went to Kennedy and talked him into buying Arctic for some three million dollars. Kravis and Kennedy then liquidated their companies, but retained their royalty interests and gradually went into drilling and exploration.[41]

Thereafter Kennedy steadily acquired other oil and gas interests in Texas. For instance, in 1952, he formed Kenoil, a Houston-based company holding leases, portions of leases, and royalties. Tax advantages lured him into drilling and developing, and he teamed up with John (Jack) Modesett, a Corpus Christi oilman. Kennedy's capital and Modesett's drilling company became the basis for Mokeen Oil Company, Inc., which took its name from the combined names of the partners. (Modesett ran the companies until his death in an automobile accident in April, 1962.) In 1962, Mokeen, described by oilmen as "very aggressive," had estimated sales of three million dollars. In the mid-fifties, Kennedy bought an interest in the Sutton Producing Company, of San Antonio, run by William Franklin (Bill) Sutton, one of the more successful independent operators in South Texas. As in the case of Mokeen, Sutton Producing Company took orders from Kennedy's Park Avenue headquarters in New York, chiefly from Tom Walsh, a tax expert and Kennedy adviser.

Surveying these Kennedy ventures, a Corpus Christi oil executive said: "He hunted up a couple of strong, small drilling companies and went in with them for the tax benefits. In a typical deal, he was allowed to take off, say, 60 percent of the intangible drilling costs, while benefiting by 60 percent interest in the oil they hit. It worked out just fine for him." In addition, his income from oil production benefited from the 27.5 percent depletion allowance.*

For all his postwar success in oil and real estate, Kennedy remained wary of other new risks. Following his term on the Civil Aeronautics Board, Jim Landis tried to interest Kennedy in buying National Airlines, but he wanted no part of operating responsibility or possible labor problems. "He told me that he didn't want his money in troubled places," Landis later recalled. To a proposed apartment building project in Caracas, Venezuela, Kennedy objected: "I'm not going into places I don't know anything about."[42]

In a modest way, Kennedy dabbled at being a sportsman. Although he did most of his wagering at the two-dollar windows, he bought a 17 percent interest in the Hialeah race track from the estate of Colonel E. R. Bradley in 1943, later selling it at a profit. He maintained a nostalgic connection with show business through such friends as actor-producer Eddie Dowling and tenor Morton Downey. In 1943, he

*During the 1960 presidential campaign, Kennedy backers in Texas spread the impression that the Kennedys were extremely heavy investors in oil, and therefore would do nothing to cut the depletion allowance so close to the heart of Texas wealth and political power.

played "angel" for the Broadway comedy "Another Love Story," explaining that he did so out of friendship for playwright Frederick Lonsdale. Kennedy was the not-too-silent financial interest behind the posh Manhattan restaurant, Le Pavillon, run by Henri Soulé; later he also backed the sumptuous La Caravelle.

Kennedy could be generous in business dealings when the mood struck him. Once, Downey outlined a proposition he had been offered. Kennedy said it sounded good and advised him to go ahead.

"But where will I get the seven hundred thousand dollars I need?" asked Downey.

"Send your figures down to my office," said Kennedy. "If they check, you've got the money."

Downey sent the figures and, within twenty-four hours, received a check for $700,000. Kennedy requested no collateral for the loan.[43]

Actually, the transaction involved a trifling sum, by Kennedy's standards. "The Kennedy fortune is different from most others," said Landis. "It isn't paper; it's real. Joe could write a check for nine million dollars just like that."

Even after Jack had gotten started in politics, Kennedy, concerned over his son's back injury, from time to time explored less demanding careers for him. In the late forties, he briefly considered buying the *New York Sun* before it was taken over by Scripps-Howard, and he made an offer for the *Boston Post,* which went instead to speculator John Fox before it folded. "He once had it in the back of his mind that Jack might make an editor," Landis remembered.

Other considerations entered into his thinking. More than a decade after his unsuccessful bid on the *Post,* a friend reminded Kennedy of his interest in buying a newspaper and asked about his plans. "I'm still waiting," he replied. "Economically, Boston is a monopoly newspaper city, like almost every city in this country. The Hearst papers are going to fold within a couple of years, and that will leave the *Globe* and *Herald-Traveler* to fight it out. After they've ruined each other, I'll come in and pick up the winner."[44]

Also in the late forties, Kennedy toyed with the idea of buying the Brooklyn Dodgers baseball team and installing his son as president. When John L. Smith, a leading Dodger stockholder, died in 1947, General Manager Branch Rickey began negotiating with Kennedy to sell him the stock owned by Smith and Rickey. The deal failed to go through because of Kennedy's bearishness; he saw the possibility of a depression and a third world war, calamities which would distract even Dodger fans.[45]

Any initial doubts Kennedy had about Jack making a career of politics were resolved by the ease with which he was reelected without working or campaigning very hard. In 1948, he had no opposition in either the Democratic primary or the general election. Two years later, he faced five opponents in the primary, and rolled up five times their combined vote. That fall, he won over his Republican opponent by almost five-to-one. Jack Kennedy's seat in Congress was "safe" for as long as he cared to occupy it.

During these years, the influence of his father's conservatism could be seen in Jack's voting record and speeches. Even though he was a down-the-line supporter of welfare legislation, he also advocated government economy, fiscal orthodoxy, and restraint on presidential power. ("How long can we continue deficit financing on such a large scale with a national debt of over two hundred and fifty-eight billion dollars?" he demanded of the House in a 1950 debate on the budget.) During the Korean War, he come out strongly for a balanced budget, even though it meant higher taxes. Like his father, he often warned against the specter of inflation. The elder Kennedy served on former President Hoover's commission on government reorganization, winning high praise for his work, and Jack introduced legislation to implement some of the commission's recommendations.

The anti-Roosevelt strain that ran through the father's public addresses also showed up in the son's. "At the Yalta Conference in 1945," Jack said in a Salem, Massachusetts, speech on January 30, 1949, "a sick Roosevelt, with the advice of General Marshall . . . gave the Kurile Island as well as control of various strategic ports . . . to the Soviet Union." Jack bolted his party to vote for the Twenty-second Amendment, limiting the President to two terms, a measure by which frustrated opponents took belated revenge on the dead Roosevelt who had been unbeatable in life. It met with Joe Kennedy's approval. In recalling his first meeting with Joe, columnist Westbrook Pegler, who made an occupation of hating the Roosevelts, wrote in 1961: "My first acquaintance happened on Park Avenue 15 years ago when a stranger stopped me and made some pleasant remark about my dogged attacks on avarice and corruption in the Roosevelt regime and household."

Added the no longer friendly Pegler: "Nowadays, I find myself drawing comparisons between the Kennedys and the Roosevelts to the moral detriment of neither."[46]

The views of the father and son on foreign policy coincided at a few points, but diverged sharply at many others. Thus, while Jack might assert that the U.S. "cannot reform the world," he consistently supported foreign aid programs, provided the Allies bore their share of the burden.

Actually, what Congressman Kennedy thought about foreign aid —or almost anything else, for that matter—was of small consequence. Later in his career, he would recall that "we were just worms over in the House—nobody pays much attention to us nationally."[47] Even if Joe Kennedy's inclination had run in that direction, which it did not, it would hardly have been worth his trouble to dictate his son's position on this bill or that. According to Jack Kennedy's biographer, James MacGregor Burns, "There is little evidence of direct paternal influence on the son's views; his files contain a number of letters from his father, but almost all relate to family and financial matters. His father states flatly today that he never asked his son to vote for or against any bill in Congress."[48]

More meaningful to Kennedy than the stand Jack took on a particular public question was the effect his son's politics had on his overall standing before the voters. His constant fear was that Jack would speak or act impulsively, and thus "hurt" himself—i.e., needlessly damage his popularity. He had been reared in the intensely personal politics of Irish Boston's wards, where the man counted for everything; the issue-centered politics of the New Deal and afterward were alien and unappealing. He railed against expanding government and onrushing socialism, but calmly accepted his son's contrary voting record, for he realized such tactical liberalism was expedient in Jack's district. Joe Kennedy admired well-organized, self-disciplined men who were physically tough and agile of mind; what they thought, or said they thought, could be disregarded. It was more important that his son win elections than that their opinions agree.

Despite his sometimes tyrannical manner, Kennedy's influence on his children had been essentially indirect, mainly by the force of example. Through ruthless independence, he had achieved formidable success, and he encouraged his sons and daughters to be equally self-reliant. Bernard Baruch once cautioned Kennedy against giving his children trust funds, pointing out that it would make them too independent. "They're already independent," said Kennedy.[49] However, while encouraging them to go one way, he forcibly impressed on them the incompleteness of his success, and thus thrust them toward public careers that would bring honors to adorn his name and fortune. Jack, obedient to his father's wish, had taken up his dead brother's career. He did not rebel against this obligation, nor did he break under it. But while the unusual solidarity of the Kennedys, girded by powerful bonds of affection and respect, made possible a joint purpose between the generations, it did not eliminate the son's need to assert his own identity. Slowly, but with quiet determination, Jack eased out of his father's shadow, until the latter, proud of him yet secretly wounded in his own pride, yielded place.

An early public sign of self-assertion on Jack Kennedy's part came in February, 1951. At his own expense, the Congressman had taken a six-week tour of Europe, visiting the chief countries of the North Atlantic Treaty Organization and gathering useful information from a number of government officials. On his return, he was invited to present his on-the-spot observations to a joint meeting of the Senate Committees on Foreign Relations and on Armed Services, then hearing testimony on the proposed assignment of U.S. troops to Europe. He was convinced of the strategic importance of Western Europe and urged that the troops be sent. At the close of Jack's testimony, courtly Senator Walter George peered over his spectacles and said:

"The question I am going to ask you I want to assure you in advance is an impersonal one, although you might at first blush think it is a personal one. . . . You come from a very distinguished American family that exercises a great influence on American public opinion. I want to ask you very impersonally, whether you remember the able speech of your father in December, 1950?"

Whereupon Senator George quoted from the elder Kennedy's address at the University of Virginia, calling for a drastic cutback of U.S. military commitments abroad. The Senator gently inquired whether the son differed with his father. Jack answered diplomatically. After reaffirming his belief that the loss of Europe and its highly developed industrial power would threaten American survival, he conceded the difficulty of swiftly building a strong, unified European military force. He could understand his father's despair. "To him and to a lot of other Americans it looks like an almost hopeless job and that we are committing troops to be lost." But, after weighing all the factors "as cold-bloodedly as I can," he believed it was a risk that should be taken.

"That is my position," he concluded. "I think you should ask my father directly as to his position."[50]

CHAPTER 23

Tea Parties and Old Scores

As early as 1949, Jack Kennedy, though scarcely more than a freshman congressman, began running hard for higher office. It had taken only one term in the House for him to become bored with the tortoiselike pace of the seniority system. Restless and impatient, he found the satisfactions of the settled legislative life distinctly inferior to the excitement of capturing higher rank. What office he wanted, when he would seek it, and who his opponent would be—these questions were left to be decided by future opportunity.

Each Thursday evening, he flew from Washington to Boston, was met at the airport by his office manager, Frank Morrissey, and set off in a chauffeur-driven car for a long weekend of speech-making across the state. On the following Monday evening, the undeclared candidate caught a plane back to the capital and resumed his congressional duties for another three days. As a leading member of the "Tuesday-to-Thursday Club" of Eastern congressmen and a notable absentee, Jack found little time to distinguish himself in the House. But by early 1952, he had crisscrossed Massachusetts dozens of times, introducing the name of Kennedy to voters in almost all of the state's three hundred and fifty-one cities and towns.

When he embarked on this long preliminary campaign, he considered trying for the governorship in 1950, when the Democratic incumbent, Paul Dever, came up for reelection. State issues and politics were uninviting, but the executive position would make an excellent springboard to national office. Gradually, however, Jack changed his mind and moved toward a direct leap to the Senate in 1952. The way was cleared when Governor Dever, the logical challenger to Republican Senator Henry Cabot Lodge, fearful of the latter's popularity, chose to stay in the governor's mansion. Thirty-four-year-old Congressman Kennedy promptly announced his candidacy.

Most of the Bay State's professional politicians regarded it as a foolhardy move, likely to end in humiliating defeat. Lodge himself was supremely confident, and passed a message to Joe Kennedy through a mutual friend. "Lodge was considered unbeatable," Kennedy later remembered. "Do you know what Lodge said? He told Arthur Krock to 'tell Joe not to waste his money on Jack because he can't win. I'm going to win by three hundred thousand votes.' "[1]

On the strength of Lodge's past performance, his boast was not extravagant. Since his first Senate victory in 1936, he had soundly beaten three popular Irish politicians—Jim Curley, Joseph Casey, and David I. Walsh. To achieve such triumphs in heavily Irish Massachusetts, it was necessary for him to attract the votes of loyal Democrats. Their defection reflected the changing Irish attitude toward the once-hated Brahmins. The envy and enmity of the nineteenth century steadily had given way to sentimental admiration and emulation. The descendants of Irish servants consciously aped the manners and outlook of the old ruling class, which kept its place on top even after its power waned. With the political emergence of late-arriving ethnic groups, such as the Italians, the Irish identified themselves with the Yankee remnant and made common cause against the newcomers. The deep-seated Irish awe of the great Yankee families both annoyed and impressed Joe Kennedy. "All I ever heard when I was growing up in Boston," he recalled, "was how Lodge's grandfather had helped to put the stained glass windows into the Gate of Heaven Church in South Boston and they were still talking about those same stained glass windows in 1952."[2]

To such would-be challengers as Governor Denver, the chief discouragement was the aura of aristocracy surrounding Lodge. His grandfather, the first Senator Henry Cabot Lodge, had held sway in Massachusetts for two decades. He had demonstrated his mastery in the Senate by leading the fight against Wilson's dream of bringing America into the League of Nations. Farther back in imposing array were the earlier founders and shapers of the Lodge family, the men who had amassed the wealth and garnered the fame on which their descendant, the present Senator Lodge, stood so securely. His high office seemed part of an established station in life which humbly born, self-made Irishmen, be they as clever as Curley or as forceful as Walsh, seemed powerless to overthrow.

In contrast, Jack Kennedy met Lodge as a self-confident equal. It was true that his grandfather, "Honey Fitz," had been defeated by Lodge's grandfather in the hard-fought 1916 election. But the following generations had seen a spectacular advance in the standing of the challenger's family, until the new riches of the Kennedys far overshadowed the ancient wealth of the Lodges. And the patina-encrusted prestige of the old Yankee family seemed dull by contrast with the glitter of the celebrated Kennedys. Moreover, the famous men from whom Lodge was descended were only austere figures in fading portraits, while Jack Kennedy's father was robustly alive, a fiercely ambitious family founder of the type not seen in Boston since the days of Lodge's great-grandfather. Those who regarded Lodge as the clear favorite failed to grasp the true nature of the Kennedy-Lodge encounter.

Sociology, not politics, would explain the campaign. The opponents might have come from the same mold, so striking were the similarities between them. Both were youthful, Harvard-bred millionaires who had dabbled in journalism early in their careers. Both had been decorated for bravery in World War II. Both were moderately liberal in their political views. As the gentlemanly campaign would reveal, there were few meaningful issues on which they differed. ("Honey Fitz," in the 1916 campaign, had made a frank appeal to class antagonism, saying of Lodge: "The robber baron is still his highest ideal and his dearest friend.")[3]

By the ordinary criteria of politics, the voters in 1952 had reason to favor the able, experienced incumbent. Paradoxically, it was the very lack of outward differences between the two men that made Jack

Kennedy an attractive candidate. He was, in Governor Dever's phrase, "the first Irish Brahmin." The Irish of Massachusetts, long a psychologically downtrodden majority, at last could purge themselves of lingering feelings of inferiority by voting for a candidate who, save for his Irish ancestry, was indistinguishable from his aristocratic Yankee opponent.

In family councils, Joe Kennedy advised his son to take on Lodge, saying, "When you've beaten him, you've beaten the best. Why try for something less?"[4] That confident remark would be widely quoted as typical of the Kennedy fighting spirit, but it disclosed only part of the truth about how Kennedy fought. He never committed himself and his resources to a quixotic battle. He fought to win, but only after being convinced there was a chance of winning. For a year and a half before the 1952 campaign, a pair of paid, full-time Kennedy advance men toured the state, sounding out opinions, wooing local politicians, lining up likely volunteer workers. In addition to their detailed reports, Kennedy carefully weighed the findings of private polls. "You wonder why we're taking on Lodge," he confided to a friend. "We've taken polls. He'll be easier to beat than Leverett Saltonstall."[5] Only after his cool head had confirmed his heart's desire did Kennedy encourage his son to go ahead.

In their recollections of 1952, father and son differed on the role the elder Kennedy played in the campaign. As Jack remembered that summer and fall, his father had stayed on the sidelines at Hyannis Port. However, Joe Kennedy recalled that he had been in Boston—and so he had. Jack's attempt to minimize his father's contribution was part of his general defensiveness about how he had won, and why. As he said several years afterward, "People say, 'Kennedy bought the election. Kennedy could never have been elected if his father hadn't been a millionaire.' Well, it wasn't the Kennedy name and the Kennedy money that won that election. I beat Lodge because I hustled for three years. I worked for what I got."[6]

Work he did. But whether or not he acknowledged it, the name and wealth bestowed on him by his father made victory possible. At the time, Joe Kennedy acted as though he was fully aware of this fact. "The father was the distinct boss in every way," said one who attended pre-campaign strategy meetings at the Kennedy home on Cape Cod in the spring of 1952. "He dominated everything, even told everyone where to sit. They [were] just children in that house."[7]

It was evident to outsiders that Jack, in his father's presence, felt the need gently to assert his authority. Running down a list of assignments at an early planning session, the candidate facetiously delegated to his father the task of making all the money. "We concede you that role," he said.[8]

As in 1946, Joe Kennedy went ahead in his usual fashion, asking no one's permission and sometimes acting without his son's knowledge. "The father was a tremendous factor in the campaign," said a Boston lawyer and campaign worker. "He remained out of public view. He didn't run things, but they happened according to his plans. He cast the die."[9]

Once again, Kennedy recruited campaign personnel. The new battle demanded the mobilization of specialized skills. The first adviser hired was Ralph Coghlan, a former St. Louis newspaperman who, while sharing Louis Lyons' sensational 1940 interview, treated it as "off-the-record" and thereby won the Ambassador's gratitude. Kennedy thought the 1952 Democratic National Convention offered an opportunity for his son to gain attention, and he assigned Coghlan to devise ways of putting the spotlight on Jack, in spite of the fact that he was a very minor party figure and not even a member of the Massachusetts delegation. With remarkable frequency, the television cameras at the Chicago convention caught the young Congressman for seemingly impromptu interviews, which duly impressed the viewers —and voters—back in the Bay State.[10]

Quiet, mild-mannered Mark Dalton, who had managed Jack's previous campaigns for the House, loyally returned to his post. By 1952, Dalton's law practice had grown to the point where he no longer could afford the sacrifice of working as an unpaid volunteer, and so he agreed to take a salary. This new arrangement lasted just two weeks. "Dalton was at his desk, smoking a pipe, when Joe Kennedy breezed in," said one who witnessed the scene. "The old man spread all the books on the desk in front of him, studied them for about five minutes without saying a word, then he shoved his finger in Dalton's face and yelled: 'Dalton, you've spent ten thousand dollars of my money and you haven't accomplished a damn thing.' The next day Dalton was gone."[11]

Money, as such, had nothing to do with Dalton's abrupt departure. Once again, Kennedy's retainer, John Ford, was serving as overseer of campaign finances, so Kennedy knew very well whom to blame if funds were misspent. His outburst may have been intended as a reminder to the hard-working Dalton that, having accepted a salary, he now became just another of Kennedy's employees.

Twenty-six-year-old Bobby Kennedy, fresh from the University of Virginia Law School, became campaign manager. "When Bobby came in," an insider said later, "we knew it was the old man taking over. What had Bobby done up to that time politically? Nothing. Not a damn thing and all of a sudden he was there as campaign manager, waving the banners."[12] At the very least, the choice provided further proof, if any was needed, that Kennedys preferred to deal with Kennedys.

The inexperienced Bobby showed little deference toward older politicians. As much a stranger in Boston as his older brother had been, he knew almost none of the local powers. One very prominent Boston political figure paid a visit to the newly opened Kennedy headquarters and was astounded to discover that no one, not even the candidate's manager, recognized him. "You're asking me who I am?" he shouted. "You mean to say nobody here knows me? And you call *this* a political headquarters?" Annoyed, Bobby threw the caller out.[13]

Some professionals found the young amateur insufferable. Governor Dever was running for reelection and his campaign was linked with Jack Kennedy's. One day, Bobby stormed into Dever's office and began to berate him for what he considered a mistake in strategy. Dever angrily cut him short and showed him the door. Then he telephoned the Ambassador: "I know you're an important man around here and all that, but I'm telling you this and I mean it. Keep that fresh kid of yours out of my sight from here on in."[14]

Early in the campaign, the elder Kennedy visited Jim Curley and asked him to make a radio speech in support of his son. On hearing this request, Curley must have looked at his caller in amazement. In 1947, Mayor Curley had been convicted of using the mails to defraud in war contracts and had been sentenced to jail despite his plea to the judge that he was suffering from nine separate ailments, including an impending cerebral hemorrhage. Still serving as mayor of Boston from behind the bars of the Danbury penitentiary, he sent out an S.O.S. to the state's sympathetic political chieftains. House Speaker John

McCormack drew up a petition to President Truman asking Curley's pardon, and promptly got the signatures of Massachusetts representatives, Republicans and Democrats alike. All of them except freshman Jack Kennedy, who regarded Curley's illness as implausible and refused to sign.[15] Freed when Truman commuted his sentence, Curley thereafter felt he owed the Kennedys less than nothing. But Joe Kennedy was persistent. "When I refused [to speak for his son] on the grounds that were I to do so I would have to do likewise for other candidates," Curley wrote in his autobiography, *I'd Do It Again,* "he [Kennedy] asked if I would agree not to speak against him. I assented. . . ."[16] Kennedy was never one to go away empty handed.

Jack Kennedy's 1952 campaign, wrote Ralph G. Martin and Ed Plaut in their book, *Front Runner, Dark Horse,* "was the most methodical, the most scientific, the most thoroughly detailed, the most intricate, the most disciplined and smoothly working statewide campaign in Massachusetts history—and possibly anywhere else." Busy behind the scenes at the center of this enterprise, incessantly demanding perfection, was Joe Kennedy. "The Ambassador worked around the clock," said one of the speech-writers he brought to Boston. "He was always consulting people, getting reports, looking into problems. Should Jack go on TV with this issue? What kind of an ad should he run on something else? He'd call in experts, get opinions, have ideas worked up."[17]

It was understood by all concerned that the candidate would make the final decisions, but the alternatives set before him usually were framed by his father's hand-picked "brain-trust." When unmade decisions piled up, as often happened in those hectic days, there was no question about where to turn. "Sometimes you couldn't get anybody to make a decision," a worker recalled. "You'd have to call the old man. Then you'd get a decision."[18]

The 1952 campaign, though broader and more complex, divided into essentially the same two sides as the race for the House six years earlier. The candidate, under the nominal managership of his brother and surrounded by a phalanx of energetic young men, carried the battle to the far corners of the state. Back in Boston, unseen but hard at work, were the specialists and professionals on the elder Kennedy's payroll. Those who slipped in and out of his suite at the Ritz-Carlton included Jim Landis; Lynn Johnson, a lawyer from the Kennedy headquarters in Manhattan; John Harriman, on leave from his job as a financial writer on the *Boston Globe*, and Sargent Shriver, formerly on the staff of *Newsweek* and more recently a dollar-a-year man at the Department of Justice, where he had assisted Eunice Kennedy in a study of juvenile delinquency. Many others also were active, coming forward as their talents were needed.

At work throughout Massachusetts were two hundred and eighty-six Kennedy "secretaries," backed by an army of more than twenty thousand volunteers. Jack Kennedy had had no opposition in the Democratic primary, thus losing an opportunity to test-run his newly built machine, but he did require twenty-five hundred signatures on his nomination papers. Someone suggested the workers should be encouraged to get as many signatures as possible. They collected more than a hundred times the number required—a record 262,324. A measure of the money spent on the campaign was the fact that each person who signed received a thank-you letter.

The magnitude of the Kennedy publicity effort was staggering. Distributed across the state were nine hundred thousand copies of an eight-page tabloid featuring drawings of Lieutenant Kennedy rescuing his shipmates in the Pacific. On the facing page was a photograph of young Joe Kennedy, whose fatal war mission was described under this headline: "John Fulfills Dream of Brother Joe Who Met Death in the Sky Over the English Channel." Inserted in each paper was a *Reader's Digest* reprint of John Hersey's article on the saga of PT-109, which originally had appeared in *The New Yorker.*

Still, the most impressive feature in this vast campaign—indeed, the Kennedy hallmark—was painstaking attention to small detail. In June, Boston's Mayor John B. Hynes appeared at a rally at the Copley-Plaza launching Jack Kennedy's campaign. "The speeches were televised," Hynes later recalled, "and for the first time I saw a teleprompter. In fact, there were *two* of them, and I wondered why." When one broke down and the other kept the show running smoothly, Hynes realized he was in the company of perfectionists.[19]

This efficient organization tried, with only limited success, to manufacture campaign issues. A major Kennedy theme was to blame Lodge for the state's industrial decline and unemployment, all the while ignoring Governor Dever's campaign claim that the economy had flourished under his leadership. Empty sloganeering was the order of the day. "KENNEDY WILL DO MORE FOR MASSACHUSETTS," proclaimed the challenger's posters. To which the Lodge forces brightly replied: "LODGE *HAS* DONE—AND *WILL* DO—THE *MOST* FOR MASSACHUSETTS."

Much more effective was the decision of the Kennedy strategists to outflank Lodge on both the left and the right, a boldly opportunistic maneuver that was feasible only because Jack Kennedy's own position was highly ambiguous. On the one hand, he criticized Lodge as a moss-back conservative, pointing to his own down-the-line support of the Truman administration's "Fair Deal" domestic program. On the other hand, Kennedy attacked his opponent for giving *too much* support to the Truman administration's foreign policy. Lodge was accused of weak-kneed bipartisanship, while Kennedy, in the words of a study prepared by his staff, "has been an outspoken critic of many elements of the Administration's Foreign Policy." In this respect, the study continued, "he has been much closer to the position of [Senator Robert A.] Taft than has Lodge...."[20]

This plea for the votes of conservative Republicans was urged by Joe Kennedy, who shrewdly guessed that the followers of Senator Taft in Massachusetts might well have a decisive influence on the Kennedy-Lodge contest. During the spring and early summer, Taft, the revered leader of the Old Guard, was locked in a bitter struggle with General Dwight D. Eisenhower for the Republican presidential nomination, and Lodge was managing the General's campaign. Conservatives, never especially fond of the liberal Senator Lodge, came to identify him as the hated symbol of their frustration. When Taft went down to defeat at the convention, his sorrowing Massachusetts supporters came home sworn to wreak vengeance on Lodge.

Joe Kennedy was waiting to exploit their anger. At his request, T. Walter Taylor, a Boston businessman and Taft backer, formed "Independents for Kennedy." A letter sent to Taft supporters over Taylor's signature read, in part:

> ... You, being a delegate for Senator Taft, I feel sure will be interested to know that something is being done to assure Senator Lodge's defeat.... Ambassador Kennedy, who by the way is a very close friend of Senator Taft's, has supported the Senator during the campaign and has spent a large amount of time with the Senator during his campaign,

requested me to open and direct a headquarters for his son whom you know is seeking election to the Senate.

Our work is to reach the Independents and Taft people in behalf of Kennedy so we have opened the Headquarters for Kennedy Independents in the Sheraton Plaza Hotel, in Parlor B, and are very happy at the privilege of bringing the Kennedy message to the people. . . .[21]

Interestingly, Kennedy in 1952 found it possible to lend generous financial support to the presidential aspirations of both the conservative Republican Taft and the liberal Democrat Stevenson. He still thought of Stevenson, not as an able reform governor or the conscience of liberalism, but rather as the young lawyer he once had "discovered" and offered a job with the SEC. In keeping with the nonideological nature of his alliance with the Kennedys, Stevenson, on a visit to Massachusetts, endorsed Jack as "my type of guy."

Always a faithful party man, Senator Taft sent word to his friends in Massachusetts that any Republican was better than any Democrat, but many of his supporters were implacably opposed to Lodge.[22] Basil Brewer, Taft's manager in the state and publisher of the influential New Bedford *Standard Times,* swung his paper from praise of Lodge to violent denunciation, calling him "a Truman socialistic New Dealer." After talking with Joe Kennedy, Brewer endorsed Jack's candidacy. That fall, Kennedy carried New Bedford by an astounding 21,000 votes, almost one-third his plurality in the state as a whole. At the same time Governor Dever squeaked through New Bedford by a margin of 328 votes. It took more than a little soul-searching for a deeply committed conservative such as Brewer to endorse a rather liberal Democrat, but always present in the background was the reassuring figure of the elder Kennedy, who seemed the very soul of conservatism and a steadying influence on his son.

Other voters, including many Jews in the Boston metropolitan area, were wary of Jack Kennedy precisely because of this presumed paternal influence. Whispers of Joe Kennedy's anti-Semitism buzzed louder than ever. Too, Lodge had built a solid base of support in the Jewish districts. "We were in a real bind with respect to the Jewish people," said Phil Fine, a lawyer and Kennedy worker. "At first, we didn't have a soul with us."[23]

This situation changed dramatically during the campaign as Jack Kennedy, by dint of charm and persuasion, won over key leaders of the Jewish community. Typical of their response was that of Jackson J.

Holtz, recently returned from the Korean War, whom Jack approached to head a committee. Holtz first had lunch with the Ambassador. His attitude toward him remained unchanged. "I wouldn't vote for Joe at any level," Holtz remarked afterward. But he gained the impression, as did others, that Jack disagreed with his father's views and came to his decisions independently. Holtz agreed to serve as chairman of the "Friends of John F. Kennedy for U.S. Senator Committee."[24]

The difficulty Jack faced was evident during a private dinner meeting of three hundred prominent Jews at the Boston Club. The candidate reviewed his voting record in the House, and recalled his 1951 visit to the new state of Israel on a trip around the world. He spoke well and forcefully, but sensed a lingering doubt in his audience. "What more do you want?" he finally asked. "Remember, I'm running for the Senate, not my father." His listeners had been waiting for that frank declaration, and they applauded warmly.[25]

Long after the campaign, a worker vividly remembered Joe Kennedy's "terrible anguish" at the possibility that the shadow of his rumored anti-Semitism would fall across his son's path. As it turned out, the steady defection of leading Jews to Kennedy caused panic among some of Lodge's supporters, and led them into a move that backfired. They flooded Jewish neighborhoods with a flier declaring, "GERMAN DOCUMENTS ALLEGE KENNEDY HELD ANTI-SEMITIC VIEWS." The flier was based on a three-year-old newspaper story reporting the State Department's publication of the dispatches of German Ambassador Dirksen, in which he had attributed pro-Nazi and anti-Semitic statements to Ambassador Kennedy.* Quickly, Kennedy's workers put out an answering leaflet: "SHAME ON YOU MR. LODGE! Lodge Endorses McCarthy in Wisconsin and Lodge Supporters Use McCarthy Tactics Here...."[26]

This indirect attack on "McCarthyism," carefully addressed to an especially receptive group of voters, marked the only time the Kennedy campaign publicly mentioned the name of Senator Joseph R. McCarthy, the explosively controversial anti-Communist crusader. In order to minimize the use of McCarthy's name, the Kennedy people hired the same men who had circulated the Lodge flier to circulate theirs to the same homes only. The determined effort to pretend that

*See Chapter 16, page 252.

McCarthy did not exist, motivated by fear of his enthusiastic following in Massachusetts, was not without a certain irony.

For McCarthy was a good friend of the Kennedy family, and particularly of the Ambassador. "In case there is any question in your mind," Joe Kennedy told an interviewer in 1961, "I liked Joe McCarthy. I always liked him. I would see him when I went down to Washington, and when he was visiting in Palm Beach he'd come around to my house for a drink. I invited him to Cape Cod."[27] At Hyannis Port one Fourth of July, McCarthy, playing shortstop for the Kennedy team ("the Barefoot Boys") in the traditional softball game on the lawn, committed four errors and was retired summarily to the porch. Another time, the Ambassador remembered, "he went out on my boat . . . and he almost drowned swimming behind it, but he never complained."[28]

It was McCarthy's unfailing good nature that commended him to Kennedy. "He was always pleasant; he was never a crab. If somebody was against him, he never tried to cut his heart out. He never said that anybody was a stinker. He was a pleasant fellow."[29]

When McCarthy began his one-man war on communism, Kennedy later said, "I thought he'd be a sensation. He was smart. But he went off the deep end." In recalling his friend's sad end, the interviewer noted, Kennedy's voice quavered and his eyes clouded.[30]

But in 1952, Kennedy saw clearly enough that McCarthy, if he came to Massachusetts on behalf of Lodge, could destroy his son's chances. According to Westbrook Pegler, Kennedy took steps to keep the Senator away. That year, McCarthy had undergone a serious operation, was almost broke, and faced a tough primary fight in Wisconsin. As Kennedy later remembered the incident, "I gave Joe McCarthy a small contribution, sure, but it was only a couple of thousand dollars, and I didn't give it to him to keep him out of Massachusetts. I gave it to him because a mutual friend of ours, Westbrook Pegler, asked me to give it to him. . . ."[31]

Wrote Pegler in 1960: "My statement is that I did not ask Kennedy to give any money to McCarthy. We were discussing McCarthy's illness and his busted condition. . . . And Joe Kennedy volunteered to send McCarthy $3,000 in currency and asked me to transmit the money myself. I took counsel of a wiser head who warned me not to touch the money or have anything to do with the deal. Therefore I kept hands off and I was told later in New York that an intimate friend of the Kennedys, and an old friend of mine, arranged to deliver the money to McCarthy. But I did not 'ask' Joe Kennedy to do anything for McCarthy, although by this time he may believe my mention of Joe's financial problem amounted to a request....

"I did not then suspect that Joe's motive in contributing to McCarthy was to keep McCarthy out of Massachusetts. But soon afterward a wise and cynical head in New York who had known Joe Kennedy of old said, 'Joe will be around to collect from McCarthy.' He was dead right. Those Kennedys are cold-blooded and long-headed but it takes experience and disillusionment to learn them." In the fall of 1952, concluded Pegler, "Joe Kennedy asked me to persuade McCarthy to keep out of Massachusetts. So my New York sage had been right. This was to be the payoff. Still, I didn't mind. I told McCarthy to let Lodge croak and foolishly ventured that Jack Kennedy, though a Democrat, was at heart a fine American....Joe Kennedy later admitted freely to me that his [McCarthy's] abstention from the fight in Massachusetts had been helpful—possibly he said decisive—in young Jack's victory over Lodge."[32]

McCarthy, for one reason or another, did not come to Massachusetts, but the question of "McCarthyism," and the candidate's attitude toward it, came up inside the Kennedy organization. When it did, Joe Kennedy put his foot down—hard.

To help him outflank Lodge on the liberal side, Jack Kennedy had recruited Gardner (Pat) Jackson, a Bostonian whose championship of liberal causes dated back to the trial of Sacco and Vanzetti. An unreconstructed New Dealer who had broken with Henry Wallace and John L. Lewis because of their imperfect devotion to liberalism, Jackson agreed to work for Jack in spite of misgivings about his father. ("Did Jack's father ask me to help?" said Jackson later. "He did NOT!") After much arguing and pleading, he was able to mobilize behind Kennedy the initially skeptical labor unions and the Americans for Democratic Action. Having sold his candidate as a liberal, Jackson, not surprisingly, wished him to behave like one. The cause then closest to his heart was the fight against "McCarthyism," and he tried to persuade Jack to take a stand. Jackson prepared a carefully worded newspaper advertisement, which quoted from a statement by ninety-nine members of the Notre Dame faculty. The headline read: "COMMUNISM AND McCARTHY: BOTH WRONG." Jack finally consented to sign it, provided Congressman McCormack would co-sign it. McCormack agreed. Triumphantly, Jackson set out the next morning, a copy of the ad in his pocket, for the small apartment Jack had rented at 122 Bowdoin Street.

"The place was a hubbub of activity," Jackson later recalled. "Jack had his coat on and went dashing out just as I arrived." The reason for the unusual early morning activity was apparent: Joe Kennedy was paying a call. Seated with him at a card table in the center of the room were three of his son's speech-writers: Jim Landis, John Harriman, and Joe Healy. Before Jack left, he asked that Jackson read the ad he had prepared.

"... I hadn't gone two sentences when Joe [Kennedy] jumped to his feet with such force that he tilted the table against the others," he remembered. For a moment, it seemed as though the enraged Kennedy would physically attack Jackson. Instead, as the others looked on in embarrassed silence, he violently berated him. "You're trying to ruin Jack. You and your sheeny friends are trying to ruin my son's career," shouted Kennedy, who said that he liked McCarthy and had contributed to his campaign. Again and again he accused the liberals and union people of hurting his son. "I can't estimate how long he poured it out on me," recalled Jackson. "It was just a stream of stuff—always referring to 'you and your sheeny friends.' " His fury spent, Kennedy stalked out.*

The McCarthy ad, of course, was dead. Next morning, Jackson and the candidate were alone in the apartment.

"I hear you really had it yesterday, didn't you?" said Jack, trying to soothe the older man.

"How do you explain your father?" Jackson asked.

"I guess there isn't a motive in it which I think you'd respect," said Jack, "except love of family." He paused for a moment, then added, "And more often than not, I think that's just pride."[33]

Whether or not Joe Kennedy encouraged McCarthy's absence from Massachusetts, he made a substantial loan to the pro-McCarthy publisher of the *Boston Post* soon after the paper's surprising editorial endorsement of his son. The transaction came to light six years after the election, in 1958, when John Fox, the former publisher of the defunct *Post,* appeared before a congressional committee to

*In interviews afterward, Joe Kennedy denied that the incident had ever occurred. "Oh, Pat Jackson has been living off that story for years," he told one reporter.

disclose the doubtful relationship between Sherman Adams, President Eisenhower's assistant, and Bernard Goldfine, a favor-seeking New England industrialist. In response to a question, Fox freely admitted that he had received a loan of $500,000 from Joe Kennedy in 1952 shortly after the *Post's* switch of support from Lodge to Kennedy. Fox denied the suggestion that a *quid pro quo* had been involved, and Kennedy's office in Manhattan issued a statement describing the loan as "a purely commercial transaction, for sixty days only, with full collateral and at full interest . . . simply one of many commercial transactions in which this office has participated."[34]

It was not quite that cut and dried.

In 1952, the flamboyant Fox, a self-made millionaire as the result of speculative triumphs in oil and gas properties and Manhattan real estate, was desperately short of cash. "Fox," recalled an associate, "was a guy who always tried to make a dollar work in three places at once." He had bought the faltering *Post* the year before mainly to have a sounding board for his enthusiasm for his strong anti-Communist views. Under Fox's direction, the traditionally Democratic *Post* became an impassioned advocate of conservative Republicanism. Parenthetically, it may be noted that the owners of the *Post*, before selling to Fox, offered the paper to Kennedy, their attorney suggesting that the property's operating loss might yield him attractive tax advantages. Kennedy studied the deal, but turned it down. Fox, intent on having the paper, sold his large holdings in Western Union stock to make the purchase, and watched, aghast, as the stock later sold for many times the price he had received.

Early in the 1952 campaign, Fox, reconciled to Taft's defeat, came out in support of Eisenhower. He also favored Lodge and even tried to persuade one of his top political reporters to direct Lodge's publicity. However, three weeks before the election, according to Fox's recollection, Basil Brewer urged him not to back Lodge, and made such a powerful case that Fox wavered in his commitment. The next day, he told two of Lodge's men that he would endorse the Senator only if Taft or McCarthy asked him to do so within a week. Neither did. Bowing to the last-minute pleas of Lodge's lieutenants, Fox himself then placed a call to McCarthy, who was in Seattle, but the message came back: "The Senator is sorry, but he cannot come to the phone."[35]

His decision confirmed by McCarthy's eloquent silence, Fox wrote for the next morning's paper a front page editorial endorsing Jack

Kennedy. He then tried to reach the candidate to break the news. When he could not, Fox instead telephoned Joe Kennedy and invited him to come over for a drink and a chat in the 99 Club, a nightclub the publisher owned. Looking apprehensive, Kennedy joined Fox at his table. Fox told him that the *Post* had chosen a candidate: it would endorse his son the next day. At that, Kennedy's eyes filled with tears.

"He told me then," Fox said, "that if I needed anything in the world, all I had to do was ask him."[36]

Then and there, as Kennedy wept for joy at his son's newly won advantage, Fox later recalled that he explained his financial plight. Kennedy, however, vigorously denied that the $500,000 loan had been "discussed or contemplated" at the time of Jack's endorsement.

Through the campaign, those around Jack often doubted his ability to bear up physically. His spinal operation had failed to heal properly, and he was in almost constant pain. On his trip with Bobby and Pat in 1951, he had become seriously ill, and was flown to a military hospital on Okinawa with a temperature above 106 degrees. ("They didn't think he would live," Bobby later recalled.) Midway through the campaign, Jack was unable to move without crutches, but he refused to admit his body's weakness. "He hated to appear in public on his crutches," said a friend who traveled with him. "When we came to the door of a hall where he was to make a speech, he'd hand the crutches to one of us and throw his shoulders back and march down the aisle as straight as a West Point cadet. How he did it, I'll never know."[37]

An unfailing source of strength was the support he received from his family. "Each Kennedy," a reporter once observed, "takes pride in the achievements of the others. Each, instinctively, had rather win the approval of the family than of outsiders. And when an outsider threatens to thwart the ambitions of any of them, the whole family forms a close-packed ring, horns lowered, like a herd of bison beset by wolves."[38] Accused of being self-centered, the Kennedys also were respected for their remarkable solidarity. "I don't worry about Jack Kennedy. I don't worry about Kennedy's money," moaned a Lodge supporter. "It's that family of his . . . they're all over the state."

Lodge, who had been busy working for Eisenhower, belatedly recognized his peril and came hurrying back to Massachusetts two months before the election. By that time, members of the Kennedy family had shaken the hands of some two million voters. During the campaign, no fewer than thirty-three formal receptions were given, attended by an estimated seventy-five thousand persons, almost all of them women. Rose Kennedy came directly from Paris for the first reception, arriving from New York's Idlewild Airport in a chauffeured limousine. Jack's standard appeal was brief and boyish. "In the first place," he told the ladies, "for some strange reason, there are more women than men in Massachusetts, and they live longer. Secondly, my grandfather, the late John F. Fitzgerald, ran for the United States Senate thirty-six years ago against my opponent's grandfather, Henry Cabot Lodge, and he lost by only thirty thousand votes in an election where women were not allowed to vote. I hope that by impressing the female electorate that I can more than take up the slack."[39]

The handsome young congressman made a dazzling impression: an estimated 80 percent of his volunteer workers were signed up at the receptions. "What is there about Jack Kennedy," a Republican visitor was heard to ask, "that makes every Catholic girl in Boston between eighteen and twenty-eight think it's a holy crusade to get him elected?" Women of all ages were awed by the family's trappings of wealth and power. A veteran newspaperman cynically remarked that "it was all they could do to keep those old gals who came to the affairs from curtsying. They had every tendency to drop to one knee."

The candidate's brothers and sisters rang doorbells, made speeches, attended house parties, and twice appeared on a family television program, "Coffee with the Kennedys." But the star of the family campaign troupe turned out to be Rose. Jack's organization was weakest in Boston, and his father summoned a seasoned professional, State Senator John Powers, to take the situation in hand.

"I told him," said Powers, "that he was right about Boston. I said to him, 'Joe, the fight's falling off and it needs something to pick it up. I asked him for permission to use Mrs. Kennedy. He answered, 'But Johnny, she's a grandmother!'*

" 'That's all right,' I told him, 'she's a Gold Star mother, the mother of a war hero and a congressman, the wife of an Ambassador, the

*A Kennedy grandchild—named Joseph—was born to Bobby and his wife, the former Ethel Skakel, during the campaign. The infant, too, played a part in the family effort. Lamented a Lodge lieutenant: "When Archbishop [now Cardinal] Cushing baptized the baby of Bobby and Ethel in a special weekday ceremony just before the election, that cut our hearts out."

daughter of a mayor and a congressman, the daughter-in-law of a state senator and representative and she's beautiful and she's a Kennedy. Let me have her.' And he thought it over and finally said, 'Well, take it slow with her.' "[40]

Joe's concern was misplaced. The daughter of "Honey Fitz" knew exactly what to say and do, no matter what the audience. Before a group of Italian women in Boston's North End, she appeared as a girl who had grown up in the neighborhood, the mother of nine children. She greeted her audience with a few words of Italian, and then showed the card index file she had used to keep track of her children's illnesses, vaccinations, and dental work. She might wear a simple black dress and a single strand of pearls. In her limousine en route to a gathering of Chestnut Hill matrons, she would don jewelry and a mink stole, as befit the Ambassador's lady. After speaking for a few minutes about her son, Rose would say, "Now, let me tell you about the new dresses I saw in Paris last month."[41]

On election night, the workers at Kennedy headquarters watched tensely as a year and a half of planning, and more than six months of unremitting effort, were put to the test. Hour by hour, the returns swayed back and forth. By early morning, it was clear that Eisenhower would sweep the state. Lodge might ride Ike's landslide to victory. But Jack Kennedy remained serene, never doubting that he would win. At six o'clock in the morning, Lodge conceded. The final returns showed that while Eisenhower was swamping Stevenson, and Dever was being narrowly defeated by Christian Herter for the governorship, Kennedy had pulled a stunning upset, defeating Lodge by more than seventy thousand votes.

Had Joe Kennedy bought his son's election? Many would argue that he had. Estimates of the Kennedy spending ran up to a wildly improbable several million dollars. It was true that Kennedy had outspent Lodge by a substantial margin. The various Kennedy committees, operating independently of the Democratic party fund-raising groups, officially reported expenses of just under $350,000. The whole cost of the Kennedy campaign was probably well above half a million dollars—how much above, no one would ever know. Officially, Lodge reported expenses of only $59,000. In addition, he benefited heavily from the Republican party's record million-dollar spending for the state ticket.[42]

"It was those damned tea parties," Lodge said afterward.[43] In a sense, he was right. He had been defeated by a young patrician whose rise was shared vicariously by thousands of Irish-Americans. Where their grandfathers dreamed of awakening as Yankee overlords, now they might dream of becoming Kennedys. Into the family's victory went money, hard work, and a long, unforgiving memory. Said Rose Fitzgerald Kennedy following the election: "At last, the Fitzgeralds have evened the score with the Lodges!"[44]

CHAPTER 24

The Way to the White House

FOLLOWING Jack's election to the Senate, Kennedy tried to retrace his steps back into obscurity. During the campaign, the furor about his past had warned him that he might become a liability to his son. "Joe knew he was controversial, so he stayed out of the way," said a friend in Boston years later. "He's sort of like a caterpillar; he couldn't quite become a butterfly, but his boys were going to fly no matter what."[1]

In explaining his "retirement" long afterward, Kennedy omitted mention of his role in the Senate campaign and merely recalled that he had made his "last speech" at the University of Virginia in 1950. "After that," he said, "I decided to keep quiet and let my children have the center of the stage. I simply stopped speaking to or seeing the press, unless Bobby or Jack requested it. And so people started calling me a mystery man."[2]

Actually, Kennedy made his last speech only a few weeks after the 1952 election. Speaking informally before the Boston Latin School Association, he drew on his business experience to sound a familiar warning against expanding government. "The pendulum has now swung, so you are entirely in the hands of the government when it comes to finance. You can know trends and the principles of the stock market, you can work out charts and tables, and in five minutes someone in Washington can knock you into a cocked hat."[3]

After his talk, Kennedy was asked what he thought of his son's views, particularly on the foreign policy issues highlighted by the Korean War. Kennedy said that he and Jack were "in complete disagreement." Describing himself as an "isolationist" because U.S. foreign aid had failed to produce "anything like the results it was supposed to produce," he concluded: "I couldn't possibly have a worse argument with anyone about foreign policy than I have had with my son."[4]

Could such statements be taken as evidence of conflict between a conservative father and a liberal son? Many were skeptical, especially committed liberals who despised Joe Kennedy and everything he stood for. To them it seemed extremely unlikely that this opinionated, domineering parent, a nineteenth-century *paterfamilias,* would tolerate real dissent under his roof.

Over the next several years, Senator Kennedy's office took pains to inform friendly reporters of the differences between Jack and his father. During debate on a natural gas bill, a lobbyist was said to have buttonholed the Senator and identified himself as a representative of some of Joe Kennedy's oil and gas holdings. Nevertheless, Jack voted against the bill. Similarly, it was pointed out that the Senator opposed the 27.5 percent oil depletion allowance, and tax relief on dividends and movie theater admissions, all of which ran counter to his family's financial interests. By 1960, Jack himself said his disagreement with his father on policy was "total," and added: "We never discuss it. There is no use, because we can't agree."[5]

Liberal suspicions of Jack Kennedy centered on a single, overriding issue: Senator Joe McCarthy and "McCarthyism." Little reassurance could be drawn from his record because he carefully avoided taking a stand. Enough was known of the motives underlying his long silence on McCarthy to inspire distrust. During the 1952 campaign, John Mallan, then a teaching fellow at Harvard, reported in the *New Republic* on a seminar at the university that Congressman Kennedy had addressed in 1950. According to Mallan, the Congressman had said, among other things, that he felt not enough had been done about removing Communists from the government, that he rather respected McCarthy, and that he thought "he knew Joe pretty well, and he may have something."[6] The article caused an uproar in intellectual circles and Mallan was rebuked for telling tales outside the lecture hall, but the substance of his report went unchallenged.

It was not until after McCarthy's censure and death that Jack Kennedy unburdened himself in an interview. "The Joe McCarthy thing? I was caught in a bad situation. My brother [Bobby] was working for Joe. I was against it, I didn't want him to work for Joe, but he wanted to. And how could I get up there and denounce Joe McCarthy when my own brother was working for him? So it wasn't so much a thing of political liability as it was a personal problem."[7]

Precisely because of family considerations, liberals found it difficult to accept Senator Kennedy as one of them. Jack himself laid only a cautious claim to the label, yet it was a justifiable one. The question was: what *kind* of liberal was he? "Some people have their liberalism 'made' by the time they reach their late twenties," he once observed almost wistfully. "I didn't. I was caught in cross currents and eddies. It was only later that I got into the stream of things."[8]

Jack Kennedy grew up unaware of the Depression and indifferent to the New Deal. He came to maturity long after the crusading days of liberalism's rise to power. Triumphant liberalism had overthrown orthodoxies and establishments only to become itself orthodox and ritualistic. Answering the needs of his ambition, Jack Kennedy adopted the attitudes and acquired the techniques of established liberalism.

There was no fundamental clash between his dispassionate liberalism and his father's temperamental conservatism. Each was a political pragmatist, alert to the moment's opportunity, heedless of the philosophical inconsistency between one action and the next. Though he attracted intellectuals, Jack did not share their conviction that ideas are the moving force of politics. Asked once why he wanted to be President, he replied: "Because that's where the power is."[9] Like his father, he was intent on the pursuit of power, and left it to the intellectuals to rationalize his deeds. He was in politics, not to advance an ideology, but to derive personal satisfaction. His politics was as self-centered as his father's fortune-building; the one was the natural successor to the other.

"The political world is so much more stimulating," he once remarked. "It's the most interesting thing you can do—it beats following the dollar. It's a very interesting life. It allows the full use of your powers. First there is the great chess game. It's the battle, the competition. There's the strategy and which piece you move and all that. And then in government you can do something about what you think."[10]

What Jack Kennedy thought and did politically arose less from adopted liberal conceptions than from instincts conditioned by inherited wealth and assured social position. Thus, while he agreed intellectually with the liberals that "McCarthyism" was deplorable, he was more comfortable emotionally with his father's wealthy and conservative friends. ". . . I had never known the sort of people who were called before the McCarthy committee," he once said. "I agree that many of them were seriously manhandled, but they all represented a different world to me. What I mean is, I did not identify with them, and so I did not get as worked up as other liberals did."[11]

For Joe Kennedy, watching his son's career from a distance was not unlike his earlier observation of the boy far offshore learning to master the sails of the *Victura.* Now Jack moved skillfully before the prevailing political wind, ready to maneuver should it shift, his only object swift forward motion. Kennedy would never fault his son's performance so long as he took both of them where they wanted to go.

Even before his son entered the Senate, Kennedy began looking ahead with characteristic directness. One day during the campaign, he appeared wearing an unusual new necktie, made of dark blue material and bearing an eye-catching silver inscription: "Kennedy for President." The gift of a friend who intended it as a joke, the tie drew amused smiles, but Kennedy's expression showed that he took the idea quite seriously.[12]

It was easy to assume from Kennedy's blunt manner that he was an uncomplicated man; and this was what he wished others to assume. Once, he made a suggestion for a television show, but one of his son's advisers shook his head and said deferentially: "Mr. Kennedy, that may seem like a good idea to you, but maybe it wouldn't appeal to the average person." Kennedy was indignant. "What do you mean?" he demanded. "I happen to be the most average guy in this whole damned outfit."[13]

But beneath this pose was an extraordinary man, complex and self-contradictory. He was at once forthright and cunning, coldly unsentimental and explosively emotional, a tough-minded realist and a Celtic dreamer. From the wellsprings of his egotism flowed an almost mystical faith in himself, his worth and his purpose. A palmist once had told him: "Your hand is a hand of destiny."[14] Unblushingly, he told friends of the palmist's discovery. What saved him from mere boastfulness was the intensity of his self-belief; the palmist only confirmed the truth he always had acted upon. Miraculously, he instilled in his children his belief in the innate distinction of the Kennedys, and imposed on them the responsibility for fulfilling the design that he believed had been foreordained. In no accepted sense of the word was Kennedy a "great" man, yet his singular achievement was to lift his children out of the common human experience of living *in* history, and to open up for them the opportunity of *making* history. When he conceived the ambition of seeing a son enter the White House, there seemed to be no chance of a Roman Catholic being elected to the Presidency. Yet Kennedy believed, with unshakable certainty, that his unattainable ambition would be a reality for his son.

Kennedy's decision to withdraw from public view—and from his son's path—was a step toward the distant goal of the Presidency. Other steps on the journey were the disclosures—calculated or not—of differences between father and son. In the beginning, none of the obvious obstacles to his son's eventual drive for the Presidency—his religion, youth, inexperience—loomed as large before Kennedy as the obstacle only the family intimately understood: Jack's uncertain health. And the answer to that problem was only partly in human hands.

Through the 1950's, the patriarch saw his family steadily expand as his children, one by one, married and returned with their wives and husbands and children to fill to overflowing the family seat at Hyannis Port. For a long time, one of the Kennedy girls remarked, it had seemed as though none of the children ever would become interested enough in anyone outside the family to get married. Interestingly, when the young Kennedys did marry, they tended to choose spouses much like themselves.

Bobby's wife, Ethel Skakel, had been Jean Kennedy's roommate at the Manhattanville College of the Sacred Heart. The large and wealthy

Skakel family controlled Great Lakes Carbon Corporation, one of the largest privately owned U.S. companies. Ethel might have been born a Kennedy, so completely did she enter into the life of her husband's family. Summer visitors at Hyannis Port watched in open-mouthed amazement as the lithe young woman, several months pregnant, asked and gave no quarter in the bruising family touch football games. Jean's husband, Stephen Smith, fitted readily into the Kennedy pattern. The quiet-spoken scion of a wealthy New York barge and tugboat operating family, he joined one of the Kennedy real estate companies and was groomed to assume many of the financial responsibilities that his brothers-in-law shunned. Similarly, Eunice's husband, Sargent Shriver, was bound closely to the Kennedy family even before marriage, serving first as assistant manager of the Merchandise Mart and later going to Washington, at her father's suggestion, to assist Eunice with her study of juvenile delinquency. Their engagement came as no surprise to Kennedy, although he vehemently rejected the suggestion that he had played matchmaker.

Of course, there were exceptions, as when Patricia chose Peter Lawford. Kennedy made no attempt to conceal his displeasure. "If there's anything I think I'd hate as a son-in-law," he told Lawford, "it's an actor, and if there's anything I think I'd hate worse than an actor as a son-in-law, it's an English actor."[15] Unperturbed, the Lawfords set up housekeeping in the palatial Santa Monica beach home of the late movie mogul, Louis B. Mayer, and became members in good standing of actor Frank Sinatra's set, variously known as "The Clan" and "the Rat Pack."*

Easily the most dazzling Kennedy in-law, and perhaps the most challenging to the head of the family, was Jack's wife, the intelligent and strong-willed former Jacqueline Lee Bouvier. The daughter of a wealthy East Hampton, Long Island, stockbroker, she was a regally poised member of America's untitled aristocracy. Hers was the small, rigorously selective world of hunt meets, country estates, and inherited Republican loyalties, a world the elder Kennedy knew well but one in which he was not at ease. When the young Kennedys had been loudly debating political questions at the Hyannis Port dinner table,

*It developed that Kennedy was not alone in his opinion of actors. In the spring of 1964, the Lawfords tried to purchase a sixteen-room suite in a cooperative apartment building on Manhattan's Upper East Side, but were rebuffed when a socially prominent tenant objected to having them as neighbors on the ground that Lawford was an actor and his wife a Democrat.

Jacqueline and her parents had been conversing by candlelight in elegant French. When she made her debut at Newport, the ecstatic society columnist "Cholly Knickerbocker" dubbed her "Queen Deb of the Year." Newport also was the scene of her wedding to Jack in September, 1953, an extravaganza attended by seven hundred guests and almost disrupted by a mob of three thousand spectators.

As a bride, Jackie shrank from the compulsive athleticism and togetherness of the Kennedy clan. ("Just watching them wore me out," she said of her hyperactive in-laws.) After injuring an ankle trying to play touch football, she withdrew from the family scrimmages. She firmly refused to attend the nightly family dinners at her father-in-law's house. "Once a week is great," she told her husband. "Not every night."[16] The inevitable head-on collision with the elder Kennedy came one day in Palm Beach when she was fifteen minutes late to lunch. "That can be fatal with Joe when he's in one of his Emperor Augustus moods," recalled a family friend who witnessed the scene. "So when she came in, he started to give her the needle, but she gave it right back. Old Joe has a lot of old-fashioned slang phrases, so Jackie told him: 'You ought to write a series of grandfather stories for children, like 'The Duck with Moxie,' and 'The Donkey Who Couldn't Fight His Way Out of a Telephone Booth.' When she said this, the old man was silent for a minute. Then he broke into a roar of laughter."[17] After that, Kennedy and his spirited daughter-in-law got along better. Some of Jackie's watercolors, painted especially for him, soon graced the walls of his home. One showed a crowd of young Kennedys on the beach, looking out to sea. "You can't take it with you," read the caption. "Dad's got it all."[18]

What should have been happy years for the newly wedded senator were filled with pain. Jack's spinal condition became progressively worse, and by the summer of 1954, he was forced to hobble about on crutches. The best chance of regaining his health, doctors said, would be through spinal fusion surgery, involving grave risk. Apparently as the result of his wartime physical ordeal and subsequent malaria and fevers, he suffered from adrenal insufficiency, and therefore lacked natural defenses against shock and infection. On the porch at Hyannis Port one day that summer, Dr. Sara Jordan, of Boston's Leahy Clinic, candidly told her patient and longtime friend that his chances of surviving an operation would be slim. When she went away, Jack punched his crutches with his fist, and, turning to a friend seated nearby, said: "I'd rather die than spend the rest of my life on these things."[19]

That October, in Manhattan's Hospital for Special Surgery, he underwent a double fusion of spinal discs. Twice his anxious wife and parents were summoned when it seemed that he would die, but, as Joe Kennedy said later, "he fought his way out of it." For several weeks, Jack lay on his back in a darkened room, showing little improvement. The doctors decided he might recuperate more rapidly in Florida. Late in December, he was flown to Palm Beach for Christmas with his family. However, his recovery was so slow that another operation was advised. In mid-February, he returned to New York. Once more, he received the last rites of the Church, and once more he survived. Late that month, he left the hospital and flew back to his father's house.

In Florida, he used five months of enforced leisure to write a book, *Profiles in Courage*, a collection of stories relating the responses of several politicians to crises arising from unpopular defense of principle. "Jack couldn't sleep for more than an hour or so at a time because his pain was so bad," Kennedy remembered. "So he'd study to get his mind off the pain. That's where the book came from."[20] During these months, the father may have reflected on how often during his son's lifetime he had seen him ill and in pain, yet how seldom he complained. In this respect, Jack resembled his mother. "I don't think I know anyone who has more courage than my wife," Joe Kennedy once said. "In all the years that we have been married, I have never heard her complain. Never. Not even once. . . . That is a quality that children are quick to see."[21] Bedridden much of the time, Jack needed, and received, a great deal of help with his book. Great stacks of reference books arrived from the Library of Congress. His devoted assistant, Theodore C. (Ted) Sorenson, sent research suggestions and drafted several chapters, which Jack rewrote. The book was not "ghost-written," but neither was it solely the author's effort.

Published by Harper and Brothers in 1956, *Profiles in Courage* quickly became a best-seller; the following year, the book won the Pulitzer Prize. Privately, Jack protested that he did not deserve this honor because the book was not based on original research. "All it was ever meant to be was a treatment of an interesting idea, the pressures that are put on a politician," he said. "I didn't expect it to have a wide appeal."[22] Pleasantly surprised, he turned the book to political advantage as only a wealthy author could: he plowed back his royalties into promotion and publicity that linked his name and photograph with the word "courage."[23] Some believed that his motive in writing the book, consciously or not, was to ingratiate himself with those liberals who had not forgiven his failure to oppose McCarthy. If so, the effort was unsuccessful, for the book gave rise to the quip among liberals that the senator should show "less profile and more courage."

As he recovered, Jack realized that his back, while still painful, would not cripple him. Now that his future had been restored, he could range freely over a world of possibilities. It was during his long convalescence, close friends later guessed, that he began to think seriously of becoming President of the United States.

As impatient as Joe Kennedy was, he recognized that timing was crucial to political success. In 1956, he was prepared to bide his time; his son, however, could not wait.

The result was that the drive for the Presidency began with a serious disagreement between them. In the spring of 1956, Sargent Shriver learned that Adlai Stevenson, who was certain to be renominated, was toying with the idea of throwing open the race for the vice-presidential nomination at that summer's Democratic convention. From Chicago, Shriver sent a memorandum alerting his father-in-law.[24] Kennedy sternly warned his son not to seek or accept this alluring but potentially disastrous prize. "I knew Adlai Stevenson was going to take a licking," he said, "and I was afraid Jack might be blamed because he was a Catholic. That would have made it much more difficult for another Catholic in years to come."[25] Four years hence, when the unbeatable Eisenhower had stepped down, the prospect would be immeasurably brighter. Before leaving for his customary sojourn on the French Riviera, Kennedy repeated his warning to Jack: *wait*.

At the convention in Chicago, Jack and Bobby, surrounded by lieutenants who also were newcomers to national politics, succumbed to the temptation of the chase and hastily organized a bid for the vice-presidential nomination. In an exciting race against Senator Estes Kefauver of Tennessee, Jack was narrowly defeated. Later he realized how close he had come to political disaster. In 1957, he was interviewed by Hearst reporter Bob Considine, who was preparing a series of articles on the Kennedy family. Jack spoke of his dead older brother. "Joe was the star of our family," he said. "He did everything better than the rest of us. If he had lived, he would have gone on in politics and he would have been elected to the House and Senate as I was. And, like me, he would have gone for the vice-presidential nomination at the 1956 convention, but, unlike me, he wouldn't have been beaten. Joe would have won the nomination." Jack paused and smiled. "And then he and Stevenson would have been beaten by Eisenhower, and today Joe's political career would be in shambles and he would be trying to pick up the pieces."[26]

Overnight the handsome young senator whom millions had watched in the televised contest gained national prominence. Crowds gathered wherever he went and fan mail and requests for speeches poured into his office. His backers had circulated among the party professionals a persuasive memorandum arguing for his nomination on the ground that he would appeal to Catholic voters in the big cities, many of whom had defected to the Republicans under Eisenhower. The presumed liability of his Catholicism thus was cleverly advanced as a prime asset, an argument that would be repeated again and again as 1960 approached.

But the advantages of the 1956 defeat were still hidden immediately following the convention. Jack was stunned by his first major political reversal. When Kennedy learned of his sons' impulsive bid for the Vice-Presidency, he telephoned from his villa at Cap d'Antibes to protest vigorously. Now a dejected and chastened Jack made his peace by telephone. "We did our best," he told his father. "I had fun and I didn't make a fool of myself." Tense and exhausted, he decided to join his father in France. Jackie, in the last months of her first pregnancy, had been lonely and miserable during the convention; she flew to her parents' home in Newport to await the birth of her baby. Her dependence was not as great as Jack's need, in his hurt and disappointment, to see his father.

Joe Kennedy and his son had a long talk. "I told him," he recalled, "that God was still with him, that he could be President if he wanted to be and worked hard." Years later, it was Kennedy's belief that his encouragement was unnecessary. "Jack had already made up his mind on the way over. He was already working on it."[27]

While Jack was sailing on the Mediterranean, an urgent message reached the Kennedy villa: Jackie had lost her baby and had undergone an operation. He flew to the Newport Hospital and stayed at her bedside for two weeks. Then he left to campaign for Stevenson. During one five-week stretch, he traveled thirty thousand miles and made one hundred and fifty speaking appearances in twenty-six states. Such heroic exertions were not explained solely by his admiration for Stevenson. When someone assured the whirlwind campaigner that he would be the favorite for the vice-presidential nomination in 1960, he replied: "I'm not running for Vice-President any more. I'm now running for President."[28]

And so he was, in a relentless, methodical fashion that would make obsolete much of the conventional wisdom of U. S. politics. In mid-December, 1956, more than three years before the convention, he and Ted Sorenson took to the road to seek out and persuade potential delegates. Before they were finished, they would visit almost every state in the Union. For they had learned from the defeat in Chicago that the national convention, for all its frantic politicking, was merely the climax of planning and preparation done far in advance; and that the work before them was to meet the hundreds of men and women on whose collective decision everything depended. On that hectic night in 1956 before the balloting for Vice-President, when the Kennedy forces were scrambling for votes, Carmine De Sapio, powerful boss of New York's Tammany Hall, had sat in an anteroom, unrecognized by the candidate's eager but unknowing supporters. At the next convention, Kennedy and his staff would know everyone. Month by month, the file in Sorenson's Washington office grew bulkier with detailed information on likely delegates and their promises of support redeemable in 1960.

Nineteen fifty-seven also saw the beginning of a publicity buildup unprecedented in U.S. political history. For the first time, a very junior and relatively unimportant member of the Senate became the subject of glowing articles that paid little attention to politics and instead presented to their readers an arresting political personality, a celebrity. With his youth, good looks, war record and wealth, not to mention his active and colorful family, Jack Kennedy made superb copy, and each article about him begot imitators. Women's magazines such as *McCall's* and *Redbook* found a perfect "angle" in the Senator's beautiful young wife.*

Joe Kennedy worked quietly on his son's behalf, wooing publishers and granting interviews to sympathetic writers. One weekend, an influential New England publisher was invited to Hyannis Port and decided to fly into a small field nearby. Bad weather delayed his arrival well past the hour set for dinner by his notoriously punctual host. As the plane landed, the publisher saw a bare-headed figure waiting beside an automobile in the gloom and drizzle, and assumed it was his host's chauffeur. It turned out to be Kennedy himself, impatient for his dinner but warmly cordial for his son's sake.[29]

In an era of television, mass magazines and "image-making," Kennedy realized that the candidate's personality had become the deciding factor in presidential politics. He candidly told a friend that "we're going to sell Jack like soap flakes," and likened his son's popular appeal to that of Hollywood's stars. "Jack is the greatest attraction in the country today," he said during an interview in 1959. "I'll tell you how to sell more copies of a 'book.' Put his picture on the cover. Why is it that when his picture is on the cover of *Life* or *Redbook* that they sell a record number of copies? You advertise the fact that he will be at a dinner and you will break all records for attendance. He can draw more people to a fund-raising dinner than Cary Grant or Jimmy Stewart. Why is that? He has more universal appeal. That is why the Democratic party is going to nominate him. The party leaders around the country realize that to win they have to nominate him."[30]

It seemed to Kennedy that his son's smoothly professional organization was running the most effective pre-convention campaign in history. "The office of the President of the United States is the greatest and the most important in the world. And yet . . . do you realize that to get the nomination for that office candidates have the worst organizations. That's because good men—men who have important jobs —don't want to give up their jobs to work for a candidate before he gets the nomination, because it's too risky. He may not get it, and then where are they? And the others—the ones you *can* hire, the ones

*Jackie Kennedy was initiated early into the publicity-centered life. When Jack proposed, she telephoned an aunt to tell her the news, but cautioned her to keep the engagement a secret. *The Saturday Evening Post* was coming out with an article on Jack, entitled "The Senate's Gay Young Bachelor," and nothing must spoil it. Jack Kennedy was indeed a gay bachelor, not marrying until he was thirty-six.

who are available—aren't any good and you can't build an organization with them anyhow."[31]

The nucleus of Jack's organization had been intact for at least four years when the drive for the nomination began; and the family stood ready to help on a moment's notice. (Even Peter Lawford got into the act during the 1956 convention, tracking down a nightclub-owner friend who was chairman of the Nevada delegation and winning his votes for Jack.) Asked where he fitted into his son's organization, Kennedy insisted he didn't. Pressed to explain, he said: "Well, I just call people. You call people that you know and ask them to help in any way they can. . . . I've made a lot of contacts all over the country. You just ask them to help. That's all."[32]

As early as 1957, Kennedy was on the telephone with Charles A. Buckley, the wizened, durable Democratic boss of the Bronx, planning the capture of New York's big bloc of convention votes. He also kept in touch with Chicago's Mayor Richard Daley, who was bound to respect Kennedy's economic power as owner of the Merchandise Mart. Kennedy took keen delight in his far-ranging acquaintanceship. One day in Palm Beach, he and a much-traveled writer whiled away an afternoon sprawled on the floor of Kennedy's living room with a map of the U.S. spread out before them. Each in turn poked a finger into the map and reeled off the names of people he knew in and about that place. Kennedy, who collected people as another would stamps, won the competition handily.

By the spring of 1958, Jack Kennedy, whose office now received more than a hundred speaking invitations a week, was the frontrunner among the undeclared Democratic presidential candidates. Some observers thought he was *too* far in front; would he "peak" and lose momentum long before the convention? Joe Kennedy scoffed at the suggestion. "The only way we can win this is to wrap it up very, very early," he said. "In our position, that's the risk we're most willing to take, and it's the least of our worries. When you start from scratch, you've got to run like the dickens all the way."[33]

Although Kennedy spoke of "our position" and "our worries," he discreetly avoided being seen in public with his son. As Jack prepared to run for reelection to the Senate that summer, Kennedy went into hiding, choosing as his retreat an apartment on Boston's Beacon Street.

It happened that the building he selected was the residence of Chief Justice Raymond S. Wilkins, a Harvard classmate. One day Mrs. Wilkins recognized Kennedy in the hall and introduced herself. He beamed and said: "I'll be down to see you at five o'clock." That afternoon, the Justice came home to find Kennedy and his wife chatting over tea. From then on, Kennedy was a frequent visitor, remarking how grateful he was to get away from the telephones and politicians upstairs.[34]

Justice Wilkins told another classmate, Oscar Haussermann, a prominent Boston lawyer, that Kennedy was in hiding and seemed lonely. Haussermann decided to act on a long-standing personal resolution to give Kennedy a dinner. He telephoned a half dozen other members of the Class of '12, and arranged to meet them in a private dining room at the Union Club. Then he telephoned the guest of honor, taking care to explain at once that he was *not* calling to solicit money for Harvard. It was a necessary precaution. On a plane only that spring, Kennedy had met a classmate from the Boston Latin School, who invited him to the fiftieth reunion of the Class of '08. Kennedy said he would attend. As they parted, he asked his companion warily: "This *is* the Latin School reunion, not Harvard College?"

His suspicions allayed by Haussermann, Kennedy appeared at the Union Club, and was delighted to find himself amid a circle of fondly remembered friends. He had been missed at the reunions over the past twenty years, and there was much to talk about. At the end of the warm, nostalgic evening, Kennedy said in a quiet voice: "This is the nicest thing anybody's done for me in years."[35]

Over tea one afternoon with Justice and Mrs. Wilkins, Kennedy spoke of the actual stake in his son's campaign for reelection to the Senate. "If we can get a plurality of a half million," he said, "they can't stop us for the Presidency."[36] Jack's unknown Republican opponent still lived on the top floor of a three-decker tenement and campaigned emotionally against the Kennedy wealth. He also found a way to make an issue of the unseen elder Kennedy. "Look how my opponent voted for the St. Lawrence Seaway—it starts right at the front door of the Merchandise Mart in Chicago, which is owned by old Joe Kennedy." It was difficult to stir voter interest in an off-year election, but the Kennedy machine, warming up for greater things, ground out a crushing victory. On election night, Jack received the returns in his father's hotel suite, and saw himself reelected by the almost incredible margin of 874,608 votes, the greatest landslide scored by any candidate for any office in either party in the history of Massachusetts. It also was the largest margin received by any senatorial candidate in the U.S. in 1958.[37]

But this brilliant vote-getting performance failed to sway many of the powerful big city bosses and officeholders in the large Eastern states who remained convinced that a Catholic could not win the Presidency. Outside the East, such party leaders as former President Truman and House Speaker Sam Rayburn anticipated a showdown at the convention that would put the young upstart in his place. Not only Jack's religion, youth, and inexperience hurt him with the party's older leaders; they also had unpleasant memories of his father. "I like Jack. He is a nice person," said Truman. "But I don't like his daddy and never did."[38]

The liberal wing of the party remained cool to Kennedy. A poll of the members of Americans for Democratic Action disclosed that most of them preferred other candidates. By and large, the liberals were secularists, suspicious of the Catholic Church and its generally conservative hierarchy. Joe Kennedy, of course, was anathema. Not long after the 1958 election, Mrs. Eleanor Roosevelt, the first lady of liberalism, warned that the elder Kennedy was "spending oodles of money all over the country" on behalf of his son, and "probably has paid representatives in every state by now." As for Jack, she described him, with a ladylike flick at his jugular vein, as "someone who understands what courage is and admires it, but has not quite the independence to have it."[39]

In addition to the party professionals and the doctrinaire liberals, other groups within the Democratic coalition had strong reservations about Senator Kennedy. Union officials were uneasy about the headlines that he and his brother had won by uncovering abuses of union power before the Senate Labor Rackets Committee. Negro leaders were unimpressed by the senator's record of compromise on civil rights, and remembered the Southern support he had enjoyed at the 1956 convention. Left to their own devices, the mutually hostile factions of the party, when they convened to perform their quadrennial miracle of accommodation, almost certainly would not choose Jack Kennedy.

To get the nomination, he would have to confront the convention with massive evidence of his popularity. Therefore he decided to go directly to the voters in key state primary elections. If he won steadily, the convention could not very well deny him the nomination without seeming to do so only because of his Catholicism. And that would alienate the Catholic voters in the big cities, without which the Democrats could not win. Thus the primary-election route promised not only to prove that Kennedy was the winner the party wanted, but also to turn "the religious issue" to his advantage.

This issue was uppermost in Joe Kennedy's mind. "A few years ago," he said during an interview in 1959, "Jack was elected to the Board of Overseers at Harvard, which would have been unheard of in my day. It seems to me that if a Catholic can be elected to the Board of Overseers at Harvard, he can be elected to anything."[40] As the primaries approached, he declared bluntly: "Let's not con ourselves. The only issue is whether a Catholic can be elected President."[41]

On January 2, 1960, Jack Kennedy announced his candidacy. Later that month, Joe Kennedy stepped off the Empire State Express at Albany and went to see an old acquaintance, Daniel P. (Uncle Dan) O'Connell, the Albany County Democratic chairman. Kennedy asked O'Connell's help for his son, but the crusty veteran balked a bit, noting that the candidate was only forty-two years old. "He's a little young, isn't he?" asked O'Connell.

"He is," Kennedy conceded, "but I'm seventy-two and I want to be around to enjoy it."

Kennedy left Albany with O'Connell's promise of the two and a half votes from his district, a modest but satisfactory start on New York's one hundred and fourteen convention votes.[42]

In such a mission, Kennedy briefly resumed his old role in his son's career, but now the roles of father and son were reversed. "Dad is a financial genius, all right," Jack told a reporter, "but in politics, he is something else."[43] Kennedy still sat among the inner circle of advisers, was privy to plans and strategy, and offered opinions and suggestions. And Jack still listened. Kennedy insisted that his son enter the Wisconsin primary. "You've got to do it, Jack," he told him during a meeting at Hyannis Port. "You've got no choice."[44] His opponent there would be Minnesota's liberal Senator Hubert Humphrey, not a major threat but one who could prove formidable in a Midwestern farm state with a number of heavily Protestant districts. Bobby Kennedy, Ted Sorenson, and others advised against entering the race. Finally, Jack took his father's advice, but only after weighing the last-minute findings of pollster Lou Harris. During the Wisconsin campaign, a friend of the family recalled coming to a political conference a few minutes before Jack arrived. A problem had come up, and Joe Kennedy sat waiting with several of his son's advisers. In former days, he would have been holding forth on what should be done. Now he sat quietly. When the candidate appeared, his father was first to speak. "Well, Jack," he asked, "what do we do now?"[45]

Kennedy urged his son to enter the California primary, but Jack refused.[46] In his anxiety over the religious issue, Kennedy at one point seriously proposed that Jack withdraw as an active candidate, a proposal he never considered for a moment.[47] Once, Jack learned that his father had called a meeting of the family and chief advisers; he brusquely informed one and all there would be no meeting.[48] When his father insisted on expounding his conservative opinions, Jack was capable of squelching him. "We've heard the former Ambassador's views," he was apt to say, "now let's get on with our business."[49]

Yet there was no question that Kennedy held unchallenged sway as head of the family. Visitors to Palm Beach remembered being shushed by the Senator as they entered the house; Jack explained that his father was watching his favorite television program. Any strain that developed as the result of tactical disagreement quickly passed as father and son pursued the strategic objective of victory at the convention.

Wisconsin did little to advance Jack Kennedy's cause, for while he won the primary there, his margin was unconvincing and he failed to knock Humphrey out of the race. An overwhelming victory was necessary on the next battleground—West Virginia. Again, Humphrey would be the opponent, and could be expected to run well in a state suffering serious economic woes and presumed to be unfriendly to a Roman Catholic candidate.

Apprehensive about the outcome, Joe Kennedy assembled a half dozen New York City and state Democratic leaders for lunch at an expensive but inconspicuous restaurant south of Central Park. "Now, my boy is going into the West Virginia primary within a few days," he told them. "All the experts say that if he wins thirty-five percent of the vote because of the religious problem, it will be considered a victory, even in defeat. . . . Will you gentlemen issue a statement calling it such if he polls that percent of the vote?"

Charles A. Buckley, the Bronx overlord, loyally said that he would. Kennedy looked around the table at his other guests: Michael H. Prendergast, the then state party chairman, Carmine G. De Sapio, Tammany Hall leader, and the remaining county leaders, Joseph T. Sharkey, of Brooklyn, Herbert Koehler, of Queens, and Joseph McKinney, of Staten Island. A commitment to a loser violated the code these men lived by. They were silent. "All right then," said Kennedy, eyeing them coldly. "You can go to blazes."[50]

The full weight of the Kennedy wealth and political expertise was brought to bear in West Virginia. Earlier in Wisconsin, Humphrey had complained half-seriously that, campaigning against all the Kennedys and their in-laws, he felt like an independent retailer competing with a chain. Addressing a dinner in New York, Jack artfully dodged criticism of his family's heavy spending. "I got a wire from my father," he said, and then read: " 'Dear Jack: Don't buy one vote more than necessary. I'll be damned if I'll pay for a landslide.' " But this good-natured banter faded as the West Virginia campaign became heated. "I don't have any daddy who can pay the bills for me," Humphrey said bitterly. "I can't afford to run around this state with a little black bag and a checkbook." The superbly organized Kennedy forces rolled up a stunning majority, carrying all but seven of the state's fifty-five counties. After this triumph, Kennedy's candidacy gained irresistible momentum. All told, he entered and won seven state primaries. In the midst of the campaign, Joe Kennedy, talking to Arthur Krock, expressed the spirit driving his son: "For the Kennedys, it's either the outhouse or the castle—no in-between."

As the Democratic convention neared, Kennedy remained in seclusion. Late in the spring, he was invited to address a dinner marking the twenty-fifth anniversary of the SEC, an honor he thought he might safely accept. At the last minute, he changed his mind, explaining to a friend that he was afraid of saying something that would hurt Jack's chances.[51] Even though he kept silent and out of sight, Kennedy was much on the minds of Democratic politicians. In Independence, Missouri, former President Truman announced to the press that he would not attend the convention because it had the appearance of "prearrangement." Truman said he had written a letter to "Senator Joseph Kennedy," asking whether he honestly thought he was ready for the Presidency. When a reporter called attention to his mistake in the Senator's name, inquiring "if that was a Freudian slip," the tart-tongued Truman said only that the name "of the young man is John."

Among the liberals, gloom prevailed. In West Virginia, the ideologically pure Humphrey had been flattened by the brute force of massed dollars. "Jack was able to use not just one political technique, but all of them—polling, TV, newspaper ads, contributions, direct mail, everything," said an aide in reviewing the campaign. Jack Kennedy also was whisked comfortably from city to city in a specially fitted Convair owned by a family corporation and leased to him at $1.75 a mile (or $15,000 to $19,000 a month). Because the family kept its $300,000 equity in the plane, it was not considered a campaign contribution, even though it contributed mightily to his success. Humphrey had bounced about Wisconsin and West Virginia in a bus, and had been forced to go deep into debt to pay for television time. Writing in the *New Republic,* Selig S. Harrison confessed to doubts about Jack Kennedy "arising from the fact that a command post of his political operations over the years has been Joe Kennedy's office in the Kennedy owned building at 230 Park Avenue. One can only imagine how many open-dated blank checks have been given to strategically placed individuals to help Kennedy get where he is. How many of these checks, if any, call for repayment by Kennedy as President, no one can foretell."[52]

The influence of the Kennedy fortune, though enormous, never approached the proportions it assumed in the imaginations of demoralized opponents. The Kennedys were not only the richest family ever to make politics their business; they also were by far the most sophisticated. They were able to demand full value for every dollar spent. It was the informed guess of close friends that, beginning in 1958, Joe Kennedy committed at least one and a half million dollars to his son's pre-convention campaign, a figure far below the guesses of outsiders. Still, this estimated outlay was huge by comparison with the resources available to Humphrey, who entered West Virginia with seventeen thousand dollars of unpaid debts. Whatever the sum Kennedy actually spent, the point was not how much money was committed, but how astutely it was used.

Spearheaded by Bobby Kennedy, a new breed of "young pros" was on the threshold of taking over the Democratic party. That canny veteran of the back rooms, Harry S Truman, had sensed the danger and moved to defend the power of the old guard, but it was too late. The Kennedy organization men were fomenting a revolution, not of substance, but of technique. Expertly using television, that costly but wondrously effective instrument of mass persuasion, and every other advanced political weapon of the electronic age, they overwhelmed their opponents. Old-line bosses, reared in a tradition of inexact political measurements and visceral decision-making, were impressed by the confident practitioners of "in-depth" polling and election analysis. The new breed looked like winners. On the eve of the convention, the cumulative force of the revolution was felt. It was reported on good authority that Jack Kennedy had committed to him more than six hundred of the seven hundred and sixty-one votes necessary for his nomination.

Almost unobserved, Joe and Rose Kennedy slipped into Los Angeles and went to the Beverly Hills mansion of Marion Davies, former movie queen and companion of William Randolph Hearst. The whitewashed, Spanish style villa lay at the end of a winding, quarter-mile long driveway, and was screened from the street by eucalyptus trees and bougainvillea. Using a battery of telephones at poolside, Kennedy kept in close touch with his sons' command post, Suite 8315 at the Biltmore, eleven miles away. His presence was felt by opposing strategists. "Where's Joe?" someone asked Sam Rayburn. Rayburn, trying desperately to perform a miracle for his fellow Texan, Senate Majority Leader Lyndon B. Johnson, replied: "I haven't seen him, but he is in the bushes around here."

Mrs. Eleanor Roosevelt arrived to lead a valiant effort for Adlai Stevenson, and found to her dismay that several leading intellectuals had quietly shifted to Kennedy's side. Noting that these defectors still thought Stevenson was the best man, but said Kennedy would win, Mrs. Roosevelt declared it was absurd for them "to accept anyone as second best until you have done all you can to get the best." Her scolding fell on deaf ears.

Senator Johnson lashed out at his young colleague, criticizing Kennedy's absenteeism and mediocre legislative record. He also assailed his wealth and family. "I haven't had anything given to me," the Texan told delegates. "Whatever I have and whatever I hope to get will be because of whatever energy and talents I have." At the Washington state caucus, Johnson, his temper blazing, attacked Joe Kennedy's prewar views, shouting: "I wasn't any Chamberlain umbrella man."

Johnson's low blow was not forgiven by the Kennedys, but it was forgotten when the moment came to make an alliance dictated by expediency. By one account, it was Joe Kennedy himself who proposed Johnson for second place on the ticket, telling his sons the Texan would help Jack by delivering the South. Then Kennedy telephoned Johnson and urged him to become Jack's running mate for the good of the party. (When it had been suggested months earlier that Jack might take the vice-presidential nomination for the same reason, Kennedy had snapped: "It's first place or nothing. Not for chalk, money or marbles will we take second place. Nobody's going to make a deal with us in a back room somewhere for second place on the ticket.")[53]

While the nominating and seconding speeches droned on at the Los Angeles Sports Arena, Jack, in a hideaway apartment on North Rossmore Boulevard, decided to visit his mother and father. Ducking reporters, he clambered down the fire escape at the rear of the building, vaulted a low concrete wall, and dashed across a backyard to a waiting car. At the Davies' mansion that afternoon, he relaxed in the pool, and later had dinner with his parents. He returned to his apartment by way of the fire escape, just in time to watch the televised balloting begin. Earlier that day, he and Bobby had compared notes on their strength; their figures checked to within a half-vote.

State by state down the roll call, the expected Kennedy votes clicked off, while those claimed by Johnson and the rest of the field did not. By the time the clerk called on Wyoming to declare the disposition of her fifteen votes, Kennedy had seven hundred and forty-eight votes. Now the antlike scurrying in the aisles stopped; the hum of whispers ceased; a hush fell over the Arena.

"Wyoming," shouted her spokesman, "casts all fifteen votes for the next President of the United States!"

John Fitzgerald Kennedy had been nominated for the nation's highest office.

That night, an exhausted Bobby Kennedy telephoned his father. "It's the best organization job I've ever seen in politics," Kennedy said jubilantly. But he could offer congratulations only from a poignant distance. While Rose and his children and their spouses went to the

Arena to appear with the nominee, Kennedy remained behind, before the television set in the Davies mansion.

Within thirty-six hours, he left Los Angeles, alone and unobserved, and streaked across the continent in a jet to New York. Soon after the plane landed in late afternoon, he began the next phase of the campaign. He telephoned the office of Henry R. Luce, Editor-in-Chief of Time, Inc., and got himself invited to dinner that evening at the Luce home in Manhattan. Afterward, they watched Jack Kennedy's televised acceptance speech before a crowd of eighty thousand in the Los Angeles Coliseum. The Luce magazines, however, did not support his candidacy.

His victory, declared a leading Republican convention planner, "proves the American dream that any boy can hope to grow up to run for President, especially if his father has four hundred million dollars." Many liberal Democrats felt a similar distaste for the outcome in Los Angeles, heightened by Kennedy's stunning choice of Johnson for second place on the ticket. Within less than a fortnight, however, the Republican convention in Chicago nominated Vice President Richard M. Nixon for the Presidency, and liberal Democrats stopped sulking. Except for the late Senator McCarthy, Nixon was the political figure that liberals hated most extravagantly; indeed, he inherited much of the anti-McCarthy hatred. The forty-seven-year-old former California Senator, an instinctive conservative, had tried to adopt a more pleasingly liberal political coloration; but the obvious masquerade disheartened his friends and inflamed his enemies. There were important doctrinal differences between his party and Kennedy's, yet these did not emerge clearly in the campaign. Their differences seemed to be almost entirely personal and stylistic. Nixon could not overcome a tendency toward mawkishness and moralizing. The word to describe his entire campaign was "strained." Kennedy, urbane, glib and seemingly relaxed, projected a much more appealing "image."

Through the late summer and fall of 1960, it seemed that the earth had swallowed Joe Kennedy, so well did he conceal himself from the press and public. The mystery of his whereabouts puzzled Republican editorial writers and inspired a couplet:

Jack and Bob will run the show
While Ted's in charge of hiding Joe.

Among friend and foe alike, the Kennedy clan provided an endless store of gossip. America's enfeebled political humor revived in a rash of father and son jokes. "Don't worry, son," Old Joe was said to have told Young Jack, "if you lose the election, I'll buy you a country." Americans had never seen anything like the small army of Kennedys and in-laws barnstorming across the land. Proclaimed an automobile bumper strip: BE THANKFUL ONLY ONE CAN WIN.

On its less amiable side, the gossip about the Kennedys attributed to them all manner of intrigue, plotted by the shadowy figure at the head of the family. Kennedy, who moved unobtrusively between New York and Hyannis Port, entertained politicians discreetly in such plush retreats as Manhattan's Hampshire House, but his participation in the campaign was limited. Early in the fall, Rose Kennedy said her husband had been working "in his own way," adding that it "seems better for Jack at this time that his father stay out of things."[54]

At the center of things was thirty-four-year-old Bobby, his sleeves rolled up, shoulders hunched, a scowl fixed on his face. Politicians who doubted that a revolution had occurred at the convention were rudely set straight by the young man who had taken charge. "Ruthless" was a word often heard along his trail, but he also left behind impressive results. Stepping between the brawling factions of New York's Democratic organization, he dealt as roughly with the high-minded reformers as with the Tammany wheelhorses. "Gentlemen," he told a group of startled reform leaders, "I don't give a damn if the state and county organizations survive after November, and I don't give a damn if *you* survive. I want to elect John F. Kennedy."[55]

In sizing up his two oldest sons, Kennedy once observed: "Bobby is more direct than Jack. Jack has always been one to persuade people what to do. . . . He [Bobby] resembles me much more than any of the other children."[56] On another occasion, he remarked of Bobby: "He's a great kid. He hates the same way I do."[57] The strong similarity between his father and younger brother had not escaped Jack. When someone mentioned his campaign manager's youth, he had a ready answer. "If I need somebody older," Jack said with a smile, "there's no need to go outside of the family. I can always get my father."[58]

Kennedy spoke frequently with his sons on the telephone, offering advice and cheering them on. The latter was especially appreciated. "The great thing about Dad," Jack said during the campaign, "is his optimism and his enthusiasm and how he's always for you. He might not always agree with what I do, just as I don't always agree with him, but as soon as I do anything, there's Dad saying: 'Smartest move you ever made.... We really got them on the run now.'"[59]

Just before and immediately after the first televised "debate" between the candidates, Kennedy was on the telephone with his son, first encouraging and later applauding him. This dramatic face-to-face encounter, witnessed by an audience of seventy million, was a turning point. Nixon, gaunt and shaky from a recent illness, appeared weak and indecisive. Kennedy, trim and fit, spoke forcefully, impressing viewers with his command of statistics. Overnight, the Vice-President lost much of the advantage he had enjoyed because of his presumably greater maturity and experience.* When some newspaper columnists wrote that the debate was a draw, Kennedy was furious. "What's the matter with all these guys?" he stormed. "If that wasn't a clear victory for Jack I never saw one." Then he paused for a moment, grinned, and said: "We'll knock their brains out."[60]

At intervals during the campaign, Kennedy relayed to Jack his latest judgments on the health of the economy and the stock market. His calculations showed a downtrend in the market and indicated poor prospects for general prosperity. These findings were incorporated into the flow of economic data from academic advisers, and added a mite to the candidate's arguments on his main theme: that only he could "get America moving again." To some of the elder Kennedy's conservative friends, Jack seemed to be moving in an alarmingly radical direction. Would he actually try to implement the utopian promises of the ultra-liberal Democratic platform? Kennedy assured them, with emphatic profanity, that the platform promises were just that—promises. A conservative newspaper columnist, pressed by Kennedy to endorse his son, replied that he saw no value in an endorsement that made either him or Jack—or both of them—appear hypocritical. Denied the favor he had taken for granted, Kennedy angrily broke off their long and intimate friendship.

It was crucial to Jack Kennedy's strategy that he carry the large

*The essential ingredient of the Kennedy revolution in political technique remained exacting preparation. For each of the last two televised debates, Kennedy rehearsed more than seven hours in the studio. Nixon, declining an offer of rehearsal time, arrived at the studio twenty-four minutes before air time for the third debate and only nine minutes before the final one.

cities of the populous Northeastern states with their heavy vote in the Electoral College. But in the city of New York, which swung the Empire State's forty-five electoral votes, there were rumblings of discontent from the Jewish population. Predominantly liberal and Democratic, the Jews were torn between allegiance to party and antipathy to Joe Kennedy. In a detailed article surveying "the Jewish vote," *The New York Times* found "a current of distrust of [Kennedy's] Catholicism and an active dislike of his father. . . ." A Democratic party worker in a Brooklyn district called the elder Kennedy "the number one bogy" in the campaign. Reported the *Times*:

> Many Jewish voters feel a personal revulsion against Joe Kennedy. They find it difficult not to transfer that dislike to the son. They agree that the sins of the father shouldn't be visited upon the son, but they are worried because this particular father has had a great influence on his children.[61]

In the closing weeks of the campaign, Kennedy broke his self-enforced silence and brought the suspicions against him to a head. From his villa on the French Riviera, he told a *Newsweek* correspondent he had no comment at the moment, but went on to promise that he would speak up after the election. "People may even see a flash of my old-time form," he declared. *What Is Joseph P. Kennedy's 'Old-Time Form'?* demanded an ad in New York newspapers, just before the election. Prepared by the "Lest We Forget Committee," which listed a Brooklyn address and Nathan D. Shapiro as treasurer, the ad consisted of quotations from newspapers, magazines, and government publications (including the Von Dirksen cables to Berlin) calculated to sustain the rumors that Kennedy was pro-Nazi, anti-Semitic, and the sinister force behind his son's career. "Study the documentation of his incredible past," the ad urged. "The future of Joseph P. Kennedy is in your hands."[62]

What occurred in the heavily Jewish districts of New York City on election day, 1960, deserves high rank among the classic ironies of U.S. politics. For the deep distrust of Joe Kennedy was neutralized by an even deeper nostalgia. A furrier, sunning himself on a park bench in East Flatbush, gave a hint of what would come when he spoke to the *Times*' reporter. "Kennedy," the furrier said, "is another Franklin D. Roosevelt."

Beginning with the West Virginia primary, Kennedy had tried to wrap himself in the mantle of Roosevelt. In that job-hungry state, pollster Lou Harris informed him that he must emphasize bread-and-butter liberalism. Presenting himself as a militant liberal, Kennedy called for a rebirth of the New Deal. He summoned to his side a former congressional colleague, Franklin D. Roosevelt, Jr., whose face and voice evoked the memory of a well-loved President. Among the Kennedy circle there was much talk of "activist" government, after the pattern of Roosevelt's whirlwind First Hundred Days. Kennedy aides encouraged the press to use the candidate's initials, a practice that helped implant in the public mind the desired association of FDR and JFK.

Thus, although Roosevelt's name was not praised in his father's house, Jack Kennedy campaigned as his political heir. So captivating was his Rooseveltian image that Jewish voters in New York, incredibly enough, supported him more heavily than did Irish Catholics.[63]

Not long after entering the White House, the President was asked about the parallel frequently drawn between himself and Roosevelt. "There is no validity to the comparison," Joe Kennedy's son said coolly.[64]

When Kennedy awoke at Hyannis Port on the morning of November 9, 1960, the dream that had been so close to fulfillment the night before still was only tentatively fulfilled.

The previous day, almost sixty-nine million Americans had cast their votes for President, the highest recorded number in any U.S. election. They had divided so evenly in their choice that the result turned on a relative handful of votes. Well into the evening, Kennedy had watched the incoming returns on television. Across the dark lawns, lights blazed in Bobby's house, the election headquarters into which filtered telephone reports from across the country. Until shortly after ten o'clock, it had seemed that Jack would win comfortably; thereafter, the trend changed slowly but dramatically. Democratic urban pluralities in the Midwest fell short of expectations, and his lead dwindled as the heavy Republican vote of mid-America and the West began coming in. By midnight, although the television screen continued to show a Kennedy triumph, the watchers in Hyannis Port, closely analyzing the returns, realized they were stalled just short of victory. One by one, they went to bed in the small hours of the morning, all except Bobby, who stayed at the telephone until dawn. At last Michigan went narrowly to Kennedy, giving him a tentative majority. Secret Service men, poised to move throughout the night, then took up positions around the house where the President-elect slept.[65]

The next morning, Kennedy and his sons, though gnawed by anxiety that the result would be reversed, showed no outward concern. Jack had been elected by the almost invisible margin of one-tenth of one percent of the popular vote. But the razor-thin margin stood up, and in mid-morning Nixon finally conceded. Now uncertainty gave way to celebration. The President-elect, his brothers and sisters, their wives and husbands—the entire family—posed for photographs in the living room of his parents' home. Joe Kennedy, released from his self-imposed exile, took the place next to his son Jack. Just before noon, a motorcade formed for the drive to the Hyannis Port Armory and the network television cameras. Suddenly Jack left his car and ran up the steps of his father's house. He emerged in a few moments and gave the signal to wait. At his son's invitation, Joe Kennedy was dressing to accompany him to the Armory and the public acknowledgment of victory.

Soon after the election, a friend telephoned Kennedy and asked him how it felt to be the father of the President. "Hell, I don't know how it feels," he replied. "Of course, I'm proud, but I don't feel any different. I don't know how I feel."[66]

Certainly his competitive attitude had not mellowed; he still wanted every vote. He confessed surprise at his son's scant plurality. "I didn't think it would be that close," he said. "I was wrong on two things. First, I thought he would get a bigger Catholic vote than he did. Second, I did not think so many would vote against him because of his religion."[67] In his ferociously partisan view, voters were only allowed to be prejudiced in *favor* of his son. When he was asked how many states Jack would have carried if he had been an Episcopalian, Kennedy unhesitatingly answered: "Fifty."

Congratulatory messages flooded into the hands of the father of the President. Among them was a letter from Chief Justice Wilkins, looking back a half-century. He wrote:

> I never gave any thought as an undergraduate as to whether any of us would have a son who would become President of the United States.

Had I done so, I am sure my choice would have fallen upon you. I congratulate you upon your success in an achievement I did not have the forethought to expect.

My prayer is that you be given the years to watch the progress of the career which is not only Jack's but also belongs to his father and mother and all his family.[68]

In his brief reply, Kennedy expressed gratitude for his classmate's thoughtful note, and then added:

Wouldn't life be dull if as undergrads we had to project destiny? Of course, like you, we glory in Jack's entire career.[69]

On the long journey from Harvard to the White House, it was fortunate that Joe Kennedy had not been able to project destiny's shifting favor and cruel caprice. Of no significance as he wrote was the date at the head of Justice Wilkins' letter: November 22. In a tragic instant three years later, that date would be etched in the hearts of a stunned family and nation.

"Jack doesn't belong any more to just a family," Kennedy told a journalist close to his son shortly after the election. "He belongs to the country. That's probably the saddest thing about all this. The family can be there, but there is not much they can do for the President of the United States."[70]

In the weeks before the inauguration, it almost seemed as though Kennedy were anticipating this separation and inadequacy, for he drew his family around him at every opportunity. Triumphantly he presided at the traditional Thanksgiving feast in Hyannis Port. A few days later, he visited Jack and Jackie in Georgetown following the birth of their son, John, Jr. Before Christmas, when the family gathered again in Palm Beach, the new President and his father were seen together attending Mass, on the golf course, and at parties. One evening, Kennedy led his son to a reception honoring his longtime friend, former President Herbert Hoover. Politely the youngest man ever elected to the Presidency asked the oldest living Chief Executive if he had any advice to offer him. "You'll hear from them all," said Hoover. "You'll have to make up your mind on what is good advice." At Joe Kennedy's request, Hoover telephoned Nixon and arranged a conciliatory public meeting between the President-elect and the opponent he had so narrowly defeated.

After their long public separation, the press noted that father and son suddenly seemed to be together almost constantly. When a reporter asked whether this was just coincidental, Joe Kennedy's terse reply was epigrammatic. "There are no accidents in politics," he said. "I can appear with him any time I want to now."[71]

CHAPTER 25

Father of the President

Eight inches of snow, a blizzard by local standards, blanketed Washington on the eve of the inauguration, bringing the capital to a standstill. But the Democrats, figuratively speaking, had been out in the cold for eight years. Bundled in overcoats and swathed in mink, they gaily struggled to the festivities heralding John F. Kennedy's New Frontier. Only half of the musicians of the National Symphony Orchestra straggled into Constitution Hall, but the inaugural concert went on as scheduled. The fund-raising extravaganza at a Washington arena began two hours late and ran hours too long, but Frank Sinatra and the Democrats of Broadway and Hollywood came handsomely to the aid of their party's treasury. Well past midnight, guests still were arriving at house parties in Georgetown and the suburbs. And in Paul Young's softly lit restaurant downtown, a very special party for the President-elect, his family, and friends began at two o'clock in the morning. The indefatigable host was seventy-two-year-old Joseph P. Kennedy.[1]

Inauguration Day was dazzling bright and bitter cold. During the night, the snow had been cleared from Capitol Plaza. Shivering in the wind, the crowd that assembled for the noon ceremony watched as high officials of the old and new administrations, and representatives of the nations of the earth, arrived to witness the formal transfer of the awesome power of the Presidency. Escorted to seats on the platform were a couple whose rank fitted none of the conventional categories of protocol. Though without office or title, this man and woman were, in a sense, the chief witnesses. Only once before, when Ulysses S. Grant entered the White House, had both parents of a President lived to see him inaugurated. Now Mr. and Mrs. Joseph P. Kennedy took their places of honor.

Joe Kennedy, ruddy-cheeked and beaming, wore a cutaway coat, put aside twenty-one years earlier when his ambassadorship ended; it had been a source of satisfaction to him that the coat needed no alteration.[2] At the inaugural balls that evening (five were to be held), Rose Kennedy would wear the same gown in which she had been presented to the Queen. "This is what I've been looking forward to for a long time," Kennedy said exultantly. "It's a great day."

It was a day when the nation, so closely divided in its choice, united hopefully behind the man who now became the President of all the people and the symbol of the world's oldest republic. Wearing no overcoat, his hand resting on a closed family Bible, John F. Kennedy, at 12:51 P.M. on January 20, 1961, recited the oath that made him the thirty-fifth President of the United States. Then, in a relatively brief address containing passages of soaring eloquence, the youngest man ever elected to the Presidency proclaimed to the world that the torch of freedom had been passed to a new generation of Americans, "born in this century, tempered by war, disciplined by a hard and bitter peace, proud of our ancient heritage. . . ." The next morning's newspapers would report that throughout the ceremony tears had glistened in Joe Kennedy's eyes.

Afterward, the mood of light-hearted celebration returned. Reporters boggled at three chartered buses parked near the Capitol, each marked "Kennedy Family." Could there possibly be *that* many Kennedys and relatives? It turned out that the red-carpeted buses were to be used to transport Joe Kennedy's luncheon guests downtown. The sparkling afternoon was filled with martial music and stirring pageantry as the inaugural parade passed over streets hastily cleared of snow with army flamethrowers. As the new President's open car approached the reviewing stand outside the White House, he rose for the first and only time. Proudly his parents rose and returned his salute.[3] Then they joined him in his new home.

In the weeks before the inauguration, there had been rumors that Joe Kennedy quietly was looking for a house in or near Washington; there were even reports that he would move into the White House itself. Seldom had the public caricature and the private man been so at odds. For now, more than ever, Kennedy intended to keep his distance from his son. "If Jack ever feels he has anything to ask me —I've had lots of different experiences in life—he knows where he can find me, and I'll tell him what I think," he said. "But I feel very strongly about older people keeping their noses out of the businesses of their children. I had a contract years ago with a couple of firms and all they paid me for was: 'for advice—when requested.' That's the way it's going to be between my son and me."[4]

Kennedy realized things never could be the same. "No matter what the previous relationship had been," he said with a trace of sadness, "the moment a man sits behind the White House desk, from then on it is 'Mr. President.'" So it always had been when Kennedy entered Roosevelt's office, and so it would be now that his son sat in the oval study. Even away from the White House, he often used the formal manner of address. "I'm certainly not going to call my son 'Mr. President' when we're alone together," he explained, "but if there are people around we don't know very well I do, and it doesn't seem at all strange."[5]

During the new administration's first year, Kennedy spent just one afternoon at the White House. However, the President and his father spoke frequently on the telephone, sometimes exchanging as many as a half-dozen calls in a single day.[6] The substance of their conversations was closely guarded, but well-informed reporters accepted the assurances of White House aides that the calls dealt mainly with family matters. Of course, politics was very much a family matter. Even with the resources at his command, the President still turned to his father occasionally for advice on such subjects as the gold outflow and for service as a political go-between with such contemporaries as Charles A. Buckley. Some conservative observers were reassured by the conversations between the President and his father. Westbrook

Pegler, the elder Kennedy's sometime crony, wrote with satisfaction: ". . . Jack can telephone Joe for the last word on politics and economics and whatever his enemies may say of Joe they can't say he has anything against riches or capitalism or in favor of Moscow or the intellectuals of the British Foreign Office who often turn up in the lee of the Kremlin."[7]

Many businessmen also found Joe Kennedy's presence in the background vaguely comforting; it was common knowledge that he laughed out loud at the suggestion that his son was a liberal. This euphoria lasted until the steel companies raised their prices in defiance of the President's wishes in April, 1962, causing Jack Kennedy angrily to recall a paternal description of the big-steel men: "My father always told me they were sons of bitches, but I never really believed him until now."[8] Later, when the price increases had been rescinded, the President adopted a more soothing tone: "Obviously these generalizations are inaccurate and unfair, and he [my father] has been a businessman, and the business system has been very generous to him. But I felt at that time that we had not been treated altogether with frankness, and, therefore, I thought that his view had merit. But that is past. Now we are working together, I hope." Whatever else businessmen learned from the episode, they were forcefully reminded that Joe Kennedy had not bred into his sons a respect for business and moneymaking. On the contrary, this independent entrepreneur had taught them that being "only" a businessman was an ambition beneath their talents.

In his first informal assignment from his son, Kennedy, by his own account, failed completely. After the election, Jack asked his father to take a month and compile a list of likely candidates for Secretary of the Treasury. "When Jack called and asked me to give him the names," Kennedy recalled, "I said, 'I can't.' "[9] Nevertheless, the President's choices for the key Cabinet posts of State and Defense, Dean Rusk and Robert S. McNamara, respectively, grew out of conversations with his father.[10] And there was no mistaking Kennedy's hand in the most controversial Cabinet appointment, that of Bobby Kennedy as Attorney General. It was Joe Kennedy's strong belief that, when the going got rough, the President would need someone near him he could trust absolutely. At first, his sons were reluctant, but he insisted that Bobby be appointed.[11]

Editorial writers called attention to Bobby's scant legal experience, l that his chief qualification was his devotion to his brother's in- To charges of "nepotism," Joe Kennedy snorted: "Nepotism, my /hy should anybody think that Bobby needs a job? He fought ...omination, fought it until he drove Jack and me crazy. A lot of people in our own camp fought it, too, and agreed with him. They wanted to see him go back to Boston and become Senator. Not me!"[12]

Kennedy was not merely insensitive to the arguments and longstanding precedent against Bobby's appointment; where his family was concerned, he simply could not see the other side of the question. This attitude troubled even those who were devoted to the family. On a stroll across midtown Manhattan one day, Kennedy said to a writer then preparing a book on his son's administration: "Bobby's the best Attorney General since Stone." He paused and nodded, underscoring the significance of his observation. Later, his companion realized that Attorney General Harlan Fiske Stone had climaxed a distinguished legal career by becoming Chief Justice of the Supreme Court, and it occurred to him that Kennedy conceivably might envisage his sons taking the leading positions in all three branches of government. The writer questioned an acquaintance of the family about Joe Kennedy's probable intentions. "I don't know," came the slow reply. "He *is* greedy."[13]

Often asked what he would do during his son's tenure in the Presidency, Kennedy invariably answered: "I'll mind the store." But he went to his Park Avenue office only infrequently, confessing that he shared his children's boredom with business. He left an able, well-paid staff to look after his interests, reviewing only the major decisions.

The exception to his indifference was show business. Kennedy once told Jimmy Roosevelt: "There are only two pursuits that get in your blood—politics and the motion-picture business."[14] Shrewdly, he saw a way to enjoy himself and boost his son's popularity. When newspaperman Robert J. Donovan's book, *PT-109,* was published, Kennedy decided Jack's World War II exploits would make a splendid movie. Renewing old Hollywood friendships, he proposed the idea to Jack Warner.[15] From start to finish, *PT-109* was a Kennedy-supervised production, the latter-day equivalent of "authorized" biography. Joe Kennedy himself negotiated the contract for the film rights, which called for one hundred and fifty thousand dollars, roughly twenty-five hundred dollars for each of the PT crew members or their widows and one hundred and twenty thousand dollars for author Donovan. The President approved the script, which *Look* magazine later described as "just this side of *The Bobbsey Twins*," and also chose actor Cliff Robertson to portray him. In the first screen test, he noticed that Robertson parted his hair on the wrong side; the actor obligingly switched it from right to left. At the completion of the picture, there was a token of the patron's favor: the President took a PT clasp from his tie and presented it to Robertson.

Bobby Kennedy also had written a book, *The Enemy Within*, describing his work as a Senate investigator of labor racketeering; when Hollywood showed interest, Joe Kennedy again took a hand. Shortly after Bobby and the studio, Twentieth Century-Fox, had agreed on a contract, the elder Kennedy telephoned and took exception to some of the wording.

"But your son, the Attorney General, said he was satisfied with the way that clause was drawn," replied a surprised studio executive.

Snapped Kennedy: "What the hell does he know about it!"

The clause in question was revised.[16]

Though semi-retired, Kennedy remained extremely active. At his farm in Osterville, on Cape Cod, he regularly rode his favorite mount, Killarney. He still played a good game of golf and boasted that none of his sons could beat him. (His closest competitor within the family was his daughter Patricia.) At Oyster Harbor Golf Club on the Cape, he was regarded as an intense, no-nonsense player. He appeared precisely on time for a match, putting on his golf shoes at the first tee. If his game was off and he flubbed a shot, he was liable to hurl his club away with an anguished bellow. After the round, instead of going on with the others to the clubhouse, he usually changed his shoes at the last green and went home. Time was too valuable to waste in idle conversation. When he went out in his fifty-two-foot cruiser, he kept an eye on his wristwatch. "He was always conscious of time," Richard Cardinal Cushing, the Archbishop of Boston, recalled. "He would allot so long a period to be out in the boat and, when the time was up, he would motion for us to go back to shore. There was always something he had to do; and he didn't want to waste a minute."[17]

Such impressions of Kennedy as unfrivolous and tightly organized contrasted with newspaper accounts that made his life seem enviably luxurious. In August, 1961, a photographer using a long-range lens snapped the father of the President strolling down a fairway at Cannes with a comely blonde at his side. Dark-eyed, twenty-two-year-old Françoise Pellegrino turned out to be his caddy. She explained to reporters that she had been pulling Kennedy's golf cart around the exclusive Biot course for five years. They had become quite friendly. "I call him 'Joe' and he calls me 'Françoise,'" she said. "I talk to him as I would to my father." Describing Kennedy as very generous, she said he had paid for her English lessons and always sent a case of champagne on her birthday.[18] Soon after the story and picture appeared in U.S. newspapers, a publicity-hungry promoter building a golf course in Miami announced that he would hire girl caddies.

Imitating the Kennedys had become the national pastime. The handsome, wealthy family seemed to satisfy a mass craving for style and elegance: Jackie Kennedy's clothing and hair styles were copied slavishly, and the administration's emphasis on youthful "vigah" created a vogue for touch football and fifty-mile hikes. But along with the adulation of the Kennedys went a degrading familiarity, as witness the leering treatment given Mme Pellegrino in the U.S. press. (The headline in the *New York Daily Mirror* winked at "Pa Joe's Nifty Caddy.") However, if the press was guilty of exploiting the Kennedys, turnabout was fair play, for the Kennedys long had exploited the press. The Kennedys were responsible for stimulating an obsessive public curiosity about themselves, for they had ushered in the era of the permanent, ever-expanding "buildup." At first the focus had been narrowly on Jack Kennedy, but it soon widened to include every member of the family, reaching the point where Teddy's young wife, Joan, wrote in the *Ladies' Home Journal* on "What It's Like to Marry a Kennedy," and Peter Lawford plaintively told the readers of *McCall's* that "The White House Is Still Wondering What to Do with Me."[19] Inevitably, there were horrors of bad taste, such as the flood of Jackie Kennedy cover stories in trashy confidential magazines favored by teenagers and love-starved housewives. Looking back on her first two years in the White House, the First Lady said hopefully: "I think that people must be as sick of hearing about us . . . as I am."[20]

Some disagreeable publicity arose from Joe Kennedy's personal associations. In the summer of 1961, with U.S.-Soviet tensions rising over Berlin, it was announced in Hollywood that the Lawfords would spend ten days at the Kennedy villa on the French Riviera. The announcement went on to say that the Lawfords planned to bring along Frank Sinatra, Janet Leigh, and the Dean Martins. The timing of the Rat Pack's visit to the father of the President brought criticism. In a front-page editorial in the movie industry trade paper, *Limelight,* the *New York Daily News*' veteran Hollywood correspondent, Florabel Muir, indignantly sounded off:

"... This is more than a summer divertissement flaunted in the worst possible taste—it is a red flag of arrogant insolence flung into the faces of friendly nations which are writhing in the agonies of attempting to survive.... We need their friendship and goodwill because we ourselves, in the words of our President, are facing our moment of truth when poisoned death may rain on us. And this is the season when one of our gaudiest multimillionaires chooses to advertise to the world a lavish exhibition of publicized high jinks.... I can remember when Joe Kennedy had a smarter head for propaganda than he's displaying with this caper."[21]

The host abruptly retracted his invitation, telling reporters: "I know they are coming to the Cote d'Azur. Certainly they will come to visit me and I'll be very happy to see them. But they will have to go to a hotel because I just don't have the room at my place to put them up."*

Still another embarrassment occurred when it was disclosed that the elder Kennedy and society columnist Igor Cassini had been involved in an episode of foreign intrigue. Cassini, whose "Cholly Knickerbocker" column for the New York *Journal-American* was widely syndicated, had known the Kennedys for several years in his role as chronicler of the Palm Beach set. His brother, the well-known dress designer Oleg, counted Jackie Kennedy among his clients. Cassini advertised his close friendship with the Kennedys shortly after the 1960 election, writing a column that set out to debunk rumors about the family. "We are accustomed to hearing all kinds of crazy things in our business," he wrote, "but feel that, in the national interest, the untrue tales about the Kennedys should be quashed immediately.[22]

*Frank Sinatra was persistent in his courtship of the first family. On the President's forty-fifth birthday, he sent to the White House a rocking chair covered with yellow chrysanthemums and white carnations. The President declined even to look at his gaudy present before it was sent to Washington's Children's Hospital.

As a lucrative sideline, Cassini and his designing brother were directors of a New York public relations firm, Martial and Company, which handled foreign government accounts and was registered with the Justice Department under the Foreign Agents Act. However, Cassini, due to what he later described as "negligence in attending to details usually handled by subordinates," had failed to register as a paid publicity agent of the Dominican Republic, long ruled with a mailed fist by Generalissimo Rafael Leonidas Trujillo Molina.

Only weeks after Jack Kennedy's inauguration, Cassini put to use his friendship with the President's father, calling on Kennedy at his Palm Beach home to deliver a warning: the Dominican Republic seemed on the verge of exploding in a leftist revolution. In 1960, Washington had broken off diplomatic relations with the Trujillo regime and had imposed severe economic sanctions. Cassini suggested that the administration send someone to Santo Domingo to confer with Trujillo. Kennedy passed on the warning to his son.

According to Trujillo's Secretary of State Security, Arturo Espaillat, Cassini's estimate of the Dominican situation was "very erroneous." No revolution was in sight.[23] However, a plot of another kind was brewing.

The President acted on Cassini's suggestion. To undertake the mission, the State Department recalled from retirement the respected career diplomat Robert Murphy. In mid-April, 1961, Murphy secretly visited the Dominican Republic and talked with Trujillo and other officials at the Presidential Palace. Cassini was also there. The dictator was urged to take steps toward liberalization of his regime. A former U.S. Marine who liked and trusted Americans, Trujillo listened closely to learn how he might get back in Washington's good graces.

Dominican officials in the U.S. sent encouraging reports. Following Cassini's first meeting with Kennedy, Luis R. Mercado, Dominican Consul General in New York, wrote to Trujillo that "he [Cassini] entertains the idea of arranging a meeting for you with Mr. Joseph Kennedy, father of the President, or with the President himself, both of whom, according to Cassini, are his intimate friends and maintain close and frequent relations."[24] Shortly after Murphy's visit, Mercado again reported: "I received a call from my friend Cassini to inform me that the father of President Kennedy had just notified him that the President had been very well impressed by the magnificent report given to him by his emissary, Mr. Robert Murphy."[25] On May 13, Mercado wrote still another letter: "Both Murphy and himself [Cassini] know from confidential talks with the eldest Kennedy that the President had already decided to act favorably in the Dominican case, even going over the heads of the adverse opinion in the Department of State."[26] In fact, the White House later said Murphy's "reporting" memorandum to the President recommended no action, and none was taken.[27] Nothing came of the Cassini-Murphy mission, except that it may have put Trujillo off guard. On May 30, 1961, on a lonely stretch of seashore highway, his car was ambushed and Trujillo died as violently as he had lived.

In July, 1962, *The New York Times* broke the story of the Cassini-Kennedy conversations leading to the Murphy mission, and quoted from the Mercado letters, which the new Dominican government had found in Trujillo's archives. Cassini denied the accuracy of the Mercado letters. However, Joe Kennedy's good friend was in deep trouble. In February, 1963, Cassini was arraigned in a Washington federal court on charges of failure to register as a foreign agent, and pleaded not guilty. Just before his trial, eight months later, he changed his plea to *nolo contendere* (no contest) and was fined ten thousand dollars and placed on six months' probation. Contemplating the scandal that wrecked his life and career, Cassini later wrote that his "cardinal mistake" had been "thinking that I was invincible, untouchable, unassailable."[28]

Trujillo, during his talk with Murphy, had complained that his enemies in the U.S. press and government never would forgive him for having been right about Fidel Castro's ties with communism as early as 1949. Murphy, according to one of those present, then offered an interesting prognostication: "Well, pretty soon there won't be any Cuban problem. Castro is a dead duck."[29] The date was April 16, 1961.

That night, in the blackness of the Bay of Pigs, fifteen hundred anti-Communist Cubans, trained and armed by the CIA, began a heroic attempt to liberate their homeland. The original invasion plan had been compromised because of political considerations. Whatever chance of success remained in the final hours vanished as the result of indecision and fear of world opinion at the White House. As the free Cubans of Brigade 2506 were defeated on the beaches and the Communists set up a worldwide clamor, the President slumped into despondency. Watching him, an aide confided to a reporter: "This is the first time that Jack Kennedy ever lost anything."[30]

In the days following the debacle, Joe Kennedy was on the telephone to his son, cutting through the gloom with words of encouragement. "Oh, hell," he told the President at one point, "if that's the way you feel, give the job to Lyndon!" He told Jack then, as he would again and again, that the Bay of Pigs fiasco, traceable to gross errors of judgment, was the best lesson he could have had early in his administration. In the agonizing postmortem, the President publicly accepted full responsibility for the invasion's failure. But Joe Kennedy, fiercely protective of his son, placed the blame squarely on the CIA, as did members of the administration. During the Eisenhower administration, he had served on a civilian watchdog committee responsible for monitoring intelligence activities. "I know that outfit," Kennedy said of CIA, "and I wouldn't pay them a hundred bucks a week. It's a lucky thing they were found out early; the best thing that could have happened, in fact. Cuba gave this Administration a chance to be great."[31]

Now well into his seventies, Kennedy understandably tried to anticipate history's verdict on his son's administration. But he was not content with speaking optimistic prophecies. Impatiently, he wrested prizes from the future for his present satisfaction. As such things were measured, the rise of the Kennedys had been extraordinary; neither the Adamses nor the Roosevelts nor any other great American family had approached it. Still it was not swift enough to satisfy the imperious founder. And so, on the heels of his eldest son's hard-won triumph, he gave impetus to his youngest son's ambitions.

Always it had been his rule within the family to treat each of his children as nearly equally as possible. Now he invoked this rule on Teddy's behalf. "You boys have what you want now, and everyone else helped you work to get it," he told Jack and Bobby. "Now it's Ted's turn. Whatever he wants, I'm going to see he gets it."[32] What Teddy wanted, although he was not yet old enough legally to take it, was Jack's former seat in the U.S. Senate.

When Teddy's candidacy became known, some expressed fear of a dynasty founded on cold cash and colder calculation. An observer in Washington, once intimate with the elder Kennedy, detected a certain brutal realism at work. "I like Joe Kennedy," he said, "but I have no illusions about him. He understands power. Everywhere he went, from Brahmin Boston to the Court of St. James's, he saw great hypocrisy about the philosophy of those who rule. Power is the end. What other delight is there but to enjoy the sheer sense of control? He would say, 'Let me see any other motive in the people who command.' Joe thinks like a king, and kings aren't always nice guys."

It was said in Washington that Jack and Bobby, for perfectly obvious reasons, were unenthusiastic about their brother's plan. Reportedly Joe Kennedy had found it necessary to lay down the law. "Look," he was said to have told them, "I spent a lot of money for that Senate seat. It belongs in the family." Apocryphal or not, the story made a point on which all the Kennedys were agreed. After entering the White House, Jack Kennedy took steps to protect his family's political domain. Massachusetts' Governor Foster Furcolo, a Democrat, was empowered by law to appoint someone to fill Jack Kennedy's vacant seat for the two-year period before the next congressional election, when the voters would choose a senator to complete the final two years of the six-year term. Furcolo, then retiring from the governorship, would have liked to appoint himself, but the President informed him that he would select the appointee. The names of several well-known Democrats were proposed, and all were turned down. Finally, the President asked the Governor to give the appointment to Ben Smith.

"Ben Smith?" Furcolo was said to have exclaimed. "Who's Ben Smith?" Benjamin A. Smith II was Mayor of Gloucester; more important, he had been Jack Kennedy's roommate in college. Innocent of serious political ambitions, he could be trusted to hold the seat until the Kennedys wanted it.[33] As Teddy told a friend: "Ben's for the family."

It was necessary for Smith to serve as a stand-in because the Constitution required that a U.S. senator be at least thirty years of age. Teddy would not be thirty until 1962. At one time, he had thought of seeking the governorship, but his father advised him to run for national office. Having decided on the Senate, Teddy considered waiting until 1964 before making his bid; but his father urged him to run as soon as possible, pointing out the advantages he would have as an incumbent.[34]

Following the presidential election, Teddy marked time by serving as an assistant district attorney for Suffolk County, Massachusetts. His evenings and weekends were spent making speeches across the state, under the watchful eye of Boston Municipal Court Judge Frank Morrissey, the President's old political tutor. Meanwhile, objections to Teddy's candidacy were raised by the President's closest political advisers, who suggested that his brother might spare him embarrassment by starting at a more modest level.[35] However, Teddy and his father were adamant, and the President did not ask his brother to desist. The deciding factor, according to White House sources, was a poll taken in Massachusetts in early 1962. The poll reportedly showed that the state's Attorney General, Edward J. (Eddie) McCormack, the favorite nephew of House Speaker John McCormack, would beat Ben Smith for the Senate nomination in the Democratic primary, but that he in turn would lose the election to the likely Republican candidate, George Lodge, son of former Senator Henry Cabot Lodge. The poll further disclosed that Teddy Kennedy could beat both McCormack and Lodge. The conclusion drawn from these findings, by the family and the President's advisers, was that Teddy must run to prevent a major Republican victory in the President's backyard.[36]

Sole hope of the party or not, Teddy, only three years out of law school, seemed an improbable senator even to cynical Massachusetts Democrats. His candidacy stunned Attorney General McCormack, the state's ranking Democratic officeholder, who had won election by an impressive 400,000 vote plurality in 1960. McCormack, a seasoned political veteran at thirty-nine, had built a solid record in a state rocked by scandals. His handling of civil rights cases had won him enthusiastic liberal support, and the state's intellectual community was behind him. Several Harvard professors issued a statement declaring that "Teddy has been aptly described as a 'fledgling in everything except ambition.'"

Unconcerned, the Kennedy organization, headed by Steve Smith, set in motion the standard operating procedures proved successful in previous campaigns: recruitment of an army of volunteers, lavish publicity and advertising, and constant exposure of the candidate to the voters. Teddy's campaign revived the nighttime street-corner rally, well suited to the candidate's outgoing personality. ("Teddy," said

Bobby, "is a better natural politician than any of us.") At the state Democratic convention, Teddy's managers strong-armed reluctant party professionals, advising them to get aboard the bandwagon before they were run over. Word came from Washington that Teddy, win or lose, would control the state's federal patronage. The McCormack forces cracked and the delegates endorsed Teddy's candidacy on the first ballot.

McCormack grimly carried the fight to the primary. Lacking the Kennedy resources (volunteers painted his posters by hand) and deserted by many who feared reprisals from Washington, he threw everything into an assault on his opponent's total inexperience, and finally succeeded in needling the reluctant Teddy into a pair of televised debates. "And I ask you," said McCormack in the first match, "if his name was Edward Moore—with his qualifications, with your qualifications, Teddy—if it was Edward Moore your candidacy would be a joke. Nobody's laughing, because his name is not Edward Moore, it's Edward Moore Kennedy." McCormack's attack was so obviously true it seemed cruel, and had the reverse effect of creating sympathy for Teddy, particularly among women voters. Turning the other handsome cheek, Teddy explained how he would fulfill the slogan he had borrowed from his brother's 1952 campaign ("He Will Do *More* for Massachusetts"), plainly implying he would not be handicapped because his name was the same as the President's.

Although McCormack never mentioned it, Teddy decided to make a public confession of a discreditable incident in his past. In 1951, he had been expelled from Harvard for cheating. As a freshman, he was struggling along as a C-minus student in Spanish when, on the spur of the moment, he asked a classmate to take a test for him. The friend was caught and both were expelled. Teddy joined the Army, and, after serving a two-year hitch, was permitted to return to Harvard.[37] According to a close friend, Joe Kennedy was more hurt than angry. That same year, he showed sympathy for other young men caught in the same situation; following the cribbing scandal at West Point, he quietly assisted thirty-one of the ousted cadets in paying tuition at other colleges.[38] While Kennedy seemed to take Teddy's misdeed in stride, one of his contemporaries made a troubled comparison of the generations. "Joe was as tough as they come," said a Harvard classmate, "but he never did anything I would consider dishonest or unethical. Teddy's cheating was a great shock to me."

Showing the familiar Kennedy stamina, Teddy marched up and down the state behind high-stepping pretty girls and a blaring brass band. Verve, excitement, and superb showmanship were the hallmarks of a Kennedy campaign. In addition, there was an indefinable quality compounded of wealth, fame, and power that exerted a magic popular appeal. Noting that some voters looked upon the Kennedys almost as royalty, Stewart Alsop identified Teddy as the newest of that breed of rich, wellborn Eastern seaboard politicians whom he called "People's Dukes." In Worchester one day, as Teddy strode by behind his band, an elderly woman darted from the curb and kissed his hand.

Eddie McCormack never had a chance. In the September, 1962, primary election, Teddy won in a runaway, rolling up 69 percent of the vote. Humiliated, McCormack announced he would quit politics. "If this is politics, if they can get away with this," he said bitterly, "then I don't want any part of politics."[39]

Many supporters of President Kennedy saw nothing to applaud in his younger brother's victory, which *The New York Times* described editorially as "demeaning to the dignity of the Senate and the democratic process." The Washington correspondent of the *Times*, James Reston, wrote a thoughtful but unsparing indictment.

> . . . the Kennedys have applied the principle of the best man available for the job to almost everyone but themselves. Teddy's victorious headlines are resented here . . . because he is demanding too much too soon on the basis of too little. . . . What is particularly surprising about all this is that the Kennedys do not see this line of criticism at all, and in fact deeply resent it. They have invoked the new pragmatism, but cannot see that, where the family was concerned, they applied the old nepotism.[40]

At his headquarters on election night, Teddy was surrounded by television newsmen brandishing microphones and shouting questions. Had he talked over his victory with his brother, the President? No, replied Teddy, but he hoped to shortly. Had he talked to his other brother, the Attorney General? No, but he hoped to shortly. Had he talked to his father? Teddy beamed. "Yes," he said, "I talked to him. He was extremely excited."

What passed from Joe Kennedy to his youngest son on that night was sensed rather than spoken. The previous December, Kennedy had suffered a stroke, leaving him partially paralyzed and unable to speak.

December 19, 1961, was a beautifully sunny day in Palm Beach, one which Kennedy could fill as his whim dictated. He had arrived eight days earlier for his usual winter vacation and the second of the family's traditional annual gatherings. Thanksgiving at Hyannis Port had seen thirty-three adults and children seated at his table. Christmas, less than a week away, would be festive and lively with most of his twenty grandchildren tumbling through the house. As always, there would be laughter over the presents. Well he remembered the time one of his daughters had given him a bathrobe bearing an embroidered warning across the back: "Danger! Explosives!" There were few occasions to explode nowadays. Old controversies had vanished like crumbling pieces of yellowed newsprint, and the world, when it thought of him at all, now thought of Joe Kennedy as a doting grandfather.

On this day, the President was to leave Palm Beach for Washington following a short visit. As Kennedy and his son entered the limousine, four-year-old Caroline Kennedy appeared at the doorway of the house. "I'm going to the airport with your father," Kennedy called. "Would you like to come along?" She climbed on her grandfather's lap in the back seat. After seeing the President off, Kennedy returned to his home with Caroline and spent a half hour playing with all his visiting grandchildren. Then, accompanied by his favorite niece, Ann Gargan, the daughter of his wife's late sister, he left for the Palm Beach Golf Club, just a few blocks away on North Ocean Boulevard.

Before teeing off, Kennedy remarked: "I really don't feel too well today, but it must be the cold I've had."[41] However, as they played the back nine holes, he walked as usual, believing the exercise was better than using an electric golf cart. On the fairway to the sixteenth hole, Kennedy sat down on the grass and said he felt ill. Quickly, his caddy brought an electric cart and took him to his car. Within a few minutes, Ann Gargan had driven him home. In the front hall, he met Jackie Kennedy and Caroline. Before going upstairs to his bedroom, he gave the order: "Don't call any doctors."[42] Several times in recent months he had had warnings of an impending stroke, and doctors had prescribed anticoagulants, but he had refused to take them. Worried by his ashen appearance, the family ignored his order. After the doctor examined him, Kennedy, still wearing a sports shirt and golf shorts, was taken from bed and sped in a private ambulance with a motorcycle escort to St. Mary's Hospital. The chaplain administered the last rites of the Roman Catholic Church. In mid-afternoon, his doctors issued a statement announcing that Ambassador Kennedy had suffered a stroke.

The President learned of his father's illness shortly after his return to the White House. The telephone call came from Bobby. After a tense conversation, Jack Kennedy put down the receiver, his face taut. "Dad's gotten sick," he said to an aide. That afternoon he returned to Florida aboard the presidential jet, *Air Force One*, accompanied by Bobby and his sister Jean.

Joe Kennedy had suffered an intracranial thrombosis, a blood clot in an artery of the brain. Doctors quickly performed an arteriogram, injecting radiopaque dye into the main artery of the neck and photographing by high-speed X ray its flow through the vessels of the brain. The thrombosis was in the left cerebral hemisphere, the dominant side in the right-handed Kennedy, and was inoperable. His right side was paralyzed, and he was unable to speak. He lay in Room 355 of St. Mary's Hospital, to which he had donated the entire third floor of the south wing. On the door of Room 354 was a bronze plaque: "In Memory of Joseph P. Kennedy, Jr. Donated by Mr. and Mrs. Joseph P. Kennedy, Sr."

When the President arrived, he conferred with his father's doctors and then went briefly to the hospital chapel, where his mother had prayed that afternoon for more than an hour. From throughout the nation, the Kennedy clan gathered in Palm Beach. Pat Kennedy Lawford flew in from California. From Washington came Eunice Kennedy Shriver. From Boston aboard a military jet came Teddy Kennedy, bringing with him a Manhattan vascular specialist. Teddy, Jean, and Ann Gargan kept an around-the-clock vigil near Room 355. On the day following his stroke, Kennedy showed some improvement, and appeared to recognize his children. However, pneumonia developed, and on Christmas Eve surgeons performed a tracheotomy to ease his breathing. Slowly he edged out of danger. Friends joined the family at his bedside, among them Richard Cardinal Cushing of Boston. "Keep up your courage," the Cardinal told his friend, "you're going to be all right." Afterward, the prelate told reporters Kennedy had replied: "I know I am."

The Cardinal had interpreted hopefully the guttural sounds he heard. These, along with smiles, frowns, and movements of his left hand, were the extent of Kennedy's ability to communicate. Long a figure of boundless energy and roaring authority, he now was mute and crippled and massively frustrated.

Within a few weeks, he was discharged from the hospital. That spring began the agonizing attempt to recover the functions he had lost. He was taken to New York's Institute of Physical Medicine and Rehabilitation, and underwent months of therapy as the patient of the Institute's director, Dr. Howard A. Rusk. A dozen years earlier, when Dr. Rusk was launching the Institute, Kennedy had made a generous contribution. When he went to Hyannis Port that summer, an elevator was installed in the house so his wheelchair could move between his second-floor room and the main floor. Later, an elaborate, glass-enclosed swimming pool, with whirlpool baths and other therapeutic devices, was built behind the house. Within a year of his stroke, stories circulated that the President's father was making a remarkable recovery, that he was talking with his family and friends on the telephone, and that he even had resumed some of his business activities.

The stories were well intended but cruelly untrue. Like many another elderly stroke victim, Kennedy was impatient with the repetitive therapy exercises and chafed under his helplessness. He enjoyed the companionship of his grandchildren and often went to watch them ride at his farm, but at other times he was depressed and difficult to manage. When the telephone rang, he insisted on picking up the receiver and trying to answer. Friends of the family were instructed to hang up and call again, in the hope that someone else would get to the telephone first. Not until two and a half years after his stroke did he take his first steps, following treatment at the Institutes for the Achievement of Human Potential in Springfield, Pennsylvania. His speech also showed marked improvement. Even before then, however, there always had been a measure of truth to the too-optimistic reports of his recovery. By sheer force of will, he retained something of his former presence. "He comes in and listens to business," his son-in-law, Steve Smith, told a visitor to the New York office, "and, don't worry, if he wants to say no to something, he can make himself known."

Kennedy had made his wishes known on Teddy's candidacy for the Senate, and Jack and Bobby were bound to respect their father's order and Teddy's turn. Even in his infirmity, Kennedy indirectly helped his youngest son's cause: the names and addresses of persons in Massachusetts who sent him get-well messages were forwarded to Teddy's campaign headquarters as likely volunteers and contributors.[43] When Teddy scored a predictably lopsided victory over Republican George Lodge in November, 1962, and took over Jack's Senate seat, Joe Kennedy's triumph was complete. The Kennedys, all of them, had won all that was worth winning.

EPILOGUE

The oldest hath borne most; we that are young
Shall never see so much, nor live so long.

—*King Lear*, V, iii

Friday, November 22, 1963, was a gentle autumn day in Hyannis Port. That morning, Joe and Rose Kennedy had been taken for a drive in their station wagon by a Secret Service man. The summer people had left more than two months ago, and the streets of the small resort village were almost deserted. This was a season of peace on the Cape, a time of year the Kennedys always had enjoyed. Later that morning, Rose, taking advantage of the balmy weather, drove her own compact car to the Hyannis Port Club to play a few holes of golf. Meanwhile, in the large white frame house overlooking Nantucket Sound, life followed its serene round. At noon, Joe Kennedy ate lunch. Afterward he rode the elevator to the second floor and retired for his nap.

In recent weeks, the routine enforced by his affliction had been broken by visits to Washington, Chicago, and New York. He had been his son's guest for a week at the White House. While in New York, he had dined in the Waldorf Towers apartment of his old friend, Herbert Hoover. Their reunion was tinged with sadness, for the years weighed heavily on both of them. His robust health failing in his eighty-ninth year, the former President was almost deaf. Kennedy could not speak. And so they had eaten in silence. Throughout the meal, Kennedy wept.

Now, as he drowsed, there were pleasures to anticipate. On Wednesday, the President and the rest of the family would arrive for Thanksgiving, and the house would echo with the laughter of children. Already there was a quiet bustle of preparation. The cook would select the turkey with great care; it was the custom to parade the golden-brown bird around the table for the family's inspection and approval before the meal began. The children would eat in the afternoon, the adults in the evening. There would be talk, now serious, now bantering, and perhaps, as in the past, skits, games, and singing. Joe Kennedy would sit at the center of it all, his eyes reflecting the love of his children.

By one-thirty, Rose had returned to the house and was eating lunch. In the chauffeur's apartment over the garage at the rear of the main house, a radio was playing. Suddenly the music was interrupted by a bulletin from Dallas, Texas. Stunned by what he heard, the chauffeur ran to the rear entrance of the big house and blurted the bulletin to a maid, who in turn hurried to tell Ann Gargan. It was Ann, her niece, who came to Rose bearing the news that defied comprehension and turned the heart cold: the President had been shot. Within minutes word arrived that the President, her son, was dead.

For the third time, death had violently taken from Rose Kennedy a child she had cherished. Soon, from the presidential jet flying her son's body back to Washington, she received a telephone call. It was the new President, seeking to comfort her. "I wish to God there was something I could do," President Johnson told her. "I just wanted you to know that."

Quickly Rose decided that her husband should not be awakened. Once he had kept from her the message reporting Jack's disappearance in the Pacific while he prayed for a miracle. This time, there was no hope of deliverance, but she would shield him until his ability to withstand the blow was known. His doctor was called and he arranged to come that evening.

After Kennedy awoke, his normal afternoon routine continued. Ann Gargan and his nurse took him for an automobile ride, which they prolonged so as to avoid the possibility that he would ask to watch television. When the doctor came, he explained to his patient that he merely was receiving his customary checkup before departing for Palm Beach at the end of the month. Afterward, the doctor advised the family that Mr. Kennedy was strong enough to take the news. Even so, it was decided to postpone the moment a while longer. Following dinner, Ann Gargan encouraged her uncle to watch a particularly long movie. Meanwhile, Teddy and Eunice arrived by plane from Washington. It was not unusual; one or more of the children visited almost every weekend. However, their sadness and hushed conversation made Kennedy restless. He seemed to sense that something was wrong but he retired as usual at nine-thirty.

The next morning, Rose went, as she did daily, to the seven o'clock Mass at St. Francis Xavier's, the small, white clapboard church in Hyannis Port. Later, as she and her husband ate breakfast together, he became more suspicious: his *New York Times* was not beside his plate. After breakfast, as Kennedy waded in the heated swimming pool, he did not respond to the forced pleasantries of his nurses.

Teddy and Eunice also attended Mass at St. Francis Xavier's and returned at about nine-thirty. By now, their father had changed clothes and was in his room. Together they climbed the stairs and joined him. His room was furnished simply—three lounge chairs, a bureau, a chest of drawers, and a hospital-size, electrically operated bed. On the bureau were photographs of the family. Three large windows looked out on the lawn and the Sound; from here Kennedy often had watched his children sail and swim.

After Teddy and Eunice came into the room, Kennedy motioned to his son to turn on the television set. Teddy hesitated, and said the set did not work. His father pointed to the unplugged power cord. Reluctantly Teddy inserted the plug, but as the set began to flicker on, he pulled the plug from the socket. It was then that he told his father that Jack was dead.

Watching from a distance, reporters could only imagine what was occurring within the white house. At the church, they had learned that the President's father had not yet been informed. Now came a sign that he knew. Just before ten o'clock, hours later than usual, the flag on the lawn before his house was raised to the top, then lowered to half mast.

Those who saw Kennedy in the days that followed found him bearing his grief with stoic calm. He understood what had happened; of that there was no question. "Joe Kennedy always understands," said a departing visitor. The newspapers were brought to him, and he watched the final honors for his son on television. But he did not break down, even when a Secret Service man sitting with him wept. Kennedy, according to his friend, Richard Cardinal Cushing, took the news with "extraordinary resignation and confidence in God." People mistakenly thought of Kennedy as a man "completely interested in accumulating money," the Cardinal said, but his friend had told him that "his idea in life was the success of his children."

Now death had stolen his success and shattered his dream. The doctor gave approval for the trip to Washington, but Kennedy chose to remain behind while the family attended the funeral on Monday. The morning was cold and bright, and as he was driven through the empty streets of Hyannis Port, he motioned for the car to go slowly, so that he might look at the store windows. Many of them displayed pictures of his son, framed in crepe and surrounded by wreaths.

Later, he and an old friend, the Reverend John Cavanaugh, president emeritus of the University of Notre Dame, watched the funeral procession on television. The muffled drums beat the grave, majestic pace of the march and the shrill bagpipes skirled dirges as the President's body was borne across the Potomac and laid to rest in Arlington. In the house at Hyannis Port, the television set was turned off and Father Cavanaugh went downstairs. Joe Kennedy sat alone in his silent room, gazing out the window.

AFTERWORD: THE KENNEDYS IN HISTORY

1.

On the morning in July 1960 after his son had won the Democratic party's presidential nomination, Joseph P. Kennedy boarded a jet alone in Los Angeles and flew to New York. From the airport, he telephoned Henry R. Luce, the editor in chief of Time Inc., and asked if he could drop by his office. They made an appointment to meet late that afternoon at the Time-Life Building. About an hour later, Kennedy called again to say he would be delayed; could the appointment be pushed back? Luce saw no alternative but to extend an invitation to dinner that evening at his apartment, which he suspected Kennedy had been angling for.

For more than thirty years, the pair had managed an on-again, off-again relationship that passed for friendship but was without real trust. They used each other without being too obvious about it. Each was conscious both of his own and the other's power and of the mutual advantages that flowed from remaining on good terms. That evening, they dined alone and through the meal kept the conversation rather deliberately general. Finally, over coffee, Luce decided it was time to come to the point, and he did so with his usual bluntness.

"Joe, I know why you're here—I'm on your list." Before Kennedy could reply, his host cut him off and continued: "Tell Jack not to worry about the way Time Inc. will treat him. We know he has to go with the liberals on domestic issues, and we'll argue with him politely. On foreign policy, we'll be fair to him—unless he listens to you and turns soft. Then we'll cut his throat."

This verbal thrust, recalling the elder Kennedy's pre-World War II support for appeasement of Nazi Germany, was delivered with a smile. Kennedy wore a look of hurt surprise. He replied: "Harry, how the hell could any son of mine be a goddamned liberal? Don't worry about Jack being a weak sister. He'll be tough."

Harry Luce told me about his evening with Joe Kennedy a couple of years later, during the October 1962 Cuban missile crisis. By then, it was evident that Luce's concern about the influence of the president's father was well founded.

The Kennedy presidency unfolded as one test after another of Jack's "toughness" under pressure. The testing began in April 1961 with the Bay of Pigs disaster, soon followed by JFK's confrontation with the blustering Nikita Khrushchev at the Vienna summit. Thereafter came a series of Berlin crises. And now, a nuclear showdown over Soviet missiles in Cuba.

In each contest, Kennedy had sought to prove himself stronger and more resolute than the previous tests had shown him to be.

I had been summoned to Luce's aerie atop the Time-Life Building to discuss with the Proprietor my *Fortune* article on the elder Kennedy. That assignment was Luce's idea and he gave it high priority. The idea had struck him as President Kennedy and Roger Blough, chairman of U.S. Steel, clashed publicly over a steel price hike during the spring of 1962. The White House leaked JFK's pungent quip: "My father always said businessmen were SOBs." Luce, a shrewd businessman and an even shrewder journalist, pounced on the president's words, telling his editors: "I think it's time to remind people what kind of a businessman Joe Kennedy was." Trim, beetle-browed, and fast-talking, Luce told me his story with the offhand manner of one reporter briefing another. He also revealed something of the personal curiosity that motivated him.

"You know," he said, "all of the men who knew Joe, including me, didn't envy him his money or his movie stars or the big political jobs. We envied his success with his family. How did he do it?" Luce paused. "And what kind of men did his sons turn out to be?"

As far as Jack was concerned, Luce clearly felt that question was still open. He had been true to his warning to old Joe. In a brilliant article, *Fortune*'s Washington editor Charles J. V. Murphy had dissected the failure of the Bay of Pigs invasion, drawing a personal protest from President Kennedy that Luce saw as confirmation of the accuracy of *Fortune*'s indictment. In the subsequent Berlin crises, Time Inc. stood in Kennedy's corner. Now, on this golden October day, as the world held its breath at the threat of nuclear war, Luce kept coming back to the same question: would Jack Kennedy measure up? Khrushchev evidently believed that he would not, that Kennedy's fear of Soviet retaliation in Berlin would cause him to submit to the entry of Soviet missiles in Cuba. He was nearly proved right.

As it turned out, the president waited much too long to warn Khrushchev against his nuclear gamble in Cuba, and then confronted him publicly, giving the Russian leader barely enough maneuvering room to back down without a war. When Khrushchev finally "blinked" and the crisis ended, seemingly on American terms, the world heaved a vast sigh of relief. Time Inc. led the media in applauding JFK as a hero. In that time of idealism, hard-boiled Harry Luce, like the rest of us, wanted to believe that what we saw in the Kennedys was real and worthy of admiration.

II.

Thirty years later, we know that Jack Kennedy's heroic "toughness" was more apparent than real. He dangerously mismanaged the Cuban missile crisis and his entire presidency, reflecting at every step his father's influence.

Jack, like Joe, had an inherited religious faith but believed in essentially nothing beyond himself and his family. Father and son alike were solitary adventurers. They were profane, cynical pragmatists and opportunists who could turn on the Irish charm instantly to attract men and seduce women but who were apt to withdraw, black-browed, in the next moment. Joe Kennedy's deep streak of pessimism and bearishness, his innate desire to nail down a quick profit and run, became, in Jack, a loner's coolly rational detachment and inability to commit himself even after he had gone through the motions of making a decision to commit.

Neither Joe nor Jack ever gave himself to a permanent enterprise demanding long-term effort and involvement. Both lived for the swift gratification of their desires. Joe Kennedy often said that the only business he ever really enjoyed was show business. In the movies, he had learned how to choose a script and a director, how to mount a publicity buildup for the star on which his investment was riding. But each production was an end in itself, a hit or a flop, and on to the next. To Joe Kennedy and his son, the family calling of politics was simply another form of show business, filled with a succession of new scripts and new roles, fleeting images and one-night stands. "In my family," Jack once said with considerable understatement, "we were interested not so much in the ideas of politics as in the mechanics of the whole thing."

In the White House, the young president discovered that ideas and decisions, made and unmade, had fateful long-term consequences. While hopelessly outnumbered invading Cubans fought on the landing beaches at the Bay of Pigs, Kennedy made and compounded grave blunders. As historian Michael Beschloss wrote in *The Crisis Years* (1991), his masterful history of Kennedy's foreign policy, President Kennedy tried to have it both ways: "Wishing to intervene without paying the price of intervention, he therefore ordained an operation too small to succeed and too big to hide America's involvement." The Soviets, amazed, pressed the newcomer harder next time.

Before the Vienna summit, his only face-to-face meeting with Khrushchev, Kennedy told an aide: "I have to show him I can be just as tough as he is." He failed. According to his aide Fyodor Burlatsky, Khrushchev thought Kennedy "had more the look of an adviser, not a political decision-maker or a president." While Kennedy was defensive and self-deprecating, Khrushchev was ruthless and bullying. He threatened to "normalize" the status of divided and encircled Berlin. He lectured and blustered and rattled his missiles. Kennedy retreated and told the Russian leader what both knew was untrue: that the two nuclear superpowers were "more or less in balance" militarily, which, according to Beschloss, "sent Khrushchev into near-ecstacy." Then, capping his misreading and mishandling of Khrushchev, Kennedy returned home and decided to close overnight the fictitious "missile gap" on which he had campaigned. He made a speech ridiculing Soviet claims to nuclear parity and disclosing the awesome details of U.S. nuclear superiority.

Khrushchev, deflated but determined to intimidate an adversary whose nerve he doubted, upped the stakes. He gave the East Germans the long-awaited approval to build their hideous wall around the western sector of Berlin. When Kennedy did not respond militarily to the Berlin Wall (the East Germans were prepared to retreat) but seemed almost relieved at this brutal "solution" to the flow of refugees westward, Khrushchev secretly set in motion his most audacious scheme: to alter the global balance of power by introducing strategic nuclear weapons into Cuba.

As Beschloss has written, Kennedy's speech to the nation during the Cuban missile crisis was given "too late to stop Khrushchev's Cuba operation" but was "so precise" in its accusations that it forced "a full-fledged confrontation" that nearly caused nuclear war. Moreover, the dramatic address did *not* reveal the actual thoughts and intentions of the president who was merely playing a role. As Kennedy saw it, according to Beschloss, the speech "was designed to divert attention from his private belief that the missiles did not seriously increase the Soviet military danger and the fact that he had not warned against them until it was too late."

A closely guarded secret at the time and for decades thereafter was the actual "deal" that ended the missile crisis. In a secret protocol, the U.S. agreed to remove missiles from Turkey, a NATO ally, in return for the withdrawal of Soviet missiles from Cuba. This dishonorable U.S. concession was made without consultation with the Turks and affected a part of the world that was not historically within the Russian "sphere."

The Cuban missile crisis had far-reaching consequences. "You Americans will never be able to do this to us again," warned veteran Soviet diplomat Vasily Kuznetsov after the agreement was signed. Khrushchev's skillful bluff that the Soviets enjoyed nuclear parity, without actually making the required heavy investment in weaponry, had now been called. The Politburo soon removed him and embarked on the massive arms buildup and geopolitical expansion that imposed on the world two more decades of Cold War.

In the remaining year of his life, President Kennedy continued to try to face in two directions at once. In his famous American University speech, apparently intended to set the stage for his second term, he signalled a left turn, calling for a reexamination of the roots of the Cold War and committing himself to the search for U.S.-Soviet arms-control agreements. At the same time, however, Kennedy gave the covert green light for U.S. complicity in the Vietnamese military's plan to assassinate authoritarian President Ngo Dinh Diem and replace him with a compliant general. That dark act entrapped the U.S. in Vietnam.

Kennedy got deeper and deeper into Vietnam as he tried to "prove" himself. As early as the Vienna summit, after his bruising encounter with Khrushchev, Kennedy had told associates: "Now we have a problem trying to make our power credible, and Vietnam looks like the place." As happened throughout his presidency, U.S. foreign policy was subordinated to Kennedy's political and personal needs, and the nation's interests became entangled and confused with his own. Had Kennedy lived, there is every reason to believe that Vietnam, his ultimate and definitive test, would have consumed his presidency as surely as it did his successor's.

III.

The historical record of the Kennedy presidency is voluminous and ever-expanding. It includes newly opened archival documents from the former Soviet side, tapes and transcripts of once highly classified White House meetings, telephone logs and personal letters, diaries and memoirs, some of which reveal JFK's secret personal life in a startling new light. It is all there for objective historians to sift and ponder as they venture fresh analyses and form new judgments about John F. Kennedy's character and conduct and the consequences of his thousand days in the White House.

In April 1968 Senator Robert F. Kennedy was assassinated as he campaigned to succeed Jack, the victim of another lone, deranged individual acting without coherent motive. A vast outpouring of public sympathy for the tragedy-scarred Kennedy family gave the legend and dynasty fresh luster. Thereafter, the embodiment of both became the youngest of Joe and

Rose's children, their only surviving son, Edward. Tall, handsome, and gregarious, he seemed destined to rise swiftly. But Teddy, to whom all had been given, including elevation at the earliest eligible age to the family's Senate seat from Massachusetts, was also reckless, undisciplined, and self-destructive. He could not live up to his role.

In the decline of the Kennedys, the incident on Chappaquiddick island in July 1969 is the fault-line dividing the dream of restoration from moral obloquy and the long slide into mere celebrity. Nothing any critic ever said or wrote, nothing any enemy ever did, was as damaging to Edward Kennedy and his family as the self-inflicted wounds of that episode. A young woman died trapped in the car that Teddy drove off a bridge in circumstances he never explained.

A conspiracy of silence among those involved covered up the facts for the next quarter-century. Kennedy family advisers, lawyers, and speechwriters flocked to Teddy's side as though, one recalled, it were the Cuban missile crisis again. They fabricated a condescending television speech for him, entirely predictable from the eulogy to the dead woman to the concluding appeal for public support ("I pray that I can have the courage to make the right decision").

A tactical success and a strategic disaster, Teddy's speech succeeded in changing the subject and drew a lopsided vote of confidence from Massachusetts viewers and voters who reelected him later that fall. But in every other respect, the speech backfired. As the world media probed the many contradictions and inconsistencies in Teddy's account, people everywhere talked about the incident. Public resentment grew at the coverup and Teddy's evasion of moral as well as legal responsibility, at the special treatment the senator received from intimidated state and local authorities, and—most of all—at the sense he gave that a Kennedy owed no one any explanation for his actions.

Teddy knew, of course, that he owed an explanation to his stricken father. With the elder Kennedy's nurse, Rita Dallas, present, Teddy told him about Chappaquiddick: "Dad, I'm in some trouble. There's been an accident and you're going to hear all sorts of things about me from now on. Terrible things. . . ." He went closer to his father's bed and the old man took his hand and held it to his chest, unable to speak. "Dad, I've done the best I can," said Teddy. "I'm sorry."

After Chappaquiddick, Teddy secluded himself at Hyannis Port and spent many long days alone with his father. Just as he outlived so many of his children, so Joe Kennedy outlived his family's legend and the dynasty he created. Even after his stroke, he remained the physical presence by which the family defined its center. He somehow made himself and his wishes understood even though he could not speak. His children and their spouses and the grandchildren came faithfully to his bedside. Rose would sit silently holding his hand for hours at a time. The president's widow, Jackie Onassis, had a special affection for "Grandpa" and she visited him frequently.

In the autumn of 1969, Joe Kennedy grew increasingly feeble. He lost his sight and could no longer watch television. The attending doctors and nurses were instructed to take no extraordinary measures to prolong his life. On November 17, 1969, as Rose, Jackie, and the surviving Kennedy children recited the Lord's Prayer, he slipped away.

IV.

The last vestige of Joe Kennedy's fierce will, which had propelled him and his family, was now spent. The fortune he had built, once concentrated in his hands and wielded as a tool of his ambition, was dispersed and locked up in estates and trusts, now a means of preserving the family's status rather than conquering it. His dream of having his name live through his children had been shattered by assassins' bullets and now seemed to have sunk beneath the black waters of Poucha Pond on Chappaquiddick.

The Kennedy legend is quite separate from JFK's presidency; it is based on the popular culture, and has a quite different, wholly subjective and transient kind of documentation: picture-filled books and magazine and newspaper articles, television docu-dramas and fictionalized films such as Oliver Stone's *JFK*. These attest the continuing public fascination with the glamorous Kennedys, figures in a real-life drama more compelling than anything imagined in Hollywood. Seen as celebrities, bearing a famous name no longer linked to any particular achievement or distinction, the Kennedys move in the same cultural context and plane of public awareness as television and film personalities.

Younger, peripheral members of the Kennedy family are sometimes caught in the spotlight of notoriety—a young man dies of drug overdose, another is acquitted of rape charges—and quickly fade away until the next sensational event briefly touches the magical family name. A handful of younger Kennedys, female as well as male, are actively engaged in politics today, but there is no longer talk of another President Kennedy.

Joe Kennedy sought to elevate the Kennedys and ensure their rank permanently, beyond the reach of probing biographers and historians who make moral judgments. His self-deception that he could do so lasted only as long as the family's formidable apparatus of self-promotion remained intact. The weapon of publicity, once so powerful in the Kennedys' hands, has now been turned against them by a new generation of serious scholars and not-so-serious tabloid historians, all determined to debunk the Kennedy legend and bury it under the cumulative weight of contrary evidence.

Some of us knew long ago what Joe Kennedy did and how he shaped his children. Even as the false legend crumbles, the facts of his life and his stunning will to power rivet our attention. His New Deal crony, Thomas G. (Tommy the Cork) Corcoran, a fellow Irishman, Catholic, and power-seeker, summed up Joe Kennedy for me in a memorable 1962 interview: "Joe sent his girls to the Church to believe and his sons to the marketplace to know better. He thought like a king and kings aren't nice guys."

NOTES

Notes

Chapter 1

1. *Boston Evening Transcript,* June 23, 1911.
2. *Ibid.*
3. Details of the game were supplied by a surviving member of the Harvard baseball team during an interview in Boston on November 8, 1962.
4. *Boston Evening Transcript,* June 24, 1911.
5. Boston interview, November 8, 1962. Interestingly, several persons volunteered the baseball anecdote, each believing it best characterized the young Joe Kennedy.
6. Tim Pat Coogan, "Sure and It's County Kennedy Now," *The New York Times Magazine,* June 23, 1963.
7. Cecil Woodham-Smith, *The Great Hunger: Ireland 1845–1849* (New York and Evanston: Harper & Row, 1963), p. 21.
8. *Ibid.*, p. 31.
9. *Ibid.*, p. 206.
10. Oscar Handlin, *The Uprooted: The Epic Story of the Great Migrations that Made the American People* (Boston: Little, Brown & Company, 1951), p. 49.
11. Woodham-Smith, *op. cit.*, p. 238.
12. Handlin, *op. cit.*, pp. 50–52.
13. Samuel P. Orth, *Our Foreigners* (New Haven: Yale University Press, 1920), p. 110.
14. George Adams, *East Boston Directory* (Boston: Adams, 1849), p. 3.
15. *Ibid.*, pp. 20–30.
16. Oscar Handlin, *Boston's Immigrants, 1790–1880: A Study in Acculturation* (Cambridge, Massachusetts: Harvard University Press, 1959), p. 109.
17. *Ibid.*, pp. 113–114.
18. *Ibid.*, p. 56.
19. *Ibid.*, p. 176.
20. *Ibid.*, p. 142.
21. William H. Sumner, *A History of East Boston* (Boston: 1858), p. 654.
22. Woodham-Smith, *op. cit.*, p. 252.
23. John Henry Cutler, *"Honey Fitz": Three Steps to the White House* (Indianapolis and New York: The Bobbs-Merrill Company, Inc., 1962), p. 72.
24. *Ibid.*, p. 50.
25. *Boston Evening Transcript,* May 20, 1929.
26. Cutler, *op. cit.*, p. 31.
27. *Ibid.*, p. 50.
28. Interview with Miss Katherine Sullivan in Canton, Massachusetts, on June 18, 1963. "My father and mother were married for forty-one years, but she knew how to gain the upper hand—by reminding him that *her* people had come over two months before his."

Chapter 2

1. Contemporary events taken from the *Boston Evening Transcript*, September 5, 1888; the *Boston Globe*, September 6, 1888; the *Boston Evening Transcript*, September 7, 1888.

2. Joe McCarthy, *The Remarkable Kennedys* (New York: The Dial Press, 1960), p. 37.

3. John Henry Cutler, *"Honey Fitz": Three Steps to the White House* (Indianapolis and New York: The Bobbs-Merrill Company, Inc., 1962), p. 73.

4. *Ibid.*, p. 73.

5. Executor's account of the estate of Patrick J. Kennedy, filed in Probate Court of Suffolk County, Massachusetts, on September 23, 1929.

6. *Boston Evening Transcript*, May 20, 1929.

7. James MacGregor Burns, *John Kennedy: A Political Profile* (New York: Harcourt, Brace & World, Inc., 1961), p. 17.

8. McCarthy, *op. cit.*, p. 37.

9. Joseph P. Kennedy recalled his job on the *Excelsior* and his fondness for Lewis' candy during an interview with George Bookman, formerly an editor of *Fortune*, on June 3, 1960.

10. Miss Katherine Sullivan, of Canton, Massachusetts, a longtime friend of the deceased Ronan Grady, related this anecdote during an interview with the author on June 18, 1963.

11. McCarthy, *op. cit.*, p. 38.

12. H. H. Martin, "The Amazing Kennedys," *The Saturday Evening Post*, September 7, 1957.

13. "Mr. Kennedy, the Chairman," *Fortune*, September, 1937.

14. Letter to the author dated September 7, 1963, from Max Levine, a classmate of Kennedy's and secretary of the Boston Latin School Association.

15. Joseph F. Dinneen, *The Kennedy Family* (Boston and Toronto: Little, Brown & Company, 1959), p. 9.

16. Levine letter, September 7, 1963.

17. Levine letter; quoted from *Boston Latin School Tercentenary Dinner: 1635–1935*, published in 1937.

18. Interview in Boston on April 12, 1963, with Raymond S. Wilkins, a graduate of Salem High School and Harvard '12, and now Chief Justice of the Massachusetts Supreme Court.

19. McCarthy, *op. cit.*, p. 45.

20. Henry Adams, *The Education of Henry Adams: An Autobiography* (Boston and New York: Houghton Mifflin Company, 1918), p. 54.

21. Cleveland Amory, *The Proper Bostonians* (New York: E. P. Dutton & Company, Inc., 1947), p. 295.

22. Kennedy-Bookman interview, June 3, 1960.

23. *Boston Record-American*, January 10, 1964.

24. Interview with Oscar Haussermann, Harvard '12, in Boston on October 10, 1962.

25. Amory, *op. cit.*, p. 308.

26. Haussermann interview; class records.

27. Margaret Kennedy Burke's reminiscences were quoted in the *Boston Record-American*, January 10, 1964. The recreations Kennedy enjoyed were recalled by a Harvard classmate during an interview with the author in New York City on December 26, 1962. One winter afternoon, this classmate and Kennedy escorted two young ladies from the cast of *The Pink Lady* to a skating party. Kennedy accidentally bumped into Rose Fitzgerald, whose greeting to her "steady" beau made the afternoon considerably chillier.

28. Cutler, *op. cit.*, p. 178.

29. Henry J. O'Meara, interviewed in Boston on March 16, 1963, was one of several friends who recalled Kennedy's antagonism toward McLaughlin.

30. Interview with a former member of the Harvard baseball team in Boston on November 8, 1962.

31. Cutler, *op. cit.*, p. 142.

32. *Ibid.*, p. 165.

33. O'Meara interview.

34. *Ibid.*

35. *Ibid.*

36. Daniel O'Connor, a Dorchester neighbor of the Fitzgeralds, related this anecdote to the author in Boston on June 20, 1963.

37. A friend who was in the accounting class told of Kennedy's difficulties during an interview in New York City on October 12, 1962.

38. The story of Kennedy's tourist-bus venture has been published previously. New details about his negotiations for the South Station franchise were related to the author by Henry J. O'Meara, whose uncle then was police commissioner, the official empowered to grant the necessary license.

39. Amory, *op. cit.*, p. 292.

Chapter 3

1. Cleveland Amory, *The Proper Bostonians* (New York: E. P. Dutton & Company, Inc., 1947), p. 23.

2. Charles Francis Adams, *An Autobiography* (Boston and New York: Houghton Mifflin Company, 1916), p. 205.

3. H. G. Wells, *The Future in America: A Search After Realities* (New York and London: Harper & Brothers, 1906), p. 227.

4. *Ibid.*, p. 230.

5. Amory, *op. cit.*, p. 50.

6. John Chamberlain, *The Enterprising Americans: A Business History of the United States* (New York, Evanston and London: Harper & Row, 1963), p. 44.

7. Karl Shriftgiesser, *The Gentleman From Massachusetts: Henry Cabot Lodge* (Boston: Little, Brown & Company [An Atlantic Monthly Press Book], 1944), p. 16.

8. Interview with Thomas G. Corcoran in Washington, D.C., on October 18, 1962.

9. James MacGregor Burns, *John Kennedy: A Political Profile* (New York: Harcourt, Brace & World, Inc., 1961), pp. 13–14.

10. Interview with Ralph Lowell in Boston on October 5, 1962.

11. Interview with Joseph L. Merrill on May 7, 1963.

12. *Ibid.*

13. Interview with Henry J. O'Meara in Boston on March 16, 1963.

14. *Ibid.*

15. *Ibid.*

16. "Mr. Kennedy, the Chairman," *Fortune*, September, 1937.

17. O'Meara interview.

18. *Ibid.*

19. *Ibid.*

20. John Henry Cutler, *"Honey Fitz": Three Steps to the White House* (Indianapolis and New York: The Bobbs-Merrill Company, Inc., 1962), p. 66.

21. *Ibid.*, p. 162.

22. *Ibid.*, pp. 162–164.

23. Miss Katherine Sullivan, who attended school at the Convent of the Sacred Heart in Boston with Eunice Fitzgerald, described the "high Irish" during an interview on June 18, 1963.

24. Cutler, *op. cit.*, p. 176.

25. *Op. cit., Fortune*, September, 1937.
26. Cutler, *"Honey Fitz,"* p. 145.
27. Quoted in the *Boston Post* in a December, 1937 series of articles by Max Grossman.
28. O'Meara interview.
29. *Op. cit., Fortune*, September, 1937.
30. *Ibid.*
31. Interview with a veteran financial writer in Boston on April 12, 1963.
32. Interview with James A. Fayne, a Kennedy financial adviser, in New York City on September 25, 1962.

Chapter 4

1. William Allen White, *A Puritan in Babylon: The Story of Calvin Coolidge* (New York: The Macmillan Company, 1938), p. 99.
2, 3. Arthur Pound and Samuel Taylor Moore (eds.), *More They Told Barron: The Notes of the Late Clarence W. Barron* (New York and London: Harper & Brothers, 1931), p. 164.
4. Interview with Clarence A. Barnes, former member of the Massachusetts legislature and former state Attorney General, in Boston on April 10, 1963.
5. White, *op. cit.*, p. 101.
6. *Ibid.*, p. 248.
7. Interview with a close friend of the late Guy Currier in Boston on April 11, 1963.
8. Interview with a contemporary member of the board of the Boston Public Library on April 11, 1963.
9. "Mr. Kennedy, the Chairman," *Fortune*, September, 1937.
10. Interview with Henry J. O'Meara in Boston on March 16, 1963.
11. *Ibid.*
12. *Ibid.*
13. "Bethlehem Ship," *Fortune*, September, 1937.
14. Ernest K. Lindley, "Will Kennedy Run for President?," *Liberty*, May 21, 1938.
15. Joe McCarthy, *The Remarkable Kennedys* (New York: The Dial Press, 1960), p. 44.
16. Interview with Oscar Haussermann, Harvard '12, in Boston on October 10, 1962.
17, 18. O'Meara interview.
19. Joseph F. Dinneen, *The Kennedy Family* (Boston and Toronto: Little, Brown & Company, 1959), p. 32.
20. *Boston Sunday Advertiser*, January 12, 1964.
21. "Mr. Kennedy, the Chairman," *Fortune*, September, 1937. Additional details were supplied by Henry J. O'Meara, to whom Kennedy related the story.
22. Interview in Boston on June 20, 1963, with a former associate of Kennedy's at the firm of Hayden, Stone and Company, hereinafter cited as Hayden, Stone interview.
23. Haussermann interview.
24. *Boston News Bureau*, December 27, 1926.
25. Hayden, Stone interview
26. *Boston News Bureau*, December 27, 1926.
27. Hayden, Stone interview.
28. Arthur Pound and Samuel Taylor Moore (eds.), *They Told Barron: The Notes of the Late Clarence W. Barron* (New York and London: Harper & Brothers, 1930), p. 36.
29. *Ibid.*, p. 95.

30. "Mr. Kennedy, the Chairman," *Fortune,* September, 1937.
31. Hayden, Stone interview.
32. "Mr. Kennedy, the Chairman," *Fortune,* September, 1937.
33. Hayden, Stone interview.
34. Interview with a former Boston business associate of Kennedy's in New York City on October 24, 1962.
35. Pound and Moore, *More They Told Barron,* p. 135.
36. "Mr. Kennedy, the Chairman," *Fortune,* September, 1937.
37. *Ibid.*
38. *Ibid.*
39. *Ibid.*
40. The number of theaters owned by Kennedy was supplied by Richard Dobbyn, an officer of Maine–New Hampshire Theaters, in Boston on October 3, 1962.
41. John Henry Cutler, *"Honey Fitz": Three Steps to the White House* (Indianapolis and New York: The Bobbs-Merrill Company, Inc., 1962), p. 201.
42. Hayden, Stone interview.
43. H. H. Martin, "The Amazing Kennedys," *The Saturday Evening Post,* September 7, 1957.
44. John F. Kennedy (ed.), *As We Remember Joe* (Cambridge, Massachusetts: The University Press, 1945), p. 45.
45. Cutler, *op. cit.,* pp. 243–44.
46. *Ibid.*
47. *Ibid.*
48. *Ibid.*
49. *Ibid.,* p. 212.
50. *Ibid.,* p. 229.
51. *Ibid.*
52. *Ibid.,* pp. 237, 238.
53. *Ibid.*
54. Interview with Kennedy's classmate in New York City on December 26, 1962.
55. Interview with Raymond S. Wilkins in Boston on April 12, 1963.
56. Interview with Ralph Lowell in Boston on October 5, 1962.

Chapter 5

1. *Boston News Bureau,* December 27, 1926.
2. Frederick Lewis Allen, *Only Yesterday: An Informal History of the Nineteen-Twenties* (New York and London: Harper & Brothers, 1931), pp. 164–165.
3. *Ibid.,* p. 109.
4. John Lloyd Parker, *Unmasking Wall Street* (Boston: The Stratford Company, 1932), p. 114.
5. *New York World-Telegram,* April 28, 1935.
6. Interview in Boston on April 10, 1963, with Francis J. Ouimet, a leading U.S. amateur golfer in the 1920's and later a stockbroker.
7. Arthur Pound and Samuel Taylor Moore (eds.), *They Told Barron: The Notes of the Late Clarence W. Barron* (New York and London: Harper & Brothers, 1930), p. 56.
8. Interview with a former associate of Kennedy's at Hayden, Stone and Company, in Boston on June 20, 1963, hereinafter cited as Hayden, Stone interview.
9. *Boston Post,* February 8, 1926.
10. Interview with Ralph Lowell in Boston on October 5, 1962.
11. Interview with Oscar Haussermann in Boston on October 10, 1962.
12. Lowell interview.

13. Interview on October 12, 1962, with a New York stockbroker and onetime associate of Kennedy.

14. Joseph P. Kennedy (as told to John B. Kennedy), "Shielding the Sheep," *The Saturday Evening Post,* January 18, 1936.

15. Joe McCarthy, *The Remarkable Kennedys* (New York: The Dial Press, 1960), pp. 46–47.

16–18. "Mr. Kennedy, the Chairman," *Fortune,* September, 1937.

19. Hayden, Stone interview.

20. Interview with Burton K. Wheeler in Washington, D.C., on October 19, 1962.

21, 22. Burton K. Wheeler (with Paul F. Healy) *Yankee From the West* (Garden City, New York: Doubleday & Company, Inc., 1962), p. 252.

23. *Ibid.*, p. 253.

24. Wheeler interview.

25. Interview with Henry J. O'Meara in Boston on March 16, 1963.

26. Allen, *op. cit.*, p. 271.

27. Pound and Moore, *op. cit.*, p. 270.

28. O'Meara interview.

29. Interview on October 22, 1962, with a Washington journalist once close to Kennedy.

30. *Boston Post,* February 8, 1926.

31. Interview with a former Kennedy business associate in New York City on October 24, 1962.

32. O'Meara interview.

33. *Ibid.*

34. *Op. cit., Fortune,* September, 1937.

35. Interview in Boston on April 3, 1963, with Frank W. Buxton, former editor of the *Boston Herald* and a friend of the late Guy Currier.

36. Letter to the author, dated May 3, 1963, from James F. Donovan, trustee of the Frederick H. Prince estate.

37. Arthur Pound and Samuel Taylor Moore (eds.), *More They Told Barron: The Notes of the Late Clarence W. Barron* (New York and London: Harper & Brothers, 1931), p. 121.

38. Fitzgerald's recollection was published as part of a series of articles that appeared in December, 1937, in the *Boston Evening American.*

39. *Boston Post,* February 8, 1926.

40. *The New York Times,* January 13, 1961. (See also the series of articles on President Kennedy's personal finances and the Kennedy family fortune, written by Fletcher Knebel, which appeared in the Minneapolis *Tribune,* November 12–20, 1962.)

41. Ralph G. Martin and Ed Plaut, *Front Runner, Dark Horse* (Garden City, New York: Doubleday & Company, Inc., 1960), p. 121.

42. McCarthy, *op. cit.*, p. 53.

43. John Henry Cutler, *"Honey Fitz": Three Steps to the White House* (Indianapolis and New York: The Bobbs-Merrill Company, Inc., 1962), p. 249.

44. Lowell interview.

Chapter 6

1. Terry Ramsaye, "Intimate Visits to the Homes of Famous Film Magnates," *Photoplay,* September, 1927.

2. Interview in Boston on June 20, 1963, with a former associate of Kennedy's at the firm of Hayden, Stone and Company.

3. Interview with Theodore H. Streibert, an associate of Kennedy's at FBO, in New York on June 14, 1962.

4. Letter to the author, dated May 3, 1963, from James F. Donovan, trustee of the Frederick H. Prince estate.
5. "Mr. Kennedy, the Chairman," *Fortune,* September, 1937.
6. Joseph P. Kennedy (ed.), *The Story of the Films* (Chicago and New York: A. W. Shaw Company, 1927), p. 27.
7. *The New York Times,* June 3, 1928.
8. "Paramount," *Fortune,* March, 1937.
9. Donald Hayne (ed.), *The Autobiography of Cecil B. DeMille* (Englewood Cliffs, N.J.: Prentice-Hall, Inc., 1959), pp. 79–80.
10. Benjamin Hampton, *A History of the Movies* (New York: Covici & Friede, Publishers, 1931), p. 130.
11. Ben M. Hall, *The Best Remaining Seats: The Story of the Golden Age of the Movie Palace* (New York: Clarkson N. Potter, Inc., 1961), p. 50.
12. James Blaine Walker, *The Epic of American Industry* (New York: Harper & Brothers, 1949), p. 327.
13. Hayne, *op. cit.,* pp. 288–289.
14. Ramsaye, *Photoplay,* September, 1927.
15. *Ibid.*
16. Streibert interview.
17. *Boston Post,* February 8, 1926.
18. "Mr. Kennedy, the Chairman," *Fortune,* September, 1937.
19. Hedda Hopper, *From Under My Hat* (Garden City, New York: Doubleday & Company, Inc., 1952), pp. 108–110.
20. Kennedy, *op. cit.,* p. 19.
21. *Ibid.*
22. Hampton, *op. cit.,* pp. 286–287.
23. Leo G. Rosten, *Hollywood: The Movie Colony, The Movie Makers* (New York: Harcourt, Brace & Company, Inc., 1941), p. 24.
24. Kennedy, *op. cit.,* pp. viii–ix.
25. *Ibid.,* p. 285.
26. The speaker was Robert H. Cochrane, then Vice-President of the Universal Pictures Corporation. Quoted in Kennedy, *op. cit.,* p. 235.
27. *Ibid.,* p. 27.
28. Terry Ramsaye, *A Million and One Nights: A History of the Motion Pictures Through 1925* (New York: Simon & Schuster, 1926), pp. 54–55.
29. Walker, *op. cit.,* p. 330.
30. Hampton, *op. cit.,* p. 379.
31. *Variety,* May 4, 1927.
32. *The New York Times,* October 23, 1927.
33. *Variety,* January 18, 1928.
34. Harold T. Lewis, *The Motion Picture Industry* (New York: D. Van Nostrand Company, Inc., 1933), p. 76.
35. *Ibid.*
36. Joe McCarthy, *The Remarkable Kennedys* (New York: The Dial Press, 1960), p. 50. The sale figure was reported in *Variety,* January 18, 1928.
37. *Variety,* January 18, 1928.
38. Douglas Gilbert, *American Vaudeville: Its Life and Times* (New York and London: Whittlesey House, McGraw-Hill Book Company, Inc., 1940), pp. 388–392.
39. *Ibid.,* pp. 392–394.
40. *Ibid.,* pp. 383–394.
41. *Variety,* May 4, 1927.
42. Gilbert, *op. cit.,* p. 387.
43. "Mr. Kennedy, the Chairman," *Fortune,* September, 1937.
44. Gilbert, *op. cit.,* p. 394.
45. *Ibid.*
46. *The New York Times,* May 17, 1928.

47. *Variety,* June 27, 1928.
48. Gilbert, *op. cit.*, p. 394.
49. *Ibid.*

Chapter 7

1. "Mr. Kennedy, the Chairman," *Fortune*, September, 1937.
2. *Variety,* June 13, 1928.
3. Frederick Lewis Allen, *Only Yesterday: An Informal History of the Nineteen-Twenties* (New York and London: Harper & Brothers, 1931), pp. 299–300.
4. Terry Ramsaye, "Intimate Visits to the Homes of Famous Film Magnates," *Photoplay,* September, 1927.
5. *The New York Times,* June 6, 1929.
6. Interview with a friend of the family in New York on October 24, 1962.
7. *Ibid.*
8. Ralph G. Martin and Ed Plaut, *Front Runner, Dark Horse* (Garden City, New York: Doubleday & Company, Inc., 1960), p. 122.
9. Interview with a close friend of the Kennedy family in Boston on March 15, 1963.
10. *Ibid.*
11. Gene Schoor, *Young John Kennedy* (New York: Harcourt, Brace & World, Inc., 1963), p. 32.
12. James MacGregor Burns, *John Kennedy: A Political Profile* (New York: Harcourt, Brace & World, Inc., 1961), p. 28.
13. *Ibid.*, p. 26.
14. John Henry Cutler, *"Honey Fitz": Three Steps to the White House* (Indianapolis and New York: The Bobbs-Merrill Company, Inc., 1962), p. 290.
15. Eunice Kennedy Shriver, "Hope for Retarded Children," *The Saturday Evening Post,* September 22, 1962.
16. Joseph P. Kennedy revealed Rosemary's condition during an interview on June 3, 1960, with George Bookman, formerly an editor of *Fortune.* Her misfortune and the family's philanthropy in the field of mental retardation were reported in *Time,* July 11, 1960.
17. Sidney Skolsky column, *New York Post,* April 30, 1941.
18. *Ibid.*
19. Interview in New York on December 26, 1962, with a Hollywood associate of Kennedy's.
20. Hedda Hopper, *From Under My Hat* (Garden City, New York: Doubleday & Company, Inc., 1952), p. 167.
21. Benjamin Hampton, *A History of the Movies* (New York: Covici & Friede, Publishers, 1931), pp. 344–345.
22. Interview with Gloria Swanson on May 7, 1963.
23. *The New York Times,* January 29, 1928.
24. Gloria Swanson interview, May 7, 1963.
25. *Ibid.*
26. *Op. cit., Fortune,* September, 1937.
27. Interview with Gloria Swanson on September 27, 1963.
28. *Ibid.*
29. Interview in New York on April 29, 1963, with Jeremiah Milbank, Sr.
30. T. A. Wise, "The Quiet Milbank Millions," *Fortune,* May, 1959.
31. Donald Hayne (ed.), *The Autobiography of Cecil B. DeMille* (Englewood Cliffs, N.J.: Prentice-Hall, Inc., 1959), p. 275.
32. Milbank interview.
33. *Ibid.*
34. *Variety,* June 13, 1928.

35. Joe McCarthy, *The Remarkable Kennedys* (New York: The Dial Press, 1960), p. 49.
36. *Variety,* June 13, 1928.
37. Interview in Boston on October 3, 1962, with a former associate of Kennedy's.
38. *Op. cit., Fortune,* September, 1937.
39. *Variety,* August 15, 1928.
40. *Ibid.*
41. Louella Parsons column, *New York Journal,* October 25, 1928.
42. *Variety,* August 22, 1928.
43. *Variety,* August 29, 1928, quoted Irving D. Rossheim, President of First National, as saying that "the consideration given Kennedy had for a long time made the company appear as if it had reached that state where artificial respiration was necessary."
44. *Variety,* August 15, 1928.
45. *Variety,* August 22, 1928.
46. Harold T. Lewis, *The Motion Picture Industry* (New York: D. Van Nostrand Company, Inc., 1933), p. 76.
47. *Boston Globe,* December 11, 1937.
48. Interview with Theodore H. Streibert in New York on June 14, 1962.
49. Interview with Stuart Webb on June 27, 1962.
50. Several interviews were conducted in Boston and New York with friends and associates of Currier and Kennedy. Currier's discovery that the deal had been made behind his back was related by his son-in-law, Robert G. Steinert, in Boston on June 18, 1963.
51. *Poor's Manual of Industrials,* 1929, p. 2906.
52. Interview in Boston on April 12, 1963, with a veteran market writer who closely followed the Currier and Kennedy operations. For an account of the RKO manipulations, see *Senate Banking & Currency Committee Investigation of Stock Exchange Practices* (72nd Congress), p. 823.
53. *Ibid.*
54. *Op. cit., Fortune,* September, 1937.

Chapter 8

1. Frederick Lewis Allen, *The Lords of Creation* (New York and London: Harper & Brothers, 1935), p. 353.
2. John Lloyd Parker, *Unmasking Wall Street* (Boston: The Stratford Company, 1932), pp. 97–98.
3. *New York World-Telegram,* April 23, 1935.
4. Frederick Lewis Allen, *Only Yesterday: An Informal History of the Nineteen-Twenties* (New York and London: Harper & Brothers, 1931), p. 324.
5. *Ibid.,* p. 180.
6. Charles Amos Dice, *New Levels in the Stock Market* (New York: McGraw-Hill Book Company, Inc., 1929), p. 257.
7. *Ibid.,* p. 260.
8. Allen, *Only Yesterday,* p. 324.
9. Interview with Henry J. O'Meara in Boston on March 16, 1963.
10. William Manchester, *Portrait of a President: John F. Kennedy in Profile* (Boston and Toronto: Little, Brown & Company, 1962), p. 174.
11. Interview with Oscar Haussermann in Boston on October 10, 1962.
12. *Boston Evening Transcript,* May 20, 1929.
13. *Boston Evening Transcript,* May 21, 1929.
14. Executor's account of estate of Patrick J. Kennedy, Probate Court, Suffolk County, Massachusetts, vol. 1482, p. 286.
15. *Ibid.,* p. 336.

16. *Ibid.*

17. Joseph F. Dinneen, *The Kennedy Family* (Boston and Toronto: Little, Brown & Company, 1959), p. 35.

18. Allen, *Only Yesterday,* pp. 329–331.

19. *Ibid.,* p. 333.

20. *New York Journal-American,* December 7, 1947.

21. Interviews in Boston, New York, and Washington with several of Kennedy's friends and with former market operators. The author discovered the names of brokers who had taken Kennedy's short-selling orders, but they would not consent to be interviewed.

22. *Ibid.*

23. Parker, *op. cit.,* pp. 148–150.

24. *Ibid.,* p. 136.

25. *The New York Times,* May 12, 1961.

26. "Profiles: Jolly Bear II," *The New Yorker,* May 21, 1932.

27. "Profiles: Jolly Bear I," *The New Yorker,* May 14, 1932.

28. Joseph P. Kennedy (as told to John B. Kennedy), "Shielding the Sheep," *The Saturday Evening Post,* January 18, 1936.

29. Interview in Boston on April 12, 1963, with one of those present during the Kennedy-Bragg exchange.

30. Interview with Burton K. Wheeler in Washington, D.C., on October 19, 1962.

31. Interview in New York on March 29, 1963, with a former associate of Kennedy's.

32. *The New York Times,* November 22, 1934.

33, 34. Interview with Stuart Webb on June 27, 1962.

35. *The New York Times,* May 8, 1930.

36. *The New York Times,* November 10, 1950.

37. Interview with Jeremiah Milbank, Sr., in New York on April 29, 1963.

38. Marquis James and Bessie Rowland James, *Biography of a Bank: The Story of the Bank of America* (New York: Harper & Brothers, 1954), pp. 1–6.

39. Interview in New York on March 29, 1963, with a former associate of Kennedy's.

40. *The New York Times,* January 8, 1932.

41, 42. Interview in New York on March 29, 1963, with a former associate of Kennedy's.

43. Gene Schoor, *Young John Kennedy* (New York: Harcourt, Brace & World, Inc., 1963), p. 37.

44. Joseph P. Kennedy, *I'm For Roosevelt* (New York: Reynal and Hitchcock, 1936), p. 3.

45. Interview in New York on December 26, 1962, with a former associate of Kennedy's.

46. *The New York Times,* August 12, 1934.

47. Joe McCarthy, *The Remarkable Kennedys* (New York: The Dial Press, 1960), p. 58.

48. Milbank interview.

Chapter 9

1. Lela Stiles, *The Man Behind Roosevelt: The Story of Louis McHenry Howe* (Cleveland and New York: The World Publishing Company, 1954), p. 136.

2. James A. Farley, *Behind the Ballots: The Personal History of a Politician* (New York: Harcourt, Brace & Company, Inc., 1938), pp. 72–73.

3. Anecdote related in Stiles' *The Man Behind Roosevelt,* p. 148.

4. Arthur M. Schlesinger, Jr., *The Crisis of the Old Order, 1919–1933* (Boston: Houghton Mifflin Company, 1957), p. 289.
5. Joe McCarthy, *The Remarkable Kennedys* (New York: The Dial Press, 1960), p. 59.
6. *Ibid.*
7. Interview in Boston on October 3, 1962, with a friend who contributed to Roosevelt through Kennedy.
8. *Ibid.*
9. Interview with Burton K. Wheeler in Washington, D.C., on March 19, 1963.
10. *Hearings on Stock Exchange Practices, Committee on Banking and Currency, U. S. Senate, 73rd Congress, First Session* (Washington: U.S. Government Printing Office, 1932), pp. 33–43.
11. *Ibid.*, p. 713.
12. *Ibid.*, p. 745.
13. *Ibid.*, p. 426.
14. Joseph P. Kennedy, *I'm For Roosevelt* (New York: Reynal and Hitchcock, 1936), p. 93.
15. W. A. Swanberg, *Citizen Hearst: A Biography of William Randolph Hearst* (New York: Charles Scribner's Sons, 1961), p. 437.
16. *The New York Times*, May 9, 1932.
17. Wheeler interview.
18. Schlesinger, *Crisis of the Old Order*, p. 300.
19. *Ibid.*, p. 304.
20. Interview in Boston on April 10, 1963, with John B. Hynes, Curley's assistant in 1932, who later defeated him for the office of mayor of Boston.
21. Arthur Krock, "Reminiscences," MS (Oral History Research Office, Columbia University, 1950), pp. 7–8.
22. Raymond Moley, *After Seven Years* (New York: Harper & Brothers, 1939), pp. 27–34.
23. *New York Herald Tribune*, October 13, 1932.
24. Elliott Roosevelt (ed.), *F.D.R.: His Personal Letters, 1928–1945* (New York: Duell, Sloan and Pearce, 1950), I, 294.
25. *The Public Papers and Addresses of Franklin D. Roosevelt*, Vol. I, *The Genesis of the New Deal* (New York: Random House, 1938), pp. 672–682.
26. Moley, *op. cit.*, p. 53.
27. Interview in New York on October 24, 1962, with a newspaperman who covered Roosevelt's 1932 campaign.
28. Marquis James and Bessie Rowland James, *Biography of a Bank: The Story of the Bank of America* (New York: Harper & Brothers, 1954), pp. 359–361.
29. *Ibid.*, p. 361.
30. *Boston Globe*, November 3, 1932.
31. *Ibid.*
32. Arthur M. Schlesinger, Jr., *The Politics of Upheaval* (Boston: Houghton Mifflin Company, 1960), p. 24.
33. *Boston Record-American*, January 17, 1964.
34. Interviews with several of Kennedy's friends in Boston, New York, and Washington.
35. Drew Pearson column, *The Washington Post*, October 1, 1960.

Chapter 10

1. Elliott Roosevelt (ed.), *F.D.R.: His Personal Letters, 1928–1945* (New York: Duell, Sloan & Pearce, 1950), I, 340.
2. Interview with Burton K. Wheeler in Washington, D.C., on March 19, 1963. Other friends also told of Kennedy's post-election disappointment.

3. Joseph P. Kennedy to Franklin D. Roosevelt, May 19, 1933 (The Roosevelt Papers, P.P.F. 207, Roosevelt Library, Hyde Park, N.Y.).

4. Interview with a former associate of Kennedy's in Boston on October 3, 1962.

5. Interview with Raymond Moley in New York on September 13, 1962. According to Moley, Howe "was suspicious of almost everyone around Roosevelt."

6. Interview in New York on December 26, 1962, with a former associate of Kennedy's.

7. *Time*, September 5, 1932; Kennedy's participation was related by a friend in an interview in New York on December 26, 1962.

8. *The New York Times*, July 19, 1932.

9. Interview with a former associate of Kennedy's in New York on October 12, 1962. See also: *Hearings on Stock Exchange Practices, Committee on Banking and Currency, U. S. Senate, 73rd Congress, Second Session* (Washington: U.S. Government Printing Office, 1934), p. 6219.

10. M. R. Werner and John Starr, *Teapot Dome* (New York: The Viking Press, 1959), p. 249.

11. *Stock Exchange Hearings*, pp. 6238–6239.

12. *Ibid.*, pp. 6221–6227.

13, 14. *Ibid.*, p. 6222.

15. *Ibid.*, p. 6225.

16. *Ibid.*, p. 6145.

17. *Ibid.*, p. 6231.

18. *Ibid.*, p. 6229.

19. *Ibid.*, p. 6228.

20. Joe McCarthy, *The Remarkable Kennedys* (New York: The Dial Press, 1960), p. 46.

21. Interview in New York on June 17, 1963, with a veteran speculator and contemporary of Kennedy's.

22. Harold L. Ickes, *The Secret Diary of Harold L. Ickes*, Vol. II, *The Inside Struggle, 1936–1939* (New York: Simon & Schuster, 1954), p. 340.

23. Alva Johnston, "Jimmy's Got It," *The Saturday Evening Post*, July 2, 1938.

24. Interview in Pittsburgh on August 28, 1963 with Colonel Willard F. Rockwell, who was a passenger on the ship.

25. Interview in New York on June 28, 1962.

26. Johnston, *op. cit.* (For Kennedy's denial, see *The New York Times*, June 29, 1938.)

27. *Ibid.*

28. Interview in Washington on October 22, 1962.

29. McCarthy, *op. cit.*, p. 60.

30. *Boston Transcript*, November 14, 1934.

31. Records show that McCarthy's suit was transferred to federal court, then "dismissed with prejudice and without costs" on October 26, 1936.

32. Arthur Krock column, *The New York Times*, March 10, 1937.

33. *The New York Times*, July 1, 1934.

34. Grace Tully, *F.D.R., My Boss* (New York: Charles Scribner's Sons, 1949), p. 192.

35. Interviews in Boston, New York, and Washington with friends to whom Kennedy expressed his disappointment at the time.

36. Arthur M. Schlesinger, Jr., *The Coming of the New Deal* (Boston: Houghton Mifflin Company, 1959), pp. 461–467.

37. "The SEC," *Fortune*, June, 1940; Schlesinger, *op. cit.*, p. 433.

38. Raymond Moley, *After Seven Years* (New York: Harper & Brothers, 1939), pp. 286–287.

39. *Boston Sunday Advertiser*, January 19, 1964.

40. Moley, *op. cit.*, p. 287.

41. *Ibid.*, pp. 285–286.

42. Quoted in "Mr. Kennedy, the Chairman," *Fortune,* September, 1937.
43. Moley, *op. cit.*, p. 288.
44. "Mr. Kennedy, the Chairman," *Fortune,* September, 1937.
45. Moley, *op. cit.*, p. 288.
46. *The New Republic,* July 11, 1934.
47. *The New Republic,* July 18, 1934.
48. Harold L. Ickes, *The Secret Diary of Harold L. Ickes,* Vol. I, *The First Thousand Days, 1933–1936* (New York: Simon & Schuster, 1953), p. 173.
49. Moley, *op. cit.*, p. 289.
50. Interview in Boston on October 10, 1962, with Oscar Haussermann, the Harvard classmate who attended the dinner.
51. *Stock Exchange Hearings,* p. 6222.

Chapter 11

1. "Mr. Kennedy, the Chairman," *Fortune,* September, 1937; *The New York Times,* July 3, 1934.
2. Raymond Moley, *After Seven Years* (New York: Harper & Brothers, 1939), pp. 288–289.
3. Interview with James A. Farley in New York on March 29, 1963.
4. *The New York Times,* July 1, 1934.
5. The comings and goings during the commission's first meeting, and Kennedy's statements, were reported in *The New York Times,* July 3, 1934.
6. "Mr. Kennedy, the Chairman," *Fortune,* September, 1937.
7. Interview with Burton K. Wheeler on March 19, 1963, in Washington, D.C.
8. Arthur Krock column, *The New York Times,* July 4, 1934.
9. Interview in Washington, D.C., on March 19, 1963.
10. Wheeler interview.
11. Interview with an associate of Kennedy's on October 18, 1962, in Washington, D.C.
12. The Kennedy interview appeared in *The New York Times,* July 4, 1934.
13. *The New York Times,* July 26, 1934.
14. Interview with James M. Landis in New York on September 21, 1962.
15. *The New York Times,* July 16, 1934.
16. Joseph P. Kennedy (as told to John B. Kennedy), "Shielding the Sheep," *The Saturday Evening Post,* January 18, 1936.
17. *Time,* September 18, 1939.
18. Elliott Roosevelt (ed.), *F.D.R.: His Personal Letters, 1928–1945* (New York: Duell, Sloan & Pearce, 1950), I, 489–490.
19. Interview with Oscar Haussermann in Boston on October 10, 1962.
20. Interview with James A. Fayne in New York on September 25, 1962.
21. Interview with Francis Currie in New York on November 14, 1962. Currie was the lawyer to whom Burns wrote.
22. Kennedy, *op. cit.*
23. Fayne interview.
24. "The SEC," *Fortune,* June, 1940; *The New York Times,* September 15, 1934.
25. *The New York Times,* August 14, 1934.
26. Kennedy, *op. cit.*
27. "The SEC," *Fortune,* June, 1940.
28. Interview with William Hickey in New York on November 14, 1962.
29. Joseph F. Dinneen, *The Kennedy Family* (Boston and Toronto: Little, Brown & Company, 1959), p. 49.
30. Kennedy, *op. cit.*
31. *The New York Times,* September 15, 1934.
32. *The New York Times,* May 3, 1935.

33. Kennedy, *op. cit.*
34. *The New York Times,* November 16, 1934.
35. Currie interview.
36. "The SEC," *Fortune,* June, 1940.
37. *The New York Times,* March 8, 1935.
38. "Mr. Kennedy, the Chairman," *Fortune,* September, 1937; *The New York Times,* March 8, 1935.
39. *The New York Times,* March 20, 1935.
40. *The New York Times,* January 20, 1935.
41. Interview with a former associate of Kennedy's on October 18, 1962, in Washington, D.C.
42. Joe McCarthy, *The Remarkable Kennedys* (New York: The Dial Press, 1960), p. 66.
43. Arthur Krock column, *The New York Times,* April 28, 1935.
44. Interview with an associate of Kennedy's on October 24, 1962, in New York.
45. Mrs. Roosevelt was quoted in Drew Pearson and Robert S. Allen column, *The Washington Times-Herald,* September 18, 1937.
46. The anecdote was related to the author by one of those present.
47. Harold L. Ickes, *The Secret Diary of Harold L. Ickes,* Vol. I, *The First Thousand Days, 1933–1936* (New York: Simon & Schuster, 1953), p. 203.
48. *Ibid.,* p. 206.
49. Quoted in Grace Tully, *F.D.R., My Boss* (New York: Charles Scribner's Sons, 1949), pp. 157–159.
50. *Ibid.,* pp. 160–161.

Chapter 12

1. Interview in Washington on October 18, 1962.
2. Francis Bacon, *The Essays or Counsels, Civil and Moral, of Francis Ld. Verulam, Viscount St. Albans* (New York: Peter Pauper Press), p. 29.
3. Ruth Montgomery column, *The Long Island Daily Press,* May 5, 1963.
4. Jerome Beatty, "Nine Kennedys and How They Grew," *Reader's Digest,* April, 1939.
5. *New York Journal-American,* July 20, 1960.
6. Interview in Washington on October 18, 1962.
7. Cleveland Amory, *The Proper Bostonians* (New York: E. P. Dutton & Company, Inc., 1947), p. 346.
8. *The New York Times,* November 13, 1963. "In Bronxville," a young matron told the *Times'* reporter, "you have the feeling of being protected." Protected from what, she was asked? "Oh, from being overrun by Negroes and Jews."
9. Gene Schoor, *Young John Kennedy* (New York: Harcourt, Brace & World, Inc., 1963), p. 34.
10. James MacGregor Burns, *John Kennedy: A Political Profile* (New York: Harcourt, Brace & World, Inc., 1961), p. 24.
11. Schoor, *op. cit.,* p. 36.
12. Burns, *op. cit.,* p. 24.
13. Schoor, *op. cit.,* p. 35.
14. *Ibid.,* p. 39.
15. *Ibid.,* p. 43.
16. Burns, *op. cit.,* p. 26.
17. *Ibid.,* pp. 26–27.
18. Interview with Henry J. O'Meara in Boston on March 16, 1963.
19. John Henry Cutler, *"Honey Fitz": Three Steps to the White House* (Indianapolis and New York: The Bobbs-Merrill Company, 1962), p. 291.
20. *Time,* December 2, 1957.

21. Burns, *op. cit.*, p. 27.

22. *Ibid.*

23. Ralph G. Martin and Ed Plaut, *Front Runner, Dark Horse* (Garden City, New York: Doubleday & Company, Inc., 1960), p. 124.

24. *Ibid.*

25. Interview in Boston on October 3, 1962.

26. Cutler, *op. cit.*, p. 247.

27. Lester Tanzer (ed.), *The Kennedy Circle* (Washington: Luce, 1961), p. 192.

28. Martin and Plaut, *op. cit.*, p. 125.

29. William Manchester, *Portrait of a President: John F. Kennedy in Profile* (Boston and Toronto: Little, Brown & Company, 1962), p. 187.

30. John F. Kennedy (ed.), *As We Remember Joe* (Cambridge, Massachusetts: The University Press, 1945), p. 43.

31. *Time*, July 11, 1960.

32. *The New York Times*, August 16, 1934.

33. Arthur M. Schlesinger, Jr., *The Politics of Upheaval* (Boston: Houghton Mifflin Company, 1960), pp. 344–345.

34. Grace Tully, *F.D.R., My Boss* (New York: Charles Scribner's Sons, 1949), pp. 161–162.

35. *Ibid.*

36. Arthur M. Schlesinger, Jr., *The Coming of the New Deal* (Boston: Houghton Mifflin Company, 1959), p. 542.

37. *The New York Times*, May 26, 1935.

38. "Mr. Kennedy, the Chairman," *Fortune*, September, 1937.

39. Frederick Lewis Allen, *The Lords of Creation* (New York and London: Harper & Brothers, 1935), pp. 266–286.

40. "The SEC," *Fortune*, June, 1940.

41. *The New York Times*, July 10, 1935.

42. Schlesinger, *The Politics of Upheaval*, p. 324.

43. *The New York Times*, September 9, 1935.

44. *The New York Times*, September 21, 1935.

45. *Ibid.*

46. *The New York Times*, May 26, 1935.

47. *The New York Times*, September 21, 1935.

Chapter 13

1. *The New York Times*, November 15, 1935.

2. W. A. Swanberg, *Citizen Hearst: A Biography of William Randolph Hearst* (New York: Charles Scribner's Sons, 1961), pp. 471–479.

3. Elliott Roosevelt (ed.), *F.D.R.: His Personal Letters, 1928–1945* (New York: Duell, Sloan & Pearce, 1950), I, 424.

4. Harold L. Ickes, *The Secret Diary of Harold L. Ickes*, Vol. I, *The First Thousand Days, 1933–1936* (New York: Simon & Schuster, 1953), p. 472.

5. John Henry Cutler, *"Honey Fitz": Three Steps to the White House* (Indianapolis and New York: The Bobbs-Merrill Company, Inc., 1962), pp. 178–179.

6. Robert I. Gannon, S.J., *The Cardinal Spellman Story* (Garden City, New York: Doubleday & Company, Inc., 1962), p. 118.

7. *The New York Times*, December 28, 1935.

8. *Time*, February 10, 1936.

9. *The New York Times*, April 8, 1936.

10. *Time*, February 10, 1936.

11. *Time*, April 20, 1936.

12. Roosevelt, *op. cit.*, p. 547.

13. Stanton Griffis, *Lying in State* (Garden City, New York: Doubleday & Company, Inc., 1952), pp. 84–88.

14. *The New York Times,* July 15, 1936.

15. Summary of the Report (June 12, 1936) and Supplemental Report (July 2, 1936) made by Joseph P. Kennedy to the Board of Directors of Paramount Pictures, Inc., p. 7. This Summary, dated July 15, 1936, consists of 25 mimeographed pages, and is hereinafter cited as Paramount Summary.

16. *Ibid.*

17. *Ibid.*, pp. 8–12.

18. *Ibid.*, p. 18.

19. *Ibid.*

20. *Ibid.*, p. 20.

21. *The New York Times,* July 3, 1936.

22. "Paramount," *Fortune,* March, 1937.

23. *The New York Times,* July 15, 1936.

24. Paramount Summary, p. 18.

25. Swanberg, *op. cit.*, pp. 485–493.

26. *Time,* July 5, 1937.

27. Roosevelt, *op. cit.*, p. 595.

28. *The New York Times,* July 26, 1936.

29. *Ibid.*

30. Joseph P. Kennedy, *I'm For Roosevelt* (New York: Reynal and Hitchcock, 1936), p. 3.

31. *Ibid.*, pp. 14–15.

32. Arthur Krock column, *The New York Times,* February 16, 1961.

33. Quoted in Joe McCarthy, *The Remarkable Kennedys* (New York: The Dial Press, 1960), p. 57.

34. *The New York Times,* August 23, 1936.

35. Joseph P. Kennedy to Marguerite LeHand, January 28, 1937 (The Roosevelt Papers, P.P.F. 207, Roosevelt Library, Hyde Park, N.Y.).

36. The text of Roosevelt's note and its place of honor were reported to the author by a visitor to the Kennedy home.

37. *The New York Times,* October 22, 1936.

38. Arthur Krock column, *The New York Times,* December 17, 1936.

39. Arthur M. Schlesinger, Jr., *The Politics of Upheaval* (Boston: Houghton Mifflin Company, 1960), pp. 623–625.

40. *The New York Times,* November 1, 1936.

41. Schlesinger, *op. cit.*, p. 24.

42. *Boston Sunday Post,* August 16, 1936.

43. Schlesinger, *op. cit.*, p. 341.

44. *The New York Times,* October 25, 1936.

45. Schlesinger, *op. cit.*, p. 639.

46. *The New York Times,* November 6, 1936.

47. Joseph F. Dinneen, *The Kennedy Family* (Boston and Toronto: Little, Brown & Company, 1959), p. 69.

48. Drew Pearson and Robert S. Allen column, *Washington Times-Herald,* September 18, 1937.

49. Quoted in McCarthy, *op. cit.*, p. 64.

50. *The New York Times,* March 10, 1937.

51. "Marine Subsidies," *Fortune,* September, 1937.

52. "H.R. 8555," *Fortune,* September, 1937.

53. *The New York Times,* March 10, 1937.

54. Interview in New York on November 14, 1962, with Francis Currie, Burns's law partner.

55. Interview in New York on October 24, 1962.

56. "H.R. 8555," *Fortune,* September, 1937.

57. *The New York Times,* June 20, 1937.
58. George Bilainkin, "The American Ambassador at Home," *The Queen,* January 12, 1939.
59. Interview in Washington on October 18, 1962.
60. *The New York Times,* May 23, 1937.
61. *The New York Times,* September 13, 1937.
62. *The New York Times,* August 17, 1937.
63. "The Maritime Unions," *Fortune,* September, 1937.
64. *The New York Times,* May 23, 1937.
65. Bill Cunningham column, *The Boston Herald,* August 16, 1942.
66. *The New York Times,* October 26, 1937.
67. McCarthy, *op. cit.,* p. 21.
68. *The New York Times,* February 13, 1938.
69. Cutler, *op. cit.,* p. 269.
70. *Ibid.,* p. 268.
71. Harvard Class of 1912, Class Report, pp. 45–46.
72. Interview with Ralph Lowell in Boston on October 5, 1962.
73. Interview with Raymond S. Wilkins in Boston on April 12, 1963.
74. *The New York Times,* December 3, 1937.
75. Henry J. Morgenthau, "The Morgenthau Diaries," *Collier's,* September 27, 1947.
76. James A. Farley, *Jim Farley's Story: The Roosevelt Years* (New York and Toronto: McGraw-Hill Book Company, Inc., 1948), p. 115.
77. Harold L. Ickes, *The Secret Diary of Harold L. Ickes,* Vol. II, *The Inside Struggle, 1936–1939* (New York: Simon & Schuster, 1954), p. 340.
78. Robert E. Sherwood, *Roosevelt and Hopkins* (New York: Harper & Brothers, 1948), p. 93.
79. Gannon, *op. cit.,* p. 119.
80. Interview in Washington on March 19, 1963, with a former associate of Kennedy's.
81. Anecdote related in McCarthy, *op. cit.,* pp. 68–69.
82. Farley, *op. cit.,* p. 114.
83. Interview with Arthur Krock in Washington on March 19, 1963.
84. Interview with Walter Trohan, chief correspondent of the *Chicago Tribune,* in Washington, D.C., on October 22, 1962.
85. *The New York Times,* February 17, 1938.
86. *The New York Times,* February 19, 1938.
87. Quoted in McCarthy, *op. cit.,* p. 66.
88. *Boston Evening Transcript,* December 10, 1937.
89. *The New York Times,* December 10, 1937.
90. Carroll Kilpatrick (ed.), *Roosevelt and Daniels: A Friendship in Politics* (Chapel Hill: University of North Carolina Press, 1952), p. 172.
91. *The New York Times,* April 18, 1937.
92. *Literary Digest,* December 25, 1937.

Chapter 14

1. William E. Leuchtenburg, *Franklin D. Roosevelt and the New Deal, 1932–1940* (New York, Evanston, and London: Harper & Row, 1963), pp. 229–230.
2. *Ibid.,* pp. 226–227.
3. John Morton Blum, *From the Morgenthau Diaries: Years of Crisis, 1928–1938* (Boston: Houghton Mifflin Company, 1959), p. 71.
4. Edward Grey, *Twenty-five Years, 1892–1916* (New York: Frederick A. Stokes, 1937), p. 110.
5. *The New York Times,* February 13, 1938.

6. *The New York Times,* February 24, 1938.
7. *The New York Times,* January 10, 1938.
8. *Time,* March 14, 1938.
9. Quoted in Joe McCarthy, *The Remarkable Kennedys* (New York: The Dial Press, 1960), p. 71.
10. Quoted in John Henry Cutler, *"Honey Fitz": Three Steps to the White House* (Indianapolis and New York: The Bobbs-Merrill Company, Inc., 1962), p. 279.
11. *The New York Times,* March 9, 1938.
12. The incident at the embassy was related to the author by a former London correspondent.
13. *The Daily Mail* (London), March 17, 1938.
14. Eunice Kennedy Shriver, "Hope for Retarded Children," *The Saturday Evening Post,* September 22, 1962.
15. Ben Robertson, "King George Strives to Please," *The Saturday Evening Post,* February 4, 1939.
16. Grace Tully, *F.D.R., My Boss* (New York: Charles Scribner's Sons, 1949), p. 157.
17. Quoted in the *Chicago Tribune,* May 12, 1938.
18. *New York World-Telegram,* May 12, 1938.
19. *The New York Times,* April 10, 1938.
20. Arthur Krock column, *The New York Times,* April 12, 1938.
21. *The New York Times,* April 10, 1938.
22. Krock, *The New York Times,* April 12, 1938.
23. *Time,* April 18, 1938.
24. Ernest K. Lindley, "Will Kennedy Run for President?" *Liberty,* May 21, 1938.
25. This off-the-record gathering was recalled by a former London correspondent, whose notes were made available to the author.
26. Interview with a former associate of Kennedy's in New York on October 24, 1962.
27. Elliott Roosevelt (ed.), *F.D.R.: His Personal Letters, 1928–1945* (New York: Duell, Sloan and Pearce, 1950), II, 769.
28. Letter to the author, dated May 5, 1963, from Julius W. Pratt, biographer of Cordell Hull.
29. The text of Kennedy's speech was printed in *The New York Times,* March 19, 1938.
30. Kennedy's letter is quoted in Marian G. McKenna, *Borah* (Ann Arbor: The University of Michigan Press, 1961), p. 354.
31. Martin Gilbert and Richard Gott, *The Appeasers* (Boston: Houghton Mifflin Company, 1963), p. 251.
32. Keith Feiling, *The Life of Neville Chamberlain* (London: Macmillan, 1947), p. 367.
33. Winston S. Churchill, *The Gathering Storm* (Boston: Houghton Mifflin Company, 1948), p. 251.
34. *Ibid.,* p. 257.
35. Gilbert and Gott, *op. cit.,* p. 76.
36. *The Nation,* December 14, 1940.
37. Interviews with friends and associates who were corresponding with Kennedy at the time.
38. Gilbert and Gott (*The Appeasers,* p. 30) quote Sir Robert Vansittart, who was Permanent Under Secretary of State at the Foreign Office from 1930 to 1938 and Chief Diplomatic Adviser to the Foreign Secretary, 1938–1941.
39. E. S. Turner, *The Phoney War* (New York: St Martin's Press, 1961), p. 182.
40. *The New York Times,* May 23, 1938.
41. Harold L. Ickes, *The Secret Diary of Harold L. Ickes,* Vol. II, *The Inside*

Struggle, 1936–1939 (New York: Simon & Schuster, 1954), p. 377.

42. *Ibid.*, p. 370.

43. Interviews in New York and Washington with newspapermen with whom Kennedy corresponded.

44. Hugh Thomas, *The Spanish Civil War* (New York: Harper & Brothers, 1961), p. 536.

45. William V. Shannon, *The American Irish* (New York: The Macmillan Company, 1963), p. 404.

46. Ickes, *op. cit.*, p. 405.

Chapter 15

1. *New York Daily News*, June 20, 1938.
2. *The New York Times*, June 21, 1938.
3. Joe McCarthy, *The Remarkable Kennedys* (New York: The Dial Press, 1960), p. 72.
4. This anecdote was related by Mrs. George de Pinto, an employee of the Harvard dining rooms since 1928, in the *Washington Star*, January 20, 1961.
5. Gene Schoor, *Young John Kennedy* (New York: Harcourt, Brace & World, Inc., 1963), p. 96.
6. *Ibid.*, p. 99.
7. James MacGregor Burns, *John Kennedy: A Political Profile* (New York: Harcourt, Brace & World, Inc., 1961), p. 32.
8. John Henry Cutler, *"Honey Fitz": Three Steps to the White House* (Indianapolis and New York: The Bobbs-Merrill Company, Inc., 1962), p. 288.
9. Interview with Oscar Haussermann in Boston on October 10, 1962.
10. *Harvard Alumni Bulletin*, Vol. XXXVII, No. 26, April 17, 1936.
11. *Harvard Alumni Bulletin*, Vol. XXXVIII, No. 35, July 3, 1936.
12. Interview with Raymond S. Wilkins in Boston on April 12, 1963.
13. *The New York Times*, May 18, 1938.
14. Haussermann interview.
15. Harold L. Ickes, *The Secret Diary of Harold L. Ickes*, Vol. II, *The Inside Struggle, 1936–1939* (New York: Simon & Schuster, 1954), pp. 415–416.
16. William Manchester, *Portrait of a President: John F. Kennedy in Profile* (Boston and Toronto: Little, Brown & Company, 1962), p. 99.
17. Schoor, *op. cit.*, pp. 106–108.
18. *Boston Evening Transcript*, June 23, 1938.
19. Ickes, *op. cit.*, p. 415.
20. Eliot Janeway, *The Struggle for Survival* (New Haven: Yale University Press, 1951), p. 24.
21. Margaret L. Coit, *Mr. Baruch* (Boston: Houghton Mifflin Company, 1957), pp. 467–468.
22. *The New York Times*, July 8, 1938.
23. U.S. Department of State, *Foreign Relations of the United States, 1938*, II, 39–42.
24. *Ibid.*, pp. 59–60.
25. *Ibid.*, p. 66.
26. *Ibid.*
27. *Ibid.*, p. 70.
28. *KEN*, October 6, 1938.
29. Quoted in William E. Leuchtenburg, *Franklin D. Roosevelt and the New Deal, 1932–1940* (New York, Evanston, and London: Harper & Row, 1963), p. 284.
30. *New York Post*, January 11, 1961.
31. Interview in New York on October 24, 1962.

32. Quoted in Martin Gilbert and Richard Gott, *The Appeasers* (Boston: Houghton Mifflin Company, 1963), p. 106.

33. William L. Shirer, *The Rise and Fall of the Third Reich: A History of Nazi Germany* (New York: Simon & Schuster, 1960), p. 423.

34. *Documents on British Foreign Policy, 1919–1939,* II, 212–213.

35. *Ibid.*

36. "The Morgenthau Diaries," *Collier's,* October 18, 1947.

37. *Boston Evening American,* August 31, 1938.

38. *Time,* September 12, 1938.

39. Elliott Roosevelt (ed.), *F.D.R.: His Personal Letters, 1928–1945* (New York: Duell, Sloan and Pearce, 1950), II, 809.

40. John Morton Blum, *From the Morgenthau Diaries: Years of Crisis, 1928–1938* (Boston: Houghton Mifflin Company, 1959), p. 518.

41. *Ibid.*

42. *The New York Times,* September 3, 1938.

43. *Ibid.*

44. *KEN,* October 6, 1938.

45. Gilbert and Gott, *op. cit.,* pp. 148–152.

46. R. J. Minney, *The Private Papers of Hore-Belisha* (Garden City, New York: Doubleday & Company, Inc., 1961), p. 146.

47. Kenneth S. Davis, *The Hero: Charles A. Lindbergh and the American Dream* (Garden City, New York: Doubleday & Company, Inc., 1959), pp. 374–379.

48. Colonel Truman Smith, U.S.A. (Ret.), "Air Intelligence Activities, Office of the Military Attaché, American Embassy, Berlin, Germany, August, 1935–April, 1939" (MS), Yale University Library. Lindbergh's letter to Kennedy appears on pp. 140–142.

49. *Ibid.,* pp. 142–143.

50. *Ibid.,* p. 144.

51. Janeway, *op. cit.,* p. 24.

52. Coit, *op. cit.,* p. 467.

53. Cordell Hull, *Memoirs* (New York: The Macmillan Company, 1948), I, 590.

54. Gilbert and Gott, *op. cit.,* p. 165.

55. Quoted in Coit, *op. cit.,* p. 467.

56. Gilbert and Gott, *op. cit.,* p. 171.

57. Hull, *op. cit.,* p. 591.

58. Gilbert and Gott, *op. cit.,* p. 174.

59. *Ibid.*

60. *Ibid.,* p. 178.

61. Shirer, *op. cit.,* p. 420.

62. Robert Graves and Alan Hodge, *The Long Week End: A Social History of Great Britain, 1918–1939* (New York: The Macmillan Company, 1941), pp. 430–431.

63. *Chicago Daily Tribune,* November 24, 1938.

64. *The New York Times,* November 24, 1938.

65. *The New York Times,* December 8, 1938.

66. *New York World-Telegram & Sun,* April 11, 1960.

Chapter 16

1. Gordon A. Craig and Felix Gilbert (eds.), *The Diplomats, 1919–1939* (Princeton: Princeton University Press, 1953), p. 662.

2. *Ibid.*

3. *The New York Times,* December 15, 1938.

4. Craig and Gilbert, *op. cit.,* p. 662.

5. *Ibid.,* p. 663.

6. Winston S. Churchill, *The Gathering Storm* (Boston: Houghton Mifflin Company, 1948), p. 330.

7. *Ibid.*, p. 339.

8. William Henry Chamberlain, *America's Second Crusade* (Chicago: Henry Regnery Company, 1950), p. 99.

9. Quoted in Joe McCarthy, *The Remarkable Kennedys* (New York: The Dial Press, 1960), p. 79.

10. *The New York Times,* October 20, 1938.

11. *The New York Times,* October 23, 1938.

12. *The New York Times,* October 20, 1938.

13. *Ibid.*

14. Quoted in John Henry Cutler, *"Honey Fitz": Three Steps to the White House* (Indianapolis and New York: The Bobbs-Merrill Company, Inc., 1962), p. 282.

15. James MacGregor Burns, *John Kennedy: A Political Profile* (New York: Harcourt, Brace & World, Inc., 1961), p. 37.

16. Interview in New York on December 26, 1962.

17. Arthur Krock column, *The New York Times,* October 23, 1938.

18. Nancy Harvison Hooker (ed.), *The Moffat Papers: Selections from the Diplomatic Journals of Jay Pierrepont Moffat, 1919–1943* (Cambridge: Harvard University Press, 1956), pp. 220–221.

19. Elliott Roosevelt (ed.), *F.D.R.: His Personal Letters, 1928–1945* (New York: Duell, Sloan & Pearce, 1950), II, 818. The letter was written to William Phillips, U.S. Ambassador in Rome.

20. Samuel I. Rosenman (comp.), *The Public Papers and Addresses of Franklin D. Roosevelt,* 1938 Volume (New York: The Macmillan Company, 1941), pp. 563–564.

21. Boake Carter column, *New York Daily Mirror,* November 12, 1938.

22. William L. Shirer, *The Rise and Fall of the Third Reich: A History of Nazi Germany* (New York: Simon & Schuster, 1960), pp. 430–432.

23. *The New York Times,* November 16, 1938.

24. *The New York Times,* November 15, 1938.

25. U. S. Department of State, *Documents on German Foreign Policy, Series D,* I, p. 713.

26. *Ibid.*

27. *Ibid.*, IV, p. 633.

28. *The New York Times,* July 22, 1938.

29. George Rublee, "Reminiscences," MS (Oral History Research Office, Columbia University, 1950–1951), pp. 283–285.

30. *The Nation,* November 26, 1938.

31. Rublee, *op. cit.*, pp. 283–284.

32. *The Nation,* November 26, 1938.

33. *The New York Times,* November 15, 1938.

34. *Ibid.*

35. *The New York Times,* November 18, 1938.

36. *The New York Times,* November 22, 1938.

37. *The New York Times,* November 27, 1938.

38. *Life,* January 16, 1939.

39. *New York Post,* January 12, 1961.

40. *The New York Times,* November 16, 1938.

41. *Ibid.*

42. Rublee, *op. cit.*, p. 287.

43. *Ibid.*, pp. 301–303.

44. *Ibid.*, p. 304.

45. *The New York Times,* December 11, 1938.

46. *The New York Times,* December 16, 1938.

47. *The New York Times,* December 17, 1938.

48. *Time,* January 16, 1939.

49. *London Daily Express,* December 28, 1938.

50. Rose Kennedy to Franklin D. Roosevelt, January 8, 1939 (The Roosevelt Papers, P.P.F. 207, Roosevelt Library, Hyde Park, N.Y.).

51. Ernest K. Lindley, "Will Kennedy Run for President?" *Liberty,* May 21, 1938.

52. Interview with a friend of the family in New York on December 26, 1962.

53. *The New York Times,* June 4, 1939.

54. John F. Kennedy (ed.), *As We Remember Joe* (Cambridge, Massachusetts: The University Press, 1945), p. 64.

55. *The New York Times,* June 4, 1939.

56. Joseph Alsop and Robert Kintner, *American White Paper: The Story of American Diplomacy and the Second World War* (New York: Simon & Schuster, 1940), p. 28.

57. Louis Fischer, *Men and Politics: An Autobiography* (New York: Duell, Sloan and Pearce, 1941), p. 586.

58. *Ibid.*

59. *The New York Times,* March 12, 1939.

60. *New York Herald Tribune,* March 14, 1939.

61. *Ibid.*

62. Robert I. Gannon, S.J., *The Cardinal Spellman Story* (Garden City, New York: Doubleday & Company, Inc., 1962), p. 159.

63. William W. Kaufmann, "The American Ambassadors: Bullitt and Kennedy," *The Diplomats,* p. 667.

64. William L. Langer and S. Everett Gleason, *The World Crisis and American Foreign Policy: The Challenge to Isolation, 1937–1940* (New York: Harper & Brothers, 1952), p. 77.

65. Quoted in Charles Callan Tansill, *Back Door to War: Roosevelt Foreign Policy, 1933–1941* (Chicago: Henry Regnery Company, 1952), p. 57.

66. *Ibid.,* p. 449.

67. Quoted in Churchill, *op. cit.,* p. 345.

68. *New York Herald Tribune,* March 25, 1939.

69. Gene Schoor, *Young John Kennedy* (New York: Harcourt, Brace & World, Inc., 1963), p. 110.

70. "The Morgenthau Diaries," *Collier's,* October 18, 1947.

71. Walter Millis (ed.), *The Forrestal Diaries* (New York: The Viking Press, 1951), p. 121.

72. Churchill, *op. cit.,* p. 349.

73. Joseph E. Davies, *Mission to Moscow* (New York: Simon & Schuster, 1941), p. 440.

74. Quoted in Langer and Gleason, *op. cit.,* p. 75.

75. Craig and Gilbert, *op. cit.,* p. 669.

76. Interview in New York on December 26, 1962.

77. Craig and Gilbert, *op. cit.,* p. 667.

78. *Ibid.*

79. *The New York Times,* June 24, 1939.

80. *The New York Times,* April 25, 1939.

81. Harold L. Ickes, *The Secret Diary of Harold L. Ickes,* Vol. II, *The Inside Struggle, 1936–1939* (New York: Simon and Schuster, 1954), p. 712.

82. *New York Herald Tribune,* May 1, 1939.

83. Arthur Krock column, *The New York Times,* July 18, 1939.

84. *The Manchester Guardian,* May 18, 1939.

85. *Washington Sunday Star,* June 25, 1939.

86. Ickes, *op. cit.,* p. 676.

87. *Ibid.*

88. *Ibid.*, p. 685.
89. Arthur Krock column, *The New York Times,* July 18, 1939.
90. *The New York Times,* July 17, 1939.
91. A. J. P. Taylor, *The Origins of the Second World War* (New York: Atheneum, 1962), pp. 272–273.
92. Hooker, *op. cit.*, p. 253.
93. Taylor, *op. cit.*, pp. 272–273.
94. McCarthy, *op. cit.*, p. 81.
95. Hooker, *op. cit.*, p. 256.
96. *Ibid.*
97. Cordell Hull, *Memoirs* (New York: The Macmillan Company, 1948), I, 671–672.
98. Quoted in R. J. Minney, *The Private Papers of Hore-Belisha* (Garden City, New York: Doubleday & Company, Inc., 1961), p. 228.
99. Alsop and Kintner, *op. cit.*, p. 68.

Chapter 17

1. Edward R. Murrow, *This Is London,* edited by Elmer Davis (New York: Simon & Schuster, 1941), pp. 9–10.
2. Winston S. Churchill, *The Gathering Storm* (Boston: Houghton Mifflin Company, 1948), p. 408.
3. Murrow, *op. cit.*, pp. 17–18.
4. *Time,* September 18, 1939.
5. *The New York Times,* September 4, 1939.
6. *Time,* September 18, 1939.
7. Joe McCarthy, *The Remarkable Kennedys* (New York: The Dial Press, 1960), p. 82.
8. Commander David D. Lewis, USN, *The Fight for the Sea* (Cleveland and New York: The World Publishing Company, 1961), p. 100.
9. McCarthy, *op. cit.*, p. 82.
10. Gene Schoor, *Young John Kennedy* (New York: Harcourt, Brace & World, Inc., 1963), p. 121.
11. *Time,* September 18, 1939.
12. *The New York Times,* September 8, 1939.
13. Interview in New York on December 26, 1962.
14. *Time,* September 18, 1939.
15. William L. Langer and S. Everett Gleason, *The World Crisis and American Foreign Policy: The Challenge to Isolation, 1937–1940* (New York: Harper & Brothers, 1952), pp. 251–252.
16. *Ibid.*, p. 259.
17. Arthur Krock column, *The New York Times,* December 12, 1939.
18. Langer and Gleason, *op. cit.*, p. 249.
19. *Ibid.*
20. *Ibid.*, pp. 249–250.
21. *Ibid.*, pp. 251–252.
22. Elliott Roosevelt (ed.), *F.D.R.: His Personal Letters, 1928–1945* (New York: Duell, Sloan & Pearce, 1950), II, 949.
23. Quoted in Harold L. Ickes, *The Secret Diary of Harold L. Ickes,* Vol. III, *The Lowering Clouds: 1939–1941* (New York: Simon & Schuster, 1955), pp. 22–23.
24. *Ibid.*, p. 23.
25. Nancy Harvison Hooker (ed.), *The Moffat Papers: Selections from the Diplomatic Journals of Jay Pierrepont Moffat, 1919–1943* (Cambridge: Harvard University Press, 1956), p. 298.
26. James A. Farley, *Jim Farley's Story: The Roosevelt Years* (New York and

Toronto: McGraw-Hill Book Company, Inc., 1948), pp. 198–199.

27. *Ibid.*, p. 199.
28. Langer and Gleason, *op. cit.*, p. 251.
29. *Ibid.*, p. 252.
30. *Ibid.*
31. Churchill, *op. cit.*, p. 410.
32. Harry Boardman, *The Glory of Parliament,* edited by Francis Boyd (New York: Taplinger Publishing Company, 1961), pp. 92–93.
33. Robert E. Sherwood, *Roosevelt and Hopkins: An Intimate History* (New York: Harper & Brothers, 1950), p. 238.
34. Quoted in Langer and Gleason, *op. cit.*, p. 491.
35. Churchill, *op. cit.*, p. 440.
36. Roosevelt, *op. cit.*, p. 950.
37. Interview with Arthur Krock in Washington, D.C., on March 19, 1963.
38. Schoor, *op. cit.*, p. 124.
39. Marguerite Higgins, "Rose Fitzgerald Kennedy," *McCall's,* May, 1961.
40. Kennedy recalled Norman's visit in *The New York Times,* May 18, 1947.
41. *The New York Times,* November 23, 1939.
42. Interview in New York on December 26, 1962.
43. *The New York Times,* December 7, 1939.
44. William E. Leuchtenburg, *Franklin D. Roosevelt and the New Deal, 1932–1940* (New York, Evanston, and London: Harper & Row, 1963), pp. 293–295.
45. Interview in New York on October 24, 1962.
46. *The New York Times,* December 9, 1939.
47. Arthur Krock column, *The New York Times,* December 12, 1939.
48. *New York Herald Tribune,* December 18, 1939.
49. Langer and Gleason, *op. cit.*, p. 345.
50. *The New York Times,* December 11, 1939.
51. Quoted in the *New York Herald Tribune,* December 16, 1939.
52. *The New York Times,* February 14, 1940.
53. Ickes, *op. cit.*, p. 147.
54. Joseph Alsop and Robert Kintner, *American White Paper: The Story of American Diplomacy and the Second World War* (New York: Simon & Schuster, 1940), p. 86.
55. Robert Murphy, *Diplomat Among Warriors* (Garden City, New York: Doubleday & Company, Inc., 1964), p. 38.
56. *The New York Times,* March 8, 1940.
57. Murrow, *op. cit.*, p. 71.
58. Quoted in McCarthy, *op. cit.*, p. 83.
59. George Bilainkin, *Diary of a Diplomatic Correspondent* (London: George Allen & Unwin, Ltd., 1942), p. 59.
60. Hooker, *op. cit.*, p. 298.
61. *Ibid.*, pp. 301–303.
62. Cordell Hull, *Memoirs* (New York: The Macmillan Company, 1948), I, 763.
63. Roosevelt, *op. cit.*, p. 1020.
64. Interview with Arthur Krock, the friend with whom Kennedy corresponded, on March 19, 1963, in Washington, D.C.

Chapter 18

1. Quoted in Martin Gilbert and Richard Gott, *The Appeasers* (Boston: Houghton Mifflin Company, 1963), p. 350.
2. Quoted in William L. Langer and S. Everett Gleason, *The World Crisis and American Foreign Policy: The Challenge to Isolation, 1937–1940* (New York: Harper & Brothers, 1952), p. 446.

3. Winston S. Churchill, *Their Finest Hour* (Boston: Houghton Mifflin Company, 1949), p. 25.

4. U. S. Department of State, *Foreign Relations of the United States, 1940,* III, 29–30.

5. *Ibid.*, I, 224–225.

6. *Ibid.*, III, 31–32.

7. *Ibid.*, I, 233.

8. Churchill, *op. cit.*, p. 118.

9. J. R. M. Butler, *Lord Lothian (Philip Kerr) 1882–1940* (New York: St Martin's Press, 1960), p. 287.

10. Walter Johnson, *The Battle Against Isolation* (Chicago: University of Chicago Press, 1944), pp. 63–71.

11. Gene Schoor, *Young John Kennedy* (New York: Harcourt, Brace & World, Inc., 1963), p. 125.

12. *Ibid.*, p. 129.

13. George Bilainkin, *Diary of a Diplomatic Correspondent* (London: George Allen & Unwin, Ltd., 1942), p. 194.

14. Ralph G. Martin and Ed Plaut, *Front Runner, Dark Horse* (Garden City, New York: Doubleday & Company, Inc., 1960), p. 127.

15. John F. Kennedy, *Why England Slept* (New York: Wilfred Funk, Inc., 1961), p. 215.

16. *Ibid.*, p. 186.

17. James MacGregor Burns, *John Kennedy: A Political Profile* (New York: Harcourt, Brace & World, Inc., 1961), p. 43.

18. Schoor, *op. cit.*, pp. 129–130.

19. Burns, *op. cit.*, p. 43.

20. *Ibid.*, p. 42.

21. Schoor, *op. cit.*, p. 130.

22. Burns, *op. cit.*, p. 44.

23. U. S. Department of State, *op. cit.*, III, 37.

24. Quoted in Langer and Gleason, *op. cit.*, p. 493.

25. U. S. Department of State, *op. cit.*, III, 32–33.

26. *Ibid.*, pp. 33–34.

27. *Ibid.*, pp. 34–35.

28. Bilainkin, *op. cit.*, pp. 105–106.

29. Langer and Gleason, *op. cit.*, pp. 486, 504.

30. William E. Leuchtenburg, *Franklin D. Roosevelt and the New Deal, 1932–1940* (New York, Evanston, and London: Harper & Row, 1963), pp. 301–302.

31. U. S. Department of State, *op. cit.*, III, 35.

32. Churchill, *op. cit.*, pp. 132–133.

33. Butler, *op. cit.*, p. 288.

34. U. S. Department of State, *op. cit.*, III, 37.

35. *Ibid.*

36. Peter Fleming, *Operation Sea Lion* (New York: Simon & Schuster, 1957), pp. 90–91.

37. Iain MacLeod, *Neville Chamberlain* (London: Frederick Muller, 1961), p. 279.

38. Churchill, *op. cit.*, pp. 400–401.

39. H. Montgomery Hyde, *Room 3603: The Story of the British Intelligence Center in New York During World War II* (New York: Farrar, Straus & Company, 1962), pp. 32–33.

40. *Ibid.*, p. 36.

41. *Ibid.*, p. 37.

42. Langer and Gleason, *op. cit.*, p. 715.

43. Forrest Davis and Ernest K. Lindley, *How War Came: An American White

Paper; From the Fall of France to Pearl Harbor (New York: Simon & Schuster, 1942), p. 96.

44. Quoted in Langer and Gleason, *op. cit.*, p. 712.

45. James A. Farley, *Jim Farley's Story: The Roosevelt Years* (New York and Toronto: McGraw-Hill Book Company, Inc., 1948), p. 264.

46. Arthur Krock, writing in *As We Remember Joe,* edited by John F. Kennedy (Cambridge: The University Press, 1945), pp. 39–41. Additional details were supplied during an interview on March 19, 1963, in Washington, D.C.

47. *Boston Record-American*, January 22, 1964.

48. Farley, *op. cit.*, p. 288.

49. Krock, in *As We Remember Joe,* p. 41.

50. Churchill, *op. cit.*, pp. 401–402.

51. Quoted in Hyde, *op. cit.*, p. 38.

52. U. S. Department of State, *op. cit.*, III, 66.

53. Elliott Roosevelt (ed.), *F.D.R.: His Personal Letters, 1928–1945* (New York: Duell, Sloan & Pearce, 1950), II, 1061–1062.

54. U. S. Department of State, *op. cit.*, III, 72–73.

55. *Ibid.*

56. *Ibid.*

57. *Ibid.*

58. Churchill, *op. cit.*, p. 404.

59. *The New York Times,* September 4, 1940.

60. *Ibid.*

61. Langer and Gleason, *op. cit.*, pp. 770–771.

62. Details of the handling of the Roosevelt-Churchill cables were supplied by Tyler G. Kent in a letter to the author dated February 3, 1964. According to informed sources, the Gray Code fell into unauthorized hands and was presumed compromised as early as 1924; thereafter foreign nationals employed in U.S. embassies were permitted access to it. One of Churchill's messages, examined by the author at the Roosevelt Library in Hyde Park, N.Y., bears the notation "Gray" before his words and "End Gray" afterward, with the remainder of the cable apparently transmitted in a different code.

63. Page 65 of the transcript of the shorthand notes of the trial of Tyler G. Kent, styled "Central Criminal Court No. 334, Rex v. Tyler Gatewood Kent." The transcript is contained in the Charles B. Parsons Collection, Historical Manuscripts Division, Yale University Library, and is hereinafter cited as Kent transcript.

64. U. S. Department of State, Press Release No. 405, September 2, 1944.

65. Letter to the author, dated March 1, 1964, from Tyler G. Kent.

66. *Washington Daily News,* September 5, 1944.

67. Letter to the author, dated February 5, 1964, from Tyler G. Kent.

68. *Ibid.*

69. *Washington Daily News,* September 5, 1944.

70. John Howland Snow, *The Case of Tyler Kent* (New York and Chicago: Published jointly by Domestic and Foreign Affairs Press, New York, and Citizens Press, Chicago, 1946), p. 5.

71. U. S. Department of State, Press Release No. 405, September 2, 1944.

72. *Ibid.*

73. *Washington Daily News,* September 5, 1944.

74. Kent transcript, pp. 46–47.

75. Kent to author, February 3, 1964.

76. *Washington Times-Herald,* June 25, 1945.

77. Kent transcript, pp. 46–47.

78. *Chicago Daily Tribune,* June 2, 1940.

79. *The New York Times,* June 2, 1940.

80. Report of a talk by Mrs. Kent at the Friend's Meeting House, Washington, D.C., on July 20, 1944, styled "Mrs. Anne H. P. Kent on Tyler Kent Case," Charles B.

Parsons Collection, Historical Manuscripts Division, Yale University Library.

81. *Washington Daily News,* September 5, 1944.

82. *New York Daily News,* December 5, 1945.

83. Charles B. Parsons Collection, Historical Manuscripts Division, Yale University Library.

84. *The New York Times,* August 2, 1940.

85. Quoted in The Earl Jowitt, *Some Were Spies* (London: Hodder & Stoughton, 1954), pp. 51–52.

86. Kent transcript, p. 19.

87. *Ibid.*, p. 20.

88. *Ibid.*, p. 51.

89. *Ibid.*, p. 188.

90. *Ibid.*, p. 127.

91. *Ibid.*

92. *Ibid.*, p. 147.

93. *Ibid.*, p. 189.

94. *Ibid.*

95. *Ibid.*, p. 132.

96. Jowitt, *op. cit.*, p. 65.

97. Kent transcript, p. 188.

98. *Washington Times-Herald,* June 25, 1945; Snow, *op. cit.*, p. 36.

99. Jowitt, *op. cit.*, p. 46.

100. Kent transcript, p. 140.

101. *Ibid.*, p. 137.

102. Jowitt, *op. cit.*, p. 57.

103. *Ibid.*, p. 58.

104. Kent to author, February 3, 1964.

105. Kent transcript, p. 138.

106. Kent transcript, p. 168.

107. *Ibid.*, p. 85.

108. Jowitt, *op. cit.*, pp. 52–53.

109. *Ibid.*, p. 53.

110. *Ibid.*, p. 64.

111. Kent transcript, pp. 198–199.

112. *Ibid.*, p. 176.

113. *Ibid.*, p. 199. "Your Lordship," said Kent, "I submit that I have not committed a felony, because I had no felonious intent. I have committed a gross indiscretion, possibly a misdemeanor . . . In closing, I should like to submit . . . that I am a loyal citizen of the United States of America, in spite of the allegations to the contrary by the Prosecution in this case. . . . I have been convicted of an offence which I did not intentionally commit. I ask your Lordship to consider that all the circumstances surrounding the case make it one unprecedented in the history of jurisprudence."

114. Charles A. Beard, *President Roosevelt and the Coming of the War, 1941: A Study in Appearances and Realities* (New Haven: Yale University Press, 1948), pp. 265–266.

115. *Ibid.*, p. 266.

116. U. S. Department of State, Press Release No. 405, September 2, 1944.

117. *Washington Daily News,* September 5, 1944.

118. *Ibid.*

119. *Ibid.*

120. *Ibid.*

121. Kent to author, February 3, 1964.

122. Letter from Mrs. A. H. P. Kent to George Seldes, editor of *In Fact,* dated January 26, 1945. Charles B. Parsons Collection, Historical Manuscripts Division, Yale University Library.

123. *New York Post,* December 4, 1945.
124. See Note 80 above.
125. See Note 80 above.

Chapter 19

1. Alexander McKee, *Strike from the Sky: The Story of the Battle of Britain* (Boston and Toronto: Little, Brown & Company, 1960), p. 215.
2. Edward R. Murrow, *This Is London,* edited by Elmer Davis (New York: Simon & Schuster, 1941), pp. 157–159.
3. Winston S. Churchill, *Their Finest Hour* (Boston: Houghton Mifflin Company, 1949), pp. 342–343.
4. George Bilainkin, *Diary of a Diplomatic Correspondent* (London: George Allen and Unwin Ltd., 1942), p. 135.
5. *The New York Times,* January 22, 1941.
6. *The New York Times,* October 2, 1940.
7. *The New York Times,* September 24, 1940.
8. Bilainkin, *op. cit.*, p. 208.
9. Murrow, *op. cit.*, p. 163.
10. Bilainkin, *op. cit.*, p. 213.
11. Interviews in New York, Washington, and Boston with friends who spoke with Kennedy on the telephone during the fall and winter of 1940.
12. Interview with Oscar Haussermann in Boston on October 10, 1962.
13. U. S. Department of State, *Foreign Relations of the United States, 1940,* III, 48–49.
14. Joseph Alsop and Robert Kintner column, *New York Herald Tribune,* December 5, 1940.
15. Churchill, *Their Finest Hour*, pp. 488–491.
16. U. S. Department of State, *op. cit.*, III, 48–49.
17. *Ibid.*
18. *Ibid.*
19. Quoted in the *New York Herald Tribune,* April 26, 1961.
20. *Ibid.*
21. *Ibid.*
22. Quoted in William L. Langer and S. Everett Gleason, *The World Crisis and American Foreign Policy: The Undeclared War, 1940–41* (New York: Harper & Brothers, 1953), p. 200.
23. *Ibid.*, p. 202.
24. Quoted in Charles A. Beard, *American Foreign Policy in the Making, 1932–1940: A Study in Responsibilities* (New Haven: Yale University Press, 1946), pp. 303–304.
25. Quoted in McKee, *op. cit.*, p. 250.
26. *The New York Times,* September 4, 1940.
27. *Boston Globe,* November 10, 1940.
28. *The New York Times,* September 22, 1940.
29. Joseph Alsop and Robert Kintner column, *Boston Globe,* October 7, 1940.
30. Arthur Krock column, *The New York Times,* October 8, 1940.
31. The friend was Arthur Krock, who prepared a memorandum of their conversation. This memorandum, dated December 1, 1940, was made available to the author.
32. Interview with Arthur Krock on March 19, 1963, in Washington, D.C.
33. *The New York Times,* October 16, 1940.
34. *Ibid.*
35. *The New York Times,* October 18, 1940.
36. Quoted in *Time,* November 4, 1940.

37. *Ibid.*
38. *Ibid.*
39. Bilainkin, *op. cit.*, p. 239.
40. *Ibid.*, p. 252.
41. Krock interview.
42. *The New York Times,* October 28, 1940.
43. *Ibid.*
44. James F. Byrnes, *All in One Lifetime* (New York: Harper & Brothers, 1958), p. 125.
45. *Ibid.*, p. 126.
46. Krock interview.
47. *Ibid.*
48. *Ibid.*
49. Byrnes, *op. cit.*, p. 126.
50. *Ibid.*
51. Krock interview.
52. *Ibid.*
53. Byrnes, *op. cit.*, p. 126; Krock interview.
54. *Ibid.*, p. 126.
55. Stewart Alsop, "Kennedy's Magic Formula," *The Saturday Evening Post,* August 13, 1960.
56. Krock interview.
57. *Boston Globe,* November 10, 1940.
58. Krock interview.
59. *Ibid.*
60. *New York Herald Tribune,* October 28, 1940.
61. *The New York Times,* October 29, 1940.
62. *New York Journal-American,* October 28, 1940.
63. Byrnes, *op. cit.*, p. 126. In a letter to the author, dated March 6, 1963, Byrnes wrote that anyone hearing only the first part of Kennedy's conservation with Roosevelt might have assumed they had come to a parting of the ways, but that before the conversation was concluded, Kennedy had agreed to make the radio speech. The eventual break between Kennedy and Roosevelt, according to Byrnes, was unrelated to what transpired at the White House on the evening of October 27, 1940.
64. The text of the speech was printed in *The New York Times,* October 30, 1940.
65. Krock interview.
66. *Life,* January 20, 1941.
67. *The New York Times,* October 31, 1940.
68. *Ibid.*
69. *Ibid.*
70. Langer and Gleason, *op. cit.*, pp. 189–190.
71. James MacGregor Burns, *John Kennedy: A Political Profile* (New York: Harcourt, Brace & World, Inc., 1961), p. 46.
72. *The New York Times,* October 31, 1940.
73. Langer and Gleason, *op. cit.*, p. 207.
74. *Ibid.*
75. William E. Leuchtenburg, *Franklin D. Roosevelt and the New Deal, 1932–1940* (New York, Evanston and London: Harper & Row, 1963), p. 321.
76. Wayne S. Cole, *America First* (Madison: University of Wisconsin Press, 1953), p. 17.
77. Joseph F. Dinneen, *The Kennedy Family* (Boston and Toronto: Little, Brown & Company, 1959), pp. 81–82.
78. *Boston Globe,* November 10, 1940.
79. *St. Louis Post-Dispatch,* November 10, 1940.
80. *The New York Times,* October 30, 1940.

81. Dinneen, *op. cit.*, pp. 84–85.
82. *Ibid.*, p. 86.
83. *The New York Times,* November 11, 1940.
84. *The New York Times,* November 12, 1940.
85. Edward Linn, "The Truth About Joe Kennedy," *Saga,* July, 1961.
86. *Ibid.*
87. In the *New York Post,* January 9, 1961, Kennedy boasted to Irwin Ross of his attempt to pressure the *Globe* into surrender.
88. *The New York Times,* December 3, 1940.
89. Interview in Boston on October 2, 1962.
90. Krock interview.
91. Interview with James M. Landis in New York on September 21, 1962.
92. Harold L. Ickes, *The Secret Diary of Harold L. Ickes,* Vol. III, *The Lowering Clouds, 1939–1941* (New York: Simon & Schuster, 1954), p. 386.
93. *The New York Times,* December 2, 1940.
94. *The New York Times,* December 3, 1940.
95. *Ibid.*
96. *New York Herald Tribune,* December 5, 1940.
97. *The Nation,* December 14, 1940.
98. Kenneth Crawford column, *PM,* December 26, 1940.
99. Drew Pearson and Robert S. Allen column, *Boston Evening Transcript,* November 26, 1940.
100. Ben Hecht, *A Child of the Century* (New York: Simon & Schuster, 1954), p. 520.
101. Quoted in *The New York Times,* December 7, 1940.
102. *The Daily Mail,* November 29, 1940.
103. *Ibid.*
104. Quoted in Bilainkin, *op. cit.*, p. 262.
105. *The New York Times,* November 30, 1940.

Chapter 20

1. Quoted in William L. Langer and S. Everett Gleason, *The World Crisis and American Foreign Policy: The Undeclared War, 1940–1941* (New York: Harper & Brothers, 1953), pp. 247–249.
2. *Ibid.*, p. 253.
3. *Life,* January 13, 1941.
4. *Christian Century,* January 29, 1941.
5. The text of Kennedy's speech was reprinted in *Life,* January 20, 1941.
6. Interview in Washington, D.C., on October 22, 1962, with one of those present.
7. For Kennedy's testimony, see *Hearings Before the Committee on Foreign Affairs, House of Representatives, Seventy-seventh Congress, First Session on H.R. 1776 (Lend-Lease), 1941,* p. 221 ff. His views were reported at length in *The New York Times,* January 22, 1941.
8. *House Lend-Lease Hearings,* p. 267.
9. *Ibid.*, p. 309.
10. Burton K. Wheeler (with Paul F. Healy) *Yankee from the West* (Garden City, New York: Doubleday & Company, Inc., 1962), p. 27.
11. *Ibid.*
12. Interview with Burton K. Wheeler on October 19, 1962, in Washington, D.C.
13. *Ibid.*
14. *New York Post,* February 18, 1941.
15. *New York Herald Tribune,* January 9, 1941. Ben Smith's trip to Vichy was reported in *The Chicago Daily News,* December 4, 1940.

16. Harold J. Laski, "British Democracy and Mr. Kennedy," *Harper's,* April, 1941.

17. *Life,* February 3, 1941.

18. *The New York Times,* May 25, 1941.

19. *Ibid.*

20. Quoted in Wheeler, *op. cit.,* p. 429.

21. Anecdote related to the author by a friend of the Kennedy family in Boston on March 17, 1963.

22. Quoted in Ralph G. Martin and Ed Plaut, *Front Runner, Dark Horse* (Garden City, New York: Doubleday & Company, Inc., 1960), pp. 124–125.

23. John F. Kennedy (ed.), *As We Remember Joe* (Cambridge, Massachusetts: The University Press, 1945), p. 52.

24. Interview with a former associate of Kennedy's in New York on October 24, 1962.

25. *Time,* December 2, 1957.

26. Gene Schoor, *Young John Kennedy* (New York: Harcourt, Brace & World, Inc., 1963), p. 144.

27. *Ibid.,* p. 155.

28. Eunice Kennedy Shriver, "Hope for Retarded Children," *The Saturday Evening Post,* September 22, 1963.

29. Joseph F. Dinneen, *The Kennedy Family* (Boston and Toronto: Little, Brown & Company, 1959), pp. 60–61.

30. Elliott Roosevelt (ed.), *F.D.R.: His Personal Letters, 1928–1945* (New York: Duell, Sloan & Pearce, 1950), II, 1290.

31. Franklin D. Roosevelt to Joseph P. Kennedy, January 12, 1942 (The Roosevelt Papers, P.P.F. 207, Roosevelt Library, Hyde Park, N.Y.).

32. Joseph P. Kennedy to Franklin D. Roosevelt, March 4, 1942 (The Roosevelt Papers, P.P.F. 207, Roosevelt Library, Hyde Park, N.Y.).

33. *Ibid.*

34. *Ibid.*

35. *Ibid.*

36. Roosevelt, *op. cit.,* pp. 1289–1290.

37. *Time,* May 4, 1942.

38. Roosevelt, *op. cit.,* p. 1290.

38a. Roosevelt's note to Land is quoted in Frederic C. Lane, *Ships for Victory: A History of Shipbuilding Under the U. S. Maritime Commission in World War II* (Baltimore: The Johns Hopkins Press, 1951), p. 167.

39. *Time,* May 4, 1942.

40. *Boston Herald,* August 16, 1942.

41. *New York Post,* April 12, 1943.

42. John Henry Cutler, *"Honey Fitz": Three Steps to the White House* (Indianapolis and New York: The Bobbs-Merrill Company, Inc., 1962), p. 295.

43. *Ibid.,* p. 296.

44. *Ibid.*

45. Robert I. Gannon, S.J., *The Cardinal Spellman Story* (Garden City, New York: Doubleday & Company, Inc., 1962), pp. 222–224.

46. *Ibid.,* p. 224.

47. James Burnham, *The Web of Subversion* (New York: The John Day Company, 1959), pp. 150–158.

48–50. Interview with Lawrence Dennis in New York on March 1, 1963.

51. James MacGregor Burns, *John Kennedy: A Political Profile* (New York: Harcourt, Brace & World, Inc., 1961), pp. 47–48.

52. *Ibid.,* pp. 48–52.

53. William Manchester, *Portrait of a President: John F. Kennedy in Profile* (Boston and Toronto: Little, Brown & Company, 1962), pp. 155–156.

54. Schoor, *op. cit.,* p. 189.

55. Samuel Eliot Morison, *The Two-Ocean War: A Short History of the United States Navy in the Second World War* (Boston and Toronto: Little, Brown & Company, 1963), p. 383.
56. Joe McCarthy, *The Remarkable Kennedys* (New York: The Dial Press, 1960), p. 110.
57. *Ibid.*, p. 111.
58. Kennedy, *op. cit.*, p. 54.
59. *Boston Record-American,* January 23, 1964.
60. *Ibid.*

Chapter 21

1. Interview in New York on December 26, 1962.
2. Bob Considine column, *New York Journal-American,* December 1, 1963.
3. John F. Kennedy (ed.), *As We Remember Joe* (Cambridge, Massachusetts: The University Press, 1945), p. 5.
4. Letter quoted in Kennedy, *op. cit.*, p. 69.
5. Arnold A. Rogow, *James Forrestal: A Study of Personality, Politics and Policy* (New York: The Macmillan Company, 1963), p. 71.
6. Kennedy, *op. cit.*, pp. 3–4.
7. *Ibid.*, pp. 53–55.
8. *Time,* September 24, 1945.
9. *Chicago Daily News,* December 6, 1945.
10. *Newsweek*, September 12, 1960.
11. Interview with Stuart Webb on June 27, 1962.
12. Interview in New York on September 21, 1962.
13. Interview in Boston with John C. Dowd on October 9, 1962.
14. Interview with Joseph L. Merrill on May 7, 1963.
15. Interview in New York on June 11, 1962.
16. These figures were supplied by Kennedy's broker, John J. Reynolds.
17. Interview with James M. Landis in New York on September 21, 1962.
18. *The New York Times,* September 29, 1944.
19. *The New York Times,* October 6, 1944.
20. *New York Herald Tribune,* February 18, 1964.
21. *New York World-Telegram & Sun,* October 9, 1957.
22. *The New York Times,* November 12, 1959.
23. *Chicago Sun,* January 15, 1946.
24. *Ibid.*
25. *The New York Times,* May 14, 1949.
26. Interview in New York on May 7, 1963.
27. Interview with James A. Fayne in New York on September 25, 1962.
28. Alva Johnston, "Jimmy's Got It," *The Saturday Evening Post,* July 2, 1938.
29. Interview with a former associate of Kennedy's in New York on November 15, 1962.
30. Interview with a former associate of Kennedy's in New York on June 28, 1962.
31. Several interviews corroborated the story of the disappointing payoff to O'Leary and Delahanty.
32. *Boston Record-American,* January 18, 1964.
33. Interview with Henry J. O'Meara in Boston on March 16, 1963.
34. Interview with James G. Colbert in Boston on April 11, 1963.
35. Drew Pearson column, *Washington Post,* December 23, 1961.
36. Landis interview.
37. Interview with Raymond S. Wilkins in Boston on April 12, 1963.
38. *Boston Record-American,* January 18, 1964.

39. Interview with a former associate of Kennedy's in New York on October 24, 1962.

40. Interview in New York on December 26, 1962.

41. Landis interview.

42. Fayne interview.

43. Interview in Boston on October 3, 1962.

44. *New York Journal-American,* January 9, 1961.

45. Joseph P. Kennedy to Harry Elmer Barnes, January 26, 1951 (Harry Elmer Barnes Papers, University of Wyoming Library, Laramie, Wyoming).

46. Robert S. Allen and Paul Scott column, Santa Barbara (California) *News Press,* September 3, 1963.

47. Barnes to author in letter dated March 11, 1963.

48. Joseph P. Kennedy and James M. Landis, *The Surrender of King Leopold* (New York: privately printed, 1950). This pamphlet consists of 61 pages and includes maps of the battlefield.

49. *The New York Times,* September 27, 1948.

50. *The New York Times,* October 27, 1944.

51. *Washington Evening Star,* April 13, 1945.

52. Quoted in Robert I. Gannon, S.J., *The Cardinal Spellman Story* (Garden City, New York: Doubleday & Company, Inc., 1962), p. 359.

53. Dinneen recalled the 1944 interview in an interview with William J. Gill on November 8, 1962, and furnished him with his original typescript of Kennedy's unpublished remarks.

54. *New York Post,* January 12, 1961.

55. Dinneen-Gill interview.

56. *Ibid.*

57. *Boston Globe,* April 25, 1945.

58. *Boston Globe,* September 17, 1945.

59. *Time,* September 24, 1945.

60. *Ibid.*

61. *Boston Herald,* September 19, 1945.

62. *Time,* September 24, 1945.

63. Eleanor Harris, "The Senator Is in a Hurry," *McCall's,* August, 1957.

64. Bob Considine column, *New York Journal-American,* December 1, 1963.

Chapter 22

1. Ralph G. Martin and Ed Plaut, *Front Runner, Dark Horse* (Garden City, New York: Doubleday & Company, Inc., 1960), p. 133.

2. John Henry Cutler, *"Honey Fitz": Three Steps to the White House* (Indianapolis and New York: The Bobbs-Merrill Company, Inc., 1962), pp. 215–216.

3. James MacGregor Burns, *John Kennedy: A Political Profile* (New York: Harcourt, Brace & World, Inc., 1961), p. 60.

4. Martin and Plaut, *op. cit.*, p. 136.

5. Joe McCarthy, *The Remarkable Kennedys* (New York: The Dial Press, 1960), p. 20.

6. Burns, *op. cit.*, p. 65.

7. Martin and Plaut, *op. cit.*, p. 131.

8. In previously published accounts of Jack Kennedy's enrollment, it has been erroneously stated that the oversight was caught *after* the deadline. In fact, the Massachusetts General Laws, Chapter 51, Sections 26 and 27, specified in 1946 that the last day for enrollment before a primary election was the twentieth day. In subsequent years the period was changed to thirty-two days.

9. *Ibid.*, p. 132.

10. Interview in Boston on October 3, 1962.

11. Interview with Mark Dalton in Boston on October 2, 1962.

12. Interview with James G. Colbert, former political writer on the *Boston Post,* on April 11, 1963.

13. Martin and Plaut, *op. cit.*, p. 138.

14. Interview with John C. Dowd in Boston on October 9, 1962.

15. Martin and Plaut, *op. cit.*, p. 141.

16. Colbert interview.

17. Martin and Plaut, *op. cit.*, p. 133.

18. Quoted in Selig S. Harrison, "Kennedy as President," *The New Republic,* June 27, 1960.

19. Martin and Plaut, *op. cit.*, p. 145.

20. Interview with William McMasters in Cambridge on April 11, 1963.

21. Quoted in George E. Herman, "The Elusive J.F.K.," *The New Leader,* December 9, 1963.

22. Harrison, *op. cit.*

23. Quoted in William Manchester, *Portrait of a President: John F. Kennedy in Profile* (Boston and Toronto: Little, Brown & Company, 1962), p. 189.

24. *The New York Times,* October 7, 1945.

25. *New York Journal-American,* November 15, 1945.

26. *Chicago Daily Tribune,* December 6, 1945.

27. Joseph P. Kennedy, "The U.S. and the World," *Life,* March 18, 1946.

28. Quoted in Walter Millis (ed.), *The Forrestal Diaries* (New York: The Viking Press, 1951), p. 153.

29. *Time,* June 17, 1946.

30. *The New York Times,* March 4, 1946.

31. *New York Journal-American,* May 25, 1947.

32. *New York Journal-American,* June 13, 1948.

33. Arthur M. Schlesinger, Jr., in *Partisan Review,* May–June, 1947.

34. Joseph P. Kennedy, "Present Policy Is Politically and Morally Bankrupt," *Vital Speeches,* January 1, 1951. The text also appears in the *Congressional Record,* Vol. 96, Part 18, December 15, 1950, p. A7723.

35. *New York Herald Tribune,* December 24, 1950.

36. *The New York Times,* December 18, 1950.

37. Kennedy's Palm Beach routine and comment were recalled by James M. Landis in an interview in New York on September 21, 1962.

38. Quoted in McCarthy, *op. cit.*, p. 12.

39. Interview with James A. Fayne in New York on September 25, 1962.

40. Interview in New York on October 24, 1962.

41. Information on Kennedy's oil holdings, never before published, was obtained from research and interviews in New York, Washington, Dallas, Houston, and Corpus Christi.

42. Landis interview.

43. *Newsweek,* September 12, 1960.

44. Quoted in Ed Linn, "The Truth About Joe Kennedy," *Saga,* July, 1961.

45. Interview with a former associate of Kennedy's in New York on October 24, 1962.

46. Westbrook Pegler column, *New York Journal-American,* March 28, 1960.

47. Burns, *op. cit.*, p. 93.

48. *Ibid.*, p. 91.

49. Quoted in Cutler, *op. cit.*, p. 247.

50. Burns, *op. cit.*, pp. 84–85.

Chapter 23

1. Ralph G. Martin and Ed Plaut, *Front Runner, Dark Horse* (Garden City, New York: Doubleday & Company, Inc., 1960), p. 168.

2. Joe McCarthy, *The Remarkable Kennedys* (New York: The Dial Press, 1960), p. 25.

3. John Henry Cutler, *"Honey Fitz": Three Steps to the White House* (Indianapolis and New York: The Bobbs-Merrill Company, Inc., 1962), p. 210.

4. *Time*, July 11, 1960.

5. Interview with Raymond S. Wilkins in Boston on April 12, 1963.

6. Martin and Plaut, *op. cit.*, p. 156.

7. *Ibid.*, p. 161.

8. *Ibid.*

9. *Ibid.*, p. 185.

10. *Ibid.*, p. 163.

11. Ed Linn, "The Truth About Joe Kennedy," *Saga*, July, 1961.

12. *Ibid.*

13. McCarthy, *op. cit.*, p. 134.

14. Linn, *op. cit.*

15. James MacGregor Burns, *John Kennedy: A Political Profile* (New York: Harcourt, Brace & World, Inc., 1961), p. 92.

16. James Michael Curley, *I'd Do It Again* (Englewood Cliffs, N.J.: Prentice-Hall, 1957), p. 355.

17. Martin and Plaut, *op. cit.*, p. 176.

18. *Ibid.*, p. 185.

19. Interview with John B. Hynes in Boston on April 10, 1963.

20. Quoted in Selig S. Harrison, "Kennedy as President," *The New Republic*, June 27, 1960.

21. Quoted in Ralph Blagden, "Cabot Lodge's Toughest Fight," *The Reporter*, September 30, 1952.

22. William S. White, *The Taft Story* (New York: Harper & Brothers, 1954), p. 182.

23. Martin and Plaut, *op. cit.*, p. 172.

24. *Ibid.*

25. Interview in Boston on October 3, 1962, with a Kennedy worker who was present.

26. Martin and Plaut, *op. cit.*, p. 173.

27. *New York Post*, January 9, 1961.

28. *Ibid.*

29. *Ibid.*

30. *Ibid.*

31. McCarthy, *op. cit.*, p. 26.

32. Westbrook Pegler column, *New York Journal-American*, December 19, 1960.

33. Two accounts of the Jackson incident have been used: *New York Post*, January 12, 1961; Martin and Plaut, *op. cit.*, pp. 174–175.

34. McCarthy, *op. cit.*, pp. 139–140.

35. Interview with John Fox in Pittsburgh on October 30, 1962.

36. *Ibid.*

37. Quoted in McCarthy, *op. cit.*, p. 136.

38. Harold H. Martin, "The Amazing Kennedys," *The Saturday Evening Post*, September 7, 1957.

39. Martin and Plaut, *op. cit.*, p. 169.

40. *Ibid.*, p. 177.

41. McCarthy, *op. cit.*, p. 135.

42. Martin and Plaut, *op. cit.*, pp. 182–184.

43. *Time*, July 11, 1960.

44. Ruth Montgomery column, *Long Island Daily Press*, May 5, 1963.

Chapter 24

1. Interview with Ralph Lowell in Boston on October 5, 1962.

2. *New York Herald Tribune,* December 12, 1960.
3. *Boston Globe,* November 25, 1952.
4. *The New York Times,* November 25, 1952.
5. *Time,* July 11, 1960.
6. John P. Mallan, "Massachusetts: Liberal and Corrupt," *The New Republic,* October 13, 1952.
7. Ralph G. Martin and Ed Plaut, *Front Runner, Dark Horse* (Garden City, New York: Doubleday & Company, Inc., 1960), p. 202.
8. James MacGregor Burns, *John Kennedy: A Political Profile* (New York: Harcourt, Brace & World, Inc., 1961), p. 155.
9. *Time,* November 29, 1963.
10. *Time,* November 7, 1960.
11. Martin and Plaut, *op. cit.,* p. 204.
12. *New York Post,* July 14, 1960.
13. Joe McCarthy, *The Remarkable Kennedys* (New York: The Dial Press, 1960), p. 190.
14. George Bilainkin, "The American Ambassador at Home," *The Queen,* January 12, 1939.
15. McCarthy, *op. cit.,* p. 146.
16. *Time,* January 20, 1961.
17. *Ibid.*
18. Robert Curran, *The Kennedy Women* (New York: Lancer Books, 1964), p. 64.
19. McCarthy, *op. cit.,* p. 150.
20. *Ibid.,* p. 151.
21. *New York Herald Tribune,* December 12, 1960.
22. Martin and Plaut, *op. cit.,* p. 199.
23. Stewart Alsop, "Kennedy's Magic Formula," *The Saturday Evening Post,* August 13, 1960.
24. Burns, *op. cit.,* pp. 183–184.
25. *New York World-Telegram & Sun,* April 7, 1960.
26. *New York Journal-American,* May 5, 1957.
27. Hugh Sidey, "Joe Kennedy's Feelings About His Son," *Life,* December 19, 1960.
28. McCarthy, *op. cit.,* p. 157.
29. Interview with William P. Loeb in Pride's Crossing, Massachusetts, on October 6, 1962.
30. Martin and Plaut, *op. cit.,* p. 461.
31. *Ibid.,* p. 463.
32. *Ibid.*
33. *Time,* May 5, 1958.
34. Interview with Raymond S. Wilkins in Boston on April 12, 1963.
35. Interview with Oscar Haussermann in Boston on October 10, 1962.
36. Wilkins interview.
37. Burns, *op. cit.,* p. 223.
38. Quoted in Associated Press Biographical Service, Sketch 4080, issued April 11, 1961.
39. *Time,* December 22, 1958.
40. Douglass Cater, "The Cool Eye of John F. Kennedy," *The Reporter,* December 10, 1959.
41. *Time,* April 18, 1960.
42. *New York Herald Tribune,* November 23, 1963.
43. *Newsweek,* September 12, 1960.
44. Alsop, *op. cit.*
45. *Ibid.*
46. *New York Post,* January 13, 1961.

47. Alsop, *op. cit.*
48. *Ibid.*
49. *Newsweek,* September 12, 1960.
50. *New York Herald Tribune,* November 23, 1963.
51. Interview with James M. Landis in New York on September 21, 1962.
52. Selig S. Harrison, "Kennedy as President," *The New Republic,* June 27, 1960.
53. *Time,* July 11, 1960.
54. *The New York Times,* October 28, 1960.
55. Robert E. Thompson and Hortense Myers, *Robert F. Kennedy: The Brother Within* (New York: The MacMillan Company, 1962), p. 204.
56. *Newsweek,* March 18, 1963.
57. *Ibid.*
58. McCarthy, *op. cit.,* p. 189.
59. *Newsweek,* September 12, 1960.
60. Sidey, *op. cit.*
61. *The New York Times,* September 1, 1960.
62. The ad appeared in the *New York World-Telegram & Sun,* November 5, 1960.
63. Nathan Glazer and Daniel Patrick Moynihan, *Beyond the Melting Pot: The Negroes, Puerto Ricans, Jews, Italians, and Irish of New York City* (Cambridge, Massachusetts: The M.I.T. Press and Harvard University Press, 1963), p. 168.
64. Quoted in William Manchester, *Portrait of a President: John F. Kennedy in Profile* (Boston and Toronto: Little, Brown & Company, 1962), p. 215.
65. Theodore H. White, *The Making of the President, 1960* (New York: Atheneum, 1961), pp. 19–24, 345–347.
66. Sidey, *op. cit.*
67. *Ibid.*
68, 69. The Wilkins-Kennedy correspondence was made available to the author during an interview with Chief Justice Wilkins in Boston on April 12, 1963.
70. *The New York Times,* January 8, 1961.

Chapter 25

1. Hugh Sidey, *John F. Kennedy: A Reporter's Inside Story* (New York: Atheneum, 1963), pp. 38–39.
2. *Ibid.,* pp. 20–21.
3. *New York World-Telegram & Sun,* January 21, 1961.
4. *New York Journal-American,* January 8, 1961.
5. William Manchester, *Portrait of a President: John F. Kennedy in Profile* (Boston and Toronto: Little, Brown & Company, 1962), pp. 29–30.
6. *Ibid.,* p. 186.
7. Westbrook Pegler column, *New York Journal-American,* March 22, 1961.
8. *The New York Times,* April 23, 1962.
9. Hugh Sidey, "Joe Kennedy's Feelings About His Son," *Life,* December 19, 1960.
10. Manchester, *op. cit.,* p. 185.
11. Sidey, *John F. Kennedy,* p. 15.
12. *New York Journal-American,* January 8, 1961.
13. Manchester, *op. cit.,* p. 174.
14. *Time,* August 12, 1940.
15. Virginia Kelly, "PT-109," *Look,* June 18, 1963.
16. Interview with a former studio executive in New York on July 14, 1963.
17. *Boston Record-American,* January 28, 1964.
18. *New York Daily Mirror,* August 24, 1961.

19. *Ladies' Home Journal,* October, 1962; *McCall's,* January, 1963.

20. Quoted in Alistair Cooke, "Too Many Kennedys?" *Show,* April, 1963.

21. *Limelight,* August 3, 1961.

22. "Cholly Knickerbocker" column, *New York Journal-American,* November 13, 1960.

23. Arturo Espaillat, *Trujillo: The Last Caesar* (Chicago: Henry Regnery Company, 1963), p. 14.

24. *The New York Times,* July 21, 1962.

25. *Ibid.*

26. *Ibid.*

27. *Ibid.*

28. Igor Cassini, "When the Sweet Life Turns Sour; A Farewell to Scandal," *Esquire,* April, 1964.

29. Espaillat, *op. cit.,* p. 15.

30. *Time,* November 29, 1963.

31. Manchester, *op. cit.,* p. 35.

32. *Time,* September 28, 1962.

33. Joe McCarthy, "One Election JFK Can't Win," *Look,* November 6, 1962.

34–36. Stewart Alsop, "What Made Teddy Run?" *The Saturday Evening Post,* October 27, 1962.

37. *Time,* September 28, 1962.

38. *Newsweek,* September 12, 1960.

39. *Time,* September 28, 1962.

40. *The New York Times,* September 21, 1962.

41. *New York Herald Tribune,* December 21, 1961.

42. *Time,* December 29, 1961.

43. Interview with James A. Fayne, at the Kennedy office in New York, on September 25, 1962.

INDEX

Index